AN INTRODUCTION TO
MONEY AND BANKING
FOURTH EDITION

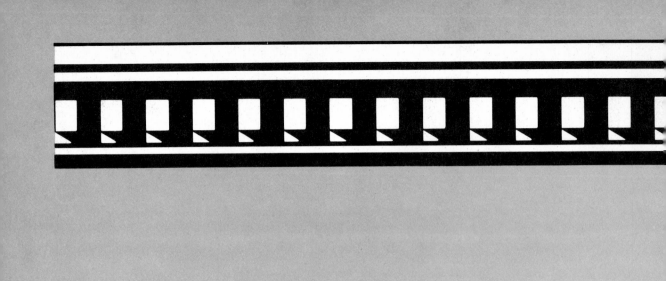

AN INTRODUCTION TO MONEY AND BANKING
FOURTH EDITION

Colin D. Campbell
Dartmouth College

Rosemary Campbell

The Dryden Press, Hinsdale, Illinois

Acquisitions Editor: Glenn Turner
Project Editors: Bernice Gordon/Brian Link Weber
Design Director: William Seabright
Production Manager: Peter Coveney

Text and cover design by Alan Wendt
Copy editing by Robin O'Connor

Address orders to:
383 Madison Avenue
New York, New York 10017

Address editorial correspondence to:
901 North Elm Street
Hinsdale, Illnois 60521

Library of Congress Catalog Card Number: 80-65792
ISBN: 0-03-058076-5
Printed in the United States of America
123 056 987654321

CBS COLLEGE PUBLISHING
The Dryden Press
Holt, Rinehart and Winston
Saunders College Publishing

PREFACE

 In writing the fourth edition of *An Introduction to Money and Banking*, the authors have again attempted to provide college students with a readable introductory text that fully reflects recent developments in the field of money and banking. In the past two decades, new facts about the historical behavior of money have been discovered; the history of monetary policy during the Great Depression has been reinterpreted; the factors affecting the supply of money have been more systematically analyzed; there has been a debate over the appropriate targets of Federal Reserve policy; new theories have been developed to explain the way changes in the quantity of money affect income and prices; monetary policy has been viewed as a more powerful type of control than it was previously thought to be; the effect of monetary policy on prices has been differentiated from its effect on real output; and inflation has become a major economic problem.

This book includes detailed descriptions of the operations of commercial banks, thrift institutions, the Federal Reserve System, the U.S. government securities market, and the market for foreign exchange. The purpose is to enable students to understand the workings of our monetary system and to give students a background for further study in economics or business administration. Throughout the text, the authors have also used historical examples in the United States and in foreign countries to illustrate the principles discussed.

The text is designed for a one-semester college course. The major topics covered are the nature of money, commercial banking, central banking, monetary theory, monetary policy, inflation, and the international monetary system. The text was written both for students majoring in economics and business administration and for nonmajors who wish to take courses in economics beyond the usual introductory course in the principles. The length of the text should allow for some supplemental reading.

The authors enthusiastically recommend a term project for the course in which each student is asked to subscribe to a major newspaper for a period of four to six weeks, read and clip the articles related to the study of money and banking, place them in a notebook, and write a commentary on them. Appropriate news articles to be included are those about commercial banking and legislation affecting it, Federal Reserve policy and actions, Treasury debt management and fiscal policy, thrift institutions, interest rate trends and the money market, exchange rate movements and developments in international finance, and inflation. This project keeps the subject matter in the course up-to-date and helps students relate the content of the course to their future careers and interests.

The fourth edition is a substantial revision of the third edition. Where possible, the statistical data in the charts and tables have been brought up-to-date through 1979. The old statistical measures of the money supply have been replaced by the new measures—particularly *M-1A* and *M-1B*—introduced in 1980. The text includes the important changes in the reserve requirements set by the Federal Reserve System and in the regulations for ceilings on interest rates on time deposits in the Depository Institutions Deregulation and Monetary Control Act of 1980. Since the publication of the third edition, there have been many new developments in commercial banking. These include the use of automatic transfers of funds from savings to checking accounts, the receiving of permission to offer six-month money market certificates with interest rates equal to the current discount yield on six-month Treasury bills, obtaining funds by selling securities under agreement to repurchase, and the expanding use of NOW accounts. There have been further changes in the way the Federal Reserve System uses its targets for the federal funds rate and the monetary aggregates and in its policy toward stabilizing foreign exchange rates.

The authors are particularly indebted to Professor Milton Friedman and Dr. Anna J. Schwartz, who have done so much to stimulate research and new ideas in the field of money and banking. They are also indebted to many persons for assistance in preparing this fourth edition: Fred A. White, President of the Dartmouth

National Bank of Hanover; Richard W. Lang, Senior
Economist of the Federal Reserve Bank of St. Louis;
Charles J. Ellard, Pan American University; George T.
Harris, University of Nebraska, Omaha; William B.
Harrison, Virginia Commonwealth University; Frances W.
Quantius, Ohio State University; Lawrence J. Rodecki,
University of Kansas; and Don Schilling, University of
Missouri. In addition, the authors owe much to their own
teachers in college and graduate school and to their
colleagues and students. Mrs. Campbell was Instructor of
Economics at Iowa State University, Ames, Iowa, from
1948 to 1951, and has done considerable research and
writing since that time. Professor Campbell has benefited
greatly from his association with the Research Department
of the Board of Governors of the Federal Reserve System
from 1954 through 1956, and from his membership on the
Board of Directors of the Dartmouth National Bank of
Hanover since 1961.

Colin D. Campbell
Rosemary G. Campbell

Hanover, New Hampshire
November, 1980

CONTENTS

Chapter One   Introduction

Different Measures of Money   4

Which Measure Is Best?   6

The Growth of the Money Supply   6

Cyclical Variations in the Money Supply   8

The Circular Flow of Money   9

Volume of Credit   10

Interest Rates   11

The Development of Our Monetary System   13

Summary   14

Notes   14

Questions   15

Chapter Two   Functions of Money

Money Unit of Account   18

Money Medium of Exchange   20

Demand Deposits as a Medium of Exchange   23

Money as a Store of Value   24

Money as a Standard of Deferred Payment   21

Motives for Holding Money   27

Summary   28

Notes   28

Questions   29

Chapter Three Currency

The Early Use of Coins and Paper Money 34
Gresham's Law 35
Token Coins 36
Our Paper Money 37
Difficulties with Coins in the Last Two Decades 39
Currency Outstanding and in Circulation 41
The Changing Status of Gold 42
Currency in Process of Retirement 45
Demand for Currency 48
Denominations of Currency 50
Reporting of Currency Transactions 51
Summary 52
Notes 53
Questions 54

Chapter Four United States Government Securities

The Government Securities Market 58
Marketable Securities 59
Dealers' Quotations 62
Variations in Yields 65
Determinants of the Bid Price 66
Nonmarketable Debt 68
Ownership of the National Debt 69
Yield Curves 72
Summary 75
Notes 75
Questions 75

Chapter Five The Commercial Banking System

History of U.S. Banking 80
National Banks and State Banks 83
Federal Reserve Member Banks and Nonmember Banks 83
Regulation of Banks 84

The Federal Deposit Insurance Corporation   86
Branch Banking   87
Foreign Banks in the United States   90
Bank Mergers   91
Bank Holding Companies   92
Correspondent Banking   93
Bank Directors and Officers   94
Summary   95
Notes   95
Questions   97

Chapter Six   The Cash Assets and Investments of Commercial Banks

Cash in Vault   102
Balances at Other Banks and Checks in Process of Collection   106
Trend of Bank Investments   110
Federal Funds Sold   111
Certificates of Deposit   113
U.S. Government Securities   114
Municipal Bonds   116
Commercial Paper   118
Corporate Bonds   120
Bank Premises, Furniture, and Fixtures   120
Summary   121
Notes   121
Questions   122

Chapter Seven   Commercial Bank Loans

Commercial Banks as Financial Intermediaries   126
Characteristics of Bank Loans   127
Commercial and Industrial Loans   129
Real Estate Loans   130
Loans to Individuals   133
Loans to Financial Institutions   136
Loans to Farmers   136
Loans for Purchasing and Carrying Securities   137

Consumerist Credit Laws   138
Summary   141
Notes   141
Questions   143

Chapter Eight   The Liabilities Side of the Balance Sheet

Demand Deposits   146
Savings and Time Deposits   147
Securitites Sold Under Agreement to Repurchase   152
Demand Notes Issued to the U.S. Treasury   154
Deposits of States and Political Subdivisions   154
Certified and Officers' Checks   155
Mortgage Indebtedness and Other Liabilities   155
Federal Funds Purchased   155
Other Borrowing   155
Capital Notes and Bonds   156
Capital Accounts   156
Bank Failures   159
Bad Loan Policies of Foreign Banks   161
Summary   162
Notes   162
Questions   163

Chapter Nine   The Creation of Deposits

Upper Limit to Deposit Creation   168
Increasing Reserves   169
Multiple Expansion of Bank Loans and Deposits   171
Leakages   177
Variations in Reserve Requirements   182
The Money Multiplier   183
Historical Variations in Excess Reserves   186
Summary   189
Notes   190
Questions   190

Chapter Ten Financial Intermediaries

Thrift Institutions   195
Regulation of Thrift Institutions   198
Insurance Companies   199
Pension Funds   201
Investment Companies   201
Finance Companies   202
Federal Financial Intermediaries   203
Rotating Credit Associations in Foreign Countries   206
Creation of Time Deposits by Thrift Institutions   206
Economic Significance of Financial Intermediaries   209
Summary   210
Notes   211
Questions   212

Chapter Eleven Structure of the Federal Reserve System

Antecedents of the Federal Reserve System   216
Panic of 1907   217
Founding of the Federal Reserve System   217
Independence of the Federal Reserve System   218
Organizational Structure of the Federal Reserve System   220
The Balance Sheet of the Twelve Federal Reserve Banks
Combined   227
Summary   232
Notes   232
Questions   233

Chapter Twelve Central Banking

Historical Function of Central Banks   238
Bank Reserve Equation   241
Factors Supplying Reserve Deposits   242
Factors Absorbing Reserve Deposits   251
Changes in the Monetary Base from March 1978
to March 1979   256

Summary   258
Notes   258
Questions   258

Chapter Thirteen   The Federal Reserve System's Instruments of Control

Open-Market Operations   262
Changes in the Discount Rate   265
Changes in Legal Reserve Requirements   269
Criticisms of Monetary Policy during the Great Depression and in the 1930s   275
Selective Credit Controls   276
Summary   279
Notes   280
Questions   281

Chapter Fourteen   Targets of Monetary Policy

Before the Targets: Interest Rate Ceilings   286
Controlling the Level of Free Reserves   288
The Dual Targets in the 1970s   292
Stable Versus Countercyclical Interest Rates   298
Summary   301
Notes   301
Questions   302

Chapter Fifteen   The Behavior of Money

Money and Business Cycles   306
Cyclical Fluctuations in the Determinants of the Money Supply   310
Growth of the Money Stock   312
The Historical Relation between Money and Income, 1870–1961   314
Money and Prices   315
Velocity of Money   317
Historical Trends in Velocity   319
Turnover of Demand Deposits   322

Summary 323
Notes 324
Questions 325

Chapter Sixteen   The Demand for Money

The Concept of Money as a Type of Wealth 328
Demand for Money Balances by Individuals 331
Demand for Money Balances by Business Enterprises 337
Changes in the Demand for Money 337
Velocity and the Demand for Real Money Balances 339
Predicting Changes in the Demand for Money 340
Other Concepts of the Demand for Money 341
Summary 344
Notes 344
Questions 345

Chapter Seventeen   The Relation of Money to Income: Part I

Measuring National Income 350
Money and Aggregate Demand 353
Equilibrium between Aggregate Demand and Aggregate
Supply 355
How Changes in the Money Supply Affect Aggregate Demand 360
Portfolio Adjustment Process 364
Reverse Effect from Income to Money 368
Summary 370
Notes 370
Questions 371

Chapter Eighteen   The Relation of Money to Income: Part II

The Money Supply and Interest Rates 374
Interest Rates and Investment 376
Investment and Income 381
Interaction between Interest Rates and Income 382
The *IS-LM* Model[4] 383

The Liquidity Trap   386
Will Investment Be Larger When Real Interest Rates Fall?   388
The Pigou Effect   390
Summary   391
Notes   391
Questions   392

Chapter Nineteen   Monetary and Fiscal Policy

Nature of Fiscal Policy   396
Fiscal Policy during World War II   397
Alternative Ways of Financing Deficits   398
Historical Relation between Fiscal and Monetary Policy   400
Measuring Fiscal Policy   401
Fiscal Policy and National Income   405
The Monetarist-Fiscalist Debate   411
Fiscal Policy and Aggregate Supply   412
Debt Management   412
Assisting the Treasury   414
Summary   415
Notes   416
Questions   417

Chapter Twenty   Alternative Monetary Systems

Monetary Systems Automatically Regulated by the
Balance of Payments   422
Discretionary Systems   430
Monetary Rules   434
Summary   441
Notes   442
Questions   443

Chapter Twenty-one   Inflation: Causes and Effects

Inflation in the United States and in Other Countries   446
The Monetary Theory of Inflation   450
The Cost-Push Theory of Inflation   454

Wealth Transfer Effects of Inflation   456
Effects of Inflation on the Distribution of Income   461
The Effect of Inflation on Government Finance   461
Some Undesirable Effects of Inflation   463
Summary   464
Notes   464
Questions   465

Chapter Twenty-two   Anti-Inflation Policies and Unemployment

Theoretical Background   470
Tight Monetary Policy   472
Reducing the Side Effects of a Tight Monetary Policy   474
Wage and Price Controls   477
The Problem of Unemployment   482
Summary   490
Notes   490
Questions   491

Chapter Twenty-three   International Finance

Foreign Exchange Markets   496
Cable Transfers and Other Means of Payment   498
Gold   501
The Dollar   504
Eurodollars   509
Special Drawing Rights   512
Summary   513
Notes   513
Questions   514

Chapter Twenty-four   Foreign Exchange Rates

Different Systems of Foreign Exchange Rates   518
Fixed Versus Floating Exchange Rates   524
Determination of the Level of Floating Exchange Rates   528
Price Movements in Countries with Fixed Exchange Rates   529
Direct Controls   532

Summary   534
Notes   535
Questions   536

Glossary   539

Name Index   553

Subject Index   555

AN INTRODUCTION TO
MONEY AND BANKING
FOURTH EDITION

1

Three fundamental subjects underlie and motivate the study of money and banking. The first is an examination of the workings of the banking and financial institutions that provide the economic system with money. The second is an evaluation of their effectiveness. And the third is a search for ways in which those institutions might be improved.

INTRODUCTION

Money and banking are so closely related that they must be studied together. The money used to carry on economic activities is provided by a complicated network of institutions—depository institutions (such as commercial banks, savings and loan associations, and mutual savings banks), the Federal Reserve banks, and the United States Treasury.

Checking accounts, the most important medium of exchange in use today, are provided primarily by commercial banks. Federal Reserve notes, the principal type of paper money in circulation, are issued by the Federal Reserve banks. To understand how the economy is supplied with checking accounts and paper money, the operations of both the commercial banks and the Federal Reserve banks must be studied.

A variety of interest-earning accounts are provided not only by commercial banks, but also by the thrift institutions—mutual savings banks, savings and loan associations, and credit unions. Although most interest-earning accounts are not part of the medium of exchange, they are included in some of the broader measures of the money supply because of their liquidity.

The United States Treasury issues coins, the only important type of money not created by banks. Other institutions involved in our monetary system in some important way are the Federal Deposit Insurance Corporation, the Office of the Comptroller of the Currency, state banking offices, and the International Monetary Fund.

Different measures of money

There are several different concepts of money and, consequently, several ways to measure the supply of money statistically. In 1980, the official measures of the money supply were revised by the Board of Governors of the Federal Reserve System. The five revised measures are:

M-1A: Currency (coins and paper money) outside banks, and demand deposits (checking accounts) at commercial banks. Currency in the vaults of commercial banks is excluded because it is held by banks as reserves for deposits. Also excluded is currency held by the Federal Reserve banks and the U.S. Treasury because it is not in use by the public.

The demand deposits included in *M-1A* are in approximately 15,000 commercial banks and are owned by persons, business firms, and units of state and local government. Three types of demand deposits are excluded—those owned by the U.S. government, by foreign banks and official institutions, and by domestic banks. The total amount of demand deposits included in *M-1A* is adjusted in several ways to allow for changes in the volume of checks in process of collection.

M-1B: *M-1A* plus NOW accounts (interest-earning accounts on which checks may be written) and ATS accounts (automatic transfer savings accounts that may be transferred to a person's checking account when the checking account is depleted or falls to a minimum level). *M-1B* includes not only NOW and ATS accounts at commercial banks, but also those at mutual savings banks and savings and loan associations. Included also are credit union share draft accounts, which are similar to NOW accounts, and demand deposits at mutual savings banks. The total amount of *M-1B* is not much larger than *M-1A*. Both *M-1A* and *M-1B* attempt to measure the total amount of money used for transactions.

M-2: *M-1B* plus most interest-earning deposits (savings deposits and small-denomination time deposits in both commercial banks and thrift institutions). The owner of an interest-earning account may be legally required to notify the bank in advance before withdrawing cash. (The types of interest-earning accounts on which checks can be written are included in *M-1B*.) The most common type of savings deposit is a passbook deposit. Savings deposits are a type of time deposit, although they are sometimes referred to separately. There are various types of time deposits with different periods to maturity and different terms for withdrawal. Small-denomination time deposits are those issued in amounts less than $100,000. *M-2* also includes shares in money market mutual funds; overnight Eurodollar deposits owned by residents of the United States (these are deposits denominated in dollars in banks in foreign countries); and overnight repurchase agreements (*RPs*) at commercial banks—an unusual new way that business firms have of keeping funds at commercial banks. Economists call time deposits and the other components of *M-2* *liquid assets* or *near money*. Like currency and demand deposits, their nominal value is certain. One hundred dollars placed in a time deposit is always worth $100 (not counting interest accumulation).

M-3: *M-2* plus large-denomination time deposits both at commercial banks and thrift institutions. It also includes term repurchase agreements at commercial banks and savings and loan associations. Large-denomination time deposits have denominations of $100,000 or more. They are excluded from *M-2* because the maturity date on most large time deposits is strictly enforced. Therefore, they cannot be cashed immediately as can most time deposits.

L: *M-3* plus U.S. savings bonds, short-term U.S. government securities, commercial paper, bankers acceptances, and term Eurodollar deposits held by U.S. residents, but not including those owned by banks. *L* is a very broad measure of the money stock and includes almost all liquid assets.

Which measure is best?

If money were defined solely as a medium of exchange, there would be little difficulty in measuring it statistically. *M-1A* and *M-1B* would be adequate. But money is also defined as a liquid asset. The broader statistical definitions of money include time deposits and other liquid assets which are not part of the medium of exchange, but do have a fixed nominal value.

How important the broader measures of the money stock (*M-2*, *M-3*, and *L*) are will depend on whether they prove to be more useful than *M-1A* and *M-1B* in explaining changes in the national income, the level of prices, interest rates, and other important economic conditions. An Advisory Committee on Monetary Statistics, appointed by the Board of Governors of the Federal Reserve System in 1974, concluded in its report that no one measure of the money supply is clearly preferable to all others. The report states that "Each has its theoretical and practical strengths and weaknesses as a guide to, or immediate target for, monetary policy operations, and as a measure of the effectiveness of such operations."[1] The narrow measures of the money supply were revised in 1980 because of the development of close substitutes for demand deposits in commercial banks, such as NOW accounts at commercial banks, savings and loan associations, and mutual savings banks, and ATS accounts. The broader measures of the money supply were revised because of the development of new liquid assets such as Eurodollars, *RPs*, and shares in money market mutual funds.

The growth of the money supply

Table 1.1 shows the growth of currency outside banks and of three of the measures of the money supply—*M-1A*, *M-1B*, and *M-2*—from 1965 to 1979. The total quantity of money in the economy is large. In December 1979, *M-1A* was equal to 15 percent of the gross national product (GNP)—the total amount of goods and services produced during the year; *M-1B* was equal to about 16 percent; and *M-2* to 62 percent.

Some increase in the money supply, no matter how measured, usually occurs each year, although the amount of the yearly increase varies. In recent decades, growth of the money stock has been a result of Federal Reserve policy. But even before the Federal Reserve System was set up, the supply of money tended to grow.

Reliable data on currency plus demand and time deposits in commercial banks go back to 1867, more than one hundred years ago. At that time, these types of money amounted to only $1.3 billion—of which a little less than half was currency and the rest was deposits of different

Table 1.1
Money Supply of the
United States,
1965–1979, Seasonally
Adjusted (in billions)

December	Currency Outside Banks	M-1A[a]	M-1B[b]	M-2[c]
1965	$36.3	$168.7	$168.8	$457.2
1966	38.3	172.8	172.9	478.5
1967	40.4	184.2	184.2	523.6
1968	43.4	198.4	198.5	566.2
1969	46.0	204.6	204.7	587.6
1970	49.0	215.3	215.4	625.2
1971	52.5	229.2	229.4	709.6
1972	56.9	250.5	250.6	801.6
1973	61.6	264.1	264.4	858.1
1974	67.8	275.3	275.7	906.2
1975	73.8	287.9	289.0	1,022.4
1976	80.8	305.0	307.7	1,166.7
1977	88.6	328.4	332.5	1,294.1
1978	97.7	351.6	359.9	1,400.8
1979	106.3	371.5	387.7	1,523.8

[a]Excludes currency in the vaults of commercial banks, the Federal Reserve banks, and the U.S. Treasury, and demand deposits owned by domestic banks, foreign banks, and the U.S. government. It is also adjusted to take account of checks in process of collection.
[b]Includes M-1A plus NOW and ATS accounts at banks and thrift institutions, credit union share draft accounts, and demand deposits at mutual savings banks.
[c]Includes M-1B plus savings and small denomination time deposits (under $100,000) at all depository institutions, money market mutual fund shares, overnight repurchase agreements (RPs) issued by commercial banks, and certain overnight Eurodollars held by U.S. residents.
Source: *Economic Report of the President, January 1980*, p. 271; *Federal Reserve Bulletin*, March 1980, p. A14; and Banking Section, Division of Research and Statistics, Board of Governors of the Federal Reserve System.

types. Available data on demand deposits at commercial banks (excluding time deposits) go back to 1914, when currency and demand deposits at commercial banks amounted to only $11.5 billion.[2]

Data on demand deposits (excluding time deposits) are not available before 1914 because commercial banks did not distinguish sharply between time deposits and demand deposits until the establishment of the Federal Reserve System. When the Federal Reserve System was established, reserve requirements were set at higher levels for demand deposits than for time deposits, and different records for the two types of deposits had to be kept. Because data on total demand and time deposits at commercial banks are available over a longer period than data on demand deposits alone, statistical series on the money supply including time deposits at commercial banks have been a particularly useful series for studies of the cyclical and secular movements of the money supply.

From 1965 through 1979, the expansion in the money stock was very rapid. Over this period, the amount of *M-1A* and *M-1B* more than doubled, and *M-2* more than tripled.

Cyclical variations in the money supply

In all of the business recessions in the United States from 1867 to the present time, the downturn in business activity has been preceded by a drop in the rate of expansion of the money stock. The opposite has been true in periods of recovery—a rise in the rate of expansion of the money supply has preceded an upturn in business activity. In Table 1.1, the increases from one year to the next in the various measures of the money supply were relatively small in 1969-1970 and in 1973-1974, and were followed by periods of recession. One of the challenging questions in the study of money and banking is whether this statistical relationship between the business cycle and the rate of increase in the money supply can be accounted for. Although movements of the money stock are interrelated with changes in the total output of the economy, there may also be a *causal* relationship between a drop in the rate of expansion of the money supply and a downturn in the level of business activity. Whether the causal link runs from the rate of change in the money stock to the business cycle or in the reverse direction is an important issue in monetary economics. While there is evidence that the connection has gone in both directions, some economists argue that the former influence is the dominant one.

The real value of money

It is important to distinguish between the nominal value and the real value of the money supply. The statistical series in Table 1.1 show the increases in the nominal value of the money stock during the past fifteen years. The real value of the money supply is its purchasing power, its command over goods and services. This real value varies inversely with changes in prices; a given nominal amount of money will buy less when prices rise. Changes in the real value of the amount of money outstanding are measured by dividing the nominal quantity of money by the price index. The lower-case m is used by economists to represent the real value of money in the economy. Using the symbol M for the nominal money supply and the symbol P for the price index:

$$m = \frac{M}{P}$$

and

$$M = mP$$

The circular flow of money

Consumers purchase the goods and services they need with money. Business firms then use the money they have received from consumers to hire labor and to obtain the machinery and the space they need to produce goods and services. As a result of these two types of transactions, money is continuously being circulated from persons to business firms and then back to persons. This circular flow of money is one of the fundamental characteristics of our economic system.

A simplified illustration of the circular flow of money is shown in Figure 1.1. The figure includes only those transactions between business firms and persons as consumers and between business firms and persons as owners of labor and capital. It is simplified because it does not show the effect on the circular flow of production of capital goods, saving by consumers, government spending and taxation, retained profit, and transactions among firms such as the purchase of materials by one business enterprise from another.

**Figure 1.1
The Circular Flow
of Money**

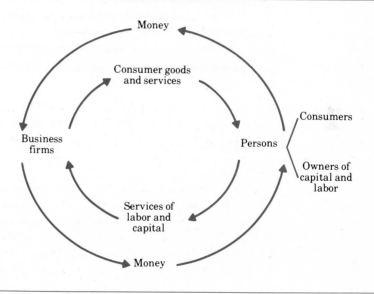

The flow of money depends on two factors: the quantity of money in circulation and how fast it circulates. Whether viewed from either the upper or the lower half of the diagram, the flow of money has significant effects on the economy. In the upper half, the flow of money affects the volume of spending by consumers; in the lower half, it affects the volume of spending by business firms. An important topic in the study of money and banking is: What determines the length of time each person holds money, and thus the speed with which it circulates.

Volume of credit

Variations in the quantity of credit may affect economic activity just as significantly as changes in the money supply. A government booklet, which was published originally in 1939 by the Board of Governors of the Federal Reserve System and went through six editions, states that "The Federal Reserve contributes to attainment of the Nation's economic and financial goals through its ability to influence the availability and the cost of money and credit in the economy. As the Nation's central bank, it attempts to ensure that money and credit growth over the longer run is sufficient to provide a rising standard of living for all of our people."[3]

Credit is involved when people borrow money. The lender is able to reserve purchasing power for later, and the borrower is able to gain purchasing power immediately. When credit is extended, there is usually formal, written evidence of the terms of the obligation. The two principal types of *credit instrument* used are (1) promises to pay (promissory notes of individuals, and notes and bonds of business firms and governments), and (2) orders to pay (bills of exchange or drafts).

When a person borrows from a commercial bank, he signs a promissory note, promising to pay back to the bank the amount of money he has borrowed, together with interest. For this note, he usually receives an addition to the balance in his checking deposit, which he then spends. People borrow money from mutual savings banks, savings and loan associations, personal finance associations, and insurance companies, as well as from commercial banks.

Economists are interested in the quantity of the different types of loans outstanding and how they vary. The principal types of credit include business loans, mortgage loans, consumer loans, financial loans, and personal loans. Table 1.2 illustrates the way the total quantity of automobile credit, which is a type of consumer credit, varied from 1965 to 1979. Automobile loans are made by sales finance companies and credit unions as well as by commercial banks. Although this is just one of the major types of credit, the way in which it has varied is typical of the other types, too.

Since most persons purchase automobiles with borrowed funds, the volume of automobile credit is large. Automobile loans are installment loans that are paid off in equal, monthly installments over a period of up to three or four years. At the same time that new automobile loans are being made, outstanding automobile loans are being paid off. An

Table 1.2
Automobile Credit
Outstanding,
1965–1979 (in billions)

End of	Amount	
1965	$28.4	
1966	30.0	
1967	29.8 ⎫	Slowdown—Jan. 1967 to May 1967
1968	32.9	
1969	35.5 ⎫	
1970	35.2 ⎭	Recession—Dec. 1969 to Nov. 1970
1971	38.8	
1972	44.3	
1973	51.3 ⎫	
1974	52.2 ⎬	Recession—Nov. 1973 to Mar. 1975
1975	53.7 ⎭	
1976*	67.7	
1977	82.9	
1978	102.5	
1979	115.0	

*New series starting in 1976.
Source: *Economic Report of the President, January 1976*, p. 240; and *Federal Reserve Bulletin*, March 1980, p. A42.

increase in the total amount of automobile credit indicates that the quantity of new loans has been larger than the amount paid off.

Variations in the quantity of automobile credit outstanding reflect conditions in the economy. During the recessions of 1969–1970 and 1973–1975, and during the slowdown of 1967, the volume of automobile credit either leveled off or declined. When prices are rising rapidly as in 1973–1974, a leveling off of the total amount of automobile loans indicates that there has been a decline in the real volume of lending. The more than 100 percent rise in prices from 1965 to 1979 accounts for a substantial portion of the increase in the amount of automobile credit.

Interest rates

Interest rates are a measure of the price of borrowed funds. If a person borrows $1,000 for one year and agrees to pay $70 interest at the end of the year, the rate of interest would be 7 percent a year. Interest rates on bank loans vary with the size, use, duration, and reliability of the loan. Table 1.3 shows the trend of the prime rate of interest for business loans by commercial banks from 1965 to 1979. An example of a bank loan made at the prime rate of interest would be a short-term loan to a large and well-established corporation. Variations in the cost of borrowing, like trends in the quantity of money and the volume of credit, reflect conditions in the economy. When business activity declined in 1967, 1969–1970, and 1973–1975, the prime interest rate, as well as

Table 1.3
Prime Rate Charged by
Banks, Annual Average,
1965–1979

Year	Rate	
1965	4.54%	
1966	5.63	
1967	5.61 ⎫	Slowdown—Jan. 1967 to May 1967
1968	6.30	
1969	7.96 ⎫	
1970	7.91 ⎭	Recession—Dec. 1969 to Nov. 1970
1971	5.72	
1972	5.25	
1973	8.03 ⎫	
1974	10.81 ⎬	Recession—Nov. 1973 to Mar. 1975
1975	7.86 ⎭	
1976	6.84	
1977	6.83	
1978	9.06	
1979	12.67	

Source: *Economic Report of the President, January 1980* (Washington, D.C.: U.S. Government Printing Office, 1980), p. 278.

interest rates on other types of loans, either stopped rising or, sooner or later, fell.

Movements in interest rates are believed to have significant effects on economic activity. Changes in interest rates are an important part of the mechanism through which monetary policy affects the output of the economy and the level of prices. How the Federal Reserve System influences movements in interest rates, and how such efforts are interrelated with changes in the quantity of money, are important questions in the study of money and banking.

Real rates of interest

Under conditions of inflation, real rates of interest must be distinguished from nominal rates of interest. The prime rate shown in Table 1.3 is a nominal rate of interest. It is the rate actually paid on certain types of loans.

If a bank lends money at 10 percent interest, but during the year prices rise by 8 percent, the purchasing power of the amount lent will have grown by only 2 percent. The real interest rate realized by the bank is 2 percent compared with the nominal rate of 10 percent. Because of the acceleration in the rate of inflation, the sharp rise in the prime rate during the past fifteen years is misleading. In 1965, when the prime rate was 4.54 percent, the rate of inflation was only 1.9 percent, while in 1979, when the prime rate was 12.67 percent, the rate of rise in consumer prices was 11.3 percent. Relative to prices, the prime rate was lower in 1979 than in 1965.

The development of our monetary system ✕

In the American colonies the currency in circulation was mainly Spanish dollars, although several of the colonies minted coins and issued paper money. The Revolutionary War was financed primarily by Continental currency printed by the Continental Congress. Continental currency depreciated sharply in value, and shortly after the war it went out of circulation. In 1789, the Constitution denied the states the power to issue money and gave the federal government the right to coin money and to regulate its value (in terms of gold and silver). Curiously, it is not clear whether the Constitution gives the federal government the right to issue paper money. (A clause in the original draft giving the federal government the right to issue "bills of credit" was struck out before the final draft.)[4]

Before the Civil War, most of the paper currency in use was issued by state-chartered commercial banks. The states could charter banks that issued paper money even though the states themselves could not issue it. These privately owned banks also accepted deposits, and by the end of the Civil War, the total quantity of demand and time deposits created by them was only slightly smaller than the total amount of currency.

The federal government first issued paper currency during the Civil War. Though the constitutionality of the Civil War "greenbacks" (United States notes) was initially a matter of dispute, in 1870 and 1874 the Supreme Court clarified the matter in several decisions, concluding that the federal government had the right to issue paper money and declare it legal tender (i.e., legally acceptable payment for debts).

During the Civil War, the federal government also established the National Banking System, a network of private banks chartered by the federal government and authorized to issue paper money called national bank notes; at the same time, they taxed notes issued by state banks. From 1865 to 1914, the principal types of paper money in use were these national bank notes, the United States notes, and silver certificates issued by the Treasury and representing silver held by it. During the latter half of the nineteenth century, bank deposits became an increasingly important type of money, and the total amount of deposits gradually became much larger than the total amount of various types of paper money.

The establishment of the Federal Reserve banks in 1914 created a system of central banking. The Federal Reserve Act authorized the Federal Reserve banks to issue Federal Reserve notes, which are now the only important type of paper money in circulation. The Federal Reserve System's principal function today is the regulation of lending and deposit-creating activities of the commercial banks. Since the activities of commercial banks are believed to have significant effects on the level of economic output and of prices, how the Federal Reserve System can most effectively use its powers to regulate the commercial banks so as to achieve broad economic objectives, such as economic prosperity and stable prices, is one of the more difficult questions in the study of Federal Reserve policy.

Deposits in commercial banks in the United States not only serve as money within the country, but have become part of the money used by foreign countries for international trade. Other types of international money have been gold and the British pound. A new type of international money—called *special drawing rights* (SDRs)—was created by the International Monetary Fund in 1970. International money is held by persons engaging in international trade and by governments to settle temporary differences between the country's total expenditures and receipts in international trade. The study of money and banking includes the international as well as the domestic monetary system.

Summary

In the study of money and banking, there are three interrelated factors: money, credit, and interest rates. We are interested in how money, credit, and interest rates have varied in the business cycle and in their historical trends, the way in which the Federal Reserve System attempts to control them, and their impact on prices, unemployment, economic growth, and the balance of international payments.

Notes

1. See Board of Governors of the Federal Reserve System, *Improving the Monetary Aggregates,* Report of the Advisory Committee on Monetary Statistics (Washington, D.C., 1976), p. 1.

2. Milton Friedman and Anna J. Schwartz, *A Monetary History of the United States, 1867–1960* (Princeton: Princeton University Press, 1963), p. 708.

3. Board of Governors of the Federal Reserve System, *The Federal Reserve System: Purposes and Functions,* 6th ed. (Washington, D.C., 1974), p. 2.

4. For an interesting account of the monetary provisions in the Constitution, see Bray Hammond, *Banks and Politics in America from the Revolution to the Civil War* (Princeton: Princeton University Press, 1957), Chapter 4.

Questions

1.1 Compare *M-1A, M-1B, M-2, M-3,* and *L.*

1.2 What does *L* include?

1.3 Which is the best statistical measure of the money supply?

1.4 Explain the meaning of the circular flow of money.

1.5 What are some of the types of paper currency that have been used in the United States?

1.6 Know the meaning and significance of the following terms and concepts: monetary system, money supply, real value of money, credit, nominal interest rate, real interest rate.

a) Monetary System - the institutional arrangement for supplying the economy with money.

b). Money Supply -

c) real value of money - what a given quantity of money will purchase - it varies w/ prices.

d) Nominal interest Rate. rate actually paid on certain types of loans

<u>See page. 12.</u>

2

Money is used as a unit of account, medium of exchange, store of value, and standard of deferred payment. The varied functions of money are important because whatever is used as money is money.

FUNCTIONS OF MONEY

The different measures of money discussed in Chapter 1 have arisen because money serves more than one function. Also, there are two distinct types of money: (1) the abstract money unit of account, and (2) money that can serve as a medium of exchange and a store of value.

The *unit of account* is used to measure the value of things—just as ounces and pounds are used to measure weight, and inches and feet to measure size. It is useful for computation and record keeping.

Coins, paper money, and demand deposits may serve as both a *medium of exchange* and a *store of value.* People use the medium of exchange to purchase the goods and services they want. They may also wish to accumulate these types of money because their nominal value is constant. Some other assets, such as time deposits and U.S. savings bonds, are similar to currency and demand deposits as stores of value because their nominal value is also constant, even though they are not part of the medium of exchange. A fourth function of money served by both the unit of account and the medium of exchange is to provide a *standard of deferred payment*—for paying debts in the future.

Money unit of account

Each country has its own unit of account. The money unit of account in the United States is the dollar; in West Germany, the deutsche mark; and in Mexico, the peso.

Having a widely accepted unit for accounting is extremely useful. By having the price of everything in dollars and cents, individuals can immediately and without effort compare values. If one item is priced at $10 and another at $5, a person knows immediately their relative cost.

Imagine an economy without a unit of account. Instead of having one price for each item expressed in terms of dollars, for example, there would be a ratio of exchange for each good and service in terms of every other good and service. If there were n number of different goods and services produced, the formula $n(n-1)/2$ gives the number of possible combinations of these goods and services taken two at a time. In a large economy, there would be so many exchange ratios that comparing the values of different goods and services would be extremely difficult. If there were only 5,000 different items produced, for example, there would be 12,497,500 possible ratios of exchange between the different goods and services.

The unit of account sometimes is different from the medium of exchange. In colonial America, the principal type of money in circulation was the Spanish peso or dollar even though the unit of account was the British pound. Officially the unit of account of the United States was changed to the dollar in 1792. The first Coinage Act passed by Congress provided for the coinage of gold eagles, half eagles, and quarter eagles (worth $10.00, $5.00, and $2.50 respectively), and silver dollars, half dollars, quarters, dimes, half dimes, copper cents, and half cents. The decimal system was an improvement over the British unit of account in

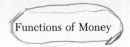
which there were 12 pence to a shilling and 20 shillings to a pound. Despite the greater convenience of the new system, customary ways of accounting were so persistent that dollars and cents were not universally used as the unit of account until after the Civil War.[1] Before that time, prices were frequently quoted in dollars and ninepence, dollars and shillings, dollars and levies, or dollars and bits. Both a levy and a bit were worth 12½ cents.

Another example occurred during a period of rapid inflation in China from 1937 to 1949, when many merchants kept their accounts in U.S. dollars but used Chinese currency to make transactions.[2] There were two prices for everything, one expressed in terms of the dollar unit of account and the other in terms of the Chinese money in circulation. The dollar prices in the merchants' accounts were relatively constant; the transactions prices in Chinese currency rose daily. Prices in Chinese currency were calculated by applying the daily exchange rate between the yen and the dollar to a price in U.S. dollars on their books. The exchange rate between the yen and the dollar rose continuously as a result of the rapid inflation. Separating the unit of account and the medium of exchange in this manner was an ingenious way of adjusting to rapid inflation. The prices expressed in Chinese currency of inputs used in production were no longer useful for accounting purposes because the value of different inputs depended on *when* the inputs were purchased.

In recent years, most countries that had nondecimal units of account have changed to a decimal system. The cost of converting to a decimal system is high; in Australia in 1966 the conversion was reported to have cost nearly $100 million. The advantage of a decimal system is that computations are simpler. Before Great Britain converted to a decimal system in 1971, a person might have been faced with adding, for example, 1 pound, 6 shillings, and 3 pence to 2 pounds, 13 shillings, and 9 pence (the sum: 4 pounds).

Monetary reforms and the unit of account

After World War II, many countries enacted monetary reforms and exchanged old bank notes and deposits for new ones with a substantially reduced nominal monetary value.[3] In the South Korean monetary reform of 1953, for example, the conversion ratio was 100 to 1. One hundred old *won* were exchanged for one new *hwan.* The principal objectives of the South Korean reform were to slow down the rate of inflation and to reduce all prices to more reasonable levels. As in some other monetary reforms, a portion of the money supply was removed from circulation and put in "blocked accounts." Persons retained their blocked holdings, but could not use them to purchase goods and services.

In a monetary reform in the Soviet Union in 1960, all circulating ruble bills were called in and replaced by new ruble bills at a ratio of 10 to 1. Prices of goods sold in the state stores were also reduced to one-tenth their former level. The *New York Times* reported that the new price of a Volga automobile was 4,500 rubles. Before the reform, the price of the same vehicle would have been 45,000 rubles.[4] The purpose of this reform was primarily to simplify the unit of account and perhaps also to put an end to the gains made by black-market operators. In the decade prior to 1960, the Soviets had little inflation, and stabilization was not a problem.

Money medium of exchange

Instead of using money, people could exchange directly the goods and services they have produced for the goods and services they want to consume. However, in specialized economies, barter is rare. It takes too much time and effort to find persons who both have what you want and want what you have to trade. There would be less trade in a system of barter. A barter exchange won't occur unless a person is better off with the goods he gets than with the goods he gives up. In contrast, monetary exchange occurs whenever a person believes there is something that he can purchase with the money received that he prefers to the goods he has sold. If barter were the only type of trade possible, there would be many situations in which people would not be able to obtain the goods and services that they wanted most.[5] The advantage of the use of money is that it provides the owner with *generalized* purchasing power. The use of money gives the owner flexibility over the type and quantities of goods he buys, the time and place of his purchases, and the parties with whom he chooses to deal.

The usefulness of a money medium of exchange increases as trade becomes more highly developed and industry more specialized. If family units are self-sufficient, there is little trade and little need for currency or checking accounts in banks. In colonial America, when most families were engaged in farming, there was much less need for a medium of exchange than there is today. As commerce and industry have developed, work has become increasingly specialized; most persons are now employees who receive their wages in currency or in checks which they put in their bank accounts. They then use the money that they have received to purchase whatever goods and services they consume.

Even in primitive societies, a medium of exchange is used if agriculture is specialized. In the Quiche Indian communities of Guatemala, some farmers grow corn, others cabbage, others onions, and others grow still different crops. On market day, usually once a week, the farmers bring their produce to market. Each farmer sells for money what he produces and then uses the money he has received to purchase what he wants. Before the arrival of the Spanish in the New World, cacao beans were used as money;[6] today, the Indians use paper money issued by the central bank in Guatemala.

An essential characteristic of a medium of exchange is that it be acceptable. It must be readily exchangeable for other things. It is usual for the government to designate certain coins or paper currency as the medium of exchange, but people have to agree on the designated medium, because unless everyone accepts it, it will not serve its purpose. Once a particular medium of exchange has been used for a long time, its acceptability becomes very firmly established.

Barter

When inflation is rapid, the use of the medium of exchange becomes very costly because the real value of money falls as prices rise. Using the customary medium of exchange is still usually preferred to barter or possibly shifting to some other medium of exchange. In Chile, for example, even though the average annual rate of inflation from 1931 to 1955 was 20 percent (at this rate of inflation, the cost of holding $100 throughout the year would be $20), Chileans still used their official currency and demand deposits at their banks. At a very high rate of inflation, it may be preferable to trade by barter or to shift to some other medium of exchange rather than to use a depreciating currency. However, the rate of inflation necessary to induce people to discard an established currency is not often reached. People are reluctant to shift to another medium of exchange because it is difficult to get agreement on what to shift to, and it takes time for a new medium of exchange to become generally acceptable.

In some countries, the preference of the public for barter over the use of money has resulted primarily from price controls rather than from rapid inflation. This was the situation in Germany from 1946 to 1948, just after World War II. Between 1936 (when the government put ceilings on prices) and 1947, the quantity of money increased approximately ten times. There was an oversupply of money compared to goods valued at their fixed 1936 prices. Under such conditions, business firms frequently had to exchange commodities for commodities in order to get the materials they needed, and there was considerable barter between urban and rural workers.[7]

It is common, but erroneous, to attribute the collapse of a monetary system during rapid inflation to the inconvenience of having to use bales of paper bills to make a purchase. Stories are told about merchants having to carry paper money in baskets or wheelbarrows. Such situations are actually quite rare. As inflation progresses, most governments simply issue paper notes in larger denominations. The possible inconvenience of having to use large quantities of bills of small denominations does not arise.

Even in countries in which most trade is carried on with money, there are often some examples of barter. A store that gives employees a discount on goods purchased or a school that gives teachers' children free tuition is giving employees a wage supplement in kind that is a type of barter. Although one purpose of such payments is to strengthen employee morale, payments in kind are also usually omitted from taxable income. There has recently been wide interest in the extent to which sectors of the U.S. economy avoid monetary transactions and thus evade taxation and government regulations.

Rationing

A possible alternative to either the use of money or barter is to pay persons in ration coupons—or for the government to distribute ration coupons to everyone, entitling them to certain quantities of specific items. Retail stores would then trade goods for ration coupons rather than money. As a practical matter, it would be difficult to distribute ration coupons for every possible item produced in a complex modern society. Another disadvantage to rationing is that it limits people's choice. Some persons would prefer a different group of commodities from those allocated to them.

Under the systems of rationing that existed in many countries during World War II, people had to pay both the governmentally controlled price in money and the requisite number of coupons in order to purchase rationed items. This arrangement made it possible for a government to control the availability of scarce goods in two ways—by changing the controlled price or by changing the rationed allotment.

In socialist ideology, the elimination of the use of money is an important goal. Although the Soviet Union experimented extensively with rationing during its first Five-Year Plan from 1928 through 1932, the Russian leaders completely discarded rationing in 1935.[8] This has led some socialist writers to accuse the Soviet Union's leadership of betraying the socialist ideal; even some leaders in the Soviet Union view their use of money as a temporary retreat.[9] Although the use of money in the Soviet Union now appears to be no different than in capitalist countries, there are actually significant differences. Journalists have reported that having money is not nearly as important in the Soviet Union as in most other countries, even though people must carry large amounts of currency with them at all times in case they have the opportunity to use it.[10] Not everyone has access to the better stores reserved for the elite (and the better housing, good schools, vacation resorts, or opportunity to travel), and many household items are frequently out of stock in the regular retail outlets where most persons must shop.

Demand deposits as a medium of exchange

In the United States, the most important type of money used to make transactions has become bank accounts called demand deposits. Demand deposits now make up more than 70 percent of *M-1A* and *M-1B*. The use of demand deposit accounts as money is a vast bookkeeping system. More than fourteen thousand commercial banks keep the books. If you have a demand deposit of $100, this is recorded on the books of your bank, and if you write a check for $10 and give it to Mr. Smith, your bank reduces by $10 the amount of your account, and Mr. Smith's bank increases his account by $10. Note that the term "deposit" is misleading. A demand deposit is no more than an account on the books of the bank. It does not represent anything deposited (and physically stored) at the bank.

A principal reason for demand deposits having become the principal medium of exchange is that demand deposits are safer to use than currency. Currency has to be stored, and it can be stolen. Also, checks are a relatively safe method of making payments by mail because they are valueless until endorsed; they are convenient because they can be written for the exact amount of the payment and they provide a record of expenditures. Checks on demand deposits are especially convenient as a method of payment for large transactions.

In Great Britain, until 1960 the use of checks was somewhat limited by a curious law that made it illegal for employers to pay their employees by check. Instead, payment had to be made in coin and currency. This law was part of the Truck Act of 1831 and was designed to prevent types of payment that might require workers to cash their checks and trade at a company store.[11]

Demand deposits have not always been considered part of the medium of exchange. Fifty years ago, economists defined money solely in terms of coins and paper currency. Even as late as 1930, when John Maynard Keynes, the leading economist of his day, included demand deposits as money in his *Treatise on Money*, H. Parker Willis, an older professor at Columbia University, was critical.[12] Demand deposits are now considered to be money because they are, in fact, used to buy goods and services. Economists have a functional conception of money: whatever is used as money is money. The public's use of demand deposits as money is not based on authorization by the federal government. Instead, demand deposits became money through common usage. Even today, legal tender—the kind of money that may be offered legally in payment of a debt and which the government will always accept in payment of taxes—does not include demand deposits. In practice, this is unimportant because demand deposits may be immediately converted into coins and paper currency that are legal tender.

Although demand deposits are now the predominant medium of exchange in the United States, they are still not as acceptable as currency because a person accepting a check usually does not know for sure that the deposit behind it is large enough to cover it. Because of this uncertainty, it is surprising that checks are accepted as readily as they are. The way in which our legal system protects those who accept checks has facilitated their use. It is a criminal offense for a person to pay for goods by check knowing that there is nothing behind the check and intending not to pay for the goods. As a criminal offense, the cost of prosecution is borne by the government rather than by the person who has been defrauded. For conviction, it is necessary to prove that fraud was intended. This is usually not too difficult to do. If, upon appropriate notice by the merchant, the purchaser does not attempt to make good the payment, evidence of intent to defraud is usually considered to exist. In countries that do not have laws of this type, checks and checking accounts are not widely used.

A check may be made more acceptable by having it certified. When a check is certified, an officer of the bank acknowledges that the bank has transferred the amount of the check from the account of the person involved to an account for certified checks. Some businesses, such as interstate trucking companies, do not wish to become involved in delays or problems of check collection, and will accept checks only if they are certified. Certified checks are also useful for international transactions.

Money as a store of value

When viewed as a store of value, currency and demand deposits cannot be sharply separated from savings and time deposits, U.S. savings bonds, short-term marketable U.S. government securities, short-term securities issued by business firms, and several other types of liquid assets. These assets also have either fixed nominal values or nominal values that vary only slightly. They can also be redeemed or sold quickly and at little cost.

The three statistical measures of the money stock that include liquid assets in addition to currency and demand deposits are M-2, M-3, and L. As shown in Table 2.1, L amounted to $1.9 trillion in December 1978. Savings and small-denomination time deposits in commercial banks and in thrift institutions—mutual savings banks, savings and loan associations, and credit unions—are the most important type of liquid asset and account for more than half of the total amount.

U.S. savings bonds are included in liquid assets because there is never the possibility of a loss in nominal terms; they may be redeemed quickly and without any redemption fee after they have been held for six months. The old Series E and the new Series EE savings bonds, which appreciate between the date of purchase and the date of maturity, have a redemption schedule showing the exact cash value of the bond for each six-month interval after the date of purchase. The old Series H and

Table 2.1
Private Liquid Assets, L,
December 1978 (not
seasonally adjusted)

Type	Amount in billions	Percent of Total
Currency, demand deposits, and other checkable deposits	$ 369.2	19.1%
Savings deposits	472.8	24.5
Small-denomination time deposits (in amounts less than $100,000)	529.8	27.4
Large-denomination time deposits (in amounts of $100,000 or more)	198.2	10.2
Overnight *RPs* and overnight Eurodollars	23.3	1.2
Money market mutual funds	10.3	.5
Term *RPs* and term Eurodollars	49.5	2.6
U.S. savings bonds	80.6	4.2
Short-term U.S. Treasury securities	98.4	5.1
Commercial paper	79.4	4.1
Bankers' acceptances	20.8	1.1
Total liquid assets	$1,932.3	100.0%

Source: *Federal Reserve Bulletin*, March 1980, p. A14; and Banking Section, Division of Research and Statistics, Board of Governors of the Federal Reserve System.

the new Series HH savings bonds, which pay the owner interest every six months, may be redeemed for their purchase price at any time after the minimum waiting period.

Short-term marketable U.S. government securities—those that had a maturity of one year or less at the time they were initially sold by the United States Treasury, and also those issues that originally had a longer maturity but have come to within one year of their maturity date—are liquid, even though they are marketable and their prices may vary. As will be explained in Chapter 4, the prices of short-term securities change very little because of the short period of time to their maturity date. Drawing a sharp line between those securities that have less than one year to maturity and those that have just slightly more than one year to maturity has little justification except that a line must be drawn somewhere.

Other important liquid assets include large-denomination time deposits, commercial paper, and bankers acceptances. Although large-denomination time deposits usually cannot be turned in for cash until their maturity date, some types can be sold. If interest rates have risen since the time they were issued, they have to be sold at a discount. However, they are still considered liquid. Because of their short maturity, the amount of the discount will be very small. Commercial paper (a type of short-term obligation of business corporations) and bankers acceptances (a short-term security related to international trade) are both similar to short-term marketable U.S. government securities and have approximately the same liquidity. Eurodollar deposits, *RPs*, and shares in money market mutual funds have grown in importance as types of liquid assets in recent years. Overnight *RP*s, overnight Eurodollars, and shares in money market mutual funds are as liquid as savings and small-denomination time deposits.

Many forms of wealth are not liquid—corporation stocks and bonds, municipal bonds, longer-term marketable U.S. government securities, and physical assets such as homes, farms, and other real estate. Corporation stock, if listed on one of the national exchanges, or if important enough to be traded frequently over the counter, can be sold quickly, but the price is uncertain. Longer-term marketable bonds—federal, municipal, or corporate—are also uncertain as to price. Bonds of solvent firms eventually have a maturity date at which they are worth their par value. But if the owner wishes to sell them prior to their maturity dates, he must take whatever he can get in the market. Houses and farms are very illiquid types of assets. It usually takes time to find a buyer, the cost of the transaction through a real estate agent is high, and the price is uncertain.

Liquid assets

Many types of liquid assets earn interest—but usually not the high rates of return that are typically received by investors in illiquid assets such as stocks, bonds, or real estate. Nevertheless, a certain amount of liquidity is so useful for emergencies—such as loss of job, sickness, or an automobile accident— that people are willing to hold part of their wealth in liquid assets. The rapid growth of time deposits in commercial banks, mutual savings banks, and savings and loan associations shows that people want to hold considerable amounts of liquid assets.

Liquidity is especially important to persons in business. Managing a business is unavoidably risky and having a sizable stock of liquid assets is necessary in order to meet contingencies such as unexpected increases in costs or disappointing sales. The balance sheets of most large corporations list relatively large amounts of liquid assets—mainly consisting of short-term marketable government securities or certificates of deposit, both of which earn interest.

When there are erratic and unexpected changes in the rate of inflation, the types of liquid assets listed in Table 2.1 do not serve well as stores of value. Although interest rates on interest-earning liquid assets tend to rise when the rate of inflation increases, persons who purchased liquid assets when rates of interest were lower prior to the acceleration in the rate of inflation would incur real losses. When the rate of inflation in a country is unstable, persons and business firms typically hold foreign currencies rather than liquid assets denominated in their own currency, or they hoard commodities such as gold and other metals. As reserves, commodities are not perfectly liquid or very reliable; but when inflation is unstable, they may be better to hold than liquid assets.

Money as a standard of deferred payment

Its use as a standard of deferred payment is a fourth function of money. This function involves the use of money both as a unit of account and as a medium of exchange. Debts are almost always stated in terms of the country's unit of account and paid off with the country's money medium of exchange. For example, both the periodic interest payments on a bond issued by a corporation in the United States and the redemption of the bond at par on its maturity date are normally made in the form of a check on a demand deposit denominated in dollars.

Under inflationary conditions, lenders may attempt to protect themselves by discarding the use of the money of their own country as a standard of deferred payment. If a creditor expects inflation, but is uncertain about how much inflation to expect, he may attempt to protect himself by requiring that the debtor pay off his debt in the money of a country that has a more stable currency, in gold, or even in commodities. In 1977, Congress enacted legislation allowing contracts based on gold prices or that call for payment in foreign currencies. There had been a federal ban on contracts tied to the price of gold ever since 1933, and the Supreme Court had prohibited contracts calling for payment in foreign money in 1938. It is still not known to what extent business firms have taken advantage of the broader types of contracts now allowed. Another more common way for lenders of money to protect themselves from rapidly rising prices is to use escalator clauses linking debt to a price index. In this case, although the amount of the debt would rise as fast as prices, lenders would still use the money of their own country as a standard of deferred payment.

Motives for holding money

Underlying the different functions of money are the different motives that people have for holding it. The famous British economist John Maynard Keynes had a threefold classification of motives—*transactions, precautionary,* and *speculative.* The same dollar held may serve all three of these purposes. Yet the differences are sufficiently distinct to warrant separate treatment.

The transactions motive results in the use of money as a medium of exchange. People need money to handle ordinary transactions and are seriously inconvenienced if they do not have money available. The amount of money needed for transactions depends in part on the volume of the purchases made. In addition, the frequency—whether weekly, monthly, or quarterly—of income received makes a difference. The more frequent the payments, the smaller the average cash balance that must be on hand to finance transactions. Regularity of payments is also important. The more certainly that one can count on receipts and payments, the less money one needs to hold.

The precautionary motive for holding money is related to the liquidity of money and the use of money as a store of value. When prices are stable, money gives people a type of protection, as insurance does, against some types of risks. Business firms also have many needs for liquidity. The amount of money held as a precaution will depend on the likelihood of future need for it. That likelihood depends significantly on the stability of the economy.

Money is also held because it provides people with the liquidity needed to shift readily to other assets. This is referred to as the speculative motive for holding money because it involves outguessing movements in the prices of securities or goods. If a person expects the prices of goods to fall, he may build up his money balances so as to take advantage of the lower prices in the future. If people expect interest rates to rise (and bond prices to fall), they will tend to build up their money balances so as to be in a position to purchase bonds when their prices reach bottom. On the other hand, if they expect interest rates to fall (and bond prices to rise), the speculative demand for money will be relatively small.

Summary

One reason money is difficult to define is that it has different functions. Some economists have based their definition primarily on the conception of money as a medium of exchange—as something to be used in trade. Others have emphasized primarily the accounting function—that it is the unit in which prices are expressed. Still others have conceived of money more broadly as any highly liquid asset with a relatively fixed nominal value. From this point of view, it is considered important that money may be used to pay off a definite amount of debt without delay. There is still a difference of opinion concerning the relative importance of the various functions of money.

Notes

1. Horace White, *Money and Banking* (Boston: Ginn and Company, 1896), p. 15.

2. Colin D. Campbell and Gordon C. Tullock, "Hyperinflation in China, 1937–49," *Journal of Political Economy* 62 (June 1954), pp. 236–245. For examples from the history of Western Europe, see Carlo M. Cipolla, *Money, Prices, and Civilization in the Mediterranean World* (Princeton, N.J.: Princeton University Press, 1956), pp. 38–51.

3. There were twenty-four monetary reforms in Europe from 1944 to 1952. See John G. Gurley, "Excess Liquidity and European Monetary Reforms, 1944 to 1952," *American Economic Review* 43 (March 1953), pp. 76–100.

4. Osgood Caruthers, "Russians Queue Up at Banks to Trade Old Rubles for New," *New York Times*, 3 January 1961, p. 9.

5. See J. Huston McCulloch, *Money and Inflation, A Monetarist Approach* (New York: Academic Press, 1975), pp. 1–7; and Armen A. Alchian, "Why Money?" *Journal of Money, Credit and Banking* (Feb. 1977), pp. 133–140, for discussions of the inadequacy of barter trade.

6. Thomas Gann, *Glories of the Maya* (New York: Charles Scribner's Sons, 1939), p. 98; and Sol Tax, *Penny Capitalism, A Guatemalan Indian Economy* (Washington, D.C.: U.S. Government Printing Office, 1953).

7. Horst Mendershausen, "Prices, Money, and the Distribution of Goods in Postwar Germany," *American Economic Review* 39 (June 1949), pp. 646–672.

8. Leonard E. Hubbard, *Soviet Money and Finance* (London: Macmillan, 1936), pp. 118–121.

9. See the last work of J. Stalin, *The Economic Problems of Socialism in the U.S.S.R.* (New York: International Publishers, 1952), pp. 16–17.

10. Hedrick Smith, *The Russians* (New York: Quadrangle, 1976), pp. 8, 62.

11. George W. Hilton, *The Truck System* (Cambridge, England: W. Heffer and Sons, 1960), pp. 150–152; and "Wages by Cheque?" *Economist*, 14 June 1958, Banking Supplement, pp. 15–16.

12. *New York Times*, 22 March 1931, Section IV, p. 10.

Questions

2.1. Compare (a) the money unit of account and the medium of exchange, and (b) the medium of exchange and money as a store of value.

2.2. How would a monetary reform affect the money unit of account, and why might this be desirable?

2.3. Explain the advantages of using money as a medium of exchange over barter or the use of ration coupons.

2.4. Will people stop using money as a medium of exchange if they expect prices to rise rapidly? Explain.

2.5. Why do merchants in the United States readily accept checks on demand deposits?

2.6. Compare the relative advantages and disadvantages of demand deposits and time deposits as a store of value.

2.7. Why do persons desire to hold not only stocks and bonds but also some money and various types of liquid assets?

2.8. How would you expect a rapid rate of inflation to affect the use of liquid assets as a store of value?

2.9. Is L a good statistical measure of the total amount of assets that serve as a monetary store of value? Explain.

2.10. Compare the transactions, precautionary, and speculative motives for holding money.

2.11. How would you define money?

2.12. Know the meaning and significance of the following terms and concepts: unit of account, medium of exchange, standard of deferred payment, monetary reform, barter, rationing, legal tender, illiquid and liquid assets.

3

For many types of transactions, people still customarily use currency rather than checks written on checking accounts. In recent years, currency in circulation has gained in relative importance. Historically, the use of currency has declined relative to the use of deposits.

CURRENCY

Many persons think of money as consisting of currency—*coins* and *paper money*. The use of currency as money has a long and interesting history, but is today less important than the use of deposit money created by the commercial banking system. The commercial banking system and the nature of the deposits it creates are explained in Chapters 5 through 9.

The early use of coins and paper money

Coins were used much earlier in history than paper money.[1] The use of coins is believed to have originated independently in both China and the ancient kingdom of Lydia in the seventh century B.C. In approximately 500 B.C. the famous Persian King Darius revolutionized the economy of his empire by adopting the use of coins as a substitute for barter. Evidence of this change has been found in the well-preserved inscriptions and rock carvings in Persepolis in Iran.[2]

Paper money in the form of warehouse receipts was first used in the eighth century in China—where printing with movable blocks was invented in about 50 B.C., and paper was first manufactured in approximately 100 A.D., both necessary to the manufacture of paper currency. The warehouse receipts were either for valuables deposited at special shops for safekeeping, for which a fee was charged, or for taxes that were paid in kind and held on deposit in a provincial center rather than being shipped to the capital. Visitors to China during the twelfth and thirteenth centuries were impressed by the use of paper money. Marco Polo regarded "the coinage of this paper money" as a novel way of doing what the alchemists had tried.[3] In the thirteenth century, counterfeiting paper money in China was a capital offense, and the government of Genghis Khan readily exchanged the paper notes for gold and silver. By the year 1500, government units in China had given up the issuance of paper money because of difficulties with oversupply and inflation, but private banks continued to issue it.

In Europe during the Middle Ages, there were important developments in banking and credit in the large trading centers of Florence, Venice, Genoa, Constantinople, and Bruges. However, they did not use paper money, even though banks transferred funds by means of letters of exchange, and extended credit in the form of delayed payments. It is believed that paper currency was first used in Europe in the seventeenth century, a development contemporary with the establishment of early commercial banks in Sweden and Great Britain.

Paper money was used quite early by settlers in the New World. In 1685, the French colonists in Canada used playing cards carrying official seals and signatures to alleviate a critical shortage of coins. In the eighteenth century, paper money was issued in most of the American colonies.

Since 1793, when the first United States mint was established in Philadelphia, the Bureau of the Mint has been supplying the country with coins. The very early American colonists had few coins and often used commodities, such as furs and tobacco, as the medium of exchange. Any British coins the colonists had were usually soon sent back to Britain to pay for imported supplies. There was quite early a favorable trade balance with the Spanish colonies, which caused an inflow of Spanish pesos, and in some colonies the legal exchange rates were raised to attract Spanish coins.[4] The colonists called the Spanish pesos, most of which were minted in Mexico City and Lima, dollars, probably because they were similar in size to the German *thaler*. Even during the first half of the nineteenth century, a substantial volume of foreign coins circulated alongside the domestically produced coins, and certain types of foreign coins were not deprived of their legal status as money until 1857.

Gresham's law

This law is helpful in explaining some of the early monetary problems of the United States, as well as some of our recent difficulties with coins. The usual statement of this law, "Bad money drives out good," is neither clear nor precise. A better statement is the following: "*Money that has value in a nonmonetary use (including use as money in another country) will tend to move, if it is free to do so, to the use (monetary or nonmonetary) in which its value is the higher.*"[5] The principle of basing a system of coinage on *token coins*—their metal content is worth less than their nominal value—is based on this law. Also, the importation into the United States of foreign coins in the first half of the nineteenth century is an example of the operation of this law. They were imported because their value as a circulating medium was higher in the United States than in the issuing country.

Gresham's Law also explains why the bimetallic standard established in the United States under the American Coinage Act of 1792 did not work. The dollar was made equivalent both to 371.25 grains of fine silver and to 24.75 grains of fine gold, a mint ratio of 15 to 1. Over time, changes in the supply of and demand for the two metals inevitably caused the ratio between the world market prices to be different from the established mint ratio. With a bimetallic standard and a fixed official ratio, whenever the price ratio in the world market differs from the official domestic price ratio, one of the two metals will necessarily be more valuable in a monetary use than the other. This makes the exportation of either silver or gold from the bimetallic country a profitable undertaking, and the bimetallic country sooner or later finds itself with only one metal. From 1792 to 1834, for example, the *market ratio* between silver and gold was approximately 15½ to 1. Since the official ratio in the United States was 15 to 1, silver was overvalued. Under these conditions, relatively little gold would be brought to the mint; it was shipped to foreign countries where its price was higher—in foreign countries it was possible to get 15½ ounces of silver, rather than 15 ounces, for 1 ounce of gold. During this period the United States was actually on a silver standard. In 1834, the official mint ratio was changed to 16 to 1. The market ratio was still nearer 15½ to 1. The official ratio now overvalued gold and created a de facto gold standard. When the official ratio overvalued gold, its value in monetary use exceeded its value in nonmonetary uses. The opposite was true for silver money, which tended to disappear from circulation under these circumstances.

Token coins

The only full-bodied coins in circulation today are ones minted many years ago. It may seem surprising, but an essential requirement of a good system of coinage is that the coins produced by the mints be token coins rather than full-bodied ones. If full-bodied, a rise in the price of the metal in the coins would cause them to be worth more as metal than the nominal value stamped on them. Even for coins that were originally token coins, if the metal in them is not worth substantially less than their nominal value, a sharp rise in the price of the metal can cause them to become worth more as metal than their face value. When this occurs, coins are hoarded and disappear from circulation, they are melted down or exported, the public is often inconvenienced by a shortage of coins, and new types of coins must be produced.

In the early history of the United States, the mints produced full-bodied coins. The weight, thickness, and metallic content of these coins were carefully watched, and some had special edges that made it difficult to shave off tiny amounts. Most of the early full-bodied coins were exported by individuals for profit, and the coins that remained in circulation consisted of a confusing variety of foreign coins. During the first half of the nineteenth century, small coins were sometimes in such short supply that postage stamps had to be used for change. These difficulties were the result of the fact that producing coins with a metallic content worth less than their nominal value was widely viewed at that time as defrauding the public. It was felt that the Treasury ought not to make a profit—called *seigniorage*—on the manufacture of coins. In 1853, these problems disappeared when Congress authorized the mint to produce token coins. This simple change is considered an important development in the history of money in the United States.[6]

Pressure for silver coinage, 1873–1900

Coinage was a major political issue in the last three decades of the nineteenth century. The Coinage Act of 1873 demonetized silver by replacing the bimetallic standard with the gold standard. The act did not provide for the minting of any standard silver dollars containing a dollar's worth of silver, but only for the minting of "trade dollars" whose silver content was similar to that of half dollars, quarters, and dimes. Thus silver was to be used for token coins but not as a standard of value. Originally, silver producers did not object because they were not interested in selling to the mint when prices were higher in the free market. Shortly thereafter, however, the attitude of the silver producers changed when increased supplies of silver from domestic and foreign mines—and the decreased demand when many countries shifted to the gold standard—drove the market price of silver down.

Only small amounts of silver were needed for the minting of token coins, and people began to agitate for free and unlimited coinage of silver. The passage of the Coinage Act of 1873 was attributed to a conspiracy and labeled the "Crime of '73." With the help of such slogans, logrolling by Western legislators, and popular support for measures that might reverse the long decline in prices, Congress passed several silver purchase bills. Under the Bland-Allison Act of 1878, $2 million of silver had to be purchased each month at the market price. Not all of the large amount acquired was coined. It was also held in vaults and used as the legally required reserve for silver certificates.

Under the Sherman Silver Purchase Act of 1890, the United States Treasury had to purchase a specified number of ounces of silver each month rather than $2 million worth, and this initially provided a large increase in revenues for silver producers. To pay for the silver purchased under the Act, Congress authorized the Treasury to issue "Treasury notes of 1890" that were redeemable in either gold or silver. Because of alarming gold drains and other financial difficulties associated with the Panic of 1893, the Sherman Silver Purchase Act was repealed in late 1893. The Treasury notes of 1890 were later retired and replaced with silver certificates.

In the bitter presidential campaign of 1896, William Jennings Bryan advocated free (unlimited) coinage of silver; it was to be purchased at a ratio very favorable to silver producers (16 to 1 at a time when the market ratio was 30 to 1). Such a price at the mints for silver undoubtedly would have meant a large increase in this type of money. Bryan was defeated by William McKinley, who ran on a platform favoring a gold standard. Improved economic conditions just before the turn of the century decreased the popular appeal of government purchases of silver. Also, gold discoveries and the increased output of gold set the stage for passage of the Gold Standard Act in 1900.

Our paper money

During the Civil War, the issuance by the Treasury of U.S. notes, popularly called "greenbacks," was an important event in the financial history of the United States. Between 1781 (when the printing of Continental currency was terminated) and 1861, no paper money was issued by the United States government; the paper money in use during this period was issued by private banks.

United States notes

The issuance of U.S. notes is an example of financing government operations by means of the printing press. Unlike the paper notes issued by private banks, they were initially not redeemable in specie. Between the outbreak of the Civil War in 1861 and its end in 1865, only 21 percent of the federal government's expenditures were financed by taxes. The rest had to be financed either by money creation or by borrowing. When the war ended in 1865, the dollar volume of U.S. notes was so large that they constituted almost half the total amount of currency in circulation. In the North, both the total money stock and prices rose approximately 2.3 times from 1861 to 1865.[7]

In the South, tax revenues were even less adequate than in the North; the Confederacy also had to issue large quantities of paper money as a method of government finance. From January 1861 to January 1864, the amount of Confederate money issued increased almost twelve times, and prices rose twenty-eight times.[8] In February 1864, the Confederate Congress enacted a currency reform, exchanging the old currency for a smaller amount of new currency and eliminating about one-third of the total amount in circulation. They still had to continue financing the war mainly by money creation, and the reform did not stabilize prices. From January 1861 to April 1865, prices in the South rose more than 92 times. After the war, the Confederate issues were worthless and disappeared from circulation.

During the late 1860s and the 1870s, there was considerable political controversy over whether the volume of greenbacks was excessive and whether they were legal tender. When the Treasury originally issued them, U.S. notes were not redeemable in gold by either the Treasury or the banks. After the Civil War, most persons considered the redeemability of these notes an important goal and regarded the contraction of their volume as necessary to achieve this. In 1866, Congress authorized the retirement of $10 million in greenbacks per month for six months and thereafter $4 million per month. Those burdened by the falling price level, such as farmers, soon opposed this currency contraction. By 1868, when Congress suspended the retirement of greenbacks, the volume had been reduced to $356 million from its wartime peak of $449 million. In later years, during periods of crisis, Secretaries of the Treasury temporarily reissued greenbacks, claiming that they were a reserve that could be drawn on. Controversies raged on both this and the question of whether Congress could legally decree that creditors must accept greenbacks in payment for debts contracted before the greenbacks were issued, or even after they were issued. There resulted numerous court decisions, new laws, and proposed laws. Even though the output of goods in the United States rose rapidly from the Civil War to 1897, the price decline during most of this period had an uneven effect on people and caused some unrest.

The period in which U.S. notes were unredeemable lasted until 1879, when the Specie Resumption Act of 1875 authorized the Treasury to redeem these notes in gold. The 1875 Act also provided that the Treasury reduce greenbacks in circulation by $4 every time there was a $5 increase in national bank notes, but this was ended three years later— about the time a new political group called the Greenback Party polled 10 percent of the votes and won fourteen seats in Congress. When U.S. notes were made redeemable in gold, the United States was said to have shifted from a paper standard to a gold standard. Under the paper standard, the price of an ounce of gold in terms of greenbacks varied. Because gold was used as foreign exchange to purchase goods from other countries, this meant that the price of foreign exchange also varied. During this period, exchange rates were uncontrolled and flexible. After 1879 the price of an ounce of gold was fixed at $20.67 and the Treasury stood ready to convert U.S. notes or other types of currency into gold at that price, ending the period of flexible exchange rates.

U.S. notes are still being issued by the U.S. Treasury. In March 1979, there were only $313 million notes of this type in circulation.

Federal Reserve notes

The authority to issue Federal Reserve notes, the principal type of paper money now in use, was granted by the Federal Reserve Act of 1913, the same act that established the Federal Reserve banks. Federal Reserve notes are liabilities of those banks. Since the establishment of the Federal Reserve System, most types of U.S. paper money that were formerly used—gold certificates, national bank notes, and silver certificates—have, one after the other, been added to the list of currencies in process of retirement. The only paper money other than Federal Reserve notes still being issued is a small quantity of United States notes. The paper money in almost all countries is today issued by their central banks.

Difficulties with coins in the last two decades

Beginning in 1959, there were frequent shortages of coins in the United States.[9] Merchants were sometimes unable to get the quantity of coins they wanted from banks—particularly around Christmas. Merchants who were unable to obtain the quantity of coins they needed from banks were willing to buy them from coin dealers at more than their face value.

The shortages were caused partly by increases in the price of silver and copper and partly by an unexpected increase in the demand for coins in the 1960s. In September 1963, the price of silver in the open market rose to $1.29 an ounce, the market value of the silver content of standard silver dollars and of the silver held as a reserve for the silver certificates that were then still in use. From 1963 to 1967, the Treasury had to sell silver to prevent the price of silver from rising above $1.29. This was done to discourage people from redeeming silver certificates for silver. It was also done to discourage hoarding of silver coins before Congress authorized new coinage and to give the mints time to manufacture enough new coins. Even though the old dimes and quarters had a lower proportion of silver than had silver dollars, if the price of silver had risen above $1.38 an ounce, they would have become worth more as silver than as coins. The Coinage Acts of 1965 and 1970 authorized the mints to produce new dimes and quarters made of copper and nickel to replace the old silver coins and to produce silverless half-dollars and dollars. In other countries, too, when the price of silver has risen sharply, recoinage has been necessary.[10]

Coinage problems occurred again in the United States for a brief period in 1973–74, when sharply rising copper prices caused hoarding and a shortage of pennies. The copper in the penny was as valuable as the coin itself when the price of copper rose above $1.51 per pound. After reaching a record of $1.52 per pound in early 1974, the price of copper dropped sharply later in the year. During the penny shortage, the Treasury Department set a maximum penalty of $10,000 and five years in prison for melting pennies or exporting them. The director of the mint also offered an Exceptional Public Service Certificate to persons bringing $25 worth of pennies to a bank. Although more than thirty million pennies a day were produced by the mints, speculation that they might be worth more as metal doubled the demand for them. In 1976, a Treasury report suggested that serious consideration be given to the elimination of the penny from our coinage system because of the high cost of producing pennies and their diminished utility. The ban on the melting of pennies was ended in 1978.

Between 1941 and 1959, the ratio of the dollar value of coins in circulation to the GNP had fallen 17 percent. The Bureau of the Mint had expected the decline in the relative importance of coins to continue and so had decreased the number of coins minted. Shortages resulted when inventories were depleted and the mints were unable to increase the supply of coins as fast as demand increased.

Table 3.1 shows the remarkable increase in the dollar value of coins in circulation from 1945 to 1979. During the 1960s, the 160 percent increase in the dollar value of coins far exceeded the 94 percent increase in the GNP. From 1970 to 1979, the value of coins increased only

86 percent compared to an increase of 141 percent in the GNP. A principal reason for the rapid increase in the volume of coins listed as in circulation was the rise in the price of silver—which caused speculation in coins and hoarding. In addition, the demand for coins has risen because of the increased use of vending machines, telephone booths, do-it-yourself laundries, parking meters, and coin-operated amusement devices. Tollways, school lunch programs, and sales taxes have also increased the demand for coins. Higher charges associated with inflation also have increased the value of coins needed for transactions involving vending machines.

Table 3.1
Coin and Paper Money in Circulation, 1945–1979 (in billions)

December	Coin	Paper Money	Total Currency
1945	$ 1.3	$ 27.2	$ 28.5
1950	1.6	26.1	27.7
1955	1.9	29.3	31.2
1960	2.4	30.5	32.9
1965	4.0	38.1	42.1
1970	6.3	50.8	57.1
1975	9.0	77.5	86.5
1979	11.7	113.9	125.6

a Outside Treasury and Federal Reserve banks.
Source: Board of Governors of the Federal Reserve System, *Banking and Monetary Statistics, 1941–1970* (Washington, D.C., 1976), pp. 622-626; and *Treasury Bulletin*, March 1976, p. 19, and March 1980, p. 19.

Because of the coin shortage, Congress took measures to sharply increase the output of coins. For several years, the mints were operated on a three-shift schedule. Congress eventually authorized the construction of a new mint that was completed in Philadelphia in 1969.

Currency outstanding and in circulation

Table 3.2 shows the amount of currency *outstanding* and *in circulation* in March 1979. The currency outstanding was issued either by the Treasury or the Federal Reserve System. The amount in circulation consists of the total amount outstanding less that held by the Treasury and the Federal Reserve banks themselves.

Treasury currency consists primarily of coins—plus a small amount of types of paper money that are in process of retirement, and U.S. notes. When new coins are produced by the mints, they are deposited in the Federal Reserve banks and held there until commercial banks withdraw them. Table 3.2 shows that at the end of March 1979, out of the total amount of Treasury currency in existence, only $395 million was held by the Federal Reserve banks. Most of the Treasury currency is held by

Type	Total Outstanding	Treasury Cash Holdings	Held by Federal Reserve Banks	Currency in Circulation
Treasury Currency[a]	$ 12,114	$363	$395	$ 11,356
Federal Reserve Notes	100,654	22	—	100,632
Total	$112,768	$385	$395	$111,988

[a] Of the total amount of Treasury currency in circulation, $10,813 million consisted of coin, $331 million consisted of U.S. notes, and $212 million consisted of types of paper currency no longer issued.
Source: *Federal Reserve Bulletin*, May 1979, pp. A4 and A12; and *Treasury Bulletin*, May 1979, p. 16.

the public, including the commercial banks. People obtain coins and paper money by cashing deposits at commercial banks, and when commercial banks need additional coins or paper money they may order them from the Federal Reserve banks, paying for them from their checking accounts at those banks.

The Treasury currency and the Federal Reserve notes that are held by the Treasury itself are called *Treasury cash holdings* and are used to carry on the activities of the operating units of the federal government. In March 1979, Treasury cash holdings amounted to $385 million —$363 million in Treasury currency and only $22 million in Federal Reserve notes.

The total amount of currency in circulation includes Federal Reserve notes issued by the Federal Reserve banks in addition to the various types of Treasury currency. Table 3.2 shows that most of the Federal Reserve notes outstanding are in circulation.

Three items in Table 3.2 are especially important: Treasury currency outstanding, Treasury cash holdings, and currency in circulation. They are factors in the bank reserve equation discussed in Chapter 12; changes in them have significant effects on the total supply of money.

The changing status of gold

Today gold does not play an important role in our domestic monetary system. In 1979 and 1980, political and economic uncertainty throughout the world made gold an attractive store of value as compared with national currencies. Gold is also used as a commodity and is still occasionally used for settling accounts between countries.

The very large stock of gold bullion owned by the United States Treasury—valued at $11,479 million in March 1979—is stored at Fort Knox, Kentucky. From 1934 to 1971, it was valued at the official price established by Congress of $35 a fine ounce. Congress raised the official price of gold to $38 an ounce in 1972 and to $42.22 an ounce in 1973 following crises in the international foreign exchange market. Each time Congress raised the official price of gold, the dollar value of the stock of gold bullion owned by the Treasury was also increased. Since 1968, there has been a free-market price for gold in the United States in addition to the official price established by Congress. In the free market, the price of gold is determined in the same way as is the price of most other commodities—by the interaction of supply and demand. In January 1980, the free-market price of gold rose to more than $800 an ounce. At the free-market price, the value of the gold owned by the U.S. Treasury would be much larger than at its official value.

Since 1971, except for auctions of gold, the United States Treasury has not purchased or sold gold, and the physical quantity of gold owned by the United States Treasury has changed very little. The U.S. Treasury sold 750,000 ounces of gold at auction from its stockpile on January 6, 1975, at an average price of approximately $165 an ounce and an additional 500,000 ounces at approximately the same unit price on June 30, 1975. Among the buyers were U.S. and foreign individuals, firms, and banks. Foreign governments were not permitted to buy the U.S. gold offered. In 1978, the Treasury initiated a regular monthly series of gold auctions. As part of a program to support the exchange rate between the dollar and other currencies, announced by President Carter in November 1978, the amount of gold sold at the auctions was increased.

It was illegal for individuals in the United States to own gold from 1933 to 1974. In 1933, two executive orders by the President and the Secretary of the Treasury required all persons, business enterprises, and banks to sell to the Federal Reserve banks or the Treasury, at the legal price then prevailing of $20.67 an ounce, their holdings of gold bullion. Rare coins were excepted. After the Treasury acquired almost all of the gold in the country, Congress then raised the price of gold to $35 an ounce.

Since 1975, American citizens have been allowed to own gold. The United States government had long opposed the removal of the ban on private ownership of gold because it was thought that the measure would encourage speculation in the gold markets and harm the international monetary system. During the rapid inflation in 1973 and 1974, there was pressure on Congress to end the ban, because it was thought that some Americans desired to purchase gold as a hedge against inflation.

Even though individuals in the United States may now own gold, people do not use gold as a medium of exchange; and, because the price of gold varies in the same way as the prices of other commodities, it can no longer serve as a liquid asset with a value that can be counted on. For international transactions, gold continues to be an acceptable type of money even though it is no longer the most important type of international money.

Gold certificates

Gold certificates were historically a type of paper money issued by the Treasury that represented the amount of gold bullion held by the Treasury. Since 1934 when gold certificates, as well as gold bullion, owned by the public had to be sold to the United States government, no new gold certificates have been put into circulation. They are obligations of the Treasury, and currently, except for the few that were not returned to the federal government in 1934, all of the gold certificates outstanding are owned by the Federal Reserve banks.

Gold certificates have become no more than accounting entries on the books of the Treasury and the Reserve banks. In March 1979, there were $11,479 million in gold certificates outstanding, an amount just equal to the official value of the gold bullion owned by the Treasury.

From 1914, when they were first established, until 1968, the Federal Reserve banks were legally required to hold gold certificates as reserves. In 1914 the gold standard existed among the major countries of the world, and the reserves of the commercial banking systems in different countries, as well as the reserves of their central banks, were expected to vary with the inflow and outflow of gold. Until 1945, when both percentages were reduced to 25 percent, the gold reserve requirements were 40 percent for Federal Reserve notes and 35 percent for the deposit liabilities of the Federal Reserve banks. In 1965, reserve requirements were dropped for deposits in Federal Reserve banks and in 1968 the same was done for Federal Reserve notes.

Reserve requirements for Federal Reserve notes had to be reduced or eliminated in 1968 if the supply of these notes was to continue to be expanded. In the previous two decades, the amount of currency in use by the public increased on the average about 3.4 percent a year. Such a rate of growth could not be continued if Federal Reserve notes—the principal type of currency—had to be based on a fixed or diminishing amount of gold certificates. The Treasury's stock of gold on which these certificates are based had declined from more than $24 billion in 1949 to less than $11 billion in 1968.

In 1979, several large commercial banks began to issue what are called "gold certificates" in denominations of $1,000 and up. These gold certificates are different from those issued by the U.S. Treasury, despite the same name. The gold certificates issued by commercial banks are simply a receipt for the purchase of a specific quantity of gold bullion. A commercial bank may buy gold and store it for its customers. This service provides customers with a convenient way to invest in gold.

Currency in process of retirement

Silver certificates, national bank notes, and Federal Reserve bank notes (the latter are different from Federal Reserve notes) are types of currency that are no longer issued.

Silver certificates

Prior to 1961, silver certificates were important, and there was no intention of removing them from circulation. They had been issued by the Treasury in $1, $2, $5, and $10 denominations, and there was three-quarters of an ounce of silver bullion stored at West Point for each dollar in silver certificates issued.

The Treasury had used the large amounts of silver acquired in the late nineteenth century under the silver purchase acts primarily as reserves for silver certificates and also for the manufacture of silver coins. Silver bullion in excess of those needs was "free silver." In the 1930s there was again pressure to increase silver purchases to help the silver mining industry and to counteract deflationary pressures. Legislation passed in 1934 required that the United States Treasury, in order to support its price, purchase both domestic and foreign silver. Silver certificates were issued to pay for much of this silver. From 1942 up to the 1960s, the Treasury continued to purchase newly mined domestic silver in order to keep the price of silver at government support levels. In the 1960s, the free-market price of silver rose above official support levels and government purchases were no longer necessary.

In 1961, the Treasury and the Federal Reserve banks started to withdraw silver certificates in $5 and $10 denominations from circulation and to replace them with Federal Reserve notes. In June 1963, legislation was passed by Congress enabling the Federal Reserve banks to issue $1 bills, and they began issuing them by the end of the year. With this change, the entire supply of silver certificates could be replaced by Federal Reserve notes. These measures were taken to expand the stock of free silver so as to assure an adequate supply for the manufacture of silver coins. In the early 1960s, the Treasury had been forced to sell a large portion of its stock of free silver to prevent the price from rising above $1.29 an ounce.

In 1965, people began to redeem silver certificates for silver. Their disappearance from circulation was another example of Gresham's Law. They were considered more valuable used to obtain silver from the mint than they were in circulation. People wanted to hold silver because they anticipated that eventually the Treasury's stock of silver would be depleted and the Treasury would be unable to keep the price of silver from rising above $1.29 an ounce. Between 1965 and 1968, silver certificates could be sold in the free market at a premium. In 1967, the

Treasury discontinued its policy of holding the price of silver at $1.29 and announced that it would discontinue converting silver certificates into silver bullion in July 1968. The rise in the price of silver above $1.29 brought about the end of the use of silver certificates as money. The metal for which they could be redeemed was worth more than their face value. The total quantity of silver certificates in circulation declined from more than $2,370 million in 1961 to $269 million in July 1968. Since July 1968, silver certificates have been included among those types of currency in process of retirement.

National bank notes

National bank notes were initially authorized by the Currency Act of 1863, the provisions of which were clarified and strengthened by the National Bank Act of 1864. These notes were an important type of currency prior to the establishment of the Federal Reserve banks in 1914. No national bank notes have been issued since 1935. Approximately $20 million are still "in circulation," although most of them have probably been lost or are in collections.

The acts of 1863 and 1864 represented an attempt at standardizing U.S. currency. Prior to 1863, paper money in circulation consisted mostly of state bank notes issued by banks operating under state charters. State bank notes had not been satisfactory. The large number of different kinds of notes was confusing, and counterfeiting was common. Banks and many merchants had to subscribe to weekly publications which described and sometimes pictured the approximately ten thousand types of genuine bank notes that were circulating, as well as numerous fraudulent ones. In addition, notes from country banks sometimes would be refused by merchants, or would be accepted only at a discount. The acts created a Currency Bureau, run by the comptroller of the currency, that granted charters for national banks and printed notes for these banks to issue. In 1865, Congress levied a tax of 10 percent on all state bank notes issued after July 1, 1866. The objective was to drive out of business the large number of banks continuing to operate under state charters or to force them to apply for national charters. In response to this tax, most state banks did apply for national charters, and the circulation of state bank notes declined sharply.

To assure the safety of national bank notes, the national banks had to deposit, with the Office of the Comptroller of the Currency, Treasury bonds equal to 90 percent of the notes issued. In addition to this limit on the amount of notes a bank might issue, banks were not permitted to issue more notes than the amount of paid-in capital of the bank. The total volume of national bank notes was not allowed to exceed $300 million and was originally to be apportioned to states on the basis of population and business indicators. The notes were not legal tender, but could be used to pay federal taxes at par.

National bank notes were a far better type of paper currency than the state bank notes. The printing of the notes by the United States Treasury reduced the risk of counterfeiting. Each national bank was obliged to redeem the notes of any other national bank at par. The reason that national bank notes were later replaced by Federal Reserve notes is that, unlike the notes of a central bank (Federal Reserve notes), national bank notes could not be expanded rapidly in times of financial crises, when people lose confidence in bank deposits. Between the time that state bank notes were retired and the time that the Federal Reserve banks were established, national bank notes were the only bank notes issued and, together with Civil War greenbacks and silver certificates issued by the Treasury, constituted the paper currency in circulation.

Notes issued by private commercial banks, such as the national bank notes and state bank notes, are similar to demand deposits. Both their notes and their deposits were liabilities of these banks. A bank making a loan could give the borrower either its own bank notes or a deposit in return for the borrower's promissory note. The borrower could purchase whatever he desired either by spending the notes he had received or by writing a check on his new demand deposit. When the 10 percent tax was placed on state bank notes, it was expected that state banks would no longer be profitable. Most banks became national banks, and by 1868 there were only 247 state banks compared to 1,640 national banks. Within the decade following 1868, state banks discovered that they could operate profitably even though they could issue only deposits. By 1887, the number of state banks exceeded the number of national banks.

Federal Reserve bank notes

The Federal Reserve Act provided for the issuance of two varieties of bank notes—*Federal Reserve bank notes* and *Federal Reserve notes*. Over the years, the Federal Reserve notes have become the predominant type of paper money in use; Federal Reserve bank notes are primarily an historical curiosity. Although Federal Reserve bank notes are in process of retirement and authority for their issuance was terminated in 1945, there are still $48 million in circulation.

The original purpose of the Federal Reserve bank notes was to replace national bank notes. It was expected that the Federal Reserve banks would purchase from the national banks the bonds backing their national bank notes and would, in turn, issue Federal Reserve bank notes on the security of the bonds. The national banks were to notify the Treasury of their willingness to sell the bonds, but none did, and the plan miscarried. Federal Reserve bank notes in circulation were issued on three occasions, in 1918, 1933, and 1942–1943, when crises required a rapid expansion of currency in circulation.

Demand for currency

During much of the history of the United States, the use of currency has declined relative to the use of deposits. Currency made up 45 percent of currency plus demand and time deposits at commercial banks in 1867 but only 8 percent in 1929. Growing industrialization and urbanization —conditions conducive to the use of checks on deposits—are probably the principal reasons for the decline in the amount of currency in use relative to demand and time deposits. In the 1930s and early 1940s, the downward trend in the ratio of currency to deposits reversed itself. In 1947, currency had risen to 17.8 percent of the total amount of currency plus demand and time deposits at commercial banks. This rate dropped from 1947 to 1960, and Table 3.3 shows that currency as a percentage of *M-2* as currently defined, has dropped over the period from 1960 to 1979 from 9.3 percent to 7 percent. As a percentage of *M-1B*, however, currency rose from 20.5 percent in 1960 to 27.4 percent in 1979. From 1970 to 1979, the dollar value of currency more than doubled—a remarkable rate of increase.

Table 3.3
Currency as a
Percentage of *M-1B* and
M-2, 1960–1979*
(dollar amounts
in billions)

December	Currency[a]	*M-1B*	Currency as a percent of *M-1B*	*M-2*	Currency as a percent of *M-2*
1960	$29.0	$141.6	20.5%	$311.2	9.3%
1965	36.3	168.8	21.5	457.2	7.9
1970	49.1	215.4	22.8	625.2	7.9
1975	75.1	289.0	26.0	1,022.4	7.3
1979	106.1	387.7	27.4	1,523.8	7.0

*Seasonally adjusted data.
[a]Excludes currency in commercial banks.
Source: *Federal Reserve Bulletin*, March 1980, p. A14; and Banking Section, Division of Research and Statistics, Board of Governors of the Federal Reserve System.

The amount of currency in circulation varies for different days of the week, days of the month, and seasons. As shown in Figure 3.1, large increases occur before Christmas and other holidays when additional currency is used for shopping and travel. After the holidays, the amount in circulation decreases. It is redeposited in commercial banks, which in turn send it to the Federal Reserve banks.

The demand for currency also varies cyclically. The annual percentage increases in currency are large in periods of business expansion when retail sales are growing, and small in periods of recession when retail sales are slack. The aggregate volume of currency responds automatically to changes in the public's desire for it, because demand deposits are convertible into currency at any time.

**Figure 3.1
Seasonal Variations in
Currency in Circulation**

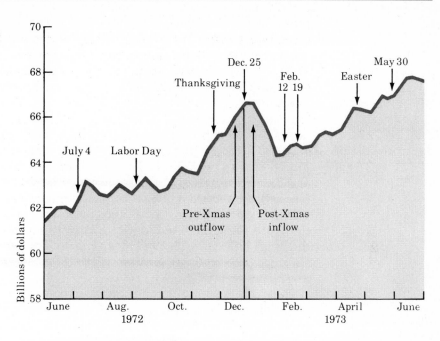

Source: Board of Governors of the Federal Reserve System, *The Federal Reserve System, Purposes and Functions*, 6th ed. (Washington, D.C., 1974), p. 46.

In addition to the regular seasonal and cyclical movements, unusual events may affect the demand for currency. During the Great Depression the holding of currency increased because many persons feared bank failures. During World War II, when workers and servicemen moved frequently, they found currency more useful than checks on demand deposits because currency is more readily accepted by strangers. In addition, the armed forces' policy during World War II of paying persons in cash rather than by check increased the use of currency. (During World War II the total number of persons in the armed forces reached over eleven million and was about one-fifth the size of the civilian labor force.)

The reasons for the phenomenal expansion of currency in the 1970s are not well understood. It has been attributed to activities carried out in cash in order to avoid detection by the government—ranging from dope peddling to babysitting. When barter is added to the volume of hidden cash transactions, it has been estimated that the "underground economy" may have reached 25 percent of the total economy by 1978.[11] Others believe that the expansion in currency in circulation has been caused by the large influx of illegal aliens from Mexico and refugees from Vietnam, persons who are reluctant to put their money in banks.

A significant aspect of the demand for currency is that changes in the proportion of the money supply held as currency can affect the total quantity of money. If currency becomes relatively more popular, and the percentage of M-1A and M-1B in currency rises, the total supply of M-1A and M-1B may decrease; and if less currency is held, the total may increase. The way in which such effects occur will be explained in later chapters.

Denominations of currency

The denominations of the currency in circulation also reflect the demands of the public. When persons or business firms obtain currency at their banks, they may specify the denominations that they desire. If they wish $5 bills, the teller gives them bills of this denomination, or if they wish $100 bills, they will receive them. The Bureau of Printing and Engraving adjusts its production of the different denominations to the inventory levels of each.

In countries with inflation, the average denomination of currency outstanding tends to rise. As prices rise, people find larger denomination currency more convenient and obtain such denominations for their use from banks. Inflation in some foreign countries has caused their small denomination coins to become a nuisance.

Table 3.4 shows the dollar value of each denomination of currency outstanding. The surprising fact is the large amount in $100 bills. They amount to almost one-third of the total dollar amount of currency. Bills of this size are not frequently used for transactions and are seldom seen. Some of these large bills may be held in the vaults of banks or hoarded by individuals. In addition, some of them are used for transactions where no record of payment is desired. Accumulations of wealth on which taxes are not paid or from illegal activities may be concealed in this way. For most other accumulations of wealth—the ownership of deposits, corporation stock, or real estate—there is a record of the acquisition and ownership of the property. During World War II the circulation of $500 and $1,000 bills increased sharply, probably because they were used to evade wartime rationing and price and production controls. When controls were discontinued after the war, the volume of the large denomination bills in circulation declined.

The $100 billion of currency in circulation in 1979 works out to about $1,200 for every American family. This surprising amount is probably related to the very large proportion of total currency in large denominations. Although the typical family does not hold anywhere near as much currency as the average indicates, a small number of persons apparently wish to accumulate wealth in a way that is easy to conceal.

In April 1976, the $2 bill was reissued. In 1966, printing of this

Table 3.4
United States Currency
Denominations in
Circulation,
September 30, 1978

Type		Amount in Millions
Coins		$ 10,504
Paper bills in denominations of:	$ 1	2,984
	2	648
	5	4,003
	10	10,768
	20	33,696
	50	10,618
	100	34,074
	500	167
	1,000	195
	5,000	2
	10,000	4
Total currency		$107,664

Source: *Statistical Appendix to Annual Report of the Secretary of the Treasury on the State of the Finances, Fiscal Year 1978* (Washington, D.C.: U.S. Government Printing Office, 1978), p. 316.

denomination had been discontinued because of the lack of demand for it. Although officials estimated that $27 million could be saved in printing costs over the next five years if $2 bills were substituted for half the $1 bills in circulation, there was again little demand for the $2 bill, and the Treasury discontinued issuing them in 1978.

In 1979, a Susan B. Anthony dollar coin was issued by the mint with the hope that it would be widely used, even though the previously minted Eisenhower dollar had been a failure. The Treasury could save money if the public would be willing to use dollar coins rather than paper dollars because the life span of paper currency is only 18 months compared to 15 years for coins. Also, because of the rising prices of merchandise, a higher denomination was considered necessary. The cost of revamping vending machines to take the new dollar coin was estimated to be $25 million. A few months after it was put in circulation, use of the new coin still had not won widespread public support.

Reporting of currency transactions

Since 1945, Treasury Department regulations have required every financial institution in the United States to file a monthly report on large and unusual currency transactions. These reports were developed for the purpose of discovering large currency transactions resorted to by racketeers, dealers in narcotics, foreign agents, and others engaged in illegal activities or seeking to avoid taxation. Banks are also required to obtain satisfactory identification of customers making large or unusual currency transactions. Financial institutions must report cash transactions involving $2,500 or more of U.S. currency in denominations of $100 or higher; $10,000 in any denomination; or any amount in any denominations which in the judgment of the financial institution may be out of proportion to the usual conduct of the customer concerned.

In 1970, Congress passed the Currency and Foreign Transactions Reporting Act, popularly known as the Bank Secrecy Act, which greatly expanded the Treasury's power to exact reports on currency transactions.[12] This law was expected to play a crucial role in the federal government's fight against white-collar crime. It requires banks to request the Social Security number of persons opening new accounts, and businesses must provide to financial institutions their IRS employer-identification number. U.S. taxpayers who have foreign bank accounts are required to file a report with the Treasury Department, and anyone who transports more than $5,000 in currency into or out of the United States must file a report with the U.S. Customs Service. In addition, financial institutions must keep extensive records, usually on microfilm, of checks in excess of $100 deposited in or drawn on the institution. Information of this type can be useful to the federal government in prosecuting cases involving tax evasion, narcotics traffic, organized crime, or political corruption.

In 1976, the Supreme Court ruled that bank records are not "a man's private papers" and therefore are not protected by the Fourth Amendment of the Constitution from unreasonable search and seizure. This blow to the privacy of the bank–customer relationship led Congress to include in the Financial Institutions Regulatory and Interest Rate Control Act of 1978 a new rule that "no government authority may have access to or obtain copies of the information contained in the financial records of any customer from a financial institution" without following strict new procedures.[13] Before the Internal Revenue Service or another governmental agency can examine your bank records, it must now advise you of an administrative subpoena and give you ten days in which to take the matter to court.

Summary

A satisfactory system of modern coinage is one that provides token coins worth much less than their nominal value. Otherwise, coins may disappear from circulation if the price of the metals used to make them rises.

Over the years, Federal Reserve notes have become the dominant type of paper money in circulation. Two types of paper money that were once important, but are now in process of retirement, are national bank notes and silver certificates.

The role of gold in the U.S. monetary system has steadily declined. From 1933 to 1974, it was illegal to circulate gold as money in the

United States. In 1968, the legal requirement that gold certificates be held as reserves for Federal Reserve notes was dropped. In 1971, the United States Treasury terminated all regular purchases and sales of gold.

Notes

1. Gordon Tullock, "Paper Money—A Cycle in Cathay," *Economic History Review* 9 (April 1957), pp. 393–407; and Fred Reinfeld, *The Story of Paper Money* (New York: Sterling, 1957).

2. Richard N. Frye, *Iran* (New York: Holt, Rinehart, and Winston, 1953), p. 37.

3. *The Travels of Marco Polo,* translated into English from the text of L. F. Benedetto by Prof. Aldo Ricci (London: George Routledge and Sons, 1931), pp. 147–149.

4. Ross M. Robertson, *History of the American Economy,* 3d ed. (New York: Harcourt Brace Jovanovich, 1973), p. 77.

5. Charles R. Whittlesey, *Principles and Practices of Money and Banking,* rev. ed. (New York: Macmillan, 1954), p. 195.

6. Whittlesey, *Principles and Practices of Money and Banking,* pp. 200–205. There are also many examples of difficulties with full-bodied coins in the history of Western Europe. See Carlo M. Cipolla, *Money, Prices, and Civilization in the Mediterranean World* (Princeton, N.J.: Princeton University Press, 1956), pp. 27–37.

7. See Milton Friedman, "Price, Income, and Monetary Changes in Three Wartime Periods," *American Economic Review, Papers and Proceedings* 42 (May 1952), pp. 612–625; reprinted in *The Optimum Quantity of Money and Other Essays* (Chicago: Aldine, 1969), pp. 157–170.

8. Eugene M. Lerner, "Inflation in the Confederacy, 1861–65," in Milton Friedman, ed., *Studies in the Quantity Theory of Money* (Chicago: University of Chicago Press, 1956), pp. 163–175.

9. Joseph J. Spengler, "Coin Shortage: Modern and Premodern," *National Banking Review* 3 (December 1965), pp. 201–216.

10. In 1903–1906, a sharp rise in the price of silver forced Japan, the Philippine Islands, the British Colony of the Straits Settlements (now Malaysia), and Mexico to change the content of their coins. See Edwin W. Kemmerer, "The Recent Rise in the Price of Silver and Some of Its Monetary Consequences," *Quarterly Journal of Economics* 26 (February 1912), pp. 215–274.

11. Edgar L. Feige, "How Big is the Irregular Economy?" *Challenge,* November-December 1979, pp. 5–13; and Peter M. Gutmann, "Statisti-

cal Illusions, Mistaken Policies, " *Challenge,* November-December 1979, pp. 14–17. See also Internal Revenue Service, *Estimates of Income Unreported on Individual Income Tax Returns,* Publication 1104 (9–79), September 1979.

12. *Public Law 91–508,* October 26, 1970. See *Federal Reserve Bulletin,* December 1970, pp. 929–939.

13. Title XI, "Right to Financial Privacy," *Public Law 95–630,* November 10, 1978, 92 STAT. 3697–3710.

Questions

3.1. What was the reason for the Coinage Act of 1965 authorizing silverless dimes and quarters?

3.2. Why is it advantageous for coins to be token coins rather than full-bodied coins?

3.3. State Gresham's Law. Give some examples of its application.

3.4. What was the nature of the bimetallic standard that existed in the United States from 1792 to 1873? Why was it replaced by the gold standard?

3.5. Explain why a shortage of pennies developed in 1974.

3.6. What was the reason for the coin shortage of the 1960s?

3.7. Explain briefly the history of U.S. notes, national bank notes, and silver certificates.

3.8. What is the difference between the total amount of currency outstanding and in circulation?

3.9. Explain the declining importance of gold bullion in our monetary system.

3.10. What have been the changes in the role of gold certificates as a type of money in the United States?

3.11. Explain the seasonal and cyclical changes in the amount of currency in circulation.

3.12. What are the uses of large-denomination currency, and what are the reasons for the government regulations requiring banks to report transactions of large-denomination currency?

3.13. Know the meaning and significance of the following terms and concepts: full-bodied coins, token coins, silver certificates, national bank notes, state bank notes, Gresham's Law, bimetallic standard, currency outstanding, currency in circulation.

4

The many different kinds of federal government securities and the market in which they are purchased and sold play an important role in our monetary system. It is through this market that the Federal Reserve System operates to control the volume of money and credit.

UNITED STATES
GOVERNMENT SECURITIES

The federal government must borrow to make up the difference when its revenues from taxation are not large enough to cover its expenses. The national debt of the United States consists of the outstanding securities that the federal government has sold as a means of borrowing. From 1975 to 1978, the gap between the expenditures of the federal government and its tax revenues was much larger than usual. This resulted in a very rapid growth in federal borrowing in these years and an increase in the national debt from $473 billion in June 1974 to $795 billion in April 1979.

The amount outstanding of each of the major categories of federal securities as of April 1979 is shown in Table 4.1.[1] The total debt of the Treasury is divided into marketable and nonmarketable issues. Although most people are familiar with U.S. savings bonds, a type of nonmarketable security, few are acquainted with the various types of marketable securities—Treasury bills, notes, and bonds—even though there has been increased consumer interest in these securities in recent years after their yields rose above interest rates paid on time deposits.

This chapter describes the types of U.S. government securities held by different groups and their yields. The market for U.S. government securities is extremely important to the Federal Reserve banks that control the reserves of the commercial banks, and to the commercial banks that provide the public with deposits, the principal type of money in the economy.

The government securities market

The primary market for marketable United States government securities is provided by twenty-five to thirty dealers. Dealers may be a department of a large commercial bank, a department of a brokerage firm, or a separate firm that specializes in this business. The market is very active. In the market provided by these dealers, government securities are typically bought and sold by banks, insurance companies, large corporations, pension funds, and foreign business firms and banks, including foreign central banks. The round lot for transactions is usually considered to be $1 million, and transactions of greater than $20 million are not unusual. The dealers in the primary market are particularly important because they are given the opportunity of dealing directly with the Federal Reserve banks in their daily operations and they report on their activities weekly to the Federal Reserve Bank of New York.

Marketable U.S. government securities can be bought and sold in the dealer market at any time after they are issued by the Treasury. Their prices fluctuate, just as do the prices of corporation stock in the stock market. If a commercial bank wishes to make a purchase, it usually contacts a dealer by phone, and the dealer quotes the price at which he is willing to sell the type of security desired. Though this market is not as well known as the stock market, Wall Street's daily, dollar volume of transactions in government securities is many times larger than the volume of transactions on the New York Stock Exchange.

In addition to the dealer market, marketable government securities can be purchased and sold by individuals through many commercial banks and brokers. The amount purchased by an individual is typically much smaller than transactions in the dealer market, and commercial banks and brokers charge a fee for this service.

Table 4.1
United States
Government
Interest-Bearing Public
Debt, End of April 1979
(in billions of dollars)

Treasury bills	$163.7	
Treasury notes	275.3	
Treasury bonds	65.5	
Total marketable debt		$504.6
U.S. savings bonds and notes	$ 80.8	
Foreign government series[a]	25.4	
Government account series	158.2	
Other[b]	26.2	
Total nonmarketable debt		290.8
Total debt		$795.4

Details do not add to totals in all cases because of rounding.
[a]Includes both dollar-denominated and foreign-currency-denominated foreign government series.
[b]Includes convertible bonds, depositary bonds, retirement plan bonds, individual retirement bonds, and state and local government series.
Source: *Federal Reserve Bulletin*, Sept. 1979, p. A32.

Marketable securities

There are many different issues outstanding of each of the three types of marketable securities—bills, notes, and bonds. The total number of the different issues outstanding varies as old issues mature and as new issues are offered for sale. In July 1979, there were weekly issues of 91-day and 182-day bills, monthly issues of 52-week bills, and more than 110 different issues of notes and bonds outstanding.

Bills are required by statute to mature within a year or less from the time they are issued. Bonds have no prescribed maturity, but currently are being issued with original maturities of over ten years and, prior to 1971, all bonds had a legal limit of 4¼ percent on their coupon rate of interest. In 1971, Congress authorized the Treasury to issue up to $10 billion in bonds without reference to this limitation, and the amount of bonds exempt from the 4¼ percent ceiling was increased to $17 billion in 1976. This was done to enable the Treasury to sell bonds when market rates were above 4¼ percent. Treasury notes have no ceiling on their coupon rates, and, prior to 1967, the maturity of notes at time of issue was always between one and five years. Starting in 1967, the Treasury sold notes with a maturity at time of issue of seven years, and in 1976 the Treasury sold an issue of notes with a maturity of ten years and a coupon rate of 8 percent. The extension of the maturity of notes up to ten years diminished the importance of the 4¼ percent legal ceiling on interest rates on Treasury bonds.

In recent years, the U.S. Treasury has sold marketable securities in book-entry form as well as in the form of a paper certificate. In January 1979, the Treasury stopped selling any bills in paper form. Eliminating the issue of paper certificates has many advantages to both the Treasury and investors in U.S. government securities. It cuts the printing costs of the Treasury and eliminates the problem of counterfeiting. It protects the investors from loss and theft of the paper certificates and reduces handling and storage costs.

Treasury bills

In April 1979, the total amount of bills outstanding was $164 billion. The Treasury always sells new issues of bills by auction. At the auction, the Treasury invites both noncompetitive and competitive tenders. Noncompetitive tenders for up to $200,000 from any one bidder are accepted in full at the average price of accepted competitive bids. Competitive tenders are made in multiples of $10,000, and the prices bid are stated on the basis of 100 and to the third decimal place (for example, 98.839). Since February 1970, bills have not been sold in denominations of less than $10,000. Upon expiration of the time set for placing bids, all tenders received are opened, the bids are arranged in descending order of price offered, and the details are communicated by wire to the office of the Secretary of the Treasury. The total amount of bills auctioned each week is usually the same as the amount maturing although there is occasionally a difference of $100 or $200 million. After the amount of the noncompetitive tenders is deducted from the total to be awarded, the Treasury awards bids in full, starting with the highest price, until obtaining the approximate amount of funds desired. At the auction of July 16, 1979, $2.9 billion of ninety-one-day bills were sold. The total amount of noncompetitive bids was $548 million and the noncompetitive price was 97.640. For competitive bids, the high bid was 97.647 and the low bid was 97.636. The low bidders received 19 percent of the amount that they bid for. The successful bidders each paid the price they bid. After the allotments are determined, the Secretary of the Treasury announces to the public the results of the auction, and the bills are dated on Thursday of that week. Payments may be made either in cash or in Treasury bills maturing on that date.

Each bill sold has an issue date, a date when it is payable, and a maturity value, but no specified rate of interest. On the day they are sold by the Treasury, the rate of interest paid by the Treasury is determined at the auction. Bills are sold for less than their maturity value, and the rate of interest received by the purchaser is the difference between the bid price that he paid for the bill and the price for which he sells it—or, if he holds it until it matures, its maturity value.

A purchaser of a ninety-one-day $1,000,000 bill at the price of $976,400 would receive $23,600 in interest if he held the bill until it matured. On an annual basis, this is a rate of 9.336 percent and is equivalent to a yield of 9.69 percent. The formula for the bill rate is:

4.1

$$r = \frac{100 - P}{100} \cdot \frac{360}{d},$$

where r = bill discount rate in decimal form, P = price paid per $100, and d = days to maturity. Thus:

$$r = \frac{100 - 97.640}{100} \cdot \frac{360}{91} = 0.09336$$

The formula for the approximate coupon issue yield equivalent for a 91-day bill is:

4.2

$$i = \frac{100 - P}{P} \cdot \frac{365}{d},$$

where i = the coupon issue yield equivalent in decimal form. Thus:

$$i = \frac{100 - 97.640}{97.640} \cdot \frac{365}{91} = 0.0969$$

The formula for the approximate coupon issue yield equivalent (formula 4.2) is based on a 365-day year and takes into account that the investor earns his return, not on the face value, but on the price paid. This calculation indicates a slightly lower return than the published yield equivalent which includes the value of reinvesting a hypothetical interest payment.

Though the most common type of bill is the ninety-one-day bill, six-month and one-year bills are issued regularly and there are occasional issues of bills that mature in only nine or fifteen days, and of tax-anticipation bills with various maturities. The three-month and six-month bills are sold on Monday of each week at the Federal Reserve banks, and the one-year bills are sold monthly. Tax-anticipation bills range in maturity up to nine months. They mature one week following the tax payment date. When used for taxes, they are in effect redeemed for par one week early.

Notes and bonds

Treasury notes and Treasury bonds are sold not only by auction, but also by cash subscription and in exchange for maturing securities (called a refunding). In recent years, the Treasury has had regular quarterly refundings in February, May, August, and November. In addition, since 1975 the Treasury has issued two-year notes monthly and four-year notes every quarter. Sales of fifteen-year bonds are becoming more regular, and the quarterly scheduling of sales of fifteen-year bonds appears to be evolving.

In a refunding, persons owning maturing securities may exchange them for one or more new issues. Owners of the maturing securities must notify the Treasury of the type and quantity of new issues they want, and they have the right to take cash if they wish. The total amount of cash taken in a refunding is called *attrition*.

The purpose of new issues sold at auction or by cash subscription is to finance a budget deficit or to make up for the attrition on a refunding. Auction sales of notes and bonds are analogous to the method of selling Treasury bills; persons submit bids and the price is set by the auction. The successful bidders receive the entire amount that they offered to buy. In a subscription sale, the Treasury announces the coupon rate of interest and other features of the issue one to three weeks in advance of the issue date, and investors subscribe for the amount they want at par value. The total amount that investors offer to buy is usually much larger than the Treasury wishes to sell. The Treasury then gives the subscribers a percentage of the amount they offered to buy. The percentage allocated is just sufficient to cover the entire amount that the Treasury desired to raise.

Dealers' quotations

Table 4.2 shows dealers' quotations at the close of the market on July 16, 1979, for United States Treasury bonds and notes maturing in 1982.

The list of dealers' quotations is prepared daily by the Federal Reserve Bank of New York by averaging the quotations from five major dealers at 3:30 P.M. It is published regularly in the financial section of major newspapers. These quotations change each day and show the prices at which dealers were willing to buy and sell these securities.

Table 4.2
Over-the-Counter Quotations on July 16, 1979 for United States Treasury Bonds and Notes Maturing in 1982

Rate	Maturity	Bid	Asked	Bid Change	Yield
6⅛s,	1982 Feb n	93.28	94.4	−.2	8.72
6⅜s,	1982 Feb	94.12	94.20	−.6	8.75
7⅞s,	1982 Mar n	97.21	97.29	−.2	8.76
7s	1982 May n	95.10	95.18	−.2	8.81
8s	1982 May n	97.28⁄30	98.4⁄30	−.2	8.76
9¼s,	1982 May n	101.10	101.18	−.1	8.62
8¼s,	1982 Jun n	98.15	98.23	−.4	8.75
8⅛s,	1982 Aug n	98	98.8	−.4	8.78
8⅜s,	1982 Sep n	98.19	98.27	−.3	8.80
7⅛s,	1982 Nov n	95.2	95.6	−.4	8.78
7⅞s,	1982 Nov n	97.3	97.11	−.4	8.81
9⅜s,	1982 Dec n	101.12	101.20	−.6	8.82

n = Treasury note.
Decimals in bid-and-asked and bid changes represent 32nds; 101.1 means 100 1/32.
Source: *Wall Street Journal*, July 17, 1979. Reprinted by permission.

Consider in detail the quotation for one issue of notes: the 8s of May 1982. This particular note was sold by the Treasury on May 15, 1975. The total amount of the issue was $2,747 million. The coupon rate is 8 percent. This means that on a $1,000,000 note, the semiannual interest payment would be $40,000. On registered notes and those in the form of book entries, the Treasury pays the interest by check to the owner. On the old notes in paper form which had coupons, the owner had to cut each coupon on the payable date. He received the interest by depositing the coupon in his checking account. The maturity date of the issue is May 15, 1982. Issues of bonds and notes are identified by their coupon rate and maturity date, and the exact day of maturity is always on the 15th of the month. On May 15, 1982, the owners of this issue are entitled to cash equal to the face value of their notes. If a person owned a $1,000,000 note, for example, he would receive $1,000,000 from the Treasury upon the surrender of his bond.

In the past, several long-term bonds had a call date as well as a maturity date. For example, if the Treasury wishes, it may pay off the owners of the 4½ percent bonds of August 1987/92 on August 15, 1987, or on any interest payment date thereafter, up until its maturity in 1992.

Under "Bid" is the price that dealers were paying for the 8s of May 1982 at the close of business on July 16, 1979. Instead of quoting the price of this note in dollars and cents, the bid price is stated as a percentage of the note's face value, with the number to the right of the decimal point indicating the fractional amount expressed in thirty-seconds. (Though unusual, it is customary business practice to express fractional amounts of the prices of Treasury notes and bonds in thirty-seconds of a dollar.) Table 4.2 shows that government securities dealers were willing to pay 97 28/32 percent of the face value—or $978,750 for a $1,000,000 note. The note is said to be selling at a discount, a price below its maturity value. When the market price of a note is higher than its maturity value, it is said to be selling at a premium.

The "Asked" price is that at which dealers would be willing to sell the note. It is slightly higher than the bid price and amounted to 98 4/32 percent or $981,250 for a $1,000,000 note. Dealers purchase securities for their own inventory and may hold them for a short time before they sell them. The difference between the bid and the asked is called the *spread.* In this example, the spread amounted to $2,500 on the purchase and sale of a $1,000,000 note, and was a source of income for the dealers.

The "Bid Change" shows the change from the bid price for the same issue on the previous day. The price of this note had fallen 2/32 or $625 on a $1,000,000 security. Dealers take losses on their inventory when prices of government securities fall. A successful dealer must manage his inventory in such a way that gains are larger than losses.

The "Yield" is the yield to maturity on the note if purchased at the asked price and held until it matures. At a price of $981,250, the purchaser would incur a capital gain equal to $18,750. For the remaining two years and 303 days until maturity, the prorated annual capital gain is approximately 35 percent of the total capital gain, or $6,625. Because the note will rise from its present value to its par value at maturity, the average value of this investment over the remaining two years and ten months is the average of the asked price and the maturity value. A very rough estimate of the yield to maturity may be made with the formula:

4.3

$$i = \frac{A + C}{(P+M)/2},$$

where i = yield, A = interest payment per year, C = prorated annual capital gain or loss, P = asked price, and M = maturity value. Thus:

$$i = \frac{80,000 + 6,625}{(981,250 + 1,000,000)/2} = 8.74\%$$

The estimated yield of 8.74 percent is slightly different from the 8.76 percent quoted in the newspaper column.

Variations in yields

A fall below par in the price of the 8s of May 1982 caused the yield on purchases of these notes to rise. If the price of this note had risen above par, its yield would have fallen. In 1975, when the 8s of May 1982 were sold by the Treasury, the prevailing market rate of interest for a seven-year government security was approximately equal to its coupon rate of 8 percent. New issues are sold by the Treasury either at par or very close to par, and the coupon rate on the note must be high enough to attract buyers. In 1979, when this note had two years and ten months to go, prevailing market rates of interest for a two-year-and-ten-month government security were about 8¾ percent. The fall in the price of this note raised its yield so that it was as attractive as other securities, including the new issues that were being offered with higher coupon rates.

Since a small change in the yield of a government security causes a relatively large change in its price, changes in yields are measured in very small units—called basis points. One basis point is equal to one one-hundredth of one percent.

Falling security prices may create problems for financial institutions which own securities that they purchased when prices were high.[2] If a bank that purchased the 8 percent note of May 1982 when it was originally sold in 1975 had to sell it in July 1979, it would incur a loss. The reason for the decline in the price of this bond is that the economy prospered between 1975 and 1979 and interest rates generally had risen. Because buyers of securities never know what the trend of interest rates will be in the future, the risk that the price of the securities they purchase may fall is unavoidable. This type of risk is called *interest risk* because it results from rising interest rates. It is different from *credit risk*, which is the risk of default. U.S. government securities lack credit risk.

Securities with short maturities have little interest risk, and differ significantly in this respect from those with long maturities. This is because prices of short-term issues do not decline much when market interest rates rise, while the prices of the longer-term issues do. As shown by the formula for the yield to maturity, the capital gain or loss that a person incurs when prices of securities fluctuate below and above par is prorated annually. To incur a similar annual capital gain and a similar rise in the yield to maturity, the price of a long-term bond that matures in the distant future must fall much further than the price of a short-term bond.

Determinants of the bid price

To obtain a better understanding of the relationship between the present value, the maturity value, and the yield to maturity of a bond, note, or bill, it is helpful to consider several formulas for the *present value* of such a security. Formula 4.3 showed how to estimate the yield to maturity, assuming that the present value is known. The formulas below show how to estimate the price of a security if the yield or expected rate of interest is known.

Formula 4.4 shows how to estimate the present value of a security maturing in one year:

4.4

$$P = \frac{M}{1 + i} \, ,$$

where P = present value; M = maturity value; and i = expected interest rate, stated decimally. The amount a person would pay now for the promise of a certain sum of money a year from now (maturity value) depends on the expected rate of interest. If he expects an annual yield to maturity of 8 percent, he would pay $92.59 now for a security worth $100.00 a year from now:

$$P = \frac{\$100}{1.08} = \$92.59.$$

The higher the yield expected on investments, the larger the gap between the present value and the maturity value. If the yield on alternative investments were 9 percent, the security would currently be worth $91.74.

If the security were a promise to pay a certain amount of money two years from now (assuming no interest payments), the formula is:

4.5

$$P = \frac{M}{(1 + i)^2}$$

Allowing for a yield of 8 percent, a buyer would pay $85.76 now for a security worth $100 two years from now. The two-year security would be worth less than the one-year so as to provide the owner with the same rate of return over a longer period of time.

$$P = \frac{\$100}{1.166} = \$85.76.$$

The formula for a security to be held n years, assuming no change in the yield and no interest payments, is:

4.6

$$P = \frac{M}{(1 + i)^a} \cdot$$

Most Treasury securities not only have a maturity value, but pay the owner fixed amounts of interest at intervals. The price would reflect the value of the interest payments as well as the maturity value. The formula for the price of such a security maturing in n years, paying interest once a year, would be:

4.7

$$P = \frac{A}{1 + i} + \frac{A}{(1 + i)^2} + \frac{A}{(1 + i)^3} + \cdots + \frac{A}{(1 + i)^a} + \frac{M}{(1 + i)^a},$$

where A = annual interest payment. If the expected rate of interest were 8 percent, the maturity three years, the annual interest payment $6, and the maturity value $100, the price would be:

$$P = \frac{\$6}{1.08} + \frac{\$6}{1.166} + \frac{\$6}{1.260} + \frac{\$100}{1.260}$$

$$= \$5.56 + \$5.15 + \$4.76 + \$79.37 = \$94.84.$$

This formula shows that the smaller the annual interest payments, the smaller the bid price of the bond. If the annual interest payments in the above example were only $5, the bid price of the bond would be only $92.26. More complicated formulas are required when interest is paid more frequently than once a year and when the bid price is computed on dates other than coupon payment dates.

Nonmarketable debt

U.S. savings bonds were designed for individual investors rather than financial institutions. They cannot be sold or transferred by the owner, but they may be redeemed for cash before the maturity date. Sales and redemptions of savings bonds are handled for the Treasury by commercial banks, business corporations operating payroll savings plans, and some mutual savings banks, savings and loan associations, credit unions, and post offices. Because of the ease with which these bonds may be cashed and because of the certainty of their redemption value, they are included in the total stock of liquid assets (see Table 2.1).

Two kinds of savings bonds—Series EE and HH—are currently offered for sale. Interest rates on savings bonds held to maturity were raised from 2.9 percent to 3 percent in 1952, 3.25 percent in 1957, 3.75 percent in 1959, 4.15 percent in 1966, 5 percent in 1969, 5.5 percent in 1970, 6 percent in 1973, and 6.5 percent in 1979, and for E and EE to 7 percent in 1980. Rates for Series H and HH remained at 6.5 percent in early 1980. The rate of return on savings bonds not held until maturity varies according to the length of time held. The interest on savings bonds is not subject to state and local government income taxes, and federal income taxes on the accrued interest on Series EE savings bonds can be deferred until the bonds mature or are redeemed.

Series EE are *appreciation* bonds. The smallest denomination is purchased for $25 and may be cashed for $50 at the time of maturity eleven years later. The difference between the price paid and the maturity value represents the accumulated interest received by the owner. An investor is permitted to purchase up to $15,000 in EE bonds each year. The full interest rate of 7 percent is earned if they are held to maturity. Series EE bonds may be redeemed at any time beginning six months after their issue date.

Series HH are *current income* bonds and are sold in four denominations—$500, $1,000, $5,000, and $10,000. Interest is paid by check semiannually. The interest payments are graduated, and the owner receives an average of 6.5 percent only if the bond is held until maturity ten years from its issue date. Series HH bonds are redeemable at par at a Federal Reserve bank or at the United States Treasury in Washington, D.C., six months after the date of issue. A person may buy no more than $20,000 (face value) of Series HH bonds annually.

The total amount of the dollar-denominated foreign series and the foreign currency series (which is denominated in the currency of the country making the purchase) increased sharply from $3.8 billion in 1969 to $28.2 billion in 1979. These securities are nonmarketable and are issued by the U.S. Treasury to foreign governments and monetary authorities. The bulk of these issues consists of the foreign series denominated in dollars. The sale of foreign series securities is related to the large deficits in the balance of payments of the United States and the accumulation of dollar balances by foreign governments. The objective of these sales was to reduce the dollar balances of foreign governments.

The securities in the government account series are sold only to federal agencies and trust funds and cannot be held by the public. The principal agencies that have accumulated these securities are the Federal Employees Retirement Funds, Federal Old-Age and Survivors Insurance Trust Fund, Federal Hospital Insurance Trust Fund, Highway Trust Fund, National Service Life Insurance Fund, and Federal Disability Insurance Trust Fund. Many agencies and trust funds are legally required to invest their funds solely in U.S. government securities. Although they may purchase marketable government issues, most of their holdings consist of the government account series. The federal agencies or trust funds may redeem government account series issues whenever they need cash. In some cases the coupon rate on these securities is related to the average interest rate that the Treasury pays on its outstanding interest-bearing debt, and in others it is regulated by legislation.

When the total amount of the government account series increases, it means that the receipts of some federal agencies have exceeded their expenditures and that they have invested the excess receipts in these securities. Through the purchase of such securities, these revenues are made available to finance the expenditures of other departments of the federal government. An increase in the volume of the government account series shows that funds have been transferred from one department to another within the federal government. In contrast, when the total volume of all types of federal securities outstanding increases, it indicates that federal expenditures have exceeded federal receipts and additional securities had to be sold to the public.

Ownership of the national debt

The important groups that own federal securities are listed in Table 4.3. From 1960 to 1970, the bulk of the increase in the total gross debt of the federal government was purchased by the Federal Reserve banks and by agencies and trust funds of the federal government. There was only a very small increase in the dollar amount of U.S. government securities owned by private investors. During the following eight years, however, from 1970 to 1978, there was a very substantial increase in the ownership of U.S. government securities by private investors, as well as an increase in the quantity of federal securities owned by the Federal Reserve banks and by federal agencies and trust funds.

In 1978, individuals held approximately 22 percent of the total fed-

Table 4.3
Ownership of U.S.
Government Securities,
End of 1960, 1970, and
1978 (par value in
billions)

Type of Holder	1960	1970	1978
Individuals	$ 66.1	$ 81.2	$110.7
Commercial banks	62.1	62.7	93.4
Nonfinancial corporations	18.7	7.3	20.6
State and local governments	18.7	27.8	68.6
Insurance companies	11.8	7.4	15.0
Mutual savings banks	6.2	3.1	5.2
Foreign and international	10.5	19.7	137.8
Other investors*	13.5	19.9	57.4
Debt held by private investors	$207.5	$229.1	$508.6
U.S. government agencies and trust funds	52.8	97.1	170.0
Federal Reserve banks	27.4	62.1	109.6
Total gross debt	$287.7	$388.3	$788.2

Details do not add to totals because of rounding.
*Includes savings and loan associations, dealers and brokers, corporate pension funds, nonprofit institutions, certain government deposit accounts, and government-sponsored agencies.
Source: Board of Governors of the Federal Reserve System, *Banking and Monetary Statistics, 1941–1970* (Washington, D.C.: Board of Governors of the Federal Reserve System, September 1976), pp.882–883; and *Federal Reserve Bulletin* (June 1979), p. A32.

eral debt held by private investors. Almost three-fourths of their securities consisted of savings bonds.

Commercial bank holdings currently amount to about 18 percent of the total debt held by the public. Commercial banks are one of the principal buyers of maturities of from one to five years. They also own a substantial amount of short-term securities maturing within a year. During and immediately following World War II, the Treasury classified securities maturing in ten years or more as "bank-restricted," and commercial banks were not permitted to purchase them. The total amount of government securities owned by commercial banks usually declines during periods of prosperity and rises during periods of recession. In periods of prosperity, banks typically get funds to lend by selling or cashing at maturity some of their U.S. government securities. In business recessions, when the demand for loans is slack, banks build up their portfolios of government securities. From the end of 1974 to the end of 1976, when the demand for bank loans was slack as a result of the recession of 1973–1975, commercial bank holdings of U.S. government securities rose very sharply—from $55.6 billion to $102.5 billion.

In recent years, foreign and international accounts in the United States have become the largest ownership group, holding in 1978 about 27 percent of the total amount of U.S. government securities held by private investors. Foreign central banks and other foreign and international institutions hold part of their dollar balances in U.S. government securities rather than in demand or time deposits. In the postwar period, the favorable balances of payments of foreign countries have caused their dollar balances to increase steadily, and in the period of international monetary turmoil from 1971 to early 1973, their holdings of U.S. government securities approximately tripled. From 1974 to 1978, the amount of U.S. government securities owned by foreigners continued to increase as a result of the accumulation of dollars by the petroleum exporting countries after the sharp rise in the price of crude oil in early 1974.

The amount of federal securities owned by industrial (nonfinancial) corporations typically varies erratically between $10 billion and $20 billion and declined from 1960 to 1970 because of increasing competition with other liquid assets such as CDs (certificates of deposit in commercial banks) and commercial paper. Large industrial and utility companies need to hold substantial liquid assets for contingencies and large anticipated outlays. Funds accumulated to pay taxes are usually held in the form of federal securities maturing around tax payment dates. Nonfinancial corporations own mainly short-term issues and intermediate issues maturing in from one to five years. Holdings of federal securities by business corporations vary inversely with their capital expenditures. From 1970 to 1978, corporations increased their holdings of federal securities because of relatively modest capital expenditures during this period.

Investments in federal securities by state and local governments have increased in most years since World War II. Retirement systems for public school teachers and other public employees have grown, and a portion of these funds is invested in federal securities, usually those maturing in over ten years. Some state and local governments invest their idle balances—accumulated between the tax payment date and the time when funds are needed—in federal securities maturing within one year, as a substitute for holding deposits. Funds obtained from the sale of state and local government bonds are usually invested in federal securities prior to the time they are spent.

The amount of government securities held by mutual savings banks and insurance companies declined sharply from 1960 to 1970, but increased from 1970 to 1978. These financial institutions invested heavily in government securities during World War II, but for many years thereafter they continuously reduced their holdings in order to accommodate the demand for mortgage loans. In the 1970s, these institutions purchased large amounts of federal securities because the demand for mortgages slackened and the interest rates on government securities rose to more attractive levels.

Other miscellaneous investors include primarily savings and loan associations, dealers and brokers, corporate pension funds, trust funds, and nonprofit institutions. The rapidly growing savings and loan associations have invested in significant amounts of government securities for liquidity purposes. The holdings of U.S. government securities by the miscellaneous investors rose sharply from 1970 to 1978.

Yield curves

The way interest yields vary with the maturity of a bond (the term structure of interest rates) may be illustrated by the yield curves shown in Figure 4.1 for February 28, 1977, and April 30, 1974. These yield curves were obtained by charting the yield for issues with maturities of up to ten years on those two dates. The rising yield curve for February 28, 1977, is typical of periods when market interest rates are relatively low and there is some economic slack. The declining yield curve for April 30, 1974, is typical of periods of prosperity when interest rates are high. Even though a recession had started in the fall of 1973, the downturn was initially very gradual, and interest rates and prices were still accelerating in 1974. The yield curves for federal securities are of particular interest because they reflect risks related to the differences in the maturity of various issues rather than differences in safety from default.

Changes in yield curves

There are several different theories to explain the changes in the yield curves for federal securities shown in Figure 4.1. According to the theory of *market segmentation,* there is a basic tendency at all times for yield curves to slope upward. This is because, when market interest rates rise or fall, short-term securities do not vary as much in price as long-term securities. When interest rates rise, for example, long-term bonds will fall much further in price than short-term securities. This makes long-term securities riskier. To offset this risk, the yield on long-term bonds must be higher than the yield on short-term securities. The fact that interest rates are lower on short-term than on long-term securities is referred to as a *liquidity premium.*[3]

The market segmentation theory is widely held among brokers and dealers. The government securities market is viewed as being divided into distinct submarkets with maturities that appeal to particular financial institutions because the riskiness of the different maturities varies. Commercial banks, for example, must invest primarily in short-term securities, while life insurance companies and pension funds prefer long-term securities because their yields are usually higher than those on short-term securities.

Although the yield curve usually slopes upward, the yield for different maturities depends on the conditions of supply and demand in each submarket, and in the latter part of a business expansion when monetary conditions are very tight, the yield curve will slope downward. At such times, commercial banks need to sell short-term federal securities in order to accommodate the demand for bank loans. This depresses the price of short-term securities and raises their yield. At the same time,

**Figure 4.1
Yields of Treasury
Securities, February 28,
1977, and April 30, 1974
(based on closing bid
quotations).**

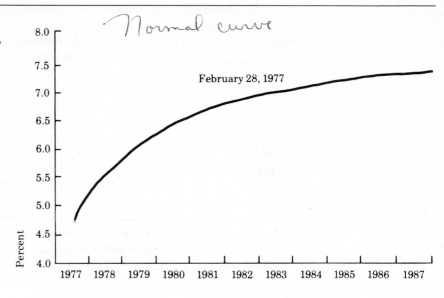

Normal curve

February 28, 1977

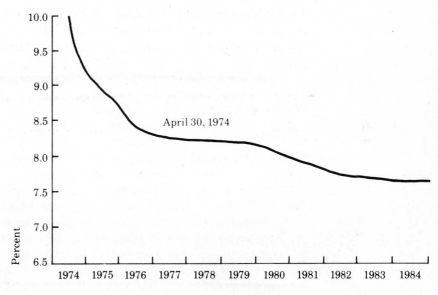

April 30, 1974

Source: *Treasury Bulletin*, March 1977, p. 80, and May 1974, p. 78.

Federal Reserve policy may be tight. These financial pressures cause short-term rates to rise temporarily above long-term rates.

The other theory explaining changes in the shape of yield curves from one period to another is known as the *expectations theory*. Most economists prefer the expectations theory to the theory of market segmentation. According to this theory, the yield curve was rising in February 1977 because interest rates were low and the economy was recovering slowly. This led people to expect that interest rates would eventually rise. As a result, borrowers would try to borrow on long-term contracts, driving long-term rates up. Lenders, on the other hand, tend to prefer short-terms if they believe interest rates may be higher later on. This drives short-term rates down. The combination of upward pressure from borrowers on long-term rates and downward pressure from lenders on short-term rates caused the February 1977 yield curve to slope upward.

According to the expectations theory, the downward-sloping yield curve for April 1974 is the result of the relatively high interest rates that existed at that time. These high interest rates caused the public to expect that interest rates would fall later on. If borrowers believe rates may be lower in the future, they tend to borrow for short terms, which drives short-term rates up. Lenders, on the other hand, try to put their funds out at long term, reducing long-term rates. If short-term rates are higher than long-term rates, this must mean that people believe that short-term securities are riskier than long-term securities. Because interest rates may fall in the future, buying a short-term security can be riskier than buying a long-term security. By the time the short-term security matures, yields on securities in the market may be very unattractive.

In the expectations theory, the various interest rates on a given yield curve are equal to the average of current and expected short-term interest rates. For example, if the current one-year rate is 10 percent and the one-year rate expected for next year is 12 percent, the current rate on two-year securities will be 11 percent—the average of the two one-year rates. This is because an investor has a choice between buying a two-year security or a one-year issue and at the end of that year reinvesting the money for another year. Although the investor does not know what the yield will be on one-year securities a year later, he will try to maximize the rate of return received over the period by basing his decision on his expectations. If the yield on a two-year issue were not equal to the average expected yield on two one-year ones, investors, by shifting, would cause them to move toward equality.

According to this theory, if the yield curve is sloping downward, investors must be anticipating lower interest rates in the future, and a rising yield curve implies that investors are anticipating higher interest rates in the future. The fact that yield curves usually slope upward when interest rates are relatively low tends to support this theory because if interest rates are relatively low one would expect investors to anticipate higher interest rates in the future. And, when interest rates are relatively high, a downward sloping yield curve seems reasonable because one would expect investors to anticipate lower interest rates in the future.

Summary

The market for United States government securities is one of the most important financial markets in the country. The yields on marketable United States government securities fall when their prices rise, and rise when their prices fall. The movements of these yields not only reflect changing conditions in the economy, but have important effects on the economy. When yields on U.S. government securities are high, interest rates on other types of securities and on loans also tend to be high, and credit generally is more costly. Both the activities of the U.S. Treasury (which issues more debt whenever its budget is out of balance) and the operations of the Federal Reserve banks (which own a large portion of the total United States debt) have significant effects on this market.

Notes

1. For a detailed description of the kinds of U.S. government securities, see *Handbook of Securities of the United States Government and Federal Agencies,* 28th ed. (New York: First Boston Corp., 1978); and William A. Hawk, *The U.S. Government Securities Market,* 3d revision (Chicago: Government Bond Division, Investment Department, Harris Trust and Savings Bank, 1976).

2. Federal tax law may alleviate these problems somewhat. It encourages banks to sell securities at a loss when prices are low. For securities other than bills, losses on security sales in any taxable year (net of all gains taken) may be deducted from income in their entirety.

3. Eli Shapiro, Ezra Solomon, and William L. White, *Money and Banking,* 5th ed. (New York: Holt, Rinehart, and Winston, 1968), pp. 334–341.

Questions

4.1. Explain the difference between marketable and nonmarketable U.S. government securities.

4.2. What are the different characteristics of United States Treasury bills, notes, and bonds?

4.3. Explain and compare the different techniques that the United States Treasury uses to market government securities.

4.4. Calculate the bill rate for a bill with ninety-one days to maturity and a price of 97.727. Calculate the coupon-issue yield equivalent for the same bill.

4.5. If a $1,000 bond, priced at $942.70, has a coupon rate of interest of 4⅛ percent and has exactly four years to its maturity date, what would be the approximate yield to maturity?

4.6. Explain why prices of bonds may fall below par and sell at a discount. At times, why may they sell at a premium?

4.7. Why are U.S. savings bonds considered to be liquid assets?

4.8. What are some of the different types of investors in U.S. government securities?

4.9. What is a yield curve? Explain why yield curves may slope downward in periods of prosperity and high interest rates generally. Why may they slope upward in periods of recession?

4.10. Know the meaning and significance of the following terms and concepts: national debt, marketable and nonmarketable securities, bill auction, refunding, cash subscription, bill rate, yield to maturity, yield curve, interest risk, credit risk.

5

Some commercial banks are national banks, and others are state banks; some are members of the Federal Reserve System, but a majority are not; some banks have branches, but most do not. In recent years, bank holding companies have grown in importance. Government regulations have significantly influenced the number of and the organization of commercial banks.

THE COMMERCIAL BANKING SYSTEM

Commercial banks create the deposits that make up the bulk of the money used in the U.S. economy. There were more than 14,700 commercial banks in the United States in 1978. Each of those banks had received a charter authorizing it to engage in banking. Chapters 5 through 9 tell about commercial banks and the nature of the deposits they create.

Historically, an essential characteristic of a commercial bank, in addition to holding demand deposits upon which customers wrote checks, was that it made short-term commercial loans. Currently, they also usually offer time deposits, rent out safe deposit boxes, exchange foreign currency, issue credit cards, and sell traveler's checks. Some banks also operate trust departments, are dealers in U.S. government securities, offer computer services, and engage in a variety of other financial activities. Today, other financial institutions engage in most of these activities, including offering demand deposits; separating commercial banks from other financial institutions is not as easy as it used to be.

According to the official count, the number of commercial banks today is less than half the number just after World War I. Table 5.1 shows that in 1921 there were 29,788 banks in the United States. By 1929 the number had declined to 24,026, as many small banks went out of business in declining agricultural areas. During the Great Depression, one-third of the banks ceased operating, and by 1934 there were only 15,519. Following World War II the banking population continued to decline, primarily because of mergers. In 1960, there were about 500 fewer commercial banks than in 1945. In the early 1960s and in the 1970s, the number of banks increased because of a more liberal government policy toward the granting of new charters. In 1979, there were over 1,200 more banks in the United States than there had been in 1960.

The distribution of banks by size of their assets in 1977 is shown in Table 5.2. One hundred and forty-one commercial banks in the United States each had total assets of greater than $1 billion. In 1979, our largest commercial banks, Citibank in New York and Bank of America in California, each had total assets of more than $100 billion.[1] Most banks, however, are small. The median size is between $10 million and $25 million in assets.

History of U.S. banking

The first modern bank in the United States was the Bank of North America established in Philadelphia in 1781. In 1800 there were twenty-nine banks in the United States, and twenty years later the number exceeded three hundred. These earliest banks were chartered by special acts of state legislatures. Before the existence of these state-chartered banks, there were colonial loan offices or private associations that made loans—usually with land as collateral—and issued paper

Table 5.1
The Number of
Commercial Banks, by
Class and Membership
in the Federal Reserve
System; Selected Years,
1921–1978

End of Year	All Commercial Banks	National Banks	State Banks	Member Banks	Nonmember Banks
1921 (June)	29,788	8,150	21,638	9,745	20,043
1929	24,026	7,403	16,623	8,522	15,504
1934	15,519	5,462	10,057	6,442	9,077
1941	14,278	5,117	9,161	6,616	7,662
1945	14,011	5,017	8,994	6,881	7,130
1950	14,121	4,958	9,163	6,870	7,251
1955	13,716	4,692	9,024	6,540	7,176
1960	13,472	4,530	8,942	6,172	7,300
1965	13,804	4,815	8,989	6,221	7,583
1970	13,688	4,621	9,067	5,768	7,920
1975	14,632	4,744	9,888	5,790	8,842
1978	14,712	4,564	⟵⟶ 10,148	5,564	9,148

14712

Source: U.S. Board of Governors of The Federal Reserve System, *Banking and Monetary Statistics* (Washington, D.C., 1943), p. 16; *Banking and Monetary Statistics, 1941–1970* (Washington, D.C.: 1976), pp. 40-41; *62nd Annual Report 1975* (Washington, D.C.: 1976), pp. 392-393; and *65th Annual Report 1978* (Washington, D.C.: 1979), p. 418.

money. They were not incorporated, were usually designed to finance specific needs, lasted only for the duration of their loans, and did not have deposits on which customers wrote checks.[2]

In the late 1830s, both Michigan and New York passed "free banking acts," making it relatively easy to establish a bank and unnecessary for state legislatures to approve each charter application. By 1860 about half of the states had adopted similar laws. Along with those changes came increased regulation by state banking commissions. Bank examinations were made on a regular basis, rather than only at times of

Table 5.2
Number and Assets of
All Insured Commercial
Banks, by Asset Size,
December 31, 1977

Asset Size (in millions)	Number of Banks	Amount of Assets (in billions)
Less than $ 5	1,197	$ 4.2
5 - 10	2,593	19.3
10 - 25	4,911	81.0
25 - 50	2,980	103.3
50 - 100	1,485	102.9
100 - 300	824	132.4
300 - 500	157	60.5
500 - 1,000	124	85.4
1,000 - 5,000	120	229.1
5,000 or more	21	315.5
Total	14,412	$1,133.4

Details do not add to totals in all cases because of rounding.
Source: Federal Deposit Insurance Corporation, *Annual Report, 1977* (Washington, D.C.: 1978), p. 145.

difficulty. Several states required a specified amount of specie reserves (gold and silver) when notes were issued by a bank, but others required only bonds and certain types of securities. As time went on, small banks began placing deposits in large urban banks as part of their reserves. Before 1863, only two states required a percentage of deposit liabilities held as reserves.

The Currency Act of 1863 and the National Bank Act of 1864 provided for the granting of national charters by the federal government. This is unusual since most corporations have charters granted by state governments. The original intention of the Civil War banking acts was to create a single system of national banks coordinated by the federal government. The national banks would issue a uniform currency, strengthen the market for federal securities, and be of assistance to the federal government in managing the relatively large national debt that had been created during the Civil War.

The federal regulations governing the chartering of new banks have not changed a great deal since the Civil War. They allow much room for judgment on the part of the comptroller of the currency, whose responsibility it is to issue charters for national banks. From 1864 to 1875 many applications for national bank charters were not approved.[3] After the Specie Resumption Act of 1875, the policy changed and banks that met certain standards were said to be "entitled" to a charter. A period of "free banking" existed from then until 1925. In the 1920s the comptrollers again became more restrictive because of the bank failures in agricultural regions of the country. After the wave of bank failures in the Great Depression of 1929–1933, it was widely believed that state bank chartering should be curtailed. In the end, states retained their privilege of chartering banks, but after the Federal Deposit Insurance Corporation was set up in 1934, federal authorities achieved some control over most state banks by being able to withhold deposit insurance if the banks did not meet certain standards. For many years after the Great Depression, comptrollers of the currency exercised extreme caution in granting national bank charters. Starting in the early 1960s, the chartering of banks became easier; in the 1970s, from 200 to 400 new charters were granted each year—mostly by state governments.

Existing banks oppose the organization of competing banks, and have often succeeded in preventing the granting of new charters. Federal authorities do not want to charter a bank that will eventually fail because of inadequate resources or incompetent management. Failure of a bank is costly and inconvenient for the public, subjects the regulatory agency to criticism, and may destabilize the banking system and the economy. The chances of failing are greater for a new bank than for an established one, and there is always a possibility that a new bank may harm an established bank. However, avoiding the risk of chartering new banks that may fail must be balanced against the gain in competition and the increase in banking facilities. Some economists are critical of the fact that charter applications are usually rejected on the basis of attempts to forecast the community's need for another bank. In recent years, the proliferation of new banks and of bank branches has increased competition among banks. This has been regarded as a cause of some of the changes favoring bank customers, such as the expansion and greater convenience of banking hours, the reduction in service charges, pay-by-phone checkless transfers, and the provision of drive-up windows and electronic computer terminals in shopping centers.

National banks and state banks

The combination of national and state chartered banks is frequently referred to as a *dual system of banking*. At the end of 1978, there were 4,564 national banks that had obtained their charters from the federal government. Although this is only 31 percent of the total number of insured commercial banks, they hold almost 57 percent of the total amount of deposits in commercial banks. The term *national* is included in the name of many banks and indicates their chartering authority. More than two-thirds of the banks are state banks that obtained their charters from their state governments. Table 5.1 shows that there has been a significant increase in the number of state banks since 1970 and a decline in the number of national banks.

Historically, one of the major requirements of a national bank was a minimum capital investment. To qualify for a charter, a national bank had to sell a minimum amount of stock and, in addition, have assets equal to 120 percent of its outstanding capital stock. For banks in communities with populations of less than 6,000, the minimum amount of capital stock is $50,000; for those in towns with between 6,000 and 50,000 people, it is $100,000; and for larger communities, it is $200,-000. For state banks, it is usually less. Today these requirements are so small that they are of little practical significance.

Federal Reserve member banks and nonmember banks

A member bank is a commercial bank that has applied and been accepted for membership in the Federal Reserve System. By law, all national banks must be members. State banks may join the system if they desire to do so and if they meet the qualifications. In 1978, only 10 percent of the state banks were members. Member banks tend to be larger than nonmember banks. In 1977, member banks accounted for only 40 percent of the total number of insured commercial banks in the country, but they held 75 percent of the total assets. Since 1950, there has been a fairly steady decline in the number of member banks and an increase in the number of nonmember banks.

Until 1980, only the national banks and the state banks that belonged to the Federal Reserve System were required to meet the System's reserve requirements. Now, the System requires all depository institutions to hold a certain percentage of their transaction and nonpersonal time deposits either as vault cash or as deposits at the Federal Reserve banks. A small fine is assessed against deficient reserves, and banks are not allowed to negotiate new loans or pay dividends until the deficiency is corrected. A member bank with prolonged or recurrent deficiencies is in danger of losing Federal Reserve membership. Previously, state banks that were not members of the Federal Reserve System were required to hold reserves, but these requirements varied from state to state, and the required ratios were usually relatively low.[4] State banks held a considerable portion of their reserves as deposits in other banks. A decided advantage that nonmember banks in some states had was that reserves could be held in the form of U.S. government securities, and in some states banks could even count cash items in process of collection as reserves. Also, the enforcement of reserve requirements was often much less strict for nonmember than for member banks. Member banks have to file reports on daily liabilities and reserve balances at the end of each reserve settlement week. In a majority of the states, nonmember banks did not have to file any reports to their state bank supervisors, but had to keep appropriate records for inspection by state bank examiners.

Now that nonmember banks are subject to the same reserve requirements as member banks under the Depository Institutions Deregulation and Monetary Control Act of 1980, nonmember banks will have access to some of the same services as member banks—including borrowing privileges. Previously, member banks had several privileges that nonmember banks did not have, but nonmember banks could arrange to use the Federal Reserve's check-clearing facilities. The checks of all banks using these facilities have numbers in the upper right corner, identifying the Federal Reserve district, its branch, the city or state, and the bank itself—information needed for routing. All banks using the Federal Reserve's check-clearing facilities must remit at par. This means that they cannot deduct an exchange charge (usually one-tenth of one percent) on checks written on themselves but presented for collection by the Federal Reserve banks. About one percent of the commercial banks do not remit at par. Checks on nonpar banks are usually cleared through correspondent banks.

Regulation of banks

A principal type of government regulation of banking consists of periodic bank examinations. The various governmental units concerned with bank examinations have divided among themselves the responsibility for making examinations, so as to avoid duplication; the reports of each agency are available to the others.

The Office of the Comptroller of the Currency uses the surprise call as one of its major ways of regulating national banks. In addition to regular calls at the end of June and December, at least twice every year, on unannounced dates, the comptroller of the currency requires each national bank to produce a complete balance sheet of its accounts. The balance sheet for the call date has to be published in a local newspaper. In order to be prepared for calls, a bank has to keep its accounts in accordance with legal regulations at all times.

The examination of state banks is divided among three groups: the Federal Reserve System examines state banks that are members of the System; the Federal Deposit Insurance Corporation examines state banks that are insured by them but are not member banks; and state bank examiners are responsible only for the small number that are not insured by the FDIC, but these state examiners may also examine any other state banks. All banks are examined at least once a year.

Bank examiners are interested in whether a bank holds the types of assets permitted, whether it has clear title to them, and whether these assets are listed at a reasonable value. The examiners must check the adequacy of collateral given by borrowers. If a loan is past due and the prospects of being paid off appear to be doubtful, the examiners require the bank to remove the loan from its reported assets. A principal concern of the examiners is to ascertain whether the bank is being thoroughly audited both by an outside accounting firm and by officers of the bank. Bank examiners also evaluate whether the bank is being properly managed and look for any possible indication of fraud. (Among other things, they seek to ascertain whether all deposit liabilities and other claims have been listed in full.) The examiners prepare a formal report that is sent to the bank's directors—who are responsible for complying with the recommendations made. Since 1933, the Board of Governors of the Federal Reserve System has had the power to remove any officer or director of a national bank who engages in unsafe or unsound practices that endanger the bank's solvency.

Few types of businesses have been subject to such extensive government regulation as have commercial banks. Much of the regulation is based on statutes legislated a generation or more ago. In the early 1960s, extensive changes were made that removed some restrictions, and in 1976 the regulation of commercial banks was one of the topics included in the broad review of financial institutions (the FINE report) made by Congress.[5] Since the early 1960s, national banks have been allowed to use preferred stock, capital debentures, and unsecured promissory notes (commercial paper) as methods of financing. Banks have also been allowed to issue stock options to their management and to organize employee stock purchase plans. They are now permitted to engage in the business of underwriting securities issued by state and local governments. The types of securities that banks are allowed to hold have been broadened. As a result of efforts by the comptroller, legislation was passed transferring authority over the trust powers of national banks from the Federal Reserve to the comptroller. These powers have been liberalized to allow banks to develop various types of collective investment funds. A more liberal approach is now taken toward the terms and variety of loans made by national banks. The limits on lending to any one borrower have been increased from 10 percent of capital stock and surplus to 10 percent of capital stock, surplus, and undivided profit. Banks are now allowed to engage in the business of providing computer and payroll services.

Almost all of these innovations were achieved by changing the rules and regulations of the administrative agencies. In only a few cases was it necessary to have new legislation passed by Congress. These changes reflected pressure from commercial banks to break through the complicated mass of restrictive controls that prevented them from developing new methods of finance suitable for a growing, more closely interrelated economy.

In the 1970s, new forms of bank regulation expanded rapidly, and the earlier trend toward less regulation was reversed. New laws were passed by Congress to protect the consumer, to assure equal opportunity, and to improve the standards of bank management.

The Federal Deposit Insurance Corporation

A system of compulsory deposit insurance had been established by the Safety Fund Act in the state of New York as early as 1829. It required banks, as their charters came up for renewal, to join a contributory fund in order to protect both depositors and the holders of notes which at that time were issued by commercial banks. Although this fund helped in the repayment of bank creditors during the depression of the late 1830s, it had to be assisted by the state. Five other states set up state-operated bank insurance systems between 1829 and 1858. After the banking difficulties in the Panic of 1907, eight states set up such plans. Most insurance systems provided for bank examinations in order that well-managed banks not be charged high premiums to cover losses due to excessive risk-taking by less carefully managed banks. All of these early insurance programs either failed or ceased operating within a few years.

The Federal Deposit Insurance Corporation was established in 1934 following the failure of a very large number of banks during the Great Depression. The establishment of deposit insurance is usually considered to be the most significant piece of banking legislation since the creation of the Federal Reserve System. Initially, it did not have the support of President Franklin D. Roosevelt's new administration and was bitterly opposed by some important interests.[6]

Banks that are members of the Federal Reserve System are required to belong to the FDIC. Although the bulk of the nonmember banks have also joined, in 1978 there were 333 state banks and trust companies that were not insured—either because they did not choose to belong or because they could not meet the minimum standards required. Some of the uninsured banks are branches of foreign banks, some of which do not accept deposits requiring FDIC insurance.

Today the FDIC insures the deposit of each individual or firm in each bank up to $100,000. The premium for coverage is paid by the bank and is one-twelfth of one percent of total deposits, although currently more than half of the premium is refunded. One criticism of this insurance is that, even though it insures each deposit only up to $100,000, the premium charged is based on the total amount of the bank's deposits. Because of the ceiling on coverage, not all of the deposits of a bank are guaranteed against loss. When a bank is closed, persons are reimbursed up to $100,000 per account. Depositors may later receive payment for amounts above this, but only to the extent that the sale of assets makes this possible. Since 1934, over 99 percent of depositors of closed banks have been paid in full. When the FDIC takes over a bank that has failed, there is usually no loss to depositors because the FDIC typically arranges for a merger with another bank. The FDIC has avoided shutting down banks whenever possible in order to assure that normal banking service can continue in the community.

The FDIC achieves more than protecting depositors against possible losses. The psychological effect of insuring deposits diminishes the prospect of having runs on banks. Prior to the establishment of the FDIC, if people feared that a bank might fail, they withdrew their deposits. Because banks typically have only a small percentage of their deposits in cash, such runs caused them extreme difficulty. In the century prior to the establishment of the FDIC, runs on banks contributed to the financial panics that accompanied most serious recessions. The removal of this incentive to withdraw deposits is an important contribution to financial stability.

Branch banking

In most foreign countries there are only a few banks, each with numerous branches. In the United States, the most common type of bank has been the *unit bank*, a bank without branches. In most states, there are now large banks with branches, together with numerous unit banks. The number of bank branches in the United States has increased rapidly since World War II. In 1947, there were only 4,161 branch offices; by 1977, the number of branches had risen to over 33,000.

A branch bank must offer the usual types of deposits in order to be classified as a branch. In recent years, large banks engaged in credit operations on a national scale have set up offices in major cities for the purpose of doing business more conveniently for their borrowers. These offices are not regarded as branches even though they engage in almost all banking activities except offering regular deposits and making loans to local customers. There is a current movement to relax further the restrictions on these interstate activities.

The regulations of some states do not allow banks to have branches. In other states, branches must be within the city or county in which the bank is located. Supervisory officials must approve both the formation of new branches and mergers with other banks. Restrictions on branch banking are gradually breaking down. The 1972 report of a presidential commission on the regulation of financial institutions (known as the Hunt Commission), and also the 1976 FINE study, recommended reducing restrictions on bank branches further.[7]

From 1869 to 1911, rulings by the comptroller of the currency severely restricted the development of branch banking even though, before the Civil War, branch banking had developed in the Middle West and in the South.[8] The legislation setting up the national banking system neither forbade nor allowed national banks to have branches, and the 1865 law which taxed state bank notes 10 percent (so as to induce state banks to become national banks) included provisions under which state banks with branches could become national banks. Even so, before 1918, the comptrollers of the currency permitted very few national banks to have branches. In 1927 the McFadden Act permitted national banks to open branches within the limits of the city, town, or village in which they were located if state laws did not forbid it. During the 1930s and 1940s, because of the Great Depression and World War II, few permits to open branches were granted. It was not until after World War II that branch banking expanded rapidly.

Resistance to branch banking is due partly to the reluctance of bankers and bank owners in rural areas to give up control of their banks. Many small communities appear to prefer local control of their banking institutions. It is a matter of dispute which type of bank, the branch bank or the unit bank, can best serve the needs of rural communities and suburbs. Unit banks can obtain many of the services that branches have by maintaining a correspondent relationship with larger banks. Several studies have concluded that the economies of scale in banking are relatively small and are less than the diseconomies of branch banking.[9] On the other hand, one important statistical study concluded that large banks with branches are, on the average, more profitable than large unit banks of comparable size.[10] This study found that average costs per $100 of loans and investments for unit banks declined as bank size increased up to $2 million in deposits, were fairly constant from a size of $2 million deposits to $50 million, and declined again for banks above that size.

Since 1965, there has been a rapid expansion of foreign branches of United States banks.[11] The Board of Governors of the Federal Reserve System must approve applications made by member banks to establish branches in foreign countries, but the branches operate under the laws of the host country. In 1979, 139 United States banks had 787 branches in 78 foreign countries and in various overseas areas of the United States. Their assets were greater than $300 billion—over 23 percent of the total U.S. assets of all commercial banks. United States banks have expanded their overseas operations in order to better serve expanding multinational corporations, but they have been discouraged somewhat by expropriation of foreign banks in some countries. Measures taken by the U.S. government to reduce our balance of payments deficit, such as the Interest Equalization Tax of 1963 and the Voluntary Foreign Credit Restraint programs had, until they were ended in 1974, the effect of stimulating the growth of foreign sources of financing.

In addition to branches in foreign countries, some U.S. banks have U.S. subsidiaries outside the bank's home state to conduct international business transactions.[12] Although such subsidiaries have been allowed since 1919 under the Edge Act, there were only 37 such operations in 1965 and 116 in 1975. To enable U.S. banks to compete with the growing number of foreign banks operating in the United States, the International Banking Act of 1978 instructed the Federal Reserve to liberalize the Edge Act regulations. Before 1979, each Edge Act corporation set up could engage in international lending activities from only one state. Now such a corporation can operate across state lines.

Electronic computer terminals

In the mid-1970s, there was disagreement among government regulators over whether automated tellers and electronic computer terminals, located in such places as supermarkets and shopping centers, were legally branches of their banks. The comptroller of the currency had ruled that, for national banks, off-premise terminals did not constitute a branch of the bank. The comptroller's original ruling was later amended and a limit of fifty miles was set as the maximum distance a terminal could be from its head office or closest branch. Later, a lower court ruled that automated tellers and electronic computer terminals were branches within the meaning of the McFadden Act and could be prohibited by state law. This ruling was allowed to stand when the Supreme Court refused to review it. These decisions were particularly significant in states such as Illinois and Texas where branches are illegal. In recent years, electronic computer terminals have become commonplace in many states.[13]

Foreign banks in the United States

In the 1970s, the number of foreign banks operating in the United States increased sharply. By 1978, there were 123 foreign banks in the United States operating 268 banking facilities. Their assets in the United States totaled $65 billion.[14]

Prior to the enactment of the International Banking Act of 1978, the regulation of foreign banks was largely determined by individual state laws, and these state laws still restrict foreign banks. Some states allow no foreign-bank operations of any kind and others do not permit extensive operations. The principal states with foreign banks are New York and California.

The laws of the State of New York allow foreign banks from reciprocating countries to accept both domestic and foreign-owned deposits and to make the same types of loans that domestic banks make. Since 1973, Illinois has allowed full-service branches of foreign banks in downtown Chicago, if reciprocity is granted. To make loans in the United States, foreign banks may establish either an *agency* (which accepts no deposits from domestic residents), or a *branch* (which can accept both foreign and domestic-owned deposits). Agencies are the dominant form of U.S.-based foreign bank organization both in number of offices and total volume of assets.

The International Banking Act of 1978 establishes for the first time specific federal regulation of foreign banks. The act attempts to provide for equal treatment of domestic and foreign banks. Domestic banks had complained that federal regulations put them at a competitive disadvantage. While the McFadden Act does not allow U.S. domestic banks to engage in interstate banking, foreign banks had been able to establish interstate banking facilities. In addition, foreign banks have been able to underwrite and sell stocks in the United States, an activity prohibited by the Banking Act of June 1933 for domestic banks. A third disadvantage was that, even though almost all of the foreign banks are very large, they were not subject to the high Federal Reserve reserve requirements for large banks. As a result, their reserve costs were much lower than those of domestic banks.

The new law provides that all branches and agencies of foreign banks shall be subject to Federal Reserve reserve requirements if their parent banks have worldwide assets of $1 billion or more. Although not classed as member banks, they will maintain reserve balances at the Federal Reserve banks and also have access to the Federal Reserve discount window. On interstate branching, each foreign bank must now select one state as its "home state" of operation, and it can establish a new branch or agency outside the home state only with the permission of the state in which it will operate. New branches and agencies outside the home state are now permitted to accept deposits only from nonresidents of that state or from activities related to international trade financing. Foreign banks still have an advantage because all of their existing out-of-state operations are exempt from the new legal restrictions.

In recent years, some foreign banks have purchased U.S. banks. Purchase of control of a U.S. bank by a foreign company must be approved by the Board of Governors of the Federal Reserve System, and approval by the state government may also be required. Britain's National Westminster Bank purchased the entire stock of the National Bank of North America, the thirty-seventh largest in the country. In 1979, the State Superintendent of Banking of New York refused to approve the attempt by the Hong Kong and Shanghai Banking Corporation to acquire control of the Marine Midland Bank, the twelfth largest in the country. At the same time, legislation was introduced in Congress to impose a six-month moratorium on foreign-bank takeovers.

Bank mergers

From 1952 through 1977, there were between 100 and 200 consolidations, mergers, or absorptions a year. In most cases, small banks are combined with large ones. For instance, in 1972, 112 banks which together had resources of $3 billion were absorbed by 100 banks which together had assets of $30 billion. A bank wishing to expand its operations often finds it easier to get permission to absorb a small bank than to set up a new branch. Mergers reduce the number of banks and are a way of eliminating competition.

The Bank Merger Act of 1960 makes federal bank regulatory agencies responsible for the approval of mergers—the comptroller of the currency for national banks that plan to absorb another bank, the Board of Governors of the Federal Reserve System for state member banks, and the FDIC for insured nonmember banks. The Bank Merger Act of 1966 forbids mergers that substantially lessen competition unless there are some other advantages which make a merger desirable. In addition, the Justice Department has used antitrust legislation to prevent several bank mergers that would have seriously threatened competition. In the important Philadelphia National Bank case of 1963, the United States Supreme Court approved of action taken by the Department of Justice to prevent a merger of the Philadelphia National Bank and the Girard Trust Corn Exchange Bank, even though the merger had been approved by the comptroller of the currency.[15] If the Justice Department intervenes, it must start proceedings within thirty days of the agency's final approval, and the merger must be suspended until the issue is resolved by litigation.

Bank holding companies

Bank holding companies—either separate corporations, or banks that own a sufficient amount of stock in one or more banks to have a controlling interest—are a means of linking together the management of a group of banks or of a group of enterprises engaged in businesses related to banking. Historically they were set up to obtain some of the advantages of branch banking, and had the unique advantage of making it possible to control a group of banks in more than one state. Western Bancorporation, one of the earliest large bank holding companies, controls banks in California, Oregon, Washington, Nevada, Arizona, Idaho, New Mexico, Utah, Colorado, Wyoming, and Montana.

Because some bank holding companies are very large and may concentrate economic power, there has been pressure to bring them under government control. Federal legislation, starting with the Banking Act of 1933, has also aimed at a basic separation of bank (and bank-related) activities from other business activities. Because the legal status of bank holding companies was for many years unclear, and because of the opposition of some banking interests, bank holding companies did not expand rapidly until the mid-1960s. The Bank Holding Company Act of 1956 provided for registration of companies holding 25 percent or more of the stock of two or more banks, barred new bank acquisitions across state lines, and set up regulations over the acquisition of additional voting stock in banks. It also prohibited registered holding companies from engaging in non-bank-related activities, and several banking corporations were required to separate their banking and nonbanking activities. After 1956, one-bank holding companies that were excluded from regulation increased rapidly in number. In 1970, new legislation extended government regulation to one-bank holding companies—usually those owning 25 percent or more of the stock of a bank.[16] The Federal Reserve Board was given authority to administer the 1970 regulations and to determine when undue control exists and when exceptions should be allowed. The bill aimed especially at preventing banks from requiring special tie-in deals in order to obtain bank loans.

Table 5.3 shows that the number of registered holding companies increased sharply in 1972 after one-bank holding companies were required to register. In 1965, there were estimated to be approximately 400 one-bank holding companies, most of which controlled small banks. Between that date and the end of 1968, the number of one-bank holding companies almost doubled.[17] A study of *multibank* holding companies showed that since 1965 such companies have expanded rapidly, if growth is measured by total deposits, number of offices, or geographic distribution.[18] Table 5.3 shows that by 1977, 72 percent of the deposits in commercial banks in the United States were in banks owned by holding companies.

Table 5.3
Number of Registered Bank Holding Companies, Banks and Branches Controlled, and Total Deposits, Selected Years, 1957–1977

End of Year	Number of Registered Holding Companies	Banks Controlled	Branches	Total Deposits (in billions)	Total Deposits as Percent of Total U.S. Commercial Bank Deposits
1957	50	417	851	$ 15.1	7.5%
1968	80	629	2,262	57.6	13.2
1970	121	895	3,260	78.1	16.2
1972	1,607	2,720	13,441	379.4	61.5
1976	1,912	3,791	19,203	553.6	66.1
1977	2,027	3,903	21,223	814.3	72.0

Source: *Federal Reserve Bulletin*, various issues; and Board of Governors of the Federal Reserve System, *Annual Statistical Digest, 1973–77* (Washington, D.C., 1978), pp. 277 and 283.

Many large banks established holding companies to get around interest rate ceilings on savings and time deposits. Federal regulations did not prevent holding companies from raising funds by selling commercial paper at rates above those set by the Federal Reserve's Regulation Q on time deposits. As a result, when market interest rates rose above the ceilings set by Regulation Q, some of the large bank holding companies were able to replace funds lost from time deposits with funds raised through the sale of commercial paper. In the early 1970s, another major objective of bank holding companies was to diversify into bank-related activities such as leasing, factoring, and investment or advisory services. The organization of bank holding companies has enabled banks to extend their operations outside the usual state boundaries.

Correspondent banking

Not as close a relationship exists between correspondent banks as between branch banks, but through their correspondent relationship, banks in an informal way have arranged themselves into a network of cooperating units. A small bank establishes a correspondent relationship by keeping deposits in a larger bank. Larger banks may establish a similar relationship by keeping deposits with each other.

Large banks compete to hold the interbank deposits of smaller banks because they provide the larger banks with funds to invest. In return for the deposit, the smaller bank receives from the larger bank advice, information, borrowed funds in time of need, help in international transactions, and some infrequently needed services that it would not pay the smaller bank to offer. Correspondent banks may lend to each other and cooperate on making loans to customers.

Bank directors and officers

The stockholders of a bank elect the bank's directors. The number of votes of each stockholder depends on the number of shares of stock owned. The chairman of the board of directors is elected by the directors. The directors usually meet at least once a month to pass on certain routine matters, to set charges, to hear and discuss reports, to approve changes in officer personnel, and to discuss problems and policies with the officers of the bank. Directors of national banks must be stockholders of the bank, and their legal responsibilities are usually greater than those of the directors of other corporations.[19]

The president, and, in some important banks, the chairman of the board and the vice-chairman, are usually the top management of the organization. They conduct the affairs of the bank and hire and supervise the employees. Other important officers are the vice-presidents in charge of the various banking activities, the trust officers, and the cashier and other officers in charge of bank operations.

Banks may be associated with each other by having one or more common directors. Independent banks linked in this way are sometimes called *chain banks* and have been most common in states that prohibit branch banking and where holding companies were not widely used to operate banks.[20] Since 1935, the Clayton Act has prohibited interlocking directorates between member banks of the Federal Reserve System located in the same or neighboring cities or towns. It was feared that such interlocks diminished competition. In the early 1970s, some states extended the prohibition against interlocking directorates in the same locality to all insured commercial banks, mutual savings banks, and savings and loan associations.

The Financial Institutions Regulatory and Interest Rate Control Act of 1978 expands federal government regulation of bank management. The act was passed by Congress in response to the banking scandal that led Bert Lance to resign as President Carter's Director of the Office of Management and Budget. The new law provides federal bank regulators with the right to fine individuals for banking-law violations and the authority to remove bank directors and officers who jeopardize the safety and soundness of a bank. It also prohibits overdrafts by bank insiders, limits the amount of loans banks can make to directors and officers—to not more than 10 percent of a bank's capital—and requires that insider loans be on a nonpreferential basis. In addition, it enables bank regulators to block changes in bank ownership that endanger the institution's safety. Interlocking directorates among large financial institutions and even among small ones in the same market are prohibited.

Summary

In past years, competition among commercial banks was reduced by the decline in the number of commercial banks, by barriers to entering the field of banking, and by restrictive government regulations. In recent years, competition has increased—chartering policy has become less restrictive, more branches have been approved, electronic computer terminals are allowed in some states, and more extensive foreign banking operations have been permitted in the United States. Also, competition has been increased by the rapid growth of other financial institutions such as the thrift institutions that provide many of the same services as commercial banks.

Most banks have some connection with other banks through a correspondent relationship, branching, or a common owner or holding company. In recent years, bank holding companies and foreign branches of United States banks have expanded rapidly.

The nature of modern commercial banking has evolved over the years and continues to change because of new regulations, new demands, opportunities for profit, tax advantages, and the development of specialized markets in which certain assets can be traded. In recent years, banks have entered several new bank-related fields—among them the credit-card and computer services fields.

Notes

1. "The Fifty Largest Commercial-Banking Companies," *Fortune* 94 (July 1979), p. 158.

2. Bray Hammond, *Banks and Politics in America* (Princeton: Princeton University Press, 1957), Chapters 1 and 6.

3. Ross M. Robertson, "The Comptroller and Bank Supervision: A Historical Appraisal," *National Banking Review* 4 (March 1967), pp. 247–261.

4. R. Alton Gilbert and Jean M. Lovati, "Bank Reserve Requirements and Their Enforcement: A Comparison Across States," *Federal Reserve Bank of St. Louis Review* (March 1978), pp. 22–31.

5. See Samuel B. Chase, Jr., "The Structure of Federal Regulation of Depository Institutions," and Donald D. Hester, "Opportunity and Responsibility in a Financial Institution," both in U.S. Committee on Banking, Currency and Housing, U.S. House, 94th Cong., 2d sess., *FINE: Financial Institutions and the Nation's Economy; Compendium of Papers Prepared for the FINE Study*, Committee Print (Washington, D.C.: USGPO, June 1976), pp. 157–170 and 185–190; and "Years of Reform:

A Prelude to Progress," in U.S. Comptroller of the Currency, *101st Annual Report, 1963* (Washington, D.C. 1964), pp. 1–32.

6. Carter H. Golembe, "The Deposit Insurance Legislation of 1933," *Political Science Quarterly* 75 (June 1960), pp. 181–200.

7. *Report of the President's Commission on Financial Structure and Regulation* (Washington, D.C.: U.S. Government Printing Office, 1972), pp. 61–62; and *FINE, op. cit.,* pp. 9 and 309.

8. Ross M. Robertson, *The Comptroller and Bank Supervision* (Washington, D.C.: Office of the Comptroller of the Currency, 1968), p. 101.

9. Paul M. Horvitz, "Economies of Scale in Banking," in Commission on Money and Credit, *Private Financial Institutions* (Englewood Cliffs, N.J.: Prentice-Hall, 1963), pp. 1–54; George J. Benston, "Economies of Scale and Marginal Costs in Banking Operations," in Kalman J. Cohen and Frederick S. Hammer, eds., *Analytical Methods in Banking* (Homewood, Ill.: Richard D. Irwin, 1966), pp. 545–574, and "Branch Banking and Economies of Scale," *Journal of Finance* 20 (May 1965), pp. 312–331; and Frederick W. Bell and Neil B. Murphy, *Economies of Scale in Commercial Banking* (Boston: Federal Reserve Bank of Boston, 1967), pp. 20–21.

10. David A. Alhadeff, *Monopoly and Competition in Banking* (Berkeley: University of California Press, 1954), pp. 77–87, 192. For a review of research on the economies of scale, see Robert C. Holland, "Research into Banking Structure and Competition," *Federal Reserve Bulletin* 50 (November 1964), pp. 1383–1399.

11. Board of Governors of the Federal Reserve System, *Annual Report, 1965* pp. 228–230, and *1978*, p. 365; and Jane D'Arista, "U.S. Banks Abroad," in *FINE, op. cit.,* pp. 801–1111.

12. Francis A. Lees, *International Banking and Finance* (New York: John Wiley and Sons, 1974), Chapter 6.

13. For a discussion of some aspects of these transfer systems, see William C. Niblack, "Development of Electronic Funds Transfer Systems," Federal Reserve Bank of St. Louis, *Review,* September 1976, pp. 1–18; and William L. Silber and Kenneth D. Garbade, "Financial Innovation and EFTS: Implications for Regulation," in *FINE, op. cit.,* pp. 193–208.

14. Federal Reserve Bank of San Francisco, "Regulating Foreign Banks," *Weekly Letter* (November 17, 1978).

15. Irwin M. Stelzer, *Selected Antitrust Cases,* 3d ed. (Homewood, Ill.: Richard D. Irwin, 1966), pp. 130–153; and Administrator of National Banks, United States Treasury, "Part One: Merger Policy: The Philadelphia Case," in *Studies in Banking Competition and the Banking Structure* (Washington, D.C., 1966), pp. 3–96.

16. See *Federal Reserve Bulletin,* January 1971, pp. 29–33; and Roy A. Schotland, "Bank Holding Companies and Public Policy Today," in *FINE, op. cit.,* pp. 233–283.

17. See Carter H. Golembe, "One-Bank Holding Companies," in Herbert V. Prochnow, ed., *The One-Bank Holding Company* (Chicago: Rand McNally, 1969), pp. 66–81.

18. Gregory E. Boczar, "The Growth of Multibank Holding Companies: 1956–73," *Federal Reserve Bulletin,* April 1976, pp. 300–301.

19. U.S. Comptroller of the Currency, *Duties and Liabilities of Directors of National Banks,* rev. ed. (Washington, D.C., 1968).

20. Jerome C. Darnell, "Determinants of Chain Banking," *National Banking Review* 4 (June 1967), pp. 459–468.

Questions

5.1 What are the arguments for and against "free banking"?

5.2. What are the functions of the comptroller of the currency?

5.3. In what ways has banking competition been limited in the United States?

5.4. Give some examples of the increasing competition in banking in the United States in recent years.

5.5. What are the differences between a national and a state bank? Between a member and a nonmember bank?

5.6 In what ways did the Depository Institutions Deregulation and Monetary Control Act of 1980 make member and nonmember banks more alike?

5.7. How does the Federal Deposit Insurance Corporation promote economic stability?

5.8. Describe bank examinations as a method of governmental regulation of banks.

5.9. How does the FDIC usually handle the failure of an insured bank?

5.10. Describe the history of the regulations preventing bank branches in the United States.

5.11. Explain the status of electronic computer terminals.

5.12. Describe some of the ways in which unit banks may achieve some of the advantages of branch banking.

5.13. What are some reasons U.S. banks have expanded their operations in foreign countries?

5.14. Describe the types of activities foreign banks engage in within the United States.

5.15. What are the objectives of bank holding companies?

5.16. Know the meaning and significance of the following terms and concepts: commercial bank, national bank, state bank, correspondent bank, deposit insurance, bank examination, bank holding company, dual banking system, chain banks, Edge Act corporation.

6

The principal financial activities engaged in by a commercial bank may be illustrated by examining each of the items on a typical balance sheet. Two of the important types of assets that banks own are their cash assets and their investments in securities.

THE CASH ASSETS AND INVESTMENTS OF COMMERCIAL BANKS

The assets held by a commercial bank are either prescribed by law or chosen by the officers of the bank to provide the mix of assets they desire. Although banks differ somewhat from one another, the balance sheet of the Dartmouth National Bank, located in Hanover, New Hampshire, may be used as an example of a small or medium-sized bank. On the date when the balance sheet was prepared, the cash in vault and the securities (valued at their purchase prices) were counted, the amount of the loans was calculated, and a value was determined for each of the other types of assets, liabilities, and capital accounts. The assets are the property that the bank owns; the liabilities are its debts; and the capital accounts show the amount originally invested by the owners, modified by retained profits and losses thereafter. The assets must equal the liabilities plus the capital accounts. Each transaction affecting a bank's operations results in two balancing entries: for example, in increasing one asset and decreasing another asset, or in increasing an asset and simultaneously increasing a liability. The fundamental technique that is involved is called double-entry bookkeeping.

The first item listed on the balance sheet in Table 6.1 consists of three types of cash assets: cash in vault, balances with other banks (including its Federal Reserve bank), and cash items in process of collection. Other important assets discussed in this chapter are federal funds sold, bank investments in certificates of deposit in other banks, U.S. government securities, and municipal bonds.

Cash in vault

Cash in vault consists of the coins and paper money in the bank's vault or cash drawers. A bank must always have coins and paper money on hand because its demand and time deposits are legally payable in cash. Each day some of the customers can be expected to request cash. A bank must have all of the various denominations of coins and paper money so that it can provide its customers with the kind as well as the quantity of cash they want.

Because, on a daily basis, the cash deposited by customers approximately balances the cash withdrawn, a bank can operate with a relatively small amount of cash in vault compared to its deposits. Excessive amounts of cash on hand are avoided because of the relative ease with which cash can be stolen and because it earns no interest income.

Commercial banks are legally required to hold as reserves a specified percentage of their deposits in certain types of liquid assets. Because they are required to hold only a percentage of their assets as reserves, commercial banks in the United States are known as *fractional reserve banks.* Since 1960, banks that are members of the Federal Reserve System have been allowed to count vault cash, in addition to deposits

**Table 6.1
Statement of Condition
of the Dartmouth
National Bank of
Hanover, June 30, 1979**

[handwritten: net Reserve, not part of nat'l funds]

Assets

	(in thousands)
Cash, balances at other banks, and checks in process of collection	$ 4,040
Federal funds sold *[handwritten: investment, excess cash banks have. Has nothing to do w/ fed'l gov.]*	1,500
Certificates of deposit	1,500
U.S. Treasury securities	4,488
Obligations of states and political subdivisions	3,395
Other securities	41
Loans *[handwritten: pay higher interest then others - more risky]*	33,854
Bank premises, furniture, fixtures, and miscellaneous	3,159
Total assets	$51,977

Liabilities

Demand deposits	$ 9,389
Time and savings deposits	32,447
Securities sold under agreement to repurchase *[handwritten: repos]*	1,950
Demand notes issued to the U.S. Treasury	406
Deposits of states and political subdivisions	1,321
Certified and officers' checks, etc.	651
Mortgage indebtedness	1,187
Other liabilities[a] *[handwritten: Deposits being process]*	669
Total liabilities	$48,020

Capital accounts

[handwritten left margin: add'l value on left side that exceds the liability]

Common stock—total par value *[handwritten: amt that bank stock sold for originally]*	$ 200
Surplus *[handwritten: pure add'l value]*	1,000
Undivided profits and reserve for contingencies and other capital reserves *[handwritten: surplus against contingencies]*	2,757
Total capital accounts	$ 3,957
Total liabilities and capital accounts	$51,977

[a]Includes a large transit account for deposits being processed.

at the Federal Reserve banks, as part of their legal reserves. This has encouraged banks to hold larger amounts of vault cash.

To illustrate the way in which the movements of cash affect a bank, we use the T-account technique. On one side of the "T" are assets, and on the other side liabilities and capital accounts. If $1,000 in currency were deposited in the bank, the balance sheet would be affected as shown in T-account 6.1:

6.1

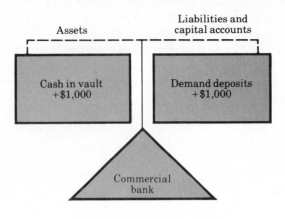

The cash in vault would be increased by $1,000, and the depositor would receive in return an increase in his deposit of $1,000.

A withdrawal of $1,000 in currency would affect the balance sheet as follows:

6.2

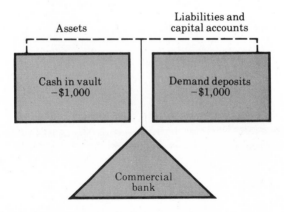

The bank would give the depositor $1,000 from its cash in vault, and the depositor would pay for it by a reduction in his demand deposit of the same amount. The T-account shows that the term "deposit" is misleading. The cash received by a bank when a person deposits currency is an asset of the bank, and the deposit is merely a recorded obligation on the books of the bank.

If the outflow of cash is more than the inflow, a bank may replenish its stock of coins and paper currency by ordering an additional amount from a Federal Reserve bank. The balance sheet changes when a bank obtains $1,000 in cash from its Federal Reserve bank are:

6.3

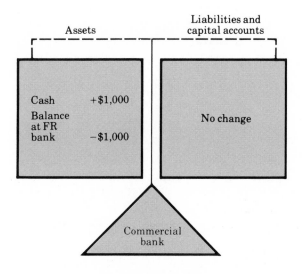

The bank would now hold more cash, but its deposit at the Federal Reserve bank would be less. Commercial banks have deposits in a Reserve bank that are basically the same as the kind of deposits persons have in commercial banks. When $1,000 in cash is deposited in the Federal Reserve bank, the commercial bank's balance at the Reserve bank is increased and its cash in vault decreased as shown in T-account 6.4:

6.4

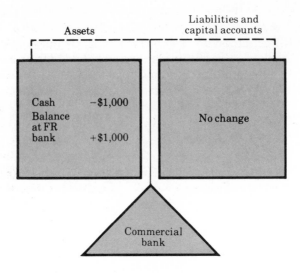

Balances at other banks and checks in process of collection

The item "balances at other banks" listed on the balance sheet of the Dartmouth National Bank includes its reserve deposit at the Federal Reserve Bank of Boston and its demand deposits at several large commercial banks.

Balances at the Federal Reserve Bank

The deposit at the Federal Reserve Bank of Boston is used for check clearing and collection in addition to being the major portion of the bank's legally required reserves. Because its reserve deposit earns no interest, a member bank typically holds in this account no more than is required, plus a small additional amount to meet check clearing needs. Except for checks requiring special attention (those on foreign banks and those on banks not on the par list), the Dartmouth National Bank sends to the Federal Reserve Bank of Boston all of the checks it receives that are written on other banks. On the way to the Federal Reserve Bank of Boston, these checks go through the computer services division of the First National Bank of Boston where the Dartmouth National Bank's deposit bookkeeping is done. (Because the computers and related machines used for processing checks are very costly, small banks find that it saves money to contract out their deposit bookkeeping.)

The checks written on other banks that have been received by the Dartmouth National Bank and are en route to the Federal Reserve Bank of Boston are assets because they represent claims to funds. The dollar amount of those checks is included on the balance sheet under *checks in process of collection.* Between the time the checks are received by the Dartmouth National Bank and the time the checks are processed by the bookkeeping division of the First National Bank of Boston, the amount of the checks in process of collection is balanced on the liability side of the balance sheet by the same amount in a transit account included in *other liabilities.* Suppose a check for $1,000 written on the National Shawmut Bank in Boston were received by the Dartmouth National Bank from one of its depositors. The immediate effect on the balance sheet of the Dartmouth National Bank is shown in T-account 6.5:

6.5

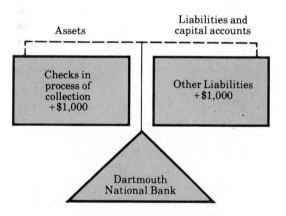

As soon as the check is processed by the computer services division of the First National Bank of Boston, the account of the person depositing the check would be increased by $1,000. Because the check is still en route to the Federal Reserve Bank of Boston, the item "checks in process of collection" is unchanged. At this stage, the effect of the check on the balance sheet of the Dartmouth National Bank would be as shown in T-account 6.6 instead of 6.5:

6.6

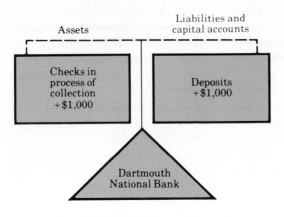

After the check is processed by the Federal Reserve Bank of Boston, the Dartmouth National Bank's balance in the Federal Reserve Bank of Boston would be increased, replacing the amount of checks in process of collection. The end result of the receipt of the check on the Dartmouth National Bank's balance sheet would be as in T-account 6.7:

6.7

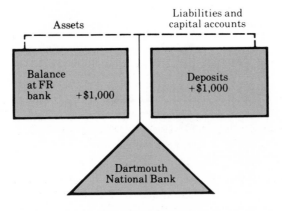

Because the check sent to the Federal Reserve Bank of Boston was written on the National Shawmut Bank, the Federal Reserve Bank of Boston would also decrease the balance of the National Shawmut Bank by $1,000 and would, in effect, collect this amount for the Dartmouth National Bank.

At the same time that the Dartmouth National Bank is receiving checks written on other banks, other banks are receiving checks written on the Dartmouth National Bank. These checks are also sent to the Federal Reserve Bank of Boston. When another bank sends a check for $1,000 written on the Dartmouth National Bank back for collection through the Federal Reserve bank, the following changes occur on the balance sheet:

6.8

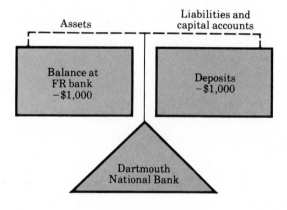

The Federal Reserve Bank of Boston decreases the Dartmouth National Bank's deposit there, and there is also a reduction in the deposit of the customer of the Dartmouth National Bank who wrote the check.

The balance of the Dartmouth National Bank at the Federal Reserve Bank of Boston increases if the total value of checks on other banks that it deposits there is greater than the value of checks on itself that other banks send to the Federal Reserve for collection. Its balance at the Federal Reserve Bank of Boston decreases if its clearing balance is unfavorable. Such changes in the size of its balance at the Federal Reserve are important because this deposit is the principal part of its legal reserve, and changes in reserves determine whether a bank expands or contracts its loans and investments. A bank will immediately invest or lend the amount of its balance at the Reserve bank in excess of its needs so as to earn additional interest. If its balance at the Reserve bank is not sufficient to meet its reserve requirements and its check clearing needs, a bank must obtain a larger balance, possibly by selling securities or letting loans run off.

Balances at correspondent banks

The Dartmouth National Bank holds deposits in large commercial banks located in Boston and New York. This establishes a *correspondent* relationship with these banks. The Dartmouth National Bank uses these correspondent balances as checking accounts, and deposits in them special checks not handled by the Reserve banks. The principal purpose of the correspondent relationship is to achieve some of the advantages of branch banking while at the same time maintaining local ownership and control. The large city banks provide the Dartmouth National Bank with advice on investments and legal matters and the credit ratings of business borrowers. They may also assist in finding officer personnel, and they may invite the Dartmouth National Bank to participate in large loans that they have arranged. The size of a bank's deposit in a correspondent bank is determined informally, but if a rural bank relies heavily on its correspondent city bank for assistance, one would expect its deposit in the urban bank to be relatively large. Although members of the Federal Reserve System are not permitted to count these interbank deposits as legal reserves, nonmember banks have usually been able to use them for this purpose. Reserve requirements for nonmembers were until 1980 established by the governments of the states in which they were located rather than by the Federal Reserve System.

Trend of bank investments

Commercial banks invest primarily in federal funds sold, certificates of deposit, U.S. Treasury securities (including those issued by agencies of the federal government), and municipal bonds; they may also invest in commercial paper and corporate bonds—but not in corporation stocks. Each of these types of investment has its particular advantages and disadvantages. The way in which the assets of a bank are distributed among the various types of investments is one of the fundamental aspects of bank management.

Commercial banks usually sell federal funds to other banks and they purchase certificates of deposit from other banks. They purchase U.S. Treasury securities and municipal bonds from dealers who are in the business of buying and selling them. The transactions with other banks and with dealers are impersonal. The dealers are middlemen. There is seldom a direct relationship between the bank, as lender, and the borrower who has issued the securities. Investing in these various types of securities may be done very promptly. Although at times yields may be unattractive, a wide variety of investments is always immediately available.

There are important cyclical changes in the total amount of bank investments as compared with the total amount of their loans. The volume of commercial bank loans is significantly determined by business conditions. In periods of recession, total bank loans drop sharply, and funds that might have been lent are then invested in securities. In periods of expansion, when commercial bank loans rise sharply in response to the increase in business demand, banks get additional funds to lend by selling off some of their securities.

Federal funds sold[1]

Table 6.1 shows that on June 30, 1979, the Dartmouth National Bank had invested $1.5 million in *federal funds sold.* Federal funds are deposits at a Federal Reserve bank, and federal funds sold is the amount of the Dartmouth National Bank's deposits at the Federal Reserve Bank of Boston which has been lent to another commercial bank or to a dealer in those funds.

The way in which the Dartmouth National Bank lends federal funds is typical of many other smaller banks. Smaller banks sell federal funds to large urban banks. The Dartmouth National Bank attempts to hold no more deposits in the Federal Reserve bank than are required as reserves, and, by a standing arrangement with the First National Bank of Boston, it lends to them any excess reserve balances that it has. Federal funds are usually lent for a period of one day so that the amount sold may, if necessary, be varied daily. The minimum unit is usually $100,000. Larger banks also may buy and sell these funds among themselves through federal funds dealers.

When the Dartmouth National Bank sells $100,000 in federal funds, the effect on its balance sheet is a reduction in its balance at the Federal Reserve bank and an increase in federal funds sold:

6.9

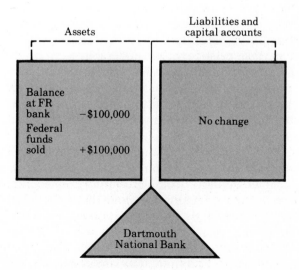

And the effect on the balance sheet of the First National Bank of Boston is to increase its balance at the Federal Reserve bank and its liability, *federal funds purchased:*

6.10

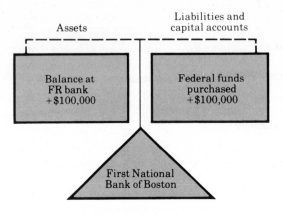

The Dartmouth National Bank gives the First National Bank of Boston a check for $100,000 on the Federal Reserve bank (this may be done by telephone). When this check is received by the Federal Reserve bank, the Dartmouth National Bank's balance there is reduced, and the First National Bank of Boston's balance is increased. To the First National Bank of Boston, federal funds purchased is a type of borrowing used to increase working funds.

The Dartmouth National Bank and other small and medium-sized banks often use federal funds sold as *secondary reserves.* It is useful to hold some type of secondary reserve because the cash assets of banks—cash in vault, balances at the Federal Reserve bank, and demand deposits at correspondent banks—are usually of little use when liquid assets are needed. Reserve assets cannot be reduced very much when total deposits decline, and correspondent balances are small and are expected to be retained at their customary level. Banks prefer to hold secondary reserves rather than excess legal reserves because secondary reserves earn interest income, and balances at the Federal Reserve and cash do not. If a bank has on hand an adequate amount of federal funds sold, should deposits decline (resulting in an equal loss of legal reserves), reserves may be replenished immediately by reducing the amount of federal funds sold. By providing for liquidity in this way, no unpleasant repercussions on lending activities will result, and there need be no forced sales, at a loss, of long-term securities. Since federal funds are sold for one day at a time, they are available promptly to replace lost reserves. Banks also must have funds available at all times to accommodate credit-worthy borrowers who are also important depositors. If a bank is unable to accommodate such borrowers, it runs the risk of losing their deposits.

The borrowing of federal funds, called federal funds purchased, has become an important source of funds for large commercial banks. Before the mid-1960s, the usual reason for borrowing federal funds was to replenish reserves to meet reserve requirements. At that time, the federal funds rate did not rise above the discount rate at which the Federal Reserve banks made loans to member banks because, if it did, banks would choose to borrow from the Federal Reserve banks rather than in the federal funds market. Banks no longer simply rely on an inflow of deposits, but aggressively expand their borrowing of federal funds and other types of borrowing, especially when the demand for credit is heavy. An advantage of federal funds as a source of funds is that except under special circumstances they have been free of reserve requirements.

Certificates of deposit

In very recent years, some commercial banks have invested relatively large amounts in certificates of deposit (CDs) at other commercial banks. On June 30, 1979, the Dartmouth National Bank had $1.5 million invested in CDs. CDs have denominations of $100,000 or more. The date of issue and the maturity of a CD may be adjusted to meet the needs of the lender, and there are no ceilings set by the Federal Reserve on their interest rates. CDs not only serve as secondary reserve because of their liquidity, but, as shown in Table 6.2, banks have usually been able to obtain a higher yield on certificates of deposit at other banks than on other short-term investments.

Table 6.2
Money Market Rates,
1975–1979

Year	Federal Funds	Prime Commercial Paper[a]	U.S. Treasury Bills, 3-month	Certificates of Deposit[b]
1975	5.82%	6.26%	5.80%	6.43%
1976	5.05	5.24	4.98	5.26
1977	5.54	5.54	5.27	5.58
1978	7.94	7.94	7.19	8.20
1979 (May)	10.24	9.95	9.61	10.15

[a]90- to 119-day.
[b]Large, negotiable, three-month, secondary market.
Source: *Federal Reserve Bulletin*, May 1978, p. A27, and June 1979, p. A27.

U.S. government securities

Commercial banks invest in large amounts of marketable U.S. government securities. In recent years, securities of federally sponsored agencies—such as the Federal National Mortgage Association, Federal Home Loan Banks, and Federal Land Banks—have grown in importance.

Since World War II, investments in U.S. Treasury securities as a type of bank asset have declined sharply in importance relative to loans. Table 6.3 shows that in 1978 commercial banks had 9 percent of their total loans and investments in U.S. Treasury securities, compared to 55 percent in 1948. During World War II, the volume of U.S. government securities outstanding had increased greatly because of the financing of the war, and banks had purchased a substantial amount of them. As shown in Table 6.1, the Dartmouth National Bank holds about 9 percent of its total assets in investments of this type.

Table 6.3
Commercial Bank Loans and Investments, Selected Years, 1948–1978, Seasonally Adjusted (in billions of dollars)

End of Year	Loans	U.S. Treasury Securities	Other Securities	Total Loans and Investments
1948	$ 41.5	$62.3	$ 9.2	$113.0
1958	95.6	65.1	20.5	181.2
1968	258.2	60.7	71.3	390.2
1978	709.0	88.4	169.9	967.3

Source: *Economic Report of the President, January 1979*, p. 252.

Commercial banks still hold large amounts of U.S. government securities for several important reasons:

1. There is a well-organized market for the purchase and sale of U.S. government securities. This market is described in Chapter 4. Although the yield on tax-exempt municipals may be higher than the after-tax yield on U.S. government securities, most municipals have the disadvantage of not having their prices quoted regularly in the newspaper. Most states and units of local government issue such small amounts of bonds that their securities are not traded often. If a bank wishes to sell a municipal bond, the price quoted by a dealer may be low partly because of the "thinness" of the market.

2. Short and intermediate maturities are available. Municipals are typically long-term. Banks invest primarily in U.S. government securities maturing in five years or less. Intermediate-term U.S. government securities are not as risky as long-term municipals because the prices of these issues do not fall as much as the prices of long-term issues when market interest rates rise.

Also, some commercial banks own short-term federal government securities, such as Treasury bills, as secondary reserves to provide liquidity. Treasury bills can usually be sold immediately without incurring a loss. Because of their very short maturity, their prices do not vary much when market interest rates fluctuate. When banks need to reduce earning assets because of a decline in their total deposits, they may sell some of these short-term U.S. government securities. This may also be a useful source of funds to lend to important customers on short notice.

Investments in short-term Treasury securities (including securities issued by agencies of the U.S. government) were stimulated in 1978 when the Federal Reserve authorized commercial banks to offer six-month money market certificates (also called T-bill certificates) carrying a much higher rate of interest than that allowed on most other types of time deposits. Money market certificates are a new type of time deposit with a minimum denomination of $10,000 and a rate of interest equal to the six-month Treasury bill rate at time of issue. By investing in securities maturing in six months, commercial banks can earn enough to pay the rate on money market certificates and still be sufficiently liquid to cover a possible loss of deposits when the six-month money market certificates mature.

3. When prices of government securities fall, banks often can realize tax losses by switching from the issues in their portfolios to other similar issues.[2] Because of their marketability, this is easier to do with U.S. government securities than with most other investments. A loss is realized when a bond is sold at a price less than the price originally paid for it. These losses will be offset later because there will be larger gains from the new securities purchased than there would have been on those that were sold. When these gains are realized, the tax liability of the bank will be larger, but in the meantime the bank has had the use of the funds that would otherwise have had to be paid in taxes. This amounts to an interest-free loan from the federal government.

4. Banks are legally required to hold an amount of U.S. government securities equal to the amount deposited by the federal government and some state governments in that bank. If a bank has large deposits of either the federal government or the state in which it is located, the amount of U.S. government securities that it must hold may be substantial. U.S. government securities are also used as collateral when borrowing from a Federal Reserve bank, and a commercial bank may hold some U.S. government securities as a safeguard for this purpose.

5. Federal securities are considered safer than most other investments. The sharp increase in the amount of U.S. government securities owned by commercial banks from $50.4 billion in December 1974 to $96.5 billion in December 1976 was partly due to the financial difficulties of New York City and a resulting loss of confidence in municipal bonds.

Municipal bonds

The "obligations of states and political subdivisions," commonly called municipals, consist of the bonds issued by states, cities, counties, towns, school districts, and turnpike authorities.[3] There are more than 91,000 separate units of state and local government that have used bond issues to finance a variety of projects, among them the construction of schools and other public buildings, water facilities, sewage plants, bridges, toll-roads, airports, subways, and low-cost public housing. These units of government finance about two-thirds of their capital expenditures through the sale of municipal bonds. The other third comes from current revenue and state and federal grants.

At the end of June 1977, there was $258 billion in state-and-local government debt outstanding, and commercial banks held about half of it. Table 6.3 shows that between 1948 and 1978 other securities (consisting primarily of municipal bonds) rose from 8 percent to about 18 percent of total loans and investments of commercial banks. The capital market for municipal securities is second in size only to the market for U.S. government securities. New issues of both municipal and corporate securities are handled by investment banks, which buy the securities from the issuer and undertake to resell them to investors for a profit. This is known as the *primary market*. The market for outstanding issues is known as the *secondary* or *trading market*. For municipal securities, the trading market consists of several hundred dealers (mostly banks) and a small number of brokers. Until 1975, the municipal bond market had little regulation. The Securities Act Amendment of 1975 established the Municipal Rulemaking Board to regulate this market.

Municipal bonds are typically issued in $5,000 denominations. Most of them have coupons attached for semiannual interest payments. Interest on municipal bonds has the special advantage of being exempt from federal income taxes. Banks are subject to the corporation income tax which taxes net income in excess of $100,000 at the rate of 46 percent. At this rate, if a bank received 5 percent on a municipal bond, this would be equivalent to a taxable yield of 9.6 percent on U.S. government or corporate bonds. In recent years, the rate of return on municipal bonds has been more attractive than on other bonds when the tax exemption is taken into account. In 1978, the average tax-exempt yield on high-grade municipals was 5.52 percent, while the taxable yield averaged 8.73 percent on high quality corporate bonds and 7.89 percent on long-term U.S. government bonds.

Most municipal bonds are long-term. However, as much as one-tenth of those held by large commercial banks have been *tax warrants*. These are notes and bills maturing within one year. They provide local governments with the funds they need before the dates when taxes are paid.

Banks tend to hold municipal bonds with the four highest ratings—Standard and Poor's listings of AAA, AA, A, and BBB, or Moody's of Aaa, Aa, A, and Baa. Municipal bond ratings are important guides to bond selection. They reflect the diversity of industry and the stability of employment in the community, and the debt load that has been incurred. Legal opinions are now commonly printed on the back of municipal bonds (for older issues, the legal opinions are attached) concerning the legality of the method of financing, the amount issued, the purpose, and the terms of the contract. These legal opinions are useful because of the diversity of state and local restrictions. Since 1975, there has been uncertainty as to the reliability of ratings of municipal bonds, and some lawsuits have been filed.

Some municipals can be retired by the issuer before maturity if the issuer wishes to do so. This call option would be used if interest rates became relatively low. Banks dislike the call feature because it could force them to relend the amount paid off at those lower rates.

Municipals that are backed by the full power to tax of the locality issuing them are called *general obligation bonds. Revenue bonds* are repaid solely from the earnings of the project financed—for instance, from the fees charged by a tollroad or a water company. From the point of view of the credit base, general obligation bonds have less risk than revenue bonds. However, the terms of revenue bonds usually limit the additional debt that can be assumed by the issuer, while the holder of a general obligation bond is given no such assurance. Probably the highest grade tax-exempt municipal bonds have been thought to be those issued by local housing agencies, but backed by federal resources through the Public Housing Administration, a federal agency.[4] These bonds are called New Housing Authority Bonds, or PHAs.

From World War II until recently, very few units of state and local government had difficulty in paying interest charges and principal on their indebtedness. (Exceptions were the bonds of the West Virginia Turnpike and Chicago's Calumet Skyway.) However, in 1975 a severe jolt occurred in the municipal market when it became apparent that New York City was in serious financial difficulty. Two major New York City banks refused to make a loan to the city without further information on expected revenues, and a group of bankers asked for a legal opinion on whether the city was exceeding its borrowing authority. City officials accused the banks of unfavorable publicity, making unprecedented demands, and contributing to the city's financial problems. Because banks throughout the country were caught holding New York City securities and because the largest seven banks in New York City held at that time $1.25 billion of these securities (9 percent of those outstanding), contingency plans were made by the Federal Reserve System in case of a default. Nonmember banks in need were to be allowed to borrow from the Federal Reserve at a rate of about 3 percent above that charged member banks. Banks were also to be allowed up to six months to reduce the value of any New York City securities held as assets on their books. During 1975 and 1976, bankruptcy was avoided—with the help of a federal loan, a group of banks renewing (at low interest) notes held and falling due, purchase of securities by the city's teachers' retirement system, increased taxes, budget cuts, a state-passed moratorium on the payment of principal on notes coming due, and other measures. In recent years, Yonkers, Philadelphia, Boston, Detroit, Buffalo, Cleveland, Chicago, and several other cities and some states have also had financial difficulties.

Commercial paper

Commercial banks are allowed to invest in commercial paper—a type of short-term security issued by both nonfinancial and financial corporations. It is unsecured, and only companies having a high credit standing can obtain funds in this way.[5] Although commercial paper is not as liquid as federal funds or 91-day U.S. Treasury bills, it is a relatively liquid investment and would be part of the secondary reserve of a commercial bank. In recent years, commercial banks have invested only a very small amount in commercial paper because the rate of interest received on CDs at other banks has been above the rate on commercial paper (see Table 6.2).

At the present time, the principal significance of commercial paper to banks is that it competes with loans from banks as a source of funds for large corporations. In 1978, the total amount of commercial paper outstanding was equal to approximately 13 percent of total loans at commercial banks, and 44 percent of their commercial and industrial loans. Whenever the commercial paper rate is less than interest rates charged by banks, corporations are encouraged to borrow less from banks.

Table 6.4 shows the rapid increase in the volume of commercial paper outstanding from 1962 to 1979—from approximately $6 billion to over $92 billion. Commercial paper was used extensively as a type of financing following World War I, until its growth was drastically curtailed by the depression of the 1930s.

Table 6.4
Commercial and
Finance Company
Paper Outstanding,
1962–1979, Selected
Years (in millions
of dollars)

End of Year	Amount
1962	$ 6,000
1967	17,085
1972	34,721
1975	48,471
1976	52,971
1977	65,101
1978	83,665
1979 (April)	92,725

Source: *Banking and Monetary Statistics, 1941–1970* (Washington, D.C.: Board of Governors of the Federal Reserve System, 1976), pp. 717-718; *Federal Reserve Bulletin*, December 1976, p. A25, and June 1979, p. A25.

Table 6.5 shows the industrial classification of the major companies issuing commercial paper in 1976. The principal issuers are industrial corporations and public utilities, although finance companies and bank holding companies also obtain large amounts of funds in this way.

**Table 6.5
Number of Companies
Having Commercial
Paper Ratings, by
Industry, October 1976[a]**

Industry Grouping	Number of Companies
Industrial	316
Public utility	173
Finance company	91
Bank holding company	80
Leasing	21
Insurance	18
Real estate investment trust	10
Transportation	4
Government	1
Total	714

[a]Based on listings of Moody's Investors Service, Standard and Poor's Corporation; and Fitch Investors Service.
Source: Evelyn M. Hurley, "The Commercial Paper Market," *Federal Reserve Bulletin*, June 1977, p. 528.

The maturity of issues of commercial paper is usually sixty days or less, and may be only a few days. To avoid the registration requirements of the Securities and Exchange Commission, issues must mature in less than nine months. Commercial paper is normally available in denominations of $50,000, $100,000, $250,000, $500,000, and $1,000,000, and a few companies offer it in denominations of $25,000. Commercial paper is sold for less than its maturity value, and the rate of interest depends on the size of the discount.

More than 60 percent (in terms of value) of commercial paper outstanding is sold directly to buyers by the issuer with a bank or sales organization acting as an agent for the sale. Sales finance companies and bank holding companies are the principal issuers of this *direct paper*. The maturity date may be negotiated.

Dealer paper is purchased mainly by ten dealers for resale to customers at a slightly higher price, with the dealer taking some risk by holding the paper for a while. He may require the company to have a line of credit with a commercial bank equal to the amount of the issues.

Purchasers of commercial paper are occasionally reminded of the risks involved—as they were when the Penn Central started bankruptcy proceedings in 1970 with $100 million in commercial paper outstanding. Most commercial paper is rated by one or more of the three rating services—Moody's, Standard and Poor, or Fitch Investors Service. The issuing companies pay a fee for this rating.

Bank holding companies were induced to sell commercial paper to obtain funds when market rates of interest were above the ceiling rates permitted on their time deposits. This inducement was curtailed sharply in 1970 and 1973 when the Federal Reserve System revised Regulation Q by eliminating ceiling rates on large certificates of deposit. After this change, banks could attract funds by offering higher rates of interest on CDs rather than by selling commercial paper.

Not only have industrial corporations borrowed through the commercial paper market, but at times they have owned as much as 60 percent of the commercial paper outstanding. Commercial paper competes with certificates of deposit and Treasury bills as a way for corporations to hold short-term funds. When the Federal Reserve's Regulation Q caused CDs to become unattractive relative to commercial paper, corporations with funds to invest shifted to the commercial paper market.

Corporate bonds

Commercial banks invest in only limited amounts of corporate bonds. Federal securities, municipal bonds, federal funds sold, and certificates of deposit either offer more attractive rates of return or are more liquid. On the Dartmouth National Bank's balance sheet, corporate bonds would be included under "other securities."

Corporate bonds have the same basic characteristics as U.S. Treasury bonds or municipal bonds. The principal difference is that they are issued by private business corporations rather than by government. They have definite maturity dates and fixed interest payments, and the yield to maturity varies with changes in their prices. The initial maturity is usually from ten to thirty years. They are an important source of corporate finance, especially for utilities. For bonds of well-established corporations, risk of default is slight. Corporate bonds that are called *debentures* are general obligations of the issuing company, and those secured by specific physical assets are called *mortgage bonds*.

Commercial banks are not allowed to invest in most types of corporation stock. Banks that are members of the Federal Reserve System are required to purchase a limited amount of stock of the Federal Reserve banks. They may also purchase the stock of certain corporations that the federal government is attempting to promote, such as the Student Loan Marketing Association and the housing corporations under the Housing Act of 1968.

Bank premises, furniture, and fixtures

The assets of a bank, in addition to its loans and investments and its cash, include its building and its furniture and equipment. Unless the bank rents part of the space in its building, these assets are not a source of money income, but the use of them by the bank provides real income.

The estimated value of these assets is based on such factors as their original cost and depreciation.

Summary

A small amount of cash in vault is always needed to meet a bank's obligation to pay deposits in cash. A bank that is a member of the Federal Reserve System is legally required to hold a certain amount of cash plus balances in its Federal Reserve bank. Though not required by law, small balances in other commercial banks are used for clearing special types of checks and for establishing correspondent relationships.

Because liquid assets (such as federal funds sold, Treasury bills, and certificates of deposit) earn interest, banks prefer to own them rather than hold amounts of cash in vault and balances in other banks larger than are needed. Many banks lend federal funds, invest in Treasury bills, or own certificates of deposit because of their liquidity despite lower rates of return than those available on other possible investments. Holding assets of this type gives a bank access to funds to cover a decline in total deposits or to accommodate important borrowers.

Banks invest in U.S. government securities with intermediate maturities because of their safety and marketability, and because banks must hold an amount of U.S. government securities equal to their U.S. Treasury deposits.

If the risk of default is low, municipal bonds are attractive investments to many banks because the interest received from them is tax-exempt, and municipal bonds usually have relatively high rates of return.

In recent years the volume of commercial paper has grown rapidly because some businesses have been able to obtain funds at lower rates through this market than by borrowing from commercial banks, and investors may receive a higher rate of return from owning commercial paper than from holding U.S. Treasury bills or certificates of deposit in commercial banks.

Notes

1. Parker B. Willis, *The Federal Funds Market,* 4th ed. (Boston: Federal Reserve Bank of Boston, 1970); and G. Walter Woodworth, *The Money Market and Monetary Management,* 2d ed. (New York: Harper & Row, 1972), Chapter 4.

2. Robert H. Parks, "Income and Tax Aspects of Commercial Bank Portfolio Operations in Treasury Securities," *National Tax Journal* 11

(March 1958), pp. 21–34. The Tax Reform Act of 1969 no longer permits banks to claim the discount earned on coupon securities as a long-term capital gain. All bank earnings from bonds are now taxed as ordinary income.

3. For a discussion of municipal bonds, see Karl M. Shelton, "Municipal Bonds: Underwriting, Trading, and Investment Portfolio Usage in Commercial Banks," in William H. Baughn and Charls E. Walker, eds., revised edition, *The Bankers' Handbook* (Homewood, Ill.: Dow-Jones-Irwin, 1978), pp. 511–521.

4. Robert Metz, "Does U.S. Back City's Housing Bonds?" *New York Times*, Dec. 10, 1976, p. D2.

5. See Evelyn M. Hurley, "The Commercial Paper Market," *Federal Reserve Bulletin*, June 1977, pp. 525–536.

Questions

6.1. How would the receipt of $100 in currency from a depositor affect the balance sheet of a commercial bank?

6.2. If a commercial bank orders $1,000 in currency from its Federal Reserve bank, how would the commercial bank's balance sheet be affected?

6.3. What uses do balances at a Federal Reserve bank have?

6.4. Explain why commercial banks have balances with correspondent banks.

6.5. How are bank investments different from bank loans?

6.6. How do total bank loans and total bank investments vary during the expansion and contraction phases of the business cycle?

6.7. What are federal funds?

6.8. Explain why some banks desire to sell federal funds and other banks desire to purchase them.

6.9. Why is it useful for a commercial bank to own some highly liquid assets such as U.S. Treasury bills, certificates of deposit, or federal funds sold?

6.10. Compare U.S. government securities with municipal bonds as types of bank investments. What are their advantages and disadvantages?

6.11. Why do banks invest substantial amounts in U.S. government securities?

6.12. Describe commercial paper as a type of investment.

6.13. Why may the amount of commercial paper outstanding increase rapidly when interest rates are very high?

6.14. Why is the amount of corporate bonds owned by commercial banks relatively small?

6.15. Summarize some of the objectives that a bank takes into consideration when managing its portfolio of investments.

6.16. Know the meaning and significance of the following terms and concepts: balance sheet, assets, liabilities, capital accounts, cash in vault, checks in process of collection, federal funds sold and purchased, investments in certificates of deposit, municipal bonds, commercial paper, secondary reserves, balance at the Federal Reserve banks.

7

The loans made by commercial banks to business enterprises are used primarily to purchase inventory goods, machinery, and buildings; those made to individuals are for the purchase of housing, automobiles, and consumer durables. An expansion in these types of spending may have an especially stimulating effect on the economy.

COMMERCIAL BANK LOANS

Deposit money is created when commercial banks expand either their loans or their investments in securities. Bankers make loans in order to obtain higher rates of return than are usually available on most securities and in order to compete for deposits of business firms. Loans take time to arrange, require judgment, and must be watched carefully. Loans offer less liquidity than some other types of assets and do not have the special tax advantages that municipal bonds have.

Commercial banks as financial intermediaries

As a type of business, commercial banks are middlemen between depositors and borrowers. These two groups are frequently not able to deal directly with each other on terms acceptable to each. As middlemen, the terms on which banks accept many of their deposits—repayment on demand—are different from the terms on which most of their loans are made—repayment on time. Depositors want to be able to transfer money by check and to get cash whenever needed. But a merchant, manufacturer, or individual borrower wants time to accumulate funds to repay his loan. His repayment schedule would not fit the demands of most depositors. As intermediaries, banks lend funds on terms different from those on which they accept them. In a general way, commercial banks can be compared to other types of middlemen. A wholesaler of goods also buys on terms different from those on which he sells. He buys in bulk from the manufacturer and sells in quantities that retailers desire.

The supply of loanable funds is a scarce resource, which bankers in their everyday activities allocate among various possible uses. Credit is wasted if loans are made to business firms that fail to use the funds productively and are unable to pay back the amount borrowed with interest. Fortunately, most loans do not turn out to be bad ones; but in order to achieve the best allocation of credit, bankers must lend funds to borrowers who can successfully pay the highest rates of return. Efficiently allocated loans, besides serving the interests of bankers who seek high profits, benefit borrowers and society as a whole. It is believed that society benefits if scarce supplies of loanable funds are used in ways that yield, for example, a real rate of return of 5 percent rather than 4 percent. To pay the higher real rate of interest, the funds borrowed would have to be used to finance investments that themselves yield a real return at least as high as the rate of interest. A capital market that efficiently processes information on the supply of and demand for loans, and achieves market and real interest rates that are accurate signals for capital allocation, is an important component of a capitalist system.[1] Bankers guide capital markets by gathering information, setting market and real interest rates for different levels of risk, and deciding to whom money will be lent.

Private ownership of banks provides an inducement for bankers to lend money successfully and in ways in which market and real rates of return are highest, because owners of banks receive maximum rates of return on their bank stock only if banks successfully lend funds at the highest possible rates of return. In both socialist and capitalist countries, it is important that scarce resources be used efficiently. Both types of economies need some means of avoiding waste and of allocating credit resources to their most productive uses. In countries in which banks are publicly owned, however, incentives other than the profit motive must be used, and other ways of evaluating management efficiency and of rationing scarce funds must be employed. In some of these countries, banks have been criticized for making loans on a political rather than on an economic basis.

Characteristics of bank loans

Most bank loans consist of *promissory notes*. A promissory note is an unconditional promise in writing, made by a private individual, business firm, or unit of government (*the maker*) to another (*the payee or bearer*), to pay a specific amount of money at a fixed or determinable future date, or upon demand. The note must be signed by the one promising to pay. It may also include the signatures of cosigners who agree to pay if the maker fails to do so. The note may provide for repayment in install-ments, on a single date, or on demand. If on demand, either the borrow-er or the lender is free to end the contract at any time. Most loans are *time loans*, and the borrower cannot be required to pay back the amount he has borrowed until the payment date of the loan. If a borrow-er fails to meet the terms of his note, the bank may start legal proceed-ings to recover the amount due.

In Britain and some other countries, bank loans may be granted in the form of overdrafts on checking accounts. The bank then charges interest on the negative balance in the borrower's account. In the United States, this method of making loans was quite rare until the recent introduction of check loans and credit cards. Banks here have traditionally preferred written evidence of the loan.

In order to obtain a loan, banks often require that they be assigned legal claims to real estate, corporation stock, savings deposits, life insur-ance policies, or automobiles and other consumer durables purchased on the installment plan. If the borrower defaults, the bank has the right to take this *collateral* and sell it to recoup the amount owed. The use of collateral reduces the risk and enables banks to lend at lower interest rates than would otherwise be possible. If collateral was required when the loan was obtained, the loan is said to be *secured*.

Normally, a national bank cannot legally lend to any one borrower more than 10 percent of its capital stock, surplus, and undivided profit. As computed from the balance sheet in Table 6.1, the maximum loan that the Dartmouth National Bank was permitted to make to one person would be approximately $400,000. The purpose of this limitation is to assure diversity among the loans made by a bank, thus reducing the risk of loss if a borrower defaults.

Some loans are called *discounts* because of the way interest is charged. On a regular 9 percent loan of $100 for one year, the borrower receives $100, and pays back $109 at the end of the year. On a 9 percent discount, he would receive $91 and pay back $100. In the latter case, the borrower is paying an interest rate slightly higher than the stated discount rate of 9 percent.

Borrowers are charged interest rates that reflect the amount of risk involved. Small businesses have a higher rate of failure than large businesses and are usually charged more. And small loans usually have higher interest rates because administrative costs per dollar lent are higher. Since the market for most types of loans is quite competitive, there is usually a similar rate of interest for a given level of risk and administrative cost.

The lowest rate charged for the least risky commercial and industrial loans is known as the *prime rate*.[2] When the prime rate is changed by one of the major banks in the country, this event is given wide publicity, and other major banks then follow, even though the prime rate need not be the same for all the large banks. Many banks in smaller communities adjust their own interest charges on commercial and industrial loans to changes in the prime rate. Originally, the prime rate was viewed as an example of monopolistic control of interest rates because it was changed only nineteen times between 1934 and 1966. Changes in the prime rate are now much more frequent. Since 1971, the prime rate set by New York's Citibank has been reviewed weekly and kept in line with the movements of interest rates in the open market. *Credit rationing* is often related to the use of the prime rate. If the prime rate is lower than would be justified by competitive conditions, the demand for bank credit by qualified borrowers would exceed the supply. Banks must then ration the available supply of loanable funds, and borrowers are not able to obtain all of the funds they would like to have at the prime rate.

In Table 7.1, bank loans are classified in the following major categories: commercial and industrial loans, real estate loans, loans to individuals (mainly personal loans and installment loans used to purchase consumer goods), loans to financial institutions, loans to farmers, and loans to security brokers and dealers and to carry securities. This classification is based on the use of the funds, not on the type of collateral. A business loan secured by real estate, for example, is a commercial and industrial loan, not a real estate loan; and a personal loan secured by stock certificates is classified as "other" rather than as a loan for carrying securities. Total bank loans have increased from only $38 billion in 1947 to approximately $675 billion in 1978.

Table 7.1
Types of Loans at All
Insured Commercial
Banks, 1968 and 1978
(In billions of dollars)

Type	Amount Dec. 31, 1968	Sept. 30, 1978
Commercial and industrial loans	$ 98.2	$213.1
Real estate loans	65.3	203.4
Loans to individuals	58.4	161.6
Loans to financial institutions	15.8	37.1
Loans to farmers	9.7	28.1
Loans to security brokers and dealers and to carry securities	10.5	15.3
Other loans	8.1[a]	17.3
Total Loans	$266.0	$675.9

[a]In 1968, other loans less reserve for bad debts.
Source: Board of Governors of the Federal Reserve System, *Banking and Monetary Statistics, 1941–1970* (Washington, D.C.: 1976), pp. 134-135; *Federal Reserve Bulletin*, June 1979, p. A18.

Commercial and industrial loans

The most important type of loan made by banks is to commercial enterprises and industries. In 1978, such loans amounted to approximately 32 percent of the banks' total loans. Most commercial and industrial loans are for the purchase of inventory goods and are for less than a year. Some of them, however, are *term loans* for as long as ten years. The latter are often used to finance purchases of machinery and are usually paid off in installments.

When feasible, commercial and industrial loans are secured by the firm's accounts receivable, by the inventory, equipment, or machinery purchased, or by the firm's plant. Whether or not they are secured, all of these loans must be supported by accounting records summarizing the financial condition of the borrower—the balance sheet and the income statement, certified by a public accountant. By examining those documents and by keeping in contact with the operations of the borrower, the bank officers can estimate the chances that the loan will be paid off when due, and they can attempt to determine whether it is advisable to continue the loan if an extension is requested. Government bank examiners also review borrowers' accounting statements. If there is some doubt whether the loan will be paid off when due, the examiners require the bank to remove the loan from the assets recorded on its balance sheet.

Some businesses that borrow often and have a good credit record are able to arrange a *line of credit*—permission to borrow up to a specified amount when needed. This reduces the time required for the customer to obtain a loan, and, for the bank, the need to make recurring credit investigations. The terms of such loans may require a deposit balance equal to a certain percentage of the loan.

The federal government's Small Business Administration has several types of programs to promote the granting of commercial loans to small businesses. Although these programs are not extensive, they enable some enterprises to obtain loans that they probably could not obtain otherwise. The Small Business Administration works with banks in making such loans and usually guarantees a substantial portion of the loan.

In the 1930s, the volume of commercial and industrial loans dropped sharply. It was commonly believed that this was the result of the growth of very large corporations which had become able to supply themselves with almost all of the funds they needed from retained profits. The expansion in commercial and industrial loans since World War II indicates that the decline in the demand for loans in the 1930s was due to the depression and was not the result of their being replaced by retained profits as a source of funds, even though this idea persists.[3]

Making short-term commercial loans used to be considered the primary function of commercial banks, and historically it is from this type of loan that commercial banks got their name. According to the *commercial loan theory* of bank liquidity, only short-term self-liquidating loans to business firms were appropriate for banks. These loans are considered to be *self-liquidating* because the merchant or manufacturer acquires the funds to repay the loan with interest when he sells his inventory or his output. From the point of view of the bank, short-term loans have the advantage that due dates can be staggered so that funds are constantly coming in. Nevertheless, to assure liquidity, most banks in recent years have relied on either borrowing or the shiftability of assets—usually federal funds sold, certificates of deposit, or Treasury bills—rather than on the cash inflow from commercial loans.[4] The basic principle of the commercial loan theory of banking—that restricting bank loans to short-term commercial loans would assure the stability of the entire banking system in times of financial crisis—is today not generally accepted.[5] According to this theory, it was appropriate for the quantity of money to decline when the demand for commercial loans decreased, but recent studies suggest that a decline in the quantity of money may contribute to recessions. It is today believed that deposit insurance and a central bank are necessary in order to avoid financial crises, and that reliance on the commercial loan theory of banking would not protect the banking system from periodic breakdowns.

Real estate loans

In 1978, real estate loans amounted to 30 percent of total bank loans. These mortgages finance the purchase, construction, and remodeling of both housing and commercial and industrial facilities. Over 70 percent of mortgage credit is provided by financial institutions, including banks. The rest is obtained from individuals or United States credit agencies.

As a source of real estate credit, commercial banks are less important than savings and loan associations, but more important than life insurance companies and mutual savings banks.[6]

It is an advantage to banks to have some funds invested over a long period without the need to renegotiate frequently as they must for commercial or consumer loans. Mortgages are also fairly safe loans because they are secured. Requiring the owner to have some equity in the house means the collateral is adequate in most circumstances even if the value of the property should go down.

Amortization

Although today most real estate loans are repaid in installments, this practice was quite rare before the 1930s. The average maturity of real estate loans being made on new homes in 1978 was twenty-eight years, but it may vary between ten and thirty years. In 1980, a down payment of 20 percent, or $12,000, would usually be required on a $60,000 house. If the rate of interest on the $48,000 lent were 17.61 percent when bank fees are included, the monthly payment for a thirty-year mortgage would be $694.07. The interest rate charged by the bank depends somewhat on whether the house is the owner's primary residence or a second home, the amount of the down payment, and whether the owner carries insurance on the property. During the life of an installment mortgage, the monthly payments are usually constant, and the mortgage is gradually paid off. The first monthly payments consist mostly of interest charges, but as time passes, the portion paying off principal gradually increases.

A new type of mortgage with a graduated mortgage payment plan (GMP) has been offered by many banks in recent years. Monthly payments start as low as 25 percent below those for a fixed rate mortgage, but then climb steeply before leveling off after five or ten years. From then on, the payments stay the same. This plan is designed to enable young home-buyers to adjust to both high real estate prices and high mortgage interest rates.

Government guarantees

About a quarter of residential mortgages are underwritten by either the Federal Housing Administration or the Veterans Administration. Banks negotiate such mortgages, although officials of the FHA or VA participate by inspecting the property. FHA-insured mortgages require a smaller down payment than is needed for conventional bank mortgages. In case of default, the ownership of the property is shifted to the FHA, and the bank is reimbursed with U.S. government securities. VA-guaranteed mortgages require no down payment, and in case of default the bank is paid in cash for any loss. These programs were designed to aid

veterans and other persons in need, and to stimulate housing construction by making housing credit more available.[7] Financial institutions
support such programs because they reduce the risk to themselves.

FHA and VA programs have been critized by students of urban
problems, since the money lent has been used mainly to purchase new
homes built in the suburbs and not to rehabilitate existing houses in the
cities.[8] As a result, these programs have subsidized the movement of the
middle class out of the central cities. The poor, who have had to live in
the older cities, have often not been able to get subsidized mortgages
of this type. The movement of people out of the city has indirectly aided
poor urban families by increasing the supply of housing available for
them in the cities.

Interest rates on mortgages

Some states have had ceiling limits on interest rates for mortgages.
When market rates of interest rose above the legal ceiling, banks tended
to shift to other types of loans and investments, and the supply of funds
for mortgages dried up.[9] FHA-insured and VA-guaranteed mortgages
also have ceiling rates, and new mortgages of this type tend to decline
sharply when market rates rise above the ceilings. For this reason, the
ceiling rates on federally underwritten mortgages have in recent years
been raised in periods of rising market interest rates—in February
1980, for example, from 11½ percent to 12 percent for single-family
homes. The Depository Institutions Deregulation and Monetary Control Act of 1980 preempted state usury ceilings on mortgage loans
unless states act within three years to reenact them.

If interest rates fall, persons who borrowed at the higher rates have
timed their borrowing badly. If they rise, the banks that lent the money
at the lower rates find themselves holding unattractive earning assets.
The sharp rise in market interest rates during the accelerated inflation
in the late 1960s and early 1970s caused difficulties for banks with large
amounts of older mortgages carrying 4 to 6 percent interest rates. The
rate of interest that banks have had to pay to acquire time deposits
exceeds the interest rates earned on many of their older mortgages. To
attempt to meet this problem, state-chartered S&Ls in California offered variable-rate mortgages in 1975, and a few commercial banks
there with national charters offered them in 1976. In 1979, federal
regulators allowed all S&Ls to offer variable-rate mortgages. Interest
rates on such mortgages are keyed to a cost-of-funds index based on
other market rates of interest and have sometimes been set at one-
quarter to one-half of one percentage point below that for a fixed-rate
loan—probably to encourage borrowers to accept the terms.[10] Variable-
rate mortgages are common in both Great Britain and Canada. In 1980,
the Federal Home Loan Bank Board went further in its efforts to enable
savings and loan associations to adjust to conditions of rapid and uncer-

tain inflation by authorizing "rollover" mortgages with interest rates that could be renegotiated every three to five years.

Loans to individuals

Commercial banks make many consumer and personal loans. Most of them are made to persons to finance purchases of consumer durable goods such as automobiles and TV sets. In 1978, the total amount of loans to individuals was approximately one-quarter of total bank loans.

Table 7.2
Percentage of Total
Consumer Installment
Credit Held by
Different Types of
Financial Institutions,
April 1979

Type of Institution	Percent of Total
Commercial banks	50%
Finance companies	21
Credit unions	16
Retail outlets	8
Other	5
Total	100%

Source: *Federal Reserve Bulletin*, June 1979, p. A42.

Most consumer credit is *installment credit.* The rest consists of single-payment loans, charge accounts, and service credit (doctors' bills and so forth). Table 7.2 shows that in 1979 commercial banks held 50 percent of the total amount of consumer installment credit outstanding. Table 7.3 shows that in the same year about 45 percent of the consumer installment credit of commercial banks consisted of loans for the financing of automobiles. In 1979 the terms of a typical loan for $4,000 for a new automobile with at least one-third equity were as follows:

Amount borrowed	$4,000.00
Life insurance on borrower	52.07
Interest	1,053.21
Total amount owed bank	$5,105.28
Monthly payment for 48 months	$106.36

In order to qualify for these terms, the price of the new car would have to be $6,000 or higher, giving the owner an equity in the car of at least one-third. Many borrowers are able to pay for most of the equity portion of the cost of a new car by trading in their old car. The terms of this loan require the borrower to pay back the loan with interest in forty-eight monthly payments of $106.36 each. In addition to the amount

Table 7.3
Types of Consumer
Installment Credit Held
by Commercial Banks,
April 1979

Type	Amount (in billions)	Percent of Total
Automobile	$62.8	45%
Revolving	24.8	18
Mobile home	9.5	7
Other	42.7	30
Total	$139.8	100.0%

Source: *Federal Reserve Bulletin*, June 1979, p. A42.

borrowed, the forty-eight monthly payments include interest amounting to $1,053 plus life insurance on the borrower costing about $52.

The coverage of the life insurance policy is equal to the unpaid portion of the loan on the automobile and declines as the loan is paid off. If the borrower dies, his estate benefits by acquiring complete title to the automobile, debt-free, and the bank gets immediate payment of the unpaid balance of the loan; the bank does not have to get involved in the probate of wills to receive payment.

If the borrower fails to meet his installment payments, the bank has the right to repossess the car. Then the bank attempts to obtain the unpaid portion of the loan by selling the car.

Because of the installment feature of automobile loans, calculating the rate of interest that the borrower pays is difficult. The important rate of interest is that based on the unpaid balance. A simple way that is sometimes used to calculate this measure of the cost of borrowing is shown in the following formula:

$$i = \frac{2mA}{P(n+1)},$$

where i = interest rate on the unpaid balance, m = number of payments a year, A = interest in dollars, P = principal, and n = number of payments needed to discharge the debt. Applying this formula to the terms of the installment loan shown on page 133, the rate of interest on the unpaid balance is 12.7 percent a year:

$$i = \frac{2 \times 12 \times \$1,053.21}{\$4,052.07\,(48+1)} = 12.7\%.$$

This is about one percentage point above the rate of 11.83 percent on a loan with these terms given in the interest rate tables used by loan officers. The formula gives better results when applied to loans with installment payments over a period of two or three years rather than four. For loans on automobiles in which the equity is less than one-third, the rate of interest charged is typically almost two percentage points higher.

Installment loans have relatively high rates of interest because of the bookkeeping involved in recording the payments and the time required in making this type of loan. There are also some losses on these loans—for example, if a car is repossessed in bad condition, or if a borrower moves to another part of the country and stops making payments.

In the loan market for financing automobiles, banks compete among themselves as well as with automobile dealers who do their own financing. Lenders cannot charge more than they do without losing customers, and they cannot lower their charges because other types of loans and investments would be more profitable if they did. Thus, the rates charged do not vary much, although they are different for old and new cars. Automobile manufacturers benefit from low interest rates that encourage more persons to buy cars.

Installment loans have been popular with consumers.[11] Historically, there has been a shift from the purchase of services outside the home and the employment of household servants to the provision of similar services by consumers themselves using highly technical equipment. Consumers have replaced laundry services with washers and dryers, taxi and bus services with automobiles, entertainment services with TV sets, and household servants with dishwashers and electric vacuum cleaners. Most people have difficulty saving the amount of money needed for the purchase of expensive durable goods. By borrowing the total and repaying it in monthly installments, they avoid the need to accumulate funds before making the purchase, and they obtain the machine's use while they would otherwise still be saving to buy it. This type of finance developed in the 1920s and coincided with the mass production of automobiles. A mass market for automobiles, based on the use of installment loans, was a necessary counterpart of mass production based on assembly-line techniques and scientific management.

Banks also make *personal loans*. These loans sometimes have collateral or cosigners, but may also be accepted simply on the signature of the borrower. In recent years, commercial banks have promoted a new type of personal loan called *cash reserve accounts*. A person with such an account may overdraw his account at any time, and the amount overdrawn is treated like a loan. The rate charged on such loans is typically 15 percent a year on the outstanding balance. The maximum limit to the amount that can be borrowed is usually $5,000 or less, depending upon the borrower's income, and is determined at the time the borrower is given the account. The borrower may repay the amount borrowed on the installment plan. The principal advantage of this method of extending credit is that it is speedy and impersonal. The borrower has credit available at all times up to the maximum limit of the account.

Many banks now also offer holders of credit cards (Master Card and VISA) credit of from $300 to $5,000, depending on the holder's income. If the amount charged is paid within twenty-five days after the monthly billing by the bank, it is not treated like a bank loan and no interest is added. Holders of these cards do not have to pay immediately for the amount charged, however, and may elect to pay on the installment plan for items purchased with the card. In some states, even federal income taxes may be paid in this way. The rate of interest on such loans is typically 18 percent on the unpaid balance. Such loans are typically paid off in installments over a period of up to ten months.

Personal loans to finance the education of college students are being encouraged by the federal government. The Higher Education Act of 1965 set up a guaranteed student loan program in which commercial banks have participated. No repayment of such loans need be made during college years. The maximum rate of interest is 7 percent. Originally, only students whose families had incomes of under $25,000 a year could qualify, but in 1978 Congress removed the earnings ceiling.

Loans to financial institutions

In 1978, 5 percent of bank loans went to other financial institutions, such as correspondent banks, finance and consumer credit companies, and brokers and dealers. Finance companies which make personal loans and loans to purchase automobiles and other consumer durables, obtain a large proportion of their funds from bank loans, although large finance companies also obtain a substantial part of their funds from the sale of commercial paper.

Both brokers financing stock purchases for customers and dealers in government securities obtain a large proportion of their funds from bank loans. These may be call loans that can be terminated by either the bank or the borrower without a waiting period. Since the mid-1930s, banks have made broker's loans only to brokers who are also depositors. The Board of Governors of the Federal Reserve System can set limits on security loans of member banks and suspend privileges to banks not observing them. As their needs and sales change, brokers and dealers typically change the amount they borrow and substitute one stock for another as collateral.

Loans to farmers

Agricultural loans now account for a smaller proportion of total loans than in previous periods. As shown in Table 7.1, in 1978 they comprised only 4 percent of total bank loans, but for banks in farming areas, agricultural loans are important.

Farmers need financing both for recurring seasonal expenses and for long-term investments in machinery and land. Farming now involves more expensive machinery; larger units of land; and the use of chemical fertilizers, sprays, hybrid seeds, and prepared foods, vitamins, and antibiotics for livestock. These agricultural costs often require financing, but not all agricultural financing is obtained from local banks. Purchases of new equipment are often financed by the seller. And when they can, farmers borrow at subsidized rates from federal credit agencies, such as the Federal Land Banks and the Banks for Cooperatives.

Loans for purchasing and carrying securities

Persons may borrow from banks to finance purchases of corporation stock and other securities. In 1978, loans amounting to 2 percent of total bank loans were of this type.

Stock market speculation, much of it financed by bank credit, caused widespread financial difficulties when stock prices fell sharply in 1929. In 1934, the Federal Reserve's Board of Governors was given the power to use selective credit controls over loans of this type. Their Regulation U applies to loans made by commercial banks for stocks listed on the national stock exchanges, and the board has the power to set minimum margin requirements which range from 25 to 100 percent. In 1972, the margin requirement for stock was set at 65 percent—meaning that the maximum amount of the loan was 35 percent of the market value of the stock. In 1974, the margin requirement was lowered to 50 percent, and from 1974 to 1980 no changes were made in these requirements.

The Federal Reserve's margin requirements apply to loans from lenders other than commercial banks and to loans which are for the purchase of stocks but which are secured by land or other physical assets. Margin requirements do not apply to loans which are secured by stocks but which are to be used for purposes other than stock purchases—for example, a loan for home improvements using common stock as collateral. In practice, it may be difficult for a bank to know whether money borrowed is being used for purchasing stock or for financing some other need.

Persons who desire funds to buy stocks or to make other expenditures sometimes prefer to borrow rather than sell their present holdings of financial assets. With their securities as collateral for loans, they are generally charged relatively low interest rates by banks. Also, they can profit from future increases in the value of their present holdings, and can postpone paying capital gains taxes on profits already made. They avoid brokerage fees and retain voting rights as stockholders.

Consumerist credit laws

A recent development in banking has been the rapid expansion of legislation designed to protect the consumer. The first of these laws was the Truth in Lending Act which became effective July 1, 1969.[12] In recent years, Congress also passed the Real Estate Settlement Procedures Act, Home Mortgage Disclosure Act, Fair Credit Billing Act, Equal Credit Opportunity Act, and the Federal Trade Commission Improvement Act.[13]

A major problem with present consumer credit regulations is that knowledge about their provisions is not widespread, even though the Administration ordered executive agencies of the government to make the language of their regulations simple enough to be understandable to the average citizen.[14] A recent survey reported that about 45 percent of borrowers with auto, appliance, or personal loans don't even know the annual percentage rate on their loans. Government regulations cannot always be simple and still be sufficiently detailed (and written in legal terminology) to adequately protect various aspects of the banks' interest.

Bank examiners have added to their duties the determination of whether banks are complying with the new consumerist legislation. The Federal Reserve banks have set up Consumer Banking Affairs Units which act as a consumer complaint clearinghouse. The Federal Reserve units investigate only complaints regarding state-chartered banks which are members of the Federal Reserve System, but forward other complaints to the proper enforcement agency: the Federal Deposit Insurance Corporation for state-chartered nonmember banks, the Comptroller of the Currency for nationally chartered banks; the Federal Home Loan Bank Board for savings and loan associations; and the Federal Trade Commission for most other creditors.

The administration of the regulations and the paperwork required are costly to banks and the government. The regulations have been criticized as not worth their large cost.

Truth in Lending Act

The Truth in Lending Act applies not just to banks, but also to savings and loan associations, department stores, credit card issuers, credit unions, automobile dealers, consumer finance companies, residential mortgage brokers, craftsmen such as plumbers and electricians, doctors, dentists, hospitals, and any other persons who extend consumer credit. Enforcement is to be shared by nine different federal agencies including the Board of Governors of the Federal Reserve System. One purpose of the regulation is to make customers aware of the cost of credit and to enable them to compare the terms available from various credit sources. The borrower must be told both the finance charges and the annual percentage rate. The finance charges include all of the various costs required by the creditor—interest plus such costs as premiums for credit life insurance. Creditors are not expected to calculate interest rates themselves; they can obtain tables that may be used to determine the annual percentage rate for each type of transaction from the Board of Governors of the Federal Reserve System. The Federal Reserve System's truth-in-lending regulation is known as Regulation Z and covers both installment credit and open-end credit such as revolving charge accounts and credit cards. It does not set minimum or maximum rates. A creditor who violates the law may face criminal penalties or suit by the customer for twice the amount of the finance charge, court costs, and a reasonable attorney's fee.

Real Estate Settlement Procedures Act

The Real Estate Settlement Procedures Act (RESPA) was passed, amended, and implemented in the mid-1970s.[15] When a borrower applies for a mortgage loan, he must be informed about settlement procedures and given a good faith estimate of settlement charges. The lender is required to prepare a Uniform Settlement Statement form for the borrower. One business day before settlement, the borrower has the right to inspect this form, and at settlement the completed statement is given to the borrower.

Home Mortgage Disclosure Act

In 1975, the Home Mortgage Disclosure Act was passed by Congress to reduce "redlining"—the practice of refusing mortgages in declining urban neighborhoods.[16] The law requires lenders to compile—and make public—information on where they have made mortgage loans. Some states also have laws of this type. The federal law applies only to institutions in Standard Metropolitan Statistical Areas and excludes very small banks. The mortgage disclosure statement is made public usually by posting it in the lobby of the institution, and the location of the mortgages is indicated by census tract (a statistical area with about 4,000 inhabitants having similar economic, social, and racial characteristics) or by zip code. Proponents of this type of legislation believe that redlining has been a primary cause of urban blight. The objective of this legislation is to discourage redlining by providing depositors with information about the lending activities of banks. If a bank were not making mortgages in a declining urban area, inhabitants of that area, it is hoped, would withdraw their savings from that bank and thus put pressure on the institution not to refuse mortgages to persons living in the declining area.

Fair Credit Billing Act

The Fair Credit Billing Act (FCBA) was part of the consumer legislation passed by Congress and implemented in the mid-1970s.[17] Its enforcement is covered under part of the Federal Reserve System's Regulation Z. The act deals with credit cards and charge accounts as well as bank credit. It requires banks and merchants to send their customers a description of their rights and of the procedures to follow in making complaints about billing errors. The borrower must notify the creditor of any billing error within 60 days of billing, and the creditor must acknowledge the customer's letter within 30 days, and then take steps to resolve the dispute within 90 days. During the period of dispute, the borrower need not pay the amount in dispute, nor be liable for interest on it. Proponents of this legislation believe that it deals with some of the problems created by increasing automation of credit facilities.

Equal Credit Opportunity Act

The Equal Credit Opportunity Act went into effect in 1975.[18] It forbids discrimination on the basis of sex or marital status by banks, retailers, and others in the granting of credit. In 1976, discrimination on the basis of age, race, color, religion, national origin, receipt of income from welfare, or exercising of rights under the Consumer Credit Protection Act of 1968 was added. "Class action" suits against creditors found guilty of using arbitrary rules to deny credit can bring damages up to $500,000 or one percent of the creditor's net worth. Starting in 1977, unsuccessful applicants for credit must be given a statement, on request, of the reasons for the denial of credit.

Married women can establish credit histories in their own names. Banks must now designate new accounts to reflect the participation of both wife and husband. On existing accounts, the law required banks, department stores, oil companies, and other credit institutions to notify their customers of the right to have credit information reported in the names of both spouses. Although several hundred million notices were mailed, a spot survey reported a response rate of only 9 percent. At some point in their lives, 85 percent of the women who are now married will become single again, either through divorce or the death of their husbands; without a credit history, these women could have difficulty borrowing.

Federal Trade Commission Improvement Act

The aim of the Federal Trade Commission Improvement Act of 1975 is to protect consumers against unfair or deceptive practices in trade or financial transactions. The regulations make money lenders liable for unsatisfactory services and defective merchandise that they finance.[19] A consumer can stop paying for a defective product even if the financing is being handled by a third party such as a bank or finance company. Financial institutions are no longer protected by the holder-in-due-course doctrine when they buy in good faith the right to collect from the contractor who originally extended the credit. Although this regulation may protect some consumers, it will mean that credit of certain types will be harder to get and more costly. After this ruling, it was reported that bank financing of used cars and of orthodontic treatment was cut.

Summary

A basic economic function of banks is to allocate a limited supply of credit among competing uses. Bank credit is allocated efficiently if banks lend to the firms and individuals who can use the funds most productively.

To make their loans secure, banks usually lend to individuals supplying collateral and to well-established firms willing to provide the bank with current accounting statements certified by a public accountant.

The calculation of the rate of interest on installment loans is more complicated than for other types of loans, because the amount of the unpaid balance keeps changing. Starting in the late 1960s, legislation passed by Congress has sought to make consumers more aware of the amount of interest and other charges they are to pay.

Other consumer legislation passed in the mid-1970s is aimed at preventing discrimination in the allocation of credit, at establishing procedures for correcting billing errors, and at protecting installment buyers from unfair trade practices.

Notes

1. Eugene F. Fama, *Foundations of Finance* (New York: Basic Books, 1976), p. 133.

2. For a description of the nature of the prime rate, see Murray E. Polakoff and Morris Budin, *The Prime Rate* (Chicago: Association of Reserve City Bankers, 1973).

3. John Kenneth Galbraith, *The New Industrial State*, 2d ed. (Boston: Houghton Mifflin, 1971), Chapter 4.

4. G. Walter Woodworth, "Theories of Cyclical Liquidity Management of Commercial Banks," *National Banking Review* 4 (June 1967), pp. 377–395.

5. For a historical analysis of the commercial loan theory of banking (also known as the *real bills doctrine*), see Lloyd W. Mints, *A History of Banking Theory* (Chicago: University of Chicago Press, 1945). Western economists have been surprised to learn that the Soviet Union adhered

to the commercial loan theory of banking long after it was discarded in the West. See Raymond P. Powell, "Recent Developments in Soviet Monetary Policy," in Franklyn D. Holzman, ed., *Readings on the Soviet Economy* (Chicago: Rand McNally, 1962), Section VIII; see also book review by Zbigniew M. Fallenbuchl, *Journal of Economic Literature* (September 1974), pp. 927–928.

6. For a more detailed survey of the market for real estate loans, see John P. Wiedemer, *Real Estate Finance*, 2nd ed. (Reston, Va.: Reston Publishing Co., 1977), Chapter 4.

7. George Break, *The Economic Impact of Federal Loan Insurance* (Washington, D.C.: National Planning Association, 1961); and Robert J. Saulnier, Harold G. Halcrow, and Neil H. Jacoby, *Federal Lending and Loan Insurance* (Princeton: Princeton University Press, 1958).

8. Edward C. Banfield, *The Unheavenly City* (Boston: Little, Brown, 1970), pp. 15–16.

9. Clifton B. Luttrell, "Interest Rate Controls—Perspective, Purpose, and Problems," Federal Reserve Bank of St. Louis, *Review* 50 (September 1968), pp. 6–14 (published also as Reprint Series No. 32).

10. Carl M. Gambs, "Variable Rate Mortgages—Their Potential in the United States," *Journal of Money, Credit and Banking* 7 (May 1975), pp. 245–251; and Mark J. Riedy, "California Experiments with VRMs," *Directors Digest* (United States League of Savings Associations), February 1977, pp. 11–14.

11. For an analysis of the historical background of the growth of consumer credit, see Board of Governors of the Federal Reserve System, *Consumer Instalment Credit*, Part 1, Vol. 1, *Growth and Import* (Washington, D.C.: U.S. Government Printing Office, 1957), Chapter 2.

12. "Truth in Lending," *Federal Reserve Bulletin* 55 (February 1969), pp. 98–103.

13. See "Consumer Affairs," *Annual Report of the Board of Governors of the Federal Reserve System, 1975* (Washington, D.C., 1976), pp. 307–346.

14. Kathleen Quenneville, "Consumers and Regulators," Federal Reserve Bank of San Francisco, *Business and Finance Letter*, September 9, 1977.

15. See *Annual Report of the Board of Governors of the Federal Reserve System, 1975*, pp. 316–318.

16. See "New Regulation C," *Federal Reserve Bulletin* 62 (June 1976), pp. 550–551.

17. See Federal Reserve Bank of San Francisco, "Consumers and Creditors," *Business and Financial Letter*, October 17, 1975; and *Annual Report of the Board of Governors of the Federal Reserve System, 1975*, pp. 311–313.

18. For a description of the regulations under this act, see "Equal Credit Opportunity," *Federal Reserve Bulletin* 63 (February 1977), pp. 101–107.

19. Robert D. Hershey, Jr., "The Shifting Onus of Consumer Credit," *New York Times,* October 7, 1976, p. 65; and *Annual Report of the Board of Governors of the Federal Reserve System, 1975,* pp. 329–335.

Questions

7.1. Explain the social role of banks in allocating loanable funds.

7.2. What is a promissory note? How are promissory notes used in banking?

7.3. What is the collateral of a loan? Why may a bank require collateral?

7.4. What is the purpose of bank laws restricting the amount lent to any one borrower?

7.5. Explain the principal characteristics of each of the following types of loans: commercial loans, real estate loans, consumer loans, personal loans, agricultural loans, loans for purchasing and carrying securities, and loans to financial institutions.

7.6. What are installment loans? What advantages do they have to borrowers as well as to banks?

7.7. What are some of the methods used by commercial banks to reduce the risk of making loans?

7.8. Why may laws setting ceiling rates of interest on mortgages cause sharp variations in the supply of mortgage credit?

7.9. What is the commercial loan theory of banking?

7.10. Describe the federal government's programs to induce banks to negotiate mortgages.

7.11. What are the purposes and principal features of the Truth in Lending Act?

7.12. Describe the provisions of the Equal Credit Opportunity Act.

7.13. Calculate the rate of interest on an installment loan of $3,500 if the total interest charged is $454.96 and there are twenty-four monthly payments of $164.79.

7.14. Why is the rate of interest charged on personal loans relatively high compared to that on other types of bank loans?

7.15. Know the meaning and significance of the following terms and concepts: commercial loan, promissory note, collateral, prime rate, line of credit, margin requirement, installment loan, variable-rate mortgage, renegotiated mortgage, consumer loan, credit rationing, overdraft, unsecured and secured loans, commercial loan theory of bank liquidity, redlining.

8

The liabilities side of the balance sheet of a commercial bank lists primarily the various types of deposits and shows the bank's sources of funds. The asset side of the balance sheet shows the ways the bank uses its funds.

THE LIABILITIES SIDE
OF THE BALANCE SHEET

The two principal types of liabilities of commercial banks are *demand deposits* and *time deposits*. Demand deposits are of particular interest because they are the principal medium of exchange in our economy. Time deposits have become by far the largest source of funds of commercial banks, and in recent years there has been an explosion in various new types of time deposits. This chapter includes a description of each of the types of liabilities and capital accounts listed on the balance sheet of the Dartmouth National Bank in Chapter 6 (see Table 6.1).

Demand deposits

Most businesses and individuals have checking accounts (demand deposits or NOW accounts) because of their usefulness—the safety and convenience of making payments by writing checks and the ability to withdraw cash on demand. The bulk of the demand deposits in commercial banks is owned by businesses—nationwide more than 60 percent of the total amount (see Table 8.1). Only 33 percent was owned by individuals, although more than two-thirds of all families now have a checking account.

Before the Great Depression from 1929 to 1933, banks typically paid interest on the demand deposits of their large depositors. This policy was changed in 1933 when the Federal Reserve System's Regulation Q made it illegal for banks to pay interest on demand deposits. In the 1970s, the restrictions on paying interest on such deposits began to break down. Banks began to offer NOW accounts (interest-bearing savings accounts on which checks may be written), automatic transfer from savings (ATS) accounts, phone transfers from savings to demand deposits, and the use of savings accounts to pay bills. In 1980, Congress enacted the Depository Institutions Deregulation and Monetary Control Act, which permanently authorizes NOW accounts in all states starting in 1981. Previously, NOW accounts had been authorized in New England, New York, and New Jersey. Also, the new law makes it legal for commercial banks to offer ATS accounts. Although commercial banks were already offering ATS accounts, the accounts had been ruled illegal by a federal court in 1979.

Despite the restrictions on paying interest on demand deposits, banks compete for business deposits by granting loans more readily to their depositors than to businesses that hold their deposits elsewhere. A business that has no deposit in the bank may have to pay a higher rate of interest than a business that is a depositor. Banks also compete for deposits by advertising, having impressive banking offices, and offering additional services such as faster check-processing.[1]

Keeping the records for each check transaction and maintaining exact accounts are costly operations. In recent years, most banks have installed more complicated, mechanized types of bookkeeping. Because of the cost of bookkeeping, many banks charge some type of service fee. Service fees for writing checks usually vary with the size of

Table 8.1
Ownership of Demand Deposits, All Commercial Banks, September 1979

Type of Holder	Amount (in billions)	Percentage of Total
Financial business	$ 26.7	9.1%
Nonfinancial business	148.8	50.9%
Consumer	99.2	33.9
Foreign	2.8	1.0
All other	14.9	5.1
Total	$292.4	100.0%

Source: *Federal Reserve Bulletin*, January 1980, p. A25.

the deposit. Depending on the amount of his deposit, a depositor receives a credit against the total fees incurred. Some banks have no service fees on each check written; instead they may require a minimum balance of several hundred dollars, and charge a fee if the depositor's balance falls below the minimum amount during the month.

Savings and time deposits

The total amount of time deposits (including savings deposits) in commercial banks has become much larger than their total demand deposits. In January 1980, total time deposits in all commercial banks amounted to $682 billion compared to about $280 billion in demand deposits. The advantage of time deposits over demand deposits is that they pay a rate of interest.

The principal types of time deposits are passbook and statement savings deposits (including automatic transfer savings accounts), NOW accounts, savings certificates (including money market certificates), open account time deposits, and certificates of deposit.

Passbook and statement savings deposits

Table 8.2 shows that in 1979, 35 percent of the total amount of time deposits in insured commercial banks consisted of savings deposits. Even though an advance notice is legally required before funds can be withdrawn from these savings deposits, banks seldom insist on a notice, and depositors generally assume that they can withdraw their funds immediately. Until 1975, these deposits could be held only by individuals and certain nonprofit organizations, but partnerships and corporations are now permitted to have savings deposits of up to $150,000 in a member bank. In 1979, the maximum interest rate allowed by Regulation Q on savings deposits in commercial banks was raised from 5 to 5¼ percent, the first increase in such rates since 1973. The Depository Institutions Deregulation and Monetary Control Act of 1980 gives the federal regulatory agencies the authority to gradually phase out the ceiling interest rates on savings and time deposits over a period of six years. *Reg Q*

Table 8.2
Types of Time Deposits, Insured Commercial Banks, Jan. 31, 1979

Type of Deposit		Amount (in billions)	Percentage of Total
Savings deposits		$214.8	35.0%
Time deposits in denominations of less than $100,000 held by domestic governmental units		3.3	0.5
Time deposits in denominations of less than $100,000 held by others:			
Less than 1 year	$32.7		
1 year to 2½ years	28.4		
2½ years to 4 years	16.4		
4 years and over	74.1		
Total		151.6	24.7
Individual Retirement Accounts and Keogh time deposits		3.5	0.6
Money market certificates		31.9	5.2
Time deposits in denominations of $100,000 or more		202.8	33.1
Non-interest-bearing time deposits[a]		4.4	0.7
Club accounts[b]		0.9	0.2
Total		$613.2	100.0%

[a]Most such deposits are believed to represent escrow accounts and compensating balances.
[b]Includes Christmas savings and vacation accounts.
Source: *Federal Reserve Bulletin*, May 1979, p. 388.

Passbook deposits are more popular than statement savings deposits. When funds are deposited or withdrawn from a passbook savings account, the passbook must be presented and the transaction recorded. With a statement savings deposit, the depositor receives a monthly record of the amount of the savings deposit plus interest earned, and deposits and withdrawals may be made by mail.

In 1978, the Federal Reserve Board and the Federal Deposit Insurance Corporation voted to allow the automatic transfer of funds from savings to checking accounts in commercial banks if authorized by the customer. Such transfers are done as needed to cover overdrafts or to maintain a minimum balance and allows the banks, in effect, to pay interest on money that would otherwise be held in checking accounts. Permitting banks to offer ATS (automatic transfer from savings) accounts has tended to blur the difference between savings and demand deposits. Before 1981, the development of ATS accounts throughout the country reduced the significance of the legal limitation of NOW accounts to banks in New England, New York, and New Jersey.

NOW accounts

NOW accounts—*negotiable orders of withdrawal*—are technically savings deposits even though the owner may write checks on them. In 1973, Congress passed an unusual law permitting banks located only in Massachusetts and New Hampshire to offer these accounts. Later this authority was extended to New York, New Jersey, and to the other four states in New England, and in 1981 to all states. Banks that are members of the Federal Reserve System may issue NOW accounts only to individuals and nonprofit associations.[2] The maximum rate of interest that commercial banks are allowed to pay on them is 5 percent. Authority to issue NOW accounts was given to commercial banks so as to enable them to compete with mutual savings banks, which were the first type of financial institution to offer them. When NOW accounts were initially authorized, an advantage to banks with NOW accounts was that the reserve requirement for such accounts was the same as for savings accounts (3 percent in 1979), rather than the much higher requirements for demand deposits (from 7 percent to 16¼ percent in 1979). The important new banking legislation passed by Congress in 1980 classifies NOW accounts as *transaction acounts*, and starting in 1981 NOW accounts will be subject to the reserve requirements for transaction accounts rather than for savings deposits.

Savings certificates

The owner of a savings certificate is given a receipt showing the amount deposited, the interest rate, the maturity date, and other terms of the contract. In 1980, maximum interest rates allowable on savings certificates were graduated according to maturity—from 5½ percent on maturities from ninety days to two years to 7¾ percent on maturities of 8 years or more (see Table 13.3 in Chapter 13). The Depository Institutions Deregulation and Monetary Control Act of 1980 provides for phasing out the interest rate ceilings on these types of deposits over a period of six years. The minimum maturity of savings certificates is usually three months. Savings certificates have grown rapidly in popularity during the past fifteen years. Table 8.2 shows that time deposits in denominations of less than $100,000 (a large portion of these are savings certificates) amounted to almost 25 percent of total time deposits.

In 1974, banks began offering special savings accounts called *Individual Retirement Accounts* (IRAs) to persons not covered by employer pension plans, following the enactment of the Employment Retirement

Income Security Act (ERISA). These accounts have been popular because persons with such accounts can reduce their taxable income during working years. Both the amount put in an IRA account and the interest earned on such an account is not taxable until it is used during retirement. These accounts are usually put in long-term savings certificates with relatively high interest rates. Payments to these accounts are limited to either 15 percent of income received or a maximum amount of $1,500 a year. Withdrawals cannot begin until age 59½.

Savings certificates may be redeemed before maturity by notifying the bank ninety days in advance and agreeing to take a cut in the interest rate. In 1979, federal regulators reduced the penalties for early withdrawal of funds to encourage savers to invest in longer-term certificates. Today there are no penalties when an account holder dies. In 1979, federal regulators eliminated the minimum denomination of $1,000 that had been required for most savings certificates with maturities over four years.

Six-Month Money Market Certificates. In 1978, federal regulators authorized a new type of savings certificate of major importance as a step toward free market determination of interest rates on time deposits. They are called money market certificates and have a maturity of six months, and a ceiling interest rate at commercial banks equal to the current discount yield on six-month Treasury bills; at thrift institutions, the ceiling rate is one-quarter of a percentage point higher except when interest rates are above 8¾ percent. Although after issuance its rate remains unchanged until maturity, the rate for new issues is adjusted weekly in line with yields at the most recent bill auction. The rate of interest paid on money market certificates has been considerably higher than on other types of savings certificates and was more than 15 percent in March 1980.

In 1979, when federal regulators eliminated the minimum denomination for some savings certificates, they retained the high minimum denomination for money market certificates ($10,000, the same as that for Treasury bills). These minimum denomination requirements have been criticized as discriminating against small savers.

The growth of this type of deposit has been phenomenal and almost 80 percent of commercial banks now offer them. A year after they were authorized, commercial banks had almost $60 billion of them—nearly 10 percent of their total time deposits. Thrift institutions also found these new certificates popular. It was hoped that the new policy of allowing depository institutions to offer money market certificates would avoid the usual slowdown in the growth of time deposits and the drying up of mortgage funds that has occurred in past periods of very high market interest rates. Although the policy appeared to be effective in 1978–79, in 1980 the very high interest rates resulted in the usual decline in the availability of mortgage credit.[3]

Floating-rate Certificates (two and one-half years or more). In January 1980, federal regulators permitted banks and thrift institutions to offer a new floating-rate certificate designed to help the small saver. No minimum denomination is required, compounding of interest is permitted, and at the same time the ceiling interest rate is tied to the yield on United States government securities maturing in two and one-half years. The maturity of the floating-rate certificates must be two and one-half years or more. The rates set are to be slightly below the yield on two-and-one-half-year federal government securities and will be one-quarter of one percent lower for commercial banks than for thrift institutions. The ceiling rate will be announced monthly by the U.S. Treasury three business days before the beginning of each month.

Open account time deposits

An open account time deposit cannot be cashed before the set date of maturity, but the amount in the account may be added to after the deposit is opened. This type of deposit has been popular with some business firms, although the number of banks offering deposits of this type is small. The maximum rate of interest payable on these deposits depends on their maturity and amount. Christmas savings funds owned by small savers are a type of open account deposit.

Certificates of deposit

Table 8.3 shows that since 1961 the volume of large negotiable certificates of deposit (CDs) with denominations of $100,000 or more has grown very rapidly. CDs are in the form of a certificate; the date of issue of a certificate and its maturity date are negotiated with the depositor, and may be adjusted to meet his specific needs. They are owned primarily by business firms with sizable amounts of funds to invest for short periods of time, charitable organizations, governmental institutions, and foreign banks. CDs which meet certain legal specifications that assure the buyer a perfect title are called negotiable and may be easily sold. A dealer-operated secondary market for CDs was established in 1961. In this market, owners in need of cash may sell their negotiable CDs before maturity. There are also nonnegotiable CDs. Most commercial banks today offer their smaller business customers nonnegotiable CDs in amounts less than $100,000.

Since 1973, there have been no interest rate ceilings on large CDs. In 1970, ceilings were suspended for large certificates of deposit with maturities of thirty to eighty-nine days, and in 1973, maximum rates of interest on all certificates of deposit in denominations of $100,000 or more were suspended.

For business firms and financial institutions with funds to invest, certificates of deposit compete with commercial paper and Treasury

Table 8.3
Large Negotiable
Certificates of Deposit,*
1961–1979
(seasonally adjusted)

December	Amount (in billions)
1961	$ 3.3
1968	23.6
1969	11.0
1970	25.5
1971	33.5
1972	43.9
1973	63.0
1974	89.0
1975	81.0
1976	62.4
1977	73.7
1978	96.6
1979 (June)	84.9

*Negotiable time CDs issued in denominations of $100,000 or more by large commercial banks reporting weekly.
Source: *Federal Reserve Bulletin*, Sept. 1979, p. A14, and earlier issues. Data for 1961 were provided by the Federal Reserve Bank of St. Louis.

bills. Table 8.3 shows that the amount of CDs outstanding declined in 1969. This was because market rates of interest on U.S. Treasury bills and commercial paper rose above the maximum rates that were allowed on CDs at that time. Even though ceilings were suspended in 1973, the volume of large-denomination CDs declined sharply in 1975–1976. In those years banks let CDs run off because short-term interest rates had fallen and banks were able to obtain funds in other ways, such as through the federal funds market, more cheaply than through the sale of CDs.

Securities sold under agreement to repurchase

In 1979, the amount of securities sold by the Dartmouth National Bank under agreement to repurchase was relatively large—almost $2 million (see Table 6.1). Repurchase agreements (RPs) have become an important new source of funds for most commercial banks, reaching approximately $80 billion for all commercial banks in 1978–1979.[4]

When a business firm has a large amount of cash to invest for a very short time, it may put the funds in an RP at a bank. The corporation benefits because it would have earned no interest at all if it had put the same amount of funds in a demand deposit. Although the rates of interest paid on RPs are slightly below those on certificates of deposit, RPs are attractive to corporations because they can be terminated at any time by the firm. To banks, RPs are significant because they permit them to get around government ceilings set on interest rates on deposits and thus to retain their sources of funds. Also, there are no insurance fees on RPs, and there usually have been no reserve requirements. (There were marginal reserve requirements on managed liabilities of large banks from November 1979 to July 1980.)

To understand how repurchase agreements work, consider the impact of issuing an RP on the T-accounts of a bank. A business firm may purchase an RP by transferring funds from its demand deposit at the bank as shown in T-account 8.1:

8.1

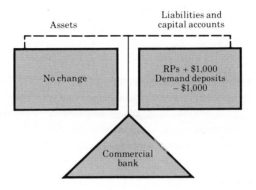

Or, the business firm may purchase an RP by giving the bank a check written on another bank. The effect of this transaction is shown in T-account 8.2:

8.2

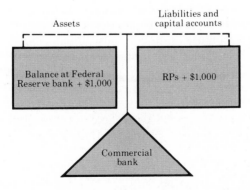

The bank will deposit the check received in payment for the RP at the Federal Reserve bank. Note that even though the issuance of an RP is tied to the sale of government securities together with an obligation to buy back the securities, there is no reduction in the amount of government securities recorded on the bank's balance sheet when an RP is issued. Also, there would be no increase in the amount of government securities owned by the business firm on its balance sheet. The role of government securities in an RP transaction is to serve solely as collateral for the RP, and the nomenclature—securities sold under agreement to repurchase—exaggerates the importance of the securities involved. However, because of the collateral, RPs are an extremely safe way for a business firm to hold liquid funds. *Not true - only as good as Co. that issues it*

Demand notes issued to the U.S. Treasury

The funds of the United States government at commercial banks and thrift institutions are now kept in the form of *interest-bearing demand notes*. When federal income taxes and Social Security taxes withheld by local business firms are deposited in commercial banks, they are immediately invested in these demand notes. Also, when banks sell U.S. savings bonds, the payments for those bonds are invested in these notes. Funds invested in these notes are transferred several times each week by the U.S. Treasury to its deposits in the Federal Reserve banks. The expenditures of the U.S. Treasury are made from the Treasury accounts in the Federal Reserve banks rather than from funds held in commercial banks and thrift institutions.

Interest-bearing demand notes were first issued by banks to the Treasury in 1978. Banks formerly held Treasury funds in interest-free demand deposits called "tax and loan accounts." No reserves need be held at the Federal Reserve banks for the demand notes issued to the Treasury, and they have not been subject to Regulation Q interest-rate ceilings. The interest rate on the demand notes is set by the federal government and varies with market interest rates on U.S. government securities. To compensate commercial banks for the services they perform for the U.S. Treasury, the banks now receive 50 cents for each federal tax deposit form they forward to the Treasury, and the banks are paid 10 cents to 70 cents on each savings bond sold and 30 cents for each bond they redeem. This is part of a movement toward *pricing* services that commercial banks and the U.S. Treasury or the Federal Reserve banks perform for each other.

Deposits of states and political subdivisions

Local units of government usually have deposits in their local banks; some banks, particularly those located in state capitals, hold the deposits of the government of the state. The Town of Hanover has a checking deposit in the Dartmouth National Bank and may at times place funds in interest-earning CDs.

Certified and officers' checks

Deposits designated to pay certified and officers' checks are listed separately from other deposits on a bank's balance sheet. When a bank certifies a check, the amount of the check is taken from the deposit of the person whose check is certified and put in a separate account. Also, when a bank writes an officer's (or cashier's) check to pay for its own expenditures, a deposit equal to the officer's check is created.

Mortgage indebtedness and other liabilities

The Dartmouth National Bank has a mortgage outstanding on the building it occupies—amounting to over $1 million. However, a large component of "other liabilities" of the Dartmouth National Bank is its *transit account*. The deposit accounting and record-keeping of the Dartmouth National Bank is done at the machine-record division of a large bank in Boston. During the time in which the checks drawn on other banks, received for deposit by the Dartmouth National Bank, are en route to Boston and have not yet been credited to the accounts of the depositors, the total amount of those checks is included in the transit account under "other liabilities." Banks that handle their own bookkeeping for checking accounts would not have a transit account. "Other liabilities" also include unearned interest on installment loans and accumulated wages and taxes owed that have not yet been paid.

Federal funds purchased

The balance sheets of some commercial banks include an item "federal funds purchased" among their liabilities. It is the amount of federal funds borrowed from other member banks. Particularly at large banks, this type of borrowing increased sharply after 1965. The Dartmouth National Bank only occasionally purchases federal funds. As described in Chapter 6, these funds are usually borrowed for only one day, but the loan may be continuously renewed. The purpose of purchasing federal funds may be either to acquire additional funds to lend or to cover a reserve deficiency.

Other borrowing

Another item on the balance sheet of some commercial banks is "borrowing." This item consists either of borrowing from the Federal Reserve banks or the amount of Eurodollars borrowed. Borrowing from the Federal Reserve banks has been available to member banks ever since the Federal Reserve System was established. The principal purpose of such borrowing is to cover a short-term deficiency of reserves.

Since the 1960s there has been a rapid expansion in Eurodollar borrowing from foreign banks and from branches of United States banks in foreign countries. Only the largest United States banks borrow in this way because most transactions are in amounts greater than $10 million. When depositors shift their deposits from banks in the United States to foreign banks or to overseas branches of United States banks to take advantage of higher interest rates there, the United States banks may, if they wish, get these funds back by borrowing from their branches. An advantage of Eurodollar borrowing is that there are currently reserve requirements only on amounts over $100 million or over the amount borrowed in a base period.

The development of the federal funds market, Eurodollar borrowing, and repurchase agreements as sources of funds has been an important change in banking. These new sources of funds provide an alternative way of supplying the liquidity needs of a bank. Traditionally, most banks assured that they had funds to cover deposit withdrawals, or to lend to important customers, by holding short-term securities. Today, most large banks meet liquidity needs by borrowing federal funds and Eurodollars, or by repurchase agreements, rather than by selling liquid assets. Heavy reliance on borrowing may in the future cause greater instability in banking. Banks lending federal funds to other banks could ask for sudden repayment and thus create unusual liquidity needs among the banks which must repay the funds.

Capital notes and bonds

A few large commercial banks have raised funds by issuing notes or bonds. Industrial corporations have customarily sold bonds as well as stock as a method of financing their activities, but financing of this type has been very rare among banks. In 1962, the comptroller of the currency ruled that debentures that are subordinate to the claims of depositors could be used to raise funds. All national banks and a number of state banks are permitted to borrow up to 100 percent of capital stock plus 50 percent of surplus in this way. An advantage of issuing notes is that, if issued by bank holding companies rather than by banks, they may legally carry interest rates above those permitted on time deposits.

Capital accounts

There are four principal types of capital accounts: capital stock, surplus, undivided profits, and reserve for contingencies and other capital reserves. The value of the *capital stock* of a bank as listed on its balance sheet is the total amount of shares of common stock outstanding, valued at par. The Dartmouth National Bank has 100,000 shares of stock outstanding, valued at $2 per share: its capital stock is listed at $200,000. Like other corporations, banks sell stock when they are initially chartered in order to raise part of the funds needed for operation. After a bank is in operation, it may sell additional shares of stock or declare dividends payable in stock, adding to the total par value of the shares outstanding. Bank stockholders receive the dividends declared by the bank, and they have voting rights enabling them to have a voice in running the bank.

Surplus is a portion of the undivided profits that has been allocated to surplus by a vote of the bank's directors. When the directors decide to increase surplus, undivided profits are reduced by an identical amount. The amount allocated to surplus is considered to be somewhat more permanently a part of the capital accounts than the undivided profits. Since 1935, national banks have been required to accumulate a surplus equal to the total value of their capital stock. Before this requirement was made, if a bank failed, each stockholder was personally liable for an amount equal to the par value of the stock he held in the bank, an arrangement called double liability.

Undivided profits is the balancing item on the balance sheet. It measures the excess in the total value of the assets over the value of all the liabilities plus other capital accounts. The total amount of the undivided profits is whatever that excess happens to be. It varies each time the balance sheet is prepared.

The difference between the balance sheet items called surplus and undivided profits is minor. Together, they measure how much the total assets of the bank exceed its total liabilities, capital stock, and reserve for contingencies.

The sum total of a bank's capital stock, surplus, undivided profits, and reserve for contingencies is significant to the bank's owners. It measures the *book value* of the shares of stock outstanding—which is related to how much an owner might be willing to sell the shares for and how much others might pay for them—as compared with the *par value* at which the value of the capital stock is listed on the balance sheet. The book value of a share of stock of the Dartmouth National Bank was about $40 when the balance sheet in Chapter 6 was prepared. If this sum increases, it means that the assets of the bank have risen relative to its liabilities, and the claims of the bank's owners are larger. The prices of the stock of large banks are quoted in major newspapers, and there is a market price for the stock. The stock of small banks is not often traded, and the price must be negotiated between the buyer and seller.

The total value of the capital accounts of a bank is expanded by retaining profits. When a bank makes profits, its gross income during the year exceeds its gross expenditures. The receipts of a bank consist primarily of interest from its loans and investments, plus service fees.

The expenses consist primarily of the wages of its employees, interest on time deposits, and other costs of operating the bank. A bank may either pay out the profits it has earned in dividends to the stockholders, or it may retain them. If the bank retains profits, undivided profits increase, and this would usually be balanced on the asset side by an increase in loans and investments. The bank's assets would be increased relative to its liabilities, and the value of its capital accounts would be larger.

Bank examiners typically require banks to keep the amount of their total capital accounts equal to approximately one-tenth of the value of their deposits. This is called the *10 percent rule*. If a bank's deposits are increasing, profits must be retained in order to maintain this ratio. An alternative way to maintain the desired capital-deposit ratio would be to sell additional stock, but this is seldom done. The capital-deposit ratio is usually smaller than 10 percent for larger banks. The appropriate capital-deposit ratio for a bank varies with the condition of the bank and is affected by the quality of a bank's assets and the proportion of its assets in loans. Historically, the capital-deposit ratio of banks has declined. For all commercial banks, it was 23 percent in 1900, 22 percent in 1910, 14 percent in 1920, 17 percent in 1930, 12 percent in 1940, and has averaged less than 10 percent since World War II.

The 10 percent rule is intended to protect depositors, because capital accounts act as a buffer to absorb bad loans. If a loan is considered bad by examiners, the bank must remove it from its recorded assets even though the loan may eventually be paid off. If a bank had to write off a bad loan for $1,000, for example, undivided profits would also be reduced, as shown in T-account 8.3:

8.3

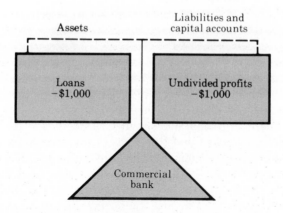

Because of the reduction in undivided profits, the value of the owners' interests in the bank is reduced. As long as bad loans are kept low enough so that they may be covered by undivided profits, the public's deposits are protected because total deposits would be smaller than the bank's total assets.

The balance sheet item *reserve for contingencies and other capital reserves* consists of reserves for expected losses on securities or reserves to supplement future obligations of employee pension programs. When the reserve for contingencies is increased, undivided profits are reduced.

Reserve items on the liabilities side of the balance sheet should be distinguished sharply from the reserve assets of a bank, consisting of its cash in vault and balance at the Federal Reserve bank. A common error is to conceive of surplus, undivided profits, or the reserve for contingencies as funds that can be used to meet expenditures. Only assets, such as cash or earning assets that can be sold for cash, can be used to cover the expenditures of the bank or to pay its debts. The capital accounts are intangible and are the way in which the balance sheet shows the amount of the claims of the bank's owners on the assets of the bank.

Bank failures

A bank fails usually because of bad loans or the decline in the value of the securities it owns. Either of these contingencies may cut into its capital accounts. When the value of its capital accounts is below zero, the bank's liabilities are larger than its assets. It is then said to be *insolvent*, and it is required by the examiners to cease operating—even though the bank may have sufficient current income to cover its current expenditures.

The most dramatic period of bank failures in the United States occurred from 1930 through 1933 when more than 9,000 banks suspended operations. The major reason for these failures was the decline in the market value of their bonds, rather than bad loans. Currently, bonds are listed on the balance sheet at their purchase price, so that a decline in the market price of bonds does not cause a reduction in the bank's assets and its capital accounts. During the 1930s, accounting practices were different. Bonds for which continuous price quotations were available had to be valued at market price. As a result, when bond prices fell during the Great Depression, the listed value of the bonds that banks had in their portfolios declined, reducing the value of their capital accounts. The runs on banks, and attempts by bankers to prepare for runs by selling securities to build up their very liquid assets, contributed to the fall in the price of bonds owned by banks.

Today when bond prices fall, undivided profits are reduced only if the bank is forced to sell its bonds at a loss. T-account 8.4 shows the effect on a commercial bank's balance sheet of the sale of a bond listed at $1,000 at a $200 loss:

8.4

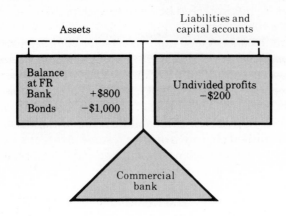

The bank's balance at the Federal Reserve bank would be increased by only $800, the sale price of the bond. The purchaser of the bond would pay for it by a check written on his bank. The bank receiving the payment for it would deposit this check in its Federal Reserve bank, thus increasing its deposit there by $800. Since the bond had been listed on the balance sheet as worth $1,000, the difference of $200 would reduce undivided profits. Banks normally are able to avoid losses of this type by holding federal funds sold or liquid securities such as U.S. Treasury bills. Liquid securities can be disposed of without incurring much of any loss. Only if a bank is caught short of liquid assets and has to sell long-term securities would it be forced to incur a loss of this type.

Banks also experience a decline in total assets and undivided profits when a loan goes bad and has to be written off. In the early part of the Great Depression, some bank loans that had been made during the prosperous 1920s turned out to be bad and contributed to the eventual failure of some banks.

The failure of banks causes losses to both stockholders and depositors. The total loss to both stockholders and depositors in the Great Depression has been estimated at $2.5 billion. While these losses were bad enough, the most serious problem caused by bank failures is the resulting decline in the total money supply. From 1929 to 1933, a decline of more than 35 percent in currency plus demand and time deposits at commercial banks caused people to cut back on their spending, contributing significantly to the length and severity of the depression.

Table 8.4 shows that from 1968 to 1977 only a few banks failed each year. Until very recently, almost all of the closed banks were small, but since 1966 several large banks have failed or been forced to merge. When the Franklin National Bank (the twentieth largest bank in the

United States) failed because of losses on loans and on foreign exchange in 1974, the FDIC published newspaper advertisements around the country to assure the public that possible losses would be covered. The European-American Bank and Trust Company—owned by six large European banks, but chartered by the state of New York—won the bid to take over the Franklin National from the FDIC.

Table 8.4 Number of Banks Closed Because of Financial Difficulties, 1968–1977	Year	Insured by FDIC	Noninsured	Total Number Closed
	1968	3	0	3
	1969	9	0	9
	1970	7	1	8
	1971	6	0	6
	1972	1	2	3
	1973	6	0	6
	1974	4	0	4
	1975	13	1	14
	1976	16	1	17
	1977	6	0	6

Source: Federal Deposit Insurance Corporation, *Annual Report, 1977* (Washington, D.C., 1978), p. 193.

In 1976, the problem of bank insolvency and near-insolvency increased—partly because of the overexpansion of certain types of housing credit. It has been suggested that FDIC premiums should be graduated according to risk to discourage banks from assuming high risks.[5]

Bad loan policies of foreign banks

Compared to the policies of many other governments regarding bad loans, those of the United States bank examiners are relatively tough. In the United States, a loan does not have to be many months behind in its repayments, nor do the prospects of repayment have to appear particularly bad, for the loan to be taken out of the recorded assets of the bank. In some other countries, bad loans may be carried on the accounts of a bank indefinitely. This practice is typical in countries where there is a considerable amount of government direction of the use of bank credit. As part of a development plan, for example, banks may be required to grant loans to certain enterprises; however, inefficient enterprises would not be able to pay back the principal of the loan. Their costs may be too high, or the price that they are able to get for their output may be too low and controlled by a government planning authority. The government may be induced to subsidize consumers by keeping the price of transportation or utilities below cost for political reasons. Under such conditions, enterprises cannot be expected to operate at a profit or to pay back the principal of bank loans with interest, and it would be unreasonable for bank examiners to require the banks to write off such loans.

Carrying worthless notes on the books of such banks does not cause difficulties in their normal operations. If a loss of public confidence starts a run on banks, it is usually not a serious problem. As long as a bank—either private or government owned—can obtain more paper money from a central bank, it can convert deposits into currency. Although the accumulation of bad loans by banks need not cause banks to fail, there may, of course, be real economic costs to the economy. If a bank makes bad loans, it has probably wasted the credit resources of the country.

Summary

Commercial banks provide people and business firms with the principal type of money that is used for making payments—demand deposits.

The variety and volume of time deposits in commercial banks have grown rapidly in recent years. Rates of interest paid on these deposits have been raised, and banks have become more aggressive in developing sources of funds.

Bank examiners require banks to have capital accounts that are considered sufficiently large to cover a substantial volume of losses from bad loans. Their objective is to ensure that the bank's total deposit liabilities are smaller than its total assets.

Notes

1. George J. Benston, "Interest Payments on Demand Deposits and Bank Investment Behavior," *Journal of Political Economy* 72 (October 1964), pp. 431–449.

2. *Federal Reserve Bulletin*, December 1973, pp. 921–923.

3. R. Alton Gilbert and Jean M. Lovati, "Disintermediation—An Old Disorder with a New Remedy," Federal Reserve Bank of St. Louis, *Review*, January 1979, pp. 10–15.

4. For a detailed description of RPs, see Marcia Stigum, *The Money Market: Myth, Reality, and Practice* (Homewood, Ill.: Dow Jones-Irwin, 1978), pp.86-87, 311-333.

5. R. Alton Gilbert, "Bank Failures and Public Policy," Federal Reserve Bank of St. Louis, *Review*, November 1975, p. 12.

Questions

8.1. Explain why demand deposits are liabilities of banks.

8.2. What are some of the different ways that banks compete for demand deposits?

8.3. Explain the rapid growth of time deposits in commercial banks during the past decade.

8.4. What is an Individual Retirement Account? What advantages do these accounts offer to individuals? Why are they of importance to banks?

8.5. Why have ceiling rates of interest on CDs been suspended?

8.6. What is a NOW account? An ATS account?

8.7. Explain the principal characteristics of passbook savings deposits, savings certificates, open account time deposits, and certificates of deposit.

8.8. What changes have recently been made in the way the U.S. Treasury holds money in commercial banks? What were the reasons for the changes?

8.9. To whom do banks sell securities under repurchase agreements, and why is this done?

8.10. Banks formerly provided for liquidity needs mainly by holding liquid assets which could be sold in time of need. How else do they obtain funds in time of need today?

8.11. What are the different types of borrowings of commercial banks?

8.12. Explain why increased reliance on the following sources of bank funds could lead to greater instability of the banking system: borrowing of federal funds and Eurodollars; large negotiable CDs; repurchase agreements.

8.13. What is the difference between a bank's surplus and its undivided profits?

8.14. Explain the way in which a bank's undivided profits may be increased. How might they be decreased?

8.15. Why do bank examiners urge banks to have capital accounts equal in total to approximately 10 percent of their deposits?

8.16. If a bank needs funds to purchase a new accounting machine, can it use its undivided profits? Explain.

8.17. Explain the ways in which banks become insolvent and fail.

8.18. Describe the recent history of bank failures.

8.19. Know the meaning and significance of the following terms and concepts: demand deposit, passbook savings deposit, capital stock, surplus, undivided profits, certificates of deposit (CDs), tax and loan account, interbank deposits, savings certificate, time deposit, reserve for bad loans, 10 percent rule for capital accounts, insolvent bank, capital notes, NOW account, ATS account, federal funds purchased, repurchase agreement (RP), demand note issued to the Treasury, Individual Retirement Account (IRA).

9

The way in which commercial banks create deposits is one of the most important processes in the monetary system. The possibility of deposit creation usually depends on an expansion in the reserves of commercial banks or on a reduction in their required reserve ratios—conditions that may be controlled by the Federal Reserve System.

THE CREATION OF DEPOSITS

To understand the way banks in a fractional reserve banking system create deposits, it is important to distinguish between an individual bank and the banking system consisting of thousands of individual banks. From the point of view of the individual bank, an obvious way in which deposits may be created is by the deposit of currency in the bank. But deposits are also destroyed when currency is withdrawn from a bank—and deposits of currency tend to be offset by withdrawals of currency. Most deposits are actually not created in this way. To the individual banker, deposits are also created by the deposit of a check written on another bank. Most of his deposits appear to be created in this way. But from the point of view of the banking system, the deposit of a check on another bank merely transfers deposits from one bank to another. For the system as a whole, total deposits are unchanged.

The principal process by which a fractional reserve banking system creates deposits, the most important type of money in our economy, occurs when a bank makes a loan or buys a security. When a bank makes a loan, it usually increases the total in the borrower's checking account by the amount of the loan. Even though the bank making the loan can expect to lose the deposit when the borrower writes a check on it, another bank, receiving that check, will experience an increase in deposits. The total amount of deposits in the banking system is increased when banks expand their total loans and investments. But this type of deposit creation can occur only when banks are in a position to expand their total loans and investments, and when a bank is required to hold as reserves only a portion of its deposits.

Upper limit to deposit creation

There is an upper limit to the amount of deposits that each bank can create by expanding its loans and investments. This limit is determined by the level of reserves required of the bank.

The total amount of reserves that a member bank is required by law to hold, either as cash in vault or as deposits at the Federal Reserve bank, is called its *required reserves*. Reserves held above the amount required are called *excess reserves*. In the simplified balance sheet shown in T-account 9.1, commercial bank A has one type of liability (demand deposits) and three types of assets (reserves, U.S. government securities, and loans). Assume that the required reserve ratio is 20 percent, a ratio somewhat higher than those that actually exist. Under these circumstances, commercial bank A would have no excess reserves, and so could not expand its earning assets beyond $80,000 or its deposits beyond $100,000. If it made a new loan, the addition to the borrower's account would increase its total demand deposits and, consequently, lower its reserve ratio below 20 percent. If bank A used funds from its reserves either to buy additional securities or to make more loans, that would reduce its reserves to less than $20,000, and its reserve ratio would again be less than the legal minimum. Only if commercial bank A acquired reserves larger than $20,000, or if its minimum reserve ratio were lowered below 20 percent, could it expand its earning assets above $80,000 and create additional deposits.

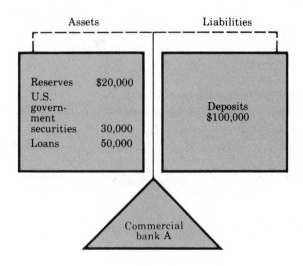

Assets | Liabilities

Reserves $20,000
U.S. government securities 30,000
Loans 50,000

Deposits $100,000

Commercial bank A

Increasing reserves

The principal type of reserves of commercial banks is deposits in Federal Reserve banks. Commercial banks obtain additional reserves when the Federal Reserve banks purchase U.S. government securities. There are other ways of increasing reserves (these are included in the bank reserve equation explained in Chapter 12), but *open-market purchases* are by far the most important. Federal Reserve banks invest in U.S. government securities and have demand deposit liabilities much as commercial banks do; the deposits in Federal Reserve banks belong mostly to commercial banks.

The way in which an open-market purchase of $1,000 would affect the balance sheets of both the Federal Reserve banks and the particular commercial bank initially affected by the open-market purchase is shown in the following T-accounts:

9.2

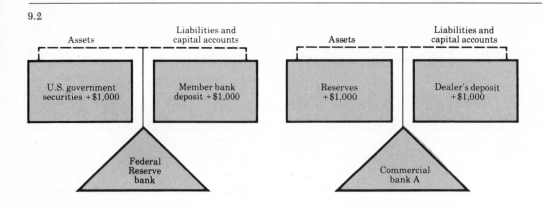

As a result of the purchase, the amount of U.S. government securities held by the Federal Reserve banks is increased by $1,000. Federal Reserve banks pay for government securities with checks written on themselves. A fundamental characteristic of the Federal Reserve banks is that they can purchase government securities in this way, and the end result of such purchases is an addition to the total reserves of the commercial banking system. Assuming that the securities were purchased from a dealer that was not a commercial bank, when the dealer deposits the check he received in payment for the securities, his balance at commercial bank A is increased by $1,000. Commercial bank A's balance at the Federal Reserve bank (its reserves) increases when it deposits the check that it received from the dealer. The simplified balance sheet of commercial bank A, originally shown in T-account 9.1, would now be as shown in T-account 9.3:

9.3

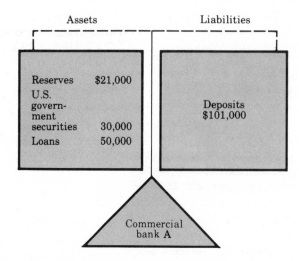

With total reserves of $21,000, commercial bank A is now in a position to expand its loans and create deposits—or it may create deposits by investing in securities. Commercial bank A's required reserves—its total deposits multiplied by its required reserve ratio—amount to $20,200. It has excess reserves of $800, which is the difference between its total reserves and its required reserves.

In the example shown in T-account 9.3, the open-market purchase was assumed to be from a nonbank dealer who deposited his check in his bank. If the dealer in U.S. government securities was a commercial bank, the purchase would have been made directly from the bank itself. In that case, there would be no increase in deposits in the commercial bank. The bank's reserves would increase, and its holdings of U.S. government securities would decrease. Its excess reserves would increase by $1,000.

Multiple expansion of bank loans and deposits

When total reserves are increased through open-market purchases, the expansion of loans and investments made by banks and the amount of deposits created will be larger than the increase in reserves. This is known as the *multiple expansion* of bank loans and deposits. A decrease in total reserves would result in a *multiple contraction* of bank loans and deposits.

A fundamental paradox in the way banks operate is that even though an individual bank cannot expand its loans or investments by any more than its excess reserves, the banking system as a whole can. When an individual bank acquires excess reserves of $800, as shown in T-account 9.3, it may expand its loans or securities by only $800. In most cases, the bank would give the borrower a deposit when it makes a loan, as shown in T-account 9.4:

9.4

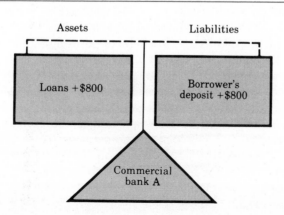

The borrower will then write a check on this deposit to make the purchase he had planned to make, and the person who receives the check will probably deposit it in another bank. When the borrower's check is sent to the Federal Reserve bank for collection, commercial bank A loses reserves equal to $800, and the deposit of the borrower— which had been increased by $800—is reduced by the same amount. The end result is shown in T-account 9.5:

9.5

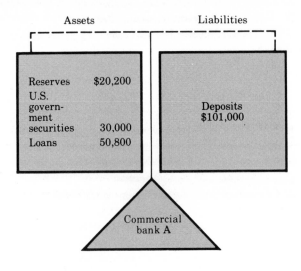

If commercial bank A had expanded its loans by more than its excess reserves, its reserves would have fallen below the legal minimum. With total deposits of $101,000, it must hold $20,200 in reserves. An individual bank's ability to expand its loans is limited because of the probability that the borrower's check will be deposited in some bank other than the one that made the original loan.

Despite the fact that an individual bank cannot safely expand its loans by more than its excess reserves, the banking system can expand its loans and investments by more than the original increase in reserves. This is because there are important effects on other banks when the person who borrows from one commercial bank spends the money lent him. The check he writes will probably be deposited in another commercial bank—for instance, commercial bank B. This will initially increase commercial bank B's deposits and reserves, as shown in T-account 9.6:

9.6

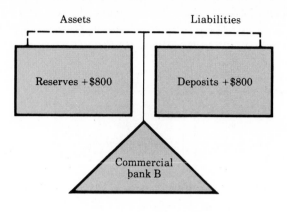

When the person receiving the check for $800 deposits it in commercial bank B, his deposit is increased by $800; and when commercial bank B deposits the check in its Federal Reserve bank, its reserve balance there is increased by the same amount.

Commercial bank B now has excess reserves of $640, and it can be expected to expand its loans or investments and its deposits by this amount, as shown in T-account 9.7:

9.7

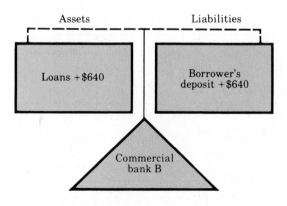

The borrower, however, will soon spend the $640 lent him. The result of this is to reduce the reserves and deposits of commercial bank B by $640—if the check he writes for $640 is deposited in another bank. The end result of this chain of events for commercial bank B is shown in T-account 9.8:

9.8

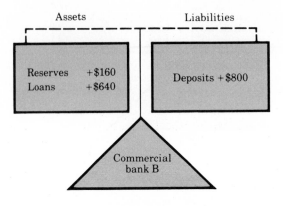

Again, when the person who borrowed from commercial bank B uses his deposit, the check that he gives to someone else will probably be deposited in a third commercial bank—let us call it commercial bank C—as shown in T-account 9.9:

9.9

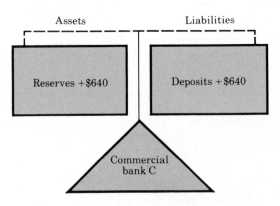

When commercial bank C deposits the check on commercial bank B in its Federal Reserve bank, its reserves there will be increased. The Federal Reserve bank will then transfer $640 from commercial bank B to commercial bank C. Now bank C has $512 in excess reserves, and when it lends the $512, the initial impact is shown in T-account 9.10:

9.10

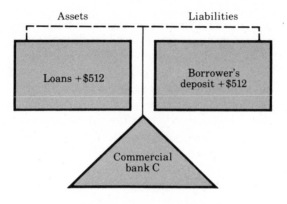

When the borrower spends the $512, bank C will probably lose $512 in both reserves and deposits. The sum total of T-accounts 9.9 and 9.10, after this loss of deposits and reserves, leaves bank C with the situation shown in T-account 9.11:

9.11

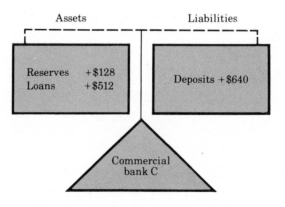

This process continues as additional banks are affected. Note that the expansion in the deposits of commercial banks A, B, and C is more than

$1,000 (the original increase in reserves in commercial bank A)—$1,000 in commercial bank A, $800 in commercial bank B, and $640 in commercial bank C.

Table 9.1 shows the expansion in loans and deposits occurring in up to ten banks as a result of an original open-market purchase of $1,000. When the first bank makes a loan for $800, a deposit of $800 is created which goes to the second bank. Each bank keeps 20 percent of the deposit it receives as reserves and lends the rest. As the process continues, the amount of the deposit received by each bank and the amount each bank can lend gets smaller. The original $1,000 of additional reserves is distributed among all of the banks affected.

The example in Table 9.1 is simplified in order to illustrate the process involved. It assumes that the initial effect of an open-market purchase is solely on one bank. This is possible, but not necessarily the case. It assumes that each bank immediately uses the excess reserves that it acquired. It assumes that the check written by the borrower was, in each case, deposited in another bank. In fact, these checks are sometimes redeposited in the same bank from which the funds were borrowed. A reserve requirement of 20 percent is used, even though legal reserve requirements are below this and vary for banks of different size and for different types of deposits. It also assumes that no other transactions affecting the reserves of the banks takes place.

Table 9.1
Illustration of the
Maximum Expansion of
Bank Loans and
Deposits Resulting
from an Open Market
Purchase of $1,000[a]

Bank	Deposited in Checking Accounts	Lent	Retained as Reserves
First	$1,000.00	$ 800.00	$ 200.00
Second	800.00	640.00	160.00
Third	640.00	512.00	128.00
Fourth	512.00	409.60	102.40
Fifth	409.60	327.70	81.90
Sixth	327.70	262.20	65.50
Seventh	262.20	209.80	52.40
Eighth	209.80	167.80	42.00
Ninth	167.80	134.20	33.60
Tenth	134.20	107.40	26.80
Total for 10 banks	$4,463.30	$3,570.70	$ 892.60
Additional banks	536.70	429.30	107.40
Total, all banks	$5,000.00	$4,000.00	$1,000.00

[a]Assuming reserve requirements equal to 20 percent of demand deposits.

The formula for the maximum expansion of demand deposits that may result from an increase in reserves is:

9.1

$$\Delta D = \frac{\Delta H}{r},$$

where Δ=increased or decreased dollar amount, D=demand deposits, H=reserves (also called the monetary base or high-powered money), and r=reserve requirement. Thus:

$$\$5,000 = \frac{\$1,000}{.20}.$$

Assuming an increase in reserves of $1,000 and a legal reserve requirement of 20 percent, the maximum expansion of *demand deposits* would be $5,000. The maximum expansion of *loans and investments* is equal to the expansion of deposits less the expansion in reserves, or $4,000. In 1980, legal reserve ratios for demand deposits varied from 7 percent to 16¼ percent, depending on the size of the bank. If an average reserve requirement of 15 percent were assumed, the maximum expansion of demand deposits would be $6,667 for a $1,000 increase in reserves.

Leakages

The actual expansion in demand deposits that occurs, given the required legal reserves, is considerably below the maximum possible because of several types of *leakage*. Leakages occur because there are several ways in which an increase in reserve deposits at the Federal Reserve banks may be used other than as reserves for demand deposits. Leakages will occur if there is an increase in currency held outside banks, in excess reserves of commercial banks, or in time deposits.

Currency drains

An expansion of bank loans (or investments) and deposits usually results in an increase in the amount of currency in circulation outside banks. When there is a multiple expansion of loans and deposits, some people who receive checks from those who have borrowed from the banks will cash them rather than deposit them. Also, if businesses borrow for payroll purposes, cash withdrawals will take place when their employees cash their checks. These withdrawals of currency from commercial banks reduce bank reserves and the amount of expansion in loans and deposits that can be created by the banking system.

Table 9.2 shows the increase in both currency outside banks and demand deposits from 1970 to 1979. As the total money supply expands, both currency and demand deposits usually increase in approximately the same proportion. This is because the percentage of total transactions paid for with currency and the percentage paid for by checks on demand deposits are based on customary ways of making payments that do not change much. Throughout much of the history of the United States, the currency-to-deposit ratio has fallen because of the growing popularity of the use of checking accounts. Since 1961, however, the ratio of currency to demand deposits has risen, and Table 9.2 shows a sharp rise in this ratio, from 29 percent in 1970 to 39 percent in 1979. There is some dispute over the reasons for the rapid increase in this ratio in the 1970s. Some economists attribute it to the rapid expansion of repurchase agreements, which are said to reduce the holding of demand deposits. Others believe that the cause is the growth of illegal transactions using currency, and the preference for currency among immigrants from Asia and Latin America. The rise in the ratio of currency to demand deposits has also been attributed to the increase in the proportion of young persons in the total population. They tend to use currency rather than checks on demand deposits as a medium of exchange.

Currency drains significantly reduce the ability of the banking system to create deposits. The expansion formula, taking into consideration the probable expansion of currency in circulation, is:

9.2

$$\ast \quad \Delta D = \frac{\Delta H}{(r + c) - \text{leakage}}$$

The variable c is the percentage of additional demand deposits that the public wishes to hold as currency. If this ratio were 35 percent, it would mean that people wish to hold thirty-five cents in currency for each additional dollar held in checking accounts. If ΔH were $1,000, the currency-deposit ratio 35 percent, and the banks' legal reserve requirement 15 percent, the estimated expansion of demand deposits would be $2,000:

$$\$2,000 = \frac{\$1,000}{(.15 + .35)}$$

Note that, of the original increase in bank reserves of $1,000, only $300—15 percent of the $2,000 increase in demand deposits—remains

Table 9.2
The Ratios of Currency, Time Deposits in
Commercial Banks, and Excess Reserves to
Demand Deposits, 1970–1979

December	Currency Outside Banks (in billions)	Demand Deposits in Commercial Banks (in billions)	Ratio of Currency to Demand Deposits	All Time Deposits (in billions)	Ratio of Time Deposits to Demand Deposits	Excess Reserves (in millions)	Ratio of Excess Reserves to Demand Deposits
	(1)	(2)	(3)	(4)	(5)	(6)	(7)
1970	$49.0	$170.7	28.7%	$229.2	134.3%	$272	0.159%
1971	52.5	181.5	28.9	271.1	149.4	165	0.091
1972	56.9	198.4	28.7	313.5	158.0	219	0.110
1973	61.6	209.0	29.5	363.7	174.0	262	0.125
1974	67.8	215.3	31.5	418.1	194.2	339	0.157
1975	73.8	221.7	33.3	450.3	203.1	264	0.119
1976	80.8	233.0	34.7	489.2	210.0	172	0.074
1977	88.6	250.1	35.4	544.4	217.7	174	0.070
1978	97.7	263.8	37.0	614.1	232.8	125	0.047
1979	106.3	275.8	38.5	664.8	241.0	503	0.182

Source: *Economic Report of the President, January 1980*; pp. 271 and 276.

as bank reserves. The amount drained into currency held by the public is $700—35 percent of the increase in demand deposits.

Holdings of excess reserves

Another type of drain that may cause the creation of demand deposits to be less than the maximum possible is an expansion of excess reserves. If the amount of excess reserves that banks desire to hold increases as their deposits expand, a loss of reserves available for the expansion of bank loans and deposits would result. Using the symbol i to refer to the percentage of their demand deposits that banks customarily hold as excess reserves, the formula for the expansion of demand deposits is:

9.3

$$\Delta D = \frac{\Delta H}{(r+c+i)} \ .$$

If the banks' usual ratio of excess reserves to demand deposits were one percent, the expansion in total demand deposits would be reduced to $1,961:

$$\$1,961 = \frac{\$1,000}{(.15+.35+.01)} \ .$$

The total excess reserves of all member banks have fallen to low levels during the past thirty years. The principal reason that banks are holding the small amounts of excess reserves shown in Table 9.2 is the growth of the federal funds market, which permits banks with excess reserves to lend them on a day-to-day basis to other banks. Banks are willing to hold smaller balances of excess reserves because additional reserves are available through the federal funds market.

Another reason for the downward trend of excess reserves is the rise in the rates of return on all types of loans and investments made by commercial banks. Higher market interest rates on their loans and investments induce banks to reduce their holdings of excess reserves.

The growth in the size of banks may also have contributed to the smaller holdings of excess reserves. Larger banks generally hold a smaller proportion of excess reserves to total reserves than do smaller banks. Banks, on the average, have expanded in size with the growth of the commercial banking system.

In 1968, the Federal Reserve System, under Regulation D, adopted new procedures for calculating reserve requirements that enable banks to cut down on their excess reserve holdings. Each bank now uses average deposits two weeks earlier to calculate *required* reserves for the week. To calculate the bank's *actual* reserves, it uses cash in vault held two weeks earlier, together with average balances at the Federal Reserve bank for the current week. In addition, the new regulations permit banks to carry forward to the next reserve week excesses or deficiencies averaging up to 2 percent of required reserves. These regulations made it easier for banks to predict the amount of required reserves needed and to avoid shortages of reserves. After the regulations became effective in 1968, average excess reserves of all member banks dropped from typical levels of about $400 million to $250 million or less.

The need for reserves for time deposits

Commercial banks create time deposits as well as demand deposits. Table 9.2 shows that from 1970 to 1979 the growth of time deposits (including all interest-bearing deposits) in commercial banks was especially large. In the expansion process, some people prefer additional time deposits rather than additional demand deposits because of the interest paid on time deposits. The almost certain increase in time deposits in commercial banks causes another drain of reserves from demand deposits, because banks must hold some of the additional time deposits as reserves. Let r' be the reserve requirement for time deposits and t be the percentage of their demand deposits that the public customarily holds in time deposits. The formula for the expansion of demand deposits would be as follows:

(9.4)

$$\Delta D = \frac{\Delta H}{[r+c+i+(r')(t)]}$$

on test ✓ *

If the reserve requirement for time deposits were 4 percent and the ratio of time deposits to demand deposits were 200 percent, the estimated total expansion in demand deposits would be $1,695:

$$* \quad \$1,695 = \frac{\$1,000}{[.15+.35+.01+(.04)(2.00)]}.$$

Although the expansion of demand deposits is smaller if people shift from demand deposits to time deposits, the increase in total deposits— demand plus time—and the increase in total bank loans and investments will be larger. If the public shifts from time deposits to demand deposits, the opposite may occur—a contraction in total deposits and bank credit. In 1980, legal reserve requirements were 3 percent for savings deposits and NOW accounts and from 1 percent to 6 percent on various maturities of time deposits. The reserve requirements for demand deposits varied from 7 percent to 16¼ percent, depending on the size of the bank. Because of the lower reserve requirements for time deposits, when the public shifts from demand deposits to time deposits, excess reserves are created which the banks may lend, and a multiple expansion of loans and deposits may result.

The formula showing the multiple expansion of demand deposits illustrates the way in which a shift from demand to time deposits increases total deposits. In Equation 9.4, when the monetary base increased by $1,000, demand deposits increased by $1,695, and one of the assumptions was that time deposits increased twice as much as demand deposits, making a total increase in deposits of $5,085. If the ratio of time deposits to demand deposits were 300 percent instead of 200 percent, demand deposits would increase by $1,587 and time deposits by three times this—a total increase in deposits of $6,348.

Variations in reserve requirements

When banks are required to raise their ratio of reserves to either demand or time deposits, the possible expansion of demand deposits is reduced; and when their reserve requirements are lowered, the expansion can be larger. The Board of Governors of the Federal Reserve System has the authority to change, within limits, these requirements for banks. Moreover, because there are different reserve requirements for banks of different size, when the public shifts deposits from one category of bank to another, it affects the average values of r and r' for the entire banking system. In 1980, there were five categories of banks based on total demand deposits: $2 million or less, over $2 million to $10 million, over $10 million to $100 million, over $100 million to $400 million, and over $400 million. There were also different reserve requirements for time deposits below and above $5 million, for savings and for time deposits, and for time deposits of different maturities. Although these reserve requirements are scheduled to be gradually changed over the next six years in accordance with the Depository Institutions Deregulation and Monetary Control Act of 1980, there will still be different reserve requirements for large and small banks, for time and transaction accounts, and for personal and nonpersonal time deposits. If people shift their deposits from small banks that have low reserve requirements to large banks which have high reserve requirements, the average values of r and r' for the entire banking system rise. If they shift deposits to banks with lower legal reserve requirements, the average values of r and r' fall.

The money multiplier ✳

In Equation 9.4, the expansion of demand deposits (ΔD) was $1,695. The increase in currency outside banks—which is added to demand deposits to calculate *M-1A*—is equal to $593 (35 percent of the expansion of demand deposits). The expansion of *M-1A* would be $2,288. The ratio $\Delta M\text{-}1A/\Delta H$ is called the *money multiplier* or the *expansion ratio*, and in this example it is equal to 2.29. The expansion of *M-1A* plus time deposits in commercial banks based on the example used in Equation 9.4 would be $5,678. An increase of time deposits equal to $3,390 would be added to the increase in *M-1A*. The money multiplier for *M-1A* plus time deposits in commercial banks would be 5.68.

The symbol H in the numerator of Equation 9.4 includes currency outside banks in addition to bank reserves and is more accurately called the *monetary base* or *high-powered* money rather than bank reserves. The monetary base consists of the total amount of those types of money that can be used as bank reserves. The portion of the monetary base in currency could be used as bank reserves but is not. The formula for the monetary base is:

9.5
$$H = C + R,$$

where C is *currency outside of banks* and R is *bank reserves*. Bank reserves include both cash in the vaults of commercial banks and their balances at the Federal Reserve banks. Thus, the monetary base is also equal to the sum of *currency in circulation* (outside the Federal Reserve banks and the United States Treasury) and the total reserve deposits of member banks at the Federal Reserve banks.

The formula for the expansion of *M-1A* is:

9.6
$$\Delta M\text{-}1A = \frac{\Delta H(1 + c)}{[r+c+i+(r')(t)]} .$$

$\Delta M\text{-}1A$ is equal to the formula for the increase in demand deposits (9.4) times $(1 + c)$:

Since $\Delta M\text{-}1A = \Delta D + \Delta C$
and $\Delta C = c(\Delta D)$,
$\Delta M\text{-}1A = \Delta D + c(\Delta D) = \Delta D(1 + c)$.

The formula for the expansion of $M\text{-}1A$ plus time deposits in commercial banks is:

9.7

$$\Delta(M\text{-}1A + TD) = \frac{\Delta H(1 + c + t)}{[r+c+i+(r')\,(t)]},$$

where TD = the amount of time deposits in commercial banks.

In recent years, the money multiplier in the United States for $M\text{-}1A$ has, in fact, been between 2 and 3.5.[1] The money multiplier for $M\text{-}1A$ + TD is somewhat larger, because the reserve requirements for time deposits are lower than for demand deposits; in 1979 this multiplier was over 6. The time it takes for an increase in the monetary base to work through the multiple expansion process is very short. A study by Professor Horwich of the expansion process concluded that the response to changes in the monetary base usually occurred within a month and often much quicker.[2]

The money multiplier in the United States is higher today than in most periods in the past. In December 1979, the public's ratio of currency to the total amount of currency plus demand and time deposits at commercial banks was 10 percent, compared to 45 percent in 1867, 32 percent in 1875, and 19 percent in 1900. As people hold proportionately less in currency, the possibilities of expansion are greater. Also, lower bank reserve requirements and smaller holdings of excess reserves would tend to cause the money multiplier to be larger. Estimates by Professor Cagan show a decline in the ratio of bank reserves to deposits from almost 40 percent in 1875 to 19 percent in 1955.[3] The larger the money multiplier, the smaller the increase in the monetary base needed to achieve a given increase in the money supply.

The formula for the total supply of money (M) in terms of the monetary base and the money multiplier is:

9.8

$$M = H \cdot m.$$

The symbol for the money multiplier is m. The formula for the *M-1A* money multiplier is:

9.9

$$m = \frac{(1 + c)}{[r+c+i+(r')\,(t)]} \; .$$

The formula for the (*M-1A* + *TD*) money multiplier is:

9.10

$$m = \frac{(1 + c + t)}{[r+c+i+(r')\,(t)]} \; .$$

Equations 9.6 and 9.7 may be used to calculate the increase in *M-1A* and (*M-1A* + *TD*) resulting from an increase in the monetary base, assuming no change in the money multiplier. However, if the money multiplier has also changed, calculations of the expansion in the money supply are more complicated than shown in those equations. Because of the inter-relationship between the monetary base and the money multiplier, the equation for a change in *M-1A* in terms of the monetary base and the money multiplier is:

9.11

$$\Delta M\text{-}1A = H\Delta m + m\Delta H + \Delta m\Delta H.$$

To estimate a change in *M-1A* resulting from simultaneous changes in both the base and the multiplier, it is necessary to determine the change in both the monetary base and the money multiplier and then to determine the change in the money supply using Equation 9.11.

Figure 9.1 shows the close long-run relationship from 1954 to 1979 between the rate of change in the monetary base and the rate of change in *M-1* as defined prior to the publication of the new *M-1A* and *M-1B* series. In the 1970s, the divergences between the rate of expansion of the monetary base and the rate of growth of *M-1* have been larger than in earlier years because currency and time deposits have expanded more rapidly than previously, causing the ratio of currency to demand deposits and the ratio of time deposits at commercial banks to demand deposits to rise (see columns 3 and 5 in Table 9.2 for trends of these ratios). As shown by equation 9.6, a rise in these ratios will cause the rate of expansion of *M-1* to be less rapid than the rate of growth of the monetary base.

Historical variations in excess reserves

A question that is frequently raised concerning the effect of monetary policy on the supply of money and credit is whether commercial banks will hold additional reserves as excess reserves rather than use them to expand loans and deposits. If additional reserves lead to an accumulation of excess reserves, an expansionary monetary policy need not increase the money supply.

Table 9.3 shows the volume of excess reserves that member banks held, and the increase in their total reserves, from 1965 to 1979. There has been no accumulation of excess reserves. As banks have acquired additional reserves, they have expanded their loans and investments. The resulting expansion in their deposits has caused their required reserves to increase as rapidly as the increase in total reserves. There was also no accumulation of excess reserves between World War II and 1965, although during this period, monetary expansion by the Federal Reserve System was based largely on reductions in legal reserve requirements rather than on expanding total reserves.

In contrast to what has happened since World War II, in the 1930s the excess reserves of banks increased sharply. During the first two years of the Great Depression, excess reserves were at the low levels that had prevailed in the 1920s. In December 1931, excess reserves were $60 million, but by the following year rose to $526 million. They continued to rise sharply from 1933 to 1935, fell in 1936 and 1937, and then rose to over $6.5 billion in December 1940. This experience in the 1930s is an interesting exception to the general rule that banks will expand their loans and investments when their reserves are increased.

The large increase in total bank reserves from 1933 to 1940 was caused primarily by a large inflow of gold. When the United States Treasury purchased gold, member bank reserves increased. The inflow of gold was the result of the 1934 increase from $20.67 per ounce to $35 in the price paid for gold by the Treasury, and also of an inflow of capital resulting from the unsettled political conditions in Europe.

There are two different views as to why the banks did not use their additional reserves in this period. One view, which was expressed in some Federal Reserve publications, is that there was little demand for loans. According to this view, the large volume of excess reserves constituted an unneeded stock of funds during a period of heavy unemploy-

Figure 9.1
The Monetary Base and
M-1 (old definition),
1954–1979
(seasonally adjusted)

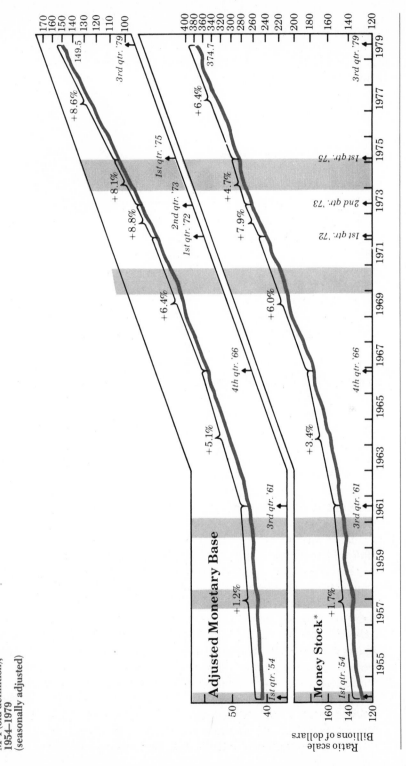

Ratio scale
Billions of dollars

*M-1 (old definition)
Percentages are annual rates of change for periods indicated.
Shaded areas represent periods of business recession.
Latest data plotted: 3rd quarter 1979.
Source: Federal Reserve Bank of St. Louis.

Table 9.3
Total, Required, and
Excess Reserves of
Member Banks,
1965–1979
(in millions)

December	Total Reserves	Required Reserves	Excess Reserves
1965	$22,719	$22,267	$452
1966	23,830	23,438	392
1967	25,260	24,915	345
1968	21,179	26,766	413
1969	28,031	27,774	257
1970	29,265	28,993	272
1971	31,329	31,164	165
1972	31,353	31,134	219
1973	35,068	34,806	262
1974	36,941	36,602	339
1975	34,991	34,727	264
1976	35,136	34,964	172
1977	36,471	36,297	174
1978	41,572	41,447	125
1979p	44,063	43,560	503

Source: Board of Governors of the Federal Reserve System, *Banking and Monetary Statistics, 1941–1970* (Washington, D.C., 1976) p. 535; Board of Governors of the Federal Reserve System, *Annual Statistical Digest, 1973–77* (Washington, D.C., 1978), pp. 18-21; and *Federal Reserve Bulletin* (December 1974), p. A6, (June 1979), p. A5, and (January 1980), p. A5.

ment. The volume of excess reserves was expected to fluctuate with changes in loan activity and gold inflows, changes over which the banks had little control. When the Federal Reserve System raised reserve requirements for member banks in 1936 and 1937, its intention was to mop up unneeded excess reserves.

An alternative point of view is held by critics of the policy adopted by the Federal Reserve in the period from 1933 to 1940, particularly Professor Friedman and Mrs. Schwartz.[4] They believe that banks held large amounts of excess reserves at this time because they wanted them. In their opinion, the structure of assets that banks hold depends on the available rates of return on various bank assets and on other conditions affecting bank operations. The critics believe that if reserves had increased above the quantity that banks desired, the total amount of bank loans and investments would have increased. It is possible that banks desired very large excess reserves in the 1930s because they had just been through an extremely severe financial crisis; from 1929 to 1933, one-third of the banks in the United States had ceased operations. Banks may have wanted to be very liquid in order to protect themselves from failure; the large amounts of excess reserves that the banks accumulated protected them against withdrawals of deposits or forced sales of securities at a loss. Another reason banks might have desired to hold large amounts of idle reserves in the 1930s is that interest rates were very low. Interest rates on three-month Treasury bills were one quarter of one percent in 1934 and reached extraordinarily low levels in 1940. Interest yields on corporate Aaa bonds fell from 4 percent in 1934 to 2.84 percent in 1940. The accumulation of excess reserves may have been related to the speculative motive for holding money; due to the rise in security prices, banks may have been unwilling to invest in them because they expected that eventually their prices would fall.

A comparison of the Canadian and United States experience during the 1930s supports the view that banks in the United States desired to hold large amounts of excess reserves because of the runs and bank failures during the Great Depression.[5] The excess reserve ratios of Canadian banks did not increase as they did in the United States, even though the decline in interest rates and the severity of the depression were similar in both countries. The major difference between the two countries appears to be that during the Great Depression the Canadian banking system experienced no bank failures and no significant runs on banks.

Moreover, banks in the United States responded to the increase in reserve requirements in 1936 and 1937 by trying to maintain their excess reserves and sold securities to do so—a further indication that banks *wanted* to hold their large excess reserves. When reserve requirements were raised at that time, yields on government securities rose, and the rate of growth in the money supply at first slowed down and then declined. In November 1941, when reserve requirements were again raised, there was no noticeable impact on the money market or the rate of growth of the money supply. By this time, the attitudes of bankers were probably changing because of the war.

Summary

There is a great deal of confusion about the deposit creation process. In an individual bank, reserves increase when deposits expand. But, in the banking system as a whole, the relationship goes in the opposite direction—deposits expand as a result of an increase in total reserves.

In the banking system, the total amount of deposits in banks will expand by several times the amount that the monetary base is increased.

Several types of leakages—increased demands for currency by the public, the desire of banks to hold larger amounts of excess reserves, and larger amounts of reserves needed for increased time deposits—reduce the amount of the expansion in demand deposits that occurs when the monetary base is increased.

Although in the 1930s banks accumulated large amounts of excess reserves, since World War II the portion of reserves held as excess reserves of banks has not expanded when the Federal Reserve has expanded the total supply of bank reserves.

Notes

1. An analysis of some of these estimates is in David I. Fand, "Some Implications of Money Supply Analysis," *American Economic Review, Papers and Proceedings* 57 (May 1967), p. 385. See also Robert E. Weintraub, *Introduction to Monetary Economics* (New York: Ronald Press, 1970), Chapter 10.

2. George Horwich, "Elements of Timing and Response in the Balance Sheet of Banking, 1953–1955," *Journal of Finance* 12 (May 1957), pp. 238–255.

3. Phillip Cagan, *Determinants and Effects of Changes in the Stock of Money, 1875–1960* (New York: Columbia University Press, 1965), pp. 366–367.

4. Milton Friedman and Anna J. Schwartz, *A Monetary History of the United States, 1867–1960* (Princeton: Princeton University Press, 1963), Chapter 9.

5. George R. Morrison, *Liquidity Preferences of Commercial Banks* (Chicago: University of Chicago Press, 1966), Chapter 5.

Questions

9.1. What is the money multiplier, and what are the principal factors determining the size of the money multiplier?

9.2. Give an example of a bank's balance sheet showing that the bank has reached the upper limit and cannot create additional deposits by making loans.

9.3. If an individual bank has excess reserves of $500, explain why it cannot normally expand its loans by more than $500.

9.4. If the reserves of the banking system are increased by $1,000, explain how the result may be an expansion in bank loans and investments and in bank deposits of several times the increase in bank reserves.

9.5. What are the two components of the monetary base, and why are they included in the monetary base?

9.6. Explain the meaning of the following equation and each of the symbols in it:

$$\Delta D = \frac{\Delta H}{[r+c+i+(r')\,(t)]} \, .$$

9.7. Explain how currency drains, the holding of larger excess reserves by member banks, and the growth of time deposits in member banks reduce the expansion ratio between the monetary base and the money supply.

9.8. Explain why an expansion of demand deposits tends to cause currency drains, increased holdings of excess reserves by member banks, and the growth of time deposits in member banks.

9.9. What are some of the factors affecting the overall ratios of reserves to demand deposits and reserves to time deposits in the banking system?

9.10. Discuss the reasons for the downward trend in the total amount of excess reserves in the banking system in recent decades.

9.11. Give the alternative explanations for the expansion of the total amount of excess reserves in the banking system in the 1930s.

9.12. Know the meaning and significance of the following terms and concepts: excess reserves, required reserves, creation of deposits, multiple expansion process, leakages, money multiplier.

10

The financial system includes, in addition to commercial banks, important types of institutions such as savings and loan associations, mutual savings banks, life insurance companies, credit unions, pension funds, investment companies, finance companies, and federal credit agencies. These institutions have grown rapidly since World War II.

FINANCIAL INTERMEDIARIES

Financial intermediaries other than commercial banks engage in many of the same activities and have many of the same characteristics as commercial banks. They are also middlemen between savers and borrowers.[1] They generally lend funds on different terms than they accept them. Mutual savings banks, for example, create their own liquid debt to obtain funds with which they buy the illiquid debt of others—e.g., these banks give people savings deposits for funds that the banks use to acquire long-term mortgages. Financial intermediaries attempt to offer rates of return and types of assets that are as attractive as possible. Although an individual might invest directly in mortgages or securities, investment through an intermediary has many advantages: highly qualified managers, opportunity for greater diversification, large-scale operation, and most of all, a basically different type of asset with greater liquidity.

Table 10.1 shows the rapid growth of the major financial institutions (including commercial banks) from 1945 to 1978, and their comparative size. In an interesting study published in 1968, it was estimated that financial institutions, as opposed to individuals, held approximately half of the total national wealth.[2] In 1800, financial institutions held less than 10 percent of the national wealth, and by 1900 still only 14 percent. The financial institutions that have grown most rapidly since 1945 are the savings and loan associations (S&Ls), credit unions, finance companies, investment companies, and pension funds. The growth of commercial banks, mutual savings banks, and life insurance companies has been much smaller. The assets of these latter institutions have expanded at about the same rate as the national income.

**Table 10.1
Total Assets of
Financial Intermediaries
at Year-End (in billions)**

Financial Intermediary	1945	1970	1978*
Commercial banks	$160.3	$ 576.2	$1,284.0
Savings and loan associations	8.7	176.2	523.6
Life insurance companies	44.8	207.3	389.0
Mutual savings banks	17.0	79.0	158.2
Finance companies	4.3	64.0	143.4
Investment companies	1.3	47.6	45.2
Credit unions	0.4	18.0	62.6
Private pension funds	2.8	110.6	205.1
State and local pension funds	2.6	60.3	146.5
Total	$242.2	$1,339.2	$2,957.6

*Preliminary
Source: '74 *Savings and Loan Fact Book* (Chicago: United States League of Savings Associations, 1974), p. 53; and '79 *Savings and Loan Fact Book* (Chicago: United States League of Savings Associations, 1979), p. 46.

The way commercial banks create deposits was described in Chapter 9. In this chapter, we are concerned with the way other financial intermediaries create time deposits. We are also interested in the characteristics of different types of nonbank intermediaries and the possible impact of their activities on the stability of the economy.

Thrift institutions

Mutual savings banks, S&Ls, and credit unions are the principal thrift institutions. They have many similarities and are subject to similar regulations.

In 1977, there were approximately 470 mutual savings banks and ten times that many S&Ls. Previously, there had been even more S&Ls, but since 1960 the number has declined 25 percent because of mergers.[3] Although there are almost 22,000 credit unions, most of them are small.[4]

Mutual savings banks

Mutual savings banks are chartered under state law and almost all of them are located in New England, New York, and New Jersey. Most were organized many years ago to encourage thrift and to provide a safe place for the savings of the general public. Their lending has been cautious, and losses from bad loans have been small. Before the Social Security System was established in 1937, they provided one of the major ways in which persons of all income levels could make provision for their old age.[5]

Mutual savings banks have no stockholders, but instead a large number of self-perpetuating incorporators—usually prominent persons in the community. The incorporators select the trustees, and the trustees select the officers. Profits are either paid out to the depositors in the form of interest or are retained. Although the Banking Act of 1933 granted mutual savings banks the right to apply for Federal Reserve membership, few have joined. About one-seventh of them belong to the Federal Home Loan Bank System, a federally sponsored agency which supplies housing credit. Two-thirds of them belong to the Federal Deposit Insurance Corporation.

Table 10.2 shows that mutual savings banks have invested about 60 percent of their assets in mortgages. They intermediate between persons who want savings deposits and persons who want to borrow to purchase homes, and they create savings deposits as rapidly as people wish them. They also invest in some corporate and U.S. government bonds, and state laws usually allow them to invest in a limited amount of corporation stock. Prior to 1951, mutual savings banks were tax-exempt and had no incentive to purchase tax-exempt state and local government securities. They still invest in very few municipals even though the Revenue Act of 1951 imposed the corporation income tax on the bulk of their retained earnings.

Table 10.2
Assets, Liabilities, and
Net Worth of Mutual
Savings Banks,
March 31, 1979

Assets	Amount (in billions)	Percent	Liabilities and Net Worth	Amount (in billions)	Percent
Cash assets	$ 3.4	2.1%	Deposits	$145.7	90.0%
Loans:			Other liabilities	5.0	3.1
Mortgages	96.1	59.4	General reserve		
Other loans	9.4	5.8	accounts	11.2	6.9
Securities:					
U.S. Govern-					
ment	4.8	3.0			
State and local	3.1	1.9			
Corporate and					
other	40.7	25.1			
Other assets	4.3	2.7			
Total	$161.9	100.0%		$161.9	100.0%

Details do not add to totals in all cases because of rounding.
Source: *Federal Reserve Bulletin*, June 1979, p. A29.

Until recently no set proportion of cash assets was prescribed for mutual savings banks. They have been able to operate successfully with very small ratios of cash assets to deposits because their deposits have been relatively stable compared to those of other types of banks. Table 10.2 shows that in 1979 their cash-to-deposit ratio was about 2.3 percent. During the Great Depression, they did not experience the runs that occurred on commercial banks, and there were almost no failures.[6]

Mutual savings banks usually cash savings deposits immediately upon presentation of a depositor's passbook, although legally they may require a notice of thirty to ninety days, depending on state laws. Some states have set limits on the size of an individual deposit, but in recent years most of these restrictions have been removed.

Savings and loan associations

Savings and loan associations operate under either state or federal charters. All federally chartered S&Ls must belong to the Federal Home Loan Bank System established by the federal government; state-chartered S&Ls may also belong if they qualify. S&Ls deal with the same types of savers and borrowers as mutual savings banks. Money deposited is legally considered as *shares* rather than as deposit liabilities, and the owner is not entitled to demand cash. In practice, any amount can usually be added to or withdrawn from a passbook account at any time. Although most S&Ls have been mutuals, a few have been owned by stockholders, and there has recently been some shift to the stock-ownership form; the stock of some S&Ls is traded on the stock exchanges.

Until the 1960s, the passbook account was the major savings instrument issued by thrift institutions. By 1977, however, S&Ls had more than 60 percent of their accounts (dollar value) in certificates and special accounts and less than 40 percent in passbook savings accounts.

Table 10.3 shows that S&Ls have a higher proportion of their assets in mortgages and own fewer corporate and other securities than mutual savings banks. In 1968, federal legislation empowered them to finance mobile homes; also, in some states consumer installment loans are becoming a more important part of their total assets. In 1979, the Federal Home Loan Bank Board authorized federally chartered savings and loan associations across the country to offer mortgages with graduated monthly payments, variable-rate mortgages, and reverse-annuity mortgages (a plan allowing older homeowners to borrow on the equity of their homes and repay it when they sell or take it out of their estate). In 1980, the Federal Home Loan Bank Board authorized mortgages that can be renegotiated every three to five years, and legislation allowed federally chartered thrift institutions to have 20 percent of their assets in consumer loans.

Table 10.3
Assets, Liabilities, and Net Worth of Savings and Loan Associations, March 31, 1979

Assets	Amount (billions)	Percent	Liabilities and Net Worth	Amount (billions)	Percent
Cash and invest-			Savings capital	$447.0	82.8%
ment securities	$ 50.1	9.3%	Borrowed money	41.6	7.7
Mortgages	441.4	81.8	Loans in process	10.3	1.9
Other	48.2	8.9	Other liabilities	10.9	2.0
			Net Worth	29.9	5.5
Total	$539.7	100.0%	Total	$539.7	100.0%

Details do not add to totals in all cases because of rounding.
Source: *Federal Reserve Bulletin*, June 1979, p. A29.

The cash plus securities held by S&Ls amount to approximately 9 percent of their savings accounts outstanding. Most of this consists of U.S. government securities, and only a small percentage is cash. The recent changes in reserves that thrift institutions are required to hold may alter the asset mix of S&Ls.

During the 1930s, many S&Ls failed; in recent years a few of them again have had financial difficulties.[7] They have their own Federal Savings and Loan Insurance Corporation, and shareholders are insured up to $100,000 per account.

Credit unions

Credit unions are typically sponsored by an occupational, labor union, religious, or other group. Ordinarily only members who have purchased at least one share in the credit union can borrow. Traditionally, their loans were for short periods, repaid in installments, and were for the purchase of consumer durables, home improvements, or personal needs. Credit unions can have low overhead costs if the sponsoring group provides them with rent-free space or if the managers receive no wages or fees—possible competitive advantages. They can sometimes charge rates of interest on consumer loans that are below those charged by commercial banks. Since they are organized mainly to serve members with a particular affiliation, the market they reach is somewhat limited and to some extent the profitability of their lending is reduced. Their risks are lessened, however, by their close contact with borrowers.

Recent changes in federal regulations have drastically changed the scope of credit union activities.[8] They can now make mortgage loans on residential property with maturities up to 30 years. They can offer both share-draft accounts which are the equivalent of interest-bearing demand deposits and variable-rate share certificates that are similar to bank CDs. Congress has created a three-member board to supervise insured credit unions. Federal regulations governing credit unions give them many advantages over other thrift institutions and commercial banks, and their growth has been more rapid than the growth of the other financial institutions. Because they are primarily cooperative, they enjoy nonprofit status and are not taxed as their competitors are. The dividend rate paid by credit unions is not limited the way interest rates on savings deposits at other financial institutions are. The average dividend rate of 6 percent paid by credit unions in 1978 was significantly above the 5 percent and 5 ¼ percent ceiling rates on savings deposits at commercial banks and S&Ls.

Regulation of thrift institutions ✓

Federal legislation has recently removed many of the restrictions on thrift institutions, and they now offer many of the services of commercial banks and compete with them for business.[9] Two major governmental studies—the Hunt Report of 1972 and the FINE study of 1975—proposed many of the changes in the regulation of financial institutions recently incorporated into law. Although historically thrift institutions have not offered checking accounts, in the 1970s they gradually moved into this type of banking. S&Ls and mutual savings banks were permitted to offer telephone transfers from savings to checking accounts, automatic transfer from savings (ATS) accounts, NOW accounts (checking accounts earning interest), and preauthorized bill-paying service from savings or checking accounts. Mutual savings banks began offering NOW accounts in 1972 in Massachusetts and New Hampshire; later in the 1970s NOW accounts were permitted in all depository institutions in New England, New York, and New Jersey, and starting in 1981 in all states. At credit unions there are similar accounts called "share draft accounts."

In 1980, major new federal legislation was passed providing for the phasing out of Regulation Q interest rate ceilings for banks and thrift institutions over a six-year period. For many years, the ceiling rates allowed on passbook deposits and different maturities of savings certificates in mutual savings banks and S&Ls were one-quarter of one percent above the rate allowed in commercial banks. This put the commercial banks at a competitive disadvantage, and they were critical of this. The reason given for the differential was that it assured an adequate flow of funds for housing and the mortgage market.

Legal restrictions on the types of assets that thrift institutions may hold have been liberalized in recent years. Instead of offering only mortgages, thrift institutions have gradually moved into consumer loans, and the Depository Institutions Deregulation and Monetary Control Act of 1980 permits them to make a limited amount of commercial loans. The objective of permitting thrift institutions to diversify their loans is to enable them to adjust to conditions of rapid inflation and rising interest rates—previously they held many long-term mortgages with interest rates lower than those they had to pay on their savings and time deposits.

Before the Depository Institutions Deregulation and Monetary Control Act of 1980, savings and loan associations that were members of the Federal Home Loan Bank System were subject to "liquidity" requirements set by the Federal Home Loan Bank Board at from 4 to 10 percent of the amount of their savings accounts. Since the passage of the important new legislation in 1980, the Board of Governors of the Federal Reserve System has set the reserve requirements on transaction accounts and nonpersonal time accounts of thrift institutions, and their reserve requirements will be increased over a period of eight years until they are the same as for commercial banks. The old liquidity requirements could be met not only by holding cash and bank deposits, but also by owning government and federal agency securities and other short-term investments earning interest. The liquidity requirement was set at 6 percent from 1950 to 1961, and 7 percent from 1961 to 1968. After 1968, the percentage required was changed more frequently and was generally raised when savings deposit growth was rapid and lowered when growth was slow.

Insurance companies

There are approximately 1,750 life insurance companies in the United States.[10] At the end of 1978, forty-nine of them had more than $1 billion each in assets, and the largest (Prudential) had assets of more than $50 billion.[11] Table 10.4 shows that in 1979, the total assets of all life insurance companies amounted to about $400 billion.

Life insurance companies appear to be very different from savings

Table 10.4
Life Insurance
Company Assets,
March 31, 1979

Assets:		Amount (in billions)	Percent
Government securities:		$ 20.1	5.0%
United States	$ 5.3		
State and local	6.1		
Foreign	8.7		
Business securities		204.0	51.1
Bonds	167.6		
Stocks	36.3		
Mortgages		108.2	27.1
Real estate		11.9	3.0
Policy loans		31.2	7.8
Other assets		24.1	6.0
Total assets		$399.5	100.0%

Source: *Federal Reserve Bulletin*, June 1979, p. A29.

institutions because of the insurance feature. In fact, they are quite similar. Their premiums are a source of funds like deposits. The owner of a regular life insurance policy is not only insured, but he also owns a potentially liquid asset with a fixed nominal value. Most life insurance policies, other than term policies, have a specified cash value and can be converted into cash immediately. In the early years of a policy, the cash value is not large because of the cost of the immediate insurance protection that is provided. As the policy becomes older, it becomes worth close to the amount paid in, plus interest.

Insurance companies are important intermediaries between persons who want life insurance on the one hand and corporate and individual borrowers on the other. In 1979, life insurance companies had about half of their assets in corporate securities (mostly bonds), as compared to the mutual savings banks with 25 percent, and the savings and loan associations with much less. Most states limit the amount of corporation *stock* that life insurance companies can hold—in some cases to 5 percent of assets. Because some insurance companies are very large, their investments in corporate securities are often negotiated directly rather than purchased in the regular securities markets. In 1979, insurance companies held over a quarter of their assets in mortgages. Their mortgages are not so closely confined to one locality as are those of most banks.

Life insurance companies hold a negligible amount of cash and in 1979 had less than 2 percent of their assets in U.S. government securities. Because their disbursements are to some extent predictable, and because premium payments and mortgage payments flow in continuously, they have less need for asset liquidity than most other financial institutions.

Pension funds

Many employers, units of government, and labor unions operate pension funds for their members. These pension funds collect savings regularly from wage earners or their employers, invest the funds received (mainly in corporation stock and in various types of bonds), and give the wage earners a contract guaranteeing a regular monthly income upon retirement. Most states and cities have pension funds for their employees similar to private pension funds. The Social Security Administration's Old-Age and Survivors Insurance System is by far the largest pension program in the United States, but it is usually not considered to be a financial intermediary. The reason is that the Social Security System is financed on a pay-as-you-go basis and does not intermediate between borrowers and lenders. It does, however, create an extremely important asset for Social Security beneficiaries.

Table 10.1 shows the growth in the assets of private and state and local government pension plans from 1945 to 1978. These plans have been popular because of the increasing emphasis on provision for retirement. There are tax incentives encouraging *employer* contributions to these plans. Employees are not taxed on that part of their current earnings that is contributed directly to a pension fund by their employer.

In the past, many pension systems earned attractive rates of return because of their investments in corporate stocks. By investing in equities, the managers of these funds hoped to be able to adjust benefits to keep up with rising prices. The slowdown in the rise in stock prices since the early 1960s has reduced the rate of return earned by many private pension systems.

Investment companies

Mutual funds (open-end investment companies) and other types of investment companies sell their own stock for the purpose of obtaining funds to buy the stocks or bonds of a diversified group of corporations, municipal bonds, or short-term money market investments. In 1978, there were more than 700 publicly offered mutual funds, and their assets were worth nearly $56 billion.[12] Investment companies offer to savers the economies of large-scale buying, diversification, and professional management. The value of a share is not fixed in nominal terms and can increase as prices rise. The amount of stock sold by an open-end mutual fund is unlimited, and more can be sold at any time. As more stock is sold, the mutual fund can expand its holdings of corporation stock or other securities. If the shareowner of an open-end mutual fund wishes to sell his shares, he sells them back to the company at a price that depends on the net asset value per share of the company's portfolio at that time.

There are also closed-end investment companies. The amount of their stock outstanding is restricted, usually to the amount originally sold, although it may later be expanded. The stock is not redeemable by the company, but is bought and sold on the national stock exchanges or over the counter. In 1977, there were fifty-seven closed-end companies, and they had total assets of more than $6 billion.

Investment companies expanded rapidly between World War II and the late 1960s. Since 1968, the conventional mutual funds—those invested in corporation stock—have had large redemptions relative to sales because of the leveling off of stock prices; in some recent years, redemptions have exceeded sales. However, a special type called money-market mutual funds—those invested in large-denomination Treasury bills, commercial paper, certificates of deposit, and other short-term instruments of one-year maturity or less—have expanded rapidly since 1974. A large portion of the investments of the money-market funds have been in CDs; even though banks lose deposits when individuals or business firms invest in money-market funds, the deposits come back to the banks through the sale of CDs to the money-market funds.

Investors in any type of mutual fund earn a return based on the fund's earnings, less a small management fee. The money-market mutual funds permit individuals with small amounts of savings to evade the ceilings set on savings deposits and the high minimum purchase requirements established by government regulations.[13] These funds typically require an initial minimum purchase amount of only $1,000 and allow subsequent purchase amounts as small as $50. In contrast, the minimum purchase requirement for certificates of deposit (which have no ceilings set on rates of interest) is $100,000; the minimum purchase requirement for Treasury bills (which also have no ceilings set) and money market certificates (whose rates of return are tied to the Treasury bill rate) is $10,000. Because money invested in these funds can be withdrawn quickly and without loss in value, shares in money-market mutual funds have become a close substitute for money, and starting in 1980 have been included in *M-2*.

Finance companies

Finance companies lend to individuals and to businesses.[14] They make relatively small installment loans to individuals in the form of consumer loans for the purchase of consumer durables (such as automobiles, mobile homes, and TV sets) and in the form of personal loans. In April 1979, they held more than $58 billion in consumer installment credit— 20 percent of this type of credit outstanding. Finance companies sometimes lend directly to consumers. They also finance consumer purchases through retailers, such as automobile dealers, by purchasing installment contracts that the retailers have negotiated with buyers. A sizable portion of their lending is to business firms for commercial vehicles and equipment; some lending to businesses is done on the basis of commercial accounts receivable.

Finance companies differ from many financial intermediaries in that they obtain most of their funds not from small savers but from other sources. They borrow from commercial banks or raise funds through the sale of their own stock or the sale of commercial paper in large denominations.

Federal financial intermediaries

A number of federally sponsored and regulated agencies sell their own securities to obtain funds to lend to cooperatives and savings institutions, and to purchase mortgages and certain types of loans originally arranged by other institutions. The objective of these agencies is not primarily to make a profit, but to promote or subsidize existing private institutions. Among them are the three principal agricultural credit agencies supervised by the Farm Credit Administration—the Banks for Cooperatives, Federal Intermediate Credit Banks, and Federal Land Banks—and the two agencies that supply housing credit—the Federal Home Loan Banks and Federal National Mortgage Association. The federal government originally held a portion of the stock of these agencies, but the goal was eventual ownership by their borrowers. Most have completed this shift and no longer receive subsidies, in the form of interest-free capital, from the government.[15] All the federal farm credit agencies have a competitive advantage in not being subject to state usury laws, and the Federal Land Banks pay no federal income taxes.

Table 10.5 shows that at the end of 1979 there was outstanding more than $137 billion in securities issued by the principal federal credit agencies. This amount has increased sharply in recent years. Government regulations permit the total amount of the securities issued by federal credit agencies to vary with the value of their capital stock and surplus. These securities are traded in the U.S. government securities market and are regarded as having little more risk than U.S. Treasury securities. Their issues, however, are not obligations of the federal government.

National banks may invest in these securities without regard to statutory limits generally applied to investment securities, and these issues may be used as security for their U.S. Treasury accounts. Banks have invested in large amounts of them because they yield slightly more than U.S. Treasury securities. The issues held by commercial banks are usually short-term or intermediate-term.

Table 10.5
Total Amount of Debt
Outstanding, Federally
Sponsored Credit
Agencies, 1960, 1970
and 1979 (in billions)

Agency	Amount outstanding at end of		
	1960	1970	1979 (Nov.)
Federal National Mortgage Assn.	$2.5	$15.2	$ 47.3
Federal Land Banks	2.2	6.4	16.0
Federal Home Loan Banks	1.3	10.2	33.3
Federal Intermediate Credit Banks	1.5	4.8	2.7
Banks for Cooperatives	0.4	1.8	0.6
Federal Home Loan Mortgage Corp.[a]			2.6
Student Loan Marketing Assn.[b]			1.4
Farm Credit Banks[c]			33.5
Total	$7.9	$38.4	$137.4

[a]Organized in 1970
[b]Organized in 1972
[c]In 1977, the Farm Credit Banks began replacing the financing activities of the Federal Land Banks, the Federal Intermediate Credit Banks, and the Banks for Cooperatives.
Source: *Federal Reserve Bulletin*, August 1961, p. 1004; May 1971, p. A39; and March 1980, p. A35.

The twelve *Banks for Cooperatives* and the Central Bank for Cooperatives were set up under the Farm Credit Act of 1933.[16] They lend to farmers' cooperatives on commodities to be marketed; on buildings and equipment needed in storing, handling, or marketing commodities; and for short-term operating needs. Since 1968 they have been owned by the private cooperative associations they serve.

The twelve *Federal Intermediate Credit Banks* were authorized by the Agricultural Credit Act of 1923. They are now owned by the Production Credit Associations. They lend to these associations and provide a secondary market for agricultural and livestock loans. Most of the securities issued by both the Banks for Cooperatives and the Federal Intermediate Credit Banks mature within one year.

The twelve *Federal Land Banks* were established by the Federal Farm Loan Act of 1916. They make first mortgages on farm properties through approximately 800 Federal Land Bank Associations. Their bonds outstanding have various maturities, with some as long as fifteen years.

The largest federal credit agency is the *Federal National Mortgage Association* (FNMA—popularly known as Fannie Mae). It was set up under the National Housing Act of 1938 to provide a secondary market for FHA-insured mortgages; it was rechartered under the Housing Act of 1954. Formerly it was supervised by the U.S. Department of Housing and Urban Development, part of its stock was held by the Treasury, and it was included in the federal budget. In 1968, it was reorganized and shifted to private ownership, but it is still subject to some government supervision.[17] Ten of its board members are elected by stockholders and five are appointed by the President of the United States; there is pressure for more government directors. Fannie Mae is able to borrow some of its funds at favorable rates from the government. The Treasury continues to have some control over the timing and amount of securities issued by FNMA. The agency sells its own securities to obtain funds to buy mortgages from private institutions—originally FHA-insured and VA-guaranteed mortgages, but since 1972 also conventional mortgages. Today conventional mortgages are about half of its annual purchases. The agency is expected to contribute to social goals by financing low and moderate income housing and giving special attention to cities. In 1978, the average FHA/VA mortgage it purchased was for $35,900, and its average conventional mortgage for $43,800. Formerly, FNMA assisted in financing special housing programs and in liquidating and managing mortgages obtained from other agencies. During the 1968 reorganization, a new agency, the Government National Mortgage Association, which is government-owned, took over some of its previous functions. Most of Fannie Mae's outstanding issues are short-term discount notes, similar to commercial paper, with a maturity range of 30 to 270 days, as arranged. Its debentures have various maturities from one to twenty-five years. The average maturity of outstanding debt issued by FNMA was under four years in 1978.

The twelve *Federal Home Loan Banks* were authorized by the Federal Home Loan Bank Act of 1932 and are supervised by the Federal Home Loan Bank Board.[18] They have been privately owned since 1951. Federally chartered S&Ls are required to hold stock in those banks; state-chartered S&Ls, mutual savings banks, and insurance companies are eligible to join the system. The Federal Home Loan Banks issue obligations (mainly short-term and intermediate-term) to obtain the funds they lend to members for unusual seasonal and cyclical needs. During a period of tight money in 1969, they substantially increased their lending to members for the purpose of preventing an excessive decline in the mortgage market.

In 1972, the federal government authorized the creation of the *Student Loan Marketing Association* (Sallie Mae). Its purpose is to stimulate the granting of guaranteed student loans by providing additional sources of funds for banks and educational institutions making these loans. Its stock is sold only to educational institutions and banks.

The *Export-Import Bank of the United States,* established in 1934, is an intermediary between savers and borrowers even though all its capital stock is owned by the U.S. Treasury and the bank is authorized to borrow up to $6 billion from the Treasury. Since 1975, it has also issued notes to the Federal Financing Bank (part of the Treasury) for medium-term needs. Many of its liabilities are held by commercial banks and the public. Its activities are intended to help the United States maintain a favorable foreign trade balance. It lends to foreign purchasers of American exports at favorable interest rates and with longer repayment periods than available commercially, it discounts loans made by commercial banks to U.S. exporters, and it guarantees and insures some foreign trade transactions.

The *Postal Savings System,* which was established by the federal government in 1911, discontinued operations in 1967. It was operated by the postal service and paid 2 percent interest. The assets of the postal savings system were invested primarily in U.S. government securities and in savings accounts in banks. The system appealed to European immigrants who were accustomed to government-run banks.

Rotating credit associations in foreign countries

Foreign countries have types of financial intermediaries not found in the United States. A curious type in the Far East is the small, rotating credit association, which is believed to have originated centuries ago in China.[19] A group of relatives or friends—often fewer than a dozen individuals—agrees to put in a stated amount each month and to assign, in advance, the monthly "kitty" to one of the members. The amounts involved are usually small, but they provide funds for weddings, home improvements, small business expenditures, clothing, or educational expenses. The arrangement ends as soon as each member has received the kitty once. Deposit schedules for these associations, specifying the amounts different members must pay, do not include any explicit mention of interest. The first member to receive the kitty, in effect, receives a loan, and the payments that he makes are the installment payments on the loan. The last member to receive the kitty is a depositor who receives back more than the total amount he deposited. Those receiving the kitty in between the first and the last have a combination of an installment loan and an interest-earning series of deposits.

In the early 1960s, rotating credit associations in South Korea allowed savers to realize more than the legal rate of interest at banks, which was below the rate of inflation and yielded a negative real rate of return. In a survey there at that time, approximately half the families were lending and borrowing through these associations.

Creation of time deposits by thrift institutions

Mutual savings banks, S&Ls, and credit unions *create* time deposits (or shares as they are called by S&Ls and credit unions) which are very similar to time deposits in commercial banks. The creation of time deposits by thrift institutions is called *intermediation.* A reduction in the volume of their time deposits is called *disintermediation.* The growth of time deposits at thrift institutions is significantly affected by the relationship between market interest rates on Treasury bills, commercial paper, and certificates of deposit and the ceiling rates on time deposits at thrift institutions set by government regulations. When the ceiling rates on time deposits are above money-market rates, the volume of time deposits in thrift institutions tends to rise rapidly. Under opposite conditions, the rise in the volume of their deposits slows down and there may be disintermediation.

The way in which intermediation occurs in mutual savings banks is illustrated in Figure 10.1. Exactly the same process occurs in savings and loan associations and credit unions. If a person shifts $1,000 from his checking account in a commercial bank to a savings deposit in a mutual savings bank, the initial impact on the balance sheets of the savings bank, the commercial bank, and the public is as shown in Figure 10.1(a). The person's deposit in the savings bank would be increased by $1,000. The savings bank would then deposit the check received in its account in a commercial bank, where savings banks hold their reserves. From the point of view of the commercial bank, the decline in the demand deposits of the public has been offset by an increase in the demand deposits of savings banks. The public's balance sheet shows fewer demand deposits and more savings deposits.

Although the savings bank will increase its reserves a small amount because of its larger deposits, the bulk of the original increase in its reserve deposit at the commercial bank will be lent. Assuming that the savings bank has a reserve ratio of 2 percent, it will keep $20 of the new deposit and expand its loans and investments by $980. When the savings bank makes a loan (usually a mortgage) of $980, the mortgages of the savings bank will increase by $980, and its balance at the commercial bank will decrease by the same amount. In return for the promissory note received from the borrower, the savings bank must give to the borrower a check for $980 written on its demand deposit at the commercial bank. When the person receiving the $980 check from the borrower deposits it in a commercial bank, his demand deposit will be increased by $980 and the savings bank demand deposit will be reduced by $980. The final result is an increase in savings bank demand deposits in commercial banks of only $20 and a decrease in public demand deposits of only $20, as shown in the commercial bank's balance sheet in Figure 10.1(b).

When a savings bank creates savings deposits for a customer, there is a difference between what the customer intended and the actual effects. The customer intended to reduce his demand deposits by an amount equal to the increase in his savings deposits. In fact, the public's demand deposits declined by only $20, its savings deposits increased by the amount intended, and its mortgage indebtedness increased by $980.

The expansion ratio for savings banks could theoretically be very large with a reserve requirement of only 2 percent, but it is not—because the person who receives the funds from the borrower from the savings bank will probably deposit them in a commercial bank rather than redeposit them in a savings bank. As a result, the mutual savings banks retain only a very small amount of the initial increase in their

Figure 10.1
Shifting Deposits from a
Commercial Bank to a
Savings Bank

(a) Initial Impact

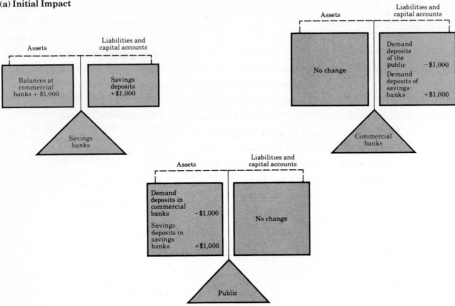

(b) Final Result

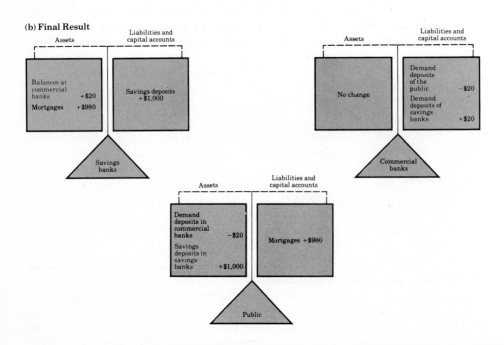

reserves. The amount that they lose is equal to the amount that they lend. If the reserve ratio is 2 percent, the amount of reserves lost will be 98 percent of the original increase in reserves. The reserves lost when the savings bank makes a loan is a type of leakage. In the savings banking system, the leakage is so large that there is little, if any, multiple expansion of deposits of the type that occurs in the commercial banking system.

Economic significance of financial intermediaries

The Federal Reserve System has not had the power to control other financial institutions in the same way that it controls member banks, even though it may influence them indirectly by affecting interest rates and the expansion of commercial bank deposits. This is considered significant because deposits in thrift institutions could rise rapidly at the same time that the Federal Reserve was cutting back on the growth of deposits in commercial banks. This could cause Federal Reserve attempts to restrain the economy during inflation to be unsuccessful.[20] The Federal Reserve might attempt to alter its own monetary policy in view of the variations in growth of the thrift institutions, but this would not be easy to do effectively.

Although the Depository Institutions Deregulation and Monetary Control Act of 1980 gives the Federal Reserve System control over the reserve requirements on transactions accounts and nonpersonal time accounts of thrift institutions and nonmember banks, the Federal Reserve System still cannot directly control the expansion of personal time accounts in thrift institutions. This is because thrift institutions will probably hold reserves for personal time accounts, if any are required, in balances in large commercial banks rather than in balances at the Federal Reserve banks. As in the past, the volume of personal time deposits created at thrift institutions will depend primarily on the extent to which the public shifts from demand deposits at member banks to personal time deposits at thrift institutions as illustrated in Figure 10.1.

In recent years, another problem has been the possibility of sharp contractions in the growth of time deposits at thrift institutions. In 1966, 1969, 1974, and 1979, interest rates on Treasury bills, commercial paper, and Eurodollar deposits in foreign banks rose above the ceiling rates allowed on time deposits. This could cause large withdrawals of deposits from thrift institutions and a sharp contraction in mortgage funds and a depressed housing industry. Although in 1966 and 1969, large withdrawals generally did not occur, the growth in savings deposits dropped sharply for a short time and caused a credit crunch. In 1968–1969, both the Federal Home Loan Banking System and the Federal National Mortgage Association took expansionary measures to counteract the effect of disintermediation. The new money market certificates which were authorized in 1978 made it possible for thrift institutions to combat disintermediation by allowing them to compete with rates of interest prevailing in the money market.

The accelerated inflation and rising market interest rates that started in 1965 have caused serious difficulties for some thrift institutions. Most of the mortgages in their portfolios were issued for long-term at relatively low interest rates. As a consequence, when higher rates of inflation caused market interest rates to rise, many thrift institutions were hard pressed to pay high enough rates on their deposits to compete with other forms of saving. Because these institutions typically hold only small amounts of liquid assets, many of them were not well prepared for a loss of deposits.

In 1966, as a precautionary move the Board of Governors of the Federal Reserve System granted temporary authority to the Federal Reserve banks to lend money to *nonmember* depository intermediaries.[21] In 1980, the Depository Institutions Deregulation and Monetary Control Act permanently extended borrowing privileges to nonmember banks and thrift institutions. With such borrowing facilities available, thrift institutions in difficulty would be able to replace a loss of deposits with funds from the Federal Reserve banks and to avoid the necessity of liquidating assets under unfavorable conditions. Without such aid, these institutions might have to liquidate some of their mortgages and investments when their deposits declined. This could result in serious difficulties because, at the time when their deposits were being withdrawn because of higher interest rates on other types of investments, the market prices of their mortgages and securities would probably also be low. If the coupon rate of interest on their securities and the rates on their mortgages were below current market rates, these assets could not be sold except at a discount. If they could not avoid taking such losses, the value of their capital accounts would decline, and these institutions would be insolvent as soon as their deposits exceeded the value of their remaining assets.

Summary

The principal financial intermediaries are mutual savings banks, savings and loan associations, insurance companies, credit unions, pension funds, and investment companies. The assets of these financial intermediaries have increased rapidly since World War II.

Time deposits in mutual savings banks and S&Ls are very similar to such deposits in commercial banks except that federal government regulations have permitted mutual savings banks and S&Ls to pay higher rates of interest than commercial banks.

Savings deposits are created in thrift institutions when individuals deposit money in them. A multiple expansion of deposits does not occur in the thrift institutions as it does when commercial banks acquire additional reserves.

The Federal Reserve System cannot directly control the expansion of thrift institutions as it can the expansion of commercial banks. Sharp variations in total time deposits in thrift institutions have a destabilizing effect on the economy by causing fluctuations in the supply of mortgage credit. Rising rates of inflation result in problems for thrift institutions because of their large holdings of long-term mortgages earning the lower interest rates that prevailed before the rate of inflation accelerated.

Notes

1. Edward S. Shaw, "Financial Intermediaries," in *International Encyclopedia of the Social Sciences*, Vol. 5 (New York: Macmillan, 1968), pp. 432–438.

2. Raymond W. Goldsmith, *Financial Institutions* (New York: Random House, 1968), pp. 4–10, 43.

3. United States League of Savings Associations, '78 *Savings and Loan Fact Book* (Chicago, 1978), p. 48.

4. Credit Union National Association, *1979 Yearbook, All Kinds of People* (Madison, Wisconsin, 1979).

5. For an analysis of the modern role of mutual savings banks, see George J. Benston, "Savings Banking and the Public Interest," *Journal of Money, Credit and Banking* 4 (February 1972), pp. 133–226.

6. Alan Teck, *Mutual Savings Banks and Savings and Loan Associations: Aspects of Growth* (New York: Columbia University Press, 1968), pp. 118–119.

7. Irwin Friend, *Study of the Savings and Loan Industry* (Washington, D.C.: Superintendent of Documents and Federal Home Loan Bank Board, 1970).

8. Joan Walsh, "Financial Co-ops," *Federal Reserve Board of San Francisco Weekly Letter* (June 16, 1978).

9. Jean M. Lovati, "The Growing Similarity Among Financial Institutions," Federal Reserve Bank of St. Louis, *Review* (October 1977), pp. 2–11.

10. Institute of Life Insurance, *Life Insurance Fact Book, 1978* (New York, 1978), p. 89.

11. "The Fifty Largest Life Insurance Companies," *Fortune* (July 16, 1979), pp. 160–161.

12. Wiesenberger Investment Companies Service, *Investment Companies, 1978* (New York: Wiesenberger Financial Services, 1978), p. 6.

13. Jack Beebe, "Pseudo Intermediaries," *Federal Reserve Bank of San Francisco Weekly Letter,* March 10, 1978.

14. For information on finance companies, see Evelyn M. Hurley, "Survey of Finance Companies, 1975," *Federal Reserve Bulletin,* March 1976, pp. 197–207.

15. D. Gale Johnson, "Agricultural Credit, Capital, and Credit Policy in the United States," in Commission on Money and Credit, *Federal Credit Programs* (Englewood Cliffs, N.J.: Prentice-Hall, 1963), pp. 355–423.

16. D. Gale Johnson, "The Credit Programs Supervised by the Farm Credit Administration," in Commission on Money and Credit, *Federal Credit Agencies* (Englewood Cliffs, N.J.: Prentice Hall, 1963), pp. 259–318.

17. John P. Wiedemer, *Real Estate Finance,* 2nd ed. (Reston, Va.: Reston Publishing Co., 1977), pp. 112–125.

18. Ernest Bloch, "The Federal Home Loan Bank System," in *Federal Credit Agencies,* pp. 159–257.

19. Colin D. Campbell and Chang Shick Ahn, "Kyes and Mujins— Financial Intermediaries in South Korea," *Economic Development and Cultural Change* 11 (October 1962), pp. 55–68; Clifford Geertz, "The Rotating Credit Association: A 'Middle Rung' in Development," *Economic Development and Cultural Change* 10 (April 1962), pp. 241–263.

20. See Jack M. Guttentag and Robert Lindsay, "The Uniqueness of Commercial Banks," *Journal of Political Economy* 76 (September-October 1968), pp. 992–993; Joseph Aschheim, "Commercial Bank Uniqueness," *Journal of Political Economy* 78 (March-April 1970), pp. 353–355; John M. Culbertson, *Macroeconomic Theory and Stabilization Policy* (New York: McGraw-Hill, 1968), pp. 196–199 and 350–365; and David E. W. Laidler, "The Definition of Money," *Journal of Money, Credit and Banking* 1 (August 1969), pp. 508–525.

21. Board of Governors of the Federal Reserve System, *Annual Report, 1966* (Washington, D.C., 1967), p. 10.

Questions

10.1. Explain why a mutual savings bank is a financial intermediary.

10.2. What are the differences between mutual savings banks and savings and loan associations?

10.3. Compare the kinds of assets in which mutual savings banks, savings and loan associations, and life insurance companies typically invest.

10.4. Describe the following types of financial institutions: credit unions, pension funds, investment companies, life insurance companies, and sales finance companies.

10.5. Describe the following federal credit agencies: Banks for Cooperatives, Federal Home Loan Banks, Federal Intermediate Credit Banks, Federal Land Banks, and the Federal National Mortgage Association.

10.6. Explain the way in which mutual savings banks create time deposits.

10.7. Even though people may decide to hold smaller amounts of demand deposits and larger amounts in deposits in mutual savings banks or savings and loan associations, actually the amount of demand deposits they hold will remain approximately the same while their deposits in mutual savings banks and savings and loan associations will increase as intended. Explain.

10.8. What is meant by disintermediation? What are some of the causes of disintermediation and some of the resulting problems?

10.9. Does the Federal Reserve System need the power to control the growth of thrift institutions?

10.10. Explain why rising interest rates may adversely affect thrift institutions.

10.11. Know the meaning and significance of the following terms and concepts: financial intermediary, mutual savings bank, savings and loan association, mutual fund, federal credit agency, disintermediation.

11

The Federal Reserve System is equivalent to the central banks in other countries, even though its organization is more complicated. The central policy-making unit of the Federal Reserve System is its Board of Governors in Washington, D.C. The operating units are the twelve Federal Reserve banks located in major cities throughout the United States.

STRUCTURE OF THE FEDERAL RESERVE SYSTEM

The Federal Reserve System was established later than most of the other major central banking systems in the world. The Bank of England was founded in 1694, the Bank of France in 1800, and the Bank of Japan in 1882. The Federal Reserve Act establishing the Federal Reserve System was passed by Congress in 1913. The System includes, in addition to the Board of Governors and the twelve Federal Reserve banks, those commercial banks (approximately 5,500 of them) that are member banks.

The Federal Reserve System is responsible for the formulation and administration of monetary policy and regulates the growth of the deposits and credit at the member banks. Chapters 11 to 14 describe the organization of the System and its instruments of control and monetary targets.

Antecedents of the Federal Reserve System

During the early history of the United States, the First Bank of the United States, which existed from 1791 to 1811, and the Second Bank of the United States, dating from 1816 to 1836, performed some central banking functions. In each case, the bank's twenty-year charter was not renewed because of political opposition. These two banks were owned partially by the federal government and partially by private individuals. Both had branches in important cities and engaged in commercial banking—they accepted deposits and made loans to individuals and business firms. Both handled federal government deposits (although government funds were withdrawn from the Second Bank of the United States by President Andrew Jackson three years before its charter ended). Because of their large size, these banks were able to regulate the lending of the numerous state banks and the quantity of notes that they issued. This is similar to the control that the Federal Reserve System has over the expansion of bank credit and deposits by the member banks. If either the First or the Second Bank of the United States wished to restrain the state banks, it could reduce the specie that the state banks held as reserves by presenting some of their outstanding notes to them for redemption. To create easy monetary conditions, the Banks of the United States would either hold the state bank notes that they had or hand them out to their own customers. The reserves of the state banks could also be reduced if the Banks of the United States cut down their lending activities. Since a loan was usually paid off with checks written on a state bank, the Bank of the United States would acquire specie reserves from the state bank. If the Banks of the United States expanded their loans, the reserves of the state banks were usually increased.

At the time of the Civil War, the idea of a central bank was still politically unpopular. However, there was enough support for an improved system of currency to allow passage of the Currency Act of 1863 and the National Bank Act of 1864. These acts provided for the creation of a system of national banks and established a relationship between the federal government and the banks that had not existed since the charter of the Second Bank of the United States expired in 1836. The acts provided for a comptroller of the currency who was authorized to grant charters to national banks and to regulate them. They also established uniform printing of national bank notes, set capital requirements for the national banks, limited the amount of the national banks' notes, and required higher reserve ratios for national banks in certain large cities (designated as "redemption cities") than for other banks.[1]

In the years just prior to the establishment of the Federal Reserve System, the Treasury intervened regularly in the money market and in effect was engaging in central banking activities. Secretary of the Treasury Leslie M. Shaw, who was appointed in 1902, was an explicit advocate of using Treasury powers to control the money market. In tight periods, when bank reserves were low relative to their deposits, the Treasury would ease conditions by increasing government deposits in the banks, purchasing government bonds, or inducing the national banks to expand the quantity of national bank notes in circulation. Secretary Shaw intervened in the market both to moderate contractions and to even out seasonal fluctuations. Although there was a small recession in 1902, he claimed that his actions prevented a panic.

Panic of 1907

The steps that eventually led to the creation of the Federal Reserve System were the result of the panic of 1907—which was associated with a short but severe recession. Several large financial institutions in New York came close to failing. There were runs on banks, and smaller banks in rural areas scrambled to get more currency from their correspondent banks in large cities.[2] During the panic, savings banks typically required notice of withdrawal. Also the New York banks, and eventually banks throughout the country, restricted the convertibility of deposits into currency. For several months, currency was traded at a premium and merchants and employers were seriously inconvenienced.

As a result of the panic, in 1908 Congress passed the Aldrich-Vreeland Act which provided for the appointment of a National Monetary Commission to study possible long-run reforms leading toward the establishment of a central bank. The commission, consisting of nine senators and nine representatives, held hearings and arranged for a large number of special studies of domestic and foreign banking. So extensive were these studies that their publication required twenty-three volumes.

Founding of the Federal Reserve System

In 1913, President Woodrow Wilson, in spite of the fact that there still was considerable opposition to a central bank, pressed for legislation

that resulted in the establishment of the Federal Reserve System. The
way the System was initially supposed to control banking activities is
different from the manner in which it operates today. As originally
conceived, it was to replace *laissez faire* with a cooperative system in
which the federal government, bankers, businessmen, and consumers
would work together. At its inception, the Federal Reserve System was
supposed to aid and supervise banks so that periodic financial panics,
such as the one that occurred in 1907, could be avoided. It was not
conceived of as an institution which controlled the quantity of bank
credit, the money supply, and interest rates. The United States was then
on the gold standard, and it was assumed that the quantity of gold in
the banking system would continue to regulate the quantity of money
and bank credit to a large extent. What was desired was a central bank
that could provide an elastic supply of currency and discounting facilities to commercial banks. The conception of the federal government
managing the economy developed later.[3]

The Federal Reserve System was also expected to provide banking
services for the United States Treasury. The Treasury keeps its active
deposits in the Federal Reserve banks; it also needs convenient loca-
tions where federal securities can be issued and redeemed, foreign
exchange handled, and U.S. currency stored.

The original Federal Reserve Act lacked a detailed blueprint of the
relationship between the twelve Federal Reserve banks and the Federal Reserve Board in Washington (renamed the Board of Governors of
the Federal Reserve System by the Banking Act of 1935). From 1914
to 1922, officials of the twelve Reserve banks held meetings at which
they determined policy for the whole System, and they tended to make
the decisions. Several factors helped the Reserve banks hold a dominant
role in the System in those early years—popular opposition to central
control, the isolation of Washington, D.C., from important financial
markets, and the leadership of Benjamin Strong, executive officer of the
New York Federal Reserve Bank, a former president of the Bankers
Trust Company of New York City, and a prominent member of the
financial community.[4] There was continuous conflict between the Federal Reserve Board in Washington and the twelve Federal Reserve
banks until, in the 1930s, the Board achieved eventual control over most
decisions.

Independence of the Federal Reserve System

The Federal Reserve System is an *independent agency* of the federal
government and is legally an agent of Congress. As such, the Federal
Reserve System is not under the direction of the executive branch of
the federal government.[5] Members of Congress have usually attempted
to guard their authority over the Federal Reserve System against en-

croachment by the executive branch and have reminded newly appointed officials of the System that they are responsible to Congress rather than to the executive. In spite of this, because of its close working relationship with the Treasury Department, one might expect a line of command from the Secretary of the Treasury to the Board of Governors. In fact, there is no such connection, and it is still widely considered that executive interference in the operations of the Federal Reserve System is improper. On several occasions, the late Congressman Wright Patman, long a member of the Banking and Currency Committee of the House of Representatives and its chairman for a decade, initiated congressional hearings into this matter.

As an agent of Congress, the Federal Reserve System submits its annual report to that body and regularly publishes several other reports requested by them. Throughout most of the history of the Federal Reserve System, the relationship between Congress and the System was actually no more than perfunctory. This weak relationship survived partly because the Federal Reserve System had an independent budget. Federal Reserve banks are supported primarily by interest on their investments in U.S. government securities, and no budgetary appropriations from Congress are necessary for their operation. The Board is supported in turn by the Federal Reserve banks. In 1975, an important new policy was initiated: The Chairman of the Board of Governors began consulting with committees of the Congress on a regular basis to discuss the Board's objectives and plans for their monetary targets.[6] This has resulted in a much closer relationship between Congress and the Federal Reserve System than formerly existed. The Federal Reserve Reform Act of 1977 and the Humphrey-Hawkins Act of 1978 require semiannual reporting by the Federal Reserve to the Congress on their planned ranges for monetary and credit aggregates.

One of the reasons given for limiting the influence of the Treasury over the Federal Reserve System is that this prevents political manipulation of the monetary system. Actually, for two decades, the Secretary of the Treasury and the comptroller of the currency were *ex officio* members of the Board of Governors, but the Banking Act of 1935 ended this arrangement.

Despite the independence of the Federal Reserve System, its monetary policy ought not to conflict with other federal governmental policies aimed at preventing inflation and promoting full employment. In fact, there are regular weekly meetings of the chairman of the Board of Governors of the Federal Reserve System, the Secretary of the Treasury, and the chairman of the Council of Economic Advisers at which these officials discuss overall economic conditions and the economic policies of the federal government.

Central banks in other countries have the same problem of relating their policies to the overall economic policies of their governments. The trend for the Federal Reserve System to coordinate its policies with those of other departments of the federal government, rather than to operate independently, is typical of the way other central banks also have developed.

Although some persons regard the independence of the Federal Reserve System highly, others are critical whenever there is a discrepancy between the economic goals of the executive and the Federal Reserve System's policies. In December 1965, for example, the Board of Governors approved a rise in the discount rate despite the objections of President Johnson and his economic advisers. The Joint Economic Committee of Congress immediately arranged for hearings at which Federal Reserve officials and several economists were asked to appear. Professor J. Kenneth Galbraith told the committee, "Men who prefer shadow to substance still speak of the independence of the Federal Reserve System. It hasn't existed for years." Professor Seymour Harris, a prominent economist at that time, stated, "I have never had much sympathy with the theory of independence. . . . The government certainly should not move in one direction and the monetary authority in another."[7]

The significance of the Federal Reserve System's legal independence from the executive branch of the government ought not to be exaggerated.[8] Independent agencies of the federal government appear to behave in much the same way as other departments and their branches. It is usually not in the interests of the officials involved, or of their organizations, to be in open conflict with top officials in the executive branch of the government, and they act accordingly. A Bank of England official, when questioned about the Bank of England's autonomy from the British Treasury, is said to have replied, "We value our independence highly and would not think of doing anything to show it."

Organizational structure of the Federal Reserve System

The Federal Reserve System consists of a Board of Governors, twelve Federal Reserve banks, and the member banks. In addition, there are two committees established by Congress which form part of the Federal Reserve System: the Federal Open Market Committee and the Federal Advisory Council.

Board of Governors

The Board of Governors consists of seven members appointed by the President of the United States with the approval of the Senate. To ensure that all areas of the country are represented, no two governors can come from the same Federal Reserve district. Each appointee may serve no more than one full fourteen-year term, but in addition may serve the remaining part of an unexpired term. One term expires every two years. The seven governors are the only officials in the Federal Reserve System appointed by the President. The President's right to appoint governors does not give him much influence over the Board, however. Each governor is appointed for a long term and, barring death or resignation, the maximum possible number of governors appointed by a President during a four-year term is two.

The Board of Governors has a chairman and a vice-chairman. Appointments to these positions are made by the President of the United States, and each holds office for a period of four years. The chairmanship of the Board of Governors of the Federal Reserve System is sometimes referred to in the press as the "nation's second most powerful office." From 1951 to 1970, the chairman of the Board was William McChesney Martin—on the Board for part of one unexpired term and one full fourteen-year term and appointed chairman by Presidents Truman, Eisenhower, Kennedy, and Johnson. In January 1970, President Nixon appointed Arthur F. Burns to the Board of Governors as its chairman; Mr. Burns served until replaced by G. William Miller, who was appointed by President Carter. In 1979, Mr. Miller was shifted to the Cabinet as Secretary of the Treasury and replaced by Paul A. Volcker, who had been President of the Federal Reserve Bank of New York.

The governing members of most independent government agencies, such as the Interstate Commerce Commission and the Federal Trade Commission, must include members of both political parties. There is no requirement of this type for governors of the Federal Reserve System. During 1977, the first year of the Carter Administration, all seven of the governors had been appointed by either President Nixon or President Ford. However, by 1979 President Carter had been able to appoint four of the seven governors. Political bias on the part of the Board of Governors could be important because tight monetary policies are politically less popular than easy monetary policies. Board members might be reluctant to pursue a policy of restraint if it would bring their party into disfavor.

The offices of the Board of Governors are located in Washington, D.C., and the Board has a large staff of economists, lawyers, examiners, and administrators. It also includes departments engaged in research on domestic and international financial trends which supply information needed by the Board to assess prevailing economic and credit conditions. These departments publish the results of their research and up-to-date statistics on money and credit in the monthly *Federal Reserve Bulletin.*

Only one of the three principal instruments used to carry out monetary policy—*changes in legal reserve requirements* of member banks—is the sole responsibility of the Board of Governors. Responsibility for the other two is shared. Policies concerning *open-market operations*—the most important of the three—are determined by the Federal Open Market Committee, on which the seven governors of the Federal Reserve System and the presidents of five Federal Reserve banks sit. *Changes in the discount rate* are initiated by the individual Federal Reserve banks but must be approved by the Board. Two other less important instruments of control are the responsibility of the Board rather than the Federal Reserve banks: control over interest rates on time deposits in member banks, and control over margin requirements on loans to purchase securities made by banks, brokers, dealers, and others. In recent years, the regulatory activities of the Board of Governors have been expanded as a result of new consumerist credit laws such as the Truth-in-Lending and the Fair Credit Billing Acts.

Some of the regulatory activities of the Board are carried on jointly with other federal agencies. Since September 1966, the Board of Governors has consulted with the Federal Deposit Insurance Corporation and the Board of the Federal Home Loan Banks in setting ceiling interest rates on time deposits. Under the Securities and Exchange Act of 1934, margin requirements are jointly regulated by the Securities and Exchange Commission and the Board of Governors.

Federal Reserve banks

The Federal Reserve Act authorized the division of the United States into twelve districts, each with a Federal Reserve bank. The boundaries of those districts and the location of the twelve Federal Reserve banks and their branches are shown in Figure 11.1.

The Federal Reserve banks are the operating units of the system. Each of the twelve banks performs routine services for its region. Each issues and supplies Federal Reserve notes, clears checks on commercial banks, processes Treasury checks, stores coins, handles the sale of government securities, examines the state-chartered member banks in its area, and administers regulations governing commercial banks.

An individual Federal Reserve bank is a federally chartered corporation with stockholders, directors, and a president. The stockholders of a Federal Reserve bank are the member banks in its district, and they select six of its nine directors. At present, a member bank purchases an amount of stock in its district Federal Reserve bank equal to 3 percent of its own capital stock and surplus, although legally it may be asked to purchase twice this amount. As the common stock and surplus of a commercial bank grow, it must purchase more Federal Reserve bank stock to keep the level at 3 percent. Dividends paid on the stock are limited to 6 percent. Earnings above this amount are returned to the Treasury.

There are three types of directors of Federal Reserve banks—Class

**Figure 11.1
The Federal Reserve
System: Boundaries of
Federal Reserve
Districts and Their
Branch Territories**

Source: Board of Governors of the Federal Reserve System, *The Federal Reserve System, Purposes and Functions* (Washington,
D.C., 1974) p. 16.

A, Class B, and Class C—and there are three of each type. Terms of all directors are for three years. One director of each type is elected (or appointed) each year.

Class A directors are elected by the member banks. They may be and usually are bankers, and it was the intention of the founders of the Federal Reserve System that they should represent the lenders of money. The member banks are divided into small, medium, and large banks, and each group selects one Class A director.

Class B directors are also elected by the member banks. They may not be bankers. They are usually prominent persons in business, commerce, or agriculture and are expected to represent the borrowers of money. The three groups of member banks, classified according to size, each select one Class B director.

The three Class C directors are appointed by the Board of Governors. It was the intention of the founders of the Federal Reserve System that the Class C directors should represent the public, and they cannot be officers of any bank. The Board of Governors also selects the chairman and the deputy chairman of the board of directors of each Federal Reserve bank from the Class C directors. Although originally the chairman was the chief executive officer of the bank, this was changed by the Banking Act of 1935. The directors of each Federal Reserve bank select the managing officials of the bank—the president, vice-president, and others. Officers are appointed for five years and must be approved by the Board of Governors.

Although some members of the board of directors of each Federal Reserve bank are bankers, the majority are not. The late Congressman Wright Patman felt that banking interests exerted too much influence over the operations of the Federal Reserve System. He was critical of the fact that banking interests were represented on the boards of directors of the Federal Reserve banks and on the Federal Advisory Council. Federal Reserve policy frequently reflects the influence of banking interests. As with most of the regulatory agencies of the federal government, a certain amount of regulation has been combined with serving the interests of those regulated.

The Federal Reserve banks are semipublic corporations. Although they are privately owned, the profits earned by the owners are limited, and the owners share control of the selection of the officials of the bank with the Board of Governors. The purpose of the Federal Reserve banks is not to maximize profit, but to implement monetary policy and supervise the member banks. Each Federal Reserve bank must submit its budget to the Board of Governors for approval.

The twelve Federal Reserve banks submit a weekly report of their financial accounts to the Board of Governors, and this information is summarized and published in newspapers at the end of each week. The Federal Reserve banks and their branches are scrutinized at least once a year by examiners from the Board of Governors. The Interdistrict Settlement Fund in Washington, D.C., maintained by the Federal Reserve banks, settles claims between these banks resulting from shifts of member bank deposits from one Federal Reserve district to another.

Most Federal Reserve banks have their own monthly bulletin containing articles on current economic problems, and some of these bulletins circulate widely. Each bank, to some extent, guards its individuality and independence. Having twelve separate Federal Reserve banks contrasts with the concentration of central banking in most other countries. Although the Federal Reserve System has been criticized by some persons as an inefficient administrative organization with excessive duplication, others believe that the present organization has the advantage of providing top government officials with greater diversity in the assessment of economic conditions and in policy proposals.

Federal Reserve banks vary in size. Ten of them have branches, which are located in twenty-four important cities. Each branch is controlled by a small board, the majority of the members of which are chosen by the district Federal Reserve bank and the rest by the Board of Governors. Branches are closely regulated by the district bank.

Member banks

All national banks are required by law to be members of the Federal Reserve System, and some state banks have voluntarily applied for admission and been accepted. Prior to 1980, banks belonging to the System had certain privileges that were not available to nonmember banks and thrift institutions, and there was some prestige attached to being a member bank. Member banks were able to borrow from the Federal Reserve banks, order and deposit currency at these banks, and obtain advice from them. Member banks could also use the Federal Reserve's check-clearing facilities and transfer funds over its leased teletype wires, although this is not an exclusive advantage because a nonmember bank could also qualify as a "clearing bank" at the district Federal Reserve bank.

The privileges and prestige of membership were not worth the costs to most state banks. State nonmember banks were subject to state reserve requirements, which varied from state to state and were usually lower than member bank reserve requirements. From the beginning, Federal Reserve authorities had hoped to enlist the state banks, but they were not successful. The state banks that chose not to belong had correspondent relationships with large urban banks and were able to obtain the same kind of services from them that they might have obtained from the Federal Reserve banks.

From 1970 to 1980, more than 500 banks withdrew from the Federal Reserve System, and the majority of the newly formed banks chose to remain outside the system.[9] As a result, the proportion of commercial bank deposits held by member banks declined from 83 percent in 1965 to 73 percent in 1978. In late 1979 and early 1980, 69 banks dropped their membership, and more than 600 other banks were reportedly considering withdrawal. The principal reason for the decline in membership was the rise in market interest rates. This increased the implicit cost of the nonearning reserves required of banks. In 1980, the Depository Institutions Deregulation and Monetary Control Act ended the attractiveness of withdrawing from the System by making transactions accounts and nonpersonal time accounts of all depository institutions subject to Federal Reserve reserve requirements. In addition, the law requires the commercial banks that left the System after July 1, 1979, to hold the same reserve requirements as the member banks. After a phase-in period of eight years, during which the reserve requirements for most member banks will be reduced and the reserve requirements for other depository institutions will be raised, the reserve requirements for all depository institutions are expected to be the same. The purpose of these changes is to solve the problem of declining Federal Reserve membership.

Federal Open Market Committee

The Federal Open Market Committee (FOMC) is responsible for determining policy concerning the purchase and sale of U.S. government securities by the Federal Reserve banks—the most important instrument of control in the Federal Reserve System.[10] The FOMC was formally established in 1935, although a committee to coordinate open-market purchases had been set up by the Federal Reserve banks in the early 1920s. The committee consists of twelve members: the seven governors and the presidents of five of the twelve Federal Reserve banks. The chairman of the Board of Governors is chairman of the committee. The president of the Federal Reserve Bank of New York is a permanent member of the committee and is its vice-chairman. The other four positions on the committee are rotated among the remaining presidents of the Federal Reserve banks. In practice, all twelve presidents attend committee meetings and take part in the discussion, although seven of them are nonvoting members. The committee meets monthly in Washington.

At the meetings of the FOMC, economic conditions are discussed, and decisions are made concerning monetary policy appropriate to the current economic situation. Staff economists of the Board of Governors and the Federal Reserve banks are called on to provide information. The policies of the FOMC are issued as a directive to the manager of the System Open Market Account, a vice-president of the Federal Reserve Bank of New York. Records of policy actions taken by the Federal Open Market Committee are currently made public about thirty days after each FOMC meeting. They are included in the *Federal Reserve Bulletin* published by the Board of Governors of the Federal Reserve System.

The Federal Reserve's policy of delaying disclosure of its monetary-policy decisions has been under attack. It is claimed that the System is obliged, under the Freedom of Information Act, to tell the public immediately after FOMC meetings what decisions were made. The case went to the Supreme Court, but it is still not definitely resolved.

The actual purchase and sale of securities is performed by the Federal Reserve Bank of New York. The transactions are made through U.S. government securities dealers, most of whom have their offices in New York. The increase or decrease in securities is apportioned among all the Federal Reserve banks according to each bank's share of total Federal Reserve bank assets.

Federal Advisory Council

The Federal Advisory Council was established under the Federal Reserve Act to provide communication between the banking industry and the Federal Reserve System. The council consists of twelve members, one selected annually by each of the Federal Reserve banks. Members usually are prominent bankers from the district. The council meets four times a year with the governors of the Federal Reserve System and confers on banking policy and the conditions of the economy. The members also carry back information to the banks in their areas. There is no obligation on the part of the Board of Governors to execute any recommendations of the council. Since this council has no power to act or set policy, it receives little public attention, and its usefulness and effectiveness are questioned by some.

The balance sheet of the twelve Federal Reserve banks combined

The principal types of assets and liabilities of the Federal Reserve banks—the operating units of the Federal Reserve System—as of March 31, 1979, are shown in Table 11.1.[11] Although each Federal Reserve bank is a separate corporation and keeps its own accounts, in this table the individual accounts of the twelve Federal Reserve banks are combined. Listed below is a description of each of the items on the balance sheet.

Federal Reserve bank assets

The *gold certificate account* shows the amount of gold certificates owned by the Federal Reserve banks. As was explained in Chapter 3, gold certificates were originally a type of paper money that was issued by the U.S. Treasury on the basis of its gold bullion stored at Fort Knox, Kentucky, but are today merely accounting obligations of the Treasury. Prior to the establishment of the Federal Reserve System, most of the gold certificates were owned by commercial banks and were used as part of their legal reserves. After the Federal Reserve System was established in 1914, the bulk of the gold certificates was acquired by the Federal Reserve banks.

Prior to 1971, the U.S. Treasury bought and sold gold bullion, and the

incr money supply
decrease in liability

if expand well
incr money supply

Table 11.1
Balance Sheet, Twelve
Federal Reserve Banks
Combined, March 31,
1979 (in millions)

Assets		Liabilities and Capital Accounts	
Gold certificate account	$ 11,479	Federal Reserve notes *MMS LIABILITY*	$100,654
Cash	395	Deposits:	
Special drawing rights		Member bank reserve *	31,714
certificate account	1,300	U.S. Treasury	5,726
U.S. government securities		Foreign and other	1,011
and federal agency		Deferred availability	
obligations	118,772	cash items	5,934
Loans	963	Other liabilities and	
Acceptances	204	accrued dividends	1,795
Cash in process of		Capital accounts	2,955
collection	10,271		
Assets denominated in foreign			
currencies	3,754		
Bank premises and other assets	2,651		
Total assets	$149,789	Total	$149,789

Source: *Federal Reserve Bulletin*, June 1979, p. A12.

amount of the gold certificate account varied with purchases and sales of gold by the U.S. Treasury. Since then, changes in the gold certificate account have occurred only when the official price of gold has been raised or when the U.S. Treasury has auctioned off gold bullion.

Before 1968, the Federal Reserve banks were legally required to hold an amount in their gold certificate account equal to 25 percent of their outstanding Federal Reserve notes. This requirement was discontinued in 1968. Three years earlier, this 25 percent reserve requirement had been dropped for the deposit liabilities of the Federal Reserve banks. Originally, the required reserve ratios for both notes and deposits had been larger than 25 percent. These requirements had set an upper limit to the expansion of the notes and deposits of the Federal Reserve banks.

Coins, the second asset listed on the balance sheet of the combined Federal Reserve banks, consist of the coins issued by the U.S. Treasury that are held by the Federal Reserve banks. The Federal Reserve banks acquire coins when new coins, manufactured by the U.S. mints, are deposited in them. Commercial banks may also deposit in the Federal Reserve banks any coins in excess of their needs.

The *special drawing rights certificate account* is based on the special drawing rights that have, since January 1970, been issued by the International Monetary Fund to member countries. SDRs at the IMF are an alternative to gold and dollars as a type of international money. They may be used by the United States Treasury to obtain the currency of other countries.

When the United States Treasury obtains SDRs from the IMF or from another government, it may issue *SDR certificates* to the Federal Reserve banks in exchange for a special Treasury deposit at the Federal Reserve banks. SDR certificates can be owned only by the Federal Reserve banks, and the amount issued by the Treasury is limited to the amount of SDRs that the Treasury owns. The amount of SDR certificates issued by the Treasury has been less than the amount of SDRs held by it. The SDR certificate *account* is a record of the SDR certificates owned by the Federal Reserve banks and is handled in the same way as the gold certificate account. Transactions between the Federal Reserve banks and the United States Treasury are carried out through book entries, rather than the issuance of paper certificates.

The *U.S. government securities and federal agency obligations* owned by the Federal Reserve banks are their most important asset. Open market operations—the Federal Reserve System's principal instrument of control—consist of buying and selling these securities. The purpose of such operations is to achieve the broad objectives of monetary policy rather than to maximize profits. The interest income received from these securities is much more than the Reserve banks need to cover their expenses and the dividend paid to stockholders, and since 1947 the bulk of their profits has been returned to the Treasury.

The *loans* of the Federal Reserve banks are made to banks rather than to businesses or private persons. One of the explicit purposes of the Federal Reserve Act was to provide member banks with facilities for borrowing from a central bank. Loans were formerly listed on the balance sheet of the Federal Reserve banks as "discounts and advances," and there is still a distinction between these two types of loans. The most commonly used type of loan is an advance—a promissory note signed by officials of a member bank with collateral in the form of U.S. government securities. Member banks may also borrow from the Federal Reserve banks by discounting commercial loans. When borrowing in this way, the member bank sells a loan that it owns at a discount to a Federal Reserve bank for a given period of time. At the end of that period, the member bank buys back the loan at its face value, recovering the loan prior to its maturity.

The rate of interest charged for loans is known as the discount rate, and raising or lowering this rate is one of the Federal Reserve banks' three major instruments of control. Normally, banks have borrowed only for very short periods—seldom more than fifteen days. All member banks must calculate reserve requirements weekly. If a bank finds itself with less than its required amount of reserves (cash in vault plus deposits in its Federal Reserve bank), it can usually borrow to make up the difference. Member banks may also borrow for seasonal needs and in emergencies. In 1980, regular borrowing privileges were extended to nonmember banks and thrift institutions.

The *acceptances* owned by the Federal Reserve banks are bills of exchange that are used primarily in international trade. They are readily marketable because they have been marked as "accepted" by the bank on which they are drawn. Federal Reserve banks purchase bankers' acceptances at prevailing interest rates in any quantity in which they are offered in order to stimulate the use of acceptances in international trade.[12] As an asset of the Federal Reserve banks, acceptances are similar to loans because the sale of acceptances to the Federal Reserve banks is done at the initiative of the member banks. A commercial bank can replenish its reserves by selling bankers' acceptances to a Reserve bank. Acceptances are short-term investments and are competitive in financial markets with U.S. Treasury bills and commercial paper. They are sold at a discount.

Cash items in process of collection is an account of the checks that have been received by the Federal Reserve banks, but which have not yet been collected from the bank on which the checks were drawn. When a Federal Reserve bank receives a check written on a bank in another Federal Reserve district, the check must be sent to the Federal Reserve bank in that district for collection, and clearing it may take several days. During the time a check is in process of collection, the amount of the check is included as an asset in cash items in process of collection.

Assets denominated in foreign currencies consist primarily of holdings of foreign currencies in the form of bank balances in foreign banks. Foreign currencies are held for the purpose of controlling exchange rates between the dollar and other currencies. This item has increased in importance in recent years. Since 1978, the Federal Reserve System has attempted to prevent the value of the dollar from falling relative to currencies of foreign countries.

Bank premises and other assets shows the value of the premises of the Federal Reserve banks, and certain operating assets such as accrued interest, other accounts receivable, and the premium on securities.

The liabilities and capital accounts of the Federal Reserve banks

The item *Federal Reserve notes* shows the total dollar amount of paper currency that has been issued by the Federal Reserve banks. Federal Reserve notes are listed on the liabilities side of the balance sheet because, when they are outstanding, these notes are liabilities of the Federal Reserve banks. Although each of the Federal Reserve banks has a large amount of brand-new notes in its own vaults ready for issue when requested by the member banks, until issued these notes are not liabilities and have no economic significance.

Member bank reserve deposits are the checking accounts of the member banks at the Reserve banks. They constitute the major portion of the member banks' legal reserves. Most member banks deposit the checks they receive which are drawn on other banks in their accounts at their

Federal Reserve banks. For each check deposited, the account of the depositing bank is credited and the account of the bank on which the check was written is debited. Also, member banks may withdraw currency from their deposit accounts if they need additional coins or paper money, or they may deposit excess currency in their accounts. Variations in the total amount of these reserve balances are significant because they affect the activity of the member banks.

The *United States Treasury deposit* is the general checking account of the United States government. Although the Treasury usually first deposits the tax payments it receives in commercial banks and other depository institutions, funds are transferred to the Federal Reserve banks and their branches several times each week. Most of the checks that the Treasury writes to pay for its expenditures are written on its deposits at the Reserve banks.

Foreign deposits are the checking accounts owned by foreign central banks, the Bank for International Settlements, and a few foreign governments. The central banks of different countries usually hold deposits in foreign countries for international settlement purposes. *Other deposits* include the deposits of some nonmember banks. A nonmember bank may have a check-clearing account with the Reserve bank in its district as a matter of convenience. Also included are deposits of the IMF and some other international organizations, a special account of the Secretary of the Treasury, and deposits of various federal corporations such as the National Railroad Passenger Corporation (AMTRAK) and the Communications Satellite Corporation (COMSAT). There are no deposits of business firms, individuals, or state and local governments in the Federal Reserve banks.

Deferred availability cash items is the amount of the checks that have been received by the Reserve banks that have not yet been added to the accounts of the member banks that deposited them. Credit for checks that must be sent to other Federal Reserve banks for collection may be postponed for up to two days; there is a time schedule based on the distance to the other bank. Crediting checks is delayed in order to reduce fluctuations in member bank reserve deposits resulting from changes in the volume of cash items in process of collection. The difference between cash items in process of collection (on the asset side) and deferred availability cash items is called *float* and will be discussed in Chapter 12.

The *other liabilities and accrued dividends* item is an estimate of the operating obligations incurred by the banks but not yet paid at the time the balance sheet is prepared.

The *capital accounts* include "capital paid in" (capital stock), "surplus," and "other capital accounts." The stock of the Federal Reserve banks is owned by the member banks. Each member bank currently subscribes to an amount of stock equal to 3 percent of its own capital stock (at par value) and surplus.

Since 1964, surplus has been maintained at an amount equal to the capital paid in. The Federal Reserve banks do not have the inducement to increase the size of their capital accounts that profit-maximizing enterprises have. If the Reserve banks were dissolved, the law provides that the surplus be paid to the U.S. government rather than to the owners—the member banks. As their capital stock expands, the Federal Reserve banks increase the amount of their surplus by retaining some of their net earnings. If they were to operate at a loss in any year, and nevertheless paid their regular dividend, their surplus would be reduced. "Other capital accounts" is an estimate of the unallocated net earnings for the year to the date of the preparation of the balance sheet.

Federal Reserve banks receive interest on their loans and on their investments in U.S. government securities. Note that when a Federal Reserve bank receives interest on a member bank loan, the deposit of the member bank is decreased and the capital accounts of the Federal Reserve bank are increased. Also, when interest is received on Treasury securities, the Treasury's deposit in the Federal Reserve bank is decreased and the capital accounts of the Federal Reserve bank are increased. Because the receipt of interest by the Federal Reserve banks is accompanied by a decline in the deposits held by them, the assets of the Federal Reserve banks are not affected.

Summary

The organization of the Federal Reserve System was designed to provide representation from borrowers, lenders, and the public living in the different geographical regions of the country. It has a high degree of participation by those its policies affect.

The Federal Reserve System is an independent agency and is not subject to supervision by the executive branch of the federal government. Although its monetary policies might conflict with other governmental economic programs, such conflicts have been rare.

By far the largest and most important type of asset of the Federal Reserve banks is their holdings of U.S. government securities.

The two most important types of liabilities of the Federal Reserve banks are the total amount of Federal Reserve notes outstanding and the member bank reserve deposits.

Notes

1. See Ross M. Robertson, *History of the American Economy*, 3d ed. (New York: Harcourt Brace Jovanovich, 1973), pp. 402–411.

2. Benjamin J. Klebaner, *Commercial Banking in the United States: A History* (Hinsdale, Illinois: Dryden Press, 1974), pp. 89–93.

3. Herbert Stein, *The Fiscal Revolution in America* (Chicago: University of Chicago Press, 1969), pp. 12–16.

4. For an account of the early history of the Federal Reserve System, see Lester V. Chandler, *Benjamin Strong, Central Banker* (Washington, D.C.: The Brookings Institution, 1958), pp. 40–48.

5. See Arthur F. Burns, "The Independence of the Federal Reserve System," *Federal Reserve Bulletin*, June 1976, pp. 493–496; and Thomas Mayer, "The Structure and Operation of the Federal Reserve System: Some Needed Reforms," in *FINE* (see notes Chapter 5), pp. 672–690.

6. House Concurrent Resolution 133, March 23, 1975.

7. U.S. Congress, Joint Economic Committee, *Recent Federal Reserve Action and Economic Policy Coordination, Hearings, Parts 1 and 2, December 13–16, 1965,* 89th Cong., 1st sess., 1966.

8. James M. Buchanan, "Easy Budgets and Tight Money," *Lloyds Bank Review* (April 1962), pp. 17–30, reprinted in Richard A. Ward, ed., *Monetary Theory and Policy* (Scranton, Pa.: International Textbook Co., 1966), pp. 164–177.

9. Robert Johnston, "Membership I—The Background," *Federal Reserve Bank of San Francisco Weekly Letter*, July 21, 1978; and "Membership II—The Proposals," *Federal Reserve Bank of San Francisco Weekly Letter*, July 28, 1978.

10. Albert E. Burger and Douglas R. Mudd describe the operations of the Federal Open Market Committee in detail in "The FOMC in 1976: Progress Against Inflation," Federal Reserve Bank of St. Louis, *Review* 59 (March 1977), pp. 2–17.

11. See Federal Reserve Bank of New York, "Consolidated Statement of Condition of all Federal Reserve Banks," *Glossary: Weekly Federal Reserve Statements* (New York: Federal Reserve Bank of New York, October 1975), pp. 3–14.

12. On the early history of Federal Reserve policy toward the acceptance market, see Charles O. Hardy, *Credit Policies of the Federal Reserve System* (Washington, D.C.: The Brookings Institution, 1932), Chapter 12. See also G. Walter Woodworth, *The Money Market and Monetary Management*, 2d ed. (New York: Harper and Row, 1972), Chapter 7.

Questions

11.1. Describe some of the attempts to establish a central bank in the United States prior to the creation of the Federal Reserve System.

11.2. What are the characteristics of the Federal Reserve System as an "independent agency"?

11.3. Give the arguments for and against the "independence" of the Federal Reserve System.

11.4. What are the different functions of the Board of Governors of the Federal Reserve System, the Federal Open Market Committee, and the Federal Reserve banks?

11.5. Which unit of the Federal Reserve System controls open market operations, changes in the discount rate, changes in reserve requirements, margin requirements, and maximum rates of interest allowed on savings and time deposits?

11.6. In what ways does the organization of the Federal Reserve System provide for some political control by the executive branch of the government?

11.7. In what way does the organization of the Federal Reserve System make possible the influence of bankers, borrowers, the public, and different geographical areas of the country?

11.8. Why in the past did some commercial banks prefer not to be member banks?

11.9. Describe each of the following assets of the Federal Reserve banks:

> Gold certificates
> Coins
> U.S. government securities
> Loans and acceptances
> Cash items in process of collection

11.10. Describe each of the following liabilities of the Federal Reserve banks:

> Federal Reserve notes
> Member bank deposits
> U.S. Treasury deposits
> Foreign and other deposits
> Deferred availability cash items

11.11. How would the receipt of the payment of interest on loans to a member bank affect the balance sheet of a Federal Reserve bank?

11.12. How would the balance sheet of the Federal Reserve banks be affected when they receive interest from the U.S. Treasury on U.S. government bonds?

11.13. Know the meaning and significance of the following terms and concepts: Board of Governors of the Federal Reserve System, member bank, Federal Open Market Committee, independent agency, Federal Reserve district, semipublic corporation, float, Federal Reserve notes.

12

Historically, central banks were intended to deal with the problem of bank runs. Modern central banking is concerned primarily with controlling aggregate demand in order to influence conditions in the economy.

CENTRAL BANKING

The first section of this chapter deals with the way in which central banks provided a means of solving one of the major financial problems of the nineteenth century—the runs on banks (or bank panics) that occurred in virtually every country in which commercial banking existed. The discovery of the way to handle this problem was a major development in banking policy. The second section of this chapter describes the bank reserve equation for the United States banking system. The bank reserve equation includes all of the major factors which affect the monetary base—member bank reserve deposits in the Federal Reserve banks plus currency in circulation. As was explained in Chapter 9, changes in the monetary base are a principal determinant of changes in the supply of money.

Historical function of central banks

Historically, the principal function of a central bank was to solve the problem of runs on the deposits of commercial banks. The way a central bank does this was first clearly described in 1874 by a British economist, Walter Bagehot, in his famous book entitled *Lombard Street*.

Normally a commercial bank can successfully operate with a very low ratio of cash in vault to deposits because its daily inflow of currency usually equals the outflow. Throughout the nineteenth century, however, there were periodic financial crises in which the public lost confidence in the solvency of banks and withdrew larger amounts of currency than it deposited. As a result, supplies of cash ran out, and many banks eventually were unable to cash checks.

Runs occurred when the public feared that banks might fail. This usually happened after some banks had actually gone bankrupt. Prior to 1934, it was a serious matter to have a deposit in a bank that failed. Deposits were not insured by the federal government and were only rarely insured by states. Depositors had to wait until the bank had gone through bankruptcy and a receiver had taken over before being paid off, and the percentage of their deposits paid off depended on the value of the bank's assets.

Prior to 1914, an important technique for handling bank runs was for the governor of a state to proclaim that because of an emergency, banks did not legally have to convert deposits into currency. When convertibility was restricted in this way, the banks would usually remain open and continue lending money. People could not cash checks, but could transfer money from one demand deposit to another by check. Although the public—especially merchants who needed currency for their cash registers and businessmen who needed currency for their payrolls—was seriously inconvenienced, as soon as people no longer attempted to convert deposits into currency, the emergency would end.

The way in which a central bank solves the problem of runs is illustrated in Figures 12.1 and 12.2. A central bank is a banker's bank and a "lender of last resort." As shown in Figure 12.1, when a member bank borrows from a Federal Reserve bank, it receives additional reserve deposits in return for its loan:

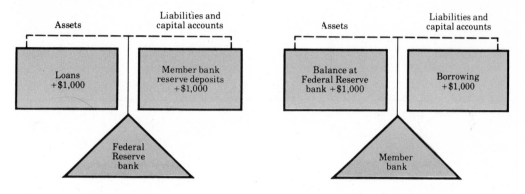

The second essential feature of a central bank is that a member bank in need of cash because of runs may convert the additional reserve balances which it has obtained at the Federal Reserve bank through borrowing into cash in vault in the form of Federal Reserve notes, as shown in the T-accounts in Figure 12.2, next page.

The Federal Reserve System was explicitly designed to provide "an elastic currency." This is the fundamental problem when there are runs on banks—more currency is needed. Federal Reserve notes have expansibility because they are *liabilities* of the Federal Reserve banks. If the paper money in circulation were an asset of the central bank, it would not be expansible because the supply of an asset can be exhausted. In contrast, there may be virtually no limit to the supply of a type of currency that is a liability. As was shown in Figures 12.1 and 12.2, with the assistance of a Federal Reserve bank, a commercial bank can obtain additional reserve deposits at the Reserve bank by borrowing and can convert deposits into Federal Reserve notes as rapidly as depositors wish.

It is also important that with the assistance of a central bank, a loss of commercial bank deposits due to runs can be offset by an increase in commercial bank borrowing at the central bank. As a result, despite the runs, there need be no reduction in the total liabilities and total assets of the commercial banking system. This has a desirable effect on the stability of the economy because any significant contraction in the

**Figure 12.2
Member Banks May
Exchange Member
Bank Reserve Deposits
for Additional Cash
in Vault**

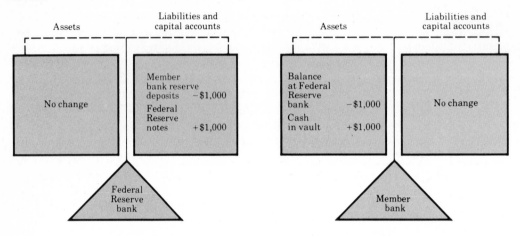

total assets and liabilities of commercial banks may depress business activity.

Historically, expansion of the quantity of Federal Reserve notes was subject to legal limitations. Federal Reserve banks were at one time required to hold reserves of gold certificates equal to a percentage of their Federal Reserve notes outstanding, and so were able to expand the amount of notes only if they had excess reserves. This restriction was discontinued in 1968. A second limitation was a collateral requirement: the Federal Reserve banks were required to hold collateral, either gold certificates or *eligible paper* (certain types of short-term commercial loans), in an amount equal to their Federal Reserve notes. Acceptable collateral has been broadened and now includes U.S. government securities. At the present time, the quantity of Federal Reserve notes issued is not restricted by the collateral requirements, because the Reserve banks' eligible collateral exceeds in value by a substantial margin the amount of Federal Reserve notes outstanding.

In the United States and most other countries, runs on banks have become very rare. However, in 1965, runs were reported on the banks in Hong Kong as the result of a rumor that checks on one of the banks there had not been honored in the United States. Also, in 1970 there were runs on banks in Santiago, Chile, following the election of a Marxist president.

The United States has not had any bank runs (panicky shifts from deposits to currency) since the Great Depression from 1929 to 1933.

Even then, the bank runs and the general financial chaos were surprising because they occurred while the Federal Reserve System was in operation. However, the existence of the Federal Reserve System did not assure that a serious financial crisis would not occur, because member banks did not increase their borrowing from the Federal Reserve banks sufficiently to offset the runs. Because of insufficient borrowing, the runs reduced bank reserves and caused a contraction of loans, investments, and deposits throughout the banking system.

Even though this experience shows that member bank borrowing from a central bank cannot always be relied on to solve the problem of runs, the Federal Reserve authorities themselves could have kept bank reserves from declining by making open-market purchases. The principal mistake made by the Federal Reserve authorities during the Great Depression was that they did not buy sufficiently large quantities of U.S. government securities to prevent the sharp decline that occurred in bank reserves. The result of not pursuing a more aggressive monetary policy was a gradual economic breakdown that was eventually ended by the banking holiday of 1933, in which every bank in the country was shut down by presidential proclamation.

The establishment of the Federal Deposit Insurance Corporation in 1934 has reduced further the likelihood of runs on banks and the possible serious consequences of runs. When deposits are insured, persons are much less anxious about the safety of their holdings, even if possible bank failures are anticipated.

Bank reserve equation

Modern central banks have evolved into governmental institutions for controlling interest rates and monetary aggregates such as the monetary base and the money supply. The important factors affecting the monetary base are included in the bank reserve equation. As was explained in Chapter 9, the monetary base is the most important variable in determining the expansion or contraction of the money supply (see Equations 9.6 and 9.7 and Figure 9.1.) If the monetary base increases, the total money stock tends to increase, and if it decreases, the money stock tends to decrease.

The bank reserve equation includes fourteen factors that may cause changes in the member bank reserve deposits at the Federal Reserve banks.[1] Eight of them *supply* reserve funds. An increase in these items tends to increase member bank reserve deposits. The other six factors *absorb* reserve funds. If they increase, a decrease in member bank reserve deposits results. The difference between the totals for factors supplying and absorbing reserves is equal to member bank reserve deposits at the Federal Reserve banks.[2]

The eight factors supplying member bank balances at the Reserve banks are the following. The first five of these items are types of Federal Reserve credit: *FR has little control over these*

U.S. government and federal agency securities owned by the
Federal Reserve banks
Acceptances owned by the Federal Reserve banks
Loans of the Federal Reserve banks
The float of the Federal Reserve banks
Other Federal Reserve assets

to miss FR has no control

The Treasury's gold stock *asset - more supply of gold cent*
The special drawing rights certificate account
Treasury currency outstanding - *more currency circulated goes back to banks as reserve*

The six factors absorbing member bank balances at the Reserve banks are:

Currency in circulation - *F.R. note - if liability goes up*
Treasury cash holdings - *anything Tr hold*
Treasury deposits in the Federal Reserve banks - *what it gets from pub*
Foreign government deposits in the Federal Reserve banks
Other deposits in the Federal Reserve banks
Other Federal Reserve liabilities and capital accounts

Note that currency in circulation—the component of the monetary base other than member bank reserve deposits at the Federal Reserve banks—is one of the six factors in the bank reserve equation absorbing reserve funds.

Table 12.1 shows the bank reserve equation published in the *Federal Reserve Bulletin* for March 1979. Most of the items in the bank reserve equation are from the balance sheet of the twelve Federal Reserve banks combined (see Table 11.1). In addition, there are the Treasury's gold stock and three items from the monetary accounts of the U.S. Treasury shown in Table 3.2 in Chapter 3: (1) Treasury currency outstanding, (2) currency in circulation, and (3) Treasury cash holdings.

Factors supplying reserve deposits

It is important to understand the way in which each of the factors in the bank reserve equation affects member bank reserve deposits. Consider first the eight factors supplying member bank reserve deposits. These are the items that if increased cause member bank reserve deposits to increase. If decreased, they cause member bank reserve deposits to decrease.

1. Changes in the quantity of *U.S. government and federal agency securities owned by the Federal Reserve banks* are the result of open-market operations. These operations are solely at the initiative of the Federal Reserve authorities and reflect attempts to achieve their broad economic objectives. This is considered the most important item in the bank reserve equation because the Federal Reserve System may control the monetary base through control of this item.

Open-market purchases increase the reserve deposits of the member banks, and sales decrease their reserve deposits. The way in which open-market sales to a nonbank dealer would decrease member bank reserves is illustrated in the T-accounts shown in Figure 12.3. When a

Table 12.1
The Bank Reserve Equation and the Monetary Base, March 31, 1979

List published every Monday.

	Amount (in millions)
Factors supplying member bank deposits at the Federal Reserve banks:	
	1982
Federal Reserve credit:	
U.S. government and federal-agency securities *141,202*	$118,772 *131,339*
Acceptances	204
Loans	963
(Float) *(Seasonal)*	4,337 *2,323*
Other Federal Reserve assets	6,405
Gold stock	11,479 *11,148*
Special drawing rights certificate account	1,300
Treasury currency outstanding	12,114
Total	$155,574
	P 23860
Factors absorbing member bank deposits at the Federal Reserve banks:	*MEMBER BANK 31,714 Res.*
Currency in circulation	$111,988
Treasury cash holdings	385
Deposits with Reserve banks:	
Treasury	5,726
Foreign	303
Other	708
Other Federal Reserve liabilities and capital accounts	4,750
Total	$123,860
The monetary base:	
Member bank deposits at Federal Reserve banks	$ 31,714[a]
Currency in circulation	111,988
Total	$143,702

Support existence of #300 Bill of Chkng Dep

[a]Equals the difference between the total amount of the factors supplying and absorbing member bank deposits at the Federal Reserve banks: $155,574 million–$123,860 million = $31,714 million.
Source: *Federal Reserve Bulletin*, June 1979, p. A4.

Federal Reserve bank sells $1,000 of securities, its holdings of government securities would be reduced. The dealer would pay for the securities with a check written on a member bank. The Federal Reserve bank, on receiving the check, would reduce the member bank's reserve deposit at the Federal Reserve bank. The check would then be sent to the member bank, which would reduce the deposit there of the dealer.

Figure 12.3
Open-Market Sales
Reduce Member Bank
Reserve Deposits
(Assume securities are sold to a nonbank dealer in government securities)

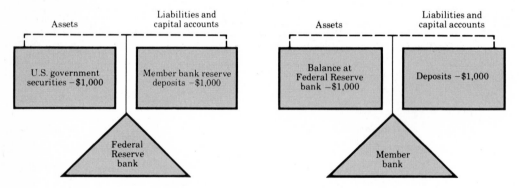

If securities were sold to a member bank that is also a dealer in government securities, the effect on the T-accounts of the member bank in Figure 12.3(b) would be slightly different. The member bank would acquire additional U.S. government securities (an asset). When the member bank pays for the securities, its balance at the Reserve bank would be decreased by the amount of the transaction. There would be no change in its deposit liabilities.

2. Federal Reserve banks purchase *acceptances* from member banks whenever the member banks wish to increase their reserve deposits by selling some of their acceptances to them. The Federal Reserve banks receive interest on the acceptances purchased; the rate at which they discount the acceptances purchased is announced in advance. An increase in acceptances owned by the Federal Reserve banks causes a similar increase in their member bank reserve deposits. The Federal Reserve banks pay for the acceptances by increasing the reserve deposits of the member banks from which they are purchased. The effect on

the balance sheets of the Federal Reserve bank and the member bank is shown in the T-accounts in Figure 12.4.

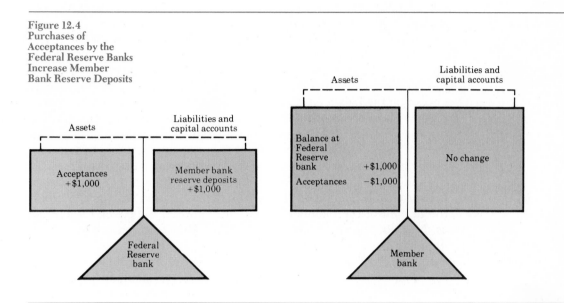

Figure 12.4
Purchases of
Acceptances by the
Federal Reserve Banks
Increase Member
Bank Reserve Deposits

3. Changes in *loans* at the Federal Reserve banks occur at the initiative of the member banks and were illustrated in Figure 12.1. An increase in member bank loans at the Federal Reserve banks causes a similar increase in their member bank reserve deposits since, in exchange for the loan from the Federal Reserve bank, the member bank receives an increase in its reserve deposit.

The Federal Reserve authorities typically lend to member banks that desire to borrow in order to meet their reserve requirements. The Federal Reserve banks may attempt to influence the volume of borrowing by changing the discount rate.

4. *Float* is the difference between two items on the Federal Reserve banks' balance sheet—cash items in process of collection and deferred availability cash items. Float is always positive because, for checks on distant banks, the Federal Reserve banks normally pay depositing banks before they collect from the banks on which the checks are written. Float is the value of all of the checks in process that have been credited to some banks prior to being collected from other banks. When float increases, bank reserves increase. Float may change sharply from week to week and often has significant short-run effects on reserve funds that are difficult for the monetary authorities to control.

Float tends to be higher toward the end of each week, when there is an increase in the volume of checks sent to the Reserve banks, and reaches a peak near the beginning and middle of most months—reflecting the bill-paying patterns of individuals and businesses. In addition, anything that causes a delay in the transfer of checks, such as a snowstorm affecting air transport, causes float to increase.

To illustrate how float affects the reserve deposits of member banks, consider the collection of an individual check for $1,000 received by the Federal Reserve Bank of Boston and written on a member bank in the San Francisco district. As shown in Figure 12.5(a), the immediate impact on the balance sheet of the FRB of Boston is that cash items in process of collection would be increased by $1,000, and for a period of two days it would credit deferred availability cash items. Thus far, float has not been increased because float is the difference between cash items in process of collection and deferred availability cash items. At the end of two days, *even though the FRB of Boston still has a cash item in process of collection of $1,000,* the FRB of Boston will have to credit the deposit of the member bank that deposited the check for $1,000, as shown in Figure 12.5(b). Because the FRB of Boston still has a cash item in process of collection, but not a balancing deferred availability cash item, float increases. There is an increase in the total reserves of the banking system because the reserves of the member bank in the Boston district have been increased, while the reserves of the member bank on the West Coast have not yet been reduced.

The float created by the movement of the single check in this example is temporary. When the check-clearing is completed, the reserve deposit of the member bank on which the check was written and the gold certificate account at the FRB of San Francisco would be reduced. At the same time, when the check is collected, cash items in process of collection at the FRB of Boston would be decreased and its gold certificate account increased. The records of the transfers of gold certificates are handled by the Interdistrict Settlement Fund. As shown by the changes in Figure 12.5(c), float declines when cash items in process of collection at the FRB of Boston are reduced and when member bank reserve deposits at the FRB of San Francisco are reduced.

5. *Other Federal Reserve assets* include assets denominated in foreign currencies, the Federal Reserve bank premises, and other assets not listed separately on the balance sheet. In recent years, the amount of assets denominated in foreign currencies owned by the Federal Reserve banks has become the most important of the other assets. An increase in foreign currency or in one of the other miscellaneous assets would tend to be balanced on the liabilities side of the balance sheet by an increase in member bank reserve deposits because the purchase of the foreign currency or other asset by a Federal Reserve bank would usually be paid for by a check written on itself. When that check was deposited in the Federal Reserve banks, total member bank deposits there would increase.

**Figure 12.5
The Effect on Federal
Reserve Float When the
Federal Reserve Bank
of Boston Collects a
Check for $1,000 from
the Federal Reserve
Bank of San Francisco**

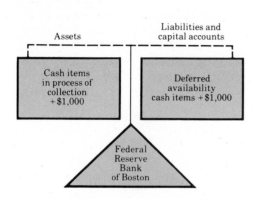

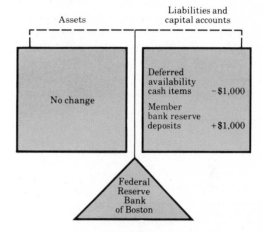

(a) The Federal Reserve Bank of Boston receives a check written on a bank in the San Francisco district.

(b) Float increases when the Federal Reserve Bank of Boston credits the member bank's reserve deposit.

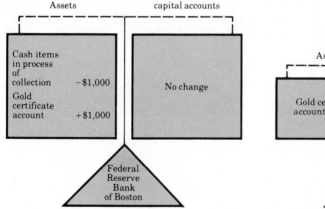

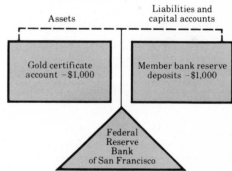

(c) The reduction of cash items in process of collection at the Federal Reserve Bank of Boston reduces float, and settlement between the two Federal Reserve banks is made through changes in their gold certificate accounts.

6. Changes in the Treasury's *gold stock* were historically an important factor affecting bank reserve deposits. Purchases of gold by the U.S. Treasury increased member bank reserve deposits at the Federal Reserve banks, and sales by the U.S. Treasury decreased them. When the Treasury sold gold, the foreign bank that bought the gold would usually pay for it by writing a check on its deposit account in a member bank.

As shown in the T-accounts in Figure 12.6(a), when the Treasury deposited the check it received in payment for the gold at the Federal Reserve bank, the Treasury account would be increased and the account of the member bank on which the check was drawn would be reduced. The Reserve bank would return the check to the member bank, which would then reduce the account of the foreign government.

Gold sales usually involved a second step. If the Treasury sold gold bullion, the amount of the gold certificate account at the Federal Re-

Figure 12.6
Treasury Sales of Gold
Decrease Member Bank
Reserve Deposits

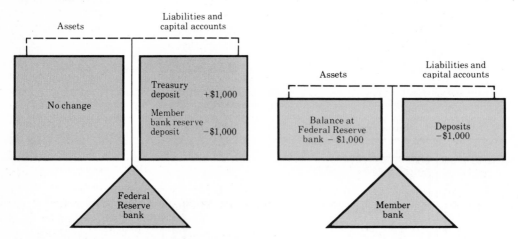

(a) The United States Treasury receives payment for the gold.

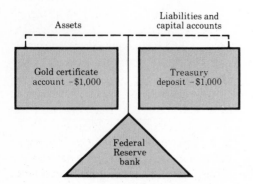

(b) The Treasury reduces its gold certificate account.

serve banks would have to be reduced. The Treasury would pay for the reduction in the gold certificate account by reducing its deposit at the Federal Reserve banks, as shown in the T-account in Figure 12.6(b). The net effect of gold sales on the balance sheet of the Federal Reserve banks was a reduction in both the gold certificate account and member bank deposits, and the amount of the Treasury's deposit at the Federal Reserve banks was unchanged.

Changes in the gold certificate account are now unimportant. The U.S. Treasury no longer purchases gold. There are only very small reductions in the gold certificate account each time the U.S. Treasury auctions gold.

7. Changes in the *special drawing rights certificate account* of the Federal Reserve banks are related to the amount of SDRs owned by the U.S. Treasury.[3] The Treasury acquires SDRs through allocations from the International Monetary Fund as well as through purchases from foreign governments. Upon receiving additional SDRs, the Treasury may issue a larger quantity of SDR certificates. If it does, both the SDR certificate account at the Reserve banks and the special Treasury account would be increased. Member bank reserve deposits will be increased when the additional funds in the special Treasury account are spent. If the Treasury does not issue additional SDR certificates when its holdings of SDRs are increased, there is no effect on the balance sheet of the Federal Reserve banks and no effect on member bank reserve deposits. In March 1979, the Treasury had issued only $1.3 billion in SDR certificates out of the $2.7 billion of SDRs that it owned.

The U.S. Treasury typically would sell SDRs when importers needed foreign exchange to pay for an excess of international payments over receipts. If pounds were needed, they would not be purchased from Great Britain, but from the government of another country with a surplus in its balance of payments, for example, West Germany. When the Treasury purchases pounds with SDRs, it will then sell the pounds it receives to a foreign exchange dealer. When the check received in payment for the pounds is deposited in the Federal Reserve bank, a special Treasury account is increased and the member bank deposit on which the check was written would be decreased, as shown in the T-account in Figure 12.7(a).

The Treasury may then decide to reduce the SDR certificate account at the Reserve banks. If so, both the SDR certificate account and the special Treasury account at the Federal Reserve banks would be reduced, as shown in the T-account in Figure 12.7(b). The net effect of the transactions shown in the T-accounts in Figure 12.7(a) and (b) is a reduction in both the SDR certificate account and in member bank reserve deposits.

If the governments of other countries use their SDRs to obtain needed foreign exchange from the United States, the effect on the

Figure 12.7
Treasury Sales of SDRs
in Exchange for Foreign
Currency Decrease
Member Bank Reserve
Deposits

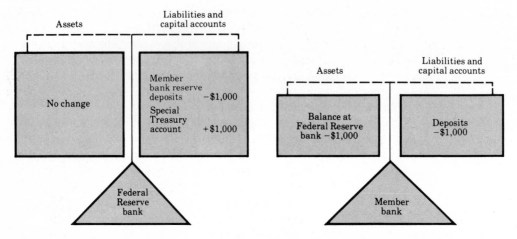

(a) The sale by the United States Treasury of foreign currency obtained in exchange for SDRs reduces member bank reserve deposits.

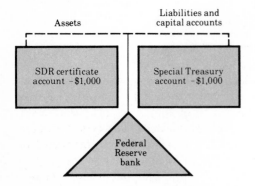

(b) When the Treasury sells SDRs, the SDR certificate account at the Federal Reserve banks may be reduced.

T-accounts would be the opposite of that illustrated in Figure 12.7. The U.S. Treasury would obtain the foreign currencies from foreign exchange dealers in the United States. The dealer receiving payment from the Treasury would deposit the check received in a member bank. Member bank reserve deposits would then be increased and the special Treasury account would be decreased. If, when the Treasury acquires SDRs, it decides to increase its SDR certificate account, both the SDR certificate account on the asset side of the balance sheet of the Federal

Reserve banks and the special Treasury account on the liability side would be increased. The net effect is an increase in the SDR certificate account at the Reserve banks and an increase in member bank reserve deposits, and there would be no net change in the special Treasury account.

8. Treasury currency outstanding consists primarily of coins, a small amount of U.S. notes, and notes in process of retirement. Coins are the only one of these types of Treasury currency being increased in amount.

When newly minted coins are deposited in the Federal Reserve banks, the amount of coin in these banks and the deposits of the Treasury increase, as shown in Figure 12.8(a). When the Treasury spends the increase in its deposits, member bank reserve deposits are increased and the Treasury's deposits are decreased. The person receiving payment from the Treasury would deposit the check received in a member bank; when the member bank deposits the check in its Federal Reserve bank, the member bank's deposit there would be increased and the Treasury's deposit decreased, as shown in the T-account in Figure 12.8(b). The Treasury would have to spend part of the additional deposit to pay for the manufacture of the new coins. In addition, it earns a profit called seigniorage—the difference between the nominal value of the coins and their cost of production. This source of government revenue will also eventually be spent.

Factors absorbing reserve deposits

An increase in any of the absorbing factors results in a decrease in member bank reserve deposits.

1. *Currency in circulation* consists of both Federal Reserve notes and Treasury currency held by persons or institutions other than the Treasury or the Federal Reserve banks.

An increase in currency in circulation will cause a decrease in member bank reserve deposits at the Federal Reserve banks. As shown in Figure 12.9(a), a member bank's balance at the Federal Reserve bank will be decreased when a member bank obtains additional cash in vault from the Reserve bank. If the increase in currency in circulation consists of Federal Reserve notes, there will be an increase in Federal Reserve notes outstanding [see Figure 12.9(b)]. On the other hand, if the increase of currency in circulation consists of coins, there will be a reduction in coin in the Federal Reserve banks [see Figure 12.9(c)]. Commercial banks would normally increase currency in circulation by reducing their holdings of reserve deposits when the public was withdrawing larger amounts of currency from its demand deposits at the commercial banks.

Note that when an increase in currency in circulation reduces mem-

**Figure 12.8
An Increase in
Treasury Currency
Outstanding Increases
Member Bank Reserve
Deposits**

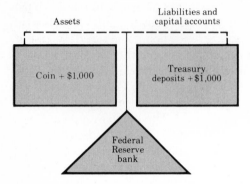

(a) The Treasury deposits newly minted coins in the Federal Reserve banks.

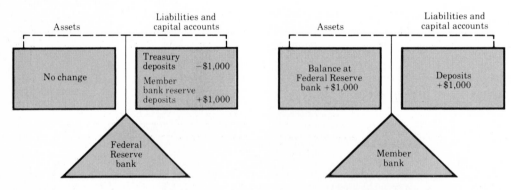

(b) When the Treasury spends the amount in its deposit, member bank reserve deposits increase.

ber bank reserve deposits, there is no change in the monetary base; when currency in circulation increases, the other component of the monetary base—member bank reserve deposits—decreases by an equal amount.

2. *Treasury cash holdings* include the amount of Federal Reserve notes and Treasury currency that the United States government holds. The principal type of money used by the Treasury consists of demand deposits in the Federal Reserve banks, but the Treasury also holds some currency for transactions that require this type of payment.

If the Treasury were to increase its holdings of either Federal Reserve notes or coins by withdrawing them from a Federal Reserve bank,

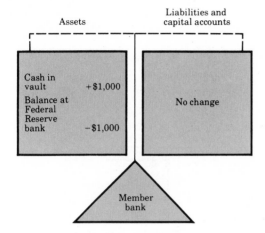

Figure 12.9
An Increase in the
Amount of Currency in
Circulation Decreases
Member Bank Reserve
Deposits

(a) Member banks exchange deposits at the Federal Reserve banks for an increase in cash in vault.

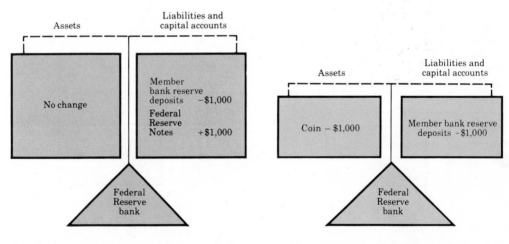

(b) Federal Reserve notes increase if the member banks want Federal Reserve notes.

(c) The cash assets of the Federal Reserve banks decrease if the member banks want coins.

the deposits of the Treasury at the Federal Reserve banks would be reduced (see Figure 12.10). Neither of these transactions directly affects member bank reserve deposits. However, the Treasury would then normally replenish its deposits at the Federal Reserve banks in order to keep them at a level sufficient to meet its needs. When the

Treasury replenishes its accounts at the Federal Reserve banks by depositing tax revenues, member bank reserve deposits are reduced, as shown in Figure 12.10(c).

Figure 12.10
An Increase in Treasury
Cash Holdings
Decreases Member
Bank Reserve Deposits

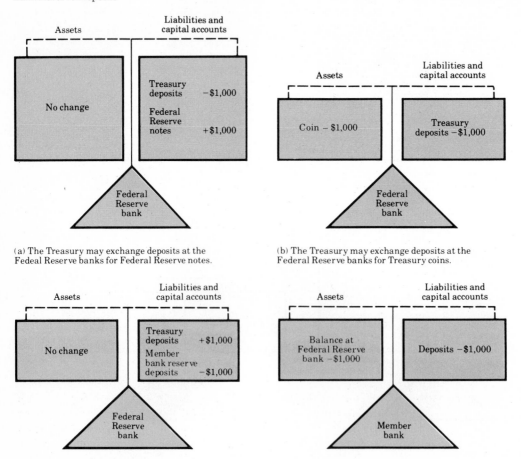

(a) The Treasury may exchange deposits at the Fedeal Reserve banks for Federal Reserve notes.

(b) The Treasury may exchange deposits at the Federal Reserve banks for Treasury coins.

(c) When the Treasury replenishes its deposits, member bank reserve deposits decrease.

3. The *U.S. Treasury deposit* consists of the amount held by the Treasury at the Federal Reserve banks. Several times a week, funds are transferred to this account from the Treasury accounts in depository

institutions. When the amount of the Treasury's deposit in the Federal Reserve banks is increased, this same amount is deducted from member bank reserve deposits (see Figure 12.11).

When the Treasury spends funds, the Treasury's account at the Federal Reserve banks decreases. At that time, member bank reserve deposits would be increased because the checks received from the government are deposited in commercial banks.

Figure 12.11
An Increase in the U.S. Treasurer's Deposit at the Federal Reserve Banks Decreases Member Bank Reserve Deposits

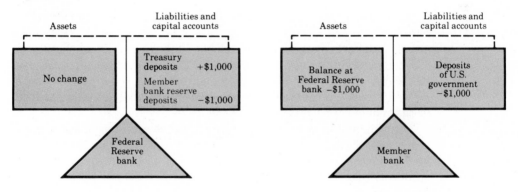

4. and 5. *Foreign* and *other deposits* are deposits of foreign central banks, nonmember banks, and various governmental institutions. Changes in these deposits have the same effect on member bank reserve deposits as changes in Treasury deposits. Foreign governments or nonmember banks increase these deposits by depositing checks written on member banks. This absorbs member bank reserves. When checks are written on these deposits in a Federal Reserve bank by foreign governments or nonmember banks, the opposite occurs. The member banks receiving the checks deposit them in a Reserve bank, and member bank reserve deposits are increased and the deposits of the foreign government or nonmember bank are reduced.

6. *Other Federal Reserve liabilities and capital accounts* includes all of the items on the liabilities side of the balance sheet that might affect member bank reserve deposits, other than Federal Reserve notes and the various types of deposits. The bulk of this item consists of the capital accounts.

If the capital accounts were to increase, this would reduce member bank reserve deposits; if they should decrease, those deposits would increase. For example, when a member bank purchases additional FRB stock, the stock would be paid for by a check written on the member bank's deposit at the Federal Reserve bank; paid-in capital would be increased, and member bank reserve deposits would be reduced. The opposite would occur when a dividend payment is made by a Federal Reserve bank; the dividend check received by a member bank would be deposited in its Federal Reserve bank. Member bank deposits would be increased and "other capital accounts" would be decreased.

Changes in the monetary base from March 1978 to March 1979

Table 12.2 shows that in the year ending March 31, 1979, the monetary base increased $13,410 million. Because changes in the base may have important effects on the money supply and thus on the level of economic activity, it is important to know the reason for increases and decreases in the monetary base. The question of what caused this increase in 1978–1979 may be answered by comparing the changes in the sources of the monetary base between these dates.

The principal reason for the increase in the monetary base was the increase of $9,002 million in the amount of U.S. government securities held by the Federal Reserve banks in March 1979 over that held a year earlier. During the year, there were both open-market purchases and open-market sales, but the purchases were considerably larger than the sales. The very large increase in the amount of U.S. government securities held by the Federal Reserve banks was still less than the increase in the monetary base. Several other factors supplying reserves also increased: other Federal Reserve assets consisting primarily of foreign currencies increased $4,077 million, float rose $1,605 million, loans increased $631 million, Treasury currency outstanding expanded $673 million, and SDR certificates increased $750 million.

The principal factors that absorbed part of the expansion in the base were an increase in the Treasury's deposit ($1,021 million), and an increase in other Federal Reserve liabilities ($890 million). There were also declines in the gold stock ($239 million) and in acceptances ($566 million).

The amount of government securities purchased by the Federal Reserve authorities is significantly affected by the changes in the other thirteen factors in the reserve equation. In the year ending March 1979, for example, the large increase in the amount of foreign currency held by the Federal Reserve banks (included in other Federal Reserve assets) supplied so much in reserves to the banking system that it was not

Table 12.2
Sources and Uses of the Monetary Base,
March 31, 1978 and March 31, 1979
(in millions of dollars)

Sources of the Base	3/31/78	3/31/79
Federal Reserve credit		
U.S. Government and federal agency securities	$109,770	$118,772
Acceptances	770	204
Loans	332	963
Float	2,732	4,337
Other Federal Reserve assets	2,328	6,405
Gold stock	11,718	11,479
Treasury currency outstanding	11,441	12,114
Special drawing rights certificate account	1,250	1,300
Treasury cash holdings	− 393	− 385
Deposits with Reserve banks:		
Treasury	−4,705	−5,726
Foreign	− 352	− 303
Other	− 740	− 708
Other Federal Reserve liabilities and capital accounts	−3,860	−4,750
Total	$130,292	$143,702

Uses of the Base	3/31/78	3/31/79
Currency in circulation	$102,392	$111,988
Member bank balances at the Federal Reserve banks	27,900	31,714
Total	$130,292	$143,702

Details do not add to totals in some cases because of rounding.
Source: *Federal Reserve Bulletin* May, 1978, p. A4, and June 1979, p. A4.

necessary for the authorities to purchase as many U.S. government securities as they would otherwise have purchased. Change in the monetary base is not left to chance, but is controlled in accordance with the objectives of the monetary authorities. An analysis of the changes in the monetary base shows that during this period the large increase in the monetary base was the result of actions taken by the Federal Reserve authorities and not the result of changes in such factors as float, the Treasury's deposit at the Federal Reserve banks, and other factors over which the Federal Reserve authorities have no control.

Summary

A central bank protects commercial banks against runs by making loans to commercial banks whenever needed and by providing an elastic supply of currency.

The Federal Reserve System can control the monetary base by buying and selling U.S. government securities—offsetting other factors in the bank reserve equation. All of the factors affecting the monetary base are from the accounts of either the Federal Reserve banks or the United States Treasury.

Notes

1. See "The Bank Reserve Equation," in Board of Governors of the Federal Reserve System, *The Federal Reserve System: Purposes and Functions*, 6th ed. (Washington, D.C., 1974), pp. 36–47; and Federal Reserve Bank of Chicago, *Modern Money Mechanics* (Chicago, 1968).

2. For a description of the factors determining bank reserves, see Federal Reserve Bank of New York, "Factors Affecting Bank Reserves," *Glossary: Weekly Federal Reserve Statement* (New York: Federal Reserve Bank of New York, October 1975), pp. 15–22.

3. "SDRs in Federal Reserve Operations and Statistics," *Federal Reserve Bulletin*, May 1970, pp. 421–424.

Questions

12.1 Explain the way in which a central bank helps commercial banks meet the problems created by runs on the banks.

12.2. Compare the following alternative methods of preventing or solving the problem of runs on banks:

> Suspending specie payment
> Federal deposit insurance
> A central bank

12.3. What is the purpose of the bank reserve equation?

12.4. Which of the factors in the bank reserve equation are from the monetary accounts of the United States Treasury, and which from the balance sheet of the Federal Reserve banks?

12.5. Explain the way in which an increase in each of the following factors in the bank reserve equation may increase member bank reserve deposits in the Federal Reserve banks:

> U.S. government securities owned by the
>   Federal Reserve banks
> Loans of the Federal Reserve banks
> Float of the Federal Reserve banks
> The gold stock
> SDR certificate account
> Treasury currency outstanding
> Holdings of foreign currencies

12.6. Explain the way an increase in each of the following factors in the bank reserve equation may decrease member bank reserve deposits at the Federal Reserve banks:

> Currency in circulation
> Treasury cash holdings
> Treasury deposits in the Federal Reserve banks
> Foreign government deposits in the Federal Reserve banks

12.7. Explain the way in which the Federal Reserve banks might offset the effect of a gold outflow on member bank reserve deposits in the Federal Reserve banks.

12.8. Explain the way in which the Federal Reserve banks might offset the effect of a decrease in currency in circulation on member bank reserve deposits at the Federal Reserve banks.

12.9. Know the meaning and significance of the following terms and concepts: bank panic, elastic currency, bank reserve equation, factors supplying member bank reserves, factors absorbing member bank reserves, Treasury currency outstanding, Treasury cash holdings, uses of the monetary base.

13

Open-market operations have become the most important instrument of control of the Federal Reserve System. Each week, some purchases and sales of U.S. government securities are made for the purpose of achieving the objectives of monetary policy.

THE FEDERAL RESERVE SYSTEM'S INSTRUMENTS OF CONTROL

Monetary policy is concerned with the way the Federal Reserve System uses its instruments of control to achieve its objectives.[1] There are three principal instruments of control: open-market operations, changes in the discount rate, and changes in the reserve requirements of the member banks. There are also two selective instruments of control currently in use: margin requirements for loans to purchase corporation stock and ceilings on interest rates paid by banks on deposits. The purpose of this chapter is to describe these major and selective instruments of control. Their relationship to the targets and goals of Federal Reserve policy are discussed in Chapter 14 and later chapters.

Open-market operations

When the Federal Reserve System was established, open-market operations were not considered as important as today. Federal Reserve banks were given the power to buy and sell certain types of securities, primarily to enable them to acquire earning assets sufficient to pay their expenses at times when very few loans were made to commercial banks. In the early years of the System, some, but not all, Federal Reserve banks found it convenient to make their securities transactions in the New York money market, and in the 1920s an informal committee consisting of officials of the Federal Reserve banks began to coordinate those transactions. It was not long before purchases and sales were used to offset gold flows and sometimes to create additional reserves for the commercial banking system. It was not until the Banking Act of 1935 that the Federal Open Market Committee (FOMC) was set up. The FOMC is now the System's most important policy-making unit.

FOMC directive

The Federal Open Market Committee prepares at its meetings a directive for the manager of the open-market account, who is a vice-president of the Federal Reserve Bank of New York.[2] The FOMC reviews available information on economic conditions and decides upon the appropriate general policy to be followed. The directive does not specify when and how much to buy or sell in the open market; these decisions are made by the manager of the open-market account. Changes in the general direction of policy are indicated by slight changes in the wording of the directive. For example, when monetary policy changed to combat the recession of 1973–1975, the directive was changed from promoting "a sustainable rate of advance in economic activity," to "supporting a resumption of real economic growth." In addition, recent directives have included specific targets to be achieved through open-market operations. The manager of the open-market account is expected to buy or sell the amount of U.S. government securities necessary to achieve, for example, its targeted federal funds rate or its targeted rates of growth of the monetary aggregates.

Manager of the open-market account

The manager of the open-market account has a staff that executes the transactions decided upon. All transactions are made with a group of well-established government securities dealer firms. As a semipublic institution, the Federal Reserve System must conduct its transactions in such a way that it gets as good a price as can be had. When the account manager decides to buy or sell, the usual procedure for outright transactions is first to brief the members of the trading staff. Then all traders simultaneously telephone dealers to ask for bids or offerings. As the traders complete their contacts with the dealers, the bids or offers are assembled and the best are selected. The entire operation is usually completed in thirty minutes.

The balance sheet of the twelve Federal Reserve banks discussed in Chapter 11 sometimes lists separately a small amount of securities owned under repurchase agreements with dealers. When this type of operation is used, the Federal Reserve Bank of New York acquires securities from a dealer under a contract which binds the dealer to repurchase the same securities, at the same price, on or before a stipulated final date. The length of the period for such agreements is usually fifteen days or less, although the contracts may be renewed. Any given repurchase agreement may be terminated virtually without notice at the option of either the Federal Reserve or the dealer, although the Federal Reserve has not found the need to use its option. The rate of interest on repurchase agreements is usually the same as the discount rate of the Federal Reserve Bank of New York, but it has at times been below this. If the account manager decides to purchase securities in this way, he contacts the dealers to find out which ones wish to sell and then allocates the total amount purchased among them. Repurchase agreements assist dealers in financing their inventories of securities by making it possible for them to sell some of their securities temporarily to the Federal Reserve banks.

Information on current open-market operations

It is possible to determine the net amount of current open-market operations by comparing two successive weekly balance sheet statements issued by the Federal Reserve System and published at the end of each week by major newspapers under the title "Federal Reserve Report" or "Federal Reserve Statement." Publication of these statements is required by law. The release of these statements does not include an explanation of the changes made.

Defensive and dynamic operations

Most Federal Reserve open-market operations are *defensive*. They are designed not to bring about a change in monetary conditions, but to offset changes in factors in the bank reserve equation not controlled by the Federal Reserve System that would cause undesired effects. *Dynamic* operations are purchases and sales of U.S. government securities made to promote economic stability or to provide for economic growth. Although there are fourteen factors in the bank reserve equation affecting member bank reserves, the Federal Reserve authorities directly control only two of them—their holdings of U.S. government securities and of foreign currencies. They may also try to influence the volume of their loans outstanding through variations in the discount rate, but lending to member banks is done at the initiative of commercial banks and cannot be precisely controlled through changes in the discount rate.

Prior to 1971, defensive operations had to be used to offset the effect of outflows of gold. In 1957, the gold stock of the United States Treasury amounted to $22.9 billion; by 1971, it had fallen to less than half that amount. If the gold outflow during this fourteen-year period had not been offset by open-market purchases, it would have caused a decrease in the monetary base and tight monetary conditions. Defensive operations have also been used to offset weekly variations in float and in the Treasury's deposits. Such changes can have disturbing short-run effects on the monetary base; the Federal Reserve authorities attempt to neutralize such effects through appropriate open-market operations.

In 1978, the scale of the Federal Reserve's combined defensive and dynamic open-market operations was enormous. Although the net increase in the amount of United States government securities owned by the Federal Reserve banks was only $7 billion, over the course of the year gross purchases of securities amounted to about $728 billion and gross sales to about $721 billion.[3]

Maturity of securities purchased

For five years starting in 1953, the FOMC limited open-market operations to bills or other short-term securities maturing within one year. Supporters of the "bills only" policy pointed out that there is an advantage to knowing which type of government securities would be affected by Federal Reserve operations. Although open-market operations are still usually in short-term securities, the limitation of open-market operations to short-term securities was criticized as unnecessarily restrictive and at times unwise.[4]

In the early 1960s, the Treasury and the Federal Reserve System attempted to lower long-term interest rates and raise short-term ones—a policy known as twisting the yield curve. The purpose of this policy was to stimulate the domestic economy, and at the same time to encourage foreign owners of dollars to keep their funds invested in short-term securities in the United States. The policy appeared to have little effect on raising short-term rates, and although long-term yields on U.S. government securities were lowered, there was little effect on mortgage rates and corporate bond yields—the real objectives of the program.

Foreign currency operations

Since 1962, the Federal Reserve has bought and sold foreign currencies as well as U.S. government securities. By having balances in foreign currencies, the Federal Reserve is in a position to purchase dollars in the foreign exchange market whenever it believes such action is necessary in order to keep exchange rates between the dollar and other currencies at the desired level. The objective of these transactions is not part of monetary policy per se, but an effort at controlling exchange rates between the dollar and foreign currencies.

Changes in the discount rate

Changing the discount rate charged on loans to member banks was the principal instrument of control initially authorized in the Federal Reserve Act. Although in the 1920s member banks regularly borrowed funds from the Reserve banks, following the Great Depression and during World War II there was very little borrowing. In 1955, the Federal Reserve System revised its Regulation A which defines the procedures and conditions for making loans to member banks, and since then member banks have actively borrowed from the Federal Reserve banks.[5]

Loans by Federal Reserve banks

Normally member banks may borrow from the Federal Reserve banks only for short periods and for the purpose of obtaining additional reserves to meet reserve requirements. However, in 1973–1974 the lending policies of the Federal Reserve banks were broadened so that smaller banks that do not have reliable access to national money markets may arrange in advance to borrow for seasonal needs. Also, banks may now borrow for unusual or emergency circumstances, and banks with heavy deposit drains or sudden loan losses may borrow relatively large amounts at a special low rate of interest for more than eight weeks.

The Federal Reserve banks discourage borrowing for profit. In practice it is not easy for a Federal Reserve bank to refuse loans to member banks which are short of reserves because of overexpansion of their loans; Federal Reserve officials would be reluctant to refuse a loan if denial reflected unfavorably on the soundness of a member bank. Also, the availability of funds for borrowing is considered an important inducement to membership. Despite these considerations, discount officers at the Federal Reserve banks will consult with banks that are borrowing excessively, and banks cannot always rely on borrowing from the Federal Reserve banks.

Discount rate policy

Figure 13.1 shows the changes in the discount rate at the Federal Reserve Bank of New York from 1971 to 1979. The discount rate is not changed more than several times a year, even though the board of directors of each Federal Reserve bank is required to either reestablish or change the existing discount rate every fourteen days. Recommended changes are immediately reported to the Board of Governors, which may either veto or approve the rate selected. As Figure 13.1 shows, the Reserve banks have kept the discount rate in line with the Treasury bill rate by raising the discount rate in periods of expansion and lowering it in periods of recession. In periods of expansion, if the discount rate were permitted to lag behind the rise in other money market rates, borrowing from the Federal Reserve banks would become very profitable. In recessions, if the discount rate were not lowered in line with money market rates, borrowing from the Federal Reserve banks would in effect be removed as a source of liquidity for most banks.

Cyclical movement of member bank borrowing

During the severe drop in economic activity in 1974–1975, member bank borrowing dropped sharply, and during the expansion from 1976 to 1979, member bank borrowing increased. Member bank borrowing has also fluctuated with the cycle during other business cycles. As shown in Figure 13.2, there is a close correlation between total member bank borrowing and the differential between the federal funds rate (the cost of borrowing funds from other commercial banks) and the discount rate (the cost of borrowing funds from the Federal Reserve banks). The cyclical changes in the differential between these two rates, and thus the cyclical variations in member bank borrowing, are the result of the tendency for changes made by the Federal Reserve banks in the discount rate to lag behind the upward movement in money market rates in periods of prosperity, and to lag behind downward movements of money market rates during periods of recession. Commercial banks obtain needed funds where the cost is lowest. If the discount rate lags behind the federal funds rate, they are induced to increase their borrowing of reserves from the Federal Reserve banks rather than from other commercial banks.

The cyclical variations in member bank loans from the Reserve banks have been criticized as having a destabilizing effect.[6] By itself, an increase in member bank borrowing increases the monetary base, and a decrease reduces the monetary base. However, Federal Reserve au-

Figure 13.1
The Discount Rate and
the Treasury Bill Rate,
1971–1979

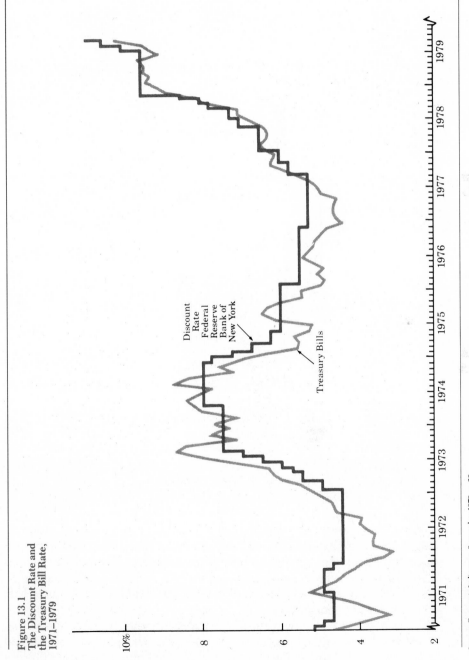

Discount
Rate
Federal
Reserve
Bank of
New York

Treasury Bills

10%

8

6

4

2

1971   1972   1973   1974   1975   1976   1977   1978   1979

Source: *Economic Indicators*, September 1979, p. 30.

Figure 13.2
Member Bank
Borrowings and Short-
Term Interest Rate
Differential,
1969–1979

Latest data plotted: February

Source: R. Alton Gilbert, "Benefits of Borrowing from the Federal Reserve When the Discount Rate is Below Market Interest
Rates," Federal Reserve Bank of St. Louis, *Review*, March 1979, p. 27.

thorities believe that it is misleading to evaluate discount rate policy in
isolation from open-market operations and changes in legal reserve
requirements. An increase in borrowing in a period of prosperity could
be offset by selling securities in the open market, and a decline in
borrowing in a period of recession could be offset by purchases of U.S.
government securities.

In order to prevent cyclical variations in member bank borrowing,
some economists have recommended that the discount rate be changed
automatically with changes in the Treasury bill rate so that the differen-

tial between the discount rate and the Treasury bill rate would be kept constant.[7] From 1956 to 1962, the discount rate in Canada was automatically adjusted each week to keep it one-fourth of one percent above the latest average tender rate for their ninety-day Treasury bills. This policy was discontinued in 1962 during a foreign exchange crisis.

Psychological effects

Changes in the discount rate may have desirable psychological effects because of the wide publicity given in the news to such changes. A rise in the discount rate would signal to the public that monetary policy is becoming tighter, and a lowering, the opposite. If a rise in the discount rate causes business firms to become more cautious about their spending plans, this in itself would have the effect desired. However, unless the Federal Reserve authorities used the other instruments of control to achieve the results indicated by changes in the discount rate, relying on discount rate changes to forecast developments in the economy could be hazardous.

Member bank borrowing and bank liquidity

Even though discount rate policy is no longer an important instrument of monetary control, a 1968 Federal Reserve study concluded that more adequate borrowing facilities were needed to assure bank liquidity.[8] Banks may provide for their liquidity by borrowing from the Federal Reserve banks, as well as by investing in liquid assets such as Treasury bills, commercial paper, or federal funds sold. Even though borrowing from the Federal Reserve banks is usually limited to fifteen days, it gives the bank time to accumulate funds by letting loans run off. In recent decades, there has been a change in the way in which many banks provide for liquidity. The importance of borrowing by commercial banks has increased, while the importance of holding liquid assets has diminished. The sharp rise in the loan-to-deposit ratio of member banks from 17 percent in 1945 to almost 82 percent in April 1979 illustrates the dramatic decline in the importance of holding liquid assets.

Still keep it, for banks to be liquid

Changes in legal reserve requirements

Early in the history of the Federal Reserve System, reserve requirements for demand deposits at member banks were fixed at 13 percent for central reserve city banks (those in New York and Chicago), 10 percent for reserve city banks, and 7 percent for banks in all other cities (country banks), and at 3 percent for time deposits in all banks. These reserve requirements were unchanged until the Great Depression.

Authority to vary reserve requirements was first given to the Federal

Reserve in 1933. In that year, the Federal Reserve Board was given emergency authority, to be exercised only with the permission of the President of the United States, to vary reserve requirements up to double the former percentages: between 13 and 26 percent for demand deposits at central reserve city banks, 10 to 20 percent at reserve city banks, 7 to 14 percent at country banks, and 3 to 6 percent for time deposits at all banks. The Banking Act of 1935 made this instrument of control permanent, and presidential approval was no longer required.

Starting in the 1960s, the Federal Reserve has shifted from a policy of setting reserve requirements according to the size or classification of the city in which the bank is located to a policy of setting requirements according to the size of the bank, regardless of its geographical location.[9] In 1972, city-size criteria were dropped completely. Banks are now classified into five categories based on the net amount of demand deposits. Banks with net demand deposits of over $400 million, the largest of the five classes, are still designated as reserve city banks, even though that designation is not based on geographical location. In 1980, the legal ranges between which reserve requirements could be set were:

	Range
Net demand deposits:	
Reserve-city banks	10–22 percent
Other banks	7–14 percent
Time deposits	3–10 percent

Measuring reserves

For demand deposits, required reserves are based on a bank's *net demand deposits*. To calculate net demand deposits, a bank deducts from its total demand deposits the amount of its balances at other commercial banks and the volume of checks it has in process of collection.

During the history of the Federal Reserve System, the treatment of cash in vault as reserves has been changed several times. In the original Federal Reserve Act, member banks were permitted to count half of their vault cash, plus their total deposits at the Federal Reserve banks, as reserves. From 1917 to 1959, only deposits at the Reserve banks had qualified as reserves. Since 1960, member banks have been permitted to include all of their vault cash as reserves.

Current reserve requirements

Table 13.1 shows the changes in reserve requirements from 1972 to 1980. Reserve requirements have become much more complicated than shown in this table because of the growth of nondeposit sources of funds at member banks. In 1969, the Federal Reserve System extended reserve requirements to cover borrowing from foreign branches—an expanding source of funds for most large commercial banks. In 1973 and 1975, however, the reserve requirements on borrowing from foreign banks were cut sharply, and in 1978 they were eliminated in order to improve the international position of the dollar.[10]

In 1970, the Federal Reserve authorities extended reserve requirements to commercial paper issued by bank holding companies.[11] The reserve ratio for commercial paper was set at 5 percent. Bank holding companies had issued commercial paper as a method of avoiding the maximum interest rates set on time deposits under Regulation Q. Market interest rates were so much higher than the ceilings on time deposits that banks were losing these deposits and issued commercial paper in order to make up the loss.

From late 1979 to July 1980, a marginal reserve requirement of 8 percent (later raised to 10 percent) was extended to the "managed liabilities" of very large banks. The requirements applied only to managed liabilities in excess of $100 million or in excess of the amount of these held by a bank in a base period. Managed liabilities (which a bank can expand on its own initiative) include large time deposits, borrowings from foreign banks, securities repurchase agreements, and federal funds borrowed. Prior to this temporary expansion in reserve requirements, there had been no required reserves for securities repurchase agreements or for federal funds purchased from other commercial banks.

The Depository Institutions Deregulation and Monetary Control Act of 1980 provides for sweeping changes in reserve requirements. The authority of the Federal Reserve to set reserve requirements on transaction accounts and nonpersonal time deposits was extended to nonmember banks and thrift institutions. Transaction accounts include demand deposits, interest bearing NOW accounts, share draft accounts, ATS accounts, phone transfer accounts, and bill paying accounts. At the end of the eight-year phase-in period, the reserve requirement for transaction balances at all depository institutions will be 3 percent on balances up to $25 million and 12 percent on balances in excess of $25 million. (This may be varied between 8 and 14 percent.) No reserves will be required for time deposits of individuals, but the reserve requirement for nonpersonal time deposits will be 3 percent. (This may be varied between 0 and 9 percent.) Under some conditions, an additional reserve of up to 4 percent may be required on transaction accounts, and interest will be paid on these additional reserves.

all banks must hold res w/ Fed Res

Differences in reserve requirements

The Federal Reserve has frequently been criticized for having different reserve requirements for different types of deposits and different sized banks. This is because whenever the public shifts demand deposits

Table 13.1
Reserve Requirements of Member Banks, November 1972–February 1980
(percent of deposits)

Date	Net demand deposits					Time deposits[a]						
	Under $2 million	Over $2 million to $10 million	Over $10 million to $100 million	Over $100 million to $400 million	Over $400 million (Reserve city)	Savings deposits	Other time deposits					
							Up to $5 million			In excess of $5 million		
							Maturing in:			Maturing in:		
							30-179 days	180 days to 4 yrs.	4 yrs. or more	30-179 days	180 days to 4 yrs.	4 yrs. or more
Nov. 16, 1972	8%	10%	12%	13%	17½%	3%	3%			5%		
July 19, 1973	8	10½	12½	13½	18	3	3			5		
Dec 12, 1974	8	10½	12½	13½	17½	3	3%	3%	3%	6%	3%	3%
Feb. 13, 1975	7½	10	12	13	16½	3	3	3	3	6	3	3
Oct. 30, 1975	7½	10	12	13	16½	3	3	3	1	6	3	1
Jan. 8, 1976	7½	10	12	13	16½	3	3	2½	1	6	2½	1
Dec. 30, 1976	7	9½	11¾	12¾	16¼	3	3	2½	1	6	2½	1

[a]The average of reserves on savings and other time deposits must be at least 3 percent.
Source: *Federal Reserve Bulletin*, December 1976, p. A7; and March 1980, p. A9.

between different sized banks, the total quantity of deposits in the banking system may change. The same may occur when the public shifts between time deposits and demand deposits, or between different types of time deposits.

Because of the increase before 1980 in the number of categories of deposits having different reserve requirements, Federal Reserve authorities were less able to precisely control the money supply than they formerly were. From 1960 to 1966, for reserve purposes there were only three categories of deposits: demand deposits in central reserve and reserve city banks, demand deposits in country banks, and time deposits in all classes of banks. In 1979, there were five categories for banks with different amounts of demand deposits and seven categories for time deposits. The Federal Reserve initiated in 1974 a new policy of varying reserve requirements with the maturity of time deposits (excluding savings deposits). Reserve requirements on longer-term time deposits were lowered relative to those on short-term time deposits in order to induce banks to rely more on long-term, less volatile sources of funds. Although the Federal Reserve authorities may attempt to offset the effect of shifts among deposits with different reserve requirements through appropriate open-market operations, the need to take such actions complicates the administration of monetary policy. There may be a lag in the time between such shifts and the time they become known to the monetary authorities.

In the past, shifts from deposits in nonmember banks (which were not required to hold reserves in the Federal Reserve banks) to member banks also affected the quantity of deposits and made it more difficult to control the money supply precisely. The new banking legislation in 1980 authorizes the Federal Reserve to set the reserve requirements for transaction accounts and nonpersonal time deposits of nonmember banks, and eventually the reserve requirements for nonmember banks will be the same as for member banks.

Effects of changes in reserve requirements on the money supply

Changes in reserve requirements can be used as a countercyclical tool, and important reductions in legal reserve ratios were made in some recent years of business slack—1953–1954, 1958, 1970, and 1974–1975. Lowering reserve requirements has the same effect on the supply of money and bank credit as open-market purchases, even though open-market purchases increase the monetary base, while lower reserve requirements permit member banks to hold a larger volume of deposits with the same monetary base.

On the other hand, the monetary authorities have been reluctant to raise legal reserve requirements—a countercyclical tool that would have effects like open-market sales. A rise could embarrass banks that are not sufficiently liquid to easily meet the higher reserve requirements. Despite its usual reluctance to raise reserve requirements, in 1973–1974, when the rate of inflation was very rapid, the Federal Reserve temporarily raised reserve requirements for banks holding net demand deposits over $2 million by one-half of one percent. Also, in some recent years, reserve requirements have been added for nondeposit sources of funds.

The principal reason the Federal Reserve authorities do not often change required reserve ratios is that changing them is a clumsy instrument of control. Small changes in reserve requirements result in large changes in the volume of bank loans and deposits. The principal argument in favor of using this instrument of control is that it may directly affect every member bank in the country. In contrast, open-market operations initially affect only a few banks—although eventually the effects are scattered throughout the system. The announcement of a change in reserve requirements is always widely publicized and may have a greater psychological impact than open-market operations. Some foreign countries have to use changes in reserve requirements as an instrument of control because their securities markets are not sufficiently developed to permit successful open-market operations.[12]

Downward trend in reserve requirements

A significant portion of the growth in the money supply since World War II has been accomplished through lowering legal reserve ratios rather than through open-market operations. This is partly because of the willingness of the Federal Reserve to lower reserve requirements during slack periods, but reluctance to use countercyclical changes during prosperity. Also, lowering reserve requirements appealed to bankers because lower requirements increased the percentage of the assets of member banks earning income and improved the competitive position of member banks relative to nonmember banks and thrift institutions. On the other hand, the U.S. Treasury would favor open-market purchases rather than lowering reserve requirements during slack periods because open-market purchases providing for the growth in the money supply would reduce the interest cost of the national debt.[13] The banking legislation in 1980 giving the Federal Reserve the power to set the same reserve requirements for transaction accounts and nonpersonal time deposits at all depository institutions may induce the Federal Reserve to use changes in reserve requirements as an instrument of control more frequently because raising reserve requirements will no longer put member banks at a competitive disadvantage compared to nonmember banks and thrift institutions.

Criticisms of monetary policy during the Great Depression and in the 1930s

Historians of monetary policy spanning the stock market boom in the late 1920s and the Great Depression have been critical of the Federal Reserve's operations during this period.[14] In the late 1920s, there was disagreement—particularly between the Board of Governors in Washington and the twelve banks—about how to deal with stock market speculation. The Board was in favor of cutting off loans to member banks that were making financial loans on securities—in order to reduce speculative activity—but was opposed to raising the discount rate for this purpose. The Board felt that raising the discount rate might be too hard on business at a time when agriculture was in a difficult situation. Officials of the Federal Reserve Bank of New York, on the other hand, held that the policy of attempting to cut off speculative loans was ineffective. In 1927, the Federal Reserve System actually purchased securities in the open market (which reduced market interest rates) and reduced the discount rate. These actions seemed to make the problem of speculation worse. Policy was then reversed in 1928 and through the summer of 1929. For sixteen months, there was no increase in *M-1* plus time deposits in commercial banks, a serious stock market crash occurred in October 1929, and the period called the Great Depression began.

During the depression, the Federal Reserve allowed the U.S. money supply to contract sharply. The money supply declined because commercial banks reduced the amount they borrowed at the Federal Reserve banks, persons withdrew currency from banks, and foreigners purchased gold from the United States because they expected the country to go off the gold standard and therefore that the price of gold in terms of dollars would rise. By 1930, the Reserve Board in Washington had become dominant and it was opposed to the more expansionist open-market policy advocated by officials of the Federal Reserve Bank of New York to combat the depression. Although large-scale open-market purchases might have been used to offset the forces causing monetary contraction, this was not done until 1932. There were several reasons that open-market purchases were not used sooner: (1) few people at the time realized the severity of the situation or had a clear understanding of the actions a central bank ought to take in a period of financial difficulties; (2) bankers opposed open-market purchases because they thought this would lower interest rates even further than they had already fallen; (3) it was thought that open-market purchases would not have a stimulating effect because they would cause banks to borrow less; (4) maintaining the quantity of money during a serious depression was not then regarded as an important objective of monetary policy; and (5) it was thought that more aggressive open-market purchases would stimulate a gold outflow.

The original purpose of the authority to vary reserve requirements introduced in 1933 was for the perceived special need of enabling the Federal Reserve System to reduce the very large amount of excess reserves that member banks had accumulated. The huge excess in reserves was viewed as a potential source of inflation. Although the Federal Reserve authorities can normally reduce excess reserves by selling securities in the open market, in the 1930s they did not own sufficient government securities to be able to eliminate the large amount of excess reserves in that way. When the official price of gold was raised from $20.67 to $35.00 per fine ounce in 1934, the value of the total gold stock owned by the United States Treasury increased, causing the excess reserves of commercial banks to rise sharply. Beginning in 1935 the political situation in Europe resulted in even more gold arriving in the United States, adding further to the volume of excess reserves.

In 1936–1937, the Federal Reserve sharply raised member bank reserve requirements. This was followed by the depression of 1937–1938, and with it came a decline in bond prices and a rise in interest yields. These events were attributed in part to the action taken by the Federal Reserve. In 1938, the Federal Reserve reversed its policy and reduced reserve requirements for the purpose of stimulating recovery.

Selective credit controls

The Federal Reserve's selective instruments of control are used primarily to influence the allocation of credit—to control the use of a particular type of credit without decreasing the total volume of money and bank credit. One of the criticisms of the use of selective controls is that they are sometimes used as substitutes for the major instruments of control, when stronger policies are needed.[15]

Margin requirements

In the Securities and Exchange Act of 1934, the Board of Governors was empowered to set margin requirements to regulate loans made for the purpose of purchasing or carrying securities. The margin is the percentage of the market value of the stocks purchased and pledged as collateral that the customer must pay for at time of purchase (always between 25 and 100 percent). With a margin of 80 percent, for example, an individual may borrow only $200 on the purchase of $1,000 of stock. If the price of the stock falls after purchase, or if the Federal Reserve raises the required margin, Federal Reserve regulations do not require the borrower to reduce the amount of the loan—but the lending institution may require this.

Table 13.2 shows changes in the margins required during the period from 1955 to 1979. Raising margin requirements, by making it more difficult for persons to borrow, is intended to dampen the demand for securities. At times, margin requirements have had the effect of inducing borrowers to obtain funds from lenders not covered by the law— before the 1968 law extended the scope of the requirements to include lenders other than banks, brokers, and dealers.

Table 13.2
Margin Requirements, 1955–1979

Effective Date	Stocks	Convertible Bonds
April 23, 1955	70%	—
Jan. 16, 1958	50	—
Aug. 5, 1958	70	—
Oct. 16, 1958	90	—
July 28, 1960	70	—
July 10, 1962	50	—
Nov. 6, 1963	70	—
Mar. 11, 1968	70	50%
June 8, 1968	80	60
May 6, 1970	65	50
Dec. 6, 1971	55	50
Nov. 24, 1972	65	50
Jan. 3, 1974	50	50

Source: Board of Governors of the Federal Reserve System, *65th Annual Report, 1978*, p. 411; and *Federal Reserve Bulletin*, March 1980, p. A28.

Regulation of interest rates on deposits

The Federal Reserve's Regulation Q—prohibiting the payment of interest on demand deposits and setting maximum rates of interest payable on time deposits in commercial banks—was established in 1933. At first these controls were largely ineffective because of the low levels of market interest rates at that time.

Regulation Q was believed necessary to restrict competition for deposits and to make it unnecessary for banks to invest in excessively risky loans and investments that would earn high enough rates of return to pay higher interest rates on time deposits than those allowed. This is not a strong argument because, even with ceilings set on interest rates, there would be an inducement for banks to maximize their profits by seeking loans and investments with the highest possible rates of return. Many commercial banks supported Regulation Q because they felt that fixed interest rates would allow them to obtain funds at a relatively low cost. After World War II, growing competition between commercial banks and the thrift institutions resulted in a change in the attitude of some commercial bankers.

The maximum interest rates allowed on time deposits in commercial banks and thrift institutions in 1980 are shown in Table 13.3. In addition to the ceilings shown in this table, member banks may not pay higher interest rates than those permitted by state laws. Prior to 1957, member banks could pay only up to 2½ percent on savings and time deposits. Since then, there has been a gradual erosion of the Regulation Q ceilings combined with a growing complexity in the regulations set. The payment of interest on transaction balances similar to demand deposits is now permitted in the case of NOW accounts, ATS accounts, and securities repurchase agreements. In 1970 and 1973, interest ceilings were suspended in two steps on all certificates of deposit of $100,000 or larger. In 1978, banks were permitted to offer six-month money market certificates with rates of return that vary with the six-month Treasury bill rate, and, in 1980, two-and-one-half-year floating rate certificates with rates that vary with the rates on two-and-one-half-year Treasury notes. In 1980, it was announced that Regulation Q interest rate ceilings would be phased out over the next six years.

Table 13.3
Maximum Interest Rates Payable on Time Deposits in Effect on February 29, 1980

Type of Deposit	Commercial Banks	Savings and Loan Associations and Mutual Savings Banks
Savings deposits	5¼%	5½%
NOW accounts	5	5
Other time deposits[a]		
Less than $100,000:		
30 to 89 days	5¼	*
90 days to 2 years	5½	5¾
2 to 2½ years	6	6½
2½ years to 4 years	6½	6¾
4 to 6 years	7¼	7½
6 to 8 years	7½	7¾
8 years or more	7¾	8
Governmental units	8	8
IRAs and Keogh plans[b]	8	8
$100,000 or more	c	c

[a]Some exceptions to maximum rates for foreign time deposits.
[b]This type of account maturing in less than 3 years subject to regular ceilings.
[c]Maximum rates on time deposits in denominations of $100,000 or more were suspended in two steps in 1970 and 1973.
* No separate account category.
Source: *Federal Reserve Bulletin*, March 1980, p. A10.

Eligibility requirements

The Federal Reserve's eligibility requirements governing the *kind of collateral* required for loans made to member banks have been made much less restrictive over the years and the requirements serve little purpose today. The original importance of eligibility requirements was related to dependence on the commercial loan theory of central banking.

Controls over consumer and real estate credit

In the World War II and Korean War periods, the Board of Governors was given the power to regulate minimum down payments and maximum maturities of credit lent for the purchase of automobiles, other consumer durables, and in 1950–1952 for housing. Because few durable consumer goods were being produced, credit regulations to reduce their demand were largely unnecessary. A principal problem in the administration of this type of control has been the extreme difficulty of eliminating evasion.[16]

Under the Credit Control Act of 1969, the President may authorize the Federal Reserve System to control any or all extensions of credit. Registration or licensing may be required and the following may be prescribed: maximum amount of individual loans, maximum rate of interest, maximum maturity, and amount of periodic payments. In March 1980, as part of an anti-inflation program that included spending cuts and tax increases, President Carter temporarily authorized the Federal Reserve to use the broad powers granted in this act to ask banks to hold growth of loans to 6 to 9 percent in 1980, and to require a marginal reserve of 15 percent on increases in total assets of money market mutual funds and on increases in credit card indebtedness or revolving credit extended by banks, thrift institutions, finance companies, retailers, gasoline companies, and credit card companies.

Summary

Purchase of U.S. government securities by the Federal Reserve banks has an expansionary effect on the monetary base, and sales have a restraining effect. Open-market policy is formulated by the Federal Open Market Committee and administered by the manager of the open-market account at the Federal Reserve Bank of New York.

Variations in the volume of member bank borrowing from the Federal Reserve banks depend on changes in the relative level of the discount rate as compared with other short-term interest rates. Member banks typically increase their borrowing from the Federal Reserve banks in periods of business expansion and decrease it during periods of business contraction.

The Federal Reserve authorities do not often use changes in the legal reserve requirements of member banks as an instrument of control, because the administration of open-market operations is simpler and the results are less severe.

The most important selective instrument of control of the Federal

Reserve System has been Regulation Q, which sets ceiling rates of interest on time deposits in commercial banks. Regulation Q controls will be phased out in the next six years.

Notes

1. Each year the Board of Governors, in its *Annual Report,* discusses its objectives for the previous year and the measures it took in attempting to achieve them. See Board of Governors of the Federal Reserve System, *65th Annual Report, 1978.*

2. For a description of the technique of open-market operations, see Paul Meek, *Open Market Operations* (New York: Federal Reserve Bank of New York, 1973).

3. William Poole, "The Monetary Deceleration: What Does It Mean and Why Is It Happening?" *Brookings Papers on Economic Activity,* 1: 1979, p. 235.

4. For the arguments for and against the bills-only policy, see Otto Eckstein and John Kareken, "A Background Memo on the Federal Reserve's 'Bills Only' Policy," in U.S. Congress, Joint Economic Committee, *Employment, Growth, and Price Levels: Hearings, July 24–30, 1959, Part 6A,* 86th Cong., 1st sess., 1959, pp. 1248–1249.

5. See "Regulation A, Advances and Discounts by Federal Reserve Banks," *Federal Reserve Bulletin* 41 (January 1955), pp. 8–14.

6. Edward C. Simmons, "A Note on the Revival of Federal Reserve Discount Policy," *Journal of Finance* 11 (December 1956), pp. 413–421; Warren L. Smith, "The Discount Rate as a Credit-Control Weapon," *Journal of Political Economy* 66 (April 1958), pp. 171–177; Charles R. Whittlesey, "Credit Policy at the Discount Window," *Quarterly Journal of Economics* 73 (May 1959), pp. 207–216; and Milton Friedman, *A Program for Monetary Stability* (New York: Fordham University Press, 1960), Chapter 2.

7. Joseph Aschheim, *Techniques of Monetary Control* (Baltimore: The Johns Hopkins Press, 1961), pp. 7–8, 83–98.

8. "Reappraisal of the Federal Reserve Discount Mechanism," *Federal Reserve Bulletin* 54 (July 1968), pp. 545–551.

9. The old policy of classifying cities for purposes of setting different reserve requirements goes back to the National Banking System. Under the National Banking System, reserve requirements for both time and demand deposits were 25 percent for banks in large and medium-sized cities, and 15 percent elsewhere.

10. Also in 1978, reserve requirements were raised for some deposit sources because of international considerations. A supplementary 2 per-

cent reserve requirement was added for all time deposits in denominations of $100,000 or more. This was done to "increase the incentive for member banks to borrow from abroad and thereby strengthen the dollar" and "to moderate the recent relatively rapid expansion in bank credit." This supplementary reserve requirement was ended in 1980.

11. "Amendments to Regulation D, Reserves of Member Banks," *57th Annual Report, 1970* (Washington, D.C.: Board of Governors of the Federal Reserve System, 1971), pp. 75–76.

12. See Peter G. Fousek, *Foreign Central Banking: The Instruments of Monetary Policy* (New York: Federal Reserve Bank of New York, 1957), pp. 10–11; and J. Aschheim, *Techniques of Monetary Control*, p. 32.

13. Increasing the money supply through open-market purchases means a larger portion of the national debt owned by the Federal Reserve banks, and a smaller amount of interest paid by the Treasury to the public. The earnings of the Federal Reserve banks, less what they need to cover operating expenses, pay the fixed rate of dividend, and build up their surplus, are required by law to be paid to the Treasury.

14. Lester V. Chandler, *American Monetary Policy, 1928–1941* (New York: Harper and Row, Publishers, 1971); and Milton Friedman and Anna J. Schwartz, *A Monetary History of the United States, 1867–1960* (Princeton: Princeton University Press, 1963), Chapters 6 and 7.

15. See Friedman, *A Program for Monetary Stability*, pp. 26–27.

16. Board of Governors of the Federal Reserve System, *Consumer Instalment Credit*, Vol. I, Part I, *Growth and Import* (Washington, D.C.: U.S. Government Printing Office, 1957), pp. 310–315.

Questions

13.1. Describe the way in which the Federal Reserve banks purchase and sell government securities.

13.2. What is the objective of defensive open-market operations?

13.3. Under what conditions is the discount rate typically lowered? Under what conditions is it raised?

13.4. Explain why the total amount of discounting may increase in a period of inflation even though the discount rate is raised. Why may total discounting decline in a period of recession even though the discount rate is lowered?

13.5. What are the shortcomings of changes in the discount rate as an instrument of control?

13.6. Should discounting at the Federal Reserve banks be eliminated?

13.7. What were some of the changes made in the 1970s in the reserve requirements of the member banks?

13.8. What changes in reserve requirements did the Depository Institutions Deregulation and Monetary Control Act of 1980 provide for?

13.9. Explain the way in which a reduction in the legal reserve ratios of the member banks makes possible an expansion in their loans and investments and in their deposits, and explain the process by which this comes about.

13.10. What are the advantages and disadvantages of changes in reserve requirements as an instrument of control?

13.11. Explain the nature of margin requirements for borrowing for the purchase of corporation stock.

13.12. What were the objectives of the Federal Reserve's controls over maximum rates of interest payable on time deposits?

13.13. Is interest currently paid on demand deposits? Explain.

13.14. Know the meaning and significance of the following terms and concepts: easy monetary policy, tight monetary policy, open-market operations, selective instruments of control, bills-only policy, defensive operations, dynamic operations, discount rate, net demand deposits, legal ranges for reserve requirements, margin requirements, twisting the yield curve, transaction accounts, nonpersonal time deposits, managed liabilities.

14

In the 1970s, the Federal Reserve System had targets for both the federal funds rate and the rate of increase in the principal monetary aggregates. The targets were used to measure the ease or tightness of monetary policy.

TARGETS OF MONETARY POLICY

To conduct monetary policy, the Federal Reserve authorities use targets that serve as gauges to guide their open-market operations.[1] They watch the targets in order to tell whether the actions they have taken are expansionary, restraining, or neutral. The targets of monetary policy are different from the basic goals—control of such economic variables as the price level, the rate of unemployment, economic growth, and the balance of payments. The goals cannot serve as targets because it takes too long for a change in monetary policy to affect them. Also, the goals may be affected by fiscal policy, government wage and price ceilings, and general economic conditions, as well as by monetary policy.

The Federal Reserve's policy instruments themselves are not useful as targets. The volume of open-market purchases or sales alone is an unsatisfactory measure of the ease or tightness of monetary policy because of the numerous other factors in the bank reserve equation that may affect the monetary base. Changes in the discount rate are also a poor indicator of the direction of monetary policy because the effect of such changes depends on the response of the member banks.

During the past 40 years, the conduct of monetary policy may be divided into three periods: (1) the years during and immediately following World War II from 1941 to 1951, in which the Federal Reserve System set ceiling interest rates on U.S. government securities; (2) the period from 1951 to 1973, in which the principal target of monetary policy was the control of the level of free reserves; and (3) the period starting in 1973, in which the Federal Reserve had two targets—the level of the federal funds rate and the rate of growth of certain monetary aggregates. In October 1979, the Federal Reserve authorities announced that they would begin placing greater emphasis on the targets for the monetary aggregates than on the target for the federal funds rate.

Before the targets: interest rate ceilings

From 1941 to 1951, the Federal Reserve's main objective was to keep market interest rates for U.S. government securities within ceiling levels that had been set at the beginning of World War II. The Federal Reserve had set the following interest rate ceilings:

Type of U.S. Government Security	Ceiling Rate of Interest
Bills, 90-day	⅜%
Certificates, 1-year*	⅞
Bonds, over 10 years	2½

*The certificates were a short-term security with a maximum maturity of one year which had a coupon rate of interest and other characteristics that were similar to U.S. Treasury bonds. No certificates have been issued since 1967.

These very low rates were based on the market rates of interest that prevailed when World War II began.

The policy of preventing market interest rates on government securities from rising originally had two major objectives: to keep interest costs in the federal budget as low as possible, and to prevent investors from speculating on a rise in interest rates during the war. It was feared that such speculation might cause investors to postpone purchases of bonds, as they had during World War I.

The ceilings were called a *bond-support program* because, in order to keep yields on U.S. government securities from rising, the authorities had to prevent security prices from falling. Yields were kept from rising by open-market purchases of government securities whenever their prices fell below the support levels.

The bond-support program was continued for several years after the war. It was thought that ending the program might cause a panic in the government securities market and would be unfair to investors who had purchased securities during the war. In addition, low market interest rates were desired as a method of stimulating the economy.

Figure 14.1 shows that efforts to keep yields on U.S. government securities from rising above the ceilings were successful. Occasionally yields fell below, but very seldom did they rise above the ceilings. The ceiling rates on Treasury bills and certificates were relaxed in 1947, but not on bonds until 1951. The relatively effective wartime price and wage controls probably contributed to the successful control of interest rates. If the prices of goods and services had risen, market interest rates also would have tended to rise in order to discount the higher expected rate of inflation. An even larger volume of open-market purchases would have been necessary in order to keep market interest rates at the ceiling levels.

During the first seven months of the Korean War in 1950–51, the bond-support program contributed to a 6 percent rise in the consumer price index (and an 11 percent increase in wholesale prices). The war-induced business expansion tended to cause market interest rates to rise. To prevent interest rates from rising, the Federal Reserve had to accelerate its purchases of U.S. government securities, and member bank reserves rose 12 percent. This was followed by an increase of nearly 20 percent in bank loans and 8 percent in demand deposits. This experience led to the termination of the bond-support program in 1951. The change was made in an announcement known as the *Treasury-Federal Reserve Accord.* The immediate effect of the Accord was to enable the Federal Reserve to stop increasing bank reserves at an inflationary rate. The most important effect was that in the future the Federal Reserve authorities would be able to use their instruments of control to attempt to stabilize the economy—by following an easy policy when the economy was slack and a tight policy when the economy needed to be slowed down.

Figure 14.1
Yields on U.S.
Government Securities,
1941-1951

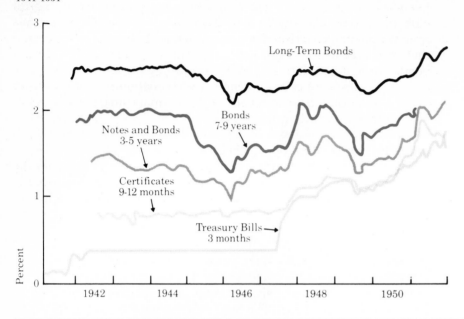

Source: Board of Governors of the Federal Reserve System, *Historical Supplement to Federal Reserve Chart Book on Financial and Business Statistics*, September 1960. p. 39.

Controlling the level of free reserves

 Free reserves—the excess reserves of member banks *less* their borrowing from the Federal Reserve banks—were an important target of monetary policy from the Accord of 1951 until the 1970s.[2] In order to stimulate the economy, the Reserve banks would purchase a sufficient quantity of securities to raise the level of free reserves. On the other hand, when inflation occurred, the account manager at the Federal Reserve Bank of New York would sell enough securities to lower the level of free reserves.

The Federal Reserve System had no difficulty controlling the level of free reserves. Open-market purchases tended to affect both components of free reserves—to increase excess reserves and to decrease member bank borrowing at the Federal Reserve banks. Open-market sales tended to decrease excess reserves and to increase member bank borrowing.

A rise in the level of free reserves was expected to lower market interest rates and to increase the rate of expansion in the money supply. (If free reserves fell, market interest rates were expected to rise and the growth of the money supply to slow down.) When the level of free reserves is low or negative, the excess reserves of banks are low, and banks are heavily in debt to the Reserve banks. This illiquidity causes banks to raise their interest rates and take steps to restrain the expansion in their loans and investments. Being heavily in debt to the Federal Reserve banks has long been regarded as a sign of weakness, and because such borrowing is usually only short-term, there is pressure for repayment. In addition, when banks are in debt, it is increasingly difficult to borrow more.

The level of free reserves would affect the rate of expansion of the money supply if it affected the willingness of banks to lend and invest. As shown below, if a higher level of free reserves induced banks to be more willing to lend and invest, a larger increase in total reserves would be needed to keep the level of free reserves on the target. The more rapid expansion in reserves would result in a more rapid rate of increase in the money supply.

The Federal Reserve raises the level of free reserves.
↓
Commercial banks become more willing to lend and invest.
↓
The actual level of free reserves falls below the target level.
↓
The Federal Reserve probably increases the rate of expansion in bank reserves in order to maintain the higher target level of free reserves.

When banks are more willing to lend and invest, they can obtain funds to lend either by using excess reserves or by borrowing from the Federal Reserve banks. Obtaining funds in either of these ways would cause the actual level of free reserves to fall, and a larger volume of open-market purchases would be necessary to keep on the target level of free reserves. The larger open-market purchases would provide the increase in bank reserves necessary to support the more rapid growth of the money supply.

Did free reserves work well as a target?

Table 14.1 shows that from 1964 to 1973, when the level of free reserves was lowered, short-term interest rates generally rose; and when the level of free reserves was raised, these rates generally fell. On the other hand, despite the drop in the level of free reserves during this

Table 14.1
Free Reserves, Interest
Rates, and the Annual
Rate of Change of *M-1*,
1964-1973*

Year	Free Reserves (December) (in millions)	Rate on 3-Month U.S. Treasury Bills (annual average)	Yield on Corporate Bonds—Aaa (Annual Average) (percent per year)	Compounded Annual Rate of Increase of *M-1*
1964	$ 168	3.5%	4.4%	4.0%
1965	− 2	4.0	4.5	4.2
1966	− 165	4.9	5.1	4.7
1967	107	4.3	5.5	3.9
1968	− 310	5.3	6.2	7.2
1969	− 829	6.7	7.0	6.1
1970	− 49	6.5	8.0	3.8
1971	58	4.3	7.4	6.7
1972	− 830	4.1	7.2	7.1
1973	− 1,036	7.0	7.4	7.5

M-1 is the same as the new *M-1A* except that the latter excludes deposits of foreign commercial banks and official institutions.
Source: *Federal Reserve Bulletin*, various issues, pp. A6, A29, and A30; Federal Reserve Bank of St. Louis, *Rates of Change in Economic Data for Ten Industrial Countries, Annual Data, 1958–1977*, June 1978, p. 51.

period, the rate of increase in the money supply rose. The lower levels of free reserves might have caused banks to become less willing to expand loans and investments and thus have caused a slower rate of expansion in the money supply, but it did not work out that way.

A principal shortcoming of the use of free reserves as a target is that other factors may affect the willingness of banks to lend and invest— especially the relationship of market rates of interest to the discount rate and the strength of the demand for loans. From 1964 to 1973, the upward trend of market interest rates relative to the discount rate probably caused a decline in the level of free reserves that the banks *desired* to hold. (Because the discount rate was relatively low, banks willingly borrowed larger amounts from the Reserve banks.) Even though the *actual* level of free reserves fell, the desired level was apparently falling even faster, and banks did not reduce the rate of expansion of their loans and investments. The divergent movements of free reserves and the rate of change in the money stock during this period caused confusion concerning the nature of monetary policy. While some persons pointed to the decline in free reserves and the high market interest rates and said that monetary policy was becoming tighter, others looked at the money stock and said that monetary policy was becoming more expansionary.

Figure 14.2 shows the movements of the two components of free reserves—excess reserves and borrowing at Federal Reserve banks— from 1950 to 1978. During recessions (1953–1954, 1957–1958, 1960–1961, 1967, 1969–1970, and 1973–1975), borrowing usually fell, causing free reserves to rise. (The unusual amount of borrowing in 1974 was the result of the large loans made to the Franklin National Bank in New York before its failure.) During periods of prosperity, borrowing has risen, causing free reserves to fall.

Figure 14.2
Excess Reserves and
Borrowings of Member
Banks, 1950–1978

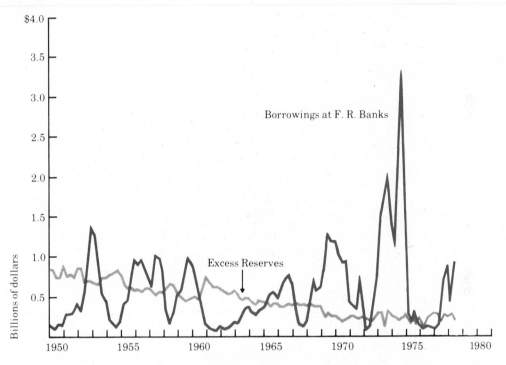

Source: Board of Governors of the Federal Reserve System, *Historical Chart Book, 1978*, p. 3.

The use of free reserves as a target may have been one of the causes of the accelerated rate of inflation that started in the 1960s. When free reserves are used as a target, the actions of banks and business firms may cause the supply of money to expand too rapidly. This is because growth in the supply of money depends both on the level of free reserves and how banks and business firms respond to the level of free reserves. When free reserves are used as a target, the Federal Reserve authorities do not have firm control over the rate of expansion in the supply of money.

The dual targets in the 1970s

In the early 1970s, the Federal Reserve shifted to two new targets—the level of the federal funds rate and the rate of expansion in certain monetary aggregates. Both targets are set by the Federal Open Market Committee in line with prevailing economic forecasts. If, for example, the forecast were for increasing unemployment, they would lower the targeted federal funds rate and raise the targeted rate of expansion in the monetary aggregates. The Federal Reserve banks would then buy sufficient government securities to reduce the federal funds rate; the lower federal funds rate was expected to cause a more rapid rate of growth of the money supply; and the more rapid rate of growth in the money supply was expected to stimulate aggregate demand and reduce the rate of unemployment.

Largely in response to the double-digit inflation of the mid-1970s, in March 1975 Congress passed a joint resolution, calling for the Federal Reserve to report to Congress periodically on its plans for the growth of the monetary aggregates.[3] The Federal Reserve System received much of the blame for the very rapid inflation. Economists pointed out that from 1965 to 1974, along with an acceleration in the rate of inflation, the rate of growth of the monetary aggregates had accelerated. The rate of growth of *M-1* (currency plus demand deposits in commercial banks) had increased from an annual rate of 1.8 percent in 1952–1962 to between 5 and 6 percent in 1963–1977. The resolution called on the Federal Reserve to "maintain long-run growth of the monetary and credit aggregates commensurate with the economy's long-run potential to increase production."

Regular consultations between the Federal Reserve authorities and Congress were formalized in the Federal Reserve Reform Act of 1977 and the Humphrey-Hawkins Act of 1978.[4] These consultations include presentation of the Federal Open Market Committee's one-year growth ranges for the money supply—from the average for the most recent quarter to the quarterly average one year later. In the first quarter of 1978, the annual range set was from 4 percent to 6½ percent for *M-1*, and from 6½ percent to 9 percent for *M-2*. (At that time, *M-2* was defined as *M-1* plus time deposits in commercial banks.) Figure 14.3 shows that during 1978, the actual levels of *M-1* were, for most months, far above the upper range that was set as the target. The actual levels of the old *M-2* were usually on or slightly above the upper range set.

In addition to the annual targets for the monetary aggregates that are reported to Congress, the Federal Reserve had short-run targets for both the federal funds rate and for *M-1* and *M-2*. The target for the federal funds rate was for one month and was set at each meeting of the Federal Open Market Committee. The targets for the monetary aggregates were for two months, and were also set at the monthly meetings.

Figure 14.3
Rates of Growth of the
Monetary Aggregates
and Announced Annual
Targets, 1st Quarter
1978 to
1st Quarter 1979

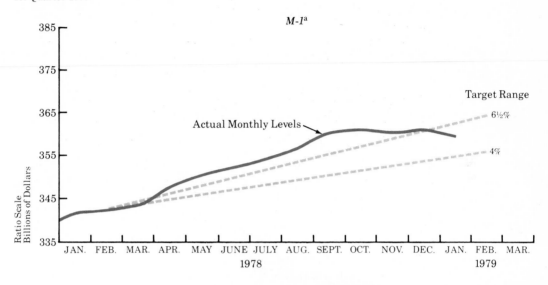

M-1[a]

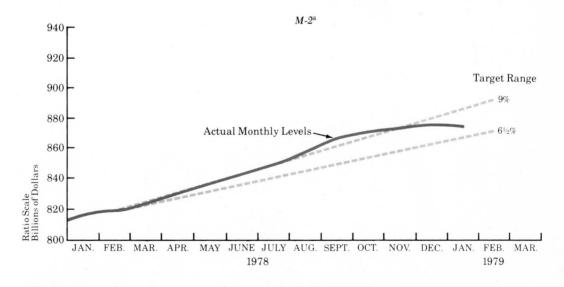

M-2[a]

[a]Old definitions of *M-1* and *M-2*.
Source: Richard W. Lang, "The FOMC in 1978: Clarifying the Role of the Aggregates," Federal Reserve Bank of St. Louis,
Review, March 1979, pp. 7, 9.

Figure 14.4 shows that the monetary authorities successfully hit their targets for the federal funds rate in most months. Figure 14.5 shows that the actual rates of growth of the monetary aggregates fell outside of the short-run targets during a significant portion of the year.

Figure 14.4
Federal Open Market Committee Ranges for the Federal Funds Rate, 1978

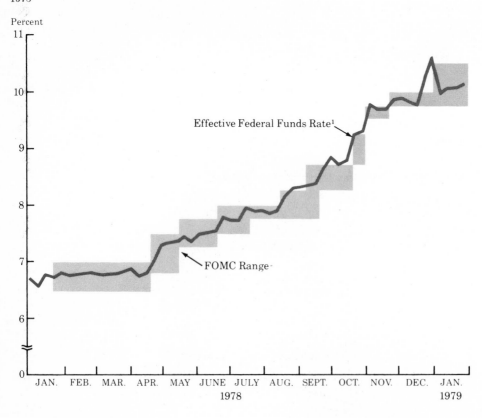

[1]Weekly averages of effective daily rates.
[2]At each meeting during 1978, the Federal Open Market Committee established a range for the federal funds rate. These ranges are indicated for the first full week during which they were in effect.
Source: Richard W. Lang, "The FOMC in 1978: Clarifying the Role of the Aggregates," Federal Reserve Bank of St. Louis, *Review*, March 1979, p. 11.

Because the Federal Reserve had two targets, a problem arose when both the federal funds rate and the growth of the monetary aggregates simultaneously reached either the upper or lower limits of their pre-scribed ranges. When this happened, the manager of the open-market account faced the dilemma of whether to let the federal funds rate exceed its prescribed limits in order to keep the growth of *M-1* and *M-2* within the set ranges, or to let the monetary aggregates overshoot or undershoot their targets in order to meet the prescribed federal funds target. The results in 1978 suggest that the principal thrust of monetary policy was to stabilize the federal funds rate, even if it meant permitting the growth of the monetary aggregates to fall outside their ranges.

In 1978, the Federal Reserve authorities were not able to keep within the *M-1* target range because this was a period in which the federal

Figure 14.5
Federal Open Market
Committee Short-Run
Ranges for the
Monetary Aggregates,
1978

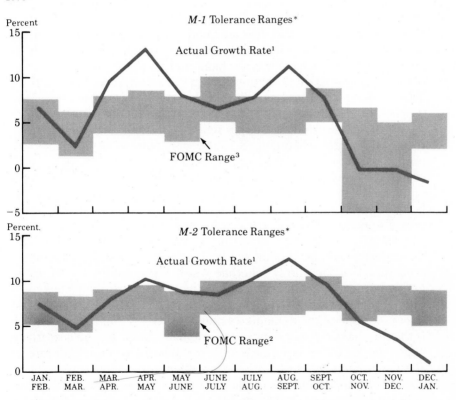

*Old definitions of *M-1* and *M-2*.
Note: Ranges and actual growth rates are in terms of two-month simple annual rates of change from the month prior to the meeting at which the ranges were adopted to the month following the meeting.
[1] Actual growth rates are revised data as of February 8, 1979, which include revisions of seasonal factors.
[2] The shaded areas represent two-month ranges adopted by the Committee at each regularly scheduled meeting. The ranges are shown for the period over which they were specified to apply.
[3] At both the October and November meetings the FOMC set only upper boundaries for *M-1*.
Source: Richard W. Lang, "The FOMC in 1978: Clarifying the Role of the Aggregates," Federal Reserve Bank of St. Louis, *Review*, March 1979, p. 10.

funds rate was rising. In such periods, in order to keep the federal funds rate from rising above its target, the monetary authorities have had to purchase large amounts of securities in the open market, causing the monetary base to expand more rapidly. In periods of falling federal funds rates, the Federal Reserve authorities were not able to reach their *M-1* target level. In such periods, the monetary authorities have not had to purchase large amounts of securities in order to keep the federal funds rate on target.

Although a reduction in the federal funds rate is supposed to cause an increase in the rate of growth of the monetary aggregates, and a rise in the rate is supposed to lower the rate of growth of the monetary aggregates, this relationship is weak, not well understood, and difficult to predict.[5] Consider the graph illustrating the market for federal funds (Figure 14.6). The federal funds rate will tend to be where the quantity demanded is equal to the quantity supplied. The demand schedule for federal funds slopes downward because banks will borrow more federal funds when they cost less. It is assumed in Figure 14.6 that the supply of federal funds does not vary with interest rates, but depends on changes in all of the factors in the bank reserve equation—and especially on the open-market operations of the Federal Reserve System. If the Federal Reserve authorities desired to lower the federal funds rate from 9 percent to 8.75 percent, they could do so by buying securities in the open market—shifting the supply schedule to the right so that it intersects the demand schedule at 8.75 percent. This would simultaneously tend to increase the money supply because the open-market purchases required to lower the federal funds rate would also increase the monetary base. Just how much the money supply will increase when the federal funds rate is lowered is uncertain because the amount of increase or decrease in the monetary base necessary to achieve a given reduction or rise in the federal funds rate varies. If, for example, the demand schedule for federal funds happened to be shifting left at the same time that the supply schedule was being shifted to the right, the Federal Reserve authorities would not have to increase the money supply very much in order to hit the target federal funds rate desired. Also, the exact slope of the demand schedule for federal funds is not known. If the demand schedule slopes very gradually, it would take a relatively large increase in the supply schedule to lower the federal funds rate. In addition, open-market operations only affect the monetary base. There may be changes in other variables in the money supply equation, such as the currency-deposit ratio and the ratio of time to demand deposits, that affect the outcome.

In the period since the Federal Reserve adopted as targets the federal funds rate and the growth of the money supply, there have been wide short-run variations in the money stock, and the money stock has continued to vary cyclically. The severity of the 1973–1975 recession

Figure 14.6
Market for Federal
Funds

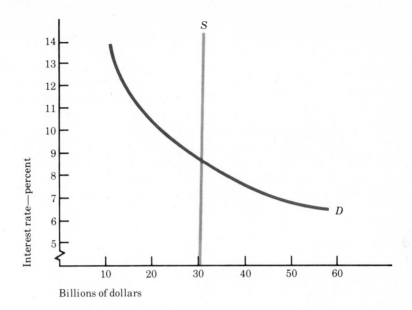

Billions of dollars

has been attributed to the Federal Reserve System's difficulties with its dual targets.[6] The rate of expansion of *M-1* dropped sharply in the latter half of 1974, despite reductions in the federal funds rate, and it is believed that the slower rate of growth of the money supply made the recession worse.

The Federal Reserve authorities might achieve greater control of the money stock if they would shift the federal funds rate target more promptly. For example, in a period in which the money stock was rising too slowly, they might have speeded up the rate of increase in the money stock by lowering the federal funds rate more rapidly than they did. In practice, this is not easy to do because the authorities do not know ahead of time how fast they must lower the funds rate to get the desired rate of expansion in the monetary aggregates.

Because of these difficulties, in October 1979 the Federal Reserve adopted a new technique of control in which the federal funds rate will have a less important role. It was announced that in the future greater emphasis will be given to keeping the monetary aggregates within their target ranges.

In the past, the Federal Reserve authorities have generally been opposed to proposals to precisely control the money supply. Doubts were frequently expressed about the significance of the statistics on different measures of the money supply, especially after the regulatory changes authorizing ATS accounts and the development of money substitutes such as securities repurchase agreements. Although new measures of the money supply—*M-1A, M-1B, M-2, M-3,* and *L*—were adopted in 1980, they may still not be ideal. Because of difficulties with the statistics on the money supply, some economists have suggested that it would be better to concentrate on controlling the monetary base.

Another objection to using the monetary aggregates as a target is that it might cause short-run interest rates to fluctuate widely. At times, banks would be short of reserves and would bid up short-term interest rates sharply; at other times they would have abundant reserves, and interest rates would fall sharply. The volatility of short-run interest rates probably could be reduced if the Federal Reserve would alter their reserve carry-over regulations so that a bank could carry over a reserve deficiency for a longer period than the present limit of one week. With less pressure on banks to immediately adjust their reserves, there would be a smaller impact on short-term interest rates.

Stable versus countercyclical interest rates

A major criticism of the Federal Reserve's attempts to control interest rates is that the monetary authorities have tended to stabilize interest rates rather than to lower them in periods of recession and raise them in periods of inflation. This is partly the result of political pressures. In periods of expansion, borrowers—the federal government, homeowners, farmers, and businesses—expect the Federal Reserve to protect them from rising interest rates. In periods of recession, bankers and other lenders have often expected the Federal Reserve System to protect them from falling interest rates.

Also, the Federal Reserve authorities view themselves as stabilizers and are naturally inclined to attempt to reduce the cyclical movements in interest rates (just as they attempt to stabilize prices, exchange rates, and rates of unemployment). To manipulate interest rates in a countercyclical manner, Federal Reserve policy would have to accentuate the cyclical movements in interest rates. The Federal Reserve authorities are usually reluctant to take such actions.

Most economists believe that the Federal Reserve authorities should not attempt to stabilize interest rates. Market interest rates tend to fall automatically in periods of recession and rise during periods of prosperity, primarily because of changes in the demand for credit. When business turns downward, firms cut down on their borrowing, and interest rates tend to fall. In periods of prosperity, business borrowing expands and interest rates rise. To understand why these automatic fluctuations in interest rates are beneficial, consider the illustration of the market for loanable funds (Figure 14.7). Assume that the market interest rates in this figure are also real interest rates. The demand schedule for credit slopes downward, indicating that borrowers will borrow larger amounts per year as borrowing becomes less costly. At lower rates of interest, more types of capital improvements become profitable.

Figure 14.7
The Credit Market

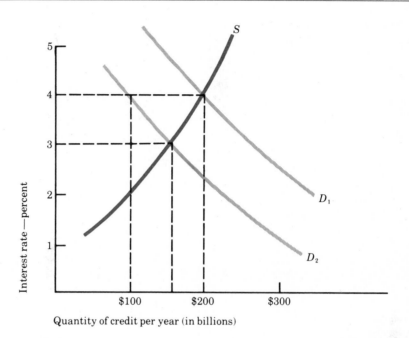

Quantity of credit per year (in billions)

The supply schedule for credit in Figure 14.7 slopes upward, indicating that the higher the rate of interest, the more savers and financial institutions are willing to lend. It slopes upward because a person pays less for a dollar delivered in the future when interest rates go up, and this makes saving more attractive. If the interest rate were 4 percent, for example, a dollar to be delivered a year from now would be worth about 96 cents today: $1/(1 + .04)$. If the interest rate rose to 6 percent, a dollar to be delivered a year from now would cost less—about 94 cents.

If the demand schedule in Figure 14.7 were D_1, the equilibrium rate of interest would be at 4 percent, where the supply of credit is equal to the demand. When business activity declines, the demand curve for loanable funds shifts downward from D_1 to D_2—only $100 billion worth of loanable funds is now demanded at 4 percent, rather than $200 billion. The supply of loanable funds at 4 percent interest is now greater than the demand. This causes interest rates to fall because some banks are willing to lend at less than 4 percent rather than not lend at all. Figure 14.7 shows that as interest rates fall, the quantity of credit demanded will increase, and at 3 percent the equilibrium quantity of loanable funds lent is now back near the original volume of $200 billion. This increase in loans would have a stabilizing effect on the economy. In a period of prosperity, if the demand for loanable funds increases, a rise in interest rates also tends to be stabilizing. As interest rates rise, the quantity of loanable funds demanded decreases. If the supply curve is unchanged, the automatic cyclical variations in interest rates will counteract cyclical movements in business activity.

Limitations to using interest rates as a measure of ease or tightness

Those economists who would deemphasize the role of interest rates in Federal Reserve policy believe that interest-rate movements can be very misleading as an indicator of the ease or tightness of monetary policy. If market interest rates decline because monetary policy has caused the supply of money and credit to increase, the lower interest rates would correctly show that Federal Reserve policy was easier. However, if market interest rates decline because of a decline in the demand for credit in a period of recession, the lower interest rates would be no indication at all that monetary policy had become easier. The Federal Reserve authorities, for example, were mistaken when, because short-term market interest rates had fallen, they described their monetary policy during the Great Depression as easy.[7] In fact, the supply of bank credit had declined and many banks were failing. During the depression, market interest rates fell because the effect of the reduction in the demand for credit was greater than that of the reduction in the supply, not because Federal Reserve policy was easy.

Using market interest rates as a measure of monetary ease or tightness can also be misleading if the market rates are not adjusted for expected inflation. Failure to distinguish between market and real interest rates in the late 1960s and early 1970s resulted in exaggerating the tightness of monetary policy. Figure 14.8 compares the market yield on highest-grade corporate bonds from 1966 to 1974 with an estimate of the yield adjusted for inflation. The estimated adjusted yield (real rate) is equal to the market yield *less* the average annual rate of change in consumer prices over the three previous years, and is based on the assumption that the rate of inflation that persons anticipate is related to the rate of inflation experienced in previous years. During this period, estimating real interest rates in this way was probably fairly accurate. Figure 14.8 shows that from 1966 to 1970, the trend of the adjusted yield did not rise even though market yields rose sharply. In 1973, when market yields rose, the adjusted yield fell.

Figure 14.8
Yields on Highest-Grade
Corporate Bonds,
1966-1974

Prepared by Federal Reserve Bank of St. Louis.

Summary

The Federal Reserve System's technique of control has been changing. Attempts by the Federal Reserve authorities to control two targets—the federal funds rate and the growth of the monetary aggregates—have been criticized by many economists both as a cause of recent recessions and of the acceleration in the rate of inflation. Just how effective the Federal Reserve authorities will be in giving greater emphasis to controlling the monetary aggregates, their new policy announced in the fall of 1979, remains to be seen.

Notes

1. See Albert E. Burger, "The Implementation Problem of Monetary Policy," Federal Reserve Bank of St. Louis, *Review* (March 1971), pp.

20–30; Jack M. Guttentag, "The Strategy of Open Market Operations," *Quarterly Journal of Economics* 80 (February 1966), pp. 1–30; and Thomas R. Saving, "Monetary-Policy Targets and Indicators," *Journal of Political Economy* 75 (August 1967), Part 2, pp. 446–465.

2. For discussions of the use of free reserves as a target, see "The Significance and Limitations of Free Reserves," Federal Reserve Bank of New York, *Monthly Review* 30 (November 1958), p. 164; William G. Dewald, "Free Reserves, Total Reserves, and Monetary Control," *Journal of Political Economy* 71 (April 1963), pp. 141–153; A. James Meigs, *Free Reserves and the Money Supply* (Chicago: University of Chicago Press, 1962); and K. Brunner and A. H. Meltzer, *The Federal Reserve's Attachment to the Free Reserve Concept*, Subcommittee Print (U.S. Congress, House, Committee on Banking and Currency, Subcommittee on Domestic Finance, 88th Cong., 2nd sess., 1964).

3. For an analysis of the initial experience with announced targets, see William Poole, "Interpreting the Fed's Monetary Target," *Brookings Papers on Economic Activity*, 1: 1976, pp. 247–259. See also Kurt Dew, "Congressional Reporting," *Business and Financial Letter* (San Francisco: Federal Reserve Bank of San Francisco, December 5, 1975); and *The Impact of the Federal Reserve System's Monetary Policies on the Nation's Economy*, Staff Report of the Subcommittee on Domestic Monetary Policy of the Committee on Banking, Currency, and Housing, House, 94th Cong., 2nd sess. (Washington, D.C.: USGPO, December 1976).

4. For the act, see *Federal Reserve Bulletin*, December 1977, pp. 1076–1078.

5. William Poole, "The Making of Monetary Policy, Description and Analysis," *Economic Inquiry* 13 (June 1975), pp. 253–265.

6. William Poole, "Monetary Policy during the Recession," *Brookings Papers on Economic Activity*, 1: 1975, pp. 123–129.

7. Milton Friedman and Anna J. Schwartz, *A Monetary History of the United States, 1867–1960* (Princeton: Princeton University Press, 1963), pp. 374–375.

Questions

14.1. Why can the goals of monetary policy not serve as targets?

14.2. Explain why a Federal Reserve System policy of supporting the prices of U.S. government securities may be inflationary.

14.3. Explain the way in which the Federal Reserve authorities may raise or lower the level of free reserves.

14.4. Why do interest rates tend to be low when the level of free reserves is high, and high when the level of free reserves is low?

14.5. Explain why the rate of growth of the money supply need not decrease when the level of free reserves falls.

14.6. Explain why a decline in interest rates in a period of recession has a desirable effect on the market for loanable funds.

14.7. Explain why using interest rates as an indicator of the ease or tightness of monetary policy may be misleading.

14.8. Know the meaning and significance of the following terms and concepts: monetary target, monetary goal, bond-support program, Treasury-Federal Reserve Accord of 1951, free reserves, easy monetary policy, tight monetary policy, desired level of free reserves, Federal Reserve dual targets, countercyclical interest rates, adjusted yield on corporate bonds.

15

Statistical data compiled for more than a hundred years show a relationship between the money supply and business cycles. There is also an important relationship between the rates of increase in the money supply and inflation.

THE BEHAVIOR OF MONEY

Recent statistical research on the money supply has added significantly to our knowledge of the relationship between changes in the money supply and fluctuations in business activity and prices. This chapter summarizes the principal findings of this research. The monetary theories explaining these relationships are presented in Chapters 16 to 18 and Chapters 21 and 22.

Money and business cycles

Probably the most important finding of the recent research on the money supply is that there is a statistical relationship between business cycles and changes in the money supply. Although it has been known for a long time that the U.S. economy has been characterized by cycles in business activity, prior to the new research, the cyclical variations in the money supply were not well understood.

Business cycles may be divided into four parts: the expansion phase, the peak, the contraction phase, and the trough. At the peak, business activity reaches a turning point at which expansion ends and a decline begins. The trough is the lower turning point where economic activity starts upward after a contraction.

Table 15.1 shows the dates of the troughs and peaks of the business cycles in the United States from 1854 to 1975. The duration of the twenty-eight expansion phases varied from ten months to 106 months, and the average length was thirty-three months. The shortest contraction lasted seven months, and the longest sixty-five months. The average duration of the twenty-nine contraction phases was nineteen months. From February 1961 to December 1969, the United States economy experienced a much longer period of unbroken expansion than at any time since 1854, although there was a slowdown in 1967.

Figures 15.1 and 15.2 show the way in which the total amount and the rate of change of *M-1* plus time deposits in commercial banks (called *M-2* before 1980) varied during the eleven peacetime business cycles that occurred in the United States from 1908 to 1961. Monthly data are available for this period. The same type of fluctuations in the money supply occurred from 1867 to 1908. However, the statistical data on the money supply for this earlier period are annual or semiannual, and the cyclical variations in the money supply cannot be measured as accurately as for the period from 1908 to 1961. These figures are from the research done by Milton Friedman and Anna Schwartz.[1]

In these figures, the eleven cycles from 1908 to 1961 have been divided into two groups, deep and mild depression cycles, depending on the severity of the decline. Figure 15.1 shows that in the three deep depression cycles, the *total amount* of *M-1* plus time deposits in commercial banks followed a regular cyclical pattern, rising during the expansion and falling during the contraction. (Table 15.2 shows the

Table 15.1
U.S. Business Cycle
Expansions and
Contractions,
1854 to 1975

Business Cycle Reference Dates		Duration in Months	
		Contraction (trough from previous peak)	Expansion (trough to peak)
Trough	**Peak**		
December 1854	June 1857		30
December 1858	October 1860	18	22
June 1861	April 1865	8	46
December 1867	June 1869	32	18
December 1870	October 1873	18	34
March 1879	March 1882	65	36
May 1885	March 1887	38	22
April 1888	July 1890	13	27
May 1891	January 1893	10	20
June 1894	December 1895	17	18
June 1897	June 1899	18	24
December 1900	September 1902	18	21
August 1904	May 1907	23	33
June 1908	January 1910	13	19
January 1912	January 1913	24	12
December 1914	August 1918	23	44
March 1919	January 1920	7	10
July 1921	May 1923	18	22
July 1924	October 1926	14	27
November 1927	August 1929	13	21
March 1933	May 1937	43	50
June 1938	February 1945	13	80
October 1945	November 1948	8	37
October 1949	July 1953	11	45
May 1954	August 1957	10	39
April 1958	April 1960	8	24
February 1961	December 1969	10	106
November 1970	November 1973	11	36
March 1975		16	
Average, all cycles:			
28 cycles, 1854–1975		19	33
12 cycles, 1919–1975		15	41
6 cycles, 1945–1975		11*	48
Average, peacetime cycles:			
23 cycles, 1854–1975		20	26
9 cycles, 1919–1975		16	30
4 cycles, 1945–1975		11	34

*Seven cycles
Source: U.S. Department of Commerce, *Business Conditions Digest* (July 1979), p. 105.

sharp percentage decline in this measure of the money supply in each of these three deep depressions.) The horizontal axis of Figure 15.1 shows the months before and after the peak in business activity. The

Figure 15.1
M-1 **plus Time Deposits in Commercial Banks:*** **Average Reference-Cycle Patterns for Mild and Deep Depression Cycles, 1908–1961**

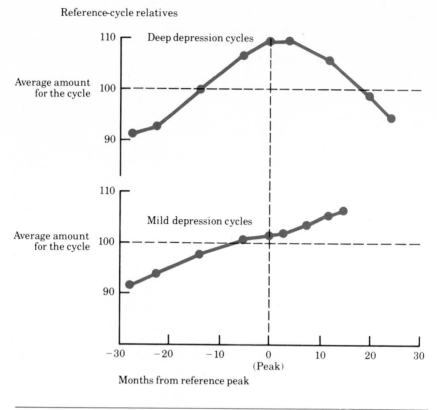

Reference-cycle relatives

Months from reference peak

*Called M-2 before 1980.

Source: Milton Friedman and Anna J. Schwartz, "Money and Business Cycles," *Review of Economics and Statistics* 45, Supplement (February 1963), p. 34.

reference-cycle relatives on the vertical axis measure the percentage above and below the average amount of the total money stock for the cycle. For example, in deep depressions, at the initial trough the money stock was, on the average, approximately 9 percent less than the average for the cycle. At the peak, it was approximately 9 percent above the cycle's average.

In mild depression cycles, changes in the total money stock do not have a cyclical pattern. In these cycles, the total money stock rises in an almost straight line, although there is some indication of a slower rate of growth from midexpansion to midcontraction. It is believed that in mild cycles the long-run upward movement of the money supply overwhelms the cyclical changes.

Figure 15.2 shows that the cyclical behavior in the *rate of change* in *M-1* plus time deposits in commercial banks during mild cycles is similar

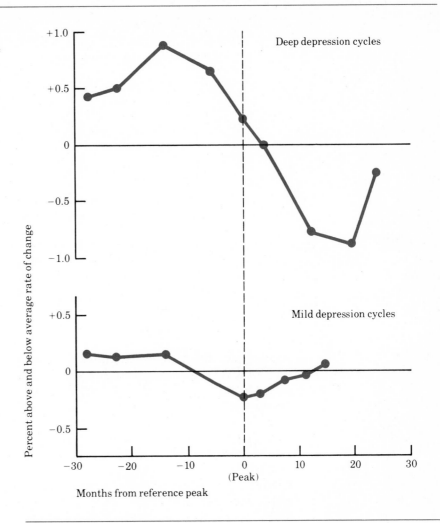

Figure 15.2
Rate of Change in *M-1*
plus Time Deposits
in Commercial Banks:*
Average Reference-
Cycle Patterns for
Mild and Deep
Depression Cycles,
1908–1961

*Called *M-2* before 1980.
Source: Milton Friedman and Anna J. Schwartz, "Money and Business Cycles," *Review of Economics and Statistics* 45,
Supplement (February 1963), p. 36.

to that in deep depression cycles, although the amplitude is larger in
deep cycles than in mild ones. Prior to this finding, it was widely
believed that cyclical fluctuations in the money supply were important
only in deep cycles.

The peak rates of change in the money supply in Figure 15.2 occur
prior to the peak in business activity, and the troughs are reached
before the bottom of the recession. When a statistical series has a pattern that conforms to the business cycle, but turns downward prior to

Table 15.2
Deep Depression
Cycles, 1908–1960*

Period	Percentage Decline in *M-1* plus Time Deposits in Commercial Banks**
1920–21	5.1%
1929–33	35.2
1937–38	2.4

*War cycles of 1914-1919 and 1938-1945 are not included.
**Called *M-2* before 1980.
Source: Milton Friedman and Anna J. Schwartz, "Money and Business Cycles," *Review of Economics and Statistics* 45, Supplement (February 1963), p. 34.

the peak in business activity and upward prior to the trough, it is called a *leading* series. Examples of other leading series are the National Bureau of Economic Research's index of stock prices and industrial material prices. Leading series are interesting because of their usefulness in forecasting.[2] The rate of change in this measure of the money supply has led all of the specific peaks and troughs in all of the cycles from 1867 to 1961. The lead is long—on the average, eighteen months at the peak and twelve months at the trough. The lead is also variable; the standard deviation of the lead is seven months at peaks and six months at troughs.[3]

The reference cycle patterns plotted in Figures 15.1 and 15.2 are designed to show statistical series that vary over a typical (or average) cycle. The major problem in illustrating average patterns for cycles is that the duration of each cycle varies. To solve this problem, every cycle is divided into the nine points shown in the figures. Starting at the left in Figure 15.1, for example, the first point shows the average reference-cycle relative for this measure of the money supply at the trough at the beginning of the cycle. The fifth point shows it at the peak. The ninth point shows the average reference-cycle relative at the trough at the end of the cycle.[4]

Cyclical fluctuations in the determinants of the money supply

The cyclical fluctuations in *M-1* plus time deposits in commercial banks are the result of fluctuations in its three principal determinants—the monetary base, the public's ratio of currency to deposits, and the banks' ratio of reserves to deposits.[5] An important study by Phillip Cagan of the eighteen cycles from 1877 to 1954 found that variations in the public's ratio of currency to deposits accounted, on the average, for half of the cyclical variations in the rate of increase in the money supply.[6] Changes in the monetary base and the banks' ratio of reserves to deposits each accounted for about 25 percent of the variations. It is significant that cyclical variations in the money supply during this period were caused primarily by factors over which the Federal Reserve System has little control—changes in the public's ratio of currency to deposits and the banks' ratios of reserves to deposits. Although, after 1914, the Federal Reserve System might have attempted to counteract the effect of these factors on the movements of the money supply through its control over the monetary base, it did not do so.

In a typical cycle, from midexpansion to midcontraction the currency-to-deposit ratio has increased and caused the rate of increase in the money supply to decrease. Just why this ratio varies in the way it does is not well understood. One possible theory is that it is the result of a shift, during periods of expansion, in money holdings from financial institutions to consumers. Since consumers typically have higher currency-to-deposit ratios than financial institutions, the aggregate currency-to-deposit ratio would rise. Initially, when the money supply expands, the increase is concentrated in the hands of financial institutions because when banks acquire additional reserves and expand their deposits, they first purchase bonds and the impact is primarily on the bond market. Only later, when banks expand their loans, is the increase in the money supply more widely distributed throughout the economy. As this shift in the distribution of the increase takes place, the point is reached, in the middle of an expansion, when the currency-to-deposit ratio begins to rise, causing the rate of expansion of the money supply to fall.

Changes in the monetary base account for part of the cyclical variations in the money stock. As an expansion progresses, the rate of growth in the monetary base slows down. Under the gold standard, the rise in prices during periods of prosperity tended to cause a reduction in exports relative to imports, which resulted in a gold outflow, and thus tended to reduce the monetary base. Since 1914, during an upswing, the slower growth of the monetary base may reflect the Federal Reserve's policy of leaning against the wind—slowing down the increase in credit and money in periods of expansion and speeding up the increase of credit and money in periods of economic contraction.

Fluctuations in the ratio of bank reserves to deposits have contributed to cyclical variations in *M-1* plus time deposits in commercial banks because this ratio has typically fallen when loan demand was strong and risen when loan demand has dropped. At first banks may reduce their excess reserves when business expands; but as the period of expansion continues, they are unwilling to reduce their excess reserves any further. This would tend to cut back on expansion of the money supply. When a recession starts, bankers probably feel that their excess reserves have fallen too far, and they take the first opportunity they have to increase those excess reserves. This would tend to cut back on the expansion in the money supply during the early months of a recession.

Growth of the money stock

In addition to its cyclical fluctuations, the money stock almost always grows from one year to the next. Figure 15.3 shows the growth of *M-1* plus time deposits in commercial banks from $1.3 billion in 1867 to more than $200 billion in 1960. By 1980, this measure of the money

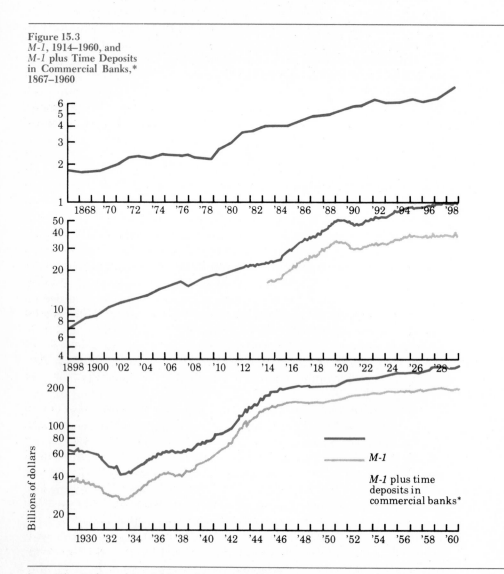

Figure 15.3
M-1, 1914–1960, and
M-1 plus Time Deposits
in Commercial Banks,*
1867–1960

M-1

M-1 plus time
deposits in
commercial banks*

Billions of dollars

Source: Milton Friedman and Anna J. Schwartz, "Money and Business Cycles," *Review of Economics and Statistics* 45, Supplement (February 1963), p. 33.

supply had risen further to more than $950 billion. Since 1914, the growth of *M-1* has closely paralleled the growth of *M-1* plus time deposits in commercial banks.

From 1875 to 1955, the average annual rate of increase in *M-1* plus time deposits in commercial banks was nearly 6 percent. The factors which caused the growth in the money supply during this long period are different from the factors which account for the cyclical variations. Cagan found that the monetary base accounted for nine-tenths of the long-run growth of the money stock. Declines in the public's ratio of currency to deposits and the banks' ratio of reserves to deposits were responsible for the remaining one-tenth.[7]

Before the Federal Reserve System was established, the money stock grew largely as a result of growth in the domestic supply of silver and gold. Cagan has estimated that between 1875 and 1914, changes in the gold stock accounted for about two-thirds of the annual changes in the monetary base. When countries were on the gold standard, the domestic supply of gold usually varied directly with the world's supply, because an increase in the world's gold supply tended to be widely distributed among all countries. The exchange rates among gold standard countries were fixed, and if the increase in the monetary base in one country lagged behind that in other countries because its domestic gold supply had not increased, its balance of payments was usually affected. Prices in the lagging country tended to be lower than those elsewhere, its exports increased relative to its imports, and a gold inflow followed. Because the money supply of each country was based primarily on bank reserves consisting of gold, if a country's gold reserves increased, the money stock also increased.

Cagan estimated that from 1915 to 1955 (after the Federal Reserve was established) changes in the gold stock accounted for only 40 percent of the changes in the monetary base. Particularly during World Wars I and II, changes in Federal Reserve credit (primarily their government securities plus loans) accounted for the substantial increases in the monetary base.

In recent years, one objective of Federal Reserve policy has been to provide for growth in the money stock. In the mid-1950s, the Federal Reserve's Chairman Martin said, "There is no firm yardstick, but we have looked on the normal growth of the country in terms of perhaps 2, 3, 4 percent, no fixed formula, and we have added to the money supply generally for that purpose. But we have to gauge things in terms of the demand and supply of credit and business activity."[8] From 1960 to 1978, the expansion of the money supply accelerated and the average compounded increase per year in *M-1* plus time deposits in commercial banks during this period was 8 percent. During this same period, the compounded annual rate of increase in *M-1* has averaged 5.1 percent.

The historical relation between money and income, 1870–1961

Historically, the relationship between the rates of change in the money supply and the rate of change in the nominal income of people in the United States has been quite close, as is shown in Figure 15.4.[9] This figure covers the period from 1870 to 1961 and excludes intracyclical effects. To eliminate intracyclical effects, the rates of change are computed from average values covering an entire cyclical phase—expansion or contraction. Note the very low rates of increase in both measures of the money supply shown in Figure 15.4 and in nominal income during the Great Depression from 1929 to 1933. Note also that during World Wars I and II, the rates of increase in both the money supply and in nominal income were very high.

Figure 15.4
The Relationship between the Rate of Change in Nominal Income and the Rate of Change in the Money Stock, 1870-1961, Excluding Intracyclical Effects

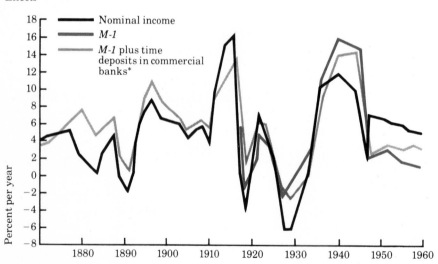

*Called *M-2* before 1980.
Source: Milton Friedman, *Dollars and Deficits* (Englewood Cliffs, N.J.: Prentice-Hall, 1968), p. 128. Reproduced by permission of Prentice-Hall, Inc.

Changes in nominal income may consist of changes in either prices or real output. The relationship between the rate of change in the money supply and the two components of nominal income—the rate of change in prices and real income—for the period from 1870 to 1961 are shown in Figure 15.5. The correlation between the money supply and the net national product in current prices is higher than for either prices or output separately. Nevertheless, the rate of change in both prices and output has usually moved up and down with the rate of change in the money supply.

Figure 15.5
The Relationship between the Rate of Change in Prices and Real Income and the Rate of Change in the Money Stock, 1870–1961, Excluding Intracyclical Effects

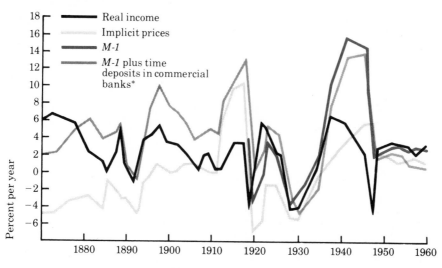

*Called *M-2* before 1980.
Source: Milton Friedman, *Dollars and Deficits* (Englewood Cliffs, N.J.: Prentice-Hall, 1968), p. 129. Reproduced by permission of Prentice-Hall, Inc.

Money and prices

Variations in the money supply are closely related to long-run movements in prices. Historically, it is difficult to find examples of countries in which inflation has occurred without an increase in the money supply, or where a substantial increase in the money supply has not been accompanied by a rise in prices.

The close relationship between monetary growth and prices in the
United States from 1961 to 1979 is shown in Table 15.3. From 1961 to
1965, the average rate of increase in *M-1B* was 2.9 percent and the
average rate of increase in prices was 1.5 percent. In the next five years,
from 1965 to 1970, the average rate of increase in the money supply
rose to 5.2 percent, and the average rate of inflation rose to 3.6 percent.
From 1970 to 1975, these rates of increase rose to 5.9 percent for the
money supply and 6.0 percent for prices. In the last five years, from
1975 to 1980, the money supply rose 6.7 percent and prices 7.4 percent. The acceleration in the rate of inflation typically lagged from 18
months to 2 years behind the rate of increase in the money supply.

Table 15.3
Monetary Growth and
Prices, 1960-1979

Year	*M-1B* Rates of Change (compounded annually)	Rate of Change in Implicit Price Deflator*
1960	−0.1%	1.7%
1961	2.1	0.9
1962	2.4	1.8
1963	3.1	1.5
1964	3.9	1.6
1965	4.2	2.2
1966	4.6	3.3
1967	3.9	2.9
1968	7.1	4.5
1969	6.0	5.0
1970	3.7	5.4
1971	6.7	5.1
1972	7.1	4.1
1973	7.3	5.8
1974	4.9	9.7
1975	4.6	9.6
1976	5.5	5.2
1977	7.5	6.0
1978	8.2	7.3
1979	7.9	8.8

*Implicit price deflator is based on Gross National Product.
Source: Federal Reserve Bank of St. Louis, *Annual U.S. Economic Data*, May 1980, pp. 3 and 10.

Table 15.4 shows the relationship between the money supply per
unit of output and price trends from 1955 to 1968 in seven Latin
American countries. Although the rates of inflation in those countries
were different, in each of them the average annual rate of growth in the
money supply per unit of output has been similar to the average annual
rate of inflation.

Table 15.4
Rates of Change in
Money and Inflation in
Seven Latin American
Countries, 1955-1968

| Country | Compound Annual Rate of Change in | |
	Money Supply/Real Gross National Production	Consumer Price Index
Brazil	35.3%	37.9%
Chile	29.0	27.6
Argentina	22.6	26.6
Colombia	11.2	10.4
Peru	7.7	9.0
Ecuador	4.4	2.3
Mexico	3.8	3.6

Source: Beryl W. Sprinkel, *Money and Markets: A Monetarist View* (Homewood, Ill.: Richard D. Irwin, 1971), p. 189. Reprinted by permission of the publisher. Data from International Monetary Fund.

Velocity of money

Statistical data on the velocity of money have attracted the interest of economists for many years. There have been significant long-run trends in velocity, and there is a cyclical relationship between velocity and business activity.

The concept of the velocity of money is based on the equation of exchange that was made famous by Professor Irving Fisher many years ago:

15.1

$$MV = PT.$$

In this equation, M represents the quantity of money in the economy; V, the velocity of money per year; P, prices; and T, total transactions, or the quantity of everything bought and sold during the year.[10] The equation states that the quantity of money in an economy multiplied by the number of times per year it is spent is equal to the sum of the quantities of all of the items sold during the year multiplied by their prices. The equation is an identity because the variables in it are defined so that it must always be true. Money that is spent by certain persons must be received by others. The left-hand side of the equation refers to the spending of money. It looks at the money used to make payments of all types. The right-hand side deals with the receipt of money. It refers to the sum of the quantity of each good and service sold per year multiplied by its price. As shown in Equation 15.2, *transactions velocity* is estimated arithmetically from data on the money stock and total transactions:

15.2

$$V = \frac{PT}{M}.$$

In recent years, Fisher's equation has been altered significantly; velocity is now based on the national income rather than on transactions, and is referred to as *income velocity* to distinguish it from transactions velocity. In its income form, the equation is as follows:

15.3

$$MV = Py.$$

The right-hand side of Equation 15.3 refers to the national income or GNP rather than to the total value of transactions. In this equation, y represents the real output of those goods and services included in the national income or GNP, P is their prices, and $Py = Y$. The national income (Y) is different from the total value of transactions in that it excludes payments for intermediate transactions and for transfers of securities. An advantage to this form of the equation of exchange is that the statistics on GNP are more accurate than those available for total transactions. Also, the national income is a more meaningful concept than total transactions because the national income measures the total payments people have received for their contribution to production, either from their own labor or from the property they own. The equation for income velocity is as follows:

15.4

$$V = \frac{Py}{M} = \frac{Y}{M}.$$

The equation of exchange is important because it shows the relationships between the quantity of money, the velocity of money, the level of prices, and real output. However, misuse of the equation is quite common because persons are tempted to view the relationships between money and prices or real output as simultaneous. Persons should not attempt to explain price movements in a given year by variations in the money supply in that year. Empirical studies have shown that price movements in any given year are influenced by the trend of the rate of increase in the money supply several years previously.

Historical trends in velocity

For many years, it seemed logical to believe that velocity was rising because of increased frequency and regularity of payments and the expansion and development of financial institutions.[11] However, data indicate that throughout the nineteenth century the velocity of *M-1* plus time deposits in commercial banks declined sharply, probably partly because the steadily increasing proportion of the nation's output passing through the market caused people to hold larger amounts of their income in money. Also, an increasing proportion of the population worked for wages, and wage earners would tend to hold more money as a reserve for bad times than farmers who have a high measure of job security.

Figure 15.6 shows the changes in income velocity in the United States during the period 1900–1960. From 1900 to 1946, the trend of income velocity was downward, although the decline was not always as rapid or continuous as shown in Table 15.5 for the nineteenth century. During the Great Depression and during World War II, velocity dropped very sharply, but from 1946 to 1960, the downward trend was reversed, and income velocity rose sharply.

Between World War II and the 1960s, the increases in the velocity of money contributed to economic expansion.[12] The rise in interest rates during this period tended to cause people to reduce the amount of money they held. Following the sudden inflation during the Korean War and the creeping inflation that occurred during 1955–1959, people probably began to anticipate inflation. In addition, there was probably a significant change in people's attitudes toward the stability of the economy. At the end of World War II, it was widely predicted that the United States would soon experience a serious depression. Secular stagnation was also feared. These predictions turned out to be wrong, and the postwar recessions were mild and short. Although changes in attitude are difficult to measure, people probably became more confident about business prospects and less fearful of losing their jobs. This also would have contributed to an increase in the velocity of money.

The ratio of gross national product to *M-1* more than doubled between 1947 and 1978, reaching 6 by 1978, as shown in Figure 15.7. The velocity of *M-1* has typically increased about 3 percent a year probably because of the long-run rise in market interest rates. When market

Figure 15.6
Income Velocity in the
United States,
1900–1960

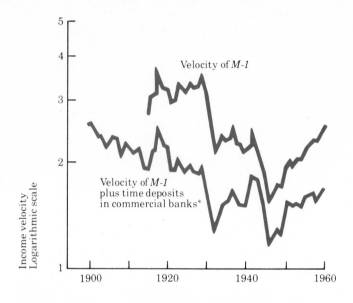

*Called *M-2* before 1980.
Source: Milton Friedman and Anna J. Schwartz, *A Monetary History of the United States, 1867–1970* (Princeton: Princeton University Press, 1963), chart 57, p. 640. Copyright © 1963 by National Bureau of Economic Research. Reprinted by permission of Princeton University Press.

interest rates rise, currency and demand deposits (which earn no interest) become relatively less attractive to hold. Figure 15.7 also shows that
the velocity of *M-1* plus time deposits in commercial banks has changed
little since 1960 probably because this measure of the money supply

Table 15.5
Income Velocity in the
United States, Selected
Years, 1799-1899

Year	Ratio of National Income to Total Deposits and Currency
1799	24.2
1809	14.1
1819	10.1
1829	7.5
1839	5.8
1849	7.7
1859	6.0
1869	3.4
1879	2.8
1889	2.1
1899	1.8

Source: Clark Warburton, "The Secular Trend in Monetary Velocity," *Quarterly Journal of Economics* 63 (February 1949), p. 76;
reprinted in Clark Warburton, *Depression, Inflation, and Monetary Policy* (Baltimore: Johns Hopkins Press, 1966), p. 200.

includes time deposits which have become more attractive to hold as interest rates on time deposits have risen.

Figure 15.7
Income Velocity,
1947–1978
(seasonally adjusted)

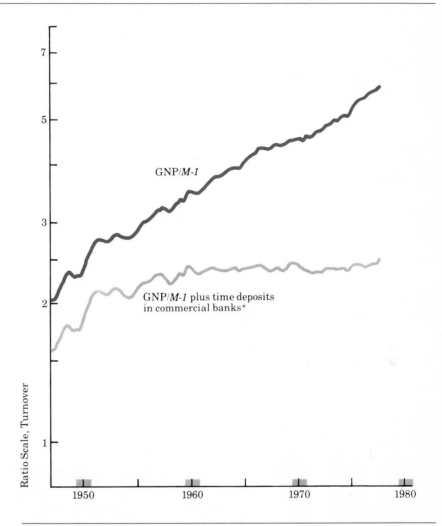

*Called *M-2* before 1980.
Source: Board of Governors of the Federal Reserve System, *Historical Chart Book*, *1978*, p. 5.

In addition to its long-run trends, velocity typically rises during business expansions and falls during contractions. In the six post-World War II recessions and in the 1966–1967 mini-recession, the yearly percentage change in *M-1* velocity dropped sharply, and in each of the subsequent recoveries it rose sharply. Changes in year-to-year velocity peaked either in the same quarter that economic activity did or one quarter earlier. In each of the recovery periods, the upward movement of velocity coincided with the upward movement of economic activity.

Movements in velocity are closely related to the demand for money, the topic of Chapter 16. When velocity declines, as it did during the nineteenth century, this indicates that the demand for money has increased. And when the velocity of money increases, as it did from 1945 to 1960, this indicates that there was a decline in the demand for money. The specific relation between the demand for money and velocity will be explained in Chapter 16.

The belief that the historical changes in velocity shown in Table 15.5 and in Figures 15.6 and 15.7 may be explained by changes in such factors as interest rates, inflationary expectations, and levels of real income is not accepted by everyone. Some economists believe that velocity is passive. To them, an increase in the money supply is offset by a decrease in velocity, and prices and incomes would be unaffected by changes in the money supply. Also, to them, if the money stock were unchanged, velocity would rise sufficiently to accommodate increases in prices or incomes. Recent studies of the statistical relationships between velocity and interest rates, the level of income, and rates of inflation do not support the concept of velocity as passive. Nevertheless, it is a possibility, and until recently it was not uncommon for economists to tacitly assume that changes in income and prices were not related to changes in the money supply. Over short periods of time, velocity may change because it takes time for changes in the money stock to affect income. Given the time necessary for changes in income to adjust to changes in the money stock, however, most fluctuations in velocity can be explained in other ways.

Turnover of demand deposits

Prior to the development of national income statistics in the 1930s, statistical data on the turnover of demand deposits were sometimes used as a measure of velocity or of the level of economic activity. The turnover of demand deposits is the total value of the checks written on demand deposits (debits to demand deposits) during the year, divided by the average quantity of demand deposits. It indicates the number of times per year that demand deposits change hands. Table 15.6 shows that, except during periods of business recession, there has been a fairly steady rise in the turnover of demand deposits from 1946 to 1979. The estimates for 1943 to 1964 are for banks in 343 Standard Metropolitan Statistical Areas, the series from 1964 to 1977 is for 232 SMSAs, and the series from 1976 to 1979 is for all commercial banks excluding major New York City banks. New York City is excluded because there the large volume of financial transactions results in a much larger turnover than occurs in the rest of the country. The volume of debits is similar

Table 15.6
The Turnover of
Demand Deposits in
Large Centers
Excluding
New York City,
1943-1964 and
1964-1979

In 343 Centers Excluding New York City			In 232 Centers Excluding New York City		
Year	Debits to Demand Deposits (in billions)	Turnover of Demand Deposits	December	Debits to Demand Deposits (in billions) (seasonally adjusted annual rates)	Turnover of Demand Deposits
1943	$ 476.3	16.2	1964	$ 2,809.9	33.4
1944	521.1	15.8	1965	3,276.3	37.5
			1966	3,567.0	39.9
1945	541.7	14.7	1967	3,960.9	41.2
1946	610.3	15.4	1968	4,736.5	45.3
1947	705.3	16.7			
1948	784.3	18.0	1969	5,430.5	50.0
1949	760.1	17.3	1970	5,915.7	52.9
			1971	6,859.9	57.3
1950	870.8	18.7	1972	8,178.9	61.8
1951	998.2	20.0	1973	10,543.6	75.8
1952	1,045.0	20.0			
1953	1,126.3	20.8	1974	12,260.6	86.6
1954	1,148.4	21.0	1975	12,594.2	84.7
			1976	15,076.1	97.0
1955	1,276.7	22.3	1977 (June)	16,296.7	97.4
1956	1,384.8	23.7			
1957	1,468.3	25.1	All Commercial Banks Excluding		
1958	1,481.0	24.9	Major New York City Banks		
1959	1,655.6	26.7			
			1976	$17,713.2	79.8
1960	1,735.9	28.2	1977	20,462.2	85.9
1961	1,832.3	29.0	1978	25,289.1	96.8
1962	2,020.6	31.3	1979	33,532.8	118.5
1963	2,198.7	33.1			
1964	2,404.9	35.2			

Source: Board of Governors of the Federal Reserve System, *Supplement to Banking and Monetary Statistics, Section 5, Bank Debits*, November 1966, pp. 6 and 12; *Federal Reserve Bulletin*, July 1972, pp. 634-635, February 1974, p. A14, and March 1980, p. A13; and *Annual Statistical Digest*, 1973-1977, pp. 46-47.

to Professor Fisher's concept of total transactions except that it excludes cash transactions. Total debits refect increases in both prices and real output.

Summary

During business cycles, the rate of change in *M-1* plus time deposits in commercial banks has tended to decline in advance of the downturn in business activity, and to rise in advance of the recovery. The cyclical movements of this measure of the money supply are related to similar movements in its three principal determinants: the monetary base, the public's ratio of currency to deposits, and the banks' ratio of reserves to deposits.

There is a close long-run relationship between money and prices, even though there is a lag of from eighteen months to two years between a change in the rate of increase in the money supply and a change in the rate of inflation.

The equation of exchange is an identity showing the relationship between money, velocity, real output, and prices. The velocity of money always rises in periods of expansion and contracts during periods of recession. During recent years, the income velocity of *M-1* plus time deposits in commercial banks has been relatively constant, while the income velocity of *M-1* has risen.

Notes

1. Milton Friedman and Anna J. Schwartz, *A Monetary History of the United States, 1867–1960* (Princeton: Princeton University Press, 1963). See also, "Money and Business Cycles," *Review of Economics and Statistics* 45, Supplement (February 1963), pp. 32–78.

2. See Geoffrey H. Moore, "The Analysis of Economic Indicators," *Scientific American* 232 (January 1975), pp. 17–23.

3. Within one standard deviation of the average are approximately 68 percent of the examples observed.

4. Each upswing (and each downswing) is divided into three equal periods of time and the second, third, and fourth (sixth, seventh, and eighth for a downswing) points show the average reference-cycle relative for each of these periods. If the upswing were thirty months long, for example, it would be divided into three ten-month periods; but if it were twenty-four months long, it would be divided into three eight-month periods.

5. Note that these three determinants are similar to the factors in Equation 9.7 for the multiple expansion of *M-1* plus time deposits in commercial banks discussed in Chapter 9. In the study by Professor Cagan, demand deposits are combined with time deposits, and required reserves are combined with excess reserves.

6. Phillip Cagan, *Determinants and Effects of Changes in the Stock of Money, 1875–1960* (New York: Columbia University Press, 1965).

7. Cagan, *Determinants and Effects*, p. 260.

8. U.S. Congress, Joint Economic Committee, Subcommittee on Economic Stabilization, *Monetary Policy: 1955–1956, December 10–11, 1956, Hearings*, 84th Congress, 2nd sess., 1956, p. 127.

9. The nominal income of the economy in this figure is based on Simon Kuznets' estimates of net national product. Net national product is similar to two other widely used measures of the level of economic activity—the gross national product (GNP) and national income (NI). In 1978, GNP was estimated to amount to about $2,100 billion, NNP to

$1,890 billion, and NI to $1,700 billion. Gross national product is the sum of the amount of each *final* good and service produced during the year multiplied by its price. A large portion of the GNP includes the production of goods that are needed to replace items that have worn out during the year. The net national product excludes the cost of replacing the manufacturing plants, machinery, housing, and other capital goods used up during the year. National income excludes both the cost of capital depreciation and the total amount of indirect business taxes—sales, excise, and property taxes.

10. Irving Fisher, *The Purchasing Power of Money*, 2d ed. (New York: Macmillan, 1926).

11. For a summary of the studies made by economists on the velocity of money, see Richard T. Selden, "Monetary Velocity in the United States," in Milton Friedman, ed., *Studies in the Quantity Theory of Money* (Chicago: University of Chicago Press, 1956), pp. 179–257.

12. Richard T. Selden, "Cost-Push versus Demand-Pull Inflation, 1955–1957," *Journal of Political Economy* 67 (February 1959), pp. 1–20.

Questions

15.1. Explain the difference between the cyclical movements of the total money supply and the rate of increase in the money supply.

15.2. Explain the reasons for the cyclical variations in the rate of increase in the money supply in terms of changes in total bank reserves, the public's ratio of currency to deposits, and the banks' ratio of reserves to deposits.

15.3. Explain the reasons for the growth of the money supply of the United States, both before and after the establishment of the Federal Reserve System.

15.4. Define each of the variables in the equation of exchange: $MV = PT$.

15.5. Explain why the equation of exchange is an identity.

15.6. What is the difference between Fisher's equation of exchange, $MV = PT$, and the equation $MV = Py$?

15.7. How has the velocity of money varied in the United States both during business cycles and over longer periods of time?

15.8. Discuss some of the different ways of measuring the velocity of money.

15.9. Know the meaning and significance of the following terms and concepts: business cycle, leading series, national income, equation of exchange, velocity of money, income velocity, transactions velocity, turnover of demand deposits, view of velocity as passive.

16

An individual's demand for money depends on his total wealth, the attractiveness of money compared to other types of wealth, and how much he desires the liquidity and other advantages of owning money.

THE DEMAND FOR MONEY

Previous chapters of this book have been concerned primarily with the supply of money. The supply of money is the amount of money people actually have. As has been explained, the commercial banks and the Federal Reserve System play a predominant role in determining the supply of money.

This chapter describes the factors affecting the demand for money—the amount of money people want to hold. Monetary theory, the topic of Chapters 16 to 18 is concerned with the relationship between the demand and supply of money and how changes in the demand and supply of money may affect prices, income, and interest rates.

The concept of money as a type of wealth

The demand for money is the amount of money people want to hold in their bank accounts or in cash. There is a demand for money because people do not want to spend the money they receive immediately. They hold money in order to bridge the period between the receipt of earnings and the spending of those earnings. There are several possible sources of confusion arising from the use of the term "demand for money." A person's salary requirement (or his demand for money income) is not the same as his demand for money. Moreover, in monetary theory the demand for money does not mean the demand for loanable funds, or the amount of money a person would like to borrow. Instead, it means the demand for money balances.

The factors that determine the quantity of money people want to hold are best understood if money is viewed as a type of wealth competing with other types of wealth such as stocks and bonds.[1] The quantity of money that people desire to hold depends largely on its potential usefulness—its convenience in making transactions, reliability when there are contingencies, and advantages in speculation. Different people wish to hold a different mix of money and other types of wealth. Also, the conditions that affect how much money and other types of wealth people want to hold may change. Under certain conditions, people will want to hold more money; under other conditions, the amount people want to hold will be smaller.

All wealth may be divided into five categories: money, bonds, equities, physical capital, and human capital. Before considering the factors that may affect the demand for money—one of the five types of wealth —it is useful to understand the particular characteristics of each of the types of wealth. The following sections describe the particular characteristics of money, bonds, equities, physical capital, and human capital.

Money

Money is the only type of wealth that has a fixed nominal value. Included in money assets are currency and demand deposits; time deposits in commercial banks, mutual savings banks, and savings and loan associations; and U.S. savings bonds. A dollar invested in any of these types of assets is always worth a dollar.

Currency and demand deposits usually do not pay interest; time deposits and U.S. savings bonds do. Even though the holding of currency and demand deposits usually does not provide the owner with a source of money income, it provides income in kind because of its usefulness, just as home ownership provides income in kind rather than money income.

Not all money assets are used for transactions. Checks cannot be written directly against most time deposits. Before using a time deposit to make a payment, it is usually necessary to transfer money out of the time deposit into a checking account.

The special characteristics of money assets are their safety and liquidity. Having money on hand avoids the inconvenience of having to sell other assets (and risk having to sell them at a loss) in order to get the money needed to make a transaction. Also, when time deposits are exchanged for demand deposits, the inconvenience and cost of making the exchange is very small compared to transferring money out of stocks, bonds, or real estate.

Bonds

An essential characteristic of a bond is that the nominal amount of its interest payments does not vary. If a $1,000 bond has a coupon rate of 6 percent, the owner receives a fixed payment of $60 a year during the life of the bond. Though interest payments on bonds do not vary, their prices do. As was explained in Chapter 4, prices of outstanding bonds fall when market interest rates rise, and they rise when interest rates fall. The return a person receives from owning bonds includes both the amount of the interest payment and any gain or loss realized when the bond matures or is sold. Because of fluctuations in bond prices, bonds may not be a reliable source of funds in time of need.

Equities

Common stock is the most widely held type of equity. An important difference between stocks and bonds is that the interest payments on bonds are fixed in amount—while dividends paid on stock vary with the profitability of the enterprise. Even though there is no promised return on stocks, if the directors of a corporation declare a dividend, each stockholder is entitled to his share. If he owns one-fourth of the outstanding stock, he is entitled to one-fourth of the dividends declared. Other types of equities are the ownership of partnerships and proprietorships. The net profit from those enterprises is the difference between their receipts and expenditures; the amount of this residual varies in amount and may be negative. A proprietor is the sole owner and receives all of the net income of the business. Partners share the net income of the enterprise in accordance with the terms of the partnership agreement.

Because prices of stocks and bonds are unstable, they are risky as assets compared to holding money. If the price of a share of common stock held rises, the owner receives a capital gain in addition to the dividends. The total annual income earned is equal to the annual dividend plus or minus the annual appreciation or depreciation in the price of the stock. Professors Fisher and Lorie estimate that for stocks listed on the New York Stock Exchange, the average nominal rates of return on stocks purchased in 1930 or in any subsequent year and held until 1965 were between 7 and 20 percent per year. (These are after-tax estimates and assume that dividends are not reinvested.) Average rates of return on stocks vary sharply with the period for which estimates are made.[2] From 1965 to 1979, average nominal rates of return on common stock dropped sharply because of a slowdown in the growth of stock prices. Also, because of inflation, in recent years the real rate of return on common stock listed on the New York Stock Exchange has, on the average, been negative.

Physical capital

Physical capital consists solely of the physical assets owned by individuals. It excludes physical capital owned by business enterprises, because this is already represented by bonds and equities. Owner-occupied homes are the most important nonbusiness physical asset, but also included are land, automobiles, antiques, art, household equipment, and jewelry. These assets usually yield the owner an income in kind rather than a money income. They may also appreciate or depreciate in price. Many persons in the United States have gained from the appreciation in the value of their homes. Wealthy persons may purchase fine pieces of art not solely for their own enjoyment, but also for financial speculation.

Human capital

The fifth category of wealth is human capital, people themselves. Human beings are not normally conceived of as capital because human beings cannot be sold. Yet human beings are the principal source of income. Wages typically amount to over 70 percent of the national income. By including human capital in this classification of the different types of wealth, the list is meant to encompass all possible sources of real and money income, and thus all wealth.

People may invest in themselves through education and training. Investment in human capital creates a valuable asset, but one that is not at all liquid. People also receive a rate of return from investments in themselves. One study estimates that the real rate of return on higher education (from money spent and forgone earnings) was approximately 14.5 percent for white males graduating from college in 1939, and 13 percent for similar persons finishing in 1949.[3] A recent study estimates that between 1968 and 1973 the real rate of return on investment in four years of college education may have declined from 11 percent to 7½ percent.[4]

Social Security wealth

A type of wealth not included in this classification of wealth, but which has been widely discussed in recent years, is Social Security wealth—the actuarial present value of the Social Security benefits to which individuals are entitled. As the Social Security System has grown, Social Security wealth has become the principal type of nonhuman wealth owned by many persons, and the total amount has become very large. Although the increase in Social Security wealth may have affected the demand for other types of wealth, this is still a matter of considerable debate.

Demand for money balances by individuals

Once money is conceived of as a type of wealth, the general factors that affect the demand for money become apparent. A person can choose how he wants to hold his wealth. If he wishes to hold more common stock and less money, he can do so. A rational person distributes his total wealth among the various types so that the marginal utility of each type of wealth is the same. As a result, the demand for money changes if the attractiveness of other types of wealth changes. If total wealth increases, one would expect an increase in the demand for each type of wealth—including the demand for money—although possibly not in exactly the same proportion. Also, the demand for money depends on how much people want the particular advantages provided by holding money—convenience in transactions and security. The analysis of the demand for money is similar to the analysis of the demand for consumer goods and services except that, as a type of wealth, money provides services in the future.

The factors that affect a person's demand for money balances may be summarized in the following equation:[5]

16.1

$$M^d = f\left(y, w; i_m, i_b, i_e, \left(\frac{\Delta P}{P}\right)^*; u\right) P$$

where M^d = the demand for money balances; y = expected real income; w = the fraction of wealth in nonhuman form; i_m = the expected rate of return on money; i_b = the expected rate of return on bonds, including expected changes in their prices; i_e = the expected rate of return on equities, including expected changes in their prices; $(\triangle P/P)^*$ = the expected rate of change in prices of goods and services, u = other factors that may affect the usefulness of money balances, and P = the expected level of prices.

Expected level of prices

Other things being equal, the higher the expected level of prices, the higher the demand for money. What matters to people is the real quantity of money that they hold rather than the nominal quantity. The higher the expected price level, the more money people will want in order to have the same real command over goods and services. If the expected price level were to double, people would probably want to hold twice as much money in order to have the same convenience in making transactions and the same security against contingencies. If the demand for money does not vary in proportion to the expected level of prices, people are said to be affected by *money illusion*—attention to the nominal quantity of money held rather than to its real value. If there is money illusion, when the expected price level rises, the demand for money would not increase as much as the rise in prices.

In equation 16.1, the quantity of money demanded (M^d) varies directly and in proportion to the expected level of prices—the variable P is outside the brackets of the formula. Statistical studies of the demand for money generally support the view that the demand for money varies directly with the expected level of prices, and that people's behavior is usually not affected by money illusion.[6] The demand for money is not assumed to vary *directly* with the other variables in the equation—there is a functional relationship between the demand for money and the variables inside the brackets.

The demand for money (M^d) is equal to the expected level of prices multiplied by the demand for real money balances (m^d):

16.2

$$M^d = P \cdot m^d.$$

The demand for real money balances (m^d) is equal to the demand for money (M^d) divided by the expected level of prices:

16.3

$$m^{\text{d}} = \frac{M^{\text{d}}}{P} .$$

In equation 16.1, changes in any of the variables inside the function $(y, w; \ i_{\text{m}}, i_{\text{b}}, i_{\text{e}}, (\Delta P/P)^*; \ u)$ may cause changes in the demand for real money balances. When these variables change, they either affect the attractiveness of holding money as compared to other assets, or they reflect an increase in total wealth. Each of these variables affects an individual's demand for real money balances in a different way.

Expected real income

Other things being equal, the higher expected real income is, the greater the demand for real money balances. Wealth and income are closely related. (Wealth is the source of all income.) When an individual's total wealth (and therefore income) is increased, he will probably want more of each type of wealth, including more money.

Expected real income may be different from the actual level of real income that persons have received. In periods of prosperity, for example, the current level of real income is often larger than the real income people expect in the future, because people realize that periods of prosperity are followed by periods of recession. Also, in recessions, when real income declines, the real income that people expect in the future may be larger than the level of real income that they are receiving. The principal factor determining expected real income is probably the real income that people have received in the past. Statistically, economists most often measure expected real income using a weighted average of past values of annual real income.

Historical experience in the United States, and in many other rapidly growing countries, indicates that when expected real income rises, the demand for real money balances increases at a faster rate than the rate of increase in real income. Table 15.5 in Chapter 15 showed a marked drop in the velocity of money during the nineteenth century, meaning that people were holding a larger proportion of their income in money balances. From the Civil War to World War II, the average annual increase in *M-1* plus time deposits in commercial banks per capita was 3.7 percent, and the average annual increase in prices was only 0.9 percent.[7] During this period, when real income per capita in the United States rose 1.0 percent, the demand for real money balances per capita rose more—about 1.7 percent. In 1869, *M-1* plus time deposits in commercial banks amounted to only 25 percent of the net national product;

in 1979, almost 43 percent. The demand for money appears to be like the demand for luxuries, such as travel and entertainment: As real income rises, people want relatively more of it.

Expected rate of return on money

Other things being equal, the higher the expected rate of return on money, the larger the demand for real money balances. Because the payment of interest on demand deposits was prohibited in the United States in 1933, some empirical studies of the demand for money (based on *M-1*) have assumed that the rate of return on money is zero. Other studies based on broader measures of the money supply have taken into account the payment of interest on time deposits. The higher the nominal rate of interest paid on time deposits (and assuming those interest rates are expected to continue in the future), the larger would be the demand for real money balances. The rate of return on money is also affected by service charges on checking accounts, loans to depositors at preferential rates, and services provided depositors without explicit charges (such as giving advice on business and tax problems). The studies that have attempted to include these factors in their measurement of the rate of return on money found that variations in the expected rate of return on money have a measurable effect on the demand for real money balances.

Expected rates of return on bonds and equities

Other things being equal, the higher the expected rates of return on bonds and equities, the less the demand for real money balances. Money competes with bonds and equities as a type of wealth. If the expected nominal rates of return on bonds and equities were low, people would want to hold larger real money balances because the lower yields on bonds and equities would not impose as large a penalty in the form of earnings forgone. Studies of the demand for money usually measure the expected rate of return on bonds by either the yield on twenty-year bonds or the four- to six-month commercial paper rate.

Several statistical studies have shown a reliable relationship between the demand for real money balances and market rates of return on bonds in the United States.[8] Professor Henry A. Latané concluded that the secular decline in the velocity of *M-1* in the United States from 1918 to 1945 (as shown by the secular rise in real money balances per unit of output) was the result of the decline in market interest rates, as measured by corporate bond yields. Professor Allan H. Meltzer examined data for the period from 1900 to 1958 and also concluded that changes in the yields on corporate bonds had an important effect on the demand for real money balances. In addition, recent studies of the demand for *M-1* have found that the rate of interest on time deposits has an important effect on the demand for real money balances.[9]

Expected rate of change in prices

Other things being equal, the higher the expected rate of inflation, the smaller the demand for real money balances. When prices rise 10 percent during a year, currency and demand deposits, which have fixed nominal values and pay no interest, are worth 10 percent less in purchasing power. Other assets, such as corporation stock and physical assets, are well-known hedges against inflation because their prices may rise with prices in general. The higher the rate of inflation, the more rapidly the value of money falls and the more attractive real assets are. The expected rate of inflation used is a weighted average of past rates of inflation, and it is based on the assumption that the rate of inflation people expect is derived from the rates of inflation they have experienced.

Statistical studies of countries with high rates of inflation have found that changes in the rate of inflation can significantly affect the amount of real money balances held.[10] In South Korea from 1953 to 1961, for example, the rate of inflation fell from 4.5 percent a month in 1953 to less than 1.0 percent a month in 1961, and the ratio of the amount of money people held relative to income more than doubled. As the rate of inflation decelerated, Koreans apparently began to expect less inflation and were willing to hold a greater proportion of their income in money. The increase in real money balances was also partly the result of the economic recovery which followed the Korean War and the per capita rise in real income.

The experience in Brazil from 1948 to 1964 is another example. There, the rate of inflation accelerated, and, as one would expect, real money balances fell. The rate of inflation rose from less than one percent a month in 1948 to 5 percent a month in 1964, and the ratio of the amount of money people held to income fell 15 percent for *M-1* and 33 percent for *M-1* plus time deposits in commercial banks. The rapid rise in per capita real income in Brazil during this period probably offset, in part, the impact of the accelerated inflation and caused the decline in real money balances to be smaller than it might have been.

Bond yields and the expected rate of inflation—two important variables affecting the demand for real money balances—are interdependent. An increase in the expected rate of inflation will raise bond yields, and the higher the expected rate of inflation, the higher the yields will be. This is caused by attempts of investors to get a real rate of return on their investments in bonds.

Division of wealth into human and nonhuman forms

Other things being equal, the higher the ratio of human to nonhuman wealth, the higher the demand for real money balances. The major asset of most persons is their own earning capacity. Although it is usually quite easy to shift from money to stocks and other types of wealth, it is not as easy to shift quickly from various types of property wealth to human wealth; it is, nevertheless, possible. An example would be a person who sold his stocks and bonds in order to pay for the cost of a medical education. Shifting in the other direction is more common. As people approach retirement, they usually use part of their earnings to invest in financial assets. As they accumulate real estate, stocks, and bonds, they come gradually to hold a larger percentage of their total assets in nonhuman forms.

The demand for real money balances is affected by that fraction of a person's total wealth which is human capital, because human capital is an extremely illiquid form of wealth. As a result, the higher the proportion of a person's wealth in human capital, the higher the demand for more liquid forms of wealth in the portfolio.

Other factors that affect tastes and preferences

There are some things which affect tastes and preferences for holding money that are important, even though difficult to measure precisely. The degree of economic instability that people expect to prevail in the future affects the size of the reserve persons wish to hold in case of sickness, the loss of a job, or business losses. If economic conditions are very unstable, as they were during the Great Depression from 1929 to 1933, one would expect people to want to hold large real money balances. During the depression, the ratio of *M-1* plus time deposits in commercial banks to income actually did rise sharply, and, although after 1932 this ratio fell, it was still higher than it had been in the 1920s. After World War II, the fact that periods of recession were short and mild probably caused persons to become less cautious. Because people had greater confidence in the security of their jobs, they held smaller real money balances.

As the United States industrialized in the nineteenth century, the use of money became more widespread. When working for wages became more common, a larger portion of the population became involved in the market economy. Family units became less self-sufficient and purchased needed goods and services in the market—and the demand for money increased.

Another factor affecting the desire for real money balances is the extent to which people move from one part of the country to another.

When geographic mobility increases, as during major wars, persons generally prefer to hold a larger fraction of their wealth in money. Real money balances relative to income rose sharply during World War II, probably because of increased travel and more frequent changes of residence. The separation of members of families during the war also resulted in less economy in the holding of real money balances.

Demand for money balances by business enterprises

Business firms have a different demand for money balances than do individuals. The business demand for money balances is large. It has been estimated that almost two-thirds of demand deposits are held by business firms, farms, and nonprofit organizations. To the business firm, money is one of the productive resources that it uses to produce its output and is listed as such in its balance sheet. The demand for real money balances by business firms is significantly related to their size, as measured by their total sales, net income, total assets, net worth, or value added. Business firms can expand the total amount of their productive assets by borrowing and by selling stock in capital markets, and they attempt to obtain the amount of resources that will maximize returns. By comparison, individuals typically allocate a given volume of total wealth among the various types of wealth. Although there are some differences between the determinants of the demand for money for individuals and for business firms, nominal rates of return on money and other assets and the rate of inflation are significant for both. Much less empirical work has been done on the business demand for money than on the aggregate demand, which includes both persons and business firms, because of the lack of data on the amount of money held solely by business firms.

Changes in the demand for money

The relationship between the demand for money and prices, assuming a constant demand for real money balances, is illustrated in Figure 16.1. In this figure, the quantity of money demanded (M^d) varies directly and in proportion to prices. The ratio of money to prices is constant and at every point on the M^d schedule is one-fourth. The demand for money schedule would slope upward in this way if, for example, when prices rose 10 percent, the amount of money people wanted to hold also increased 10 percent.

Figure 16.2 illustrates a decrease in the demand for money. The M^d schedule shifts to the left from M^d_0 to M^d_1. When the demand schedule

Figure 16.1
Aggregate Demand
for Money

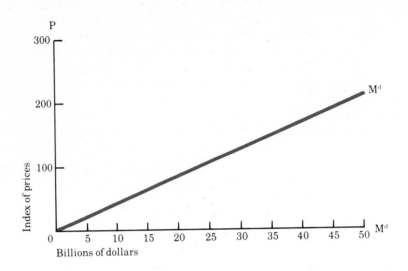

for money decreases, people wish to hold smaller real money balances. When the index of prices was at 100, people wanted to hold $25 billion; after the decrease in the demand for money, they wanted to hold less, only $20 billion, even though there was no change in prices. A decrease in the demand for money may be caused by a decrease in expected real income in the economy, higher expected rates of return on stocks and

Figure 16.2
Decrease in the
Demand for Money

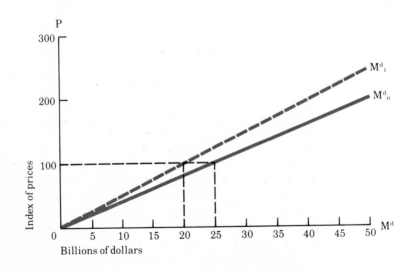

bonds, lower expected rates of return on money, a higher expected rate of inflation, a change in preferences (such as a greater feeling of security), or a decrease in the portion of wealth owned in human forms.

Figure 16.3 illustrates an increase in the demand for money. The M^d schedule shifts to the right from $M^d{}_0$ to $M^d{}_1$. When the demand for money increases, people want to hold more money relative to prices. When the price index was at 100, people wanted to hold $25 billion. After the increase in the demand for money, they wanted to hold more, $30 billion, even though prices had not changed. The factors causing an increase in the M^d schedule are the opposite of those causing a decrease: an increase in expected real income, higher expected rates of return on money, lower expected rates of return on bonds and equities, a low expected rate of inflation, a feeling of insecurity, or a larger fraction of wealth in human forms.

**Figure 16.3
Increase in the
Demand for Money**

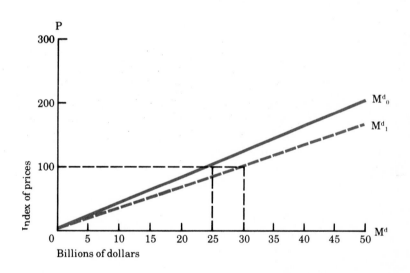

Velocity and the demand for real money balances

The shifts in the demand for money schedule shown in Figures 16.2 and 16.3 occurred because of changes in the demand for real money balances, to which changes in the velocity of money are closely related. The velocity of money tends to increase when the demand for real money balances decreases, and velocity tends to decrease when the demand for real money balances increases. This relationship is shown in Equation 16.4. The usual equation for velocity is Py/M (see Equation

15.4). If we divide both the numerator and the denominator of this equation by prices, the result is that velocity is also equal to real output (y) divided by real cash balances (m):

16.4

$$V = \frac{Py}{M} = \frac{y}{\dfrac{M}{P}} = \frac{y}{m} \; .$$

This form of the equation for velocity shows that if there is no change in real output, a decrease in real money balances would cause velocity to rise. An increase in real money balances by itself would cause velocity to fall.

Predicting changes in the demand for money

If the factors affecting it were perfectly understood, economists would be able to predict changes in the demand for money.[11] An ability to predict such changes, combined with control over the money stock, would add significantly to the Federal Reserve System's ability not only to control inflation, but also to control short-run fluctuations in real output. As will be explained in Chapter 17, an increase in the demand for money tends to depress spending, and a decrease in the demand for money has a stimulating effect on spending. Economists still have a long way to go before they can predict changes in the demand for money, even though in recent years many statistical studies of the demand for money have been made. Statistical data are available for many of the variables affecting the demand, and correlation tests of their relationship to this demand can be carried out. The statistical studies have shown that such factors as per capita real income, interest rates, and rates of inflation affect the demand for money, although much is still to be learned about the exact relationships. One of the problems in making these studies is that it is necessary to make estimates of expected real income, expected rates of return, and expected inflation from the available data on actual rates. Although statistical techniques have been developed to estimate expected series, these are based on the assumption that expectations can be projected from recent experience, and these techniques are not able to take into account all of the possible conditions affecting expectations. Another problem is that the factors affecting tastes and preferences are often difficult to quantify.

Other concepts of the demand for money

The transactions demand for money

Some economists conceive of money as demanded exclusively for a medium of exchange rather than as a type of wealth. In accordance with this point of view, the demand for money is expected to expand in proportion to increases in income, and shifts in the demand for money relative to income are attributed primarily to changes in the frequency, regularity, and coordination of receipts and payments, and to the stage of development of the credit and financial system.[12]

If the demand for money depended primarily on its use in transactions, then the shorter the interval between receipts, the smaller would be the demand for money. For example, consider a person who is paid $600 monthly on the first day of each month and spends his income at a uniform rate of $20 per day for thirty days. The amount of money he needs to hold would decline uniformly over the course of the month, and his average balance would be $300, half his monthly income. However, if this same person were paid every fifteen days, he would receive $300 twice a month, and his average balance would be only $150. Also, a decrease in the frequency of disbursements for consumption may increase the average amount of money held because people would hold larger amounts between the times when expenditures are made.

The demand for money may also be influenced by the regularity of income receipts. The more irregular the receipt of money, the larger the amount of money a person needs to tide him over relatively long periods between paydays or to see him through periods when income is relatively low. If the timing and amount of a person's receipts and expenditures correspond, less money is needed. If, for example, because of more widespread use of charge accounts, people customarily pay off their debts on payday rather than spreading their expenditures throughout the income period, the demand for money would decrease.

Another factor affecting the demand for money for transactions is the development of credit institutions. If people can borrow money easily and quickly, it is not necessary for them to hold as much money for contingencies or transactions. Also, if well-developed credit markets are available, owners of excess funds would be more likely to lend them rather than to hold them as money.

The demand for money as a type of asset is related to the demand for money for transactions. For example, an increase in the expected rate of inflation might reduce the demand for money as a type of asset, by affecting payment practices. This would occur if during rapid inflation pay periods become more frequent so as to avoid longer-term contracts.

The principal shortcoming of the transactions conception of the demand for money is that the historical trend toward more frequent payments to workers and toward a larger variety of credit facilities, particularly in the nineteenth century, would lead one to expect that people would hold less money relative to their incomes. Instead, people now hold larger amounts of money than in the past.

The transactions plus asset demand for money

The theory of the demand for money in Keynes' famous work, *The General Theory of Employment, Interest and Money*, separates the demand for money into two parts: the *transactions* demand and the *asset* demand.[13] According to this theory, money includes only the medium of exchange—currency and demand deposits—and would be measured by *M-1A* or *M-1B*. The transactions demand is determined primarily by the level of the national income, as shown in Figure 16.4(a). The transactions demand for money is designated as L_0 to distinguish it from the asset demand for money which is designated as L_1.

Figure 16.4
The Demand for Money

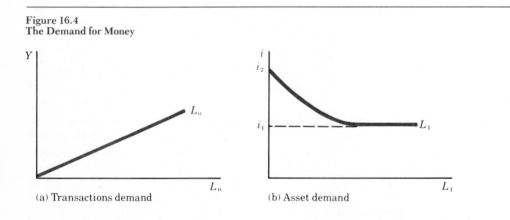

(a) Transactions demand   (b) Asset demand

People are expected to increase their holdings of money for transactions approximately in proportion to increases in their income so as to have the same convenience in making current expenditures and to have additional security in providing for possible future contingencies. Underlying the transactions demand are both the transactions and precautionary motives for holding money. The demand schedule, L_0, may shift upward or downward if the *transactions costs* involved in converting other assets into money change. It is useful to have some money on hand in order to avoid the inconvenience of having to cash a savings deposit or to sell bonds every time one needs money. There may also be fees charged for selling bonds, or lower rates of return received on time deposits cashed before their maturity date. The less inconvenient and costly it becomes to convert interest-earning assets into money, the smaller would be the demand for money for transactions and the larger would be the demand for savings deposits and bonds. This would cause the L_0 schedule to shift upward. Or, if it should become more costly and time-consuming to convert interest-earning assets into money, the L_0 schedule would shift downward. The demand for money for transactions also varies with the frequency, regularity, and coordination of receipts and payments and with the development of new types of credit.

The asset demand for money depends primarily on market interest rates and is illustrated in Figure 16.4(b). It is based on the speculative motive for holding money. This figure shows that if market interest rates are as high as i_2 there would be no demand for money as an asset. The speculative objective of holding money is to be in a position to purchase stocks, long-term bonds, inventory goods, and other types of real property when their prices are low or are expected to rise. The principal alternative to holding money for this purpose is to hold short-term government securities. If the market yield on short-term government securities is very high, persons interested in speculating would hold those securities rather than money. There are two reasons: (1) the high rate of return on the short-term securities is attractive; and (2) if their yield were high, the prices of those securities would be low, and the risk of capital loss would be minimal because there would be little chance that their prices would fall further.

Figure 16.4(b) also shows that, if market interest rates are as low as i_1, the demand for money as an asset would be infinite. For the speculator, there would be two reasons for this preference for holding money rather than short-term government securities: (1) the low yield on the short-term securities would be unattractive; and (2) since the prices of these securities would be very high, there would be a great risk of incurring a capital loss if one wished to sell these securities to obtain funds with which to purchase other assets. In between i_2 and i_1, the demand for money as an asset would increase as market interest rates fell because it would be more attractive to hold money for speculative purposes than to hold short-term bonds.

Because all money holdings may be used either for transactions or for asset purposes, the separation of money holdings into balances held for transactions and balances held for speculation has been criticized as unrealistic. The justification for the separation is theoretical and is based on the belief that the demand for money for transactions is primarily determined by income, and the demand for speculation is determined primarily by interest rates. There is a difference of opinion concerning whether the conception of money should be restricted to currency and demand deposits or broadened to include all assets with a fixed nominal value. The transactions plus asset demand for money is based on the narrower definition of money. There is also a difference of opinion concerning the spectrum of assets with which money competes. Should this spectrum include long-term bonds, equities, physical assets, and even human capital, or should it be restricted primarily to short-term securities? In the transactions plus asset demand for money, the holding of money competes primarily with the holding of short-term securities. Another question is whether the demand for money should be related to current income or to expected income. In the conception of money as a type of wealth, the demand for money is related to expected income.

Summary

If the demand for real money balances is constant, the demand for money varies in proportion to the expected level of prices.

The demand for real money balances will decrease if people expect a more rapid rate of inflation, if they expect higher market rates of interest, if expected real income declines, and if the ratio of human to nonhuman wealth decreases. The demand for real money balances will increase if people expect less inflation, lower market rates of interest and higher real incomes, and if the ratio of human to nonhuman wealth increases.

There are several different conceptions of the demand for money. In addition to the demand for money as a type of wealth, there is the transactions demand for money and the transactions plus asset demand for money.

Notes

1. Milton Friedman, "The Quantity Theory of Money—A Restatement," in *Studies in the Quantity Theory of Money* (Chicago: University of Chicago Press, 1956), pp. 3–21.

2. Lawrence Fisher and James H. Lorie, "Rates of Return on Investments in Common Stock, The Year-by-Year Record, 1926–1965," Table 2, *Journal of Business* 41 (July 1968); and James H. Lorie and Mary T. Hamilton, *The Stock Market, Theories and Evidence* (Homewood, Ill.: Richard D. Irwin, Inc., 1973), Chapter 2.

3. Gary S. Becker, *Human Capital,* 2nd ed. (New York: Columbia University Press, 1975), pp. 148–157.

4. Richard B. Freeman, *The Over-Educated American* (New York: Academic Press, 1976), pp. 26–27.

5. Milton Friedman, "Money, Quantity Theory," in *International Encyclopedia of the Social Sciences,* Vol. 10 (New York: Macmillan, 1968), p. 440.

6. For a summary of the results of statistical studies of the demand for money, see David E. W. Laidler, *The Demand for Money: Theories and Evidence,* 2nd ed. (New York: Dun-Donnelley, 1977), pp. 119–152.

7. Milton Friedman and Anna J. Schwartz, *A Monetary History of the United States, 1867–1960* (Princeton: Princeton University Press, 1963), p. 5; and Milton Friedman, "The Demand for Money," in *Dollars and Deficits* (Englewood Cliffs, N.J.: Prentice-Hall, 1968), p. 199.

8. Henry A. Latané, "Income Velocity and Interest Rates, A Pragmatic Approach," *Review of Economics and Statistics* 42 (November 1960), pp. 445–449; and Allan H. Meltzer, "The Demand for Money: The Evidence from the Time Series," *Journal of Political Economy* 71 (June 1963), pp. 219–246.

9. Stephen M. Goldfeld, "The Demand for Money Revisited," *Brookings Papers on Economic Activity, 3,* 1973, pp. 577–638.

10. See Phillip Cagan, "The Monetary Dynamics of Hyperinflation," in Milton Friedman, ed., *Studies in the Quantity Theory of Money* (Chicago: University of Chicago Press, 1956), pp. 25–117, for examples of the effect of hyperinflation on real cash balances in seven European countries after World War I and during World War II. See also John V. Deaver, "The Chilean Inflation and the Demand for Money," and Colin D. Campbell, "The Velocity of Money and the Rate of Inflation: Recent Experience in South Korea and Brazil," in David Meiselman, ed., *Varieties of Monetary Experience* (Chicago: University of Chicago Press, 1970), pp. 7–67 and 339–386.

11. Carl Brunner and Allan H. Meltzer, "Predicting Velocity: Implications for Theory and Policy," *Journal of Finance* 18 (May 1963), pp. 319–354; and Stephen M. Goldfeld, "The Case of Missing Money," *Brookings Papers on Economic Activity, 3:* 1976, pp. 683–730.

12. Irving Fisher, *The Purchasing Power of Money* (New York: Macmillan, 1926), pp. 79–89; and Lester V. Chandler, *Introduction to Monetary Theory* (New York: Harper & Row, 1940), pp. 34–40.

13. See Robert E. Weintraub, *Introduction to Monetary Economics* (New York: Ronald Press Company, 1970), Chapter 13, "Keynesian Money Demand," pp. 249–266.

Questions

16.1. What is the difference between the supply of money and the demand for money?

16.2. Explain the unique characteristics of each of the following types of wealth: money, bonds, equities, physical capital, human capital.

16.3. Why would you expect the demand for money to vary with the price level?

16.4. Explain the difference between actual real income and expected real income.

16.5. Explain the way in which the demand for real money balances is affected by:
  (a) a rise in expected real income,
  (b) a fall in expected interest rates,
  (c) a rise in the expected rate of inflation,
  (d) a rise in the expected rate of return on money,
  (e) an increase in human wealth relative to nonhuman wealth.

16.6. Name some factors, other than those listed in question 16.5, that may affect the demand for real money balances.

16.7. Draw a schedule on a graph showing the relationship between the demand for money and prices. Explain the meaning of an increase in the demand schedule for money. Explain the meaning of a decrease in the demand schedule for money.

16.8. Explain the decrease in the demand for money in the United States from 1945 to 1960.

16.9. Compare the different concepts of the demand for money:
  (a) the demand for money as a type of wealth,
  (b) the transactions demand for money,
  (c) the transactions plus asset demand for money.

16.10. Know the meaning and significance of the following terms and concepts: demand for money, wealth, equities, human capital, Social Security wealth, real money balances, expected income, expected inflation, transactions costs, increase in the demand for money, transactions demand for money, asset demand for money.

17

This chapter is concerned with the way in which changes in the quantity of money cause portfolio adjustments which lead to changes in total spending and thus in the national income.

THE RELATION
OF MONEY TO
INCOME: PART I

Monetary theory attempts to explain how an increase in the money supply may raise the national income or how a decrease in the money supply may lower it. This is the subject of Chapters 17 and 18.

The national income is a measure of the level of economic activity in a country. When the national income increases, it means that the economy has probably grown; when the national income decreases, there has usually been a decline in economic activity. Governments attempt to control the national income of their countries through their control of monetary policy.

To affect the national income, changes in the money supply must increase or decrease aggregate demand. This chapter explains the way money affects aggregate demand through its effect on the relationship between the supply and demand for money and through its effect on the portfolios of both commercial banks and the public.

Measuring national income

There are two ways of measuring national income—by distributive shares and by type of expenditure. The statistical data for these two measures of national income in 1979 are given in Table 17.1.

Table 17.1
National Income of the United States, 1979 (in billions of dollars)

By Distributive Shares		By Type of Expenditure	
Compensation of employees	$1,459.1	Personal consumption expenditures	$1,509.8
Proprietors' income	130.0	Gross private domestic investment	386.2
Rental income	26.9	Net exports of goods and services	– 3.5
Net interest	129.7		
Corporation profits	178.5		
		Government purchases of goods and services	476.1
National income	$1,924.2		
		Gross National Product	$2,368.5
		Less: Capital consumption allowances	243.0
		Indirect business taxes, etc.	201.4
		National Income	$1,924.2

Columns do not add to totals because of rounding.
Source: *Economic Report of the President, January 1980*, pp. 212–13, 222, and 224–5.

The national income is composed of five different types of income: compensation of employees, proprietors' income, rental income, net interest, and corporation profits. By far the largest type is the *compensa-*

tion of employees—wages and salaries. *Proprietors' income* is the profit received by persons who run businesses organized as proprietorships and partnerships. *Rental income* consists of both the net rent (after payments for depreciation, property taxes, and operating costs) that people receive from leases on real estate, and the implicit rent from home ownership—the estimated amount persons would have to pay to rent the homes they live in if they did not own them. *Net interest* is the income that people receive on funds lent to others. It consists primarily of interest from time deposits at banks and from bonds—corporate, municipal, and U.S. government. Net interest excludes interest received on loans to consumers to buy automobiles and other consumer goods. This is because conceptually interest is viewed as a payment for the use of capital, and consumer goods are not capital. For the same reason, interest payments on U.S. government securities were formerly not included, but are now. Until recent years, because most of the national debt was incurred during World Wars I and II, interest on the national debt was not a payment for the use of capital equipment. *Corporation profits* include the total amount of the profits of business enterprises that are organized as corporations. Part of the total amount of corporation profits is paid in corporation income taxes, part is retained by the enterprises, and part is paid as dividends to the stockholders. Dividends distributed to stockholders usually amount to approximately 30 percent of total corporate profits before corporation income taxes are deducted.

The gross national product (GNP) is the sum of four different types of expenditures—consumption, investment, net exports, and government purchases. *Personal consumption expenditures* include primarily expenditures for food, clothing, housing, transportation, and entertainment. *Gross private domestic investment* consists of expenditures for new housing, business plants, machinery and equipment, and changes in business inventories—types of capital goods which are used to produce other goods and services. Gross investment includes the replacement of capital goods which have depreciated during the year (called capital consumption allowances), as well as additions to the total stock of capital. *Net exports* are the difference between total exports and imports of goods and services. Usually, exports are larger than imports. Only net exports are included in this category because imports equal to the bulk of exports are already included in total personal consumption, gross private domestic investment, or government purchases. *Government purchases* of goods and services consist of the amount spent by federal, state, and local government. Welfare payments are excluded because they are not payments to people for their contribution to production either from their own labor or from the capital they own.

The gross national product is larger than the national income for two reasons. Part of gross domestic investment consists of the replacement of plant or machinery that has depreciated during the year. This causes the GNP to be larger than the national income because rental income, corporate profits, and the income of proprietors—types of income shown on the left-hand side of Table 17.1—are estimated net of the costs of depreciation. In the United States, the total amount spent to cover depreciation usually amounts to about one-tenth of GNP. The second reason that GNP is larger than national income is that expenditures for property taxes and sales taxes (called indirect business taxes) are included in the prices of the goods and services in the GNP, but are costs which, like depreciation, are deducted before estimating rental income, corporate profits, and the income of proprietors. When the amount of capital consumption allowances and indirect business taxes are deducted from the GNP, the measure of the national income by type of expenditures is equal to the measure by distributive shares. The two ways of measuring national income—by type of expenditure and by distributive shares—must be equal. This is because the amount received for the goods and services produced, after deducting the appropriate amounts for capital consumption allowances and indirect business taxes, is distributed to the owners of labor and capital. Although the retained profits of business firms are not paid out to the owners, they are retained in the business to the benefit of the owners.

There are several types of transactions that are not included in the GNP. The GNP does not include purchases of securities or of houses that were built in previous years. Neither of these would represent payments for current production. Also, some goods are *intermediate goods* that are sold by one producer to another. The purchase of steel by the automobile manufacturer is an example. It would be double counting to include in the national income both the value of the steel sold to the automobile companies and the value of the automobiles produced with the steel. Only *final goods* are included in the national income. Because of the need to distinguish intermediate goods from final goods, the calculation of the GNP by type of expenditure is a difficult task.

GNP in 1972 prices

Statistical data on the GNP are published both in current prices and in 1972 prices. Annual data from 1970 to 1979 are shown in Table 17.2. Changes in the GNP in current prices reflect not only changes in real output, but also changes in prices because of inflation. The series on the GNP in 1972 prices measures solely changes in real output—1972 prices are used in calculating the GNP for each year. In this way prices are held constant from year to year.

The statistical series on the GNP are the best estimates available of the country's economic growth and the changes in the total output of the economy. Table 17.2 shows that there were small percentage declines in real GNP in 1970 and in 1974 and 1975. Recessions occurred in these years. Table 17.2 also shows that in every year from 1970 to 1979, the percentage increases in GNP in current prices were larger than the percentage increases in 1972 prices. Over the entire period, there was considerable inflation.

Table 17.2
Gross National Product,
1970–1979

Year	GNP in Current Prices (in billions)	Change from Previous Year (Percent)	GNP in 1972 Prices (in billions)	Change from Previous Year (Percent)
1970	$ 982.4	5.0%	$1,075.3	–0.3%
1971	1,063.4	8.2	1,107.5	3.0
1972	1,171.1	10.1	1,171.1	5.7
1973	1,306.6	11.6	1,235.0	5.5
1974	1,412.9	8.1	1,217.8	–1.4
1975	1,528.8	8.2	1,202.3	–1.3
1976	1,702.2	11.3	1,273.0	5.9
1977	1,899.5	11.6	1,340.5	5.3
1978	2,127.6	12.0	1,399.2	4.4
1979P	2,368.5	11.3	1,431.1	2.3

Source: *Economic Report of the President, January 1980*, pp. 203, 205, and 215.

Money and aggregate demand

The important economic diagram in Figure 17.1 is used by economists to explain the way in which changes in the money supply may cause changes in the national income. This diagram includes two schedules— an aggregate demand schedule and an aggregate supply schedule. For an increase in the money supply to increase the national income, it must raise the aggregate demand schedule without any change in the aggregate supply schedule. To decrease the national income, a decrease in the money supply must lower the aggregate demand schedule without any change in the aggregate supply schedule. To comprehend this relationship, it is necessary to understand why the equilibrium level of the national income is where aggregate demand is equal to aggregate supply and why changes in the money supply may shift the aggregate demand schedule up or down.

Aggregate demand

Aggregate demand is the total amount that people, business enterprises, and governments *desire* to spend for consumer goods and services, investment goods, and government goods and services. The vertical axis of Figure 17.1 measures total desired spending ($C + I + G$). C is the

symbol for consumption; I represents investment and combines investment spending with net exports of goods and services; and G stands for
government expenditures. The horizontal axis of Figure 17.1 measures
the national income (Y). Note that the two axes have the same scale.

Figure 17.1
The Equilibrium Level
of National Income

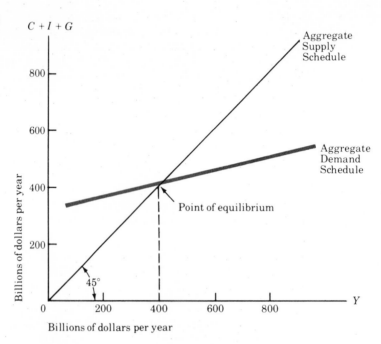

The aggregate demand schedule slopes upward, indicating that total
desired spending becomes larger as the national income increases. One
would expect people to want to consume more as their incomes increase. The amount spent by most people depends on their income, and
if their income increases they spend more. However, when income
increases, aggregate demand does not increase as fast as income; and
when income decreases, aggregate demand does not decline as rapidly
as income. This relationship between income and aggregate demand is
based on the relationship between income and consumption. Aggregate
demand also includes investment and government spending, but these
do not have the same close relationship to income as does consumption.
Empirical research by economists has shown that, in periods of business
expansion, consumption does not increase as fast as income. Because
people do not desire to increase their spending for consumer goods and
services in periods of prosperity as fast as their income rises, the average

propensity to consume (C/Y) falls. On the other hand, when income falls in a recession, people do not desire to reduce their consumption as much as their income, so the average propensity to consume increases. This relationship between income and consumption is a short-run relationship that occurs during periods of business expansion and recession—it does not occur in the long run.

There are several theories explaining this relationship—the permanent income theory, the life-cycle theory, and the relative income theory.[1] According to the *permanent income theory*, in periods of prosperity, the decline in consumption relative to income is thought to reflect the belief by individuals that when incomes rise, not all of the increase will last. They view the increase in their incomes as temporary. Unless the increase in income is expected to last, one would not expect consumption to increase as much as income. Eventually, as higher levels of income continue, consumption does rise as rapidly as income. According to the *life-cycle theory*, people plan their consumption over their lifetime. It is assumed that people seek to smooth their consumption, making its variations during their lifetime less than variations in income. The *relative income theory* states that consumption depends on one's income in the past as well as on current income. Once people have established a particular consumption standard, they will be reluctant to reduce that standard. As a result, when income declines, consumption does not decline nearly as much.

Equilibrium between aggregate demand and aggregate supply

The aggregate supply schedule in Figure 17.1 shows the level of the national output at each level of national income. The vertical axis of Figure 17.1 measures total output as well as total desired spending. The slope of the aggregate supply schedule is 45 degrees. Since both axes of Figure 17.1 have the same scale, the total output of goods and services is equal to the total income that people received to produce the output at each point on the aggregate supply schedule.

The aggregate demand schedule crosses the aggregate supply schedule at a level of national income of $400 billion. At a national income of $400 billion, aggregate demand is equal to the national output. At levels of national income smaller than $400 billion, aggregate demand is greater than the national output—the aggregate demand schedule is above the aggregate supply schedule. To the right of $400 billion, aggregate demand is smaller than the national output—the aggregate demand schedule is below the aggregate supply schedule—and the difference between the two becomes larger as national income increases.

In Figure 17.1, a level of national income equal to $400 billion is the *equilibrium* level of national income. At equilibrium, there is no tendency for the national income either to increase or decrease. The national income would fall to $400 billion if it happened to be larger than $400 billion, and it would rise to $400 billion if it happened to be smaller. It is possible for people to buy more than the economy is producing by using up inventories. The inventories of merchants and manufacturers are buffers between desired spending and output. Inventories fall if aggregate demand exceeds output; they rise if output is larger than total spending.

The impact on inventories of a difference between aggregate demand and aggregate supply is very important. Conditions in which inventories are falling cannot last long. Inventories would soon be depleted. Business firms cannot operate effectively without adequate inventories. It is necessary to have goods on hand to avoid delays in delivery to customers, because businesses compete to give good service. As a result, if aggregate demand exceeds the annual output of the economy, output will rise, because only in this way can an eventual depletion of inventories be avoided. In addition, when desired spending exceeds the output of the economy, firms are strongly induced to expand output because of high profits and expansion in the market. When inventories are low, profits tend to be high because of the lower storage costs and the lower credit costs of financing inventories. The opposite conditions prevail if output is larger than desired spending: People desire to buy less than is being produced, and inventories are growing. Firms react quite quickly to larger stockpiles by cutting down their output. The carrying of large inventories is costly. To avoid a drop in their profits, they are forced to reduce output in order to get inventories back to normal levels.

An increase in the aggregate demand schedule

For monetary policy to be expansionary, it must raise the aggregate demand schedule—for example, from AD_1 to AD_2 as in Figure 17.2. At the original equilibrium level of national income of $400 billion, aggregate demand is now $410 billion. In this example, the imbalance between aggregate demand and aggregate supply would cause the level of national income to rise to $425 billion.

In order to raise the aggregate demand schedule, an increase in the rate of expansion of the money supply must cause people to spend more even though their incomes are the same. Most increases in spending are the result of increases in the income people have received. In Figure 17.2, the upward slope of the aggregate demand schedule shows that total spending increases as the national income increases. But what is required of monetary policy is more than this. There must be an increase in total desired spending for some reason other than an increase in income. The terms used to describe this type of increase in spending are *autonomous* or *exogenous*.

Figure 17.2
Effect on National
Income of an Increase in
the Aggregate Demand
Schedule

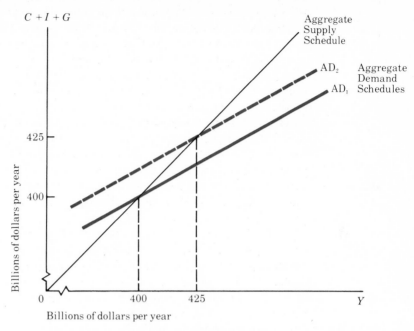

The strength of monetary policy depends on whether it is able to create sources of desired spending in addition to the normal increase in spending caused by an expansion in income. Evidence that the banking system can do this, either by providing additional supplies of credit or by providing the public with additional amounts of money, is the reason that monetary policy is important. Changes in investment spending are more apt to be autonomous than changes in consumption. It is believed that consumption is determined predominantly by the amount of income people have received. Much investment spending is financed by bank loans or by money saved in the past. Investment spending financed in either of these ways, since they are not based on income changes, would be autonomous and would shift the aggregate demand schedule upward. If government expenditures are financed by new money, they also would probably cause an autonomous increase in spending and an upward shift in the aggregate demand schedule.

The multiplier

If monetary policy causes an autonomous increase in spending, the national income would tend to expand by more than that increase. There is a multiplier relationship between an autonomous increase in spending and the resulting increase in the national income. The *multiplier* is the ratio of an increase in income (Y) to an autonomous increase in spending (I) and may be expressed as $\triangle Y/\triangle I$. The symbol I is used for autonomous increases in spending, because such spending is frequently in the form of purchases of capital goods. The multiplier relationship between autonomous increases in spending and income is illustrated in Figure 17.2. The increase in income—$25 billion—is larger than the $10 billion rise in the aggregate demand schedule. The results of statistical studies indicate that in the United States the multiplier is approximately two: If the increase in autonomous spending were $1 billion, the increase in national income would be $2 billion.

The way in which an autonomous increase in spending may cause an even larger expansion in real output, assuming no change in prices, is illustrated in Table 17.3. In this example, each period is equal to three months, and there is only one increment in investment (in the first period). The first period shows the effects of the autonomous increase in planned spending for capital goods in the first quarter, the second period shows the effects in the second quarter, and so on.

As shown in Table 17.3, in period 1 the increase in planned investment causes an equal increase in national income in the form of wages, rent, interest, and profits, because someone was paid to produce the additional investment goods. In the first period, because people have larger incomes, there would also be an increase in spending for consumer goods. Assuming that people have a *marginal propensity to consume* ($\triangle C/\triangle Y$) of 60 percent, consumption spending would rise by $600, and saving—which is anything that people do with their income other than spending it for consumption—increases by $400. If people have a 60 percent marginal propensity to consume, it means that they would spend for consumption 60 percent of the increase in their income. The increase in consumer spending in period 1 does not affect the production of consumer goods until the second period. The effect of the increase in consumption spending in period 1 is to reduce inventories of consumer goods by the amount of the increase in consumption. It should be noted that in period 1, measured investment (defined as planned investment less the reduction in inventories) increased only $400, the same amount as the increase in saving.

If business firms wish to maintain their inventories at the same level as existed prior to the increase in investment, they have to replenish the $600 worth of inventories lost in period 1. This is the reason for the increase in the output of consumer goods in period 2. Additional persons are hired to produce the consumer goods needed to replenish inventories, and the national income rises by $600 in this period. With a 60 percent marginal propensity to consume, these persons would increase consumption spending in period 2 by $360 and save $240. Although merchants had attempted to replace the inventories they had

Table 17.3
The Multiplier Process
for a Single Increment of
Investment

Period	Δ Planned Investment	Δ Consumer Goods Production	Δ National Income	Δ Consumer Spending	Δ Saving	Amount that Inventories Are Below Original Level
1	$1,000	–	$1,000	$ 600	$ 400	$ 600
2	–	$ 600	600	360	240	360
3	–	360	360	216	144	216
4	–	216	216	130	86	130
5	–	130	130	78	52	78
6	–	78	78	47	31	47
7	–	47	47	28	19	28
All subsequent periods	–	69	69	41	28	
Total	$1,000	$1,500	$2,500	$1,500	$1,000	0

lost because of the increase in investment in period 1, their inventory levels in period 2 would still be $360 below customary levels. As a result, the process continues. Merchants order $360 worth of consumer goods in period 3; the output of consumer goods increases; there is an increase in the national income, consumer spending, and saving—and inventories are still below customary levels. The final result, accumulating the effects in all periods, is an increase of $1,500 in consumption, $2,500 in national income, and $1,000 in saving. The multiplier is equal to 2.5.

The amount of the increase in national income depends on people's marginal propensity to consume (MPC). The formula is as follows:

17.1

$$\Delta Y = \frac{\Delta I}{1 - MPC} ,$$

where ΔY = increase in income, ΔI = increase in planned investment, and MPC = marginal propensity to consume. Thus,

$$\Delta Y = \frac{\$1,000}{1 - .60} = \$2,500 .$$

The smaller the MPC, the smaller the multiplier.

In Table 17.3, accumulated saving amounted to $1,000—equal to the increase in planned investment in period 1. In period 1, people had desired to invest more than the increase in saving. This caused inventories to fall. The replacement of those inventories then increased income sufficiently to create a volume of saving equal to the larger amount of planned investment.

In the illustration of the multiplier in Table 17.3, it should be noted that it is assumed that business firms maintain the inventory levels they desire by replacing the reduction in inventories rather than by raising prices. If merchants raised their prices, the effect of the increase in aggregate demand on real output would be reduced.

How changes in the money supply affect aggregate demand

An important question in monetary theory is how changes in the money supply affect aggregate demand and thus the national income. In the quantity theory of money, Figure 17.3 is of fundamental importance in explaining this relationship.[2] In this figure, the vertical axis measures the national income, the horizontal axis measures the quantity of money, and there is a money supply schedule and a money demand schedule. If the demand for money is not equal to the supply, there will be changes in aggregate demand that will cause changes in the national income. If the demand for money is less than the supply of money, aggregate demand will increase, causing national income to rise. And if the demand for money is larger than the supply, aggregate demand will decrease, causing national income to fall.

In Figure 17.3, the money supply (M^S) in the economy is $400 billion. The money supply schedule is vertical, on the assumption that the money supply is controlled by the monetary authorities. The money demand schedule shows that the quantity of money demanded (M^D) varies directly and in proportion to the national income. The schedule is drawn so that it is a straight line rising from the intersection of the two axes. The ratio of money to income is constant and at every point on the M^D schedule is equal to one-half.

In Figure 17.3, the equilibrium level of national income is the point at which the quantity of money demanded is equal to the quantity supplied, at $800 billion. At this income, the quantity of money people have is just equal to the amount they want. The national income will have a tendency to change unless the demand for money is equal to the supply. Consider why the national income would rise if it were at $600 billion: At that level of income people would want to hold only $300 billion in money—half of their income; they would have more money than they want. The *individual* who has excess money balances will spend them for goods and services, lend them, or buy stocks and bonds. His money balance will go down to the level he desires. However, when one person attempts to reduce his money balance, he increases the amount of money held by someone else. The public has $400 billion in

Figure 17.3
The Demand and
Supply of Money and the
Equilibrium Level of
National Income

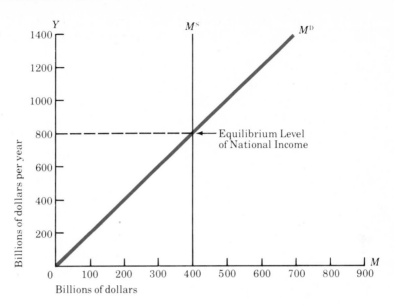

money, and the public cannot reduce this amount by spending it. In the process of trying to reduce their excess money balances, people spend more, and this spending increases aggregate demand and thus the national income. The increase in national income may be the result of a larger real output or higher prices. In either case, an increase in the national income increases the quantity of money demanded, and eventually desired money balances are brought into equality with actual money balances. As soon as the level of income rises to $800 billion, the ratio of the money people have to their income is one-half, and they no longer have excess money balances.

Consider why the national income would fall if it were at $1,000 billion. At this level, people desire to hold $500 billion even though they have only $400 billion. (Although they want the ratio of their money holdings to their income to be 50 percent, they are actually holding a ratio of only 40 percent.) If persons want to hold more money than they have, they can cut down on their spending for goods and services or they can sell stocks, bonds, or physical assets. Both of these would tend to reduce the national income. Consuming less and saving more out of any given level of income directly reduces spending. Selling bonds and stocks causes their prices to fall and raises their yields and interest rates generally. This tends to reduce investment spending and thus the level of income.

Even though an individual can increase his own money balances by saving more or by selling other assets, the public as a whole cannot increase the total money balances in the economy in this way. When one person increases his balance, the balance of another person must be reduced. There is a conflict between what the individual can do and what the public as a whole can do. The attempted adjustments by individuals lower the income of the economy and eventually eliminate this conflict. When income falls from $1,000 billion to $800 billion, the public's ratio of money to income rises from 40 percent to 50 percent, which is the desired ratio.

Effect on national income of changes in the supply of and demand for money

In Figure 17.4, an increase in the money supply from $400 billion to $500 billion raises the level of national income in the economy from $800 billion to $1,000 billion. At the initial level of income of $800 billion, the supply of money would be $500 billion and the demand for money only $400 billion. People would have excess money balances; they would increase their spending, and the level of national income would rise to $1,000 billion, thus increasing the amount of money demanded to $500 billion. A change in any of the factors in the money supply function, such as an increase in the monetary base or a decrease in the ratio of currency to demand deposits, could shift the M^s schedule to the right.

**Figure 17.4
Effect on National
Income of an Increase in
the Supply of Money**

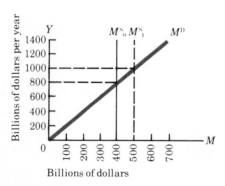

If there were no change in the supply schedule, but instead the demand schedule shifted upward, as in Figure 17.5, national income would again increase. The M^D schedule would shift upward if people expected higher interest rates, a more rapid rate of inflation, or more stable conditions in the economy, the factors causing changes in the demand for real cash balances discussed in Chapter 16.

In Figure 17.4, when the supply of money increases, causing the national income to rise, at the points of equilibrium where $M^S = M^D$ there is no change in the income velocity of money, Y/M. The income velocity of money is 2 per year both when Y is equal to $800 billion and when Y is equal to $1,000 billion. In Figure 17.5, however, when the demand for money schedule decreases, causing the national income to rise, at the higher level of income the velocity of money, Y/M, is larger. The velocity of money is 2 when Y is equal to $800 billion, and rises to 2½ when Y is equal to $1,000 billion. Whether or not statistical data on income velocity represent points of equilibrium of the type shown in Figures 17.4 and 17.5 depends on how quickly the economy reaches equilibrium conditions. If equilibrium conditions are reached quickly, increases in velocity, as measured by statistical data, will reflect an upward shift in the M^D schedule shown in Figure 17.5, and decreases in measured velocity will reflect a downward shift in this schedule.

Figure 17.5
Effect on National Income of a Decrease in the Demand for Money

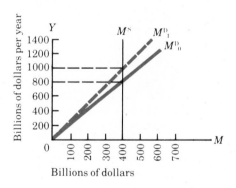

The relationships illustrated in Figures 17.4 and 17.5 are based on the equation of exchange: $MV = Py$. As is true in the equation of exchange, in Figures 17.4 and 17.5, changes in Py are the result of changes in either M or V. Whether or not it can be concluded that changes in the national income are in fact the result of changes in the money supply depends on the empirical evidence of this relationship. Also, how important we can consider changes in velocity or in the demand for money to be in explaining changes in the national income depends on the evidence provided by studies of the velocity of money. Quantity theorists believe that, in explaining changes in the national income, the evidence shows that changes in the money supply are more important than changes in the demand for money. They believe that changes in velocity tend to be gradual and may also be affected by changes in the money supply. For example, an increase in the money supply could result in inflationary expectations which would cause the M^D schedule to shift upward, thus adding to the stimulating effect on income of an increase in the money supply. Another possibility is that interest rates could fall temporarily when the money supply is increased. If people expected lower interest rates in the future, the M^D schedule would shift downward. This would lessen the stimulating effect on income that an increase in the money supply would be expected to have. Although the quantity theorists believe that changes in the M^S schedule in Figure 17.4 may cause the M^D schedule to shift, they doubt that the reverse relationship is very common, i.e., that changes in the M^D schedule cause the M^S schedule to shift.

Portfolio adjustment process

The way in which an increase in the money supply may cause an increase in aggregate demand may be explained in greater detail than in Figure 17.4 by examining the effect of increasing the money supply on the portfolios of banks and the public.[3] (An additional explanation of the relationship in terms of interest rates and investment is presented in Chapter 18.) This portfolio adjustment explanation is part of the new quantity theory of money that was developed in the 1950s and 1960s. In this portfolio adjustment approach, when there is an increase in the money supply, both individuals and banks experience an increase in the ratio of money holdings to the other assets they own. This change in their portfolios tends to cause them to make adjustments that result in an increase in spending.

The most common way in which the portfolio adjustment process is set in motion is by open-market purchases—the principal instrument of monetary control. As was explained in Chapter 13, when the Federal Reserve purchases securities in the open market, the action usually affects the portfolios of both the member banks and the public. If the purchase is from a nonbank dealer, the total deposits owned by the public will be increased by the amount of the open-market purchase. The public's portfolio has been changed: It now has less in bonds and more in money. In addition, such an open-market purchase affects the portfolios of the member banks. Their reserve deposits at the Federal Reserve banks have been increased, and there has been no change in their other assets. The increase in bank reserves will almost always result in a multiple expansion of the deposits of the member banks, and this expansion will have further effects on the portfolios of the public.

Adjustments of the commercial banks

Assume that commercial banks have a certain *structure of assets*—reserves, bonds, and loans—which they consider the best possible distribution among the different types of assets that they might own, as shown below:

Type	Desired Distribution of Bank Assets
Reserves	15%
Bonds	30
Loans	55
Total	100%

This desired structure of bank assets is partly the result of legal reserve requirements and partly the result of the banks' objectives of maximizing the rates of return received on their assets, avoiding losses on their loans and investments, and providing for adequate liquidity. Chapters 6 and 7, which describe the different types of assets of commercial banks, explain the various considerations that affect the management of their portfolios. The desired structure is not rigidly fixed. It changes over time as the banks adjust to changing conditions and changing yields on different types of assets.

Open-market operations cause the actual structure to be different from the desired structure. Suppose the Federal Reserve System, through open-market purchases, increased bank reserves by $1.5 billion but did not purchase the securities from commercial banks. The banks' bonds and loans would be unaffected. They would now hold a higher proportion of their total assets in reserves than formerly. Will the individual banks attempt to reduce the amount of reserves they hold? If they do, there will be portfolio adjustments that will almost certainly stimulate total spending in the economy. As was pointed out in Chapter 9, when banks have received additional reserves, they have usually reacted by expanding their investments and their loans.

What are some of the conditions under which the disturbance of bank portfolios might not affect national income? Much depends on how strongly banks try to maintain a particular portfolio distribution. When the actual structure is changed, there might be a simultaneous change in the desired structure. Because the increase in reserves created by the Federal Reserve is usually not supplied in response to a desire of the banks for additional reserves, such a possibility would be unusual.

If open-market purchases altered the desired structure of bank assets, it would be through their effects on interest rates. When the Federal Reserve buys securities in the open market, it bids up their prices (lowers their yields). If the Federal Reserve banks purchased bills, the bill rate would be slightly lower than it otherwise would be. If the bill rate declined, banks might wish to hold a somewhat larger quantity of excess reserves. Even if there was some impact, it would probably be small. The bulk of the additional reserves received by the banks is used to make loans and investments for two reasons: (1) the additional reserves earn no interest, and (2) the banks can purchase Treasury bills that are virtually riskless, yield a rate of return, and are practically as liquid as excess reserves. Banks with excess reserves may also lend them to other banks through the federal funds market.

When banks attempt to return to their normal structure of assets, they will probably first invest in Treasury bills or lend federal funds. This would cause either the bill rate or the federal funds rate to fall, and this decline would cause those investments to become less attractive than they had been as compared to longer-term securities or loans. This would induce banks to move into intermediate- or long-term securities. As a result, the higher prices of these securities would lower their interest yields. Interest yields on investments would then be lower than those on loans; this would induce banks to expand their loans and then interest rates on loans would also fall.

If, when banks get an increase in reserves, they eventually expand their loans, there is little doubt that this would raise the aggregate demand schedule. The proceeds of the loans are almost always spent, and the increase in the spending of those who borrowed from the banks would not be offset by a decrease in the spending of anyone else. Even when banks buy outstanding securities, the effect may be expansionary, because the persons who receive payment for the securities now have money which they will probably spend—or lend to someone else who will spend it. The market for bank credit is an important channel through which open-market purchases and other tools of monetary policy affect the level of economic activity.

The portfolio adjustment approach stresses the willingness of the lenders to lend rather than the willingness of borrowers to borrow. According to this approach, it is usually assumed that there is an array of borrowers willing to borrow at various interest rates, and if banks are more willing to lend and lower their interest charges, the volume of borrowing will increase. In order to increase their loans, there must be borrowers. Critics who are skeptical of the power of monetary policy believe that borrowers are insensitive to changes in interest rates, and have doubted whether lending would be increased when interest rates are lowered.

The individual bank gets rid of reserves it does not wish to hold by lending or investing them. The banking system as a whole cannot get rid of reserves by increasing loans and investments, although there may be a currency drain as deposits expand. The bulk of the reserves lent by one bank will be deposited in another bank. Banks as a whole return to their original structure of assets by expanding their total loans and investments. In the example above, if reserves are increased by $1.5 billion and remain at that level, investments must be increased by $3.0 billion, and loans by $5.5 billion, in order to retain the same percentage of total assets in reserves. Although interest rates play an important part in this process (as relative interest rates decline, different assets become, in turn, desirable to own), the expansion in bank portfolios is more important in this approach than changes in interest rates.

The process by which an increase in reserves is transmitted into an increase in spending takes time. The initial impact is probably on financial markets. Banks can expand their investments immediately, but it takes time to process loans. Probably, one reason the power of monetary policy control measures has been underestimated is that they take time to produce their effects. If one looks for immediate results, monetary control measures may appear ineffective.

Adjustments of the public

Like the banks, the public has a variety of different assets, including money, bonds, stocks, physical assets, and consumer goods, and it probably has a certain structure of assets that it considers to be most desirable. If the Federal Reserve increased the money supply, people would probably respond by attempting to reduce their money holdings and by purchasing other assets.

However, when additional money is injected into the system by open-market purchases, the public's holdings of bonds would decrease at the same time that their holdings of money increased. There would be no increase in total wealth, and thus no wealth effect on total spending. The open-market purchases would also raise security prices and lower interest rates. It is the rise in bond prices that induces people to sell their securities. The high bond prices could cause the public to change the desired structure of their assets, tending to increase the demand for money and reduce the demand for bonds. But more is involved than just the relative attractiveness of money and bonds. The increased supply of money and the lower yields on bonds would increase the relative attractiveness of other assets such as corporation stock, capital goods, and consumer goods.

Changes in the relative prices of different assets may have a stimulating effect on spending. When the public gets additional money, some persons shift to bonds. This causes bond prices to rise further (their interest yields to fall). As a result, bonds become relatively unattractive compared to stocks, and the public is then induced to purchase the latter. The higher prices of stocks reduce their earnings-to-price ratios, and cause stocks to become relatively unattractive compared to physical assets. Then, as people purchase physical assets, prices of those assets rise. As a result, it becomes a better bargain for some persons to purchase the services of capital rather than the capital itself. For example, if the prices of houses rise, some persons would be induced to rent rather than purchase a house.

An increase in the money stock may also increase the demand for consumer goods and services directly, rather than by first increasing the demand for financial assets and capital assets. Whether an increase in the money stock initially affects financial markets or the market for goods and services probably depends on who gets the increase in the money stock. If it is primarily in the hands of financial institutions, the initial impact would be on financial assets. But if it is in the hands of consumers (many of whom seldom invest in financial securities), it may have its initial effect on the market for consumer goods and services. Both during the mini-recession of 1967 and in 1968, when an expansionary monetary policy offset the impact of a 10 percent income-tax surcharge that was designed to combat inflation, consumption appeared to be more sensitive to changes in monetary policy than was generally expected.[4]

For an increase in the money stock to have no impact on spending, the immediate decline in interest rates because of the open-market purchase must induce the public to want to hold all of the additional money rather than other assets, or to adjust their portfolios in such a way as to affect only financial markets. Those who doubt the power of monetary policy believe that there may be a wide gap between the desire for financial assets and the desire for physical assets and consumer goods and services. Under such conditions, even though the prices of financial assets are raised and their rates of return are reduced, it would not induce persons to add to their holdings of physical assets.

The extent to which the supply of capital goods and consumer goods responds to the increase in the demand for them determines the impact of monetary policy on income. If an increase in the money supply adds to the demand for existing houses and raises their prices relative to the cost of constructing them, this probably would stimulate the output of new houses. If the prices of bonds and stocks rise, interest rates fall, and it becomes less costly for corporations to finance capital expenditures by issuing bonds. This could stimulate investment in the same way that a lower rate of interest on bank loans would.

Reverse effect from income to money

The explanation thus far has shown how changes in the money supply affect income. Changes in income may also affect the expansion of the money supply unless the Federal Reserve System prevents this by trying to control the money supply in a precise way. Changes in the level of business activity, for example, may affect the public's currency-to-deposit ratio and thus the total money supply. The studies done by Professor Phillip Cagan showed that historically the cyclical behavior of the currency-to-deposit ratio has had a significant effect on the supply of money.

Under the gold standard, changes in the level of income also had significant monetary effects. Higher incomes caused a deficit in the balance of payments, a loss of gold, and a decline in the amount of money. A fall in income had the opposite effect. The resulting surplus in the balance of payments led to an inflow of gold and an increase in money.

Variations in income may also affect the money supply through their effect on interest rates. When income rises, interest rates tend to rise, and when income falls, interest rates tend to fall. When interest rates are higher, banks may tend to economize on their excess reserves and reduce the ratio of their reserves to their deposits, thus increasing the amount of money. On the other hand, when interest rates are low, banks are likely to hold a larger proportion of deposits as reserves, thus causing a monetary contraction. These effects would accentuate cyclical ups and downs. Another possible result of an increase in interest rates resulting from a rise in national income is that it may induce people to hold more time deposits relative to demand deposits. An increase in t, the ratio of time deposits to demand deposits, would tend to increase M-1 plus time deposits in commercial banks, but to decrease M-1.

Historically, relatively large changes in the amount of money in the United States have usually not been the result of changes in income. Prior to the 1970s, the periods of rapid monetary expansion and inflation all occurred during wars, when the money supply was increased by the government to finance military expenditures. The gradually rising quantity of money from 1896 to 1913 was a result of the increase in the gold stock rather than an increase in income. This increase occurred because of the discovery of new mines and improved techniques of extracting gold from low-grade ore. In the 1970s, the Federal Reserve System continued the rapid expansion in the money supply that was started during the 1960s. The monetary authorities appear to be reluctant to risk the adverse effects on unemployment that could occur if the rate of expansion in the money supply were slowed.

In serious depressions, the relatively large declines in the amount of money have almost always been caused primarily by financial panics—bank failures, currency runs on the banks, and bank hoarding of reserves—rather than by declines in income. In 1920–1921, the decline in the money stock was largely the result of Federal Reserve policy rather than changes in income. The Federal Reserve raised the discount rate sharply. This was followed by a sharp decline in borrowing at the Federal Reserve banks and a decline in bank reserves. In 1937–1938 Federal Reserve policy again had the same effect. At that time, the reserve requirements of the member banks were doubled. Although it was thought that unwanted excess reserves would be absorbed, the banks reacted by increasing the ratio of their reserves to deposits. Although there have been important interrelationships between money and income during minor recessions, changes in income during major depressions and in periods of inflation have not been a major cause of changes in the money supply.

Summary

Statistical data on the national income in current prices measure the dollar value of the total output of the economy. Monetary theory attempts to explain how variations in the money supply may stimulate or restrain the growth of the national income.

Under conditions of equilibrium, aggregate demand will be equal to aggregate supply. Otherwise, levels of inventories will be growing or contracting.

When the national income is in equilibrium, the demand for money must also be equal to the supply. Prices or real output will increase if people have more money than they want to hold. Prices or real output will decrease if people want to hold more money than they have.

People and banks own a variety of different types of assets. An increase in the money supply may cause people to have a larger portion of their total assets in money than they desire. The attempt to shift to other types of assets may have a stimulating effect on the demand for both financial and real assets. According to the portfolio approach, an increase in the real money supply will have a stimulating effect on the national income by causing an expansion in the total assets of the entire commercial banking system as well as in the total assets of the public.

Notes

1. Milton Friedman, *A Theory of the Consumption Function* (Princeton, N.J.: Princeton University Press, 1957); Albert Ando and Franco Modigliani, "The 'Life Cycle' Hypothesis of Saving: Aggregate Implications and Tests," *American Economic Review* (March 1963), pp. 55–84; and James Duesenberry, *Income, Savings and the Theory of Consumer Behavior* (Cambridge, Mass.: Harvard University Press, 1952).

2. Milton Friedman, "Money, Quantity Theory," *International Encyclopedia of the Social Sciences*, Vol. 10 (New York: Macmillan, 1968), p. 434.

3. Milton Friedman and Anna J. Schwartz, "Money and Business Cycles," *Review of Economics and Statistics* 45, Supplement (February 1963), pp. 32–78; reprinted in *The Optimum Quantity of Money and Other Essays* (Chicago: Aldine, 1969), pp. 189–235. See particularly Section 3, "A Tentative Sketch of the Mechanism Transmitting Monetary Changes."

4. A. James Meigs, *Money Matters* (New York: Harper and Row Publishers, 1972), pp. 50–52, 58–60.

Questions

17.1. Compare the two ways of measuring the national income: by distributive shares and by types of expenditures.

17.2. What accounts for the difference between gross national product and national income?

17.3. Draw a graph showing the relationship between the national income and aggregate demand.

17.4. Why does the average propensity to consume decrease when total income increases?

17.5. What is the meaning of an increase in autonomous spending? Illustrate by using a graph showing the relationship between aggregate demand and aggregate supply.

17.6. What is the formula for the multiplier? Explain why an increase in autonomous spending results in an increase in national income larger than the increase in autonomous spending.

17.7 If the quantity of money demanded is less than the supply of money, why will the national income rise? What determines how much the rise in income will be?

17.8 If the supply of money is less than that demanded, why will national income fall? What determines how much the fall in income will be?

17.9. Assuming no change in the supply of money, if the demand for money decreases, what would be the effect on the national income?

17.10. Explain the way an open-market purchase initially may affect the portfolios of both the member banks and the public.

17.11. If open-market operations increase bank reserves relative to their loans and securities, will the banks respond so as to increase total spending? Why?

17.12. If open-market operations increase the money holdings of persons relative to their other assets, will the response of persons increase total spending? Why?

17.13. Explain how changes in income may affect the supply of money.

17.14. Know the meaning and significance of the following terms and concepts: personal consumption expenditures, gross private domestic investment, net exports of goods and services, income of proprietors, rental income, net interest, intermediate goods, capital consumption allowances, aggregate demand, aggregate supply, autonomous increase in aggregate demand, permanent income, marginal propensity to consume, average propensity to consume, equilibrium level of national income, multiplier, structure of assets, portfolios of banks.

18

This chapter explains the way in which an increase in the money supply may lower interest rates, lower interest rates may increase investment, and more investment may increase the national income.

THE RELATION OF MONEY TO INCOME: PART II

Changes in the money supply may have significant effects on interest rates, and changes in interest rates may have significant effects on investment spending by business firms. This chapter examines these relationships. The latter part of the chapter presents the widely used *IS-LM* model centered around the effects of money on interest rates and interest rates on investment.[1]

Under inflationary conditions, it is important to distinguish between real and nominal changes in both the money supply and interest rates. When prices are rising, the amount of real money balances held need not increase when the money supply increases, and real interest rates need not rise when market interest rates rise.

The money supply and interest rates

The liquidity preference schedule (L) in Figure 18.1 shows the relationship between nominal interest rates and the demand for real money balances. This schedule slopes downward from left to right, indicating that the quantity of real money balances (M/P) people wish to hold will be larger at lower nominal interest rates (i). As was explained in Chapter 16, persons choose between holding money and securities, and the relative attractiveness of the two depends on nominal rates of interest. When nominal interest rates are high, people wish to hold smaller amounts of real money balances and more securities; when nominal interest rates are low, the demand for real money balances is greater.

Other factors that affect the demand for real money balances, such as changes in expected real income or changes in views on the economic outlook, would cause the liquidity preference schedule to shift. An increase in expected real income would cause it to shift to the right; at all possible levels of nominal interest rates, the demand for real money balances would be greater. On the other hand, if people feel that the contingencies of doing business have become less hazardous, the schedule would shift to the left, and at all possible nominal interest rates, people would want to hold less real money balances.

In Figure 18.1, the schedules for the real money supply (M/P) are vertical. This is based on the assumption that the quantity of money (M) is controlled by the Federal Reserve System and that the price level is constant at P. Given the price level, if the Federal Reserve System increases the money supply, the real money supply schedule would shift to the right; if the money supply were decreased, the M/P schedule would shift to the left.

If the real money supply schedule were at $(M/P)_1$, the equilibrium level of interest rates in Figure 18.1 would be at the point where the $(M/P)_1$ schedule (the supply schedule) intersects the liquidity preference schedule (the demand schedule)—at 6 percent. If nominal interest rates were above 6 percent, the supply of real money balances would be greater than that demanded. Some persons with excess money balances would use them to purchase securities. The resulting higher prices of securities would lower their yields. As yields declined toward

Figure 18.1
Determination of
Nominal Interest Rates

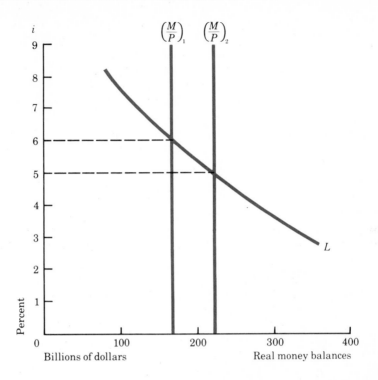

6 percent, the amount of real money balances demanded would increase until the point of equilibrium was reached. Or, if nominal interest
rates were below the equilibrium level, the quantity of real money
balances demanded would be greater than that supplied. To get larger
real money balances, some persons would sell securities. The resulting
lower prices of securities would raise their yields.

When the total demand for real money balances is different from the
supply, the possibilities for adjustment confronting an individual are not
available for the public as a whole. Although an individual can build up
his real money balances by selling securities, such selling merely
reduces the real money balances of someone else. Conversely, if an
individual tries to reduce his real money holdings by spending them, he
simply adds to the balances of others. Equilibrium conditions in the
economy as a whole are restored only when yields change, causing the
quantity of real money balances demanded to equal the supply.

In Figure 18.1, an increase in the money supply would shift the real
money supply schedule from $(M/P)_1$ to $(M/P)_2$. In order to get people
to hold the larger quantity of real money balances, nominal interest
rates must fall. Only at the lower yields are people willing to hold more
real money balances relative to their holdings of other financial assets.

The decline in nominal interest rates in Figure 18.1 when the M/P

schedule shifts to the right is known as the *liquidity effect* on interest rates.[2] The liquidity effect occurs only in the first three to five months following an expansion of the supply of real money balances.[3] In the long run, the lower nominal interest rates may cause an increase in income which would shift the liquidity preference schedule to the right and cause a reversal in the downward movement of interest rates.

Interest rates and investment

A reduction in real interest rates would tend to increase the volume of spending for investment, and conversely an increase in real interest rates would tend to cut investment spending. The real interest rate is the nominal rate of interest on a loan, for example, minus the expected rate of inflation over the period of the loan. If the nominal rate of interest on a loan was 10 percent and the expected rate of inflation was 7 percent a year, the real rate of interest would be 3 percent. As indicated in Figure 18.1, the Federal Reserve System is able to lower nominal interest rates by increasing the supply of real money balances. The Federal Reserve System's control of real interest rates is more limited than its control of nominal interest rates because real rates of interest are affected by changes in the rate of inflation expected by the public, as well as by the supply of real money balances.

Table 18.1 shows that the amount of investment varies with business conditions. Both gross and net investment declined in 1974 and 1975— years in which the economy was in a recession. In 1979, gross private domestic investment amounted to $386 billion and consisted of the four major components shown in Table 18.2—nonresidential structures, producers' durable equipment, residential fixed investment, and changes

Table 18.1
Investment in the
United States,
1970–1979 (in billions)

Year	Spending for Depreciation	Net Investment	Gross Private Domestic Investment
1970	$ 90.8	$ 50.0	$140.8
1971	98.8	61.2	160.0
1972	105.4	82.9	188.3
1973	117.7	102.3	220.0
1974	137.7	76.9	214.6
1975	162.0	28.9	190.9
1976	177.8	65.2	243.0
1977	195.4	107.9	303.3
1978	216.9	134.6	351.5
1979P	243.0	143.2	386.2

Source: *Economic Report of the President, January 1980*, pp. 219 and 222.

in business inventories. Depreciation expenditures that year to replace worn-out equipment and to repair building structures amounted to about 63 percent of gross private domestic investment. Net investment consists of that portion of capital expenditures in excess of depreciation. In 1979, net private investment, the addition to the total stock of capital in the economy, amounted to $143 billion.

The amount of investment spending made during the year depends on how much business enterprises desire to increase the stock of capital —plants, equipment, inventory, and housing. The desired capital stock depends on both the *marginal product of capital* and the *user cost of capital.*

Table 18.2
Private Investment,
1979

Type of Investment	Amount in Billions
Nonresidential structures	$ 92.3
Producers' durable equipment	161.6
Residential fixed investment	113.9
Change in business inventories	18.4
Total gross private domestic investment	$386.2
Less: depreciation	243.0
Total net private domestic investment	$143.2

Source: *Economic Report of the President, January 1980,* pp. 219 and 222.

The marginal product of capital

The marginal product of capital is the additional amount of output that can be produced by a unit of capital. It is, for example, the annual amount of income that a business firm expects to get from the use of a newly purchased machine. If the marginal product per year was equal to 20 percent of the total cost of the capital, the annual marginal product of an additional dollar's worth of capital would be 20 cents. Capital is a resource that, like labor, has a marginal product—it produces goods and services that people will pay for.

The productivity of a given quantity of a resource depends on what is used with it. It is commonly recognized that the productivity of labor depends on the amount of capital and other resources used with labor, and the high standard of living in the United States is usually attributed primarily to the large amount of highly technical machinery and equipment used with labor in producing the gross national product. In the same way, the productivity of capital depends on the amount of labor and other resources used with it. If a larger amount of other resources (the quantity and quality of labor, technical and scientific knowledge, and government services) is used with a given quantity of capital, the productivity of capital will increase, and if fewer other resources are used with a given quantity of capital, the marginal product of capital will decrease.

The vertical axis in Figure 18.2 measures the value of the marginal product of capital, and the horizontal axis measures the amount of capital stock. In this figure, if the GNP is equal to $600 billion and the capital stock (K) is equal to $3 trillion, the marginal product of a dollar's worth of capital would be 20 cents. The MPK schedule slopes downward—if GNP is unchanged at $600 billion, the marginal product of capital will be less if the stock of capital is increased. This is because if the GNP is the same when more capital is used, it is not necessary to use as much of other resources to produce the same GNP. The use of fewer other resources with the capital would cause the marginal product of capital to decline.

If GNP increases from $600 to $620 billion, the MPK schedule shifts to the right. (If GNP decreases, it shifts to the left.) In order to produce a larger GNP, more resources—either capital or other resources—would be needed. If the quantity of capital used is still $3 trillion, larger amounts of other resources would have to be used, and in Figure 18.2 the marginal product of a dollar's worth of capital would rise to 25 cents. On the other hand, if the amount of capital used is increased when GNP rises from $600 to $620 billion, the marginal product of capital would be less than 25 cents, and could even fall below 20 cents.

**Figure 18.2
The Marginal Product of
Capital and the Capital
Stock**

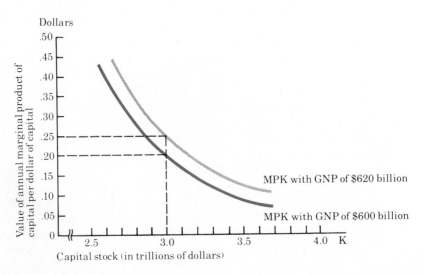

Capital stock (in trillions of dollars)

The user cost of capital

The user cost of capital (also called the rental cost of capital) depends primarily on the market rate of interest, depreciation costs, and the expected rate of inflation.

Business firms often must borrow in order to obtain the funds needed to purchase capital. However, even if a firm finances the purchase of capital equipment with retained earnings, the cost would include the market interest rate because the firm could have earned that rate if it had lent its retained earnings to someone else. If the rate of interest were 10 percent a year, the annual interest cost per dollar of capital would be 10 cents.

The user cost of capital must also take into account depreciation—the replacement of machines as they wear out and the repair of structures. The marginal product of capital is normally large enough to more than cover the cost of depreciation, and if capital is maintained in its original condition, the productivity of a given capital investment may continue indefinitely in the future. During the period of a year, only a portion of most types of capital is used up. When the rate of depreciation is 15 percent, the depreciation cost per dollar of capital is 15 cents.

A third factor affecting the user cost of capital is the expected rate of inflation. With a given nominal interest rate, expected inflation reduces the user cost of capital. If the market rate of interest were 10 percent, for example, at the end of a year a person borrowing $1.00 would have to pay back to the lender $1.10. However, if prices rose 10 percent during the year, the $1.10 paid back would purchase no more than the $1.00 originally borrowed, and the real rate of interest would be zero. The formula for the user cost of capital, taking into account the expected rate of inflation, is:

18.1

$$i_c = i - \left(\frac{\Delta P}{P}\right)^* + d \,,$$

where i_c = the user cost of capital, i = the market interest rate, $(\Delta P/P)^*$ = expected annual increase in prices, and d = the annual cost of depreciation. If the nominal interest rate were 10 percent, the depreciation rate 15 percent, and the rate of inflation 5 percent, the user cost of a dollar's worth of capital would be 20 cents.

Since the formula for the real rate of interest (i_r) is

18.2

$$i_r = i - \left(\frac{\Delta P}{P}\right)^*,$$

Equation 18.1 may be rewritten as follows:

18.3

$$i_c = i_r + d.$$

In Figure 18.3, the horizontal axis measures the desired capital stock, and the user cost of capital is 20 cents. The amount of capital stock desired will be where the marginal product of capital is equal to the user cost of capital because it is profitable for firms to add to the stock of capital if the marginal product of capital covers the user cost. If GNP is $600 billion, Figure 18.3 shows that at a user cost of 20 cents, the maximum amount of capital stock desired would be $3 trillion. If more capital stock than this were used, the marginal product of capital would be lower than the 20-cent user cost of capital.

If the expected rate of inflation is unchanged, a monetary policy lowering nominal interest rates would reduce real interest rates. This would reduce the user cost of capital relative to its marginal product and, as shown by the *MPK* schedules in Figure 18.3, would increase the desired stock of capital. An increase in the desired stock of capital relative to the stock of capital in existence induces business firms to increase the volume of investment spending.

Figure 18.3 shows that if GNP rises to $620 billion, but the user cost of capital remains constant at 20 cents, the amount of capital stock desired will increase to $3.1 trillion. If there were no increase in the capital stock when GNP rose to $620 billion, the marginal product of capital would rise above 20 cents and be larger than the user cost of capital. This stimulates investment by increasing the profitability of using more capital goods. As the stock of capital increases, the marginal product of capital decreases until it is equal to the user cost.

Because many investments have a long life, the desired stock of capital is based on the output *expected* in the future, rather than simply on current output. Expected output depends primarily on the current level of output and the growth in output from year to year that firms are accustomed to. But, expected output may also be affected by changes in psychological attitude. When people are optimistic, this will increase the expected level of output and have a stimulating effect on invest-

Figure 18.3
The Desired Capital
Stock and the User Cost
of Capital

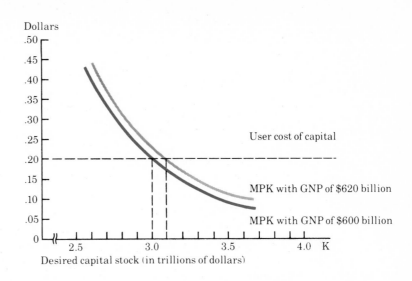

ment. On the other hand, if people are pessimistic, it will reduce the volume of investment spending.

An additional factor that may affect the desired stock of capital and thus the volume of investment spending is government tax policies. Corporation income taxes reduce the after-tax marginal product of capital. If the corporation income tax rate was 50 percent and the marginal product of a dollar's worth of new capital was 20 cents, the after-tax marginal product would be only 10 cents. Higher corporate income taxes shift the *MPK* schedule in Figure 18.3 downward. Because of the reduction in the after-tax marginal product, a given quantity of capital stock will be desired only at a lower user cost. A reduction in corporation income tax rates would increase the amount of capital stock desired.

Investment and income

If an increase in the money supply lowers real interest rates and increases investment, the increase in investment will result in a higher level of national income in the economy. As illustrated in Figure 17.2 in the previous chapter, an increase in investment would raise the aggregate demand schedule and there would be a new higher equilibrium level of national income. The rise in the aggregate demand schedule has a stimulating effect on total output because inventories fall when aggregate demand is greater than aggregate supply. To prevent inventories from being depleted, firms will increase output. As output is increased, aggregate demand will not increase as fast as aggregate supply, and eventually aggregate demand will be equal to aggregate supply at a higher level of national income.

Interaction between interest rates and income

As has been explained thus far, an increase in the real money supply tends to lower nominal interest rates and, if expected prices are unchanged, would also tend to lower real interest rates; lower real interest rates would probably increase investment, and an increase in investment tends to increase income. This is not a complete explanation of the relationship between changes in the real money supply and changes in income. When income rises, it will cause the liquidity preference schedule (L) in Figure 18.1 to shift to the right. This is because the higher the level of income people expect, the larger the quantity of real money balances they want to hold for convenience in making transactions and for security against contingencies. The interaction between interest rates and income is illustrated in Figure 18.4. Because the increase in income shifts the L schedule to the right, interest rates would eventually fall no further than to i_3. This would mean that aggregate demand (which includes investment) would rise only to AD_3 and national income to Y_3. Still, the final result of an increase in the real money supply is a reduction in nominal and real interest rates from i_1 to i_3, and an increase in the level of income from Y_1 to Y_3.

Figure 18.4
Graphic Description of
the Sequence of Interest
Rate-Investment Effects

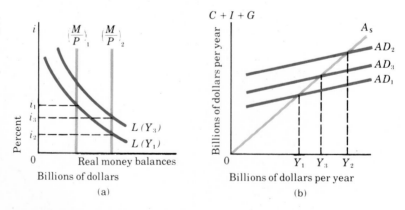

The fact that an expansionary monetary policy tends eventually to result in a reversal of the downward movement of nominal interest rates is called the *income effect* on interest rates (in contrast with the initial decline called the liquidity effect). Nominal interest rates cannot go back to the original level that existed prior to the expansion in the money supply. This is because the downward movement of nominal interest rates would not be reversed at all unless there were an increase in income, and an increase in income depends on nominal interest rates being below their original level.

The IS-LM model[4]

Figure 18.5 consolidates the two graphs of Figure 18.4 into one graph based on six variables: the demand for real money balances (L), the supply of real money balances (M/P), aggregate demand (AD), aggregate supply (AS), nominal interest rates (i), and national income (Y). The vertical axis of Figure 18.5 represents nominal interest rates; the horizontal axis, the national income. The IS schedule is based on points of equilibrium between aggregate demand and aggregate supply. The LM schedule is based on points of equilibrium between the demand for and supply of real money balances. At the point where the IS schedule crosses the LM schedule, taking into account both national income and nominal interest rates, the demand for real money balances is equal to the supply, and aggregate demand is equal to aggregate supply.

The downward-sloping IS schedule in Figure 18.5 is related to Figure 17.2. If nominal and thus real interest rates fall, the aggregate demand schedule would shift upward, causing aggregate demand to be equal to aggregate supply at a higher level of income. The reason the

Figure 18.5
Income and Nominal
Interest Rate
Determination

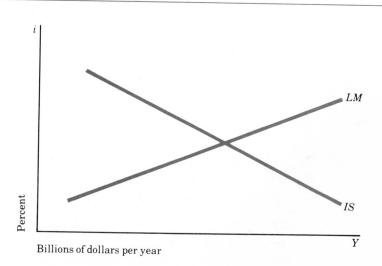

Billions of dollars per year

LM schedule slopes upward is shown in Figure 18.6. An increase in income would cause the L schedule to shift to the right from $L(Y_1)$ to $L(Y_2)$. The increase in the demand for real money balances relative to the supply would cause nominal interest rates to rise from i_1 to i_2. This relationship between nominal interest rates and the national income is that usually found in the different phases of the business cycle. In the expansion phase of the cycle, when the national income is increasing, nominal interest rates usually do actually rise, and in the contraction phase, nominal interest rates fall.

Figure 18.6
Effect on Nominal
Interest Rates of an
Increase in the Demand
for Real Money
Balances

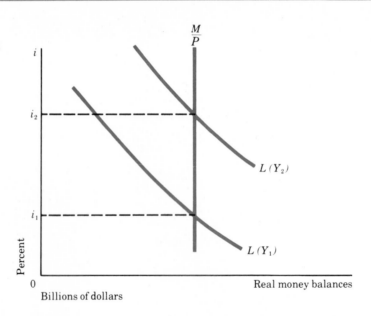

In Figure 18.5, shifts in either the *IS* or the *LM* schedule affect both income and nominal interest rates. If the *IS* schedule shifts to the right, both income and nominal interest rates rise. If the *LM* schedule shifts to the right, income rises and nominal interest rates fall. The point of equilibrium is the one at which the *LM* schedule intersects the *IS* schedule.

A shift of the *IS* schedule to the right occurs when aggregate demand increases because of changes other than a reduction in nominal and real interest rates. When income rises because of lower nominal and real interest rates, aggregate demand would be equal to aggregate supply at a lower point on a given *IS* schedule. An important factor that would shift the *IS* schedule to the right is an increase in the marginal product of capital. An increase in the marginal product of capital raises the aggregate demand schedule in Figure 17.1 and causes income to rise. The marginal product of capital would increase if more and better trained workers were used with capital or as a result of scientific and technological development. As will be explained in Chapter 19, the federal government's fiscal policy is another important factor that may shift the *IS* schedule to the right.

A principal cause of the shift in the *LM* schedule such as from LM_1 to LM_2 in Figure 18.7 is an expansionary monetary policy. Note that a shift in the *LM* schedule to the right indicates either that at a given level of income (Y_1) the demand and supply of real money balances are now equal at a lower nominal rate of interest, or that at a given nominal rate of interest the demand and supply of real money balances are equal at a higher level of income. It was shown earlier (in Figure 18.1) that if the real money supply schedule were shifted to the right, the supply and demand for real money balances would be in equilibrium at a lower nominal rate of interest, assuming no change in the *L* schedule and no change in income. Also, if a shift of the real money supply schedule to the right in Figure 18.1 were matched by a shift of the *L* schedule to the right because of an increase in income, the demand and supply of real money balances would be in equilibrium at a higher level of income, but with no change in nominal interest rates.

The *LM* schedule in Figure 18.7 may shift to the right even when the real money supply schedule in Figure 18.1 is unchanged, if the demand schedule shifts to the left because of some reason other than a fall in income. Equilibrium between the demand for and supply of real money balances would then be at a lower nominal interest rate than formerly.

Figure 18.7
Effects on Income and Nominal Interest Rates of an Increase in the Real Money Supply

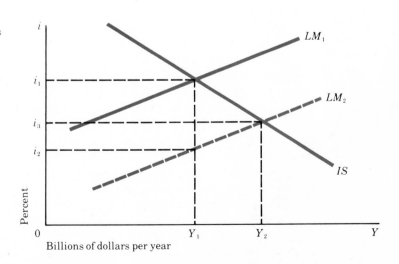

The factors that might cause the demand schedule to shift to the left are greater confidence in the stability of the economy, the expectation of more rapid inflation, or an expected fall in nominal interest rates (rise in bond prices).

In Figure 18.7, the effect of an expansionary monetary policy shifting the *LM* schedule to the right is to lower nominal interest rates and increase income. If the *IS* schedule is unchanged, the initial effect of the increase in the *LM* schedule is to lower nominal interest rates from i_1 to i_2. But at i_2, *LM* is not equal to *IS*. Neither nominal interest rates nor income are at the point of equilibrium. The lower nominal interest rates increase investment, and the increase in aggregate demand relative to aggregate supply raises the level of income from Y_1 to Y_2. The higher level of income would limit the fall in nominal interest rates by causing the *L* schedule to shift to the right, as shown in Figure 18.4(a). When nominal interest rates are at i_3 in Figure 18.7, income is at equilibrium at Y_2 because *IS* is then equal to *LM*.

The liquidity trap

Under certain circumstances, an expansion in the real money supply and a shift of the *LM* schedule to the right need not have the stimulating effect on income shown in Figure 18.7. When market interest rates are very low, for example, the *L* schedule might become horizontal, as shown in Figure 18.8, rather than sloping downward to the right, as in Figure 18.1. The area in which the *L* schedule is horizontal is called the liquidity trap. In that region, a shift in the *M/P* schedule to the right would not cause a fall in nominal interest rates. The reason the *L* schedule may be horizontal is that at very low nominal rates of interest, people might not attempt to shift from money to bonds, even though their real money holdings are increased. When nominal interest rates are at bottom levels, bond prices are at peak levels. If people expect that bond prices will eventually fall, they would prefer to hold larger real money balances rather than buy bonds.

When nominal rates of interest are in the liquidity trap, a shift to the right in the *M/P* schedule does not shift the *LM* schedule to the right, and it would have no effect on nominal interest rates, investment, or the level of income. In addition, an increase in income, which would shift the *L* schedule to the right as in Figure 18.9, would not affect nominal interest rates. Because of the trap, the quantity of real money balances demanded would not exceed the supply and there would not be upward pressure on nominal interest rates. An *LM* schedule based on Figure 18.9 would be perfectly elastic at a very low level of market interest rates, as shown in Figure 18.10. With such an *LM* schedule, a shift of

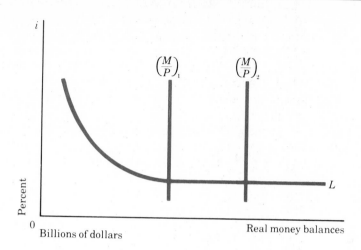

Figure 18.8
The Effect of an
Increase in the Real
Money Supply,
Assuming a Liquidity
Trap

the *IS* schedule to the right would cause income to rise, but it would not raise market interest rates.

Recent statistical studies of the shape of the *L* schedule in the United States find little evidence that there ever has been a liquidity trap. From 1900 to 1958, one study estimates an *interest elasticity* in the demand for *M-1* (the percentage change in the quantity of money demanded

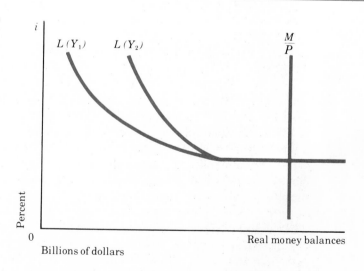

Figure 18.9
Nominal Interest Rates
Are Unaffected When
the Liquidity
Preference Schedule
Rises, Assuming a
Liquidity Trap

divided by the percentage change in market interest rates) of about
-0.7 percent.[5] This estimated elasticity means that the demand for
money would rise 7 percent if the rate of interest fell 10 percent. Since
World War II, nominal interest rates have been rising and have become
relatively high. The conditions under which one might expect a liquidity trap have not existed. The slope of the L schedule is no longer
considered an important reason for questioning the effectiveness of
monetary policy in influencing income. There is little doubt that the L
schedule slopes downward and the LM schedule slopes upward.

**Figure 18.10
The LM Schedule Is
Perfectly Elastic When
There Is a
Liquidity Trap**

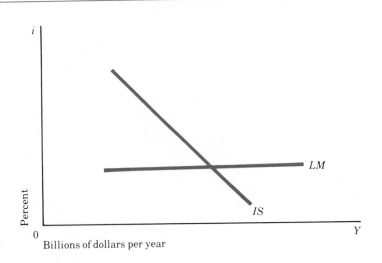

Will investment be larger when real interest rates fall?

Another possible problem is whether or not the volume of investment
will increase when real interest rates fall. Even without a liquidity trap,
if investment does not increase when real interest rates fall, an increase
in the M/P schedule might not affect income. If the investment
schedule were perfectly inelastic, as shown in Figure 18.11, the volume
of investment would not vary with changes in the real cost of borrowing
money, aggregate demand would not increase relative to aggregate
supply, and the level of income would be unaffected.

An IS schedule based on the perfectly inelastic I schedule in Figure
18.11 is also perfectly inelastic, as shown in Figure 18.12. Under these
conditions, an increase in the LM schedule as a result of monetary
policy would lower nominal interest rates, but would not raise the level
of income.

**Figure 18.11
Changes in Real Interest
Rates Have No Effect on
Investment, Assuming
an Inelastic Investment
Schedule**

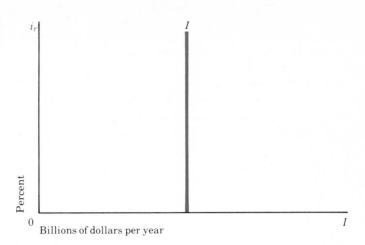

Many economists have maintained that investment is not significantly affected by changes in nominal and thus real interest rates. For
short-term investments, it is felt that interest costs are too unimportant
to affect the volume of investment. Although interest costs are admitted
to be important for long-term investment, it is said that, compared to
the other uncertainties, interest rates do not significantly affect decisions to invest—especially that large portion of capital spending
financed with undistributed profits and depreciation reserves.

**Figure 18.12
An Increase in the LM
Schedule Lowers
Nominal Interest Rates,
But Has No Effect on
Income, Assuming an
Inelastic IS Schedule**

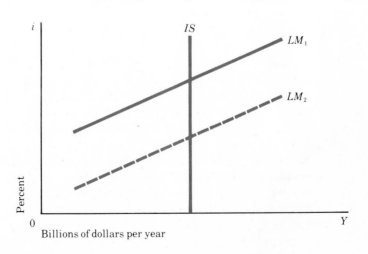

The earliest surveys asking businessmen whether their investment plans were contingent on the market rate of interest concluded that there was little effect. Also, in the early regression studies attempting to discover the determinants of investment, the market rate of interest did not turn out to be an important variable.[6] Recent studies have questioned the results of some of the earlier regression studies, and a growing number of studies have shown certain types of investment to be affected by market interest rates.

The Pigou effect

In Figure 18.7, monetary policy affected the *LM* schedule, but not the *IS* schedule. In fact, an increase in the quantity of real money balances as a result of a fall in prices may shift the *IS* schedule to the right. This type of shift in the *IS* schedule is known as the *Pigou effect.*[7]

An increase in real money balances as a result of a fall in prices will tend to stimulate spending by increasing people's wealth. When wealthier, people would be expected to spend a larger percentage of their income for consumption and save less, because there is less need to save. This would raise the aggregate demand schedule in Figure 17.2, causing aggregate demand to be equal to aggregate supply at a higher level of income. Also, this would cause the *IS* schedule to shift to the right. On the other hand, if wealth were decreased because of a decline in real money balances associated with a rise in prices, it would have the opposite effect—the public would consume less of their current income and save more because of the greater need to accumulate additional wealth in order to provide adequately for the future. This would shift the *IS* schedule to the left.

The Pigou effect is significant because it means that even if the economy were in a liquidity trap and the investment schedule were perfectly inelastic, a rise in real money balances because of a fall in prices would stimulate output. By holding the money supply constant while prices are falling, the monetary authorities could stimulate spending.

Price flexibility plays a very important role in the Pigou effect—price flexibility automatically sets in motion forces to counteract cyclical movements in the economy. It tends to eliminate persistent excess unemployment because unemployment would tend to cause prices to fall. The Pigou effect is operative only if the Federal Reserve System prevents fluctuations in the money supply. If the Federal Reserve System let the money supply decline in periods of recession when prices were falling, there would be no increase in real money balances. And, if they let the money supply increase in periods of rising prices, there would be no decrease in real money balances. Some economists believe that as a practical matter it would be unwise for the government to rely on the Pigou effect to stabilize the economy and prevent unemployment. They believe that there is not sufficient downward price flexibility in the economy to cause the change in real cash balances needed for this effect.

Summary

According to the interest rate-investment analysis of the relation of money to income, an increase in the real money supply will have a stimulating effect on the national income by lowering real interest rates and increasing investment. Although the interest rate-investment analysis overlaps the portfolio approach explained in Chapter 17, the emphasis of the two approaches differs.

The immediate effect of an increase in the real money supply is to lower nominal interest rates. By causing the real supply of money to be greater than the demand for real money balances, an expansionary monetary policy induces people to purchase bonds and thus lower their yields.

Lower real interest rates may increase the amount of investment spending by increasing the desired stock of capital. Lower real interest rates reduce the user cost of capital relative to the marginal product of capital.

Real money balances will rise when prices fall, and decline when prices go up. By affecting the amount of wealth that people have, changes in real money balances may have significant effects on total spending—causing spending to rise when real money balances get larger and to fall when real money balances get smaller. If prices were flexible, changes in real money balances would have important effects on total spending.

Notes

1. For recent advanced studies of macroeconomic theory, see Rudiger Dornbusch and Stanley Fischer, *Macroeconomics* (New York: McGraw-Hill, 1978); Michael R. Darby, *Macroeconomics, The Theory of Income, Employment, and the Price Level* (New York: McGraw-Hill, 1976); and Robert J. Gordon, *Macroeconomics* (Boston: Little, Brown and Company, 1978).

2. See Milton Friedman, "Factors Affecting the Level of Interest Rates," *Savings and Residential Financing, 1968 Conference Proceedings* (Chicago: United States Savings and Loan League, 1968), pp. 10–27.

3. William E. Gibson, "Interest Rates and Monetary Policy," *Journal of Political Economy* 78 (May–June 1970), p. 453.

4. See Robert L. Crouch, *Macroeconomics* (New York: Harcourt Brace Jovanovich, Inc., 1972), Chapter 13.

5. David E. W. Laidler, *The Demand for Money: Theories and Evidence*, 2nd ed. (New York: Dun-Donnelley, 1977), p. 125. This summarizes the results in Allan Meltzer, "The Demand for Money: The Evidence from the Time Series," *Journal of Political Economy* 71 (June 1963), pp. 219–246.

6. See the summary of these studies in Thomas Mayer, *Monetary Policy in the United States* (New York: Random House, 1968), pp. 120–123.

7. See A. C. Pigou, "The Classical Stationary State," *Economic Journal* 53 (December 1943), pp. 343–351.

Questions

18.1. Why does the liquidity preference schedule slope downward?

18.2. What are some factors that can cause the liquidity preference schedule to shift to the right? Explain why.

18.3. Explain the way in which an increase in the real money supply may lower nominal interest rates.

18.4. What are the different types of investment spending?

18.5. What will cause the marginal product of capital to increase?

18.6. Why does investment increase when real interest rates fall?

18.7. Draw a graph showing the *IS* and *LM* schedules. Why does the *LM* schedule slope upward to the right? Why does the *IS* schedule slope downward to the right?

18.8. What are some factors that may cause the *IS* schedule to shift to the right? Explain why.

18.9. Explain how an increase in the real money supply may cause the *LM* schedule to shift to the right.

18.10. If interest rates are in the liquidity trap, explain why monetary policy would be unable to affect income.

18.11. If the investment function is inelastic, explain why monetary policy would be unable to affect the level of income.

18.12. Define the Pigou effect.

18.13. It is claimed that the Pigou effect would stimulate recovery in a period of depression if the Federal Reserve System prevented a decline in the money stock. Explain.

18.14. Explain the factors affecting the user cost of capital.

18.15. Explain why the desired stock of capital will be where the marginal product of capital is equal to the user cost of capital.

18.16. What will be the effect on the desired stock of capital of an increase in the national income?

18.17. Know the meaning and significance of the following terms and concepts: liquidity preference schedule, net private domestic investment, marginal product of capital, user cost of capital, desired stock of capital, real interest rate, liquidity trap, inelastic investment schedule, Pigou effect, liquidity effect on interest rates, income effect on interest rates.

19

If budget deficits are financed by new money, there is an automatic relationship between fiscal and monetary policy—the larger the deficit, the larger the expansion in the money supply. When budget deficits are financed by borrowing, fiscal and monetary policy may be independent.

MONETARY AND FISCAL POLICY

This chapter is concerned with the relationship between fiscal policy and monetary policy. Fiscal policy involves primarily the use of the powers of the federal government to tax and spend so as to influence aggregate demand. If expenditures are increased without an equivalent increase in taxes, the funds to pay for the excess expenditures must be obtained in some way. The government may raise the funds needed either by borrowing, thus increasing the amount of its debt, or by creating additional money. On the other hand, when taxes exceed expenditures, the surplus can be used either to retire outstanding government securities or to reduce the money supply. There is little disagreement among economists that fiscal deficits financed by new money will increase aggregate demand. But there are differences of opinion concerning the effects on aggregate demand of deficits financed by borrowing.

Nature of fiscal policy

When the government increases its tax revenues, it takes from individuals and businesses some of the income they would otherwise have had. With lower incomes, they have less money available to spend for consumption and investment. If the reduction in private spending because of the heavier taxes were just equal to an increase in government expenditures for public services and transfers, total spending would probably be unaffected. But there is not always such a balance.

The objective of fiscal policy is to control the relationship between taxes and government expenditures, sometimes increasing and sometimes decreasing total spending in the economy. A stimulating fiscal policy involves either reducing taxes or increasing government expenditures. To restrain the economy, the federal government would do the opposite: increase taxes or reduce government spending.

Over the years, the nature of what is considered appropriate fiscal policy has changed.[1] In the 1930s, the primary emphasis was on increasing government expenditures, such as public works, as a method of stimulating employment. At that time, income taxes did not cover many persons, and because income taxes were not withheld, reducing taxes would not have had the immediate effect it has today. During World War II, budget deficits became more widely accepted as the way to achieve full employment. Changes in taxes as well as in expenditures became a central part of fiscal policy. Near the end of the war, it was widely feared that the period following would see a serious depression unless appropriate fiscal policies were used to stimulate the economy.[2] This led to the enactment of the Employment Act of 1946—"to promote maximum employment, production, and purchasing power." The Council of Economic Advisers, established by this act, is the principal group in the executive branch of the federal government responsible for the formation of fiscal policy, and its members assist the President in making a required economic report to Congress at the beginning of each year.

A principal difficulty in administering fiscal policy has been its inflexibility. Most decisions to make changes in taxes and expenditures must go through Congress. The process is slow, and by the time action is taken, it is often less appropriate than it was when first proposed. It has often taken over a year for a change in taxes first proposed by the President to be enacted. Until recently, a major problem was that Congress voted only on individual pieces of the budget, and there was no process for considering how the sum of the individual actions would affect the economy. In 1974, Congress passed the Congressional and Impoundment Control Act, which ought to bring a major improvement in implementing fiscal policy. Both the House and the Senate now have Budget Committees which are responsible for developing overall targets for fiscal policy and seeing to it that appropriations and revenues conform with these targets once they are agreed upon by Congress.

The way in which tax revenues and government expenditures are affected by changes in business conditions complicates the administration of fiscal policy. When the economy prospers, tax receipts rise automatically, tending to create a budget surplus. When there is a recession, tax receipts fall off and some government expenditures (such as those for relief) rise automatically, creating a budget deficit. For many years, these changes were referred to as *automatic stabilizers*. It was felt that they helped to restrain inflationary pressures and to moderate recessions, and they were believed to be particularly desirable because congressional changes in taxes and government spending occurred slowly. In the 1960s, the attitude toward the automatic stabilizers changed. The tendency of taxes to rise while unemployment was still above 4 percent was referred to as a *fiscal drag*. It was felt that the decline in total spending resulting from the rapid rise in taxes was keeping the economy from operating at its full potential. The problems associated with automatic stabilizers changed again in the 1970s. Because of the automatic stabilizers, during the recession of 1973–1975, the federal government's budget deficits became much larger than they had been during past recessions and the national debt expanded sharply. Despite the problems of fiscal drag and abnormally large deficits, the automatic movements of taxes and expenditures probably have a stabilizing effect on the economy.

Fiscal policy during World War II

The development of widespread confidence in the power of fiscal policy was largely the result of experience during World War II. Table 19.1 shows that government outlays rose sharply from 1940 to 1945. Tax receipts also rose rapidly, but not by as much as government outlays. The federal government had very large deficits. In 1940 the rate of unemployment in the United States was 14.6 percent. By 1945 it had fallen to only 1.9 percent.

Table 19.1
Federal Budget,
Consolidated Cash
Statement, 1940–1948
(in billions)

Year	Receipts	Outlays	Surplus (+) or Deficit (−)
1940	$ 6.9	$ 9.6	−$ 2.7
1941	9.2	14.0	− 4.8
1942	15.1	34.5	− 19.4
1943	25.1	78.9	− 53.8
1944	47.8	94.0	− 46.1
1945	50.2	95.2	− 45.0
1946	43.5	61.7	− 18.2
1947	43.5	36.9	+ 6.6
1948	45.4	36.5	+ 8.9

Source: U.S. Bureau of the Census, *Historical Statistics of the United States, Colonial Times to 1970*, Bicentennial edition, Part 2, page 1105.

Although the large deficits from 1940 to 1945 would be expected to have a stimulating effect on the economy, the experience in World War II does not provide a test of the possible expansionary effects of a deficit financed by borrowing. A significant portion of the wartime deficits were financed by money creation. *M-1* rose from $40 billion in 1940 to about $100 billion five years later—two and a half times. In the early years of the war, the commercial banks were able to expand their total assets and liabilities by using excess reserves that they had acquired in the latter part of the 1930s. The ratio of their reserves to their deposits fell sharply. As the war progressed, the Federal Reserve banks purchased enough securities in the open market and increased bank reserves sufficiently to enable the banks to create the money the United States Treasury needed to finance its deficits.

Experience in the period following World War II raised some doubts concerning the strength of fiscal policy. As shown in Table 19.1, there was a sharp change from a deficit of $45 billion in 1945 to a surplus two years later. The federal government reduced expenditures much more sharply than taxes. Some economists predicted that this restraining fiscal policy would cause a serious depression, but their predictions turned out to be wrong. From 1945 to 1947, *M-1* rose from $102 billion to $113 billion.

Alternative ways of financing deficits

When nations finance a deficit by borrowing from the public, the sale of government securities provides the funds needed to pay for an excess of expenditures over tax revenues. When deficits are financed in this way, the amount of the national debt is increased. The owners of the new securities receive interest, and there is an increase in the government's expenditures for interest.

Nations may also finance deficits by creating money. During the Revolutionary War, the colonies financed the shortfall in revenues with the printing press. The Continental currency issued at that time involved this type of finance. Under modern conditions, the way a country finances fiscal deficits by creating money (demand deposits as well as paper notes) involves cooperation with its central bank. The treasury department of a country would finance a deficit in this way by selling its bonds directly to its central bank in return for either deposits or paper notes. Assume that the treasury department wishes the new money to be half in deposits and half in central bank notes. The effect on the central bank's balance sheet is shown in Figure 19.1. The central bank receives interest on the government securities it has acquired, but this is usually unimportant because modern central banks are almost always public institutions, and the additional income they receive would be returned to the treasury. The treasury spends the new central bank notes and deposits to finance its deficit. The persons acquiring the notes and deposits would in turn spend them again, and the notes and deposits would continue to circulate in the economy.

Figure 19.1
Sales of Government Securities to the Central Bank

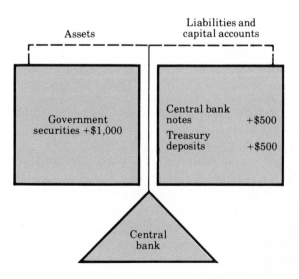

The way in which the United States Treasury finances a fiscal deficit with new money is slightly different from the process just described. But the result is the same, even though money-creation to finance the deficit appears to be borrowing. Such money-creation occurs if, at the same time that the Treasury is selling new securities to the public, the Federal Reserve banks are purchasing them in the open market. When the Federal Reserve banks and the United States Treasury act together in this way, no additional U.S. government securities need be sold to the public, and there is no additional borrowing from the public. There is, however, an expansion in the U.S. Treasury's deposits at the Federal Reserve banks. The Treasury will use these deposits to pay for the excess in its expenditures over its tax receipts, and the deposits will then continue to circulate as bank reserve deposits at the Federal Reserve banks.

Historical relation between fiscal and monetary policy

The expansion of the money supply in the United States during the past two decades has been quite closely related to the size of the Treasury's fiscal deficits.[3] Figure 19.2 shows the similar upward trends from 1954 to 1979 in (1) the total federal government debt less the portion of this held by U.S. government agencies and trust funds, (2) the total federal government debt held by the Federal Reserve System alone, and (3) M-1. From 1954 to 1961, the average annual rate of growth in federal government debt was only 0.8 percent because of small budget deficits in those years. In the 1960s, budget deficits increased because both defense and nondefense expenditures grew more rapidly than tax receipts. The rate of growth of the federal debt rose to 1.6 percent a year for the period from 1961 to 1966, 3.9 percent a year from 1966 to 1972, 5.2 percent from 1972 to 1973, 3.6 percent from 1973 to 1975, and 13.7 percent from 1975 to 1979. The accelerated expansion in federal government debt has been accompanied by a more rapid expansion in the amount of government debt purchased by the Federal Reserve banks, and consequently a more rapid expansion in the money supply.

Larger budget deficits have led to larger open-market purchases because the short-run effect of issuing additional government securities is to raise market interest rates. Because the Federal Reserve has had specific targets for interest rates, larger fiscal deficits that tend to raise interest rates would lead to actions by the Federal Reserve to keep interest rates on their target. To counteract upward pressure on interest rates, the Federal Reserve would purchase securities in the open market, thus increasing the monetary base and the money supply.

Although there has been an upward trend in both the rate of increase in the federal government debt and the money supply, they do not always vary together. From 1975 to 1979, the expansion in the money stock has not risen as rapidly as the expansion in the federal government debt.

**Figure 19.2
Influence of Federal
Government Debt on
Monetary Expansion
(seasonally adjusted
data)**

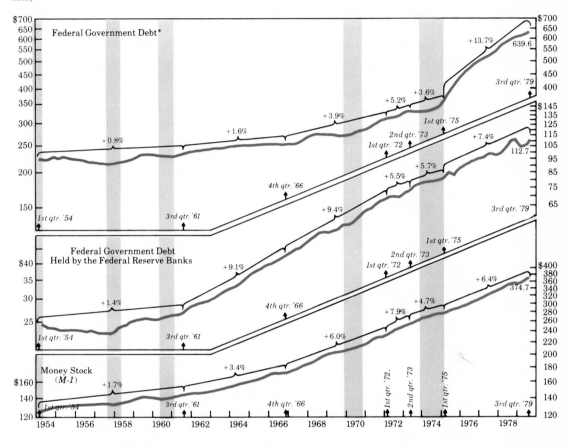

*Total gross public debt less debt held by U.S. government agencies and trust funds.
Shaded areas represent periods of business recession.
Percentages are annual rates of change.
Source: Federal Reserve Bank of St. Louis

Measuring fiscal policy

The federal government has three types of budgets showing the changes in its expenditures and receipts: the unified budget, the national income accounts budget, and the high-employment budget.[4]

Unified budget

The unified-budget concept replaced several other budget concepts in fiscal year 1969. The amounts of the principal types of receipts and outlays in the unified budget for the fiscal year 1978 are shown in Table 19.2. The objective of this budget is to show the cash flows of the United States Treasury. A major change from the previous budget concepts was the inclusion of the trust accounts, such as those of the Social Security Administration. Both the employment taxes used to finance Social Security and the payments to those receiving Social Security benefits were added. The expenditures in the unified budget also include the lending of various federal credit agencies for housing, agriculture, and international assistance. Net lending is equal to the excess of loan disbursements over loan repayments and has become important because of the expansion in the activities of the federal credit agencies. Total receipts and total expenditures in the unified budget from 1970 to 1979 are shown in Table 19.3. The United States has had a deficit in the unified budget in all of these years.

Table 19.2
Receipts and Outlays in the Unified Budget of the United States, Fiscal Year 1978 (in billions)

Receipts:	
Individual income taxes	$181.0
Social insurance taxes	123.4
Corporation income taxes	60.0
Excise taxes	18.4
All other	19.3
Total	$402.0
Outlays:	
Defense, space, foreign affairs	$115.6
Agriculture, energy, natural resources, transportation, commerce and housing credit, community and regional development	54.2
Education, employment, social services, health, income security, veterans	235.4
Justice and general government	7.6
Revenue sharing	9.6
Interest	44.0
Undistributed offsetting receipts (mainly intergovernmental transactions)	−15.8
Total	$450.8
Budget deficit	$ 48.8

Source: *Treasury Bulletin*, September 1979, pp. 1, 3, and 4; and *Economic Report of the President*, January 1979, p. 265.

National income accounts budget

The national income accounts budget is similar to the unified budget, but is based on a conception of output used in the national income accounts. Like the unified budget, it includes the regular government transactions and trust fund accounts. The government's contributions to government employee retirement are included as part of compensation.

Table 19.3
Unified Budget of the
United States,
1970–1979 (in billions)

Fiscal Year[a]	Receipts	Outlays	Surplus (+) or Deficit (−)
1970	$193.7	$196.6	− $ 2.8
1971	188.4	211.4	− 23.0
1972	208.6	232.0	− 23.4
1973	232.2	247.1	− 14.8
1974	264.9	269.6	− 4.7
1975	281.0	326.2	− 45.2
1976	300.0	366.4	− 66.4
1977	357.8	402.7	− 45.0
1978	402.0	450.8	− 48.8
1979	465.9	493.6	− 27.7

Details do not add to totals because of rounding.
[a]Starting in October 1976 (fiscal year 1977), the federal government's fiscal year was fixed to run from October 1 through September 30. In earlier years, the fiscal year was from July 1 through June 30. The 3-month period from July 1, 1976 through September 30, 1976 is a separate fiscal period known as the transition quarter.
Source: Federal Reserve Bank of St. Louis, *Federal Budget Trends*, Feb. 15, 1978, p. 2, and *Monetary Trends*, March 26, 1980, p. 14.

The expenditures also include both income-generating purchases of goods and services and transfer payments that enhance the purchasing power of the private sector. Net lending is not included in expenditures, as it is in the unified budget. The purchase and sale of existing real and financial assets are also excluded because they do not represent current income or production. Expenditures are recorded when delivery is made to the government, and taxes are usually recorded when the tax liability is incurred.

High-employment budget

The high-employment budget shown in Table 19.4 was developed in the 1960s. If this budget shows a growing deficit, it means that the federal government has shifted to an easier fiscal policy. If it shows a growing surplus, it means that the federal government has adopted a more restraining fiscal policy. In this budget, both the estimated tax revenues and expenditures of the national income accounts budget are adjusted to show what they would be if the economy were operating at a steady and high level of employment. For example, although tax receipts might be relatively low because unemployment was high, this budget would show what the level of tax receipts would be if the level of unemployment were, for example, 4 or 5 percent. By holding the level of resource use constant, the high-employment budget attempts to measure the effect solely of the changes in fiscal policy made by the governmental authorities. The concept of the high-employment budget was developed to provide a measure of fiscal policy that does not reflect changes in the level of the national income. Such a measure is useful for planning fiscal and monetary policy and for appraising past policy decisions.

Table 19.4
High-Employment
Budget, United States,
1970-1979 (in billions of
dollars)

Fiscal Year	Receipts	Expenditures	Surplus (+) or Deficit (−)
1970	$205.9	$203.7	+$ 2.2
1971	211.0	219.5	− 8.5
1972	227.3	244.0	− 16.7
1973	258.4	265.1	− 6.7
1974	295.6	298.6	− 3.0
1975	318.8	349.9	− 31.1
1976	353.0	379.8	− 26.8
1977	384.2	418.3	− 34.1
1978	435.3	458.4	− 23.1
1979	501.1	507.6	− 6.5

Source: Federal Reserve Bank of St. Louis, *Monetary Trends*, November 17, 1978, p. 14, September 26, 1979, p. 14, and March 26, 1980, p. 14.

Although changes in the high-employment budget are a better measure of the direction of fiscal policy than changes in the unified or national income accounts budgets, use of the high-employment budget has several limitations.[5] The impact of government expenditures begins when business firms start producing to fill government contracts, but the high-employment budget shows the effects only when government expenditures are made. On the revenue side, taxes probably have an impact on private expenditures when persons and business firms start to accrue funds to pay taxes rather than when they pay the taxes. The national income accounts treat corporate taxes on an accrual basis, but personal taxes are on a cash basis. There are also problems in measuring high-employment expenditures and receipts. Although 4 percent unemployment was used for many years to calculate the high-employment budget, it is not always the proper target for high employment. In recent years, the rate of unemployment consistent with high employment has risen above 5 percent, and the basis for estimating high-employment expenditures and receipts has had to be changed.

Measuring budgetary effects

The usual way of measuring the effect of fiscal policy on spending is by calculating the change in the deficit or surplus from one year to the next. Consider the change from 1972 to 1973 in the unified budget shown in Table 19.3. The deficit fell from $23 billion to $15 billion. Taxes increased almost $24 billion, but expenditures increased less—by $15 billion. The fact that the increase in taxes was larger than the increase in government expenditures withdrew funds from the spending stream. The net deflationary effect on total spending was almost $9 billion. The larger the decrease in the deficit, the more deflationary the impact would be. Note that having a deficit does not necessarily indicate that fiscal policy is expansionary, and that having a surplus does not necessarily indicate that fiscal policy is restraining. Fiscal policy is expansionary only if the deficit is getting larger or the surplus is getting smaller, and it would be restraining only if the deficit is becoming smaller or the surplus larger.

Another way in which some economists measure the economic impact of fiscal policy is by changes in government expenditures. The larger the increase in such spending, the larger the expected impact on the national income. The use of this measure of fiscal policy is the result of the development of econometric forecasting models. Using these models with historical data, it has been found that the increase in total government expenditures is more closely related to the national income than changes either in taxes or in the budget deficit. An interesting study by Andersen and Jordan at the Federal Reserve Bank of St. Louis found that an increase in government spending is mildly stimulative in the quarter in which spending is increased and in the following quarter.[6] In the subsequent two quarters, there are offsetting negative influences, and the overall effect is relatively small. This study found no evidence that fiscal actions, as measured by the high-employment budget or changes in tax receipts due to changes in tax rates, have a significant effect on GNP.

Fiscal policy and national income

The way changes in fiscal policy may cause changes in total spending may be explained with the same figures as those used in Chapters 17 and 18. Consider first the effect on the national income and on nominal interest rates when an expansionary fiscal policy is financed by borrowing.

Fiscal deficits financed by borrowing

The analysis of the effect of fiscal deficits financed by borrowing is of particular interest because there is disagreement among economists as to how expansionary such a fiscal policy may be. Figure 19.3 presents graphically the usual explanation of the way in which an expansionary fiscal policy financed by borrowing would raise nominal interest rates and increase the national income.

**Figure 19.3
The Effect of an
Expansionary Fiscal
Policy Financed by
Borrowing**

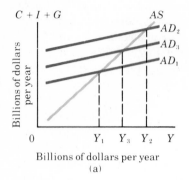

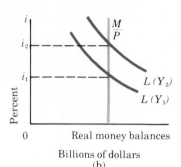

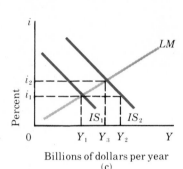

The initial effect of either an increase in government spending or a reduction in tax revenues would be to raise the aggregate demand schedule in Figure 19.3(a) from AD_1 to AD_2. An increase in government purchases of goods and services would raise the aggregate demand schedule because increases in government spending are autonomous (not the result of an increase in national income). A reduction in tax revenues would also raise the aggregate demand schedule because people would be able to spend a larger proportion of their incomes because their taxes are lower. As shown in Figure 19.3(a), the rise in the aggregate demand schedule would cause aggregate demand to be greater than aggregate supply at Y_1. To prevent a depletion of their inventories, business firms would increase output, raising the national income to Y_3.

Thus far, the analysis is incomplete because it has not taken into consideration the way in which the deficit is financed. As Figure 19.3(b) shows, an expansionary fiscal policy financed by borrowing will tend to raise nominal interest rates. In Figure 19.3(b), the real money supply schedule (M/P) is unchanged because it is assumed that the deficit was not financed by newly created money. The increase in the national income caused by the expansionary fiscal policy would shift the demand for real money balances schedule (L) to the right by increasing the amount of real money balances people want to hold for transactions and for precautionary needs. This would raise nominal interest rates from i_1 to i_2. At the original level of nominal interest rates, i_1, the quantity of real money balances demanded would be larger than the supply. As interest rates rise, the quantity of real money balances demanded decreases until the demand for real money balances is equal to the supply at i_2.

If the rise in nominal interest rates were also a rise in real interest rates, the rise in interest rates in Figure 19.3(b) would then tend to reduce investment. In Figure 19.3(a), this would cause the aggregate demand schedule to shift downward to AD_3. This would limit the increase in income to Y_3.

Even though the rise in nominal interest rates causes a smaller expansion in income, interest rates would not have risen in the first place unless income were larger. The aggregate demand schedule cannot fall back to its original level. On the IS-LM graph in Figure 19.3(c), the final equilibrium between IS and LM is at Y_3 and i_2. An expansionary fiscal policy will shift the IS schedule to the right because the rise in the aggregate demand schedule in Figure 19.3(a) was not the result of a reduction in interest rates. Given an upward-sloping LM schedule, a shift of the IS schedule to the right must increase both the national income and interest rates. Note that before interest rates rise from i_1 to i_2, the IS_2 schedule is not in equilibrium with the LM schedule. In Figure 19.3(c), the demand for real cash balances is equal to the supply, and aggregate demand is equal to aggregate supply only when market interest rates are at i_2 and national income at Y_3.

The precise effect of fiscal policy on national income depends on the shapes of the IS and LM schedules. To take an extreme case, suppose the LM schedule were horizontal as shown in Figure 19.4(a). If the LM schedule is perfectly elastic, it means that when an increase in income shifts the L schedule to the right as in Figure 19.4(b), nominal interest rates would be unaffected because of the liquidity trap. Compare this with the rise in nominal interest rates resulting from an increase in income shown in Figure 19.3(b). If fiscal policy does not cause nominal and thus real interest rates to rise, it would have the maximum effect on income because a decline in investment would not offset in part the increase in government spending. The LM schedule would not be perfectly horizontal unless nominal interest rates were very low and the economy very depressed. Although such conditions would be extreme, the purpose of this example is to show that the smaller the rise of nominal interest rates, the more expansionary fiscal policy will be.

Consider another possibility—a vertical IS schedule as in Figure 19.5. The IS schedule would be perfectly inelastic if investment were completely unaffected by nominal and real interest rates. Even if real interest rates rose because of an expansionary fiscal policy, the rise would have no effect on investment. Under these conditions, a shift of the IS schedule to the right, because of increased government spending, would have the maximum possible effect on income. Although it is unlikely that changes in real interest rates would have no effect on investment, the purpose of this illustration is also to show that the smaller the decline in investment because of the rise in real interest rates, the more expansionary the fiscal policy financed by borrowing from the public will be. Note that the examples in Figures 19.4 and 19.5

Figure 19.4
Effect of Fiscal Policy on
Income, Assuming a
Liquidity Trap

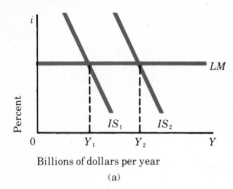

(a)

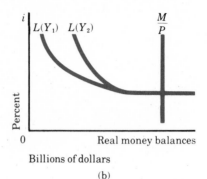

(b)

show that the conditions in which fiscal policy is most expansionary—nominal interest rates at liquidity trap levels and an inelastic investment schedule—are the same as those in which monetary policy is least effective. (Compare with Figures 18.8, 18.9, 18.10, and 18.12).

Figure 19.5
Effect of Fiscal Policy or
Income, Assuming an
Inelastic Investment
Schedule

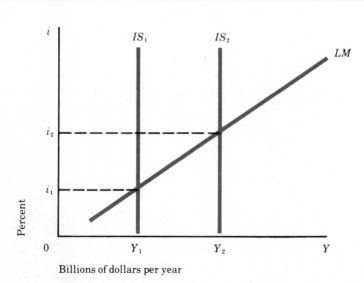

Fiscal deficits financed by newly created money

Figure 19.6 shows that a fiscal deficit financed by newly created money is more expansionary than when financed by borrowing. In both cases, an increase in government spending or a reduction in tax receipts would raise the aggregate demand schedule from AD_1 to AD_2. However, as shown in Figure 19.6(b), if a deficit is financed by newly created money, a shift to the right of the real money supply schedule could keep nominal interest rates from rising. As a result, the aggregate demand schedule in Figure 19.6(a) could rise the maximum amount. The stimulating effects of the increase in government spending or reduction in taxes would not be offset by a decrease in investment caused by rising nominal, and thus real interest rates. In the *IS-LM* graph in Figure 19.6(c), an increase in the money supply would shift the *LM* schedule to the right. The *IS* schedule and the *LM* schedule would intersect at a higher level of national income, and there need be no rise in nominal interest rates.

Figure 19.6
The Effect of an
Expansionary Fiscal
Policy Financed by New
Money

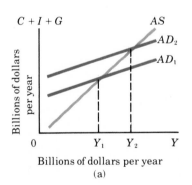
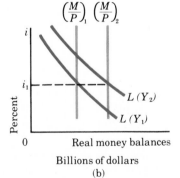
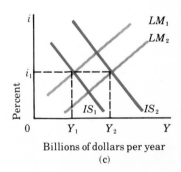

Figure 19.6 can be used to illustrate why the role of monetary policy has often been viewed as supplementary to fiscal policy. According to this view, fiscal policy was thought to be the primary means of controlling the output of the economy. The unique contribution of monetary policy was to prevent a possible rise in interest rates that might result from an expansionary fiscal policy.

Is a fiscal deficit financed by borrowing always expansionary?

Even though a fiscal deficit financed by borrowing from the public is not as expansionary as one financed by new money, according to the analysis in Figure 19.3 it would still be expansionary. Some economists have rejected this analysis and believe that the stimulating effect on national income of a deficit financed by borrowing from the public would last only a short time. These critics claim that if there is a deficit, nominal and real interest rates may rise because of the need to sell additional securities to finance the deficit, and not solely because of an increase in income. In Figure 19.3, there would be no rise in nominal interest rates unless income rose. However, if nominal interest rates rise because a deficit is being financed by selling securities rather than because income has increased, the increase in spending because of an expansionary fiscal policy may be completely offset by a decrease in private spending because of higher interest rates.

The critics also believe that sales of additional Treasury bonds take funds away from private borrowers. This is known as the *crowding-out effect.*[7] Consider the effect of deficit financing when bonds are sold to commercial banks. If the Federal Reserve banks made no open-market purchases during a period in which the Treasury was financing a deficit, bank reserves and the total amount of bank credit would be unchanged. Commercial banks would have to cut down on the volume of loans made to the private sector of the economy if they purchased additional government securities. This would reduce the private capital expenditures that might have been financed by these loans.

There may also be crowding-out effects on the spending of other financial institutions and the public. Funds that might have been invested in other ways would now be invested in U.S. government securities. Because of the increased supply of federal government securities on the market, nominal interest rates generally would tend to rise. The higher rates of return would reduce the supply of other assets such as stocks, bonds, and physical assets because it is more difficult to earn these higher rates of return. As a result, the issue of additional U.S. government securities would tend to be offset by a decline in the supply of some of those other assets and thus in private investment.

A third concern of the critics is the usual assumption that higher nominal and real interest rates will not affect saving. In the model in Figure 19.3, it is assumed that saving is not affected by the rise in real interest rates. It is possible that higher real interest rates increase saving, either because of the higher rate of return or by reducing consumption of items purchased on credit. This would lower the aggregate demand schedule and lower the level of income. Many economists believe that the effect of real interest rates on saving is small, but little is known about the exact relationship.

The monetarist-fiscalist debate

There is disagreement among economists over whether the national income is more affected by changes in the money supply or by fiscal changes.[8] The *monetarists* believe that more money means more spending, and less money the opposite, although some monetarists doubt that monetary policy can be effectively administered so as to control national income. *Fiscalists* believe a growing budget deficit would induce more spending and income-creation, while a shift toward a surplus would be restraining. The relative importance of fiscal and monetary policy is still a matter of debate. Econometric tests of their relative importance have been inconclusive.[9]

Ultimately, the test of a theory depends primarily on its predictive ability. In the latter half of the 1960s, there was greater popular acceptance of the monetarist approach because of its apparent superiority as a basis for forecasting.[10] There were three occasions that tested the relative importance of fiscal and monetary policy quite well, and in each test the monetary models seemed to predict best. To test the relative strength of the two policies, there must be occasions when their indicators move in opposite directions.

Experience in 1966–1967

For a period of seven months beginning in the spring of 1966, monetary growth dropped to near zero while the high-employment deficit continued to grow larger. Monetarist predictions for 1967 ranged from pause to recession. Fiscal policy indicated a continued rapid growth in spending. In fact, the economy slowed abruptly, real GNP declined for one quarter, industrial production dipped moderately, and inflation slowed. The period has been characterized as a mini-recession.

Experience in 1968–1969

A second test occurred in 1968 when Congress passed a 10 percent surtax at about midyear. A $19 billion shift in the high-employment budget, from a $6 billion deficit in fiscal 1968 to a $13 billion surplus in fiscal 1969, resulted. At the same time, monetary growth accelerated because Federal Reserve officials feared a possible "overkill" resulting from the tax increase. Fiscal policy indicated an abrupt slowing in the economy, a reduced rate of inflation, and lower market interest rates, while monetary policy indicated the opposite. In fact, the economy remained strong, inflation became more severe, and market interest rates rose.

Experience in 1970

Monetarists uniformly projected a recession for 1970, whereas most fiscalists expected real output to increase at a rate of approximately 2 percent. From June to December of 1969, there had been only a very small increase in *M-1*, and *M-1* plus time deposits in commercial banks declined by more than $5 billion. The year 1970 turned out to be a year of recession.

Fiscal policy and aggregate supply

In recent years, there has been growing interest in the possible effect of fiscal policy on aggregate supply. If higher government expenditures together with higher taxes discourage work effort or reduce the supply of capital, they would lower the real output of the economy. The interest in the effect of fiscal policy on aggregate supply is the result of rising tax rates.[11] In 1978, total federal, state, and local government expenditures amounted to 44 percent of the national income.

The possible depressing effects of an expansion in government spending on aggregate supply would offset the stimulating effects on aggregate demand. The combined effects are particularly undesirable—if fiscal policies expanding government spending both increase aggregate demand and reduce aggregate supply, the result would be both higher inflation and higher unemployment. Higher marginal tax rates affect the supply of labor and capital in two ways. High taxes on income affect the choice between additional leisure and additional earnings because leisure is not taxed and earnings are. The higher the tax rate on additional earnings, the more attractive retirement, shorter hours of work, and long vacations become. High taxes on income also affect the choice between additional future income from saving and additional current consumption. Income from savings is taxed, while current expenditures escape this type of taxation. As a result, the higher the tax rate, the more attractive current consumption becomes relative to saving. Economists who believe that the supply side of fiscal policy has been neglected believe that high tax rates are a reason for the slow growth of labor productivity in the United States in the 1970s.

Debt management

When the United States Treasury finances a fiscal deficit by selling new securities, it must decide what kind to issue—short-term, intermediate-term, or long-term. Decisions about the composition of the debt may have economic effects on output and prices, in addition to the effects of fiscal policy that have already been discussed.

The Treasury is continuously faced with the problem of replacing maturing securities. Budget surpluses have been infrequent, and these have been more than offset by deficits. A large portion of the total national debt matures each year. The 91-day regular bills have to be "rolled over" four times during the year, the 180-day bills twice, and the one-year bills once. The substantial amounts of notes and bonds coming due each year must also be replaced.

It is sometimes suggested that the Treasury ought to manage the maturity of the debt so as to counteract the ups and downs of business activity.[12] To have a countercyclical effect, the Treasury must issue long-term debt when it wishes to restrain inflation and short-term debt when there is slack in the economy.

The sale of additional long-term bonds is restraining because it tends to lower the prices of long-term bonds and increase nominal interest rates not only for bonds but also for mortgages and other long-term investments that compete with bonds. Higher nominal and thus real interest rates would tend to discourage private borrowing and invest-ment spending. The fall in bond prices also causes capital losses for bondholders, which may have a further restraining effect. In addition, when maturing issues are replaced by long-term bonds, the total supply of liquid assets tends to be reduced.

The impact is different when short-term securities are offered. If maturing issues (always short-term as they near maturity) were replaced by new short-term securities, the quantity of liquid assets would be unchanged. Moreover, if short-term securities were sold to finance a budget deficit, the total supply of liquid assets would be increased. Although the increase in the supply of liquid assets would tend to raise short-term interest rates, it might tend to lower long-term interest rates because financial institutions would be more willing to purchase long-term bonds because of the increase in their liquid assets. If the econom-ic effect of the decline in long-term market interest rates more than offsets the effect of the rise in short-term rates, the net effect could be expansionary.

The principal measure of the variations in the maturity of the debt is the average maturity of the marketable interest-bearing debt held by private investors. The average maturity of the marketable debt tends to fall automatically as outstanding securities gradually approach their maturity dates. When the Treasury issues long-term debt, the average maturity of the debt tends to rise.

Despite the proposals to manage the debt so as to stabilize aggregate demand, the debt has not been managed in this way. In the recession years of 1953–1954, 1957–1958, and 1960–1961, the Treasury issued longer-term securities, raising the average maturity of the debt. In the intervening periods of prosperity, the average maturity of the debt typically decreased. From 1961 to 1965, the average maturity of the debt was increased substantially, although this was a period of relatively high unemployment. Despite fluctuations in economic activity from 1969 to 1976, Table 19.5 shows that the average maturity of the debt decreased steadily—from over four years to about two and a half years. From 1976 to 1978, the average maturity of the debt rose, and was consistent with an anti-inflationary policy.

The Treasury manages the maturity of the debt the way it does because it wants to keep its own interest costs as low as possible and thus is hesitant to create long-term debt in periods of prosperity when market interest rates are high. At the same time, the Treasury usually tries to lengthen the maturity of the debt whenever it seems feasible. One of the traditional views of Treasury officials is that "good government requires lengthening the maturity of the debt." Whenever the average maturity of the debt is lengthened, it is pointed to with pride.

Table 19.5
Average Length of Marketable Interest-Bearing Public Debt Held by Private Investors, 1969-1978

End of Fiscal Year	Average Length	
	Years	Months
1969	4	2
1970	3	8
1971	3	6
1972	3	3
1973	3	1
1974	2	11
1975	2	8
1976	2	7
1977	2	11
1978	3	3

Source: *Treasury Bulletin*, September 1979, page 26.

If, because of the Treasury's other objectives, debt management accentuated undesired cyclical trends in market interest rates or the stock of liquid assets, appropriate monetary policy could offset these effects. But the need to counteract the impact of changes in the maturity of the debt and the difficulty of determining how much of an offset is necessary makes the administration of monetary policy more complicated.

Assisting the Treasury

In most countries, central banks assist their treasuries with the sale of government debt. After the Federal Reserve System had been operating for only three years, the monetary authorities were faced with the problem of helping to finance the large Treasury deficits caused by World War I. During World War I and for several years afterward,

Federal Reserve loans to commercial banks were expanded rapidly. This enabled the banks to purchase some of the bonds issued to finance the war. During World War II, the Federal Reserve System also expanded bank reserves in order to help finance the large budget deficits and to make possible the selling of government securities at low market rates of interest. During both world wars, these efforts by the Federal Reserve System to assist Treasury wartime financing resulted in a rapid expansion of the money supply—and inflation.

In recent years, during periods of refunding, the Federal Reserve has maintained an *even-keel policy* designed to keep changes in monetary policy from interfering with the success of Treasury debt operations. At the time of the refunding, the Treasury announces the rate of interest on the new issues prior to the date of the exchange. The quantity that investors are willing to purchase at the rate set cannot be known in advance and may be more or less than desired. Because the owners of the maturing issues may desire cash instead of the new issues offered, the exchange may be only partially successful. The Treasury sets coupon rates on new issues as low as possible. As a result, if there were a small rise in market interest rates, the new issues would be unattractive compared to other available investments. To keep attrition relatively low, the Federal Reserve usually purchases securities in the open market during Treasury refundings so as to prevent market interest rates from rising.

In recent years, the Treasury has made greater use of the auction technique in marketing federal securities and less use of refundings and subscriptions. This has made the implementation of monetary policy simpler. With the auction technique, the Treasury always sells the amount of securities it wishes to sell because it is willing to accept the best price that it can get; assistance from the Federal Reserve is not needed. The even-keel policy occasionally conflicts with attempts by the Federal Reserve authorities to achieve their targets. During periods when the Federal Reserve is assisting the Treasury, monetary policy would have to depart from its usual target, and it would later be necessary to overcompensate to get back on the target. Such actions would either be destabilizing in the short run or result in missing the long-run target.

Summary

The rate of expansion of the money supply in the United States is often closely related to the rate of expansion of the national debt. There has been an important relationship between fiscal and monetary policy.

A budget deficit financed by new money is more expansionary than a deficit financed by borrowing. A budget deficit financed by borrowing causes nominal interest rates to rise, and lenders are induced to purchase government securities rather than to make loans to private borrowers.

The combination of a tight money policy and an easy fiscal policy occurs when the rate of increase in the money supply declines at the same time that there is an increase in the high-employment budget deficit. The opposite combination occurs when the rate of increase in the money supply rises at the same time that the high-employment budget deficit gets smaller. For many years, it was generally accepted that fiscal policy had a more powerful effect on the national income than monetary policy. Recent experience has resulted in a reevaluation of the relative power of these two policies—with the viewpoint of the monetarists gaining support.

The Treasury could manage the maturity of the debt in such a way as to increase the supply of liquid assets during recessions and reduce the supply during booms, but usually it has not done so.

Notes

1. Herbert Stein, *The Fiscal Revolution in America* (Chicago: University of Chicago Press, 1969), Chapter 9. For a description of the operation of fiscal policy, see Lester C. Thurow, ed., *American Fiscal Policy, Experiment for Prosperity* (Englewood Cliffs, N.J.: Prentice-Hall, 1967), pp. 1–27.

2. See, for example, Henry A. Wallace, *Sixty Million Jobs* (New York: Simon and Schuster, 1945).

3. Kenneth Stewart, "Government Debt, Money, and Economic Activity," Federal Reserve Bank of St. Louis, *Review*, January 1972, pp. 2–9.

4. For an analysis of the federal budget for the fiscal year 1979, see Michael E. Levy, *The Federal Budget, Its Impact on the Economy*, No. 1 (New York: The Conference Board, 1978). Before 1978, this analysis was published annually, but it is now issued three times a year.

5. For a description of an alternative measure of fiscal policy, the *instant stimulus* measure, see E. Gerald Corrigan. "The Measurement and Importance of Fiscal Policy Changes," Federal Reserve Bank of New York, *Monthly Review*, June 1970, pp. 133–145. The expenditure component of this measure is the quarter-to-quarter change in total federal outlays as recorded in the national income accounts budget. The revenue component measures the initial dollar impact of discretionary changes in the various tax rates and their bases.

6. Leonall C. Andersen and Jerry L. Jordan, "Monetary and Fiscal Actions: A Test of Their Relative Importance in Economic Stabilization," Federal Reserve Bank of St. Louis, *Review*, November 1968, p. 18.

7. See John M. Culbertson, *Macroeconomic Theory and Stabilization Policy* (New York: McGraw-Hill, 1968), pp. 462–463; and Roger W. Spencer and William P. Yohe, "The 'Crowding-Out' of Private Expenditures by Fiscal Policy Actions," Federal Reserve Bank of St. Louis, *Review*, October 1970, pp. 12–24.

8. For a debate on this issue, see Milton Friedman and Walter W. Heller, *Monetary vs. Fiscal Policy* (New York: W. W. Norton and Company, 1969). For the monetarist point of view, see Beryl W. Sprinkel, *Money and Markets: A Monetarist View* (Homewood, Ill.: Richard D. Irwin, 1971), pp. 8–16; and A. James Meigs, *Money Matters* (New York: Harper and Row, 1972). For the fiscalist point of view, see Arthur M. Okun, *The Political Economy of Prosperity* (New York: W. W. Norton and Company, 1970).

9. Andersen and Jordan, "Monetary and Fiscal Actions," pp. 11–24; and Benjamin M. Friedman, "Even the St. Louis Model Now Believes in Fiscal Policy," *Journal of Money, Credit and Banking* 9 (May 1977), pp. 365–367.

10. In newspapers and news magazines, interest in the monetarist approach centered on articles about Professor Milton Friedman, the leading theorist responsible for its development. See *Time* (December 19, 1969), pp. 66–72; and Milton Viorst, "Friedmanism," *New York Times Magazine*, January 25, 1970, pp. 22–23 and 80–84.

11. U.S. Joint Economic Committee, *The 1978 Joint Economic Report*, 95th Cong., 2nd sess., Union Calendar No. 498, House Report No. 95-995 (Washington, D.C.: U.S. Government Printing Office, 1978), pp. 93–100, 140–141.

12. John M. Culbertson, *Full Employment or Stagnation?* (New York: McGraw-Hill, 1964), Chapter 9.

Questions

19.1. What is the meaning of an expansionary fiscal policy? A restraining fiscal policy?

19.2. What are some of the difficulties encountered in administering fiscal policy?

19.3. Compare the financing of a fiscal deficit in the United States by borrowing with financing a deficit by an expansion in the supply of money.

19.4. What are the differences between the unified budget, the national income accounts budget, and the high-employment budget?

19.5. What is the special usefulness of the high-employment budget?

19.6. What are some ways of measuring how expansionary fiscal policy is?

19.7. Explain with the use of graphs the way either an increase in government expenditures or a decrease in taxes is expected to increase national income—disregarding the question of how the deficit may be financed.

19.8. Explain with the use of graphs why a fiscal deficit financed by new money has a more expansionary effect on income than a fiscal deficit financed by borrowing.

19.9. Explain some of the factors that determine how expansionary deficit financing through borrowing may be.

19.10. Would it be possible for deficit financing through borrowing to have no effect on income?

19.11. Explain the differences in the point of view of the monetarists and fiscalists toward fiscal and monetary policy.

19.12. Explain the reasons for the Federal Reserve's "even-keel" policy during periods of debt financing by the Treasury.

19.13. How were the commercial banks enabled to buy many of the government bonds issued to finance World Wars I and II?

19.14. If the Treasury wished to manage the maturity of the debt in an expansionary way, what would it do?

19.15. What are some of the reasons the United States Treasury does not manage the maturity of the national debt in a countercyclical way?

19.16. How do the effects of fiscal policy on aggregate demand and aggregate supply differ?

19.17. Know the meaning and significance of the following terms and concepts: budget deficit, budget surplus, unified budget, national income accounts budget, high-employment budget, automatic stabilizers, fiscal drag, crowding-out effect, the supply side of fiscal policy, the Federal Reserve's even-keel policy, managing the maturity of the debt, monetarist, fiscalist.

20

There are three principal types of monetary systems: automatic systems in which monetary policy depends largely on the balance of international payments, discretionary systems in which monetary policy is determined by government authorities, and those in which monetary policy is based on a rule.

ALTERNATIVE
MONETARY SYSTEMS

Many countries have a type of monetary system in which changes in the money supply are *automatic*—the quantity of money varies with the balance of international payments. The best example of this type of system was the gold standard as it operated in the nineteenth century. In the United States today, the monetary system is not automatic. It is a *discretionary* system regulated by the authorities of the Federal Reserve System. The monetary authorities are provided with instruments of control, such as open-market operations. The authorities have considerable latitude in determining policy objectives and actions. Several economists have proposed a third type of monetary system, one in which monetary policy is *based on a rule.* In a system of this type, the monetary authorities would have at their disposal means of controlling the monetary base, but the purposes and targets of monetary policy would be narrowly defined. Congress might prescribe by law that the monetary authorities increase the money supply at a particular rate, or stabilize a price index. This chapter is concerned with these different types of monetary systems, and how our present system has developed.

Monetary systems automatically regulated by the balance of payments

Monetary policy is sometimes tied in with balancing a country's international payments. In most countries, international payments must eventually be balanced by receipts. If a country had continuous deficits, its supply of international reserves (international money primarily in the form of gold and foreign exchange denominated in U.S. dollars) would soon be exhausted. To avoid such a contingency, each country must have some technique of adjustment. The objective of having a monetary system based on the balance of payments is that such a system provides a country with a fairly efficient technique for keeping payments in balance. Monetary restraint tends to correct a deficit in the balance of payments and monetary ease tends to bring an end to a surplus—the money supply automatically begins to increase when there is a surplus in the balance of payments and to decrease when there is a deficit. As was explained in Chapters 17 and 18, a policy of monetary restraint eventually slows down the economy, and in the short run raises interest rates; a tight policy also may lower prices. Monetary ease raises income and prices, and in the short run lowers interest rates. These effects tend to change the flow of international trade and bring about a reversal of the conditions that caused the imbalance. In such a system, there could be little discretion, and establishing a monetary rule would not be possible.

An automatic system based on international payments existed when the gold standard was used in the nineteenth century. If international receipts exceeded payments, there was an inflow of gold which caused an automatic increase in bank reserves and made possible an increase in the money supply; if payments exceeded receipts, there would be an outflow of gold and a decrease in bank reserves. Today, the dollar has largely replaced gold as international money, but the gain or loss of dollars has the same important effect today on bank reserves in many countries as the gain or loss of gold did previously.

Reliance on gold and commodity money before 1914

Before 1914, the United States had a monetary system guided primarily by the balance of payments. At that time, gold and gold certificates were held directly by commercial banks, and an outflow of gold caused a decline in their gold reserves. Importers in need of foreign exchange could purchase gold from commercial banks. For every dollar of gold reserves lost to another country, there tended to be a multiple contraction of bank loans and deposits throughout the banking system. On the other hand, if there was a surplus in the balance of payments, the opposite occurred. Gold flowed into the United States, increasing bank reserves and permitting the multiple expansion of bank loans and deposits.

For several decades after the Civil War, increases in the world production of gold did not keep up with increases in the production of other goods. This was one factor causing the worldwide decline in prices during this period because gold was then the principal determinant of bank reserves and of the expansion in the supply of money. From 1890 to 1914, the world gold stock doubled because of new discoveries and improved processes of extracting gold, which was probably a cause of the worldwide price rise that occurred at that time. Wholesale prices in the United States rose 49 percent from 1897 to 1914. The rise in prices in that period started later in the United States than in most countries, possibly because of monetary difficulties caused by agitation for unlimited coinage of silver. The political movement to coin more silver money probably had the opposite effect on prices than that intended by its supporters. It threatened inflation and discouraged foreigners from holding dollars. This meant smaller capital inflows, larger outflows of gold, and a deflationary monetary policy. The upturn in prices started in 1897, when the United States acquired gold because of sharply increased exports, owing in part to good harvests in the United States when there were crop difficulties elsewhere.

When the Federal Reserve was established in 1914, the founders visualized the continuation of a monetary system based on gold. Open-market operations were not expected to be an instrument of control, and legal reserve ratios of member banks could not be changed. The only types of discretionary control available were changes in the discount rate and variations in the volume of lending to member banks. The system was not purely automatic, but it was expected that changes in the amount of gold would be the predominant factor determining member bank reserves, and that an excess of imports over exports would be paid for primarily with gold. At that time, gold and the British pound were the two important types of international money. The dollar itself had not yet achieved the important position that it has today as an international currency.

In the first three decades of the 1900s, many countries throughout the world were anxious to revise their monetary arrangements and hired British or American consultants to help them. Professor Edwin Kemmerer of Princeton, a leading economist of his day, was one of the principal consultants hired. Relatively early he had gone as a "money doctor" to the Philippines (1903–1906) and soon to Poland, Germany, Turkey, China, and the Union of South Africa. Between 1917 and 1931, he advised the governments of Mexico, Guatemala, Colombia, Chile, Ecuador, Bolivia, and Peru. He was paid by the countries that hired him, but otherwise his missions were similar to some of our more recent foreign-aid programs. His blueprint for the monetary system of those countries was a system similar to the original conception of the Federal Reserve System, a central bank based on the gold standard. Many countries set up central banks in this period, and although many of them went off the gold standard in the 1930s, some of their monetary systems have been guided to a large extent by balance of payments considerations even since then.

Limits to the quantity of commodity money

Automatic systems based on the use of gold have the advantage that the quantity of such commodity money would be limited and the system need not be regulated extensively. With a *pure commodity standard,* the only type of money would be that commodity—usually gold or silver—or paper money representing that commodity. Although the government would have to designate the particular commodity used as money and see to it that there was no other type of money in the economy, the production of money could be left to private enterprises operating under competitive conditions. If gold were the commodity money, for example, any enterprise that desired to produce gold would be allowed to do so, and private firms would be expected to produce gold if it were profitable enough. The unit of account might also be gold, and the price of everything would be in ounces of gold. Or the prices could be in dollars or another unit of account defined as equal to a certain quantity of gold.

Although there would be no legal limit to the amount of gold mined in such a system, there would be an effective limit. This is because a rapid increase in the production of gold would cause a rise in the prices of all other goods and services in terms of gold. This would cause the production of other goods to become more profitable than mining gold and bring about a decline in gold production. Although accelerated inflation is impossible with a commodity standard, there may be gradual inflation. This occurred under the gold standard whenever, because of the discovery of new resources or improvements in technology, it became cheaper to produce gold.

People in some countries have historically had a strong preference for commodity money because of the limits to its quantity and the protection this provides against depreciation in its value. In Panama, when the United States government started construction of the canal in 1904, canal employers were surprised to discover that the native employees expected to be paid in silver coins and would not accept dollar bills even though they were legally convertible into gold.

A very desirable characteristic of commodity money is that it would work well in periods of business recession, provided that prices were flexible downward. Suppose prices fell because of a decline in business activity. The relative profitability of producing gold would increase. Employment would be stimulated among the producers of the commodity money, providing jobs for the unemployed. Also, a more rapid increase in the money supply would have a stimulating effect on the output of goods and services and bring the recession to an end. This stabilizing feature of a pure commodity standard has attracted the interest of several economists, and attempts have been made to conceive of pure commodity standards that would be an improvement over existing monetary systems.[1]

Cost of using commodity money

Despite some attractive characteristics, commodity money has disadvantages. It is costly in terms of the use of real resources. The cost of mining additional quantities of the monetary metal is higher than one would expect. To keep prices stable in the United States, the money supply would probably have to be increased about 4 percent a year to match the growth in real output and a possible decline in velocity. In 1979, a 4 percent increase in *M-1* would have amounted to more than $15 billion. It is an advantage to have a type of money that requires a much smaller amount of real resources to produce.

Automatic systems with fractional reserve banks

As modern banking developed, a monetary system based on a type of commodity money such as gold was usually combined with fractional reserve banking, i.e., commercial banks with reserves equal to only a fraction of their notes or deposits. Although in the eighteenth century money usually consisted solely of gold and silver coins, increasingly commodity money was replaced by paper money and deposits, and fractional reserve banks became a common type of business in all countries.

A pure commodity standard tends to break down and evolve into a mixture of commodity and paper or deposit money. Roughly, this is what occurred historically with the development of fractional reserve banking. If a commodity standard bank held an amount of the commodity (specie) equal to 100 percent of the value of the paper money (bank notes) it issued, its balance sheet would be of the following type:

Commodity Standard Bank

Assets		Liabilities	
Specie	$100,000	Notes	$100,000

The notes of the bank would be "warehouse receipts." The bank would store the commodity and issue paper money equal to 100 percent of the commodity. Although the notes issued by a bank of this type would legally be convertible into specie, in practice most people would not attempt to convert them because of the greater convenience of using paper money rather than specie. As a result, a bank would discover that it could get along by holding specie reserves equal to only a fraction of its outstanding notes, and it would use some of its specie to purchase securities or make loans. Because of the interest income received from the loans and investments, it would be able to issue paper money at a lower cost than banks that attempted to operate with 100 percent reserves. The balance sheet of such a bank might be as follows:

Fractional Reserve Bank

Assets		Liabilities	
Specie	$10,000	Notes	$100,000
Loans and investments	90,000		

It would be a fractional reserve bank because its specie reserves would be equal to only a fraction of its notes. In the United States, the state bank notes issued prior to the Civil War and the national bank notes that were issued later were money of this type.

The quantity of money with fractional reserve banks

In the early fractional reserve banking systems, there was an upper limit to the quantity of paper money, in the form of bank notes, that the banks could issue. Assume that the banks held $100,000 in specie and had issued $1,000,000 of notes, a reserve ratio of 10 percent. Assume also that the public held $250,000 in specie as well as the $1,000,000 of notes, a ratio of specie to paper money of 25 percent. The public would not put all of its specie in banks because it would still be more convenient to make some payments in specie rather than in paper money; specie would also be more acceptable for some uses than paper money. Under such conditions, as shown in the following formula, the maximum quantity of bank notes that banks could issue would be $1,000,000:

$$\text{Notes} = \frac{\text{Specie}}{(r + c)} = \frac{\$350,000}{(.10 + .25)} = \$1,000,000 \, ,$$

where r = the bank's reserve ratio, and c = the public's ratio of specie to paper money. The banks could not issue more than $1,000,000 in notes because if they did, their ratio of specie to notes would fall below 10 percent. The maximum amount of notes that the banks could issue would vary, depending on changes in the quantity of specie in the system, the bank's reserve ratio, and the public's ratio of specie to paper money. Note that this formula is similar to Equations 9.6 and 9.7 for increases in the money supply in today's banking system.

A fractional reserve bank must keep a certain percentage of its notes in specie reserves because notes are legally convertible into specie on demand. In the above example, if the public should wish to hold $300,000 rather than $250,000 in specie, the bank's holdings of specie would fall by $50,000. The reserve ratio that fractional reserve banks have to keep—assuming no government legal reserve requirements—depends on the variations in the public's demand for specie that the bankers believe necessary for them to be prepared for. A major problem in a fractional reserve banking system is that if banks misgauge the size of the variation in the public's ratio of specie to notes and run out of specie, they could be in difficulty. One reason for the historical instability of fractional reserve banking was that fractional reserve banks made contracts that they were not always able to keep because they did not hold enough specie. To make matters worse, banks were induced to issue more and more notes and to hold very little specie as reserves. The smaller their reserve ratio, the larger the profits; but the smaller the reserve ratio, the more vulnerable banks were to changes in the amount of specie the public wished to hold relative to notes. As was explained in Chapter 12, this inherent weakness eventually led to the establishment of central banking and deposit insurance.

During the nineteenth century, the principal legislative measure taken in the United States to strengthen fractional reserve banks in times of crisis was to legally require banks to hold reserves equal to a percentage of their notes and deposits. Although such laws were enacted in most states, they were based on a misunderstanding of the problem. In a fractional reserve banking system, banks hold reserves both to meet ordinary demands for cash and to provide for unusual demands for cash whenever they might arise. The legislated reserve requirements prohibited banks from using reserves for unusual demands for cash—a major purpose for which they were originally held.

As was explained in Chapter 12, a fractional reserve banking system requires a large amount of government regulation. In a system with fractional reserves, the quantity of money may vary sharply because of changes in the banks' reserve ratios or in the public's ratio of specie to notes. These ratios typically increase in serious depressions, which makes matters worse. One of the important features of a central bank is that it may manipulate total bank reserves so as to offset the undesired effect on the money supply of changes in the banks' reserve ratios or the public's ratio of specie to notes. In addition, government regulation, through periodic bank examinations, is necessary because of the opportunities for fraud in fractional reserve banking. The notes issued may not be backed by sound loans. This is difficult to regulate, because some bank loans are inherently risky. Bank examiners attempt to ascertain that the loans and investments that fractional reserve banks hold as assets are worth the amount stated on the bank's balance sheet.

A modern automatic system

Guatemala provides an example of a small country that still has a monetary system controlled primarily by its balance of payments, even though gold and other types of specie are not as important as they were in the nineteenth century. The bulk of this central American country's international reserves currently consists of dollar deposits owned by the central bank (the Bank of Guatemala) and held in United States banks. The amount of these dollar deposits varies with the country's balance of payments—and the gain or loss of dollars affects bank reserves just as the gain or loss of gold affected bank reserves under the gold standard.

In Guatemala, when a local exporter receives dollars in payment for goods he has sold, he sells the dollars through a commercial bank to the Bank of Guatemala for deposits denominated in *quetzals*, the money of his own country. A surplus in Guatemala's balance of payments results in an increase in the dollar reserves of the Bank of Guatemala. This surplus also increases the deposits of commercial banks—their reserves —at the central bank. When their reserves are increased, the commercial banks in Guatemala may expand their own loans and deposits. On the other hand, when there is a deficit in the balance of payments, importers' banks purchase dollars from the Bank of Guatemala and this causes a decrease in the reserves of both the Bank of Guatemala and the commercial banks when those dollars are spent for foreign goods.

Guatemala's monetary system has kept the international payments of the nation in balance. Guatemalan monetary authorities do not attempt to adjust their balance of payments through variations in exchange rates. The exchange rate between the *quetzal* and the dollar has been one for one since 1925. In recent years, there have been some official restrictions on the exchange by Guatemalans of *quetzals* for dollars, but such controls can usually be evaded to some extent.

Domestic conditions in countries with automatic systems

When a country has a deficit in its balance of payments, monetary tightness as an adjustment technique usually slows down economic activity. Because of this, it might seem unwise ever to allow a restraining policy. Actually, having a monetary system geared primarily to equating a country's balance of payments does not necessarily retard a country's economic development. Mexico, for example, had the highest average growth rate in Latin America from 1940 to 1970, 6 percent annually in real terms, despite the fact that the country allowed its bank reserves to fluctuate with changes in the balance of payments and had no changes in its exchange rate from 1954 to 1976.[2]

Suppose a country had a deficit in its balance of payments. The resulting monetary conditions would reduce imports and expand exports in the following ways:

1. A loss of bank reserves would cause monetary tightness; domestic prices would fall in comparison with the prices of international goods. This would provide an incentive for business enterprises to produce for export. The prices of international goods would not fall as a result of the tight domestic monetary policy, because their prices depend on international market conditions. Lower domestic prices would also make the country relatively attractive for foreign tourists and thus stimulate tourism as a type of export. Imports of all types would be discouraged, since they would now have to compete with cheaper local goods; and the lower costs resulting from the tight money policies would make it easier for domestically produced goods to compete in foreign countries.

2. Tight monetary conditions would tend to correct a deficit in the balance of payments by reducing the national income. Lower incomes would reduce the consumption of imported goods and travel in foreign countries.

3. The rise in interest rates resulting from tight money conditions would increase receipts and decrease payments in the capital markets. High domestic interest rates would discourage the purchase of foreign securities or investment in enterprises in other countries. The higher rates of return on investments in a country with a deficit in its balance of payments would induce foreigners to purchase its securities.

In an attempt to avoid the depressing effects when income and price movements are used to balance international payments, some countries have tried direct controls over foreign exchange; they attempt to reduce imports by placing restrictions on the purchase of foreign exchange. These measures usually are not reliable. Ultimately, most countries either have to use monetary controls to keep payments in balance or have flexible exchange rates.

Discretionary systems

Most major industrial countries now have discretionary monetary systems. The shift from automatic to discretionary monetary systems has significantly affected not only the domestic economies of these countries, but also their international financial arrangements.

Discretionary system in the United States

The shift in the United States from an automatic system with fractional reserve banking to a discretionary system was the result of special circumstances. During the period between World War I and World War II, surpluses in the balance of payments meant there was not the problem of running out of international reserves and made it possible to use monetary policy for goals other than avoiding a deficit in the balance of payments. During the same period, in order to stabilize prices, gold inflows were sterilized (that is, their expansionary impact on bank reserves was offset through open-market sales by the Federal Reserve banks). This was a step away from reliance on an automatic monetary system, because gold flows no longer determined our domestic monetary policies. At this time, many foreign countries also went off the gold standard, and their economies were no longer automatically regulated by gold flows. In the 1920s, the point of view of Governor Strong of the Federal Reserve Bank of New York was that although other countries should go back on the gold standard, the United States should not allow gold inflows to cause domestic inflation.

After World War II, the United States was still able to adhere to a discretionary monetary system. Even though the balance of payments of the United States shifted to a deficit, the large amount of gold that the Treasury had accumulated during the 1930s and 1940s was available to cover the deficit. Also, the use of U.S. dollars as international money was becoming more common. This made it possible to cover a large portion of the deficits by expanding the volume of dollars held by foreigners.

In the 1970s, the historical trend away from automatic to discretionary monetary systems continued with the adoption of systems of flexible exchange rates by most large countries. As will be explained in Chapter 24, it is widely believed by economists that with flexible exchange rates it is not necessary to use monetary policy to balance a country's international payments.

Since World War II, the Federal Reserve System's policy goals have been conceived of as both broad and flexible, allowing much discretion. The Federal Reserve authorities are legally independent of the executive departments of the government. Until recently, they were also relatively free of control by Congress, even though the chairman of the Board of Governors of the Federal Reserve System now regularly reports to Congress on the Federal Reserve's targets for monetary policy.

The principal group that determines the goals of Federal Reserve policy at any particular time and changes its goals as conditions change is the Federal Open Market Committee. A major goal of monetary policy during much of the post-World War II period has been to reduce unemployment. At other times, the principal goal has been to combat inflation. In recent years, there has been increasing concern about protecting the value of the dollar relative to other currencies of important industrial countries. Because the Federal Reserve System has several important goals, a major difficulty in administering a discretionary monetary policy is that the goals may conflict. At times the authorities may have to decide which they prefer, less inflation or less unemployment. An expansionary policy designed to reduce unemployment may also result in balance of payments problems.

The broad goals of monetary policy are also not easy to define.[3] Some of the issues connected with defining goals are:

1. Economists differ on what rate of unemployment should be the goal. Should it be 3 percent, 4 percent, or 5 percent? Some economists believe there should be no set goal for the rate of unemployment.

2. There are several price indexes—consumer prices, producer prices, and the GNP deflator. These do not always move in the same direction. If the producer price index is steady, but the GNP deflator is rising, should Federal Reserve policy become tighter? There has been considerable discussion among economists of upward biases in the consumer price index that are difficult to measure.

3. For the United States, a reasonable balance of payments is a particularly difficult objective to define because the dollar is used as a type of international money. A policy of balancing payments would eliminate any growth of international money in the form of U.S. dollars. If international payments should not be balanced, how large a deficit in the balance of payments is desirable?

4. The appropriate rate of economic growth is difficult to define. Growth should be sufficiently rapid to prevent a rise in unemployment; but beyond this how rapidly should per capita income rise? Should the goal be 1, 2, or 3 percent a year? Although rapid economic growth used to be considered a cure-all for many social and economic problems, in recent years public attitudes toward the desirability of rapid growth have changed.

In a discretionary system, once the goal of monetary policy has been decided upon, monetary policy may move toward either ease or tightness. Since World War II, the principal measures of ease and tightness used by the Federal Reserve have been the level of free reserves, the level of certain market interest rates, and the rate of growth of various monetary aggregates. For many years, even though the particular measure of ease or tightness used by the Federal Reserve System was known to the public, the Federal Reserve authorities did not announce whether its policy was supposed to be easy or tight. During this period, financial analysts were usually uncertain about what the direction or end goal of monetary policy was and spent considerable effort trying to determine its nature. Without an announced target, it was difficult to evaluate Federal Reserve actions. Also, unless it is clear what the Reserve System is trying to do, it cannot be ascertained whether the target is appropriate in terms of the Federal Reserve's broad goals. Although targets are now announced, until recently it was still not always possible to determine the direction of Federal Reserve policy because the Federal Reserve had two targets—the rate of increase in the monetary aggregates and the federal funds rate. If a rise in the federal funds rate occurred simultaneously with a more rapid expansion in the money supply, for example, whether monetary policy was viewed as easy or tight depended on what you were looking at. The change in Federal Reserve policy announced in October 1979—stressing control of monetary aggregates and deemphasizing control of the federal funds rate—should make it easier for the public to follow the direction of monetary policy.

Controlling the monetary aggregates

Effectively controlling the growth of the money supply so as to provide easier conditions at certain times and tighter conditions at other times depends primarily on how precisely the Federal Reserve authorities can control the monetary base. Even though the Federal Reserve authorities do not control most of the factors in the bank reserve equation, they can attempt to control the monetary base through open-market operations by offsetting changes in the other factors in the bank reserve equation that also affect the monetary base. Control of the monetary base could be made more exact if the Federal Reserve made certain changes in its operating procedures that would reduce variations in the volume of member bank borrowing from the Reserve banks and speed up the collection of checks to reduce variations in float.

As was explained in Chapter 9, a change in the monetary base will result in a predictable change in the money supply only if factors affecting the money multiplier remain constant or offset each other. Although the Federal Reserve authorities have considerable control over the ratio of reserves to demand deposits(r) and the reserve requirement for time deposits(r'), they have almost no control over the ratio of currency to demand deposits(c), the ratio of excess reserves to demand deposits(i), and quite limited control of the ratio of time deposits to demand deposits(t). Although the Federal Reserve sets the various reserve require-ments, shifts in deposits among banks with different reserve require-ments affect the average ratio of reserves in the banking system for both demand and time deposits. In addition, although the Federal Reserve could attempt to control the ratio of time to demand deposits by varying the maximum rates of interest payable on time deposits under Regula-tion Q, their control of this ratio was probably limited.[4]

To control the money stock by controlling the monetary base, the Reserve authorities would have to accurately predict the money multi-plier. If they cannot predict the money multiplier correctly, the in-crease in the money supply resulting from an increase in the monetary base will be different than anticipated. They might then attempt to offset the error, but to do so would require time, and there would be a lag in achieving the desired rate of expansion in the quantity of money. Table 20.1 shows that the M-1 multiplier has fallen from 2.95 to 2.48 from 1970 to 1979. The decline in the money multiplier has been the result of relatively large increases in both the currency-deposit ratio and the ratio of time to demand deposits.

Table 20.1
Monetary Multiplier for
M-1*, 1970–1979
(seasonally adjusted)

December	Adjusted Monetary Base (in billions)	M-1 (in billions)	M-1 Multiplier
1970	$ 74.5	$219.7	2.95
1971	79.9	233.9	2.93
1972	87.0	255.3	2.93
1973	93.9	270.5	2.88
1974	102.6	283.2	2.71
1975	110.5	295.4	2.67
1976	119.5	313.8	2.63
1977	130.0	338.7	2.61
1978	142.2	361.5	2.54
1979	154.0	382.1	2.48

*Definition used before 1980.
Source: Federal Reserve Bank of St. Louis.

A problem that might arise if the Federal Reserve attempted to implement monetary policy by controlling the monetary base is that a change in the monetary base could itself affect the money multiplier through its effect on the ratio of excess reserves to demand deposits and the ratio of time to demand deposits. An increase in the monetary base might lower interest rates—which in turn might increase the quantity of excess reserves that banks desire to hold. This would cause the money supply to rise by a smaller proportion than the monetary base. Lowering interest rates might reduce the ratio of time to demand deposits by making time deposits less attractive in relation to demand deposits. Because of the lower reserve ratio for time deposits, a decline in t would tend to reduce the volume of *M-1* plus time deposits in commercial banks, but increase *M-1*. The effect of changes in the monetary base on the multiplier could conceivably be large enough to make it impossible to control the money supply by manipulating the monetary base. Increases in the monetary base might be completely offset by decreases in the money multiplier. Despite these possibilities, there has usually been a close relationship between the monetary base and the money supply. Table 20.2 shows that the month-to-month changes in 1979 in the multiplier for *M-1B* have been small. In general, when the base increases at a rapid rate, *M-1B* also increases rapidly.[5]

Table 20.2
Money Multiplier for
M-1B, 1979
(seasonally adjusted)

Month	Adjusted Monetary Base (in billions)	*M-1B* (in billions)	*M-1B* Multiplier
Jan.	$143.2	$360.0	2.51
Feb.	143.8	360.7	2.51
Mar.	144.2	363.9	2.52
Apr.	145.2	369.7	2.55
May	145.9	369.5	2.53
June	147.2	374.3	2.54
July	148.5	378.0	2.55
Aug.	149.7	380.7	2.54
Sept.	151.1	383.2	2.54
Oct.	152.3	383.9	2.52
Nov.	152.7	385.3	2.52
Dec.	154.0	387.7	2.52

Source: Federal Reserve Bank of St. Louis, *Monetary Trends*, March 26, 1980, pp. 2, 7.

Monetary rules

A monetary system based on rules is a possible alternative to either an automatic system or a discretionary system. If monetary policy were based on a rule, the present discretion of the monetary authorities would be replaced by a relatively precise regulation that would govern any monetary actions taken. The rule that is most often suggested is to increase the money supply at a fixed rate.[6]

Fixed rate of increase per year in the money supply

If monetary policy were based on a rule, one rule that has been proposed is for the Federal Reserve authorities to increase *M-1* plus time deposits in commercial banks at a rate of 4 percent a year. During the 1960s and 1970s, the velocity of this measure of the money supply changed little; an annual rate of increase in *M-1* plus time deposits in commercial banks of 4 percent (equal to the rate of increase in real output) would be roughly consistent with long-run price stability. Because this measure of the money supply has been increasing at an annual rate of nearly 10 percent in recent years, there would be a need for a transition program to a noninflationary policy, but the eventual goal would be a fixed rate of expansion of 4 percent.

Professor Milton Friedman's proposal for a monetary policy based on a rule includes flexible exchange rates to provide an adjustment technique for balancing international payments and receipts. If monetary policy is based on a rule, it cannot be used to keep a country's international payments in balance. The way in which flexible exchange rates may be used to adjust imports to exports is explained in Chapter 24.

Other possible rules

Two other rules that have been proposed as guides to monetary policy are to stabilize a price index and to fix the quantity of money at a given level. The first of these was advocated by Irving Fisher, and in the 1920s and early 1930s several bills were introduced in Congress to enact such a rule.[7] The second rule, to fix the quantity of money at a given level, was advocated by Henry C. Simons in the 1930s, although he also advocated stabilizing the producer (wholesale) price index because it seemed more feasible.[8]

If a rule to stabilize a price index were adopted, when prices fell the monetary authorities would be required to expand the money supply sufficiently to bring the price index back to the prescribed level. If prices rose, the money supply would have to be reduced until prices returned to their original level. The principal argument against this rule is that the time lag between changes in the money supply and changes in prices is so long that it would be difficult to implement. Statistical studies indicate that the average time lag is as long as two years.

Professor Simons' rule to fix the quantity of money would be much simpler to administer than attempting to stabilize a price index. The authorities would have to use open-market operations with sufficient skill to offset both the effect on the monetary base of changes in the other items in the bank reserve equation, and the effect of changes in the currency-deposit and reserve-deposit ratios on the money supply. But this could probably be done reasonably well. The disadvantage of this rule is that it would result in gradual deflation. As output rose and the money supply was held constant, prices would gradually fall.

Eliminating "fine-tuning"

The enactment of a monetary policy based on a rule would mean a radical change in current Federal Reserve policy. The monetary authorities would no longer have to *fine-tune* monetary policy—forecast economic trends, choose among alternative goals, and then vary the ease or tightness of monetary policy. According to Professor Friedman, the reason for establishing a monetary rule is that it is "the best we can do in the light of our present knowledge." At the present time, to operate a discretionary system effectively, it is necessary for the monetary authorities to forecast future economic trends accurately. The actions taken by the Federal Reserve do not affect income immediately. Because forecasting is seldom perfect, the chances are high that a discretionary monetary policy will be misdirected. For instance, if the authorities predicted rapid inflation and took appropriate restraining actions, these actions would turn out to be inappropriate and make conditions worse rather than better if, instead of rapid inflation, the economy turned downward.

Also, studies show that the lag in the number of months between changes in the money supply and changes in income is variable. Six to nine months is the average lag, but experience in past business cycles shows a significant deviation from the average, and the causes of these deviations in lags are not well understood. If the estimated lag is incorrect, monetary policy may be destabilizing rather than stabilizing, even if the forecast is correct.

A third problem is that estimating the rate of increase in the money supply necessary to achieve a given increase in income is difficult. This would depend on the relationships between the demand for real money balances and nominal interest rates, between real interest rates and investment, and between investment and income. Without precise knowledge of each of those relationships, one would not know exactly how much the money supply ought to be increased.

Avoiding monetary instability caused by political pressures

A second argument in favor of a rule is that it would avoid monetary instability resulting from short-run political and economic considerations. An extreme example of such instability occurred during the Great Depression. If any of the major rules—increasing the quantity of money at a fixed rate, stabilizing prices, or fixing the quantity of money—had been in effect at the time, the unfortunate monetary policy of that period would not have occurred.

The errors in monetary policy made during the Great Depression were the result of a series of policies that changed as the short-run problems facing the monetary authorities changed. Sixteen months prior to the crash in 1929, monetary policy shifted from providing for a gradual expansion in the money supply to allowing for no increase in the money supply. The reason for the change was that the monetary authorities were attempting to combat speculation in the stock market —a matter of great public concern at that time. Unfortunately, the failure of the money supply to expand was almost certain to bring on a recession eventually. Income was still rising rapidly, and the ratio of the money balances held by the public to their incomes fell. This caused people to want to hold more money than was available and eventually led to a decline in spending.

From the October 1929 stock market crash until 1933, the quantity of money declined continuously. The standard explanation of this monetary contraction used to be that there were no willing borrowers despite the Federal Reserve authorities' expansionary policy. The recent studies made by Milton Friedman and Anna Schwartz have concluded that the Federal Reserve authorities could have prevented the decline in the money supply if they had wished to do so.[9]

During the first year of the depression, from October 1929 to October 1930, the monetary base and the money supply declined because there was less discounting by member banks at the Federal Reserve banks. The decline in borrowing occurred even though the monetary authorities had lowered the discount rate. Despite the drop in borrowing, the monetary authorities could have prevented the decline in the monetary base by making open-market purchases, but they did not do so.

In October 1930, a financial panic started and the reason for the declining money supply changed. Large numbers of banks failed. Runs on banks became common, and banks started to hoard reserves. From October 1930 through March 1933, both the public's ratio of currency to deposits and the banks' ratio of reserves to deposits rose sharply, reducing the quantity of money. The authorities might have increased the monetary base sufficiently to offset the effects of runs and hoarding, but they did not.

In September 1931, when Great Britain went off the gold standard, the Federal Reserve authorities shifted from what had been a relatively laissez-faire policy to one of restraint. The discount rate was raised from 2½ percent to 3½ percent. This surprising policy in view of the seriousness of the depression was in response to the panicky effect that Britain's going off the gold standard had on the public. Gold had started to flow out of the country. Foreigners were buying gold because they expected that the United States would also go off the gold standard and that the price of gold would rise. The Federal Reserve's tight policy led to an intensification of runs on banks, a rise in the public's ratio of currency to deposits, and a further decline in the money supply.

For several months starting in April 1932, the Federal Reserve purchased large amounts of U.S. government securities. This action appeared to have a desirable effect, but it was not continued, and at the beginning of 1933 another wave of bank failures and runs began. Another gold drain followed, and the Federal Reserve authorities again reacted by raising the discount rate. The financial panic became so bad that on March 6, President Roosevelt declared a bank holiday, and all banks in the United States were closed for a period of seven days. Following the holiday, the banks were gradually opened, monetary policy was reversed, and a long period of monetary expansion began.

Monetary policy during the Great Depression might have been different, even if not guided by a rule, if the authorities had taken a less passive attitude and had had a better understanding of the nature of bank panics and the importance of money. But it can still be argued that a rule would have been useful, because it would have kept the authorities from being misled by short-run problems such as stock market speculation or a gold drain. There were undoubtedly strong political pressures on the authorities to do something to meet those problems, and these pressures caused them to neglect their primary objectives.

Some critics have felt that in recent years as well as during the Great Depression a monetary rule would have been superior to the kind of discretionary policy that we have had. Particularly since the early 1960s, the Federal Reserve has been criticized for expanding the money supply too rapidly. It is believed that if there had been a rule setting an upper limit to the rate of increase in the money supply, the excessive expansion in the money supply that has occurred, and the subsequent acceleration in the rate of inflation, would have been prevented. In a simulation analysis of the period from 1962 to 1972, Professor Otto Eckstein concluded that much of the instability of the economy was caused by monetary and fiscal policies that were at times too restrictive and at other times too accommodating.[10] Using econometric models that were designed for forecasting and are composed of equations derived from historical experience, he substituted stable monetary and fiscal policies for the actual policy record. The result was substantially less inflation, smoother real growth, and smaller variations, but little change in the rate of unemployment for the entire period.

100 percent reserve banking

Closely related to the proposal that monetary policy be based on a rule is a basic reform known as *100 percent reserve banking.* This reform was originally proposed by Irving Fisher as a fundamental way of avoiding bank panics.[11] In recent years, proponents of this reform have argued that it would allow the monetary authorities to control the money supply more effectively than they can under present arrangements. As has been explained, under present conditions, the Federal Reserve System might have some difficulty assuring that the money supply increased at a constant rate of 4 percent a year. Such a reform would also make it unnecessary for the government to regulate the lending and investing activities of banks.

The way in which this proposal would work may be illustrated by comparing the balance sheet of a 100 percent reserve bank with that of a fractional reserve bank. In each of the examples, deposits are the same.

---

100 Percent Reserve Bank

Assets		Liabilities	
Reserves	$100,000	Deposits	$100,000
Loans and investments	100,000	Capital stock	100,000

Fractional Reserve Bank

Assets		Liabilities	
Reserves	$ 10,000	Deposits	$100,000
Loans and investments	100,000	Capital stock	10,000

In both types of banks, reserves would consist of cash in vault and balances at the Federal Reserve banks. In the 100 percent reserve bank, reserves are equal to 100 percent of deposits, persons would write checks on deposits as at present, and deposits could be cashed on demand. Under the plan as proposed by Professor Friedman, banks would be paid interest (roughly equal to the prevailing Treasury bill rate) on their reserve deposits at the Federal Reserve banks.[12] This expense could be met with the interest that the Reserve banks earn on their investments in U.S. government securities. Currently, the bulk of this income is returned to the Treasury.

Paying interest on these deposits appears to be a subsidy to the commercial banks, paid for ultimately by the taxpayers. Although commercial bank profits would increase in the short run, in the long run the subsidy would probably be passed on to the depositors. Because of increased bank profits, banks would compete for additional deposits by offering higher rates of interest on time deposits (assuming no federal ceilings) and lower service fees to owners of demand deposits.

If the Federal Reserve did not pay interest on the deposits of the member banks, the 100 percent reserve system would appear very unattractive to bankers. They would not be permitted to invest part of their depositors' funds in earning assets. To cover the cost of processing checks and keeping deposit records, they would have to charge much higher service fees than they do at present. This would have the unfortunate effect of discouraging the use of demand deposits as money. Persons and business firms would be induced to spend time and effort keeping their deposit balances at a minimum and investing instead in interest-earning short-term securities.

Every dollar lent by a 100 percent reserve bank would come from the sale of equity shares. Currently, banks obtain only a very small portion of their loanable funds through the sale of bank stock. Banks would have to obtain funds for lending in much the same way as mutual funds now do. It is expected that bank stock would become a very common type of investment. As with other types of stock, there would be a market for bank stocks, and if a person wished to sell his bank stock, he would have to sell it in the market for whatever price it would bring. Bank stock would not be redeemable at the bank for cash.

The advantage of 100 percent reserve banking, which was stressed by Irving Fisher, is stability. When Fisher advocated this idea, bank failures were a major problem. For a 100 percent reserve bank, runs are never a problem because its reserves are equal to its deposits and a decline in deposits would have no repercussions on its lending and investing activities. Also, with 100 percent reserve banking, bad loans would depress the price of the bank's stock; but since the stockholders cannot cash their stock at the bank, the reserves of the bank would be unaffected.

It might appear that one of the disadvantages of 100 percent reserve banking is that it would reduce the supply of bank credit and thus the volume of funds for real investment. Actually this need not be a problem. The money supply could be increased sufficiently to induce persons to purchase enough bank stock or other types of securities to provide a sufficient quantity of credit to keep the economy booming. The Federal Reserve banks would increase the money supply in the same way as they currently do, by open-market purchases.

The 100 percent reserve banks would temporarily have more than 100 percent reserves whenever they sold additional stock, a loan was paid off, or they sold securities from their portfolios. These transactions would cause their deposits to decline relative to their reserves. Such banks would not need to hold excess reserves to cover unfavorable clearing balances or to assure that they have sufficient liquidity. It is doubtful whether they would ever want to hold more than 100 percent reserves. However, if holding excess reserves did, for some reason, become a problem, the plan might include a fine on excess amounts held.

In a system of fractional reserve banking, whenever the public desires to hold a larger ratio of currency to demand deposits, whenever banks wish to hold larger excess reserves relative to demand deposits, or whenever time or demand deposits are shifted to banks with higher required reserve ratios, the money supply declines. If the public or the banks wish to hold smaller ratios of currency or reserves to deposits, the money supply tends to increase. To control the money supply with a system of fractional reserve banking, changes in these ratios have to be offset by appropriate changes in the total amount of the monetary base.

The principal advantage of 100 percent reserve banking is that the ability of the monetary authorities to control the rate of increase in the money stock precisely would be greater. At present, forecasting changes in the public's currency ratio, the ratio of excess reserves to demand deposits, and the ratios of required reserves to demand and time deposits for the overall banking system is not easy, and adjustments have to be made after the changes become known. As a result, some delay in achieving the intended increase in the money stock is probably unavoidable. With 100 percent reserve banking, the increase in the money stock would always be equal to the increase in high-powered money. Changes in the public's ratio of currency to deposits would not affect the total money supply.

Another advantage of 100 percent reserve banking is that it would no longer be necessary for the government to protect depositors by assuring that bank loans and investments were sound and free of any type of fraud. Because deposits would be invested solely in cash in vault and deposits at the Federal Reserve banks, a principal function of government bank examiners would be eliminated. This would make it possible to reduce the amount of regulation of banks by the government.

Summary

A principal advantage of an automatic monetary system, in which monetary policy varies with a country's balance of payments, is that it provides an adjustment mechanism for avoiding continuous balance-of-payments deficits or surpluses.

With a pure commodity standard, the only type of money in use would consist of a commodity such as gold, and there could be a minimum of government regulation of the monetary system.

The monetary system of the United States has become discretionary, because the United States has not had to use monetary policy to keep its international payments in balance.

Advocates of basing monetary policy on a rule, such as requiring the Federal Reserve authorities to increase the money supply at a fixed rate, believe that such a policy would result in greater stability of prices and less unemployment than a discretionary policy.

With 100 percent reserve banking, the Federal Reserve System would have greater control of the money supply, because variations in the public's currency-deposit ratio would not affect the supply of money, and the reserve-deposit ratios of banks would no longer vary.

Notes

1. Frank D. Graham, *Social Goals and Economic Institutions* (Princeton: Princeton University Press, 1942), pp. 94–119; and Milton Friedman, "Commodity-Reserve Currency," *Essays in Positive Economics* (Chicago: University of Chicago Press, 1953), pp. 204–250.

2. See Dwight S. Brothers and Leopoldo Solis, *Mexican Financial Development* (Austin: University of Texas Press, 1966), p. 128; and B. Griffiths, *Mexican Monetary Policy and Economic Development* (New York: Praeger, 1972), pp. 77–83.

3. Thomas Mayer, *Monetary Policy in the United States* (New York: Random House, 1968), pp. 3–22.

4. James Tobin, "Deposit Interest Ceilings as a Monetary Control," pp. 4–14; and Milton Friedman, "Controls of Interest Rates Paid by Banks," pp. 15–32, both in *Journal of Money, Credit and Banking* 2 (February 1970).

5. See Robert H. Rasche, "A Review of Empirical Studies of the Money Supply Mechanism," Federal Reserve Bank of St. Louis, *Review* (July 1972), pp. 11–19; and Albert E. Burger, "Money Stock Control," in Federal Reserve Bank of Boston, Conference Series No. 9, *Controlling Monetary Aggregates II: The Implementation* (September 1972), pp. 33–55.

6. Milton Friedman, *A Program for Monetary Stability* (New York: Fordham University Press, 1960), pp. 84–99; and "How Much Monetary Growth?" *Morgan Guaranty Survey*, February 1973; pp. 5–10.

7. For a discussion of this legislation, see Charles O. Hardy, *Credit Policies of the Federal Reserve System* (Washington, D.C.: The Brookings Institution, 1932), pp. 199–226.

8. Henry C. Simons, "Rules versus Authorities in Monetary Policy," *Journal of Political Economy* 44 (February 1936), pp. 1–30.

9. Milton Friedman and Anna J. Schwartz, *A Monetary History of the United States, 1867–1960* (Princeton: Princeton University Press, 1963), Chapter 7.

10. Otto Eckstein, "Instability in the Private and Public Sectors," *Swedish Journal of Economics*, March 1973, pp. 19–26.

11. Irving Fisher, *100 Percent Money* (New York: Adelphi Company, 1935).

12. Friedman, *A Program for Monetary Stability*, pp. 65–76.

Questions

20.1. Why do some countries have a relatively automatic monetary system based on the balance of payments?

20.2. Explain the way a restraining monetary policy would correct a deficit in the balance of payments.

20.3. What is the upper limit to the increase in the quantity of money in a pure commodity standard?

20.4. Why does a pure commodity standard tend to break down?

20.5. Why does fractional reserve banking require considerable governmental regulation?

20.6. Explain the nature of a discretionary monetary system and how it differs from an automatic system.

20.7. Why has the United States been able to have a discretionary monetary system?

20.8. Explain the difference between a monetary system based on a rule and a discretionary monetary system.

20.9. What are the arguments for and against a monetary system based on a rule?

20.10. Explain the reasons for the sharp decline in the money supply during the Great Depression.

20.11. Explain the differences between a 100 percent reserve bank and a fractional reserve bank.

20.12. What were the objectives of the early proposals for 100 percent reserve banking?

20.13. What are the objectives of current proposals for 100 percent reserve banking?

20.14. Know the meaning and significance of the following terms and concepts: automatic monetary system, discretionary monetary system, pure commodity standard, fractional reserve bank, 100 percent reserve bank, gold standard, monetary goals, fine-tuning, monetary rules.

21

Inflation has become a major economic problem in the United States and in many other countries. According to the monetary theory of inflation, inflation is caused by excessively expansionary fiscal and monetary policies. According to the cost-push theory of inflation, the causes of rising prices are excessive union wage demands, higher oil prices, a rise in the price of imports, or other factors that might raise costs.

INFLATION:
CAUSES AND EFFECTS

Attitudes toward the problem of inflation have changed. Inflation is now considered to be a more important problem than previously. When World War II ended, it was thought that deflation, rather than continued inflation, would be the major threat for the postwar period. (After the inflation occurring during World War I, there was a sharp drop in prices in the depression of 1920–1921; after the Civil War, there had been almost three decades of declining prices.) Instead of the expected deflation, in the 1950s prices gradually rose and the theory that some inflation was necessary to maintain a high level of employment was widely accepted. It was thought that the government should adopt vigorous economic policies to keep employment high even though such policies would occasionally cause inflation by overshooting. It was also believed that if inflation could be kept slow and irregular enough to cause people to think that they were better off than they actually were, it would help solve conflicts over the distribution of income and serve as a "social lubricant." In the 1960s, when the rate of inflation accelerated, interest shifted from the possible beneficial effects of slow inflation to methods of keeping inflation from getting out of hand and to ways of reducing the rate of inflation without causing a rise in the rate of unemployment.

This chapter surveys the different theories of inflation and analyzes the effects of inflation on different groups in our society.

Inflation in the United States and in other countries

In the United States, continuous inflation at rates above 1 to 2 percent a year started in 1965. From 1952 to 1965, the average annual rise in the consumer price index was only 1.3 percent. Table 21.1 shows that from 1965 to 1979, there has been a tendency for the rate of inflation to accelerate, even though the rate of inflation declined following the mini-recession of 1967 and the recessions of 1969–1970, and 1973–1975. Special circumstances may have contributed to the very high rates of inflation in 1973–1974: the termination of the wage-price controls enacted in August 1971; the decline in the value of the dollar relative to some other currencies following the shift from fixed to floating exchange rates in early 1973; and the success of the OPEC oil cartel in raising the price of oil in 1974. Higher oil prices also contributed to the high rates of inflation in 1978–1979.

The problem of inflation is worldwide. The annual rate of depreciation of money in 1978 for fifty countries is shown in Table 21.2. In most countries, prices rose 6 to 12 percent a year. In Argentina they rose more than 66 percent, and in Turkey, Israel, Uruguay, and Chile more than 30 percent.

Measures of price trends

There are three principal measures of changes in the general level of prices that are widely used in the United States: the consumer price

Table 21.1.
Consumer Price Index,
1965–1979

Year	Index (1967 = 100)	Percent Change, Dec. to Dec.
1965	94.5	1.9%
1966	97.2	3.4
1967	100.0	3.0
1968	104.2	4.7
1969	109.8	6.1
1970	116.3	5.5
1971	121.3	3.4
1972	125.3	3.4
1973	133.1	8.8
1974	147.7	12.2
1975	161.2	7.0
1976	170.5	4.8
1977	181.5	6.8
1978	195.4	9.0
1979	217.4	13.3

Source: *Economic Report of the President, January 1980*, pp. 259 and 263.

index, the producer price index, and the GNP deflator. The first two are published by the Bureau of Labor Statistics, and the third by the Department of Commerce.

The *consumer price index* (CPI) has been published regularly since 1921. To make the index, each month retail prices for each of the items included in a "market basket of goods and services" are gathered in a large number of cities from the kinds of establishments in which typical persons shop. The last major revision in the CPI was made in 1978. Before the 1978 revision, it covered prices of about 400 specific goods and services purchased by typical urban wage earners and clerical workers, including families and single persons—roughly half of the urban population.[1] In the 1978 revision, the items included were defined so as to cover broader categories, and the weighting of the items and the sampling method used were improved. Also a new and expanded consumer price index covering all urban consumers—80 percent of the population—was published. Both the old index as revised and the expanded index will be published at least through 1980 while they are under further study. The accuracy of the consumer price index has become increasingly important. Many union contracts now include escalator clauses providing for automatic wage increases as the CPI rises, and since 1975 Social Security benefits received by more than 30 million persons have been automatically increased each year to reflect changes in the CPI.

Table 21.2
Annual Rate of
Depreciation of Money
in 1978*

Industrialized countries		Less-developed countries	
Switzerland	1.3%	Panama	2.3%
West Germany	2.7	India	3.2
Luxembourg	3.0	Malaysia	4.2
Austria	3.5	Costa Rica	4.8
Netherlands	3.7	Singapore	5.0
Japan	3.9	China (Taiwan)	6.2
Belgium	4.6	Venezuela	6.4
United States	6.5	Paraguay	6.6
Ireland	6.7	Philippines	6.6
Portugal	7.5	Bolivia	7.4
Australia	7.6	Thailand	8.3
Norway	7.6	Indonesia	8.8
United Kingdom	7.9	Kenya	10.9
Canada	8.2	Ecuador	11.1
France	8.3	South Korea	11.6
Finland	8.5	Iran	13.3
South Africa	9.1	Mexico	15.2
Denmark	10.5	Jamaica	15.7
Sweden	10.6	Colombia	18.8
Italy	11.1	Brazil	27.5
Yugoslavia	11.2	Peru	29.0
Greece	11.7	Chile	31.4
New Zealand	11.8	Uruguay	32.2
Spain	16.2	Israel	33.7
Turkey	37.5	Argentina	66.5
Median rates	7.9	Median rates	10.9

*Based on average monthly data for 1978 compared with corresponding period of 1977.
Source: Citibank, *Monthly Economic Letter*, October 1978, p. 7

Prior to 1978, the *producer price index* (PPI) was known as the wholesale price index. This index is based primarily on prices paid by businesses, although it includes some prices paid by consumers. Nearly 2,800 commodities are included.[2] In the new PPI, the weighting of the items included is significantly different from that in the old wholesale price index. The change was made as a result of defects in the old wholesale price index that became apparent during the double-digit inflation in 1973–1974.[3] Wholesale prices rose 15.4 percent in 1973 and 20.9 percent in 1974, while the CPI increased only 8.8 percent and 12.2 percent in those years. Although higher wholesale prices normally show up eventually in higher consumer prices, this did not occur. One would expect some differences in the two indexes because the producer price index does not include services. In addition, important housing expenditures such as the purchase price of houses, financing charges, taxes, insurance, rent, and utilities are included in the consumer price index, but not in the producer price index. Even after making an allowance for these differences, it was discovered that the very rapid rise in the wholesale price index in 1973–1974 was exaggerating the rate of inflation by double or triple counting the prices of raw materials. The commodities in the old wholesale price index were weighted by the relative dollar value of the sales of each item. As a result, a rise in the price of petroleum, for example, would show up first in the value of crude petroleum, then in the price of refined petroleum products, and again in the price of plastics and other products requiring the use of petroleum. The new producer price index eliminates this double counting by including each commodity in only one stage of production. With this change, excessively large differences in the two indexes ought not to occur, and changes in the producer price index ought to provide a better indication of future changes in the consumer price index.

The *GNP deflator* is a measure of changes in the prices of all the goods and services that make up the GNP. One of the major differences between the GNP deflator and the indexes is that it includes the cost of government services. As its name indicates, the GNP deflator is a by-product of estimates of the GNP in terms of constant dollars made by the Department of Commerce. It is calculated by dividing the current dollar GNP by the estimate of the GNP in constant dollars.

A major difficulty with price indexes as compared to the GNP deflator is taking into account quality changes resulting from improvements in technology. The items included in an index are not supposed to change. If the quality of an item does in fact improve, the rise in its price may reflect that improvement rather than a "true" increase in price. A higher-priced new model automobile would be an example. What portion of the higher price should be attributed to the model changes? Because it is difficult for price indexes to take into account improvements in quality, the price indexes usually have a small upward bias that exaggerates inflation.

Another difficulty is that changes in the major components of the indexes may vary considerably. In the producer price index, food prices sometimes move in the opposite direction from industrial prices. When relative prices change, one would expect consumers to change their buying habits and substitute other things for those goods with the most inflated prices. If the kinds of goods and services purchased change, ideally the weights in the consumer price index and in the producer price index ought to be changed. As a practical matter, weights are seldom changed, because when weights are altered, changes in the index reflect both price movements and the changes in weights.

An advantage of the GNP deflator is that it is not a fixed-weight index. In 1978–1979, the consumer price index overstated the rate of inflation because of its fixed weights. The consumer price index accelerated from 9 percent in 1978 to 13.3 percent in 1979, compared to a change in the deflator for the personal consumption expenditure component of the GNP from 7.1 percent in 1978 to 9.9 percent in 1979. The principal reason for the difference in the two measures of inflation is that the consumer price index did not incorporate changes in the pattern of consumer expenditures resulting from the more rapid rise in the prices of products affected by the sharp rise in oil prices compared to the prices of other products. In these years, the consumer price index also overstated the rate of inflation because the sharp rise in the prices of houses and in mortgage interest rates are treated as costs for both prospective and current homeowners. To current homeowners, higher housing prices and mortgage interest rates do not represent an increase in the cost of living.

When governments set the prices of most goods and services—as in socialist countries or when there are general wage and price controls—price indexes measure the overall level of prices as established by the government rather than the level of prices that would be established if prices were determined by supply and demand in free markets. Under such conditions, increases in aggregate demand would have little effect on the price index, and inflation is said to be *suppressed*.

The monetary theory of inflation

Table 15.3 in Chapter 15 showed the close long-run relationship between money and prices in the United States from 1961 to 1979. There is a lag of between eighteen months and two years between a change in the rate of increase in the money supply and the rate of inflation. The monetary theory of inflation is an explanation of this long-run relationship. As was also explained in Chapter 15, business cycles are also significantly related to changes in the rate of expansion in the money supply. In addition to the long-run relationship between money and prices, prices tend to rise in periods of prosperity and fall in periods of recession, although the movements in prices do not always coincide with the business cycle. Recessions are accompanied by a reduction in the rate of inflation because firms often cannot raise prices when business activity is declining. Raising prices would make it even more difficult to get rid of heavy inventories, and banks may be urging repayment of loans. In recessions, some firms fail and sell out for what they can get. When business conditions are bad, there is an inducement for firms to cut costs and thus prices. During periods of prosperity, the opposite conditions make it easy for firms to raise prices.

Equilibrium between the demand for and supply of money

The theoretical analysis of the way changes in the money supply affect the price level in the long run is based on the supply and demand diagram shown in Figure 21.1.[4] This figure is similar to Figure 17.3 in Chapter 17 except that the price level, rather than national income, is on the vertical axis. The price level will be where the money supply schedule and the money demand schedule intersect. The supply schedule is vertical on the assumption that the money supply is controlled by the monetary authorities. The money demand schedule slopes upward showing that as prices rise, the quantity of money demanded increases. As was explained in previous discussions of the demand for money, the basic assumption behind the money demand schedule in Figure 21.1 is that what is important to people is the real value of their money balances, not the nominal value. If prices are higher, people must hold more money in order to have the same real convenience in purchasing goods and services, and the same real protection should there be contingencies.

Figure 21.1
A Rise in Prices Caused by an Increase in the Supply of Money

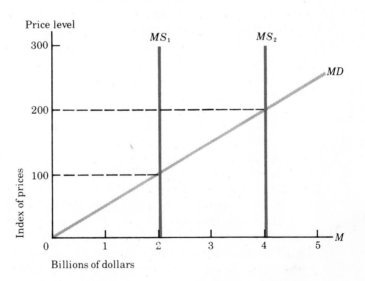

In Figure 21.1, if the price index is at 100, the demand for money would be $2 billion. The upward slope of the schedule shows that if prices double, the demand for money would also double from $2 billion to $4 billion. This is because if prices doubled, the total value of the transactions made with money would double, and people would have to hold twice as much money in order to purchase the larger volume of transactions. At all points on a given demand schedule for money in the figure, the average length of time each dollar is held is constant. For example, if the total value of transactions were $102 billion a year and the turnover of each dollar was 52 times a year (in this example, each dollar is held on the average for a week between its receipt and its use for expenditures), the demand for money would be $2 billion. If transactions rose to $208 billion because prices doubled and people still held each dollar for the same length of time, the demand for money would be $4 billion.

If the length of time each dollar is held increases, the money demand schedule would shift downward to the right; and if dollars move more rapidly from person to person, the money demand schedule would shift upward to the left. Also, increases in real output affect total transactions and cause the money demand schedule to shift downward to the right; decreases in real output would cause the schedule to shift upward to the left.

In Figure 21.1, an increase in the money supply from M^S_1 to M^S_2 causes prices to rise from a price level of 100 to a level of 200; at 100, the quantity of money supplied would exceed the demand. This causes prices to start rising because if people have more money than they want, they will spend it, causing an increase in aggregate demand. Although an individual who has more money than he wants may decrease the amount of money he holds, this will not cause any reduction in the total amount of money held by all individuals together. Rising prices increase the demand for money until the demand for money is equal to the supply of money at a price level of 200.

In Figure 21.1, it was assumed that the schedule for the demand for money does not shift downward when the money supply schedule shifts to the right. Actually, an increase in the supply of money would tend to lower nominal interest rates because some of the additional supply of money would be used to purchase bonds. This would raise the prices of bonds and lower their yields. If the fall in nominal interest rates had a very large effect on the schedule for the demand for money (by causing people to hold money for a shorter period of time between the receipt of money and its expenditure), there need not be much of a rise in prices as a result of an increase in the money supply. The monetary theory of inflation assumes that the schedule for the demand for money is not very sensitive to changes in nominal interest rates.

Inflation may be caused by a decrease in the demand for money, rather than by an increase in the supply. A decreased demand for money would raise the M^D schedule in Figure 21.1, causing the supply of money to exceed the demand at a price level of 100. A factor that could cause the M^D schedule to shift upward is higher nominal interest rates. If market interest rates rise, persons are induced to invest in securities rather than hold as much money. Also, if people anticipate a more rapid rate of inflation, the demand for money will decrease and inflation will be more rapid than it would otherwise have been.

The inflationary gap

The way in which an increase in the money supply may cause inflation is also illustrated in Figure 21.2. Assume that there is full employment—no further increase in real output is possible—at the level of income (Y_F) where aggregate demand (AD^1) is equal to aggregate supply. As was explained in Chapter 18, if an expansion in the money supply causes real money balances to increase, and if the increase in real money balances reduces real interest rates, investment would probably increase the aggregate demand schedule. In Figure 21.2, a rise in the aggregate demand schedule from AD_1 to AD_2 would create an *inflationary gap*, x. At Y_F, people would now desire to spend more than the maximum real output of the economy at existing prices. Prices would rise because of the increase in the demand for goods and services relative to the supply. Persons who found themselves unable to get the goods and services they wanted would offer to pay higher prices, and one would expect sellers to agree to higher prices.

Figure 21.2
The Inflationary Gap
Caused by an Increase
in the Money Supply,
Lower Interest Rates,
and an Increase in
Aggregate Demand

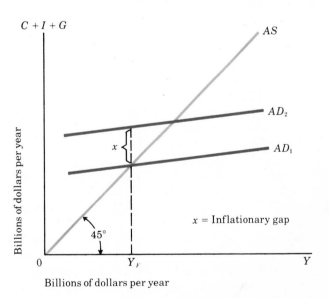

An inflationary gap may be created by anything that raises the AD schedule after full employment has been reached, not just by an increase in the money supply. An inflationary gap may be the result of optimistic expectations, new technological developments, lower taxes on business profits, or government fiscal policy.

Fiscal policy as a cause of monetary expansion

Although an expansion in the money supply is an essential component of the monetary theory of inflation, there are various possible reasons for an expansion in the money supply. The rise in the rate of inflation in the United States that began in the mid-1960s appears to be related to the federal government's fiscal policy.[5] During this period, the federal government's budget deficits and the publicly held national debt got larger and larger, as was shown in Figure 19.2. The more rapid growth of the national debt probably caused the more rapid growth of the money supply. This is because the growth in the national debt would tend to raise market rates of interest—a larger volume of bonds can be sold only at higher interest rates. The Federal Reserve's traditional policy of controlling market interest rates would tend to cause them to automatically make larger open-market purchases of government securities whenever the Treasury debt management policies were tending to raise interest rates. This would increase bank reserves and the money supply.

The cost-push theory of inflation

The cost-push theory explains inflation in terms of factors other than an increase in the money supply. Instead of the traditional *demand-pull* forces affecting aggregate demand, the cause of inflation according to this theory is primarily higher costs—union demands for higher wages, price increases by large producers, or higher oil prices. This view of inflation became popular during the 1960s. In 1973–1974, some economists stressed higher commodity prices as a cause of inflation and referred to the inflation as a *commodity inflation.*

According to the *cost-push* theory, unless wages in the nonunion sector fall when union wages are raised, a rise in union wages would result in an overall rise in wages. Employers would pass through the increase in wages to prices, and inflation would result. If higher union wages and the higher prices of the products produced by unionized firms were offset by lower wages and prices in the nonunionized sector of the economy, large union wage demands would not cause inflation. The higher union wages would merely lead to a change in relative prices and a reallocation of resources. The lower wages in the nonunion sector would provide an incentive for those employers to hire more labor and increase output. The higher wages in the union sector would dispose such employers to cut down on their hiring and to produce less.

Cost-push inflation involves a rise in the rate of unemployment as well as higher prices. Because of the rise in the cost of labor, the number of persons employed would be reduced. Also, at the higher prices, the amount of real output that could be sold at a given level of aggregate demand would be reduced—and fewer people would be needed to produce the smaller output.

There is considerable agreement among economists that union wage movements, higher oil prices, and other factors affecting costs have short-run effects on inflation. Economists differ on how long such effects will last, particularly if there is no increase in the rate of expansion in the money supply. Cost-push factors, however, may themselves cause an increase in the rate of expansion in the money supply if the unemployment caused by cost-push inflation affects the monetary and fiscal policies of the government. One would expect monetary and fiscal policy to become more expansionary if unemployment rises as a result of cost-push inflation. Wage pressures may be considered the basic cause of this type of inflation, even though a more rapid expansion in the money supply is essential to the process. The inflationary forces initiated by unions are said to be validated by monetary policy.

If the monetary authorities did not attempt to prevent the unemployment resulting from cost-push inflation, the more rapid inflation might soon end. The rate of inflation would slow down if the unemployment caused wages to rise less rapidly. Economists differ on the strength of cost-push inflation in the absence of monetary support, primarily because of different conceptions of the labor market. If wages were flexible enough so that they tended to move to an equilibrium position where the quantity of labor demanded was equal to the quantity supplied, the unemployment caused by union wage increases would fairly soon lower the rate of growth of nonunion wages. On the other hand, if wages are inflexible (the rate of increase in wages is not determined by market conditions), the impact of cost-push forces on the rate of inflation would be very different and would last longer.

Structuralist theory

The structuralist theory of inflation has been used to explain inflation in South America, primarily in Argentina, Brazil, and Chile.[6] The rate of inflation in these countries has typically been higher than in most other countries, and all three of these countries have had rapid inflation for many years. The structuralist theory is similar to the cost-push theory of inflation.

The structuralists believe that inflation is a necessary accompaniment of growth. Although they agree that inflation could be curbed by monetary or fiscal policy, these policies are rejected because an excessive amount of unemployment might result. Initially, according to this theory, rising incomes and population growth tend to raise the prices of food or of imports. The supply of both of these groups of products is believed to be inelastic. The supply of imports does not increase as a result of higher prices paid for them because it is said that the volume of imports depends on the volume of exports and the volume of exports does not expand when the prices of imports rise. Also, it is claimed that the output of food does not increase when prices rise, because of feudal land-tenure systems or various government controls removing incentives to increase output.

The structuralist theory assumes that the rise in the prices of imports and of agricultural commodities causes prices in general to rise, because prices in other sectors of the economy are not flexible downward. This inflexibility is partly the result of the fact that wage and price movements in those countries tend to become adjusted to the rate of inflation that people expect, and these expectations are slow to change. Any governmental attempts to force prices down in other sectors of the economy would cause unemployment. Because prices tend to be inflexible in the short run, when aggregate demand is cut back, real output falls. Moreover, to prevent a rise in unemployment, the money supply must be expanded rapidly enough to accommodate the overall rise in prices caused by economic growth. The structuralist theory of inflation does not claim that inflation is possible without rapid increases in the money stock. The basic cause of inflation is said to be economic growth combined with supply inelasticites and downward inflexibility of prices. Growth in the money stock is essential, but still supplementary and permissive.

To some extent, the money supply in these South American countries automatically expands when prices rise. Firms need larger loans from banks as prices rise. The total volume of bank loans and that of deposits rise together, assuming that bank reserves are not rigidly controlled. Also, as prices rise, more money may be needed to finance larger government deficits. This will happen if government wages and expenditures rise more rapidly than tax revenues. Such conditions tend to occur when government wages are tied to cost-of-living indexes by wage contracts with escalator clauses and when import and export duties are a major source of revenue. Tax receipts from import and export duties may not be very sensitive to changes in prices.

Wealth transfer effects of inflation

When prices in general rise, some persons are hurt and others benefited. The retired person with a fixed private pension is often cited as an example of one who is hurt by inflation.[7] The person with a fixed monthly payment on his mortgage is usually believed to benefit from inflation.

Identifying the effects of inflation is not as easy as it might seem at first, despite these familiar examples. In order to know who is harmed and who helped, it is necessary to distinguish between anticipated and unanticipated inflation. When people foresee inflation, the effects are different than when it is unexpected. When prices rose 4 percent, for example, did people *expect* that prices would rise this fast and in advance adjust their actions and decisions accordingly? Or did prices rise 4 percent even though people expected that prices would be stable? Sometimes prices rise 4 percent when people are anticipating a 2 percent increase. Probably the anticipated rate of inflation is only rarely exactly the same as the actual rate of inflation.

It is a common error to assume that in countries that have had inflation, people do not expect any inflation. The steadiness of an inflation determines how fully inflation is anticipated. An inflation need not be perfectly steady, but if the rate of inflation remains approximately the same for a long period of time, the public will come to expect prices to rise at that rate, and they will adjust their economic activities to take inflation into account. The effects of intermittent inflation are probably different. Inflations of this type are seldom correctly anticipated because people are usually slow to recognize the change that has occurred and are not certain the inflation will continue.

Unanticipated inflation— effects on the distribution of wealth

In an unanticipated inflation, wealth is transferred from net monetary creditors to net monetary debtors. Unanticipated inflation occurs because it is usually impossible for people to anticipate changes in the rate of inflation. The following example illustrates the effect of unanticipated inflation on a net monetary debtor. In order to analyze how inflation affects such a person, it is necessary to calculate his net holdings of wealth before and after inflation. This may be done by combining his assets, liabilities, and residual wealth in the form of a balance sheet. A person's wealth (the difference between his total assets and his total monetary debts) is the balancing item. The person in this example is a net monetary debtor because his total monetary debts are larger than his total monetary assets.

Net Monetary Debtor

	Assets			Liabilities and Wealth	
	Original	After 100% Inflation		Original	After 100% Inflation
Monetary assets	$ 5,000	$ 5,000	Monetary debts	$20,000	$20,000
Real assets	30,000	60,000	Net wealth	$15,000	$45,000
Total	$35,000	$65,000	Total	$35,000	$65,000

Monetary assets consist of currency, demand deposits, time deposits, U.S. savings bonds, corporation, municipal, and U.S. government bonds, and private pensions. All of these are claims to a fixed amount of money now or in the future, and the amounts claimed would be unaffected by inflation. Real assets include houses, automobiles, the equity in a business, real estate, and corporation stock. These are not claims to a fixed amount of money. If prices in general rise, the value of these assets usually rises. Social Security wealth is similar to real assets in that future payments are not fixed, but are indexed to reflect changes in prices. Monetary debts consist of the amounts a person has borrowed. These may consist of a mortgage, automobile loan, or a personal debt, all contracts to pay a fixed amount of money.

In this example, it is assumed that prices have doubled and that during this period there has been no change in the assets owned by the net monetary debtor or in his liabilities. The value of the net monetary debtor's real assets would probably double, rising from $30,000 to $60,000. The amounts of his monetary assets and monetary liabilities would not be affected. His net wealth triples, rising to $45,000. He has benefited because the rise in his net wealth is greater than the rise in prices. The reason is that his monetary debts are larger than his monetary assets. He had *borrowed* to buy real assets. Note that owning real assets helps a person to keep up with inflation, but only those who borrow to buy real assets can expect their net wealth to rise more rapidly than prices.

The way inflation affects monetary creditors—those whose monetary assets are larger than their monetary debts—is the opposite:

Net Monetary Creditor

		Assets			Liabilities and Wealth
	Original	After 100% Inflation		Original	After 100% Inflation
Monetary assets	$13,000	$13,000	Monetary debts	—	—
Real assets	2,000	4,000	Net wealth	$15,000	$17,000
Total	$15,000	$17,000	Total	$15,000	$17,000

In the above example of the balance sheet of a net monetary creditor, the creditor has no debts, but $13,000 in monetary assets. His original net wealth is $15,000, the same as that of the net monetary debtor in the previous example. If prices doubled, his real assets would probably rise from $2,000 to $4,000, and his wealth would rise to $17,000. The rise in his net wealth would not have kept up with the rise in prices.

There are many familiar examples of net monetary debtors, e.g., persons who bought their homes by taking out mortgages. Examples of net monetary creditors are also familiar—persons who saved cautiously, never borrowed, and preferred to rent rather than buy a home. Young persons who have recently purchased a house with the aid of a mortgage are typically net monetary debtors, while older persons who have paid off their mortgages are typically net monetary creditors.[8] When it is unanticipated, inflation transfers wealth from people who are net monetary creditors to those who are net monetary debtors.

Before the 1960s and 1970s, it was usually assumed that one way to protect oneself against inflation was to own corporation stock because the price of the stock would tend to rise as fast as prices. Actually, corporations, like persons, may be either net monetary creditors or net monetary debtors, and a rise in the price of a particular stock may be more or less than prices in general. Of course, many factors affect stock prices, but only if a corporation is a net monetary debtor can the stockholder expect to benefit in real terms from unanticipated inflation. The monetary assets of corporations consist of bank deposits, short-term marketable securities, and accounts receivable. Their real assets consist of plant, equipment, and inventory. Monetary debts of business firms include their debt to banks, bonds outstanding, commercial paper outstanding, accounts payable, and income taxes payable. If a corporation has financed enough real assets by borrowing, it would be a net monetary debtor, and during inflation the value of its equity would increase more rapidly than prices. But those corporations that have financed their activities primarily by the sale of stock or with retained earnings are typically net monetary creditors. They would not benefit from inflation.

In an interesting economic study, the performance from 1914 to 1952 of the stock of corporations that were net monetary debtors was compared with that of net monetary creditors.[9] The results were that in periods of inflation, on the average, the price of the stocks of the net debtor corporations rose more than the price of the stocks of the net creditors. In periods of deflation, the net creditors did better than the net debtors. The corporations included in this study were those listed on the major exchanges. About half of them were net monetary creditors, and half were net monetary debtors.

In the 1960s and 1970s, stocks of corporations that were net monetary debtors as well as of corporations that were net monetary creditors would not have been an effective hedge against inflation. The reason is not easy to explain because normally profits rise with inflation and stock prices rise with profits. The reason may be that the recent rapid growth in governmental regulation of corporations—environmental, safety, pensions, personnel practices, and others—have been a jolt to the future prospects of most large corporations.

Effects of anticipated inflation

An important consequence of anticipated inflation is that interest yields on securities tend to discount the expected rate of inflation. If, for example, prices rise 7 percent a year, nominal yields must be 10 percent in order to give people a real return of 3 percent. As a result, if people expect to earn a real return of 3 percent and also expect 7 percent inflation, the demand for securities with nominal yields lower than 10 percent would decline, and their prices would fall until their yields rose to 10 percent. Also, if borrowers anticipate a rate of inflation of 7 percent, they would expect to be able to afford to pay 10 percent. They could realize a rate of return of 7 percent by holding goods the prices of which were rising at that rate, and in addition they might expect to earn a real rate of return of 3 percent.

There are some striking examples of the effect of inflation on nominal interest rates. In China in 1947, when inflation was 600 percent a year, interest rates on bank deposits were 2 percent a day compounded daily. In South Korea, when inflation ranged from 100 percent a year during the Korean War to 40 percent immediately following the war, nominal interest rates of 5 to 10 percent a month were typical.

Historically, when prices have risen, market interest rates have risen, and when prices have fallen, market interest rates have fallen. This relationship was noted by economists in the early nineteenth century and was called the *Gibson paradox* because it contradicted the classical theory in which an increase in the money supply would cause prices to rise and interest rates to fall. At least a partial explanation of the Gibson paradox is that it is necessary to take into consideration the difference between nominal and real interest rates.

In the 1970s, although nominal interest rates in the United States were high, they did not always fully discount the inflation, possibly because people in the United States have not been accustomed to inflation and have not yet adjusted to living with it. Negative real interest rates are a new phenomenon that economists have not yet adequately explained.

If nominal rates of interest were to rise enough so that they fully discounted the rate of inflation, the wealth transfer effects of inflation would be sharply reduced. The interest received on monetary assets would be large enough so that the value of such assets plus the interest received would keep up with inflation. Also, the high nominal rates of interest that borrowers would have to pay on monetary liabilities would remove any gain that such borrowers might have made because of inflation. There would, however, still be some transfer of wealth because persons are not always able to obtain nominal interest rates which fully discount the rate of inflation, and there may be lags. The law has not permitted banks to pay interest on most checking accounts. Also, interest rates on time deposits have been regulated by the federal government and have not been permitted to rise sufficiently to protect the owner from being harmed by inflation.

Effects of inflation on the distribution of income

If, when prices rose 7 percent, all of the different types of income—wages and salaries, dividends, interest, rental income, profits from unincorporated enterprises, and pensions—were to rise by the same percentage, there would be no redistribution of income. But some types of income, such as interest and rent, tend to be inflexible. Since profits are a residual type of income, dependent upon whatever is left after meeting all other expenses, owners of enterprises would benefit from inflation if some of their costs did not rise. Persons whose income is governed by a contract for a specific period of time are generally hurt by inflation, because their income remains unchanged when prices rise. Rent covered by a lease, interest on government bonds, and wages under a union contract are examples. An analysis of the effects of inflation on the distribution of personal income and on the distribution of wealth overlaps, because wealth is the source of income.

The effects of inflation on the distribution of income may be different from those commonly expected. As we have seen, it is not true that owners of business firms as a group benefit from inflation because their income consists of profits. Instead, it may depend on whether the firms are creditors or debtors. Also, although the idea that wages lag behind prices is often taken for granted, some historical research has questioned this point of view.[10]

The effect of inflation on government finance

In the United States, inflation automatically, and without any necessary action by Congress, increases sharply the tax revenue received by the federal government, i.e., the amount of tax revenue collected increases more rapidly than the rate of inflation, giving the federal government greater command over real resources.[11] Inflation does this by pushing individuals and corporations into higher tax brackets although they may be no better off in real terms. The rate schedules for individual and corporation income taxes are progressive. If prices rose 20 percent, for example, the taxable income of a person originally receiving $1,000, where the marginal tax rate is 14 percent, would tend to rise to $1,200, where the marginal tax rate is 15 percent. In addition, the fixed amount of the $750 personal exemption shrinks in real value when prices rise. A rise in prices may also cause the net income of some corporations to rise from $25,000, at which point the marginal tax is 17 percent, into a higher bracket. Rates of the corporation income tax are graduated, with a top marginal tax rate of 46 percent on earnings over $100,000.

Inflation also results in higher tax receipts for the federal government because it increases the revenue collected through the capital gains tax. The base of this tax is the difference between the purchase price and the sale price of a capital asset such as a house, real estate, or corporation stock. When no adjustment is allowed for inflation, persons are taxed on increases in the value of their property because of inflation as well as on real gains. The once-in-a-lifetime exclusion from federal income taxes enacted in 1978 for persons age 55 and over on capital gains up to $100,000 on one's residence is an adjustment made partly because of inflation.

Inflation has sharply increased federal revenues from the corporation income tax not only because of the progression in the tax rate, but also for other reasons. The base of the corporation income tax is the profits of corporations. Inflation results in an increase in corporate profits and therefore corporate income taxes because depreciation allowances, inventory gains, and capital gains are based on purchase prices and are not adjusted for inflation. As a result, inventory gains and capital gains are inflated and depreciation allowances are smaller than they would have to be in order to cover the real cost of replacing capital equipment.

The effect of inflation on tax revenues could be avoided if Congress would enact a policy of indexation for personal and corporate income taxes. If these taxes were indexed, the personal exemption, the brackets in the tax tables for both the personal and corporate income tax, and the base for calculating capital gains, the cost of inventories, and depreciation on fixed capital assets would be increased in step with increases in the consumer price index. If, for example, prices rose 10 percent during the year, all of these would be increased by 10 percent. Indexation would slow down "tax-bracket creep" and the growth of federal government expenditures.

The effect of inflation on the national debt

A rise in the rate of inflation has important effects on the financing of the national debt. As has been explained, a rise in the rate of inflation tends to cause nominal interest rates to rise; but the higher interest rates apply only to that debt issued after interest rates rise. As a result, when the rate of inflation rises, the average interest rate that the federal government is paying on the national debt becomes less than it would be if interest rates on all of the national debt fully discounted the rise in the rate of inflation. In 1979, for example, much of the national debt had been issued in earlier years when interest rates were lower than they were in 1979. People had not foreseen that the rate of inflation was going to become more rapid, and the low interest rates in earlier years did not allow for the higher rate of inflation in 1979. Because of the failure of people to anticipate the higher rate of inflation, the federal government's interest expenditures in 1979 were less than they would otherwise have been.

Some undesirable effects of inflation

A problem resulting from the rising rate of inflation in the United States since the mid-1960s is that it has become difficult for many persons to find ways to save that yield a real rate of return. Yet, people must save for such things as their old age, possible illness, periods of unemployment, the education of their children, and other needs. Real after-tax rates of interest on savings deposits and on most types of bonds have typically been near or below zero. Although nominal interest rates might have risen sufficiently to provide persons with a real rate of return, in many years they have not, and government policy has kept nominal interest rates on many important types of savings below the rate of inflation.

Another objectionable aspect of inflation is that unanticipated fluctuations in the rate of inflation may hinder the effective operation of credit markets because the risk of borrowing and lending is increased. Although interest rates tend to adjust to the rate of inflation, every time there is a change in the rate of inflation, there is confusion and loss for some persons. When the rate of inflation rises unexpectedly, debtors gain; when the rate of inflation falls unexpectedly, creditors gain. Under these circumstances, business success depends primarily on the ability to forecast changes in prices and to adjust rapidly to them. This involves a waste of resources because persons must use considerable time (and often other resources) monitoring the inflation in order to avoid incurring losses or to take advantage of changes in the rate of inflation.

Even a steady, anticipated inflation should be avoided if possible. Cost accounting becomes complicated, and it becomes difficult to keep meaningful records. If prices are rising rapidly, nominal prices do not give an accurate picture of the costs of items purchased at different times. Under extreme circumstances, bookkeeping becomes very complicated, requiring substantial readjustments in order to make the accounts meaningful.

During periods of inflation, the usefulness of money declines because it becomes more costly to hold in real terms. As people begin to anticipate the rise in prices, they will attempt to hold other real or financial assets instead of money. Real assets are expensive to store and handle, however, and do not serve well as liquid resources because their prices usually do not rise in exactly the same proportion as prices in general. Holding financial assets, even when interest rates discount inflation, is risky because the market seldom discounts the rate of inflation exactly.

Only if inflation is avoided does money maintain its real value and provide the kind of liquidity that people want. There are no fully adequate substitutes.

Despite the long-run problems created by inflation, in the short run the political appeal of a policy of inflation may be very great because of the benefits to debtors and governments. On the subject of the prevalence of inflation, the famous British economist Keynes wrote as follows: "... this progressive deterioration in the value of money through history is not an accident, and has behind it two great driving forces—the impecuniosity of Governments and the superior political influence of the debtor class."[12]

Summary

A price index is not a perfect measure of the rate of inflation because of quality changes and different variations in the prices of the items included in the index.

An increase in the money supply may cause inflation by increasing the supply of money relative to the demand. Rising prices increase the quantity of money demanded until it is equal to the supply.

In the cost-push theory of inflation, excessive union wage demands may cause inflation by inducing employers to raise prices. In addition, the unemployment caused by the rise in union wages may induce the federal government to make fiscal and monetary policy more expansionary.

Inflation tends to transfer wealth from creditors to debtors, although the transfer diminishes sharply when inflation is anticipated. Inflation is also an important source of gain for governments. Tax receipts rise more rapidly than the rate of inflation, and the interest costs on outstanding debt remain unchanged when market interest rates rise as a result of inflation.

Notes

1. U.S. Department of Labor, Bureau of Labor Statistics, *The Consumer Price Index: Concepts and Content over the Years* (May 1978, Revised), Report 517.

2. U.S. Department of Labor, Bureau of Labor Statisics, *Producer Prices and Price Indexes, Supplement, 1979, Data for 1978,* pp. 1 and 108.

3. William Nordhaus and John Shoven, "Inflation 1973: The Year of Infamy," *Challenge,* May-June 1974, pp. 14–22.

4. J. Huston McCulloch, *Money and Inflation, A Monetarist Approach* (New York: Academic Press, 1975), pp. 65–81.

5. Darryl R. Francis, "How and Why Fiscal Actions Matter to a Monetarist," Federal Reserve Bank of St. Louis, *Review,* May 1974, pp. 2–7.

6. Roberto de Oliveira Campos, "Two Views on Inflation in Latin America"; David Felix, "An Alternative View of the 'Monetarist'— 'Structuralist' Controversy"; and Joseph Grunwald, "The 'Structuralist' School on Price Stability and Development: The Chilean Case," in Albert O. Hirschman, ed., *Latin American Issues* (New York: Twentieth Century Fund, 1961), pp. 69–123.

7. However, since 1972, Social Security benefits have been automatically indexed to reflect recent changes in prices. For an analysis of the effects of inflation, see Armen A. Alchian and William R. Allen, *University Economics,* 3d ed. (Belmont, Calif.: Wadsworth Publishing Company, 1972), pp. 673–681.

8. Nancy A. Jianakoplus, "Are You Protected From Inflation?" Federal Reserve Bank of St. Louis, *Review,* January 1977, pp. 2–8.

9. Armen A. Alchian and Reuben A. Kessel, "Redistribution of Wealth through Inflation," *Science* 130 (September 4, 1959), pp. 535–539.

10. Reuben A. Kessel and Armen A. Alchian, "The Meaning and Validity of the Inflation-Induced Lag of Wages Behind Prices," *American Economic Review* 50 (March 1960), pp. 43–66.

11. Milton Friedman, "Using Escalators to Help Fight Inflation," *Fortune* 90 (July 1974), pp. 94–97 and 174–176; reprinted in Herbert Giersch, et al. *Essays on Inflation and Indexation* (Washington, D.C.: American Enterprise Institute, 1974), pp. 25–61.

12. John M. Keynes, *Monetary Reform* (New York: Harcourt, Brace and Company, 1924), p. 12.

Questions

21.1. Compare the consumer price index, producer price index, and GNP deflator.

21.2. What are some of the problems in constructing indexes to measure changes in the price level?

21.3. Using a graph, explain the meaning of an *inflationary gap.*

21.4. Using a graph of the supply and demand for money, explain how an increase in the money supply may cause inflation. Under what conditions would an increase in the money supply not cause inflation?

21.5. How do aggressive union wage demands cause inflation? Could unions cause inflation if at the same time the Federal Reserve System had a tight money policy?

21.6. Explain the structuralist theory of inflation.

21.7. If people expect 5 percent inflation a year, how will this affect nominal interest rates?

21.8. Define and give some examples of monetary assets, real assets, and monetary liabilities.

21.9. What is the relationship between a person's net wealth and his monetary assets, real assets, and monetary liabilities?

21.10. Using figures, give an example of the balance sheet of both a net monetary debtor and a net monetary creditor.

21.11. Explain why an unanticipated inflation of 100 percent would harm net monetary creditors. Why would an unanticipated inflation of the same amount benefit net monetary debtors?

21.12. Why is the effect of inflation on the distribution of wealth much less when inflation is anticipated?

21.13. Explain how inflation causes tax revenues to increase faster than the increase in prices.

21.14. What harm is done by inflation?

21.15. How does inflation affect the interest expenditures of the federal government?

21.16. Know the meaning and significance of the following terms and concepts: price index, GNP deflator, negative interest rate, inflationary gap, cost-push inflation, demand-pull inflation, wealth transfer effects of inflation, net monetary debtor, net monetary creditor, wealth, anticipated inflation, Gibson paradox, escalator clauses, indexation.

22

The government has two principal programs for combatting inflation: reducing aggregate demand by adopting tighter fiscal and monetary policies and setting controls over wages and prices. The initial effect of attempts to cut back on inflation by reducing aggregate demand is to cause a recession.

ANTI-INFLATION POLICIES AND UNEMPLOYMENT

This chapter starts with a theoretical explanation of the way changes in aggregate demand and aggregate supply affect both real output and prices. Although a tight monetary policy lowers prices in the long run, its initial effect is to reduce real output. Conversely, although an expansionary monetary policy eventually raises prices, it initially increases real output. This chapter also covers proposals to lessen the effects of anti-inflation monetary policies on real output, the use of wage and price controls to combat inflation, and the problem of reducing unemployment.

Theoretical background

The graph in Figure 22.1 is used to analyze whether a change in monetary and fiscal policy affects real output or prices. Chapters 17 and 18 included explanations of how changes in monetary and fiscal policy may affect the national income, but did not attempt to break down the effect into the impact on real output and prices, the two components of nominal national income.

Figure 22.1
The Equilibrium Level
of Prices and Real
Output

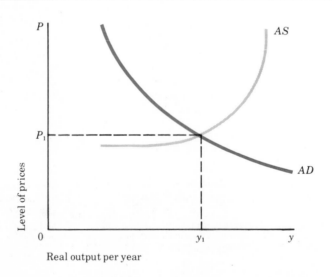

The aggregate demand schedule in Figure 22.1 assumes a given level of national income and shows that, given the level of national income, real output varies inversely with prices—the higher prices are, the smaller the quantity of real goods and services that people would be able to purchase and business firms would be able to sell. The aggregate demand schedule is a rectangular hyperbole. The national income is equal to prices times real output, the two axes of the graph. A rectangle drawn under the schedule would be equal to the national income, and all rectangles from different points on the same demand curve would be equal in area. If the national income increases, the aggregate demand schedule in Figure 22.1 would shift to the right; and if national income decreases, it would shift to the left. The factors affecting the level of the national income were discussed in Chapters 17 and 18.

The aggregate supply schedule in Figure 22.1 shows the amount of goods and services that firms would be willing to sell at various prices. It assumes that the level of money wage rates and that the technological and resource conditions affecting the productivity of labor are given. If money wage rates rise, the schedule would shift upward. Firms would be willing to sell the same real output only at higher prices because of the increase in their costs per unit of output. On the other hand, increases in the productivity of labor because of greater amounts of capital used with labor and improvements in education and technology cause the aggregate supply schedule to fall. Firms would be willing to sell the same real output at lower prices because of the decrease in their costs per unit of output.

At low levels of real output, the aggregate supply schedule is horizontal. If there is idle capacity in plants, costs per unit of output do not rise as more labor is hired and output is expanded. Eventually, however, the aggregate supply schedule slopes upward, indicating that as real output increases, costs per unit of output and prices rise. This is because the use of some resources can no longer be expanded, and it becomes necessary to use additional variable resources with a given quantity of the fixed resources. According to the law of diminishing returns, the productivity of the variable resources declines when such resources have smaller amounts of other resources to work with, and costs per unit of output would rise. As real output expands, the supply schedule in Figure 22.1 eventually becomes vertical. This is because there is a limit to the increase in real output when resources are fully employed.

In Figure 22.1, the point of equilibrium which determines the level of prices and the level of real output is where the aggregate supply and demand schedules intersect. To be in equilibrium, prices must be at a level where people are able to purchase the entire real output of the economy. If prices were higher than P_1, aggregate demand would be less than aggregate supply. People would not have large enough incomes to purchase the output of the economy, and prices would fall to P_1 as producers lowered their prices so as to sell their entire real output. If prices were below P_1, aggregate demand would be greater than aggregate supply. People would be able to purchase the entire output of the economy and still have some income left to spend. With excess income, they would bid up prices until the value of the goods purchased was just equal to the income they had to spend.

Tight monetary policy

Figure 22.2(a) shows the effects of a tight monetary policy on real output and the level of prices in the short run, and Figure 22.2(b) shows these effects in the long run. In the short run, it is assumed that the reduction in the rate of expansion in the money supply reduces the national income and shifts the aggregate demand schedule to the left. The principal short-run effect of the decrease in the aggregate demand schedule is to reduce real output from y_1 to y_2. Prices fall only very slightly from P_1 to P_2. If prices don't fall when aggregate demand declines, real output must be smaller because there will be fewer real goods and services sold. The decline in real output will cause the rate of unemployment to increase. The aggregate supply schedule does not fall in the short run because producers do not immediately lower prices when there is a decline in aggregate demand, and employees do not immediately offer to work for lower wages. To producers, a decrease in total spending because of the tight money policy means smaller sales. The immediate response of firms to smaller sales is usually either to allow inventories to rise above their customary levels or to decrease real output. Producers hesitate to lower prices because they are not certain that the decrease in sales is permanent, and they are not sure that other

Figure 22.2
The Effect of
Anti-Inflation Monetary
Policies on Real Output
and Prices

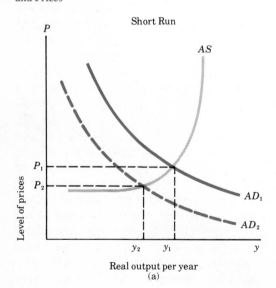

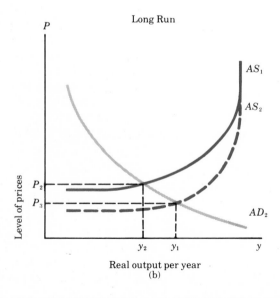

producers have also had decreased sales. In addition, because their costs have not fallen, producers are reluctant to lower prices.

To employees, a decrease in total spending means a weaker job market and possible unemployment. Instead of offering to work for lower wages, at first workers work fewer hours per week and spend more time looking for jobs. They probably view the unemployment as temporary, and they do not realize that there has been a general decline in the market.

Prices may fall slightly when the aggregate demand schedule shifts to the left if it is assumed that at y_1 plants are operating at a relatively high level of production; then, when real output is decreased, fewer variable resources need to be employed with a relatively fixed quantity of other nonexpansible resources. This would cause the average productivity of the variable resources to increase, resulting in lower costs per unit of output and prompting firms to lower their prices.

In the long run, the aggregate supply schedule will probably fall as a result of the decrease in the aggregate demand schedule. This is shown in Figure 22.2(b). The decrease in the aggregate supply schedule lowers prices from P_2 to P_3, and increases real output from y_2 back to y_1. The rate of inflation eventually drops because of the unemployment and recession caused by the decrease in aggregate demand. Producers find that they must lower prices in order to keep inventories at desired levels and production at normal rates of output. Workers do not want to work fewer hours per week permanently, and they eventually take the customary amount of time looking for jobs. The increase in unemployment causes the supply of labor to be greater than the demand, resulting in a drop in the rate of increase in wages. Because of lower labor costs, firms cut prices, shifting the supply schedule downward. When prices fall, firms are able to sell more, and real output increases. The long-run effect of a decrease in aggregate demand is a lower rate of inflation, and the effect on real output is temporary.

This theoretical explanation of the effects of anti-inflation monetary policy on real output and prices is consistent with recent experience in the United States. A principal way in which the federal government has attempted to combat inflation is by using fiscal and monetary policy to reduce aggregate demand. In 1959–1960, when the Federal Reserve System attempted to halt inflation through restrictive monetary and fiscal policies, a recession followed and the rate of unemployment rose from 5.5 percent in 1959 to 6.7 percent in 1961. In 1969–1970, when measures were taken to combat inflation, there was another recession, and the rate of unemployment rose from 3.5 percent in 1969 to 6.0 percent in December 1970. From 1972 to 1974, when the rate of increase in M-1 was reduced from more than 9 percent a year to 4.6 percent, a relatively severe recession started in late 1973, and the rate of unemployment rose from less than 5 percent in 1973 to more than 8 percent in 1975.

Each of these anti-inflation efforts eventually slowed up the rise in prices. After the restrictive policies of 1959–1960, the early 1960s were years of relative price stability. Also, after a restrictive policy in 1969–1970, the rate of inflation dropped from more than 6 percent in 1969 to approximately 3.5 percent a year in 1971–1972. There was a similar reduction in the rate of inflation from more than 12 percent a year in 1974 to 4.8 percent in 1976, following the anti-inflation policy of 1973–1974.

Although many economists believe that it is not possible to reduce inflation by monetary or fiscal policy without provoking a recession, Congress has not yet faced this issue.[1] In 1978, Congress passed the Humphrey-Hawkins Act (Full Employment and Balanced Growth Act of 1978) which calls for reducing the rate of inflation to not more than 3 percent by 1983 and to do so in such a way that it does not impede reducing the rate of unemployment among adults to 3 percent and among teenagers to 4 percent. In the first year following the Humphrey-Hawkins Act, the consumer price index rose from 9 percent to 13.3 percent and the unemployment rate fell from 6 percent to 5.8 percent.

When there is a recession, the Federal Reserve authorities follow an easy rather than a tight monetary policy. Their objective would be to shift the aggregate demand schedule in Figure 22.2 to the right. The effects of an easy monetary policy on real output and prices are the opposite of a tight money policy. Initially the results are very good. Real output increases and prices rise very slightly. There is no change in the aggregate supply schedule because, in the short run, prices and wages are inflexible. However, in the long run, the effect of an easier monetary policy is to raise prices rather than to increase real output. After a period of time, the aggregate supply schedule will rise. Eventually producers realize that they can raise prices and still keep inventories at desired levels and production at normal rates of output. Also, employees will not want to work overtime permanently; and they will take the customary, longer amount of time looking for jobs. The relatively low rate of unemployment causes the demand for labor to be greater than the supply, and results in higher wages and thus higher prices.

Reducing the side effects of a tight monetary policy

Even though it may not be possible to reduce inflation by monetary and fiscal policy without causing a recession, it might be possible to reduce the extent of the recession. One proposal is to encourage the use of escalator clauses in union wage agreements and in private financial and business contracts. Another is to reduce the rate of expansion of the money supply very gradually over a period of several years. Also, it has been proposed that it would be useful if government officials publicized in advance the anti-inflation program. Finally, it is believed by some that the side effects would be less harmful if tight monetary policies were combined with controls over wages and prices in such a way that these programs reinforced each other.

Indexation

The principal purpose of indexation is to increase the downward flexibility of prices when a tight money policy reduces the rate of expansion in total spending. Escalator clauses in union contracts are already very common. Under these contracts, if the rate of inflation slows down, the amount of the automatic increases in wages is also reduced. Financial and business contracts may also be indexed to changes in prices. Business rental contracts may be varied with the gross receipts of the tenant. The interest and principal of business loans may be varied with the rate of inflation. With wages and other costs indexed, a firm would be more able to reduce prices when sales declined in a recession. This would mean greater flexibility of prices, a shorter time for a tight monetary policy to cut down inflation, and less unemployment associated with the tight conditions.

Using a more gradual policy

Advocates of the proposal to gradually reduce the rate of expansion of the money supply believe that it would result in a smaller slowdown in economic activity. It is hoped that this would make it possible for the Federal Reserve to stick to its anti-inflation program rather than to reverse itself as it has in the past when there has been a sharp rise in the rate of unemployment. The Federal Reserve's policy of alternating between a tight policy to combat inflation and then an easy policy to combat unemployment has lowered the rate of inflation only temporarily. During the 14 years following 1965, the rate of inflation reached new peaks after each recession. Because the Federal Reserve was not able to stick to its anti-inflation policies, the economy went through the recessions in order to lower the rate of inflation without achieving the long-run goal of less inflation.

A second argument for a gradual policy is that a sharp reduction in the rate of inflation would cause bankruptcies and financial difficulties for many business firms. Current business contracts for wages and interest rates are based on the assumption that the rate of inflation will continue at 6 percent to 10 percent. If the future rate of inflation were much lower than the rate currently expected, many firms would have difficulty paying the interest and the wages that they have contracted to pay, and many would probably fail. Business instability of this type would also make it difficult for the Federal Reserve to stick to an anti-inflation policy.

Announcing monetary policy in advance

The objective of widely publicizing a tight monetary policy is to increase the downward flexibility of wages and prices and make expectations more accurate. One reason firms are reluctant to lower their prices when their sales decline is that they don't know the reason for the decline. Sales may have declined because of a drop in the demand for the firm's product relative to other products, rather than because of a decline in total spending. If a businessman knew that the reduction in his sales was part of a general trend caused by a shift in monetary policy, he would probably lower his prices more quickly.

Announcing a tight monetary policy in advance might also affect long-term wage and financial contracts so that possible financial difficulties would be less serious. If firms believe that the rate of inflation is going to slow down, market interest rates will be lower and wage increases scheduled for future years will be smaller. The success of such a policy would depend on whether the Federal Reserve achieved its objective. If rates of inflation did not decline despite the announcement of a tighter monetary policy, publicizing monetary policy in advance would increase, rather than decrease, the riskiness of long-term contracts.

Combining tight monetary policy with wage and price controls

The purpose of combining wage and price controls with tight monetary policy would be to increase the downward flexibility of prices and thus reduce the slowdown in the economy. If at the same time that a tight monetary policy shifted the aggregate demand schedule in Figure 22.2 to the left, wage and price controls lowered the aggregate supply schedule, real output would not decline, and prices would be lowered. In order to be successful, such a program would require careful coordination.

Past efforts to combat inflation with wage and price controls have been different from this proposal. Wage and price controls have usually been combined with expansionary fiscal and monetary policies. During World War II, it was not possible to pursue restrictive fiscal and monetary policies. In the postwar period, although the Federal Reserve System might have pursued a tight monetary policy at the same time that the government tried to control wages and prices, it did not. Because pursuing an anti-inflation policy is an unpleasant job, the Federal Reserve authorities may tend to avoid such a policy if they think some other department of the government is doing it.

Wage and price controls

An alternative to monetary policy as a method of controlling inflation is government wage and price controls. The purpose of wage and price controls is to lower the aggregate supply schedule. In Figure 22.3, an effective governmental program to lower wages and prices would shift the aggregate supply schedule downward from AS_1 to AS_2. Because of the lower wages, firms would be willing to produce at lower prices because their costs would be reduced. Given no change in the aggregate demand schedule, a drop in the aggregate supply schedule would both lower prices from P_1 to P_2 and increase real output from y_1 to y_2. At the lower level of prices, consumers would be able to purchase a larger real output. Although this explanation of the way wage and price controls work appears simple, in fact wage and price controls are very difficult to administer, they impede the functioning of the market system for controlling the allocation of resources, and they are sooner or later discarded.

Figure 22.3
The Effect of Wage and
Price Controls on Real
Output and Prices

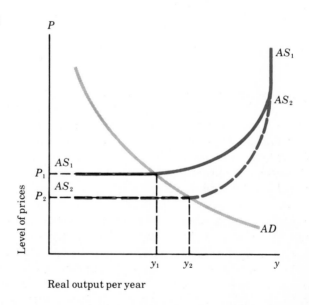

Wage and price controls in World War II

The United States government enacted an extensive program of wage and price controls during World War II and has revived such programs periodically in the years since then. The World War II policies are an example of combining wage and price controls with very expansionary fiscal and monetary policies. During the war, government expenditures had to be greatly expanded, it was not possible to tax heavily enough to avoid very large budget deficits, and a large portion of the deficits was financed by the creation of money. *M-1* increased from $40 billion in 1940 to $99 billion in 1945.

The control of wages during World War II was administered by the National War Labor Board. The Board froze most wages and salaries at the levels of September 1942. In addition, President Roosevelt set up the Defense Mediation Board to keep industry functioning smoothly, and he appointed the War Manpower Commission to mobilize the nation's manpower for the war effort. Management and labor agreed that there would be no strikes and that all disputes would be settled by the National War Labor Board. Congress also passed the Smith-Connally Act authorizing the government to take over private plants in which there were strikes and to maintain the same working conditions as prevailed under private operation.

The problem of keeping retail prices under control was put in the hands of the Office of Price Administration. Ceiling prices on retail commodities were set at levels that prevailed on a certain date, generally in late 1942. To avoid shortages, the Office of Price Administration also instituted a system of rationing. A ration book containing stamps was issued to each individual, and the proper number of stamps had to be given to a merchant whenever any of the rationed commodities, such as sugar and meat, were purchased.

One of the problems resulting from the wartime rationing and price controls was a decline in the quality of certain types of goods. Labor costs rose in spite of the wage freeze because of the upgrading of labor and the use of overtime. Some business enterprises were able to continue to operate profitably without price increases only by reducing quality. Another problem was the development of black markets, where rationed goods were sold at prices above the legal ceilings and without ration stamps. Black markets sprang up for meat, gasoline, radios, and a number of other commodities. In addition, the red tape associated with the controls was annoying and the programs were so unpopular that they were terminated very quickly following the war.

The price and wage controls established during World War II were quite effective. From 1941 to 1945, consumer prices rose only 20 percent, although some economists believe that this estimate of the rise in the cost of living is too low. From 1945 to 1948, after price and wage controls were lifted, consumer prices rose 33 percent, even though fiscal and monetary policies were no longer inflationary. A principal effect of the wartime controls was to delay the rise in prices. Average hourly earnings in manufacturing rose almost 40 percent from 1941 to 1945, and then another 30 percent from 1945 to 1948.

Wage and price guidelines in the 1960s

A mild program of guidelines for prices and wages was established by the federal government in 1962.[2] Appeals were made to labor unions to be moderate in their wage demands and to business enterprises not to raise prices. Critics referred to the guidelines as a "policy of exhortation." The guidelines for wages attempted to limit annual hikes to the rise in labor productivity. It was thought that wage increases that did not exceed gains in productivity would not be inflationary. Although exceeding the guidelines for wages was not illegal, the federal government used its influence to persuade unions and business enterprises not to do so.

Experience with the guidelines indicated that the federal government had quite effective powers over the pricing policies of some large corporations. In 1962, when the steel companies raised prices, President Kennedy was able to force them to retract. Many large corporations are sensitive to adverse publicity and dislike being accused of social irresponsibility. Through its own contracts with business enterprises and by varying the rigorousness of the enforcement of the government regulations over business activities, the federal government could have exerted much more power than it did. Government contracts are so important to most large corporations that the fear of losing them for failure to comply with the wishes of the federal government would keep them in line. It is doubtful, however, whether controlling the prices charged by some of the large corporations is an effective way to control prices in general. If certain prices are kept down, people are left with more to spend on other products whose prices cannot so easily be controlled. These uncontrolled prices will tend to rise more than they otherwise would have, and the rise may offset the effect of the lower prices in the controlled sector.

Despite the guidelines, the rate of inflation became more rapid in 1965 and 1966. As a result, unions would not limit their annual wage increases to productivity gains, and the guideline targets had to be discarded in 1966. Unless governmental efforts to control the prices of goods and services are successful, ceilings on wages will not be observed by labor unions. Unions expect wages to rise enough both to keep up with inflation and to reflect productivity gains. One reason the 1962–1966 wage guidelines had to be given up is that they were accompanied by expansionary fiscal and monetary policies. Prior to 1961, M-1 increased at an average annual rate of 1.8 percent. From 1961 to 1966, the average annual increase in M-1 rose to 3.4 percent. Starting in 1961, there was also a significant increase in the size of the annual budget deficits of the federal government. The resulting increases in aggregate demand kept the economy booming and caused prices to rise despite the controls.

Wage and price controls in the 1970s

In August 1971, at a time of international monetary crisis, President Nixon initiated another program to directly control wages and prices. Phase I of the program consisted of a ninety-day freeze of wages and prices.[3] The freeze was supposed to curtail inflation and help solve the balance of payments problem. The freeze was followed by Phase II, which consisted of a mixture of voluntary and mandatory regulations. Stores were required to post their retail prices, guidelines were set for wages, and firms were permitted to increase prices without approval only if they could show that profit rates were not above those for two of the three previous fiscal years. During 1972, the rate of inflation declined. Because it appeared that the wage and price controls had been quite effective, at the beginning of 1973, controls were relaxed somewhat. The new regulations were known as Phase III and were considered to be a step back toward the long-run goal of a free market. Phase III removed rent controls, and smaller firms no longer had to keep the records which were being used by the federal government to audit their price and wage decisions.

The initial success of the program was short-lived. In 1973, the rate of inflation rose to new peaks. In June 1973, the President announced the beginning of a second price freeze lasting sixty days. In July, the freeze was replaced by Phase IV, which stipulated that firms could raise their prices only if their costs rose. Larger firms were required to notify the federal government of planned price increases. Smaller firms were required to submit quarterly or annual reports, depending on their size. Only very small firms were exempt from reporting. The policy toward wages was to continue the guidelines that had already been established: a 5.5 percent increase in wages per year plus 0.7 percent for fringe benefits. It was hoped that the tightening of price controls in Phase IV would keep wage demands moderate and reduce the danger of an upward wage-price spiral. Even though Congress had originally urged the President to use wage and price controls to combat inflation, in 1974 Congress permitted the controls to expire.

During the period of wage and price controls in the early 1970s, monetary policy was very expansionary. From the first quarter of 1972 to the second quarter of 1973, *M-1* had increased at an average annual rate of 8 percent, the most rapid rate of increase in *M-1* that had occurred since World War II. The rapid increase in the money supply was probably one of the reasons the 1971–1974 wage and price controls had only a temporary impact on the rate of inflation. As shown in Figure 22.2(b), the long-run effect of changes in monetary policy is to shift the aggregate supply schedule; if monetary policy was made more expansionary, the aggregate supply schedule would tend to shift upward, offsetting the downward effect of wage and price controls on the aggregate supply schedule.

In 1978, a new program of wage-price guidelines was announced. It was called a program of voluntary standards for pay and prices. A Pay Advisory Committee and a Price Advisory Committee were appointed by the President to review and make recommendations on pay and price standards. Initially, the standard for annual wage increases was set at 7 percent or below, and the standard for price increases was set at 6 to 6½ percent. These limits were soon exceeded in one way or another and had to be revised. Just how effective this program has been is uncertain. Failure to hold to the limits was attributed to the rise in oil prices.

Inefficiencies caused by wage and price controls

Except during wartime periods, programs of wage and price controls appear to result in serious diseconomies. This is because wage and price controls not only fix the maximum prices that can legally be charged, but also fix *relative prices and wages*—the ratio of the price of A to the price of B.

In an economy in which consumer demands are changing and techniques of production are continuously improved and vary from one good to another, changes in relative prices and wages guide the reallocation of resources from uses that are declining in importance to those that are increasing in importance, and from goods that are expensive to produce to those that are cheaper to produce. For example, if people want or need more wood-burning stoves, their price rises relative to the prices of other goods, and they become relatively profitable to produce. Or, if the economy needed more chemical engineers, the salaries of chemical engineers would rise compared with the salaries of other types of engineers. This would encourage more engineering students to choose chemical engineering as their special field of study, and the supply of chemical engineers would soon be adjusted to the larger demand. Without such changes in relative wages and prices, the economic system would not adjust promptly to changes in consumer demand. With controls, the process that the market system uses to guide the allocation of scarce resources so that they are used to produce those goods and services that people want most breaks down.

When relative prices are frozen and the market system is not permitted to work, the allocation of resources must be taken over by government administrators. During a major war, government administrators would be expected to guide the allocation of resources to support the military effort. However, in normal times, the policy in the United States has been to let consumers through the market system guide production, rather than to have the allocation of resources determined by government officials.

A dramatic example of the diseconomies caused by wage and price controls occurred in West Germany in 1948.[4] In the six months following the abolition of their system of rationing and price controls, industrial production rose by about 46 percent. Following World War II, there were similar experiences in Italy and Japan. The economies of these countries were not able to operate efficiently under peacetime conditions until their wartime wage and price controls were discarded.[5]

The problem of unemployment

High rates of unemployment are a major problem in our economy. Since World War II, the annual rate of unemployment has varied from less than 3 percent in 1953 to almost 9 percent in 1975, as shown in Figure 22.4. The rate of unemployment varies inversely with the business cycle, falling in periods of expansion and rising in periods of contraction. The rate of unemployment has typically been quite high. From 1948 to 1979 the average rate of unemployment was about 5.1 percent. In 1975–1976, the rate of unemployment rose to its highest levels in the post-World War II period.

Figure 22.4
Unemployment Rate,
1948–1979

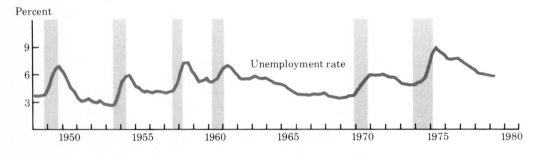

Unemployment rates shown are quarterly averages of monthly figures, seasonally adjusted. Shaded areas represent periods of business recession.
Source: Board of Governors of the Federal Reserve System, *1979 Historical Chart Book*, p. 20.

The *unemployment rate* is the ratio of the total number of unemployed to the total labor force.[6] The *labor force* consists of those who are working and those who want to work. Not counted in the labor force are children under sixteen years of age, students, retired persons, the disabled, and wives who are not looking for work. Estimates of unemployment are based on direct interviews with a sample of the total population. A person is counted as employed if he did any work at all during the sample week. In addition to those who are fully unemployed, there are persons who would like to work more hours a week. Estimates of unemployment do not include partial unemployment.

The meaning of a particular level of unemployment may be illustrated by examining the rate of unemployment for a given month. In December 1979, for example, the unemployment rate was 5.9 percent. This corresponds to 6,087,000 unemployed. Table 22.1 shows that one-fourth of the unemployed were teenagers, many looking for their first job. Thirty-seven percent were women workers twenty years of age and over, many of whom do not work continuously. The remaining 38 percent consisted of men twenty years old and older. The period of unemployment for many of those without jobs was short. Forty-nine percent had been unemployed less than five weeks, and the average duration of unemployment was less than eleven weeks. The total number of hard-core unemployed who had been out of work for six months was estimated to be 519,000 persons, 8 percent of the total number of unemployed.

Table 22.1
Total Unemployment, Persons 16 Years of Age and Over, December 1979

Age Group	Thousands of Persons (seasonally adjusted)
16 to 19 years	1,527
20 years and over:	
Females	2,257
Males	2,303
Total	6,087

Source: *Economic Report of the President, January 1980* (Washington, D.C.: U.S. Government Printing Office, 1980), p. 236.

People are counted as unemployed while they are negotiating for a job or moving from one position to another. This kind of unemployment is caused by the mobility of labor and is called *frictional unemployment.* Unemployment of this type need not be undesirable, because the economy benefits when people shift from lower-paying to higher-paying jobs. Changes in consumer demand also cause much unemployment that is not considered undesirable. When the demand for a particular product declines, workers who had been manufacturing that product will be laid off and will have to look for jobs in other types of firms. In addition, certain types of employment are unavoidably seasonal and require a regular inflow and outflow of labor. To allow for this frictional unemployment, government policymakers for many years expected that the unemployment rate would be at least 4 percent.

In recent years, government policymakers have raised their estimate of the minimum acceptable rate of unemployment to between 5 and 6 percent. The reason given for this is that the structure of the labor force has changed. The percentage of men twenty years and over in the labor force has declined in recent decades and the percentage of women and teenagers in the labor force has increased sharply (see Figure 22.5). This would have the effect of raising the overall rate of unemployment even though there were no change in the rate of unemployment for any of the three component groups: women, teenagers, and men over twenty. This is because women and teenagers, who tend to work intermittently, have a higher rate of unemployment than do men over twenty. Teenagers, for example, may work only for a few months in the summer and spend the rest of the year in school. At least once a year they are looking for a job, and between the time they begin looking and the time they start work, they are counted as unemployed.

Figure 22.5
A Comparison of the Trend in Labor Force Participation Rates for Men 20 Years and Over with Rates for Women and Teenagers, 1948–1976

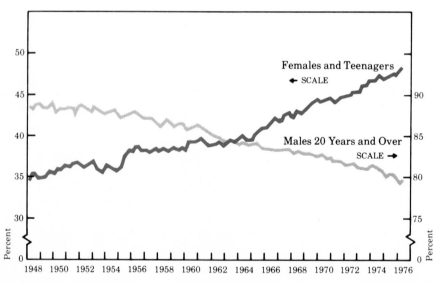

Quarterly averages of monthly rates, seasonally adjusted.
Source: Jean M. Lovati, "The Unemployment Rate as an Economic Indicator," Federal Reserve Bank of St. Louis, *Review*, September 1976, p. 7.

Another reason for raising the minimum acceptable rate of unemployment is that recent changes in the welfare system in the United States may have caused current rates of unemployment to be different in significance from rates of unemployment in previous years. In 1975, Congress established a temporary special unemployment assistance program which extended the period over which persons may draw unemployment insurance benefits. This may have had the effect of encouraging persons to take a longer time to locate new jobs, thus raising the unemployment rate. In addition, the recent expansion of new welfare programs, such as the food stamp program and aid to families with dependent children, which require persons to register for work in order to qualify for welfare benefits may have increased the labor force, as statistically measured, and thus the rate of unemployment.[7] It is believed that many persons who now must register for employment in order to get welfare are not really looking for jobs.

The recent rise in the rate of unemployment could also be related to a relatively rapid growth in the 1970s of the underground economy—unmeasured economic activities such as the narcotics trade, prostitution, gambling, loan sharking, acquisition and sale of stolen goods, illegal alien employment, unreported employment, covert rentals, skimming of retail sales, and barter.[8] Although some of these activities are illegal, the purpose of a good many of them is to evade taxes and various types of government regulation. If the underground economy has grown faster than the official economy and real resources have been shifted from the official economy to the underground economy, some persons counted as unemployed would actually be employed in the underground economy and the official statistics on unemployment would overstate the rate of unemployment.

From 1970 to 1979, there was an exceptionally rapid increase from 78.6 million to 96.9 million in the number of persons employed. In addition, Figure 22.6 shows that in the 1970s the percentage of the noninstitutional population sixteen years of age and over in the labor force has risen to the highest levels in the post-World War II period. These statistics on rising employment appear to contradict the statistics on the high rate of unemployment during the past decade and raise questions concerning the high rates of unemployment that have prevailed during periods of prosperity.

Lowering the long-run rate of unemployment

There are two divergent points of view about the high rates of unemployment in the United States during periods of prosperity as well as periods of recession.[9] (Figure 22.4 shows the rate of unemployment from 1948 to 1979.) The older view is that the growth of aggregate demand has not kept up with the expansion of the labor force and the rise in labor productivity. It is believed that an unnecessarily high rate of unemployment results because firms do not hire the expanding labor force rapidly enough. Those who hold this view advocate a more aggressive fiscal and monetary policy so that aggregate demand will increase as fast as the growth of the labor force even though the effects of such policies on unemployment may be only temporary. The more recent view is that the high *long-run rates of unemployment* (the average rate

Figure 22.6
Total Civilian Labor
Force as a Percentage
of Civilian
Noninstitutional
Population Age 16 and
Over, 1948–1979

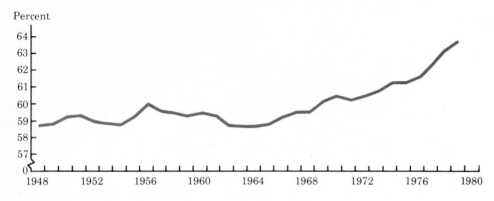

Source: *Economic Report of the President, January 1980*, p. 234.

of unemployment during periods of prosperity and recession) have been the result of the difficulties new entrants into the labor force have in finding out where the jobs are, the low job attachment among those at work, and unnecessary seasonal and cyclical fluctuations in labor demand. This point of view rejects the conception of the labor market as one in which the number of job seekers is typically larger than the number of jobs available. Instead, the labor market is conceived of as operating effectively enough so that eventually the supply of labor becomes equal to the demand.

Recent statistical studies of unemployment have uncovered information that appears to support the new point of view that high long-run rates of unemployment are not the result of inadequate total spending. It has been found that less than half of the unemployed were laid off by their employers. The bulk of the unemployed either had voluntarily left their jobs, were reentering the labor force, or were looking for their first jobs. Also, even if expansionary government policies reduced the rate of unemployment for men over twenty-four years of age to very low levels, there would still be excessively high rates of unemployment among other groups of workers such as teenagers and women. Advocates of the new point of view believe that an important way in which the long-run rate of unemployment could be reduced is by creating a special Youth Employment Service primarily concerned with the transition of young workers from school to permanent employment. Another proposal is to encourage firms to provide young workers with training on the job and opportunities for significant advancement, in order to reduce labor turnover by making jobs more attractive. Also, it has been suggested that the minimum wage rates set by the government be kept relatively low so that young and inexperienced workers will be able to find jobs more easily and that the system of unemployment compensation be reformed so as to remove the present incentive to the unemployed to take as long as possible before locating a new job.

The inflation-unemployment trade-off

In the 1960s, it was widely believed that one way to reduce unemployment was to have a little inflation. If the rate of inflation were zero, for example, it was believed that the lowest rate of unemployment possible was about 5 percent. If, however, the rate of inflation were 3 percent, it was claimed that the rate of unemployment could be reduced to less than 4 percent. It was believed by many that the benefits of less than 4 percent unemployment were worth the cost of a little inflation, and when the rate of inflation actually rose to 3 percent in 1967 and the rate of unemployment fell to less than 4 percent, this was not viewed as an unexpected problem, but the result of a conscious choice.

Table 22.2 shows the relationship between the rate of unemployment and the rate of inflation in the United States from 1960 to 1979. From 1960 to 1963, both the rate of inflation and the rate of unemployment were fairly steady. From 1963 to 1966, as the rate of inflation became more rapid, the rate of unemployment fell. Then from 1966 to 1969, despite a more rapid rate of inflation, the rate of unemployment fell very little. When unemployment gets relatively low, it probably cannot be reduced much further. Although experience in the 1960s appeared to support the trade-off theory, in the 1970s the relationship broke down. In 1970 and in 1974, instead of an inverse relationship between inflation and unemployment, when the rate of unemployment rose, the rate of inflation, as measured by the GNP deflator, rose. Also, in 1972 and in 1976, both prices and the rate of unemployment fell. In 1975–1976, there did not appear to be much of a trade-off; rates of inflation were over 5 percent a year, unemployment was 8 percent. In 1977–1978, however, when the rate of inflation accelerated, the rate of unemployment dropped.

The relationship between unemployment and the rate of increase in wages is illustrated in Figure 22.7—with the *Phillips curve,* named for Professor A. W. Phillips.[10] In this graph the higher the rate of unemployment, the less rapid the rise in wages. This relationship between unemployment and wages is believed to underlie the trade-off between inflation and unemployment. One would expect wages to rise more slowly when many people are unemployed. The supply of labor would be large relative to the demand. Some persons would accept lower wages rather than not work at all. On the other hand, when there is little unemployment, there would be upward pressure on wages. The de-

Table 22.2
The Rate of
Unemployment and the
Rate of Change in the
GNP Deflator,
1960–1979

Year	Rate of Unemployment	Rate of Inflation (GNP Deflator)
1960	5.5%	1.7%
1961	6.7	0.9
1962	5.5	1.8
1963	5.7	1.5
1964	5.2	1.6
1965	4.5	2.2
1966	3.8	3.3
1967	3.8	2.9
1968	3.6	4.5
1969	3.5	5.0
1970	4.9	5.4
1971	5.9	5.1
1972	5.6	4.1
1973	4.9	5.8
1974	5.6	9.7
1975	8.5	9.6
1976	7.7	5.2
1977	7.0	6.0
1978	6.0	7.3
1979	5.8	8.8

Source: *Economic Report of the President, January 1980* (Washington, D.C.: U.S. Government Printing Office, 1980), pp. 207, 237.

mand for labor would probably be greater than the supply. Rather than not get the labor they want, business firms would bid up wages.

The relationship between unemployment and wage rates shown in Figure 22.7 may reflect the effect of inflation on unemployment rather than the effect of unemployment on wages, as originally expected. A recently developed explanation of this relationship states that although there is a trade-off between inflation and unemployment in the short run, there is no trade-off in the long run.[11] According to this point of view, when inflation accelerates and is unexpected, the higher wages offered in the labor market appear very attractive, persons spend less time looking for jobs, and this causes the rate of unemployment to fall. The opposite would occur if the rate of inflation slowed down. The wages offered would appear to be unattractive. Persons would take longer looking for jobs, and the rate of unemployment would rise. In the long run, as soon as persons expect the higher rate of inflation, there is no trade-off. The job offers would not look particularly attractive, workers would take the normal amount of time looking for jobs, and the rate of unemployment would increase until it reached its normal level.

Although the short-run relationship between unemployment and wage rates is as shown in Figure 22.7, according to this point of view, in the long run the rate of unemployment is unaffected by inflation. The long-run rate of unemployment is determined primarily by institutional arrangements affecting the speed with which persons shift from one job to another—such institutional factors as the efficiency of employment offices and the amount and availability of unemployment insurance.

Figure 22.7
The Rate of Increase in
Wages and
Unemployment

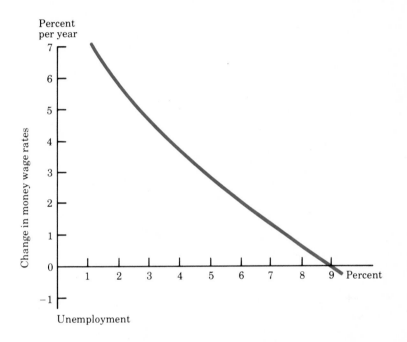

According to this explanation of the relationship between unemployment and inflation, attempts by the monetary authorities to keep the rate of unemployment below its normal long-run rate could cause a continuous acceleration in the rate of inflation.[12] Suppose the aim of the federal government was to reduce unemployment to 3 percent and that 4 percent was the long-run rate of unemployment. At first, if the rate of increase in the money supply were raised, for example, from 2 percent to 3 percent a year and prices also rose more rapidly, unemployment might fall to 3 percent. But as people became adjusted to the new rate of inflation, unemployment would rise back to 4 percent. To again attempt to reduce the rate of unemployment to 3 percent, the rate of increase in the money supply would have to be increased further, for example from 3 percent to 4 percent. This kind of situation may have occurred during the late 1960s when there was both a relatively low rate of unemployment and an accelerated expansion in the rate of increase in prices.

Summary

The immediate impact of decreases in total spending resulting from anti-inflation monetary policies is to increase unemployment because wages and prices do not fall immediately when total spending declines.

The immediate impact of increases in total spending resulting from expansionary monetary policies is to decrease unemployment because wages and prices do not rise immediately when total spending rises.

In the long run, expansionary monetary policies increase and tight money policies reduce the rate of inflation. However, because of the unemployment it causes in the short run, the Federal Reserve System has reversed its tight money policies so that the achievement of a lower rate of inflation has been only temporary.

Most programs to combat inflation through wage and price controls have had only a temporary effect on inflation because these programs have been combined with expansionary fiscal and monetary policies. Wage and price controls have important side effects on the free market system and may impede efficient adjustments to changes in demand and in costs of production.

Notes

1. Milton Friedman, "Using Escalators to Help Fight Inflation," *Fortune* 90 (July 1974), pp. 94–97 and 174–176; reprinted in Herbert Giersch et al., *Essays on Inflation and Indexation* (Washington, D.C.: American Enterprise Institute, 1974), pp. 25–61.

2. For a description and evaluation of this program, see George P. Shultz and Robert Z. Aliber, eds., *Guidelines, Informal Controls, and the Marketplace* (Chicago: University of Chicago Press, 1966).

3. Marten Estey, "Wage Stabilization Policy and the Nixon Administration," in *A New Look at Inflation* (Washington, D.C.: American Enterprise Institute, 1973), pp. 107–133.

4. Egon Sohmen, "Competition and Growth: The Lesson of West Germany," *American Economic Review* 49 (December 1959), pp. 986–1003.

5. See Walter Eucken, "On the Theory of the Centrally Administered Economy: An Analysis of the German Experiment; Part I," *Economica*, May 1948, pp. 79–100.

6. U.S. Department of Labor, Bureau of Labor Statistics, *BLS Handbook of Methods for Surveys and Studies,* Bulletin No. 1910 (1976), Chapter 1.

7. Kenneth W. Clarkson and Roger E. Meiners, *Inflated Unemployment Statistics, The Effect of Welfare Work Registration Requirements,* Law and Economics Center Study (Coral Gables, Fla.: University of Miami School of Law, March 1977).

8. Edgar L. Feige, "How Big Is the Irregular Economy?" *Challenge,* November-December 1979, pp. 5–17.

9. Martin S. Feldstein, *Lowering the Permanent Rate of Unemployment,* Joint Committee Print, Joint Economic Committee, 93rd Cong., 1st sess. (Washington, D.C.: U.S. Government Printing Office, September 18, 1973); and "The Economics of the New Unemployment," *Public Interest,* Fall 1973, pp. 3–42.

10. A. W. Phillips, "The Relation between Unemployment and the Rate of Change in Money Wage Rates in the United Kingdom, 1861–1957," *Economica* 25 (November 1958), pp. 283–299.

11. J. Huston McCulloch, *Money and Inflation, A Monetarist Approach* (New York: Academic Press, 1975), pp. 83–94.

12. Milton Friedman, "The Role of Monetary Policy," *American Economic Review* 58 (March 1968), pp. 1–17, reprinted in *The Optimum Quantity of Money and Other Essays* (Chicago: Aldine, 1969), pp. 95–110.

Questions

22.1. Draw an aggregate demand schedule on a graph and explain its shape.

22.2. Graph an aggregate supply schedule and explain its shape.

22.3. The equilibrium level of prices and real output is where the aggregate demand schedule intersects the aggregate supply schedule. If prices are above the equilibrium level, explain why they will fall to that level. If prices are below the equilibrium level, explain why they will rise to that level.

22.4. Given the aggregate supply schedule, explain why a shift in the aggregate demand schedule to the right will cause an increase in output but little increase in prices.

22.5. Given the aggregate demand schedule, explain why a rise in the aggregate supply schedule will cause prices to rise and real output to fall.

22.6. Explain why an increase in the productivity of labor would shift the aggregate supply schedule downward.

22.7. Explain why an anti-inflation monetary policy, designed to reduce the rate of inflation, causes an increase in the rate of unemployment.

22.8. "A more expansionary monetary policy may reduce the rate of unemployment in the short run, but not in the long run." Explain and discuss.

22.9. How is the rate of unemployment measured?

22.10. Discuss some of the factors affecting the rate of unemployment.

22.11. Should efforts be made to avoid frictional unemployment?

22.12. Is the high long-run rate of unemployment in the United States caused by insufficient aggregate demand?

22.13. Explain why a rise in the rate of inflation may result in a lower rate of unemployment in the short run, but not in the long run.

22.14. Explain why a policy of freezing wages and prices is an impediment to the use of the market system for allocating resources.

22.15. What were some of the problems associated with the freezing of wages and prices during World War II?

22.16. Discuss and evaluate the use of wage and price guidelines as a method of preventing inflation.

22.17. Know the meaning and significance of the following terms and concepts: rate of unemployment, labor force, frictional unemployment, full employment, long-run rate of unemployment, Phillips curve, wage and price guidelines, wage and price freeze, the inflation-unemployment trade-off.

23

The dollar has become widely used as a type of international money. It is used by business firms for international transactions. It is also held as international reserves by the governments of most countries in case the country's international payments exceed its receipts.

INTERNATIONAL FINANCE

This chapter includes a description of the ways in which international payments are transacted and the different types of international money that are currently used and were used in the past. Transactions in international trade involve exchanging the money of different countries. In addition, the governments of most countries typically hold a reserve of international money (gold; dollar deposits; deposits of some other currencies such as the deutschemark, yen, Swiss franc, and British pound; and special drawing rights). This enables business firms engaged in international trade to obtain foreign exchange when there is an excess of international payments over receipts.

Foreign exchange markets

In the New York foreign exchange market, American importers who need foreign money of any kind can get it, and American exporters who have received payment in foreign money can exchange it for dollars. The exchange of money may take place in either the importing or the exporting country. It is not necessary for an American importer to acquire foreign money in order to purchase foreign goods. He may pay for the goods he has imported with dollars. But then the foreign exporter from whom the goods were purchased will usually exchange the dollars he has received for his own money.

The two largest foreign exchange markets in the world are located in London and New York, but there are a dozen or so others of lesser importance. The New York market is somewhat different from the others, but it is illustrative of the basic operations involved. It has no centralized meeting place, no fixed opening or closing time, and no formal requirements for participation. There are three groups dealing in foreign exchange: (1) commercial banks which exchange money for their customers, (2) the foreign exchange brokers located in New York, and (3) the trading banks—a small number of commercial banks that have departments operating foreign exchange markets—that deal with banks in other countries.[1]

Importers and exporters buy and sell foreign exchange at commercial banks rather than from each other. Exchanging foreign money is one of the services of most commercial banks. Even though most banks do not have relationships with foreign banks, they can accommodate their own customers through one of the trading banks. An importer in New Hampshire who needs pounds, for example, can exchange dollars for pounds at his local bank. His local bank would purchase the pounds from a trading bank (probably one of its correspondent banks). The trading bank has deposits in pounds in a correspondent bank or in one of its own branches in Great Britain, and it can arrange for the payment of pounds to the British firm that is owed money by the New Hampshire importer.

Currently, eight foreign exchange brokers in New York serve as middlemen under certain circumstances for the trading banks. They handle the important types of foreign money in which most trade is transacted, especially the pound sterling, the Canadian dollar, the West German deutschemark, the Japanese yen, and the Swiss franc. On some days, a trading bank's purchases of a particular type of foreign money will exceed its sales of that money, and on other days sales will be higher than purchases. When the bank accumulates more foreign money than its customers are demanding, it will have funds tied up which do not provide an immediate source of income. On the other hand, when the demands for a type of foreign money are greater than the supply coming from its clients, the bank runs the risk of losing business by being unable to satisfy its customers. The brokers provide a wholesale, inter-bank market at which these banks may buy and sell foreign exchange. The trading banks do not trade with each other directly. The brokers receive a commission for their services paid by the selling bank. The banks seek the best terms available, and the brokers are able to match bids and offers from various banks.

Several dozen United States banks operate as traders in foreign exchange. Branches of foreign banks in the United States and a few dealers that are not banks also operate in this field. To engage in this type of trading, a bank must have balances in banks in foreign countries. When a New York bank sells a type of foreign money, it sells deposits that it owns in a foreign bank; and when it buys a type of foreign money, it acquires additional deposits in a foreign bank. These international transactions are carried on primarily by telephone, but also by telegraph, cable, and mail.

Consider the impact on the balance sheet of a trading bank in New York when it sells $1,000 worth of British pounds to an American importer. As shown in Figure 23.1, the New York bank's deposit in the British bank would decline by $1,000 when it sold this amount to the importer. If the importer were also a depositor of the same New York bank, his own deposit would be reduced to pay for the pounds, as shown in Figure 23.1. If the British pounds were paid for by a check on another bank, the decline in the New York bank's balance in a British bank would be offset by an increase in the New York bank's balances at the Federal Reserve bank, and there would be no changes on the liabilities side.

When a trading bank in New York purchases pounds from an exporter in the United States, the impact on its balance sheet is the opposite. Figure 23.2 shows that the New York bank's deposit at the British bank increases. If the exporter had a deposit at the New York bank, the bank would pay the exporter for the pounds by increasing his deposit by $1,000.

The trading banks in the United States do not have to own balances in correspondent banks in all foreign countries. To obtain the money of many of the smaller countries, the procedure is different. Important foreign banks have dollar balances in banks in New York. To obtain the money of Colombia, for example, the New York bank would probably

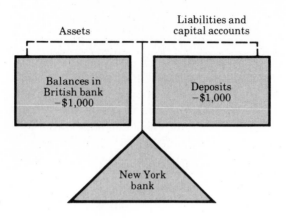

Figure 23.1
A Bank in New York
Sells British Pounds to
an American Importer

make a payment to the dollar account of a Colombian bank in this
country in exchange for a peso account in the Colombian bank.

Each type of foreign money has its price in terms of the dollar. In
September 1979, the exchange rate between the dollar and the pound
was $2.20 per pound; a French franc was exchanged for approximately
24 cents, and the Mexican peso for approximately 4.4 cents.

For each type of foreign exchange, the New York trading banks buy
at a different rate than they sell at—they have a small spread between
these rates, rather than charging a commission for each transaction.
There are also *spot* and *forward* exchange rates. Spot exchange is delivered within one or two business days and applies mostly to cable
transfers. In a forward exchange transaction, the buyer purchases a
foreign currency for delivery in the future. Forward exchange rates
depend on the exchange rate that is expected in the future. They are
quoted either at a discount or at a premium from the spot rate. Forward
exchange rates are useful guides to various types of transactions.

Cable transfers and other means of payment

The principal way in which money is exchanged is by cable (telegraph-
ic) transfer. When an American exporter wishes to exchange pounds
that he has received for dollars, he would cable the importer from whom
payment is due to transfer pounds to his New York bank's deposit in a
bank in London. He would then receive a dollar deposit in the New
York bank equivalent to the pounds sold. When an American importer
purchases pounds from a New York bank, this bank would cable its

**Figure 23.2
A Bank In New York
Purchases British
Pounds from an
American Exporter**

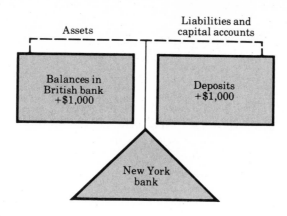

Assets

Liabilities and
capital accounts

Balances in
British bank
+$1,000

Deposits
+$1,000

New York
bank

branch or correspondent in London to transfer pounds from its account
to the British exporter's account. The New York bank then collects the
equivalent amount of dollars from the importer. The transfer of funds
by cable is usually completed on the first or second day following the
purchase or sale, and same-day transfers may in some cases be arranged.

Bills of exchange

A type of document that has been used in the foreign exchange market
for many years is the *bill of exchange,* though the speed and ease of
cable transfers have reduced their use. An American exporter may draw
a bill of exchange (or draft) on a foreign buyer. The bill of exchange is
an order (similar to a bank check) on the foreign buyer to pay a certain
amount of money to the exporter on a certain date. The American
exporter has the right to draw up such a bill of exchange because he has
sold goods to the foreign firm. A bill of exchange is similar to the usual
type of bill that is sent to persons who owe money. In foreign transactions, the bill of exchange is for payment in a foreign money. The date
on the bill may give the foreign importer some time to pay it, as is
typical of many business transactions. Bills that are payable 30, 60, 90,
or 180 days after a specified date are known as *time drafts.* Those that
must be paid immediately are called *sight drafts.*

For greater security, many bills of exchange are written on the importer's bank rather than on the importer himself and are known as
bankers' bills of exchange. In order to write a bill of exchange on the
importer's bank, the exporter must have received a *letter of credit* from
the importer. The latter would obtain this from his bank. It is the bank's
assurance to the exporter that the bank will accept his bill of exchange.

The exporter has greater assurance of payment because of the superior credit of a bank.

The exporter often attaches to a bill of exchange the shipping documents. Bills of exchange are then exchanged for dollar deposits at a trading bank. The New York bank that buys the bill has legal title to the products sold until it is assured of payment by the importer. To get possession of the goods, the importer in the foreign country must have made certain arrangements to pay for them. The New York bank sends the bill of exchange to its foreign branch or correspondent bank, and the latter will collect the amount due on the appropriate date.

If a bank purchases a bill of exchange that is payable thirty days or so in the future, it will purchase the bill at a discount. A New York bank that purchased one payable in thirty days, for example, would use the forward exchange rate in calculating the price to be paid for that bill of exchange. The bank is in effect lending the exporter money, and the bank would expect to receive interest on the money lent. It is a loan because the exporter receives payment for the bill of exchange immediately, while the bank must wait thirty days or more before it can demand payment from the importer or the bank on which the bill of exchange was drawn. If the bank that purchased the bill of exchange would like to be reimbursed immediately, it may ask the bank on which it is drawn to accept the bill. After an officer of the bank acknowledges that it has been accepted and "Accepted" is written on the face of it, the bill of exchange becomes a *bankers' acceptance* and may be sold on the open market at a discount. From the point of view of investors, bankers' acceptances are a type of short-term paper similar to United States Treasury bills and commercial paper.

Bills of exchange may also be used by importers as a method of paying for goods that they have purchased. An American importer would purchase a bill of exchange designated in foreign money from one of the trading banks that has deposits in a foreign bank. The bill of exchange would be written by the trading bank in this country on its correspondent bank in the foreign country. The importer would then mail the bill of exchange to the foreign exporter. The foreign exporter gets paid when he presents the bill of exchange to his bank.

Foreign bank notes

In addition to the exchange of deposits, part of the international market for foreign exchange consists of the purchase and sale of foreign bank notes and coins. The foreign exchange dealers that are not banks typically trade in this type of exchange. The demand for foreign bank notes comes mainly from American tourists, and the supply comes from foreign tourists visiting the United States. A fairly large volume of Canadian bank notes is also acquired by United States merchants in the border areas.

Traveler's checks

The use of traveler's checks by tourists is another way of exchanging money. An American may purchase traveler's checks in dollars from the American Express Company, Cook's, or one of the large banks that issue these checks. When cashing them in a foreign country, the tourist receives foreign currency for the dollar traveler's checks at the going exchange rate. The foreign person or bank that accepts the check may return it to New York for dollars. Such checks are obligations of the issuer—such as the American Express Company or Citibank in New York. The financial standing of the issuers of traveler's checks is usually beyond question so that any foreign person or bank cashing them can be sure of receiving payment. An American may purchase traveler's checks in pounds, francs, or other foreign currencies rather than in dollars. By purchasing traveler's checks in a foreign currency, a person may protect himself from any adverse change in the exchange rate between the time the checks are purchased and the time he uses them.

Gold

Gold is much less important today as a type of international money than it was in the nineteenth century. It has become less important than the dollar and other major foreign currencies.

The United States operated on an international gold standard from 1834 until the early part of this century, except during and following the Civil War (from 1861 to 1879), when the dollar was not convertible into a fixed quantity of gold. Under the international gold standard, in addition to using gold as international money, the quantity of gold bullion in the United States significantly determined the reserves of the banks, and banks could create additional deposits and credit if they acquired additional gold. After the Federal Reserve System was established in 1914, the effect of international gold flows on bank reserves diminished as the Federal Reserve System's control of bank reserves through open-market operations became increasingly important.

Under the international gold standard, the dollar was defined in terms of a physical quantity of gold. From 1832 to 1934, the dollar was valued at approximately 1/21 of an ounce of fine gold, and the official price of an ounce of fine gold was $20.66. When the dollar was devalued in 1934, the dollar was valued at 1/35 of an ounce of gold, and the price of an ounce of fine gold was raised to $35. Other major countries also specified that their money was equal to a certain physical quantity of gold. As a result of fixing the value of each type of money in terms of gold, the values of different types of money were fixed in relation to each other. From 1819 to 1931, the weight of the British pound in gold was 4.76 times that of the U.S. dollar, and for most of this period the exchange rate between the dollar and the pound was $4.76 to the pound.

When the gold standard was in operation, most governments were willing to buy and sell gold at their official gold prices. An American importer, for example, could get pounds by buying gold from the U.S. Treasury at the official U.S. price, shipping the gold to Great Britain, and selling it to the Bank of England for pounds at their official price. Although the bulk of the pounds needed by American importers came from the receipts of American exporters, the fact that pounds could be obtained in Great Britain in exchange for a certain quantity of gold established an upper limit on the price that importers would pay for pounds, as well as a lower limit. Because there were costs involved in shipping gold, the price of foreign exchange varied within what was known as the *gold points*. These were the upper and lower limits for the price of a foreign currency set by the cost of shipping gold. The cost of shipping gold made American importers desiring pounds willing to pay a little more than the fixed rates; and American exporters who had pounds to be exchanged for dollars were willing to receive a little less than the fixed rate. From 1819 to 1914, the gold export point for the pound was approximately $4.78 and the gold import point was approximately $4.74.

Between World War II and 1968, even though the international gold standard was no longer in operation, the world price of gold was kept at $35 an ounce primarily because the U.S. Treasury would buy and sell gold at that price. From 1961 to 1968, the major industrial countries of the world operated a "gold pool" in London for the purpose of keeping the world price of gold at $35, i.e., equal to the official United States price at that time. The gold pool was established because it was feared that if gold could be sold at a price far above the official price, foreign owners of dollars might try to convert their dollars into gold at the U.S. Treasury at the official price of $35 an ounce. The gold pool had to be given up in 1968. The ceiling price of $35 an ounce was significantly below the equilibrium price. As illustrated by the supply and demand graph in Figure 23.3, at $35 an ounce, the supply of gold from private sources was less than the demand. To prevent a rise in the price, the participating governments had to sell from their stocks an amount of gold equal to the amount of the shortage (X). Without this increase in supply from government stocks, demand would have been greater than supply, and the price would have been bid above $35 by those buyers who were willing to pay more than $35 an ounce rather than to go without gold. In the six months preceding the dissolution of the gold pool, the United States had to sell more than $2.5 billion in gold as its share in the pool (60 percent). Rather than deplete their stocks of gold completely, in 1968 the partners decided to dissolve the pool.

After the gold pool was given up in 1968, the United States permitted private companies that mined gold and manufacturers that used gold as a raw material to buy and sell gold at free-market prices. The U.S. Treasury continued to sell gold to foreign governments for international reserve purposes at the official price. This attempt to maintain a two-price system for gold was discontinued in August 1971, when the U.S. Treasury stopped selling gold to foreign governments.

Figure 23.3
Market for Gold,
1961–1968

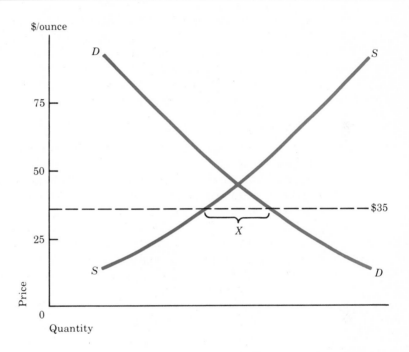

In 1969, a year after the dissolution of the gold pool, the free-market price of gold moved downward, much to the surprise of speculators who had purchased gold expecting the price to rise. This caused a reversal in the gold policy of the major trading countries. In place of the previous efforts to prevent the price of gold from rising, they took measures to keep the free-market price of gold from falling below $35 an ounce. The International Monetary Fund agreed to purchase gold from South Africa when the price fell to $35 or lower, or when South Africa had a deficit in its balance of payments. In 1970, $640 million worth of gold was purchased from South Africa. This agreement with South Africa was terminated in 1973.

In the fall of 1971, the free-market price of gold began a spectacular ascent, climbing to over $175 an ounce in April 1974. Then, in September 1975, the market price of gold fell from $160 an ounce to $129. This decline followed the release of official IMF recommendations: (1) to cease pegging the official price of gold at $42.22 an ounce, the price that had been set in 1973, (2) to cease requiring the use of gold in transactions between members of the fund, (3) to return 1/6 of the gold held by the IMF to its member countries, and (4) to begin selling at a series of auctions another 1/6 of the IMF's holdings of gold at the market price to benefit sixty-one less developed countries. The IMF auctions began on June 2, 1976, and were to be held periodically until the portion to be sold was disposed of.

In 1977, the price of gold again began to rise, and by early 1980 rose for a short time to over $800 an ounce. A reason for part of the remarkable rise in the price of gold is that higher rates of inflation in the United States and in other major countries have reduced the attractiveness of holding the dollar and other foreign currencies as international money compared to gold.

Table 23.1 shows the total amount of the different types of international reserves held by the governments of member countries of the International Monetary Fund in 1979. In this table, gold is valued at only SDR 35 per ounce (approximately $46), and its listed value does not reflect its market price. (SDRs are the new type of international money first discussed in Chapter 11.) The recent rise in the price of gold has caused the actual market value of the gold reserves held to rise. Gold continues to be used as a type of international money, and today a nation may sell gold at its market value to settle its accounts with other countries if the value of the country's international payments should exceed receipts.

Table 23.1
Official International
Reserves, End of April
1979 (in billions of SDRs)

	All Member Countries, IMF	United States
Gold[a]	SDR 32.3	SDR 9.3
SDRs	12.4	2.1
Reserve positions in fund [b]	12.4	1.0
Foreign exchange	233.5	3.7
Total reserve assets held by governments	SDR 290.6	SDR 16.1

[a]Gold is valued at SDR 35 per ounce.
[b]Arise primarily from the use of IMF credit and gold subscriptions to the fund.
Source: *International Financial Statistics*, November 1979, pp. 28, 29, 32, 33, and 37.

The dollar

Table 23.1 shows that a major portion of the official reserves of national governments consists of foreign exchange. About four-fifths of these holdings of foreign exchange consist of U.S. dollars. Part of them are held as deposits in U.S. banks and part as Eurodollar deposits in banks in foreign countries. As shown in Table 23.1, the United States government still holds relatively little foreign exchange (currency of other countries) as a type of international reserve compared to the amount held by most other national governments, even though the amount of currency of other countries owned by the United States government was increased sharply in 1979.

Although the dollar has become the most important type of foreign exchange held as international money, before World War II the pound was more important than the dollar. In the 1970s, holdings of foreign exchange in pounds declined further, and holdings of deutschemarks and other currencies increased. The dollar became the predominant type of international money for several reasons: the United States plays a major role in international trade; prior to 1971 the dollar could be converted into gold; there are few restrictions on the convertibility of the dollar into other assets; and the value of the dollar was relatively stable prior to 1965. This expanding role of the dollar developed informally and was not the result of a governmental or international decision or plan.

Table 23.2 shows the increase in U.S. liabilities owed to foreigners as reported by banks in the United States from 1950 to 1978. These liquid liabilities consist of demand deposits, time deposits, short-term U.S. government securities, and other short-term securities, and they are used as international money. Slightly more than half of these liquid liabilities are owned by foreign governments, and the rest by banks and foreign businesses engaged in international trade.

Table 23.2
Liabilities to
Foreigners,
Reported by Banks
in the United States,
Selected Years,
1950–1978[a]

December	Amount (in billions)
1950	$ 7.3
1955	11.9
1960	18.6
1965	25.5
1970	41.4
1975	93.8
1976	110.7
1977	126.2
1978	167.1

[a]Payable in U.S. dollars excluding the International Monetary Fund. Data for time deposits prior to April 1978 were for short-term issues only.
Source: *Federal Reserve Bulletin* (October 1979), p. A59; and Board of Governors of the Federal Reserve System, *Banking and Monetary Statistics, 1941–1970* (Washington, D.C.: United States Government Printing Office, 1976), p. 936.

Inconvertibility of the dollar into gold

During the 1950s, the value of the gold stock owned by the United States government was larger than the amount of liquid dollar holdings owned by foreigners shown in Table 23.2. After 1959, this was no longer true—foreign liquid dollar holdings then exceeded the value of our gold stock. This change eventually led the United States government to end the convertibility of dollars into gold—because the United States no longer had enough gold to satisfy all the claims that might be made against it. Under such circumstances, whenever foreigners believed that the official price of gold might have to be raised or that the United States was in danger of running out of gold, they would want to hold gold rather than dollars, and there could be a scramble for it. Intense speculation in gold and widespread hoarding did in fact occur in 1967 and in 1970–1971. The crisis in 1971 ended when the United States government declared the dollar inconvertible into gold.

Table 23.3 U.S. International Transactions, 1978 (in billions)		
Trade flows:		
Merchandise exports		$142.1
Merchandise imports		175.8
Service exports		79.0
Service imports		53.6
Unilateral transfers, net balance		− 5.1
Current account balance		− 13.5
Capital flows:		
Direct investment in the United States		$ 6.3
Direct investment abroad		16.7
Security purchases in the United States		5.0
Security purchases abroad		3.5
Bank liabilities to foreigners		17.0
Bank claims on foreigners		33.0
Foreign official assets in the United States		33.8
U.S. government assets abroad		3.9

Note: The surplus items in this table do not exactly balance the deficit items. It is not possible to obtain data on all international transactions.

Source: Federal Reserve Bank of St. Louis, *International Economic Conditions*, January 22, 1980, p. 7.

The role of deficits in the U.S. balance of payments

The increase in the amount of foreign-owned dollars, shown in Table 23.2, is the result of deficits in the U.S. balance of payments. The *balance of payments* of the United States is a listing of the principal types of international transactions of the United States for the year. By far the largest type of transaction is for *exports and imports of merchan-*

dise. As shown by the first two items in Table 23.3, in 1978 the United States had a deficit in its *trade balance*—the dollar value of physical goods exported by the United States was $142 billion compared to $176 billion imported.

A second type of international transaction is *service exports and imports.* An important type of service import and export is the payments and receipts associated with foreign travel and transportation. When Americans travel in other countries, they must exchange dollars for the foreign currencies needed to pay for hotel accommodations, transportation, and other expenses involved in foreign travel. On the other hand, when foreigners travel in the United States, they need to exchange their currencies for dollars, and their expenditures are classified as service exports in our balance of payments. This category of international transactions also includes sales and purchases of military equipment and expenditures for maintaining U.S. military stations abroad. The cost of hiring foreigners for the operation of United States military installations in foreign countries is a service import. Service exports include the payment of interest and dividends to American owners of foreign stocks and bonds; such payments to foreigners who own stocks and bonds of U.S. corporations are service imports.

A third type of international payment listed in Table 23.3 is *unilateral transfers.* This item includes private gifts of money to persons or organizations in foreign countries and aid given to foreign governments under the federal government's foreign aid programs, less the amount of such gifts given to persons in the United States by foreigners. When gifts or aid are given to persons in foreign countries, payment of dollars to foreigners results, and this payment has the same effect on exchange markets as the import of goods and services. The sum of the merchandise exports and imports, service exports and imports, and unilateral transfers is the *current account* of the balance of payments. There was a deficit in the current account balance in 1978.

The capital flows in the balance of payments consist of direct investment, security purchases, changes in bank liabilities and claims, and changes in government assets. *Direct investment in the United States* includes expenditures made by foreign corporations for capital equipment in this country, and *direct investment abroad* includes primarily earnings reinvested by U.S. corporations in new plants and equipment in foreign countries. Direct investment abroad has tended to be larger than direct investment in the United States by foreign corporations. During the past thirty years the rapid growth of large multinational corporations has resulted in large amounts of international transactions of this type.

Security purchases in the United States consist of net sales of U.S. stocks and bonds to foreigners from persons in the United States, and *security purchases abroad* consist of net purchases of foreign stocks and bonds by United States citizens from persons in foreign countries. In

1978, security purchases by foreigners in the United States were larger than security purchases abroad by U.S. citizens. Transactions of this type do not include the purchase and sale of securities with a maturity of less than one year.

Bank liabilities to foreigners consist primarily of changes in the amount of demand and time deposits owned by foreigners, excluding those owned by foreign official agencies. *Bank claims on foreigners* consist of changes in the amount of loans by U.S. banks to foreigners, investments by U.S. banks in foreign securities, and deposits by them in foreign banks. Expansions in these transactions are deficit items because they give rise to payments by banks in the United States to foreigners. Table 23.3 shows that in 1978 a significant portion of the funds that foreigners received from the deficit in the U.S. current account balance, in direct investment, and from borrowing from U.S. banks was used to increase their deposits at U.S. banks. When dollars owned by foreigners are accumulated in this way, the quantity of international money in the form of dollars owned by foreign individuals and businesses for international transactions is increased.

Foreign official assets in the United States include primarily United States government securities and bank deposits owned by foreign governments and central banks. Table 23.3 shows the very large amount of such assets acquired by foreign governments and central banks in 1978. When foreign governments accumulate assets of this type, the quantity of international reserves in the form of dollars owned by foreign governments is increased. As will be explained in Chapter 24, the large accumulation of United States government securities and deposits by foreign central banks is related to their efforts to control the exchange rate between their currencies and the dollar.

U.S. government assets abroad consist primarily of changes in foreign currency owned by the U.S. government, although changes in this item may also reflect sales of gold and SDRs and borrowing from the IMF. A possible way to cover deficits in the current and capital accounts would be to use some of this government-owned foreign currency.

Note that Table 23.3 does not include any overall measure of the deficit or surplus in the balance of payments. Instead, it shows the deficit or surplus in the major different types of transactions. In 1976, the Department of Commerce discontinued attempts to measure the overall deficit or surplus.

The rise of the dollar standard

The United States has had deficits in its balance of payments accounts in almost every year from 1950 to 1979. Although there have usually been surpluses in the current account, the capital accounts have had large deficits. These deficits came as a surprise to most students of international trade. It was thought in the late 1940s that there had been certain structural changes in the international economy which would cause the United States to have continuous surpluses in its balance of payments. The United States, it was said, would import little because we were well stocked with goods and because of tariff protection. On the other hand, American exports were expected to be large because Europe needed the primary commodities produced in the United States and because of the rapid development of American exports of manufactured goods. These conditions were expected to create a "dollar shortage" because our imports, which supply others with dollars, would be less than our exports.[2]

The use of the dollar as the principal type of international money has been a major reason for the continuous deficits in our balance of payments; the expected surpluses did not develop.[3] Following World War II, world trade expanded rapidly and foreign governments needed international reserves to cover their own deficits; the larger the volume of a country's international trade, the larger the occasional deficits a country can expect to have. Also, the larger the number of enterprises engaged in international trade, the larger the number of firms needing dollar balances or some other type of foreign exchange to cover their regular needs for international money. Prior to 1968, gold did not provide for the expanding need for international money because the price was fixed at $35 an ounce, and the quantity of newly mined gold was relatively small.

Because the dollar has become an international type of money, the significance of deficits in the current and capital accounts in the balance of payments is different for the United States than for other countries. When other countries have deficits, their government's international reserves get smaller. Their balance of international payments is now in need of adjustment so as to avoid a continuous deficit that would deplete their reserves. A principal way in which such countries have corrected a deficit in their balance of payments is through tight money policies as described in Chapter 20. When the United States has a deficit, instead of a loss of some of our international reserves, other countries have usually built up larger holdings of dollar balances—although prior to 1971 deficits in the U.S. balance of payments also resulted in the loss of a large amount of U.S. gold. An important consequence of the use of the dollar as international money is that the United States has been able to pursue domestic economic policies with little regard for their effects on the balance of international payments.

Eurodollars

The growth in the amount of Eurodollar deposits from approximately $10 billion in 1964 to $348 billion in 1978 (see Table 23.4) is related to the expansion in the role of the U.S. dollar as a type of international money for business transactions.[4] Eurodollar deposits are deposits in foreign commercial banks and foreign branches of American commercial banks denominated in dollars. Foreign banks that have deposits denominated in dollars are called Eurodollar banks. A Eurodollar deposit is created when a person deposits a check on a bank in the United States in a Eurodollar bank. Because Eurodollars represent obligations to pay dollars, foreign banks offering deposits denominated in dollars must hold some reserves in the form of demand deposits in banks in the United States. For each dollar held in reserve, there may be a small multiple expansion of Eurodollar loans and Eurodollar deposits.

Eurodollar deposits have expanded rapidly because the rates of interest paid on these deposits have often been above those on time deposits in banks in the United States. This expansion has also been stimulated by the fact that reserve requirements for Eurodollar deposits are lower than they are for deposits in the United States. In addition, prior to 1974 when the foreign credit restraint program was discontinued, the Eurodollar market made it possible for American banks to finance the activities of large American firms in foreign countries without violating United States government regulations.

Table 23.4 Total Eurodollar Deposits in Banks in Reporting European Countries, 1964–1978a	End of December	Total Amount (in billions)
	1964	$ 9.7
	1965	11.4
	1966	14.8
	1967	18.1
	1968	26.9
	1969	46.2
	1970	58.7
	1971	70.1
	1972	96.7
	1973	131.4
	1974	156.4
	1975	189.5
	1976	230.0
	1977	278.8
	1978	348.6

aIncluded banks in 8 reporting European countries in earlier years. Austria, Denmark, and Ireland added starting in 1977.
Source: Bank for International Settlements, *40th Annual Report, April 1, 1969 to March 31, 1970* (Basle, Switzerland, June 1970), p. 151; and *49th Annual Report, April 1, 1978 to March 31, 1979* (June 1979), pp. 103 and 118; and other years.

The bulk of deposits received by Eurodollar banks are invested or used to make Eurodollar loans. There is much interbank lending among Eurodollar banks, even across national boundaries to areas most willing to pay for capital. Funds acquired by foreign branches of American banks have often been lent to their head offices in the United States. Fluctuations in the volume of this borrowing of Eurodollars by U.S. banks have often been related to changes in the spread between Eurodollar interest rates and interest rates on certificates of deposit in the United States. As shown in Figure 23.4, in 1968–1970 Eurodollar borrowing by U.S. banks rose sharply because Eurodollar rates for ninety-day time deposits rose to over 10 percent at the same time that Regulation Q ceilings on short-term CDs in the United States were 5½ to 6 percent. In these years, although Eurodollar deposits rose sharply, the amount of funds available to U.S. banks were not affected very much because the Eurodollar banks lent to the banks in the United States a large portion of the funds that had been shifted to them. After the suspension of Regulation Q interest rate ceilings on large CDs in 1973, when Eurodollar rates rose CD rates in the United States also rose, depositors did not shift deposits from the United States to Eurodollar banks, and there was no large expansion in Eurodollar borrowings by U.S. banks.

Figure 23.4
Eurodollar Borrowing
by United States Banks
and Eurodollar Rates,
1965–1973

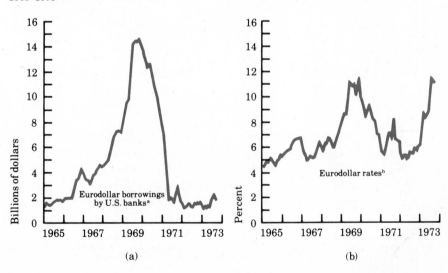

(a)   (b)

aMonthly averages of Wednesday figures. Eurodollar borrowing represents gross liabilities of United States banks to their foreign branches.
bMonthly averages of Friday figures for ninety-day Eurodollar rates.
Latest data plotted: September 1973.
Source: Federal Reserve Bank of St. Louis, *U.S. Balance of Payments Trends*, October 24, 1973, p.7

Special drawing rights

Special drawing rights are a new type of international money that was first created in 1970.[5] SDRs consist of a bookkeeping account kept by the IMF. When the IMF makes an allocation, the recorded amount of the SDRs owned by each national government is increased; when a government uses its SDRs, the amount of SDRs owned by it declines and the amount owned by the national government receiving them is increased. The allocation of SDRs to national governments is based on the government's present quota in the fund. The quota for the United States has been over 20 percent of the total. Once they have been issued, the total amount of SDRs in existence cannot be reduced by any member government.

SDRs are the first deliberately created international monetary reserves. There were approximately 3 billion SDRs issued each year from 1970 through 1972. Further issues were discontinued between 1972 and 1979 because of the very large expansion that occurred in other types of international reserves. Then, 4 billion more were issued in January 1979. Although it was initially intended that the SDR would replace gold in international reserve transactions between governments (and possibly also replace the dollar), this objective has not been realized. In 1979, the total amount of SDRs held by member countries was SDR 12.4 billion, only a very small percentage of the total amount of official international reserve money (see Table 23.1).

SDRs are used by national governments to obtain foreign exchange. They cannot be used for private transactions. The government of a country wishing to use its SDRs to purchase pounds, for example, may notify the IMF, and they then arrange for an exchange with the government of a country, such as West Germany, that has accumulated large surplus holdings of pounds. The government of the country receiving the pounds would then sell them to its importers in need of foreign exchange.

The government of a country receiving additional SDRs earns a rate of interest on the amount that it owns in excess of its allocation. The governments of countries that have used their SDRs pay interest at the same rate on the difference between their allocations of SDRs and the amount held by them. The rate of interest on SDRs is now changed periodically and was set at 6.5 percent in mid-1979. The government of a country holding a surplus is not required to accept unlimited SDRs; it may refuse to take them if its holdings are equal to two times its own allocation. The government of a country can use only 70 percent of its total SDR allotment to settle its accounts for the first three years, and must hold the remainder in reserve.

At its inception in 1970, the SDR was valued at one U.S. dollar. Since 1974, because of the shift to floating exchange rates, the value of the SDR has been set daily by the IMF according to a fixed formula which involves the exchange rates between the dollar and the currency of sixteen countries. The currencies of these countries are known as "SDR-basket" currencies. Relative weights for each currency are roughly proportional to the country's exports. The value of the SDR now fluctuates from day to day as foreign exchange rates change. In late 1979, the SDR was worth about $1.32. Because of the new method of valuing SDRs, there has been increasing use of the SDR as an international unit of account. Some securities and some internationally traded commodities such as oil may be priced in SDRs rather than in dollars. When exchange rates are floating, the SDR is attractive as a unit of account because of its broad currency composition. Interest in the SDR as a unit of account has increased because the value of the dollar has depreciated against other currencies. By denominating prices in SDRs, persons hoped to avoid losses resulting from the decline in the purchasing power of the dollar relative to other major currencies such as the deutschemark.

Summary

International transactions require foreign exchange markets in which the money of each country may be exchanged for the money of other countries. Providing markets where the money of different countries may be exchanged for one another is one of the functions of commercial banks.

The principal types of international money are gold, the dollar, and SDRs. Although deposits denominated in the currency of some other countries such as West Germany, Switzerland, Great Britain, and Japan are also used as international money, the use of the dollar predominates.

The use of gold as international reserves has declined sharply compared to its use in the nineteenth century. Since 1968, the market price of gold has fluctuated widely, and gold is no longer convertible into any major currency at a fixed price.

In 1970, special drawing rights were created by the International Monetary Fund to serve as a new type of international reserves. They could eventually replace the use of the dollar and other types of international reserves. The use of the SDR as international reserves is restricted to transactions among national governments; the volume of SDRs is still relatively small.

Notes

1. See Alan R. Holmes and Francis H. Schott, *The New York Foreign Exchange Market* (New York: Federal Reserve Bank of New York, 1965).

2. Charles P. Kindleberger, *The Dollar Shortage* (New York: John Wiley and Sons, 1950).

3. Gottfried Haberler, "Prospects for the Dollar Standard," *Lloyds Bank Review*, July 1972, pp. 1–17; reprinted by American Enterprise Institute, Reprint Number 3, August 1972.

4. See U.S. Joint Economic Committee, *Some Questions and Brief Answers About the Eurodollar Market*, A Staff Study Prepared for the Use of the Joint Economic Committee, Congress of the United States, 95th Cong., 1st sess., Joint Committee Print (Washington: United States Government Printing Office, February 7, 1977); and Milton Friedman, "The Eurodollar Market: Some First Principles," *The Morgan Guaranty Survey*, October 1969, pp. 4–14.

5. For a history of the development of SDRs, see Fritz Machlup, *Remaking the International Monetary System* (Baltimore: The Johns Hopkins Press, 1968).

Questions

23.1. Describe the role in the foreign exchange market of trading banks and foreign exchange brokers.

23.2. Explain the way in which imports affect the foreign exchange balances of the trading banks. Do the same for exports.

23.3. How are bills of exchange used by exporters in foreign exchange transactions?

23.4. What is a bankers' acceptance, and why are they used in foreign exchange transactions?

23.5. Explain the way in which exchange rates were fixed under the international gold standard.

23.6. What was the function of the "gold pool"? Why was the pool given up?

23.7. Why did the United States give up buying and selling gold at a fixed price?

23.8. How has the supply of international money in the form of foreign exchange denominated in dollars been increased?

23.9. Contrast the effect on the United States and on most other countries of deficits in their balance of payments.

23.10. What is a Eurodollar bank, and why have these banks grown in recent years?

23.11. Explain the nature of special drawing rights. What is the objective of the IMF's allocations of SDRs?

23.12. Would it be desirable to replace the dollar as an international money with the SDR?

23.13. Know the meaning and significance of the following terms and concepts: foreign exchange, foreign exchange market, bill of exchange, deficit or surplus in the balance of payments, trading bank, foreign exchange brokers, exchange rate, international gold standard, official international reserves, current account balance, trade balance, U.S. liabilities owed to foreigners, Eurodollar banks, special drawing rights (SDRs).

24

There was an important change in the international system of foreign exchange rates in 1973. Many major countries now have floating or managed exchange rates. Some other countries have fixed exchange rates.

FOREIGN EXCHANGE RATES

There are several systems for setting exchange rates between the dollar and other currencies. This chapter includes a discussion of the arguments for and against fixed exchange rates as opposed to floating exchange rates, the causes of changes in floating exchange rates, the reasons for parallel movements of prices in countries with fixed exchange rates, and the use of direct controls under systems of fixed exchange rates.

Different systems of foreign exchange rates

There are three principal systems of foreign exchange rates—fixed exchange rates, floating exchange rates, and managed exchange rates.

The IMF system of fixed exchange rates

From 1944 to 1973, the exchange rates between the dollar and the currencies of all other countries of the world were, except for a few special exceptions, fixed. The system of fixed exchange rates during this period was administered by the International Monetary Fund (IMF) which was established at an international conference in Bretton Woods, New Hampshire, in 1944, and which has its offices in Washington, D.C. In addition to administering the system of fixed exchange rates, the objective of the IMF is to promote multilateral trade among nations and the ending of direct restrictions on trade and discriminatory practices.[1] The staff of the Fund provides advice to countries having balance of payments difficulties. Its monthly publication, *International Financial Statistics,* is a major source of economic statistics on the 138 member countries.

Under the IMF system, the way in which the exchange rate between a country's currency and the dollar was fixed was for the country to buy dollars with its own currency whenever the exchange rate between its currency and the dollar fell below the fixed rate, and to sell dollars in return for its own currency whenever the exchange rate rose above the fixed rate. In 1972, for example, there was a tendency for the price of a dollar in terms of deutschemarks to fall below the fixed rate of 3.2 *DM*. At that exchange rate, receipts of dollars by West Germany were greater than that country's payments of dollars to other nations; the supply of dollars in West Germany exceeded the demand. To keep the official exchange rate for a dollar from falling to less than 3.2 *DM*, the West German Bundesbank bought dollars. By bidding up the price of dollars, such purchases kept the exchange rate for dollars at its fixed level of 3.2 *DM*.

Although West Germany was usually faced with the problem of keeping its exchange rate from falling below the fixed level, many other countries were faced with the opposite problem—of keeping their exchange rate for dollars from rising above the fixed level. In order to keep its exchange rate from rising above the fixed level, the government of each country had to maintain a reserve of international money (mostly dollars) which could be sold to keep the exchange rate from rising.

A principal problem in a system of fixed exchange rates is the possibility that a country might find itself with insufficient international reserves to keep its exchange rate from rising above the fixed level. The IMF holds a stock of currency that it has obtained from the member countries which it can lend to those member countries in need of additional international reserves. The IMF balance sheet for 1979 in Table 24.1 shows the amount of gold and currencies held by the IMF, contributed by member countries. The IMF has a quota system for determining the amount of currency to be contributed by each country, and the amount each country can borrow. Periodically, the quotas have been increased so as to provide for the expanding needs of the member countries as world trade has grown. On the liabilities side of this balance sheet, the amounts of gold and currencies received are balanced by member subscriptions.

A country borrowing from the IMF pays for the currency received by replacing it with its own currency. There is no change in the total assets of the IMF, and member subscriptions are unchanged. A country is ordinarily limited to borrowing or drawing an amount equal to its own quota; however, additional amounts may be obtained, under certain circumstances. There are different types of regular drawing rights. The *ordinary gold tranche right* is equal to 25 percent of the country's total quota and is virtually available on demand. The *credit tranche rights* are those for the remaining 75 percent of a country's quota. These rights become less available as the amount drawn increases. The amount drawn by a country is a type of credit and is expected to be paid back by the borrowing country as soon as its balance of payments position improves.

Table 24.1
International Monetary Fund: Major Balance Sheet Items, April 30, 1979 (in millions of SDRs)

Assets		Capital and Liabilities	
Gold	SDR 4,055	Member subscriptions	SDR 39,011
Currencies and securities[a]	39,567	Indebtedness	5,034
Special drawing rights	1,290	Reserves and other liabilities	1,036
Other assets	169		
Total	SDR 45,081	Total	SDR 45,081

[a]Converted into equivalent amounts of SDRs on the basis of representative rates of exchange.
Source: International Monetary Fund, *1979 Annual Report*, pp. 156 and 160.

Although changes in exchange rates were very rare under the IMF system of fixed exchange rates, the IMF system allowed a country to unilaterally change its rate in either direction by 5 percent. However, most countries typically postponed needed changes for so long that a

5 percent change was not sufficient. For larger changes, a country was expected to discuss adjustments in its exchange rate with the IMF and reach a mutual agreement with the countries primarily involved. This was to avoid a chain of competitive devaluations. Countries did not always adhere to these procedures because of the fear that any discussions concerning a possible change would become known to the public and lead to adverse speculation.

An example of a change in the exchange rate of a major currency under the IMF occurred in 1949 when Great Britain *devalued* the pound by reducing the rate of exchange from $4.00 to $2.80 a pound. In 1967, the pound was again devalued—to $2.40 a pound. An important *upward revaluation* under the IMF system occurred in 1961 when West Germany raised the value of the mark by changing its exchange rate from 23.8 U.S. cents to 24 U.S. cents per deutschemark. West Germany revalued its currency upward again in 1969 and 1971.

Floating exchange rates

When a currency is floated, the country's central bank ceases to buy and sell foreign currencies for the purpose of keeping its exchange rate within certain limits. Although floating of exchange rates was not consistent with the system agreed to by members of the IMF, there was some floating before 1973. The exchange rate between the United States and Canada floated from 1951 to 1962. It was then fixed at 92.5 American cents for one Canadian dollar; in June 1970, it was again allowed to float. In 1969, when West Germany revalued the deutschemark upward, its exchange rate was also permitted to float for almost a month before setting a new official rate of approximately 27 U.S. cents per deutschemark. In 1971, most major industrial countries permitted their exchange rates to float for several months before the Smithsonian Agreement of late 1971 set new official rates and widened allowable fluctuations of exchange rates above and below their fixed rate from 1 percent to 2¼ percent. Statistical demand and supply schedules for a country's money are difficult to estimate, and they vary over time with changing conditions. Rather than attempt to estimate the equilibrium rate, it was sometimes more effective to let the market determine the rate by permitting exchange rates to float.

In 1972, Great Britain allowed the pound to float because of continuing difficulties after the large devaluations in 1949 and 1967. After a foreign exchange crisis in 1973, West Germany, France, Japan, Switzerland, and some other countries announced they too would let their exchange rates float, and their currencies have floated ever since.[2] The IMF rules were changed to permit floating by the Jamaica Agreement of 1976. Because some countries continued to fix their exchange rates, the world exchange rate system became a mixture, with some rates floating and others fixed.

The principal reason for the shift to floating exchange rates was the need to avoid the periodic foreign exchange crises that had developed under the system of fixed exchange rates. During these crises, the central banks of countries that had surpluses in their balance of payments, primarily West Germany and Japan, would initially buy dollars to prevent the price of the dollar in terms of their currencies from falling. Persons then began to speculate that the governments of these countries would soon have to raise their official fixed exchange rate. They speculated by shifting from dollars to deutschemarks and yen, and the tendency for the value of the dollar to fall became even stronger. The amount of dollars that the central banks had to purchase in order to keep the exchange rate fixed became so large that they eventually gave up the attempt and the official exchange rate was changed.

When a currency such as the deutschemark became undervalued and it appeared that an upward revaluation might be necessary, speculators would naturally shift from holding other types of currency to holding deutschemarks. There appeared to be almost no chance that the price of the undervalued deutschemark would decline; it could either stay fixed or rise. If the price were raised, those holding deutschemarks would make a large profit. If it stayed fixed, the speculator could lose only a little—transaction costs and the interest forgone. Following the adoption of a system of floating exchange rates, the foreign exchange crises and excessive speculation that had formerly been frequent ceased. With floating exchange rates, speculation causes changes in exchange rates, and rates may either fall or rise.

A fixed exchange rate that is changed frequently is not much different from a floating exchange rate. In 1968, Brazil adopted a policy known as the *trotting peg*.[3] Under this system, the cruzeiro has usually been devalued by 1½ to 4 percent almost every month or so. These frequent adjustments in the exchange rate appear to have worked well. The necessary changes are so small that speculation is discouraged. In countries with continuous rapid inflation, frequent changes in exchange rates have the advantage of preventing the harmful effects that exchange rates which are badly out of line have on their international trade.

Figure 24.1 shows the changes in the exchange rates between the dollar and the deutschemark, the pound, and the Canadian dollar from 1972 to 1979. While the deutschemark has risen from less than 32 cents per *DM* to over 52 cents per *DM*, the value of the pound dropped sharply from $2.60 in 1972 to less than $1.70 in 1976, but then rose to $2.08 in 1979. The value of the Canadian dollar was relatively stable from 1972 to 1976, but then dropped sharply to about 85 cents in 1979.

Managed exchange rates

The floating exchange rates for Canada, West Germany, and Britain shown in Figure 24.1 have to some extent been managed so as to keep

**Figure 24.1
Exchange Rates,
1972–1979**

(a) Canada

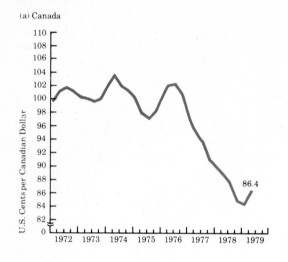

(b) Germany

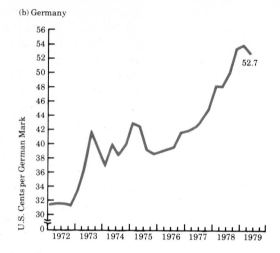

(c) United Kingdom

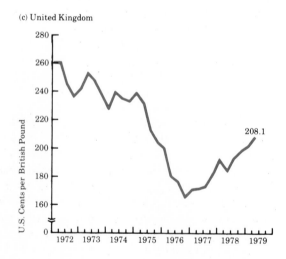

Latest data plotted: 2nd quarter, 1979.
Source: Federal Reserve Bank of St. Louis, *International Economic Conditions*, October 9, 1979, pp. 3 and 4.

the rate of exchange from rising or falling more than desired by the governments concerned. Although these exchange rates are no longer fixed, the central banks in countries with floating exchange rates still buy and sell their currency so as to influence the exchange rate. The system that has been adopted is known as a managed or dirty float.

In 1978, the Federal Reserve authorities began to take a more active role than they previously had in preventing the value of the dollar from falling relative to the deutschemark and other strong currencies. Their objectives were to "counter disorderly conditions in the exchange markets" and to halt the speculative action that they believed had reduced the value of the dollar. It was claimed that as the value of the dollar declined, the prices of imports into the United States increased and made it more difficult for the federal government to combat inflation.

Intervention in foreign exchange markets has now become a regular part of the operations of the Federal Reserve System. In the fall of 1978, several special policies to expand the capacity of the Federal Reserve banks to support the dollar were included in a new economic program announced by the federal government. The sale in foreign markets of up to $10 billion worth of U.S. Treasury securities denominated in foreign currencies was authorized. The Treasury's monthly gold sales were increased. Three billion dollars worth of deutschemarks, yen, and francs were temporarily withdrawn from the U.S. reserve account at the IMF. The sale of $2 billion worth of Special Drawing Rights to foreign central banks was authorized. The upper limit on swap arrangements with foreign central banks was expanded. All of these measures would enable the Federal Reserve banks to acquire larger amounts of foreign currencies to be used to purchase and support the dollar in foreign exchange markets.

European monetary system

In 1979, the principal countries in Western Europe agreed to a new system of exchange rates known as the European Monetary System. (An exchange rate system called the European Currency Snake preceded the European Monetary System and was similar to it.) The key feature of the European Monetary System is that the member countries have agreed to maintain fixed exchange rates between each other's currencies. This means that when the deutschemark goes up relative to the dollar, other currencies such as the Italian lira or the French franc must appreciate proportionally. Previously, when the deutschemark rose relative to the dollar, it usually also rose relative to other European currencies, and German goods were priced out of world markets compared with the goods of other European countries. This put pressure on the German authorities to inflate. Supporting the dollar in order to keep their goods competitive increased West Germany's monetary reserves and was inflationary. Under the European Monetary System, instead of supporting the dollar, the European countries as a group can let their currencies rise relative to the dollar when a higher rate of inflation in the United States than in the European countries tends to cause the dollar to decline in value. For this system to work, it will be necessary for member countries to have similar rates of inflation. Otherwise, readjustments in the exchange rates among the member countries will have to be made in order to keep their international payments in balance.

Fixed versus floating exchange rates

There is still some dispute over the desirability of floating exchange rates, as compared with fixed exchange rates, even though the type of crisis in foreign exchange markets that led countries to discard the fixing of exchange rates has been effectively avoided. The principal argument in support of fixed exchange rates is that they facilitate international trade.[4] It is feared that floating exchange rates may impede the growth of international trade, thereby placing a limit on an important factor in economic development throughout the world. Fixing exchange rates does eliminate uncertainties that exist when exchange rates are permitted to fluctuate. If the exchange rate falls between the time an exporter and an importer sign a contract and the time when the exporter is paid, the exporter would receive less in payment than he had expected. Protection against adverse movements of a free exchange rate is possible through hedging on the *forward exchange markets* that exist among the major currencies, but such markets are not available for all currencies, and the need to use markets of this type makes foreign trade complicated.

Hedging can be used as protection against losses resulting from changes in the price of foreign exchange, in the same way that *futures markets* are used for commodities.[5] With a forward exchange market, an American exporter to West Germany, for example, could protect himself against loss by simultaneously *selling* deutschemarks in the forward market. If the value of the goods sold was 100,000 *DM*, and payment was to be made on a date three months later, he would contract to sell 100,000 *DM* in the futures market on that date. Then, if the deutschemark, for example, became worth 5 percent less (if the exchange rate fell from 55.3 cents to 52.5 cents to the deutschemark), the American exporter would gain 5 percent in the forward market and lose 5 percent on the amount received for his exports. The payment of 100,00 *DM* received by the American exporter would be worth 5 percent less because of the fall in the price of the deutschemark, but in the forward market he would gain because of the decline in the price of deutschemarks in terms of dollars. On the date of payment, he would be able to purchase deutschemarks for a lower price than the price at which he had contracted to sell them.

The argument that floating rates may impede the growth of international trade would be stronger if countries had been able to keep their exchange rates fixed without periodically changing them. The frequent changes in fixed exchange rates in the early 1970s were probably more disruptive than floating exchange rates would have been because the changes were large, unexpected, and accompanied by financial crises.

It is often claimed that a major advantage of floating exchange rates is that monetary policy no longer need be used to keep international payments in balance. Instead, changes in exchange rates will keep trade in equilibrium. When exchange rates are fixed, countries are expected to correct a deficit by tightening their monetary policy. This usually has the undesirable effect of temporarily increasing unemployment. Also, a country with a payments surplus was expected to follow an easier monetary policy, probably resulting in inflation. Some countries have adopted flexible exchange rates in order to facilitate the pursuit of their own domestic goals apart from international conditions.

If exchange rates are fixed, countries having unusual trends in prices and rates of growth often end up with imbalances in their international payments and receipts. A system of fixed exchange rates requires a certain degree of harmony in the domestic policies of different countries in order to work satisfactorily. Countries such as Argentina, Brazil, and Chile that have more rapid inflation than most countries have had to change their exchange rates quite often. Inflation has reduced their receipts and increased their payments, creating deficits in their balance of payments. To correct the deficits, these countries have devalued their currency, reducing the value of their own money in relation to the money of other countries, instead of using monetary policy to bring a halt to the inflation.

Another disadvantage of a system of fixed exchange rates is that it leads to the adoption of direct controls. Countries attempt to correct the imbalances that arise by enacting restrictions over imports and exports. This hampers free trade and capital flows. A system with fixed exchange rates plus an elaborate system of direct controls may actually impede the development of international trade more than a system of flexible rates.

Some countries have sought to benefit by fixing their exchange rates so as to stimulate their exports. Before floating their currencies in 1973, Germany, Japan, and some other countries were usually reluctant to revalue their currency upward even though they were accumulating large surpluses in their balance of payments. They feared that a revaluation would harm their prospering export industries.[6] Their exchange rate policies have had the same objectives as the mercantilist policies of former times. A country can just as effectively stimulate exports, discourage imports, and create an inflow of international money through setting a favorable exchange rate as through raising tariffs or subsidizing export industries. This type of international policy had a stimulating effect on the economies of those countries, and is one of the reasons for their rapid economic growth following World War II. The inflow of international money increased their monetary base and resulted in a continuous increase in the supply of credit and money.

Graphical comparison of fixed and flexible exchange rates

Figure 24.2 illustrates both the way in which freely floating exchange rates would keep international payments and receipts in balance and the way fixed exchange rates would cause the supply of dollars to be greater than the demand. In this figure, the exchange rate between the dollar and the deutschemark is on the vertical axis. Although there are different exchange rates for each foreign currency, the price of dollars is, for convenience, stated here in terms of deutschemarks. The quantity of dollars demanded and supplied is measured on the horizontal axis. In foreign exchange markets, the amount of dollars demanded and supplied is the amount desired per year to make payments for international transactions. In this figure, at the rate of 2 *DM* per dollar the amount of dollars demanded is equal to the supply.

The demand for dollars is based on the demand for U.S. exports of

Figure 24.2
Market for Dollars

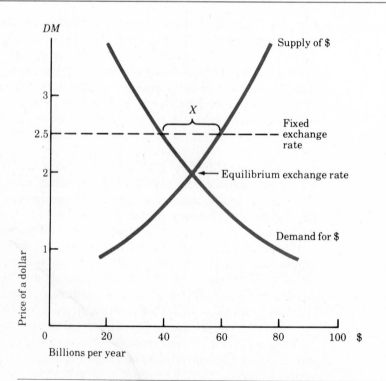

goods and services and the demand for investments (direct and port-folio) in the United States. Foreigners need to acquire dollars to pur-chase our exports and in order to make investments in the United States. If the exchange rate fell from 2.5 *DM* per dollar to 2 *DM* per dollar, for example, the demand for U.S. exports would increase. To foreigners, American goods would be cheaper, and they would almost certainly want to purchase more American exports.

Underlying the supply of dollars is the demand for imports into the United States of goods and services, transfers abroad by Americans, and investments abroad (direct and portfolio) by Americans. When Ameri-cans buy foreign goods, they pay for those imports by exchanging dol-lars for foreign currency, thus supplying dollars in the foreign exchange market. When the exchange rate changes from 2 *DM* per dollar to 3 *DM* per dollar, imports from Europe tend to increase because one dollar can now buy 3 *DM*'s worth of goods instead of 2 *DM*'s worth, and each item imported into the United States is cheaper. The upward-sloping supply schedule for dollars assumes that the demand for imports is elastic. This means that when the price of dollars changes and imports become cheaper for Americans to buy, the quantity of imports demanded in-creases enough so that, despite the lower price, the total amount spent for them is larger.

If exchange rates were free to fluctuate, there would be an equilibri-um exchange rate where the demand for dollars would be equal to the supply. If, for example, the supply of dollars were larger than the de-mand, some foreign holders of dollars would be unable to exchange them at the current exchange rate. Rather than hold dollars, they would probably be willing to sell them for fewer deutschemarks. On the other hand, if the demand for dollars exceeded the supply, some foreign importers who wanted dollars and were unable to obtain them would bid up the price, offering more deutschemarks per dollar. Only when the quantity of dollars demanded was equal to the supply would there be no tendency for the rate to change. Changes in free exchange rates would occur as a result of shifts in either the demand or supply schedule for dollars. Although one would not expect international payments to be in perfect balance in the managed floats that have existed since 1973, some degree of floating probably contributes to a better balance of international payments than would result with a system of fixed rates.

Figure 24.2 shows that if a fixed exchange rate were set above the equilibrium rate, U.S. payments would be larger than receipts, and the quantity of dollars supplied would be larger than that demanded. The surplus of dollars, X, would represent primarily the increase in dollar balances accumulated by foreigners plus, prior to 1971, the increase in their holdings of gold acquired from the United States.

If a fixed exchange rate were set below the equilibrium rate, receipts would be larger than payments, and the quantity of dollars demanded would be greater than the supply. Under these circumstances, the dollar balances owned by foreigners would diminish or, prior to 1971, the United States might have acquired larger international reserves in the form of gold.

Figure 24.2 shows that if a dollar cost 2.5 *DM*, a devaluation of the dollar—a lower price of the dollar in terms of deutschemarks—would correct an imbalance between payments and receipts. At the lower exchange rate, the demand for dollars by West Germans would increase because exports from the United States to Germany would be larger with the lower exchange rate, and the supply of dollars held by West Germans would decrease because imports into the United States from Germany would be smaller at that exchange rate. Note that there would be no improvement in the balance between international payments and receipts, if, at the same time that a currency was devalued, the demand schedule for some reason shifted to the left enough to compensate, or the supply schedule shifted to the right. The devaluation of a currency could cause the demand schedule for that currency to shift to the left, for example, if people believed that the amount of the devaluation was insufficient and that the currency would have to be devalued again in the near future.

Determination of the level of floating exchange rates

Different rates of inflation from one country to another are the major cause of changes in floating exchange rates. Suppose prices were stable in the United States but doubled in Argentina. Changes in the exchange rate between the dollar and the Argentine peso would tend to reflect the different price movements in the two countries. The price of a dollar in terms of Argentine pesos would tend to double. Instead of an exchange rate of, for example, 3.5 pesos to the dollar, the price of a dollar would rise to 7 pesos. This is known as the principle of *purchasing-power parity*. When exchange rates are free to fluctuate, people will exchange one type of money for another at rates that roughly express their relative purchasing powers.[7]

Floating exchange rates reflect the purchasing power of different types of money because the demand for a currency depends on what it will buy in real goods and services. The worth of dollars to a person in Argentina depends on the things he can buy with them. So does the worth of his own pesos. Therefore, the number of pesos that he will give for a dollar must depend on the quantity of goods and services that he can get for the pesos and for a dollar. If the exchange rate did not reflect accurately the purchasing power of each currency in the two countries, persons engaged in foreign trade would profit by taking advantage of the discrepancy. For example, if the exchange rate were 3.5 pesos per dollar and traders could (allowing for transportation costs and tariffs) purchase more wheat in the United States for a dollar than in Argentina for 3.5 pesos, they would be induced to purchase wheat in the United States and sell it in Argentina. The demand for dollars to purchase wheat in the United States would increase, causing the exchange rate to rise above 3.5 pesos per dollar to a point where this type of trade was no longer profitable.

Although many goods and services that are produced and sold in a country are not traded internationally and consequently would have little effect on exchange rates, enough are traded so that exchange rates roughly reflect varying price movements in different countries. A floating exchange rate would not be expected to vary exactly with fluctuations in the official price indexes of the two countries because the prices that affect exchange rates are not exactly the same as those included in official price indexes.

Figure 24.3 shows the relationships between exchange rate changes and the relative rates of inflation in eight major foreign countries and in the United States from 1973 to 1976. On the horizontal axis is shown the percentage change in the exchange rates between the currencies of each of these countries and the dollar. For example, Figure 24.3 shows that from 1973 to 1976 the cost of Swiss francs in terms of dollars rose 25 percent. In contrast, the cost of British pounds in terms of dollars fell 20 percent. On the vertical axis is shown the relative change in wholesale prices in these countries as compared to the change in wholesale prices in the United States. Figure 24.3 shows, for example, that in Switzerland wholesale prices rose approximately 21 percent less than in the United States, and in Great Britain, wholesale prices rose almost 40 percent more than in the United States. The relationships shown in Figure 24.3 support the purchasing-power parity theory of exchange rates. For each of the eight countries, when compared with the United States, there is a negative relationship between exchange rates and the relative rates of inflation; the larger the increase in prices in the country relative to the rate of inflation in the United States, the larger will be the decline in the country's exchange rate in terms of dollars. The smaller the increase in prices in the country relative to the rate of inflation in the United States, the larger will be the rise in the country's exchange rate in terms of dollars.

Price movements in countries with fixed exchange rates

Latin American countries that have had fixed exchange rates with the dollar and do the bulk of their trading with the United States constitute what is sometimes called a *dollar bloc.* Small countries that have had fixed exchange rates with the pound and trade extensively with Great Britain have been known as the *sterling bloc.* Price movements in the countries in the dollar bloc have roughly paralleled price movements in the United States. For example, when prices in the United States rose

Figure 24.3
Relationship between
Exchange Rate Changes
and Relative Rates of
Inflation, Eight
Countries Compared
with the United States,
March 1973 to
March 1976

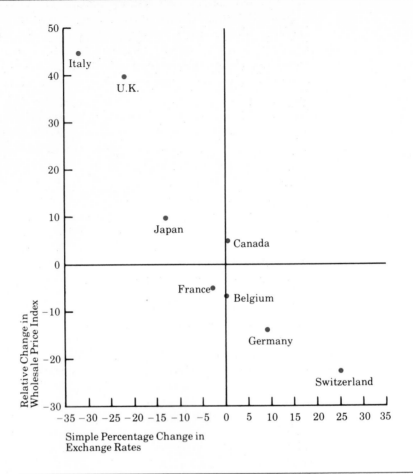

Source: Donald S. Kemp, "The U.S. Dollar in International Markets: Mid-1970 to Mid-1976," Federal Reserve Bank of St. Louis, *Review*, August 1976, p. 14.

sharply in the 1940s because of the financing of World War II, countries such as Mexico, Costa Rica, El Salvador, and Honduras experienced a somewhat similar rise in prices, as shown in Table 24.2. In none of those countries could inflation be attributed to war finance. Instead, given their fixed exchange rates with the dollar, U.S. wartime inflation was transmitted to them. When prices rose in the United States, those countries were able to sell more to the United States because their prices had not yet risen and their exchange rates were fixed. They tended to have a surplus in their balance of payments. As a result, their international reserves increased, their money supply expanded, and eventually their prices also rose. Although the exchange rates between the currencies of Costa Rica, El Salvador, and Honduras were not changed substantially from 1940 to 1950, Mexico devalued its peso in 1948 and 1949. This accounts for the relatively large rise in prices in Mexico compared to the inflation in the other countries. If Mexico had not devalued, its price trends would probably have been closer to those of the United States and of the other countries. The deflation in the United States during the Great Depression was transmitted to other countries in the same way as the World War II inflation.

Table 24.2
Cost of Living Indexes: United States, Mexico, and Three Central American Republics, 1940–1950 (1940 = 100)

Year	United States	Mexico	Costa Rica	El Salvador	Honduras
1940	100	100	100	100	100
1941	106	105	105	112	104
1942	117	123	127	115	109
1943	125	159	162	126	125
1944	127	200	170	165	135
1945	129	214	181	185	144
1946	140	268	189	182	145
1947	160	305	216	194	149
1948	173	323	222	197	151
1949	171	336	238	206	158
1950	173	359	262	241	165

Source: United Nations, *Statistical Yearbook, 1955*, pp. 446-447. Copyright, United Nations (1955). Reproduced by permission.

Although the exchange rates for many of the major currencies of the world are now floating, most small countries still have fixed exchange rates between their currency and other major currencies. It is useful for small countries to have rigid convertibility at a fixed price between their currency and the currency of a major country with which the small country trades extensively or on which it depends for capital for investment. An advantage of dependence on the currency of a large country is that, in contrast to the currency of a small country, the currency of a large country can be used directly to purchase a great diversity of goods and assets. By having a fixed exchange rate with the currency of a larger country, the smaller country will not risk a change in the value of its currency because of fluctuating exchange rates, and its currency will be more acceptable both internationally and domestically.[8] Another advantage of fixed exchange rates for a small country is that its monetary policy may be more stable when guided by its balance of payments than if left to the discretion of its central bankers.[9] When monetary policy is controlled by government officials, there is always the temptation to inflate, because inflation provides additional sources of revenue for the government. Although with fixed exchange rates inflation or deflation in the major country will be transmitted to the smaller country, if prices are stable in the major country, prices will also be stable in the smaller country. There will probably be greater stability because, in general, monetary policy has been less inflationary in larger countries than in smaller countries that are attempting to follow an independent domestic economic policy.

Direct controls

Although countries may keep their international payments in balance by letting exchange rates float or by changes in monetary policy, an alternative way is through the use of direct controls. The use of direct controls was the principal adjustment technique available to the United States when the exchange rates between the dollar and other major currencies were fixed. In the late 1960s, the United States government was frequently concerned about the outflow of gold and the excessive size of the deficits in the country's balance of payments. During this period, the federal government used monetary policy and fiscal policy primarily to influence unemployment, and it was unwilling to deemphasize this objective in order to use these policies to balance international payments. Direct controls were adopted with reluctance because the United States was also attempting to promote free international trade. Such controls include tariffs, quotas, voluntary guidelines, and limitations on investments—all types of restrictions that make the economic system less flexible, reduce competition, and prevent gains that countries might achieve through specialization and trade.

Free trade, fixed exchange rates, and stabilization of the national income cannot all be achieved simultaneously. If a country with fixed exchange rates wishes to maintain stable domestic conditions, it must use direct controls to balance its payments. If a country with fixed exchange rates has free trade, it must use monetary policy to balance its payments. But if a country has free trade and uses its techniques of control to stabilize domestic economic conditions, it must attempt to adjust its balance of payments through variations in exchange rates.

Government control of the purchase and sale of foreign exchange

In its most extreme form, the government of a country may directly control sales and purchases of foreign exchange. All exporters would be required to sell their foreign exchange to the government, and all purchases of foreign exchange would have to be from the government. Even though the demand for foreign exchange at the official exchange rate might be much larger than the supply, the government could limit the amount sold to the amount that it had available by rationing it for those imports that were considered most important. This type of regulation was characteristic of some European economies following World War II, although by 1958 most currencies had become freely exchangeable in a foreign exchange market. The dollar has always had *market convertibility*—foreigners have been able to use dollars as they wish, to buy American goods, to invest in American securities, and also to convert dollars into other currencies at the prevailing rate. This convertibility of the dollar contributed to the growth of world trade in the period since World War II.

Direct controls in the United States

The most important type of direct control used by the United States has been *restraint on foreign investment*. In March 1965, the Federal Reserve initiated a "voluntary restraint" program in which banks and other financial institutions were asked to increase their lending to foreigners in that year by only 5 percent over the amount at the end of 1964. The Department of Commerce asked more than 600 large industrial and commercial corporations engaged in international trade and investment to repatriate their liquid funds and whatever earnings they could. These companies operating in twenty-two developed countries were also asked, in 1965 and 1966, to limit dollar outflows plus reinvested earnings from the United States to 35 percent more than in the 1962–1964 base period. Investment financed by borrowing abroad was exempt, since it would not harm our balance of payments and eventually might improve it when earnings flowed back to the United States. The program was initially made voluntary, in order to make it possible to act quickly to stop the abnormally large outflow of long-term capital loans and funds for direct foreign investment, which had shown a 20 percent increase in 1964.

In 1966, the targets for banks were set at 109 percent of the 1964 base and revised guidelines for direct investment by industrial and commercial corporations were also established. In 1968, participation was made mandatory, and permissible increases above the end-of-1964 base were reduced to 3 percent for most banks. Banks were requested not to make any new loans of more than one-year maturity in Western European countries and not to renew loans when paid off. In 1968, industrial and commercial corporations operating overseas were required to observe annual limits on the transfer of new capital, repatriate a specified share of total annual earnings, and reduce short-term financial assets held abroad to their 1965–1966 level.

From 1963 to 1974, another important type of direct control over capital imports was the *interest equalization tax*. The rate of the tax was initially 15 percent of the purchase price of foreign stocks, and from about 1 percent on notes and bonds maturing in one year to 15 percent on those maturing in twenty-eight and a half years or more. The tax also applied to bank loans. Excluded from the tax were the securities of Canada and many underdeveloped countries.

The interest equalization tax and the restrictions on foreign investment were among the main factors that stimulated the development of the Eurodollar banks. By borrowing from Eurodollar banks, international corporations could avoid these restrictions. The usefulness of these controls was increasingly questioned and in 1974 they were discontinued. Both the Commerce Department's program of controls over the amount of money American companies could send abroad for new plants and equipment, and the Federal Reserve Board's program of guidelines limiting lending and investments overseas by American banks, were terminated.

There has been a variety of other programs meant to encourage American exports and discourage imports. The United States Department of Commerce has given awards to manufacturers who have expanded their exports by a sizable amount. Tourist offices have been set up in important European capitals, in order to stimulate foreign travel to the United States. The duty-free limit on foreign purchases by American tourists was reduced from $500 to $100 per person in the 1960s, explicitly for the purpose of cutting down on imports. Both the leveling off of the foreign aid program and some reductions in our armed forces stationed in foreign countries have had balance-of-payments considerations as one of their objectives. One of the justifications given in recent years for smaller quotas for imports of many basic commodities is that it would benefit our balance of payments. The way direct controls may eliminate a deficit may be illustrated by referring again to Figure 24.2. Direct controls that were designed to expand exports would reduce the gap between the supply of and demand for dollars by shifting the demand schedule to the right. Direct controls designed to reduce imports would achieve the same objective by shifting the supply schedule to the left.

Summary

The system of exchange rates is currently mixed—with some countries having floating exchange rates and other countries having fixed exchange rates. The reason for floating exchange rates is to avoid the periodic foreign exchange crises that had developed under the fixed exchange rate system. The exchange rates of the currencies that were floated have been managed and not allowed to float freely.

Floating exchange rates tend to vary inversely with the relative rates of inflation in different countries; the currency of a country with a relatively high rate of inflation, for example, would tend to fall in value relative to other currencies.

Loss of international reserves because a country's payments are larger than its receipts causes monetary tightness, and the resulting rise in interest rates, lower prices, and lower levels of income would tend to cause imports to decrease and exports to increase until they are again in balance. Changes in monetary conditions are an alternative to both fluctuations in exchange rates and direct controls as a method of keeping a country's international payments in balance.

Notes

1. For a history of the International Monetary Fund and its policies, see W. M. Scammell, *International Monetary Policy*, 2d ed. (New York: St. Martin's Press, 1961), Chapters 5 to 7. See also J. Carter Murphy, *The International Monetary System, Beyond the First Stage of Reform* (Washington, D.C.: American Enterprise Institute, 1979).

2. Robert Solomon, *The International Monetary System, 1945–1976* (New York: Harper and Row, Publishers, 1977). See also Harry G. Johnson, "The World Monetary Crisis," *Encounter*, August 1970, pp. 43–52; and Gottfried Haberler, *The Dollar-Mark-Yen Crisis, 1973*, Reprint Number 16 (Washington, D.C.: American Enterprise Institute, 1973).

3. Juergen B. Donges, *Brazil's Trotting Peg, A New Approach to Greater Exchange Rate Flexibility in Less Developed Countries* (Washington, D.C.: American Enterprise Institute, 1971).

4. For further discussion of the issues, see Meredith O. Clement, Richard L. Pfister, and Kenneth J. Rothwell, *Theoretical Issues in International Economics* (Boston: Houghton Mifflin Company, 1967), Chapter 6; and Fritz Machlup, Gottfried Haberler, Henry C. Wallich, Peter B. Kenen, and Milton Friedman, "Round Table on Exchange Rate Policy," *American Economic Review, Papers and Proceedings* 59 (May 1969), pp. 357–369.

5. Egon Sohmen, *Flexible Exchange Rates, Theory and Controversy* (Chicago: University of Chicago Press, 1961), Chapter 4.

6. Harry G. Johnson, "The International Monetary System and the Rule of Law," *Journal of Law and Economics* 15 (October 1972), pp. 289–290.

7. See Leland B. Yeager, "A Rehabilitation of Purchasing-Power Parity," *Journal of Political Economy* 66 (December 1958), pp. 516–530.

8. Harry G. Johnson, "The Case for Flexible Exchange Rates, 1969," Federal Reserve Bank of St. Louis, *Review*, June 1969, p. 16.

9. Milton Friedman, *Money and Economic Development, The Horowitz Lectures of 1972* (New York: Praeger, 1973), pp. 44–48.

Questions

24.1. What are the objectives of the International Monetary Fund?

24.2. Explain how member countries may obtain foreign exchange from the IMF.

24.3. What are the limits to the amount of foreign exchange that a country may obtain from the IMF?

24.4. Explain how the monetary authorities of a country may prevent the exchange rate between their money and the money of other countries from rising above its fixed level.

24.5. Draw a supply schedule for dollars in the foreign exchange market. Explain its shape.

24.6. Draw a demand schedule for dollars in the foreign exchange market. Explain its shape.

24.7. If exchange rates are free to fluctuate, why will exchange rates in the exchange market for dollars be where the demand for dollars is equal to the supply of dollars?

24.8. Why will a country's international payments be larger than its receipts if its fixed exchange rate is relatively high? Why will its international receipts be larger than its payments if its fixed exchange rate is relatively low?

24.9. Explain why the demand for dollars in the foreign exchange markets would increase if the exchange rate is lowered. Why would the supply of dollars decrease?

24.10. What are the arguments for a fixed exchange rate?

24.11. When Great Britain devalued the pound in 1949 and 1967, how was this expected to correct the imbalance between its payments and receipts?

24.12. What are the principal reasons the monetary authorities of some of the major countries of the world let their exchange rates float in 1973?

24.13. Following the floating of the exchange rate between the pound and the dollar, why would the cost of the pound in terms of dollars be expected to fall if prices rise more rapidly in Great Britain than in the United States?

24.14. What steps has the United States government recently taken to enable it to manage the exchange rate between the dollar and other currencies?

24.15. Explain why prices in countries with fixed exchange rates move in the same direction.

24.16. Give some examples of direct controls over international transactions and explain their purpose.

24.17. Explain, with the use of a supply and demand graph, the way in which direct controls attempt to influence a country's international payments and receipts.

24.18. Know the meaning and significance of the following terms and concepts: International Monetary Fund, fixed exchange rates, floating exchange rates, managed float, hedging, forward exchange market, devaluation, revaluation upward, trotting peg, purchasing power parity, interest equalization tax, foreign credit restraint program, dollar bloc, European Monetary System.

GLOSSARY*

aggregate demand Total spending for consumption, investment, and government goods and services. It increases as the national income increases. (17)

appreciation bonds Bonds such as Series E savings bonds which are purchased for less than their maturity value. The interest received consists of the difference between the purchase price and the redemption value of the bond. (4)

asked price The price at which dealers are willing to sell marketable United States government securities. It is slightly higher than the dealer's bid price. (4)

attrition The amount of securities not exchanged when new securities are offered to owners of maturing issues in an exchange or refunding by the United States Treasury. Attrition is the amount of cash taken by such owners. (4)

automatic stabilizers Types of taxes which automatically increase more rapidly than increases in national income—thus tending to reduce total spending in prosperity. Also, some types of federal spending may automatically decrease when national income rises. (19)

automatic transfer from savings (ATS) accounts Deposits that allow the automatic transfer of funds from savings accounts paying interest to checking accounts as needed to cover overdrafts or to maintain a minimum balance. Such accounts allow banks, in effect, to pay interest on money that would otherwise be held in checking accounts. (8)

autonomous increase in spending An increase in total spending that is not the result of an increase in income. Examples of autonomous spending are increases in spending financed from savings, increases in government spending, and increases in investment resulting from lower interest rates. (17)

average propensity to save (APS) Ratio of total saving to the national income—S/Y. (18)

balance of payments An account of international transactions of a country which give rise to money payments and receipts. (23)

bank-holding company A separate corporation that owns enough of the stock of one or more banks to exert control. Such companies are subject to special government regulations. (5)

Bank Holiday of 1933 A period of seven days during which all banks in the United States were ordered closed by President Franklin D. Roosevelt. Before the holiday there were runs on banks and many bank failures. (12)

---

*Numbers in parentheses after each item indicate the chapter in which the concept is discussed.

Bank for International Settlements Located in Basle, Switzerland. Its principal purposes are to aid governments of countries in their efforts to stabilize their exchange rates and to provide a forum for discussing international financial problems. (23)

bank reserve equation Shows factors determining the amount of member bank reserve deposits at the Federal Reserve banks. (12)

bank runs Panicky shifts by the public from bank deposits to currency. (12)

bankers' acceptance A negotiable bill of exchange on which a foreign importer's bank has written "accepted." (13)

barter Trading a good or service for another without the use of money. (2)

basis point A change in the yield of a government security of 1/100 of one percent. (4)

bill of exchange A bill written by a creditor on the person or enterprise owing him money. It is an order to pay on demand or after a specified period of time. Bills of exchange are also called drafts. (23)

bill rate The rate of return, adjusted to an annual basis, received by investors in United States Treasury bills. (4)

bills-only policy Limiting open-market operations of the Federal Reserve System to United States Treasury bills or other short-term securities. (13)

bimetallic standard Existed in the United States when the dollar was defined in terms of both a certain weight of gold and a certain weight of silver. The United States had such a standard until the Coinage Act of 1873 demonetized silver. Under the bimetallic standard, the United States Treasury would purchase gold and silver at their official prices. (3)

bond-support program The Federal Reserve's policy of keeping bond prices up and interest rates low. A bond-support program existed during and following World War II—from 1941 to 1951. (14)

book value of a share of corporate stock Based on the value of the capital accounts on the balance sheet of the corporation. It is equal to the total value of the following items listed on the balance sheet divided by the number of shares of stock outstanding: capital stock, surplus, undivided profits, and various types of reserves for contingencies. (8)

branch banking A type of banking organization in which a bank has more than one banking outlet. (5)

budget deficit Government expenditures in excess of tax receipts. (19)

business saving Retained profits of business enterprises. It may be defined to include expenditures to maintain depreciating capital equipment. (18)

capital accounts The items on the liabilities side of the balance sheet of a company showing the claims of the owners on the assets. These items include the par value of the stock issued, surplus, undivided profits, and reserves for various contingencies. (8)

capital consumption allowances The part of gross private domestic investment representing expenditures to cover depreciation. (17)

capital stock The amount of a corporation's stock outstanding. It is listed under capital accounts on the liabilities side of the balance sheet. (8)

central bank The official bank of a country which regulates monetary policy, lends to commercial banks, issues currency, regulates foreign exchange, and acts as a country's fiscal agent. (12)

central reserve cities New York and Chicago. Member banks in central reserve cities used to be required to hold higher reserve requirements than member banks in reserve cities or elsewhere. This classification was dropped in 1960. (13)

certificates of deposit (CDs) A type of time deposit which matures at an agreed-upon date and which is typically issued to business enterprises. They often have denominations of $100,000 or more and their interest rates depend upon money market conditions at time of issue. (8)

check loan A type of personal loan available to a bank depositor who has arranged with the bank to be able to borrow a limited amount of funds immediately by overdrawing his checking account. (7)

closed-end investment company Similar to a mutual fund, but the number of shares is fixed. Shares can be sold to other investors, but are not redeemed by the company. (10)

collateral Security given by a borrower to a lender as a pledge for repayment of a loan. It usually consists of real estate, an automobile, equipment, securities, or a passbook. (7)

commercial bank A bank offering checking accounts. It may also offer time and savings deposits and engage in other types of banking activities. (5)

commercial loans Short-term loans to businesses, usually for the financing of inventory. (7)

commercial loan theory of bank liquidity A theory of banking that was based on the belief that only short-term, self-liquidating loans were appropriate for banks. (7)

commercial paper Short-term securities issued mainly by industrial corporations, utilities, finance companies, and bank-holding companies. This paper usually has a maturity of less than nine months and is sold at a discount. (6)

common stocks A financial security issued by corporations to raise capital. The owners of common stock share in the profits and the control of the corporation. (16)

Comptroller of the Currency The head of the office of the Comptroller of the Currency in the United States Treasury Department. He is appointed by the President and supervises the regulation and examination of national banks. (5)

constant dollars Dollars adjusted for changes in buying power. (21)

correspondent banks Banks connected through interbank deposits. The bank holding the deposit usually provides advice and special services for the bank making the deposit. (5)

cost-push theory of inflation Attributes inflation to excessive wage demands by unions or price demands by large producers. (21)

country banks All member banks of the Federal Reserve System except those classified as central reserve city or reserve city banks. (13)

creation of deposits The ability of the commercial banking system to expand its deposits by several times the amount of an increase in its reserves. The process of creating deposits is called the multiple expansion process. (9)

credit Loans made by lenders to borrowers. Examples are bank loans; corporate, municipal, and United States government bonds; doctors' bills; and charge accounts. (1)

credit instrument A written statement that a person, business firm, or government will pay a specified amount of money either on demand or on a certain date in the future. Examples are promissory notes, bonds, and checks. (7)

credit risk The risk that the borrower may default. (4)

crowding-out effect The effect on other

lending and investing when newly created federal securities are purchased. (19)

currency Coins and paper money. (3)

currency in circulation Currency outstanding, excluding the amount held by the United States Treasury and the Federal Reserve banks. (3)

currency outstanding All United States coins and paper money issued, whether held by the U.S. Treasury, the Federal Reserve banks, or the public. It includes money held by persons and banks in foreign countries and some that has been lost or destroyed after issuance. (3)

debt management Policies of the United States Treasury designed to influence economic activity by altering the maturity of the United States government debt. (19)

defensive operations Federal Reserve open-market operations to prevent changes in items in the bank reserve equation, such as float and gold flows, from causing undesired changes in member bank reserve deposits. (13)

deferred availability cash items A liability account on a Federal Reserve bank's balance sheet. When member banks deposit checks on banks in other Federal Reserve districts in a Federal Reserve bank, this item is temporarily increased for a period of up to two days. (12)

demand deposits Deposits in a commercial bank that usually pay no interest and may be transferred by check or converted into currency at any time. (8)

demand-pull theory of inflation Attributes inflation to excessive aggregate demand. (21)

depository intermediary A financial institution that creates deposits for savers and lends the money so acquired out at interest to business firms and investors. (10)

deposits at a Federal Reserve bank Checking accounts which may be drawn on or converted into Federal Reserve notes. These accounts pay no interest. Ownership is limited to member banks, some nonmember banks, foreign governments or their central banks, the United States Treasury, and a few federal government agencies. (6)

depreciation The wearing out of plant and equipment, machinery, and housing. (17)

desired investment The amount of expenditures for capital goods that enterprises desire to make. This may be different from the actual amount of investment because of unintended declines in inventories. (21)

devaluation A rise in exchange rates, usually as a result of government action. In 1971, for example, the dollar was devalued when the dollar price of deutschemarks rose from 27.5¢ to 30.0¢. (24)

dirty float A flexible exchange rate that is being manipulated by government intervention in the foreign exchange markets. (24)

discount rate Rate charged by the Federal Reserve banks for member bank loans. (13)

discounted loan A type of loan in which the amount received by the borrower is less than the principal amount of the loan. The interest paid consists of the difference between those two amounts. (7)

disintermediation A reduction in the amount of deposits in mutual savings banks and savings and loan associations, in the value of insurance policies owned by persons, or in the activity of other financial institutions outside the commercial banking system. (10)

disposable income Personal income less the amount paid in personal taxes. (18)

dollar bloc Countries that have fixed exchange rates with the dollar and do a large portion of their foreign trading with the United States. (24)

Edge Act corporation A company chartered and regulated by the Federal Reserve System and owned by a bank to provide its customers with international banking services in another state. (5)

elastic currency An expansible supply of currency. An objective of establishing the Federal Reserve System was to create a central banking system that could provide additional currency whenever the banks and the public desired it. (12)

eligibility requirements Federal Reserve regulations determining the types of commercial bank loans or securities that can be used as collateral for loans made by Federal Reserve banks to member banks. (13)

equation of exchange An identity stating that the total amount of money multiplied by the velocity of money (the number of times money is spent per year) is equal to the annual output of goods and services sold multiplied by their prices. In symbols the equation is expressed either as $MV = PT$ or as $MV = Py$, depending on whether the annual output of goods and services sold consists of all transactions or only of those items included in the national income. (15)

equilibrium level of national income Exists when total planned spending is equal to the economy's total output. (17)

equities A type of asset providing a variable amount of income and with a variable sale price. The principal examples of equities are corporation stock and the ownership of unincorporated enterprises. (16)

Eurodollar deposits Deposits denominated in dollars, held in banks outside the United States—usually in overseas branches of American banks. (23)

even keel policy Actions of the Federal Reserve banks to keep interest rates from rising during periods of exchanges or refundings of United States Treasury securities. (14)

excess reserves Bank reserves above the amount legally required. (9)

exchange rate The price of a foreign currency in terms of a country's own money. (24)

exchange-rate band The limits below and above its official fixed exchange rate that a government permits its exchange rate to vary. (24)

Federal Deposit Insurance Corporation (FDIC) A federal deposit insurance system of which all banks belonging to the Federal Reserve System must be members, and which other banks that qualify may join. Each deposit in a bank it insures is covered up to $100,000. (5)

federal funds sold A member bank's deposits at the Federal Reserve bank that have been lent to another bank. (6)

Federal Open Market Committee An important policy-making unit of the Federal Reserve System. Its membership includes the seven members of the Board of Governors of the Federal Reserve System plus the presidents of five of the Federal Reserve banks. (11)

Federal Reserve notes The most common type of paper currency in use in the United States today. They are issued by the Federal Reserve banks and are liabilities of these banks. (3)

finance company Makes personal loans and loans to purchasers of automobiles and other consumer durables. It may also buy installment loans negotiated by automobile dealers and other retailers. (10)

financial assets Stocks, bonds, commercial paper, CDs, or similar claims to physical assets or money. (17)

financial intermediaries Financial institutions including commercial banks that create deposits or other types of liquid debt to obtain funds which are invested in less liquid types of loans and securities. (10)

flexible exchange rates Also called floating exchange rates. They are determined in a free market by demand and supply rather than fixed by the government. (24)

float The difference between cash items in process of collection (on the asset side of the Federal Reserve banks' combined statement) and deferred availability cash items. (12)

floating-rate certificates Time deposits with a maturity of 2½-years or more, no minimum denomination, and a rate of interest (announced monthly) slightly below the current rate on 2½-year U.S. government securities. These certificates were designed to make higher interest rates available to small savers. (8)

foreign credit restraint program Restrictions established by the United States between 1965 and 1974 on bank lending to foreigners, foreign investment, and the holding of liquid funds and earnings overseas by large American corporations. (24)

fractional coins Coins with denominations less than one dollar—pennies, nickels, dimes, quarters, and fifty-cent pieces. (3)

fractional reserve bank Holds reserves equal to only a portion of its deposits. (20)

free banking acts Laws of the early 1800s that made it easy for entrepreneurs to obtain charters from state government authorities to form banks. (5)

free reserves Excess reserves of member banks less their borrowings from the Federal Reserve banks. They were in the past used as a target of Federal Reserve actions. (14)

free trade International transactions unrestricted by quotas, tariffs, and direct controls. (24)

frictional unemployment Short-term unemployment caused by the search for a first job and the shifting of persons between jobs. (22)

full employment Usually considered to exist when the rate of unemployment is between 4 and 5 percent. This allows for job shifting and other types of frictional unemployment. (22)

general obligation bonds Bonds whose interest and principal will be paid primarily by future taxes collected by the state or local unit of government issuing the bond. (6)

Gibson paradox Evidence that interest rates are higher at higher rates of inflation, contradicting the theoretical expectation that a more expansionary monetary policy would lower interest rates. (21)

gliding bands A proposal to allow both the fixed exchange rate and the bands set by a government to vary periodically with the average levels of exchange rates within the bands. (24)

GNP deflator An index of the prices of the goods and services that make up the GNP. (21)

gold certificates A type of paper money which has not been in circulation in the United States since 1933 and is currently issued by the United States Treasury only to the Federal Reserve banks. They represent gold bullion owned by the United States Treasury. (3)

gold certificate account An asset on the combined balance sheet of the Federal Reserve banks representing the amount of gold certificates owned by the Federal Reserve banks. (12)

gold pool Operated in London from 1961 to 1968 by the major trading countries of the world. The pool sold gold whenever necessary to keep the price of gold from rising above $35 an ounce. (23)

gold standard Exists when a national government defines its currency in terms of a given weight of gold and will convert its currency into gold at that rate on demand. From 1879 to 1933 when the United States was on the gold standard, the United States defined the dollar as equal to approximately 1/21 of an ounce of gold. (23)

Gresham's law A very old principle stating that any type of money that becomes more valuable in some other use than as money will cease to be used as money. (3)

gross national product (GNP) The value of all the final goods and services produced in a country during the year. (17)

gross private domestic investment Purchases of newly created capital goods—machinery, plant, and houses—and changes in inventories. Includes replacements of depreciated capital goods as well as additions to the total amount of capital goods. (17)

hard-core unemployed Persons who have been out of work for at least six months. (22)

hedging Done by exporters and importers to protect themselves from possible losses from unanticipated variations in exchange rates. This is done through forward exchange markets. (24)

high-employment budget Federal revenues and expenditures estimated at the level they would have reached if there were full employment. This budget is used as a measure of the ease or tightness of fiscal policy. (19)

high-powered money The monetary base. (9)

human capital The capitalized value of the earning capacity of individuals. It is increased by education and training. (16)

income velocity The ratio of the national income during a year to the amount of money in the economy. It is equal to Y/M. (15)

index of unemployment severity Product of the unemployment rate in decimal terms and the average number of days the unemployed have been out of work in that year. (22)

indirect business taxes Sales, excise, and property taxes. (17)

individual retirement accounts (IRAs) Savings accounts (limited in amount) offering tax advantages for persons not covered by employer pension plans. (8)

inflation A decrease in the real value of a unit of money. It is usually measured by a rise in a price index covering a wide variety of goods. (21)

inflationary gap The amount by which aggregate demand exceeds the output of the economy at full employment. (21)

insolvent bank A bank whose deposit liabilities plus borrowings are larger than its assets. (8)

interbank deposit A deposit of a bank in another bank. (8)

interest equalization tax Tax imposed by the United States from 1963 to 1974 on the purchase price of foreign stocks, notes, and bonds. (24)

interest rate The annual percentage rate of return received for lending or investing money. (1)

interest risk The risk that the price of a security will fall because of a rise in interest rates. (4)

interlocking directors Directors of one company who are directors of one or more other companies in the same or a similar line of business. (5)

International Monetary Fund (IMF) An international organization whose principal purpose is to assist the governments of countries experiencing balance-of-payments difficulties. (23)

IMF credit tranche A type of borrowing rights at the International Monetary Fund. It is less available than the gold tranche right and is equal to three-fourths of a country's quota of its own currency and gold paid in to the IMF. (23)

IMF gold tranche A type of borrowing rights at the International Monetary Fund. It is equal to one-fourth of a country's quota of its own currency and gold paid to the IMF and is available almost on call. (23)

international money The types of money used in international trade—gold, dollars, pounds, and special drawing rights. (23)

L The broadest monetary aggregate. It includes *M-3* plus certain other liquid assets—savings bonds, short-term U.S. government securities, commercial paper, bankers acceptances, and some types of Eurodollars held by U.S. residents. (1)

labor force Persons working plus those seeking work. (22)

law of diminishing returns A basic principle stating that when larger amounts of one resource are used in combination with a fixed amount of another resource, eventually both the marginal productivity and the average productivity of the variable resource will get smaller. (18)

leakages Uses of the monetary base that lower the size of the money multiplier. The principal leakages result from expansions of currency in circulation, time deposits, and excess reserves. (9)

legal tender Legally approved types of money which must be accepted in payment of debts and which the government will accept in discharge of debts and for taxes due to itself. (2)

line of credit An agreement by a bank to lend over a period of time in the future up to a given limit to a business borrower without detailed negotiations. (7)

liquid assets Assets that may be converted into money quickly and without loss in nominal value. (2)

liquidity preference The demand for money at different interest rates. The demand for money tends to be larger at lower rates of interest. (18)

liquidity trap May exist when interest rates are so low that persons will not invest additional money holdings in securities because of the expectation that security prices will fall as interest rates rise. (18)

managed float A flexible exchange rate that is being manipulated by government intervention in the foreign exchange markets. (24)

managed liabilities Certain sources of funds that a commercial bank can expand on its own initiative—large time deposits, Eurodollar borrowings, securities repurchase agreements, and federal funds borrowed. (8 and 13)

margin requirement Percentage of the purchase price of stocks or bonds that a customer must pay when there is borrowing for the purchase. (7 and 13)

marginal product of capital The addition to annual income that a business firm expects for a dollar of additional investment. (18)

marginal propensity to consume (MPC) The percentage of additional income that persons spend for consumption—$\Delta C / \Delta Y$. (17)

marketability Exists when a security can be sold quickly with relatively low transactions costs and at a price regularly determined in active markets. (6)

marketable United States government security One that can be transferred from one owner to another by sale. (4)

maturity date The date on which the principal value of a bond, loan, savings certificate, or similar debt instrument will be repaid to the lender. (4)

medium of exchange Money used to purchase goods and services and to pay debts. (2)

mercantilist policies Governmental policies aimed at maintaining an excess of exports over imports. (24)

mint ratio The ratio of the official value of one unit of gold (usually one ounce) to the same weight of silver when a country is on a bimetallic standard. (3)

monetary aggregates A type of target used to guide Federal Reserve policy. The principal monetary aggregates used are total member bank reserves, the monetary base, *M-1A*, *M-1B*, and *M-2*. (14)

monetary base (H) Total member bank reserve deposits with the Federal Reserve banks plus currency in circulation. The monetary base is also called high-powered money. (9)

monetary reform A conversion from one unit of account to another, involving a reduction in the quantity of money. (2)

monetary system The institutional arrangements for supplying the economy with money. (1)

monetary theory of inflation Attributes inflation to excessive increases in the money supply per unit of output. (21)

money market certificates A type of time deposit with a maturity of six months, a minimum denomination of $10,000, and a rate of interest equal to the six-month Treasury bill rate at time of issue. (8)

money market mutual fund A type of investment company that holds CDs, large denomination Treasury bills, commerical paper, or other short-term credit instruments. (10)

money multiplier (*m*) The ratio of the amount of money to the monetary base. Also called the expansion ratio. (9)

M-1A Demand deposits in commercial banks (excluding deposits owned by domestic banks, foreign banks, and the U.S. government) plus currency outside banks. (1)

M-1B *M-1A* plus NOW accounts and ATS accounts at commercial banks; and demand deposits, NOW accounts, ATS accounts, and credit union share draft balances at thrift institutions. (1)

M-2 *M-1B* plus savings and small denomination time deposits (under $100,000) at all depository institutions, money market mutual fund shares, overnight repurchase agreements (RPs) issued by commercial banks, and certain overnight Eurodollars held by U.S. residents. (1)

M-3 *M-2* plus large-denomination time deposits in all depository institutions, and term RPs issued by commercial banks and savings and loan associations. (1)

municipal bonds Bonds issued by states and by units of local government. Interest from municipal bonds is exempt from federal income taxes. (6)

mutual fund An open-end investment company that offers to sell an unlimited amount of its shares to obtain funds to invest—usually in corporation stock. The company redeems its shares on demand at a price that reflects the value of its asset holdings. (10)

national bank One that has received its charter from the United States Comptroller of the Currency. National banks have been required to be members of the Federal Reserve System since 1914 and to be insured by the FDIC since 1933. (5)

national bank notes A major type of paper currency used in the United States from 1863 until 1914. They were issued by national banks in accordance with the terms of the national bank acts of 1863 and 1864, and were liabilities of the banks that issued them. (3)

national debt The total amount of United States government securities outstanding. The federal government issues securities as a means of borrowing to meet its expenditures when the federal budget is in deficit. (4)

national income (NI) The total amount of wages, proprietors' income, rental income, net interest, and corporation profits received per year. It is equal to gross national product less the cost of depreciation and less the total amount of indirect business taxes. (17)

national income accounts budget A record of the expenditures and receipts of the federal government, adjusted in accordance with the concept of expenditures for goods and services used in the national income accounts. (19)

near money Liquid assets other than money. (2)

negotiable Applies to a credit instrument that meets certain legal standards that assure a buyer a perfect title. Some negotiable instruments are payable to the bearer and others are payable to a specific person and must be endorsed. (7)

net borrowed reserves A negative level of free reserves. (14)

net investment Gross private domestic investment minus capital expenditures to cover depreciation. (18)

net monetary creditor A person whose monetary assets exceed his monetary debts. Also applicable to business enterprises. (21)

net monetary debtor A person whose monetary debts exceed his monetary assets. Also applicable to business enterprises. (21)

net national product Gross national product less the cost of depreciation. (15)

net wealth The value of a person's total assets minus his debts. (21)

noncompetitive bidders Investors who do not submit a bid price, but offer to pay the average price of accepted competitive bids in an auction of United States Treasury bills. The amount sold to a noncompetitive bidder is limited to $200,000. (4)

nonpersonal time deposits Those not owned by individuals. They are owned mainly by businesses. (13)

NOW accounts Interest-earning deposits using negotiable orders of withdrawal that are similar to checks. (8)

100% reserve bank Holds an amount of reserves equal to its deposits. (20)

operation twist Federal Reserve open-market operations attempting to change the relative yields of short-term and long-term United States government securities. These operations were important in the early 1960s. (13)

OECD Organization for Economic Cooperation and Development, an international organization set up in Paris in 1960 to further economic progress and trade. Twenty-four nations belong. (24)

overdraft A negative balance in a checking account. Overdrafts are sometimes treated like loans, the depositor being charged interest on the amount overdrawn. (7)

permanent income The level of income expected by a person. When incomes are rising, permanent income tends to be less than the income actually received. (18)

personal consumption expenditures Spending for food, clothing, housing, transportation, and entertainment. (17)

Phillips curve A curve showing lower annual percentage increases in wage rates at higher rates of unemployment. (22)

Pigou effect The effect on total spending of a change in real cash balances, M/P. (18)

portfolio The real and financial assets owned by a person or financial institution. (17)

price index A measure of changes in prices in general. (21)

prime rate The lowest interest rate charged by banks on short-term business loans. Announcements of changes in the prime rate by large banks are widely publicized. (7)

purchasing-power parity The principle that freely fluctuating exchange rates will vary so that the currencies of different countries have roughly similar purchasing power. (24)

pure commodity standard A monetary system in which the only type of money consists of a commodity that circulates. (20)

rationing A system of distributing goods and services in which there is a maximum limit to the quantity of a good or service that a consuming unit can purchase or obtain. (2)

real cash balances The quantity of money relative to the level of prices. Real cash balances rise when prices fall. In symbols it is M/P. (16)

real interest rates Nominal interest rates less the rate of inflation. (14)

real value of money What a given quantity of money will purchase. It varies inversely with prices. (1)

refunding An exchange in which new United States government securities are offered to owners of maturing United States government securities. (4)

Regulation Q A Federal Reserve regulation that prohibited the payment of interest on checking accounts and set interest rate ceilings for banks from 1933 to 1980. Legislation passed in 1980 allows interest on certain checking accounts and phases out interest rate ceilings over a six-year period. (13)

remit at par Policy required of member banks of the Federal Reserve System. Banks that remit at par do not deduct an exchange charge on checks written by their depositors and returned for payment by the recipient of the check through clearing channels. (11)

repurchase agreements at commercial banks (RPs) Business funds lent to commercial banks under an agreement that can be terminated at any time and secured by U.S. government securities. (8)

required reserves The percentage of a bank's deposits and other sources of funds that must be held in the form of certain liquid assets. (9 and 13)

reserve cities Certain large cities designated by the Federal Reserve System as areas in which member banks were required to hold higher reserve requirements than banks in communities that were less important as financial centers. After 1972 when a new policy for reserve requirements based on bank size rather than geographical location was adopted, this classification ceased to be important. (13)

revenue bonds The interest and principal of these bonds are paid from earnings of the state or local government project financed. They are secured by the property of the enterprise. (6)

savings bonds A type of United States government security. They are nonmarketable and available in both appreciation and current-income forms. (4)

savings certificates A type of time deposit. The owner receives a certificate showing the amount deposited, interest rate, maturity date, and other terms. They are sold only to individuals, nonprofit organizations, and fiduciaries. (8)

savings deposits Interest-bearing time deposits with no set maturity date. The principal type is called passbook deposits. They cannot legally be withdrawn without written notice thirty days or more in advance, but they are usually convertible into currency or demand deposits on demand. (8)

secondary reserves Liquid assets held by banks in excess of their legally required reserves. These usually consist of short-term United States government securities, commercial paper, or federal funds sold. (6)

seigniorage The profit that the treasury of a country makes on its coinage. It is the difference between the nominal value of the coin and its cost of production. (3)

selective instruments of control Federal Reserve controls that affect the use of a particular type of credit. Examples are margin requirements on loans for purchasing corporate stock, the regulation of interest rates on time deposits, and marginal reserve requirements on credit extended by some retailers and others. (13)

silver certificates Treasury-issued paper currency in process of retirement since 1968. For each dollar of silver certificates issued, three-quarters of an ounce of silver was stored at West Point. (3)

special drawing rights (SDRs) A new type of international money usable as international reserves. (23)

standard silver dollars Dollar coins that contain three-quarters of an ounce of silver. Following the rise in the price of silver above $1.29 an ounce in the 1960s, they became collectors' items and were no longer used as a medium of exchange. (3)

state bank A bank that has received its charter from its state government. (5)

state bank notes A major type of paper currency used in the United States prior to 1865. They were issued by state-chartered banks and were liabilities of the banks. The issuance of state bank notes was discontinued after 1865 as a result of the levying of a federal tax on them. (3)

sterilization of gold flows A central bank policy of taking actions to offset the effect of gold flows on the quantity of bank reserves. (21)

sterling bloc Countries that have fixed exchange rates with the pound and do a large portion of their trading with Great Britain. (24)

structuralist theory of inflation Attributes inflation to economic growth combined with supply inelasticities usually of food and imports. (21)

subscription An offering of new issues of United States Treasury notes or bonds at announced coupon rates. (4)

surplus A type of capital account on a company's balance sheet. Together with undivided profits, it shows the amount that the total assets of a company exceed its total liabilities, capital stock, and various reserves for contingencies. When surplus is increased by the directors of a company, the undivided profits are reduced by the same amount. (8)

surplus, balance of payments Excess of international receipts over payments of a country. (23)

surplus, budget Excess of revenues over expenditures in the federal budget. (19)

swap arrangements Used between governments of countries to obtain foreign currencies on call through the Bank for International Settlements. (23)

tax and loan account Demand notes issued by a commercial bank or other depository institution to the United States Treasury. (8)

tax-anticipation bills United States Treasury bills that mature one week after federal tax-payment dates and are accepted in payment for federal taxes a week before their maturity date at their maturity value. (4)

tax-exempt securities Municipal bonds. Under federal income tax laws their interest payments are not taxable. (6)

ten-percent rule A requirement used by bank examiners that banks keep capital accounts equal to approximately 10 percent of their deposit liabilities. (8)

thrift institutions Mutual savings banks, savings and loan associations, and credit unions. (10)

time deposits Interest-bearing bank deposits. These include savings deposits, savings certificates, and certificates of deposit. Types having a stated maturity date usually cannot be withdrawn before maturity without penalty. (8)

token coins Coins whose metal content is worth less than their face value. (3)

transaction account Bank demand deposits, interest-bearing NOW accounts, ATS accounts, credit union share draft accounts, and telephone transfers and other accounts subject to transfer to third parties. (8, 10, and 13)

transactions costs The costs of shifting from one type of asset to another or to money. They include the fees paid to brokers or dealers handling the transaction as well as the value of any time and effort required of the owner. (16)

transactions velocity The number of times per year that money changes hands and is used for all types of monetary transactions. (15)

transfer payments Personal gifts and government welfare payments. They are payments of money that are not made in return for any services or for the use of real property. (17)

transfer payments between countries Private gifts of money to persons and organizations in foreign countries plus government aid given under the foreign aid program. (23)

Treasury bills A short-term, marketable United States government security sold at a discount. They are typically issued in maturities of 3 months, 6 months, 9 months, and 1 year. They are always sold by auction when issued. (4)

Treasury cash holdings Coins and paper money held by the United States Treasury. There tends to be an inverse relationship between Treasury cash holdings and member bank reserve deposits at the Federal Reserve banks. (12)

Treasury-Federal Reserve Accord An agreement reached in 1951 to drop the Federal Reserve's bond-support program that had been initiated during World War II. (14)

Treasury notes A type of marketable United States government security having an initial maturity of one to ten years. There is no legal ceiling to the coupon rates on these notes. (4)

trotting peg Fixed exchange rates that are frequently changed—as used by Brazil. (24)

turnover of demand deposits Total value of checks written during the year divided by the average quantity of demand deposits—used as a rough measure of transactions velocity. (15)

undivided profits A type of capital account on the balance sheet of a company. It is similar to surplus. Undivided profits increase when the total assets of the company expand more than the sum of its liabilities, the par value of its capital stock outstanding, surplus, and the amount of the various reserves for contingencies. (8)

unemployment rate The percentage of the labor force that is not working. (22)

unified budget The record of all the expenditures and receipts of the federal government, including the trust accounts. (19)

unit of account Used to measure and compare the value of goods or services. Prices are expressed in the unit of account. (2)

unit bank A bank without branches. (5)

United States liquid liabilities to foreigners Foreign holdings primarily of demand and time deposits in American banks plus their holdings of nonmarketable and short-term marketable United States government securities. (23)

U.S. notes A type of paper money initially issued by the United States Treasury during the Civil War. They were popularly called greenbacks. (3)

unsecured loan A loan not backed by collateral. (7)

user cost of capital The annual cost of investing a dollar in physical capital. It is the sum of the annual real interest rate and the depreciation rate. (18)

value added The amount spent by a business enterprise for labor and the use of capital. (16)

variable-rate mortgages Real estate loans whose interest rates are changed periodically in line with a cost-of-funds index based on other market rates of interest. (7)

wage-price guidelines Goals set by the federal government to limit increases in wages and prices. (22)

world liquidity Total amount of international money available for international trade and for settling accounts between nations. (24)

yield curve A curve showing the comparative yields on a certain date of United States Treasury securities of different maturities. (4)

NAME INDEX

Ahn, Chang Shick, 212
Alchian, Armen A., 29, 465
Alhadeff, David A., 96
Aliber, Robert Z., 490
Allen, William R., 465
Andersen, Leonall C., 405, 416
Ando, Albert, 370
Aschheim, Joseph, 212, 280–1

Banfield, Edward C., 142
Bagehot, Walter, 238
Becker, Gary S., 344
Beebe, Jack, 212
Bell, Frederick W., 96
Benston, George J., 96, 162, 211
Bloch, Ernest, 212
Boczar, Gregory E., 97
Break, George, 142
Brothers, Dwight S., 442
Brunner, Karl, 302, 345
Bryan, William Jennings, 37
Buchanan, James M., 233
Budin, Morris, 141
Burger, Albert E., 233, 301, 442
Burns, Arthur F., 221, 233

Cagan, Phillip, 184, 190, 310, 313, 324, 345, 368
Campbell, Colin D., 28, 212, 345
Campos, Roberto de Oliveira, 465
Carter, Jimmy, 94, 221, 279
Caruthers, Osgood, 29
Chandler, Lester V., 233, 281, 345
Chase, Samuel B., Jr., 95
Cipolla, Carlo M., 28, 53
Clarkson, Kenneth W., 491
Clement, Meredith O., 535
Corrigan, E. Gerald, 416
Crouch, Robert L., 392
Culbertson, John M., 212, 417

Darby, Michael R., 391
D'Arista, Jane, 96
Darius the Great, 34
Darnell, Jerome C., 97
Deaver, John V., 345
Dew, Kurt, 302
Dewald, William G., 302
Donges, Juergen B., 535
Dornbusch, Rudiger, 391
Duesenberry, James, 370

Eckstein, Otto, 280, 438, 442
Eisenhower, Dwight D., 221
Estey, Marten, 490
Eucken, Walter, 490

Fallenbuchl, Zbigniew M., 142
Fama, Eugene F., 141
Fand, David I., 190
Feige, Edgar L., 53, 491
Feldstein, Martin S., 491
Felix, David, 465
Fischer, Stanley, 391
Fisher, Irving, 317–18, 323, 325, 345, 435, 440, 442
Fisher, Lawrence, 330, 344
Ford, Gerald R., 221
Fousek, Peter G., 281
Francis, Darryl R., 465
Freeman, Richard B., 344
Friedman, Benjamin, 417
Friedman, Milton, 14, 53, 188, 280–1, 302, 306–15, 320, 344–5, 370, 391, 417, 435–7, 442, 465, 490–1, 535
Friend, Irwin, 211
Frye, Richard N., 53

Galbraith, J. Kenneth, 141, 220
Gambs, Carl M., 142
Gann, Thomas, 29
Garbade, Kenneth D., 96
Geertz, Clifford, 212
Gibson, William E., 392
Gilbert, R. Alton, 95, 162–3, 268
Goldfeld, Stephen M., 345
Goldsmith, Raymond W., 211
Golembe, Carter H., 96–7
Gordon, Robert J., 391
Graham, Frank D., 442
Gresham, Thomas, 35, 45
Griffiths, Brian, 442
Grunwald, Joseph, 465
Gurley, John G., 29
Guttentag, Jack M., 212, 302
Guttmann, Peter M., 53

Haberler, Gottfried, 514, 535
Halcrow, Harold G., 142
Hamilton, Mary T., 344
Hammond, Bray, 14, 95
Hardy, Charles O., 233, 442
Harris, Seymour, 220
Hawk, William A., 75
Heller, Walter W., 417
Hershey, Robert D., Jr., 143
Hester, Donald D., 95
Hilton, George W., 29
Holland, Robert C., 96
Holmes, Alan R., 513
Horvitz, Paul M., 96
Horwich, George, 184, 190
Hubbard, Leonard E., 29
Hurley, Evelyn M., 119, 122, 212

Jackson, Andrew, 216
Jacoby, Neil H., 142
Jianakoplus, Nancy A., 465
Johnson, D. Gale, 212
Johnson, Harry G., 535
Johnson Lyndon B., 220–1
Johnston, Robert, 233
Jordan, Jerry L., 405, 416

Kareken, John, 280
Kemmerer, Edwin W., 53, 424
Kemp, Donald S., 530
Kenen, Peter B., 535
Kennedy, John F., 221, 479
Kessel, Reuben A., 465
Keynes, John Maynard, 23, 27, 342, 464–5
Kindleberger, Charles P., 514
Klebaner, Benjamin J., 233
Kuznets, Simon, 325

Laidler, David E. W., 212, 345, 392
Lance, Bert, 94
Lang, Richard W., 293–5
Latané, Henry A., 334–5
Lees, Francis A., 96
Lerner, Eugene M., 53
Levy, Michael E., 416
Lindsay, Robert, 212
Lorie, James H., 330, 344
Lovati, Jean M., 95, 162, 211, 484
Luttrell, Clifton B., 142

Machlup, Fritz, 514, 535
Martin, William McChesney, 221, 313
Mayer, Thomas, 233, 392, 442
McCulloch, J. Huston, 29, 464, 491
McKinley, William, 37
Meek, Paul, 280
Meigs, A. James, 302, 370, 417
Meiners, Roger E., 491
Meiselman, David, 345
Meltzer, Allan H., 302, 345, 392
Mendershausen, Horst, 29
Metz, Robert, 122
Miller, G. William, 221
Mints, Lloyd W., 141
Modigliani, Franco, 370
Moore, Geoffrey H., 324
Morrison, George R., 190
Mudd, Douglas R., 233
Murphy, J. Carter, 535
Murphy Neil B., 96

Niblack, William C., 96
Nixon, Richard M., 221, 480
Nordhaus, William, 464

Okun, Arthur M., 417

Parks, Robert H., 121
Patman, Wright, 219, 224
Pfister, Richard L., 535
Phillips, A. W., 487, 491
Pigou, A. C., 390–2
Polakoff, Murray E., 141
Polo, Marco, 34, 53
Poole, William, 280, 302
Powell, Raymond P., 142

Quenneville, Kathleen, 142

Rasche, Robert H., 442
Reinfeld, Fred, 53
Riedy, Mark J., 142
Robertson, Ross M., 53, 95, 96, 232
Roosevelt, Franklin D., 87, 438, 478, 539
Rothwell, Kenneth J., 535

Saving, Thomas R., 302
Saulnier, Robert J., 142
Scammell, W. M., 535
Schotland, Roy A., 97
Schott, Francis H., 513
Schwartz, Anna J., 14, 188, 281, 302, 306–12, 320, 345, 370, 437
Selden, Richard T., 325
Shapiro, Eli, 75
Shaw, Edward S., 211
Shaw, Leslie M., 217
Shelton, Karl M., 122
Shoven, John, 464
Shultz, George P., 490
Silber, William L., 96
Simmons, Edward C., 280
Simons, Henry C., 435, 442
Smith, Hedrick, 29
Smith, Warren L., 280
Sohmen, Egon, 490, 535
Solis, Leopoldo, 442
Solomon, Ezra, 75
Solomon, Robert, 535
Spencer, Roger W., 417
Spengler, Joseph J., 53
Sprinkel Beryl W., 317, 417
Stalin, Joseph, 29
Stein, Herbert, 233, 416
Stelzer, Irwin M., 96
Stewart, Kenneth, 416
Stigum, Marcia, 162
Strong, Benjamin, 218, 430

Tax, Sol, 29
Teck, Alan, 211
Thurow, Lester C., 416
Tobin, James, 442
Truman, Harry S., 221
Tullock, Gordon C., 28, 53

Viorst, Milton, 417
Volker, Paul A., 221

Wallace, Henry A., 416
Wallich, Henry C., 535
Walsh, Joan, 211
Warburton, Clark, 320
Weintraub, Robert E., 190, 345
White, Horace, 28
White, William L., 75
Whittlesey, Charles R., 53, 280
Wiedemer, John P., 142, 212
Willis, H. Parker, 23
Willis, Parker B., 121
Wilson, Woodrow, 217
Woodworth, G. Walter, 121, 141, 233

Yeager, Leland B., 535
Yohe, William P., 417

SUBJECT INDEX

Acceptances, 229–230, 244–245
Accord, Treasury-Federal Reserve in 1951, 287, 551
Advances, 229
Advisory Committee on Monetary Statistics, 6
Aggregate demand and supply, 292, 353–362, 470–471, 539
Agricultural Credit Act of 1923, 204
Aldrich-Vreeland Act of 1908, 217
AMTRAK, 231
Anthony, Susan B., dollars, 51
Attrition, 62, 415, 539
Automatic stabilizers, 397, 539
Automatic transfer service accounts (ATS accounts), 146, 198, 271, 539
Autonomous spending, 356–360, 539

Balance of payments, adjustment mechanisms,
  changes in fixed exchange rates, 519–520
    devaluations, 501, 520, 542
    direct controls over imports and exports, 89, 525, 532–534
    flexible exchange rates, 430, 520–521, 524–529, 544–546
    under gold standard, 422–423
    monetary regulation, 430–431, 525
    upward revaluations, 520, 525
  deficits and surpluses, 430–431, 547, 550
  United States in 1978, 506–508
  See also International Monetary Fund; Reserves, international
Bank for International Settlements, 231, 540
Bank holding companies, 92–93, 119–120, 539
Bank mergers, 91
Bank reserve equation, 241–256, 540
"Bank Secrecy Act" of 1970, 52
Bankers' acceptances, 500, 540
Banking Act of 1933, 92, 195
  of 1935, 218–219, 224, 262, 270
Banking holiday of 1933, 241, 438, 539
Banks for Cooperatives, 137, 203
Barter, 21–22, 49, 540
  in Germany after World War II, 21
Basis point, 65, 540
Bid price, computation of, 66–67
Bill rate, 61, 540
Bills of exchange, 499, 540
"Bills only" policy, 264, 540
Bimetallic standard, 35–36, 540
Black markets (see Price controls, evasion)
Bland-Allison Act, 37
Board of Governors of the Federal Reserve System, 182, 218–222, 224, 226
Bond support program from 1941 to 1951, 287–288, 540, 541
Bonds, corporate, 120, 329
Bonds, government (see Government securities; also see Municipal bonds)
Branch banking, 87–89, 540
Budget, federal, 397, 401–405, 540
  deficit financing, 398–400
    by borrowing, 399, 405–408, 410
    by money creation, 399–400, 409
  high-employment, 403, 545
  national income accounts, 402, 548
  unified, 402, 551

Business cycles, changes in money supply during, 306–310, 450
  velocity of money in, 321–322

Capital accounts, commercial banks, 156–159, 540
  Federal Reserve banks, 231–232
Capital consumption allowances (see Depreciation)
Capital-deposit ratio, 158, 551
Capital gains tax, 462
Capital notes, 156
Capital requirements, 83
  See also Commercial banks, government regulation of
Cash in vault (see Commercial banks, assets)
Cash items in process of collection, 106–109, 245
Central banks, early U.S. banks acting as, 216
  foreign, 216, 231
  functions of, 238–241, 427–8, 540
  opposition to in U.S., 216–218
Central reserve cities, 269–270, 540
Certificates, floating rate, 151
  money market, 115, 150, 202
Certificates of deposit (CDs), 113, 151, 541
  growth of, 152
  ownership, 110
Charters, bank, 80–83
Checks, acceptability, 24, 49
  certified, 155
  clearing of, 84, 230–231, 245–246
  See also Cash items in process of collection
Civil War, money creation during, 38
  See also United States notes
Clayton Act, 94
Clearing systems, 225, 245–246
Coinage Act of 1792, 35
  of 1873, 36
  of 1965 and 1970, 40
Coins, 544
  demand for, 40–41
  early U.S., 35
  early use of, 34
  newly minted, 41, 251
  problems with supply of, 36, 39–41
  token, 36
  use of foreign in U.S., 35–36
Collateral, 127, 278, 541
Commercial banks, 541
  assets, 102–121, 269
  balance sheet, 102–103
  borrowings from Federal Reserve banks, 155–156, 239, 288–291
    collateral for, 278–279
    emergency provisions for, 210, 229, 265
    pressure for repayment, 265–266, 289
  branches, 87–89
    foreign, 87, 89–91
  capital accounts, 156–159, 540
  capital-deposit ratio, 158, 551
  charters, 80–83
  competition, 82–83
  correspondent banks, 84, 93, 110, 225, 497, 499, 541
  deposits (see Deposits, commercial bank)

directors, 85, 94
early U.S., 80–83
examinations, 81–82, 84–85, 428, 441
failures, 82, 159–161, 188–189, 238–241, 369, 437
  in Canada in Great Depression, 189
foreign in U.S., 87
government regulation, 81–86, 92–93
interlocking directors, 94
as intermediaries, 126–127, 194
investments, 110–121
  cyclical variations in, 110–111
liabilities, 146–156
  managed, 271, 546
liquidity, 110–113, 156, 269
loans, 127–137
  cyclical variations in, 110–111
  limits on size, 86, 94
managed liabilities, 271, 546
member banks, 83–87, 225–226
mergers, 91
national banks, 82–83, 225–226, 547
nonmember banks, 83–84, 210
nonpar, 84, 106, 549
numbers of, 80–81
officers, 85, 94
profitability, 88–89
repurchase agreements, 152–154, 549
reserve for bad loans, 159
runs on, 87, 189, 238, 369, 437, 540
size, 80–81
state banks, 82–84, 87, 550
  before Civil War, 80–82
  Federal Reserve membership, 83, 225
  notes, 46–47, 550
stock, 83, 157, 540
surplus, 157, 550
taxation of, 115–116
undivided profits, 157, 160, 551
unit banks, 87, 552
See also Loans, Reserve requirements
Commercial loan theory of banking (real bills doctrine), 130, 279, 541
Commercial paper, 118–120, 541
  issued by bank holding companies, 93, 119–120
    reserve requirements for, 271
  ownership, 118–120
  rates on, 119–120
  ratings, 119
Comptroller of the Currency, 85–86, 88–89, 138, 217, 219, 541, 547
COMSAT, 231
Confederacy, currency of, 38
Congress, relationship to Federal Reserve System, 218–220
Constitution, U.S., 13
Consumer price index, 431, 447
  stabilization of, proposed, 435
Consumerist credit laws, 86, 138–141, 222
Correspondent banks, 84, 93, 110, 225, 497, 499, 541
Cost-push inflation, 454–455, 541
Council of Economic Advisers, 219–220, 396
Counterfeiting, 46
Country banks, 269, 541
Credit, 10–11, 541
  allocation of, 126–128
  consumer, 133–135, 197–198, 202–203, 279
  variations in volume of, 10–11, 299
Credit cards, 136, 279
Credit Control Act of 1969, 279
Credit instruments, 10, 548
Credit unions, 194, 197–198
"Crowding out" effect, 410, 541
Currency, 34, 542
  in circulation, 41–42, 251–252, 542
  confederate, 38
  Continental, 13, 38, 399
  cyclical fluctuations, 39–40, 48–49
  demand for, 48–50
  denominations, 50–51
  elasticity of supply, 239, 543
  Federal Reserve bank notes, 47
  Federal Reserve notes, 39, 47, 543

greenbacks (see U.S. notes)
national bank notes, 46–47, 426, 547
outstanding 41–42, 542
paper, 13, 34–35, 39, 45–47, 50–51
per family, 50
in process of retirement, 39, 45–47
seasonal fluctuations, 48–49
silver certificates, 13, 37, 45–46, 550
state bank notes, 13, 46–47, 426, 550
transactions, reporting of, 51–52
Treasury notes of 1890, 37
United States notes, 13, 37–39, 251, 552
Currency Act of 1863, 46, 82, 216
Currency-deposit ratio, 48, 178, 310–311
  and changes in money supply, 177–178, 310–311
  in Great Depression, 437
Currency, foreign, stabilization operations, 230, 246, 265, 508, 523
Debentures, 120
Debt, types of, 58–59, 413
  See also Government securities
Debt management, 412–414, 542
Deferred availability cash items, 231, 245, 542
Deficits, budget (see Budget, federal)
Deficits, in balance of payments (see Balance of payments)
Demand, aggregate, 353–362, 470–471
  effects of changes in money stock on, 292
Depository Institutions Deregulation and Monetary Control Act of
    1980, 84, 132, 146, 148, 182, 199, 209, 225
Deposits, commercial bank, creation of, 126, 168–189
    limits to, 168–177
  demand deposits, 23–24, 146–147, 542
    interest payments on, 146, 277, 549
    ownership of, 147
    service fees, 146–147
    turnover of, 322–323, 551
  Eurodollar, 510, 543
  insurance on, 86–87, 161
  interbank, 93, 110, 545
  nature of, 104–105
  savings of time deposits, 147–152, 549, 550
    certificates of deposit, 151–152, 541
    interest rates on, 147–151, 278
    open-account, 151
    reserve requirements for, 149, 272–273
    savings certificates, 149–151, 549
  of state and local governments, 154
  of U.S. Treasury, 154
  security for, 115, 203
Depreciation, 377, 379, 542
Devaluations (see Balance of payments, adjustment mechanisms)
Discount rate, 113, 229, 542
  in Canada, 269
  changes in, 265–269, 266
  control over, 222, 266
  cyclical fluctuations, 266–269
Discounts, commercial banks, 128, 542
  at Federal Reserve banks, 229
Discrimination, rules against, 139–140
Disintermediation, 206, 209–210, 542
Dollar as an international reserve currency, 430, 504–509
Dollar bloc, 529, 542
Drafts, sight and time, 499

Edge Act Corporations, 89, 543
Elasticity of currency, 239, 543
Electronic banking terminals, 89
Eligibility requirements, 240, 278–279, 543
Employment Act of 1946, 396
Employment Retirement Income Security Act of 1974 (ERISA),
    149–150
Equal Credit Opportunity Act, 138, 140
Equation of exchange, 317–319, 339–340, 363–364, 543
Eurodollar banks, 509–511, 543
  borrowings by U.S. banks from, 156, 511
    reserves required for, 156
European Monetary System, 523
"Even-keel" policy, 415, 543
Examinations, bank, 81–82, 84–85, 428, 441

Excess reserves, 168, 179–181, 186–189, 290–291, 311, 543
  during 1930s, 186–189, 276, 437
Exchange rates, 518–532, 543
  determinants of, 528–529
  equilibrium rate, 526–528
  fixed, 518–520, 524–531, 543
    changes in, 519–520
    under IMF, 518–519
    speculation over changes, 521
  flexible, 430, 524–529, 544
  managed, 265, 521–523, 542, 546
  See also Balance of payments, adjustment mechanisms
Export-Import Bank, 205

Failures, bank, 82, 159–161, 188–189, 238–241, 369
Fair Credit Billing Act, 138, 140
Farm Credit Act of 1933, 204
Federal Advisory Council, 227
Federal Deposit Insurance Corporation (FDIC), 82, 86–87, 138, 161, 195, 222, 241, 543
Federal Farm Loan Act of 1916, 204
Federal funds, 110–113, 155, 271, 543
  rate, 113, 266, 292–297
Federal Home Loan Banks, 114, 195, 197, 199, 203–205, 209–210, 222
Federal Intermediate Credit Banks, 203–204
Federal Land Banks, 114, 137, 203
Federal National Mortgage Association (Fannie Mae), 114, 203–205, 209–210
Federal Open Market Committee (FOMC), 226–227, 262, 292, 543
  See also Open market operations; Federal Reserve Bank of New York
Federal Reserve Act, 216–218
Federal Reserve bank notes, 47
Federal Reserve Bank of New York, 218, 226, 262–263
Federal Reserve banks, 222–225
  assets, 227–230
  branches, 223, 225
  capital accounts, 231–232
  cash and currency held, 238
  deposits of, 542
    owned by foreign governments, 231, 255
    owned by member banks, 169, 230–231
    owned by nonmember banks, 84, 231
    owned by U.S. Treasurer, 231, 252–255
  directors, 222–224
  discounts and advances, 229
  float, 231, 245–246
  investments, 229, 243
  loans to member banks, 156, 229, 245, 265–269, 289
  liabilities, 230–231
  ownership, 222, 224, 231
  presidents, 224, 226
  profits, 222, 224, 229, 439
  reserves, 44
Federal Reserve notes, 47, 230, 239–240, 543
  reserves required for, 44, 228
  held by Federal Reserve banks, 230
Federal Reserve Reform Act of 1977, 219, 292
Federal Reserve System, 216–227
  assistance to Treasury, 218, 222, 414–415
  control of monetary base, 296, 340
  decentralization, 222–225
  defensive operations, 263–264
  goals, 286, 292–298, 430–431
  independence of, 218–220, 292, 431
  member banks (see Commercial banks)
  original functions, 218
  relation to Congress, 218–220, 292, 431
  relations with Treasury, 219, 287
  reporting by, 226, 263, 292, 432
  selective instruments of control, 222, 276–279, 550
Federal Trade Commission, 140
Finance companies, 136, 194, 202–203, 543
Financial Institutions Regulatory and Interest Rate Control Act of 1978, 52, 94
Financial intermediaries, 194–211, 542, 543
  banks as, 126–127
  creation of near money, 194, 206–210
  depository, 195–199

  federal, 203–206
  foreign, 206
  growth of, 194–195
  impact on economy, 206–210
  rotating credit associations, 206
  thrift institutions, 195–199
Financial panics, 238, 369, 437
  avoidance of, 87
  panic of 1907, 86, 217
Financial record-keeping, required, 51–52
FINE study (Financial Institutions and the National Economy), 88, 198
First Bank of the United States, 216
Fiscal policy, 396–398, 412
  "automatic stabilizers", 397, 539
  effects on national income, 400, 405–410, 412
  disagreement of effectiveness, 411–412
    recent experience, 411–412
  measures of (see Budget, federal)
  relation to monetary policy, 400–401
Fiscalists, 411
Float, 231, 245–246, 544
Floating-rate certificates, 151, 544
Foreign banks in U.S., 87
Foreign branches of U.S. banks, 87, 89–91
Foreign credit restraint programs, 533–534, 544
Foreign currency, stabilization of, 230, 246, 265, 508, 523
Foreign exchange, dealers, 496–498
  markets, 496–498
  speculation, 521
Forward exchange rates, 498, 524
Fractional reserve banking systems, 102, 168, 425–428, 544
Free banking acts, 81–82, 544
Free reserves, 288–291, 544, 548

Germany, use of barter in after World War II, 21
Gibson paradox, 460, 544
Glossary, 539
G N P (national income), 350–353, 545
G N P deflator, 449–450, 544
Gold, 501–504
  offsetting flows of, 430, 550
  price of, 42–44, 228, 501–504
  sales and purchases by U.S., 43, 228, 248–249
  speculation, 43, 503
Gold certificates, 44, 227–228, 248–249, 544
Gold points, 502
Gold pool, 502–503, 544
Gold standard, 36–37, 422–425, 544
Gold tranche, 519, 546
Government securities, U.S., appreciation bonds 68, 539
  auctions of, 60, 62, 415
  as security for government deposits, 115, 203
  bank restricted, 70
  bills, 59–62, 202, 551
  bonds, 59, 62
    call date, 63
  book-entry option, 60, 63
  E-bonds, 68
  exchange, 62
  foreign series, 68
  government series, 69
  interest rate ceilings on, 59, 286–288
  marketable, 58–62, 115, 413, 546
  maturity of, 59–60, 412–414, 542, 546
  nonmarketable, 68–69, 549
  notes, 59–60, 62, 551
  ownership of, 69–71, 114
  prices of, 62–67
  refundings, 62, 415, 549
    attrition, 62, 415, 539
  repurchase agreements, 152–154, 263
  risk on, 65, 115, 541, 545
  savings bonds, 68–69, 549
  as security for Treasury deposits, 115, 203
  short-term, 59–62, 115, 412–414
  subscriptions, 62, 415
  tax-anticipation bills, 62, 550
  taxation of income from, 114
  yields on, 61, 64–65, 72–74

Great Depression, bank failures, 159–160, 188, 437
demand for loans, 130, 300
excess reserves, 186–188, 276, 437
Federal Reserve actions, 241, 275–276, 436–438
interest rates, 188–189, 300
money supply, 437
real cash balances, 319, 336
Greenbacks, 13, 37–39, 552
Gresham's Law, 35–36, 45, 545
Gross national product (GNP) (see National income)
Guidelines, wage-price, 479, 552

Hedging, against loss on foreign exchange, 524, 545
High-employment budget (see Budget, federal)
Higher Education Act of 1965, 136
Holder-in-due-course doctrine, 141
Holding companies, 92–93, 119–120, 539
Home Mortgage Disclosure Act, 138–139
Human capital, return from investment in, 330–331, 336, 545
Humphrey Hawkins Act, 219, 292, 474
Hunt Commission, 88, 198
Hyperinflation (see Inflation, rapid)

Income, Permanent, 355, 548
Income effect on interest rates, 382–383
Income velocity, 318–322, 545
Indexation, Proposals for, 462, 475
Individual Retirement Accounts (IRAs), 149–150, 545
Inflation, accounting in, 463
adjustments to, 338–339
anticipated, 460–461
beneficiaries of, 457–459, 461
effects on demand for money, 338–339
in Brazil, 455, 521, 525
in Chile, 21, 446, 455, 525
cost-push, 454–455, 541
demand-pull, 450–454, 542
effects of anti-inflationary policies, 472–474
effects on, distribution of wealth and income, 456–61, 464
government finance, 461–464
interest rates, 209, 460
in major countries, 446, 448
rapid, 21, 335, 446
reasons for avoiding, 463–464
theories of, cost-push, 454–455, 541
interest rate-investment, 374–383
portfolio adjustment (monetary), 450–454, 547
structuralist, 455–456, 550
unanticipated, 457–459
Inflationary gap, 453–454, 545
Insurance on deposits, 86–87, 241, 427
early, 86, 238
Insurance companies, life, 194, 199–200
Interdistrict Settlement Fund, 224
Interest elasticity of demand for money, 388
Interest Equalization Tax of 1963, 533–534, 545
Interest rate-investment theory, 374–383
Interest rates, 11–12, 545
ceilings, 12, 209, 286–288
and demand for money, 299–300, 374
during inflation, 12, 132; 210, 300–301, 460, 462–463
effects of debt management on, 413
equilibrium rates, 299–300
expectations theory, 73–74
Gibson paradox, 460, 544
in Great Depression, 300
as indicators of monetary policy, 300–301
on installment loans, 133–135
in interest rate-investment theory, 374–383
in portfolio adjustment theory, 365–368
prime rate, 128, 549
real, 376, 549
regulation of, on demand deposits 146, 277
on deposits in thrift institutions, 209
effects on allocation of credit, 209
effects on housing starts, 209
evasion, 271
on government securities, 286–288

on savings and time deposits (see Regulation Q)
on real estate credit, 132
relation to investment, 376–377, 388–390
stabilizing effects of cyclical changes in, 298–300
theory of market segmentation, 72
variable, 132–133
See also Discount rate; Bill rate; Federal funds, rate; Commercial paper, rates on
Interlocking directors, bank, 94, 545
International Banking Act of 1978, 90
International Monetary Fund (IMF), 231, 545
balance sheet, 519
purchases and sales of gold, 503
regulation of exchange rates, 518–519
services for members, 518–519
Special Drawing Rights (SDRs), 228–229, 249–251, 512
International reserves, 504, 546
Inventories, in theories of income determination, 356–360, 376–377, 381
Investment, determinants of, 376–377, 380–381, 388–389, 548
foreign, controls on, 533
gross private domestic, 351, 545
relation to saving, 358–360
Investment companies, 194, 201–202, 541, 547
IS-LM model, 383–386

Jamaica Agreement, 520

Leading series, 310
Legal tender, 38, 546
Letter of Credit, 499
Liabilities, bank, 146–156
managed, 271
Life insurance, cash value, 200
Liquid assets, 5, 413, 546
creation of, 194, 206–210
held by banks, 112–113, 115
held by business firms, 154
types, 24–26
See also Stores of value; Commercial banks, liquidity
Liquid liabilities owed to foreigners, 505–506, 552
Liquidity effect on interest rates, 376, 383
Liquidity preference schedule (see Money, demand for)
Liquidity trap, 386–388, 546
Loans, 127–137
agricultural, 136–137
call, 136
collateral 127, 278, 541
commercial, 129–130, 541
consumer, 133–135, 197–198, 202–203, 279
in default, 85, 129
demand for, 110–111, 130, 135
discounts, 128, 542
federal funds sold, 111–113, 543
from Federal Reserve banks to member banks, 229, 265–269, 278
pressure for repayment, 265–266, 289
Federal Trade Commission regulations on, 140
to financial institutions, 136
guaranteed, 130–132
holder-in-due-course doctrine, 140
installment, 133–135, 197–198, 202–203
limits on size, 86, 94, 127
lines of credit, 129
margin requirements, 137, 222, 276–277, 546
overdrafts, 94, 127, 135
overseas loans, restraint on, 533
personal, 135
promissory note, 127
real estate, 129–131, 195, 197–198, 200, 204–205, 209–210, 552
government guarantees, 131–132, 204–205
government regulations, 132, 279
on securities, 136–137
student, 136

Managed exchange rates, 265, 542, 546
Managed liabilities, 271, 546
Margin requirements, 137, 222, 276–277, 546

Marginal product of capital, 377–378, 381, 546
Marginal propensity to consume, 358–359, 546
McFadden Act of 1927, 88–90
Medium of exchange, 20–21, 341–344, 546
  during inflation, 21
Mergers, bank, 91
Mexico, changes in exchange rates, 429, 530–531
  inflation in, 448
  monetary regulation in, 429
Mint ratio, 35–36, 547
Mint, U.S., 40–41
Monetarists, 411
Monetary aggregates, as targets, 292–298, 547
Monetary base, 183–185, 187, 547
  causes of changes in, 312–313, 369–370, 546
  control over, 296, 340, 432–434
  effects of changes in, 315–317
  rate of change in, 187, 316–317
Monetary policy, discretionary, 423, 430–434
  easy, 422
  lags in effects of, 436
  recent experience, 411–412
  rules, 434–438
  targets, 286–301, 313
  tight, 429–430, 472–476
Monetary reforms, 19–20, 547
Monetary regulation, automatic, 422–426
    early U.S., 216–217
    in Guatemala, 428–429
    under pure commodity standard, 424–426
  based on balance of payments, 422–423, 428–430
  based on a rule, 434–438
    fixed quantity of money, 435
    price stabilization, 435
    steady increases in money stock, 434–435
  discretionary, 423, 430–434
Money, causes of changes in, 310–311, 364–367, 369–370
  commodity, 423–426
  control of, 209, 256–257, 436, 441
  creation of, 126, 168
  cyclical variations in, 8, 306–310
  definitions of, 4–6, 23
  demand for, 322, 546
  by businesses, 337
  determinants of, 331–332, 341–344, 360–362
  income elasticity of, 333–334
  by individuals, 331–337
  interest elasticity of, 387–388
  nature of, 328, 341–344
  effect of change in supply of, on interest rates, 365–367
    on national income (see Portfolio adjustment theory; Interest
      rate-investment theory)
  growth in volume of, 6–7, 312–313
  high-powered (see Monetary base)
  international, 228, 430, 504–505, 508–509, 546
  as medium of exchange, 20–21, 23–24, 341–344
  measures of, 4–6, 297–298, 547
  money multiplier, 183–186, 433–434, 546
  motives for holding, 27–28, 341–344
  multiple expansion and contraction of, 171–177
  paper money, 13, 34–35
  in primitive societies, 20–21
  relationship to monetary base, 310–311
  relationship to trend of national income, 314–315
  real value of, 8
  as standard of deferred payment, 27–28
  as store of value, 24–26, 343–344
  supply, from 1867 to 1960, 6–7, 306–310
  recent trends, 7
  tight, 429–430, 472–476
    effects on balance of payments, 422, 429
  as unit of account, 18–20
  velocity of, 9–10, 317–323
    determinants of, 319–322, 339–342
    measures of, 317–323
    trends, 319–322, 363
  as wealth, 328–329, 341–344
Money market certificates, 115, 150, 202, 547
Money market mutual funds, 279, 547

Mortgages (see Loans, real estate)
Multiple expansion and contraction process, 171–177
Multiplier, money, 183–186, 433–434, 546, 547
Multiplier, theory of, 357–360
Municipal bonds, 114, 116–118, 547
  ratings, 116–117
  risk of default, 115, 117
  taxation of, 114, 116, 550
Mutual funds (see Investment companies)
Mutual savings banks, 194–196
  taxation of, 195

National Bank Act, 46, 82, 216
National bank notes, 46–47, 547
National banks, 46–47, 82–83, 225, 547
National debt, 548
  See also Government securities
National income, determinants of 360–364
  equilibrium level, 353–357, 543
  measures of, 350–353, 548
  relation of, to demand for money, 360–362
  reverse effects on money supply, 368–370
  See also Portfolio adjustment theory; INterest rate-investment theory
National income accounts budget (see Budget, federal)
Near money, 5, 548
  See also Stores of value; Liquid assets
Nonmember banks, 83–84, 210
Notes, promissory, 127
NOW accounts, 146, 149, 198, 271, 548

Office of Price Administration (OPA) (see Price controls)
100 percent reserve banking systems, 438–441, 548
Open market operations, 169–171, 222, 226–227, 243–244, 262–265, 364
  to control free reserves 288
  to control interest rates, 296
  defensive operations, 263–264, 542
  during 1930s, 241, 275, 438
  during refundings, 415
  early use by Treasury, 217
  in foreign countries, 274
  mechanics of transactions, 227, 263
  to offset gold flows, 262, 264, 430
  See also Federal Open Market Committee: Federal Reserve Bank of
    New York: Foreign currency, stabilization of
Overdrafts, 94, 127, 135

Panic of 1907, 86, 217
Paper money, denominations of, 50–51
  early, 34–35
  early U.S., 13
  in process of retirement, 39, 45–47
Paper standard, 39
Penny shortage, 40
Pension funds, 194, 201
  individual, 149–150, 545
Phillips curve, 487–489, 548
Pigou effect, 390–391, 548
Portfolio adjustment theory, 364–368
  interest rates in, 365–368
Postal Savings System, 206
Price controls, 477–482
  and allocation of resources, 481–482
  effects, 450
  evasion of, 478, 481
  in Germany, 481–482
Price indexes, biases, 431
  consumer price index, 431, 447
  GNP deflator, 431
  producer, 431, 448
  stabilization of, proposed, 435
  wholesale, 448
Prime rate, 128, 549
Producer price index 448
Promissory note, 127
Purchasing power parity, 528–529, 549
Pure commodity standard, 424–425, 549

Quantity theory of money (*see* Equation of exchange)

Rationing, 22, 549
   in Soviet Union, 22
Real Bills doctrine (*see* Commercial loan theory of banking)
Real Estate Settlements Procedures Act, 138–139
Real money balances, 332–333, 549
   cyclical fluctuations, 335–339
   determinants of quantity held, 331–340, 360–362, 374–376, 390–391
   holding of, by business firms, 337
   long-run trends, 334
   See also Money, demand for
Redlining, 139
Regulation Q, 93, 120, 146, 148, 271, 549
   effects on quantity of time deposits, 209
   phasing out of, 199
   setting of ceilings, 199, 222, 277–278
Regulation U, 137
Regulation Z, 139–140
Repurchase agreements, 152–154, 263, 271, 549
Reserve cities, 269–270, 549
Reserve-deposit ratio, 310–311
Reserve requirements, for certificates of deposit, 271
   for commercial paper issued by bank holding companies, 271
   early, 82, 269–270, 423
   effects of nonuniformity of, 181–183, 271–273
   effects on liquidity of banks, 373–374, 427–428
   for Eurodollars borrowed by U.S. banks, 271
   for Federal Reserve banks, 44, 228
   for managed liabilities, 153, 271, 546
   for member banks, 84, 113, 149, 168–169, 221, 269–274, 549
      effects of changes in, 189, 273, 369
      methods of calculating, 103, 180–181, 270
   for nonmember banks, 84, 110, 209, 273
   for thrift institutions, 84, 209, 274
   in foreign countries, 274
Reserves for bad loans, 159
Reserves, creation of, 169–171
   deficiencies in, 181, 298
   excess, 168, 179–181, 186–189, 276, 290–291, 311, 369, 437, 543
   factors absorbing, 242, 251–256
   factors supplying, 241–251
   historical variations in, 186–189
      during 1930s, 186–189
   leakages of, 177–182, 546
   member bank, 84, 103
   of nonmember banks, 110, 209
   100 percent, 438–441, 548
   ratio to deposits, 310–311
   secondary, 112–113, 115, 118, 550
   of thrift institutions, 199
   use of, 427–428
Reserves, international, 501, 504–505, 512–513
Revenue Act of 1951, 195
Risk, credit, 65, 541
   interest, 65, 545
Runs on banks, 87, 189, 238–241, 369, 437, 540

Saving, relation to investment, 358–360
Savings and loan associations, 194, 196–197, 205
Savings bonds, 68–69
Savings certificates, 149–151
Savings deposits, 147–152
   individual retirement accounts, 149–150
   NOW accounts, 146, 149, 198, 271, 548
   See also Deposits, commercial banks, savings and time
Second Bank of the United States, 216
Securities Act Amendment of 1975, 116
Securities and Exchange Act of 1934, 222, 276
Securities and Exchange Commission, 222
Seigniorage, 36, 251, 550
Selective instruments of control, 222, 276–279, 550
Silver, "free" silver, 45
   price of, 45–46
   standard, 36, 550
Silver certificates, 45–46, 550
Silver purchase acts, 37, 45

Small Business Administration, 130
Smithsonian agreement, 520
South Africa, gold purchases from, 503
Special Drawing Rights (SDRs), 228–229, 249–251, 512, 550
Specie Resumption Act of 1875, 39, 82
State banks, 82–84, 110, 225, 550
   early, 80–83
   notes, 13, 46–47, 426, 550
   See also Commercial banks
Stock, bank purchases of, 120
   book value, 157, 540
   capital stock of banks, 83, 540
Stores of value, 24–26, 343–344
   during inflation, 26
Student Loan Marketing Association, 120, 205
Surplus, commercial bank, 157
   Federal Reserve bank, 231–232

Targets of monetary policy, 286–301, 432
   conflicts, 294–297, 415
Tax and loan accounts (*see* Deposits, commercial bank; Treasury, U.S. deposits)
Tax warrants, 116
Thrift institutions, 195–199, 551
Time deposits (*see* Deposits, savings and time; Savings deposits)
Transaction accounts, 149, 182, 199, 209, 271, 551
Transactions costs, effects of, 342–343
Transactions demand for money, 341–344
Transactions velocity, 317–318, 551
Transit account, 155
Travelers checks, 501
Treasury, U.S., as beneficiary of inflation, 461–463
   cash holdings, 42, 252–254, 551
   currency issued by, 38–42, 251
   debt management decisions, 412–414, 542
   deposits of, 154, 231, 254–255, 550
      in statistics on money supply, 4
      security for, 115, 203
   gold policy, 42–44
   monetary accounts of, 242
   notes of 1890, 37
   relation of Federal Reserve System to, 219, 287
   silver policy, 36–37, 45–46
Treasury-Federal Reserve Accord of 1951, 287, 551
Truck Act, British, 23
Truth in Lending Act, 138–139

Underground economy, 49, 485
Undivided profits, 157, 160, 551
Unemployment, 482–490
   effects of anti-inflation policies on, 473–474
   effects on wage changes, 487–489
   frictional, 544
   prevention of, 474–476
   relation of, to rate of change in prices, 487–490
   target level of, 431, 471
Unified budget (*see* Budget, federal)
Unit of account, 18–20, 551
   decimal system, 19
United States notes, 13, 37–39, 251, 552
   convertibility into gold, 38–39
User cost of capital, 377, 552
USSR, use of money in, 23
   monetary reform, 19–20
   monetary regulation, 141–142

Velocity of money, determinants of, 319–322, 339–340
   in inflation, 319–322, 341–342
   measures of, 317–323, 545, 551
   trends, 319–322, 363
Voluntary foreign credit restraint programs, 533–534

Wage changes, determinants of, 481, 487–490
Wage controls, 477–482
   and allocation of resources, 481–482
Wage-price guidelines, 479, 552

Wealth, 328–331, 390–391
   money as a type of, 328–329, 341–344
Wholesale price index, 448
World liquidity (*see* Dollar, as an international reserve currency; Gold;
   SDRs)

Yield curves, 72–74, 264, 552
Yields, on bank investments, 113
   changes in, effects on demand for money, 334–335
   computation of, 61, 64
   on different maturities, 72–74